Frommer's

S0-ARE-542

Northern Italy
including Venice, Milan & the Lakes

2nd Edition

by Reid Bramblett

Here's what the critics say about Frommer's:

"Amazingly easy to use. Very portable, very complete."

—Booklist

"Detailed, accurate, and easy-to-read information for all price ranges."
—Glamour Magazine

"Hotel information is close to encyclopedic."

—Des Moines Sunday Register

"Frommer's Guides have a way of giving you a real feel for a place."
—Knight Ridder Newspapers

WILEY

Wiley Publishing, Inc.

Travelgum

Smettilla!

Published by:

Wiley Publishing, Inc.

111 River St.

Hoboken, NJ 07030-5774

Copyright © 2004 Wiley Publishing, Inc., Hoboken, New Jersey. All rights reserved. No part of this publication may be reproduced, stored in a retrieval system or transmitted in any form or by any means, electronic, mechanical, photocopying, recording, scanning or otherwise, except as permitted under Sections 107 or 108 of the 1976 United States Copyright Act, without either the prior written permission of the Publisher, or authorization through payment of the appropriate per-copy fee to the Copyright Clearance Center, 222 Rosewood Drive, Danvers, MA 01923, 978/750-8400, fax 978/646-8600. Requests to the Publisher for permission should be addressed to the Legal Department, Wiley Publishing, Inc., 10475 Crosspoint Blvd., Indianapolis, IN 46256, 317/572-3447, fax 317/572-4447, E-Mail: permcoordinator@wiley.com.

Wiley and the Wiley Publishing logo are trademarks or registered trademarks of John Wiley & Sons, Inc. and/or its affiliates. Frommer's is a trademark or registered trademark of Arthur Frommer. Used under license. All other trademarks are the property of their respective owners. Wiley Publishing, Inc. is not associated with any product or vendor mentioned in this book.

ISBN 0-7645-4293-1

Editor: Kendra L. Falkenstein
Production Editor: Bethany André
Cartographer: Nick Trotter
Photo Editor: Richard Fox
Production by Wiley Indianapolis Composition Services

Front cover photo: View of Lake Como, Corenno Plinio
Back cover photo: Historical Regatta on Venice's Grand Canal

For information on our other products and services or to obtain technical support, please contact our Customer Care Department within the U.S. at 800/762-2974, outside the U.S. at 317/572-3993 or fax 317/572-4002.

Wiley also publishes its books in a variety of electronic formats. Some content that appears in print may not be available in electronic formats.

Manufactured in the United States of America

5 4 3 2

Contents

4   The Veneto   154

5   Trentino–Alto Adige: The Dolomites & South Tirol   205

6   Friuli-Venezia Giulia   239

7   Milan & Lombardy   255

List of Maps

An Invitation to the Reader

In researching this book, we discovered many wonderful places—hotels, restaurants, shops, and more. We're sure you'll find others. Please tell us about them, so we can share the information with your fellow travelers in upcoming editions. If you were disappointed with a recommendation, we'd love to know that, too. Please write to:

Frommer's Northern Italy, 2nd Edition
Wiley Publishing, Inc. • 111 River St. • Hoboken, NJ 07030-5774

An Additional Note

Please be advised that travel information is subject to change at any time—and this is especially true of prices. We therefore suggest that you write or call ahead for confirmation when making your travel plans. The authors, editors, and publisher cannot be held responsible for the experiences of readers while traveling. Your safety is important to us, however, so we encourage you to stay alert and be aware of your surroundings. Keep a close eye on cameras, purses, and wallets, all favorite targets of thieves and pickpockets.

About the Author

Reid Bramblett learned Italian on the playground of a Roman parochial school when he was 12, explored Italy with his parents for two years in a hippie-orange VW camper, and spent a year studying there during a break from the anthropology department at Cornell. After a stint in Frommer's editorial offices, Reid vaulted over the desk to write Frommer's first guide to Tuscany and Umbria and hasn't stopped exploring, learning, interviewing, taking notes, and reporting it all in guidebooks since. He has also written *Frommer's Portable Florence, Frommer's Memorable Walks in New York, Europe For Dummies,* is co-author of *Frommer's Italy from $70 a Day,* and contributes to *Frommer's Europe from $70 a Day.* When not on the road, he lives in Maspeth, Queens, with two cats and the brilliant and beautiful Frances Sayers, without whose invaluable help and stupendous patience none of those books listed above (to say nothing of this one) could have been written.

Other Great Guides for Your Trip:

Frommer's Italy
Frommer's Italy from $70 a Day
Italy For Dummies
Frommer's Tuscany & Umbria
Frommer's Europe
Frommer's Italy's Best-Loved Driving Tours
Frommer's Northern Italy's Best-Loved Driving Tours
Frommer's Italy's Best Bed & Breakfasts and Country Inns
Suzy Gershman's Born to Shop Italy

Frommer's Star Ratings, Icons & Abbreviations

Every hotel, restaurant, and attraction listing in this guide has been ranked for quality, value, service, amenities, and special features using a **star-rating system.** In country, state, and regional guides, we also rate towns and regions to help you narrow down your choices and budget your time accordingly. Hotels and restaurants are rated on a scale of zero (recommended) to three stars (exceptional). Attractions, shopping, nightlife, towns, and regions are rated according to the following scale: zero stars (recommended), one star (highly recommended), two stars (very highly recommended), and three stars (must-see).

In addition to the star-rating system, we also use **seven feature icons** that point you to the great deals, in-the-know advice, and unique experiences that separate travelers from tourists. Throughout the book, look for:

Finds	Special finds—those places only insiders know about
Fun Fact	Fun facts—details that make travelers more informed and their trips more fun
Kids	Best bets for kids, and advice for the whole family
Moments	Special moments—those experiences that memories are made of
Overrated	Places or experiences not worth your time or money
Tips	Insider tips—great ways to save time and money
Value	Great values—where to get the best deals

The following **abbreviations** are used for credit cards:

AE	American Express	DISC	Discover	V	Visa
DC	Diners Club	MC	MasterCard		

Frommers.com

Now that you have the guidebook to a great trip, visit our website at **www.frommers.com** for travel information on more than 3,000 destinations. With features updated regularly, we give you instant access to the most current trip-planning information available. At Frommers.com, you'll also find the best prices on airfares, accommodations, and car rentals—and you can even book travel online through our travel booking partners. At Frommers.com, you'll also find the following:

- Online updates to our most popular guidebooks
- Vacation sweepstakes and contest giveaways
- Newsletter highlighting the hottest travel trends
- Online travel message boards with featured travel discussions

What's New in Northern Italy

After the flurry of renovations and new museums and monuments that came along with Jubilee Year 2000, and the continent-wide price hikes that accompanied the introduction of the Euro in 2002, Italy seems to be taking a bit of a breather on large-scale changes. The overall downturn in tourism figures since the September 11, 2001, terrorist attacks and the war in Iraq have hurt hotels and other local businesses, but have also meant that prices on tourism facilities have largely held steady-ish over the past two years (or at least didn't rise as fast as local inflation). As for smaller and more specific changes and novelties in Northern Italy, here they are, region by region.

VENICE There's a new Venice Card on offer that gets you significant discounts on sightseeing and transportation all across town.

The campanile in St. Mark's Square—with its brilliant view over the piazza, the domes of St. Mark's Cathedral, the striped Doge's Palace, and the boats bobbing in the *bacino* (bay) where the Grand Canal empties into the Venetian lagoon—has reopened to the public (Apr–Sept; 6€/$6.90)—and, unlike most bell towers in Italy, it has an elevator, so you don't have to climb endless spiral stairs.

The Associazione Chiesa di Venezia, which curates most of Venice's top churches, now offers audio guides at some of the churches for just .50€ (60¢).

The wonderful family-run Hotel Bernardi-Semenzato has opened a second annex—just four rooms, but any increase in the number of rooms available at this gem of a budget hotel is welcome.

For complete details on Venice, see chapter 3.

THE VENETO **Padua** The brilliant and beautiful frescoes by Giotto that carpet the interior of the Scrovegni Chapel, which are head and shoulders above the Gothic master's far more famous frescoes in Assisi, have finally been fully restored to their vibrant, glorious colors and tones. That's the good news. The bad news is that they've gone from being in a dusty chapel beloved by art aficionados into a major tourism turnstile where bus groups disgorge to shuffle through just like at *The Last Supper* in Milan. And they now limit the number of people who can enter the chapel to 25 at a time and then shoo them out after just 15 minutes! You'll have to visit after 7pm if you want a special ticket that gets you half an hour inside. If you don't book ahead at this one, you probably won't get in.

The *centralissimo* Hotel Leon Biano was closed in 2002 for extensive renovations that will keep this top hotel in the center of Padua out of the game until at least late 2004. At least we can still stay at the owner's nearby Hotel Majestic Toscanelli in the interim.

Treviso The Museo Civico has largely shut down for a massive renovation. Many of the works it used to house may stay permanently in what was, when we went to press, a temporary home in the newly renovated Santa Caterina. The restoration of Santa Caterina (in the summer of 2003) is great news, for this monastery with wonderful frescoes by Tomaso de Modena was for a long time virtually inaccessible by dint of opening only 1 day a month; now it's open 6 days a week.

For more information on the Veneto, see chapter 4.

TRENTINO–ALTO ADIGE: THE DOLOMITES & SOUTH TIROL

Bozen (Bolzano) In August 2003 a research team determined that the final moments of Ötzi—the famous ice man whose body and accouterments were preserved for 5,300 years inside a glacier, then, since 1998, in a museum in Bolzano—were anything but calm. The Ice Man was apparently caught in a thrilling battle, shot at least once in the back by an enemy arrow, and dragged away by a valiant companion who patched up Ötzi's wounds before our hero gasped his last breath in an icy crevasse high in the Alps. For more on Bozen and Trentino–Alto Adige, see chapter 5.

MILAN & LOMBARDY

Milan The facade of the Duomo in Milan has gone under scaffolding for a thorough cleaning of indeterminate length (though at press time they're saying "end of 2004").

A new museum, the Museo Diocesano, has opened on Corso di Porta Ticinese to display all the best works collected from small churches throughout Milan and the surrounding region in one place. There are medieval sculpture, paintings, and crucifixes galore, along with Flemish tapestries, Renaissance paintings by Tintoretto, and Romantic ones by Francesco Hayez.

Meanwhile, the inimitable 18th-century opera house La Scala, home turf to Giuseppe Verdi, Arturo Toscanini, and Maria Callas, has closed its doors yet again for another renovation (it pulled this same stunt from 1999 to 2001). Until the gala reopening of the '06 season on December 7, 2005, performances are being held at a venue way out in the 'burbs, and La Scala's noted theatrical museum (lots of costumes, Verdi scores, and old record players) has been moved temporarily to digs near *The Last Supper.* Learn more about Milan and Lombardy in chapter 7.

THE LAKES

Lake Como The sweet old lady who ran the Milano hotel in Varenna since time immemorial has retired. This tiny inn was long the best value on any lake, with tiny, simple rooms overlooking gorgeous Lake Como and costing virtually nothing. The new owners are busily renovating the spot into a three-star boutique hotel—and prices have already jumped by more than 30%. At less than $140 for a double room, it's still a reasonably priced place to stay, the new owners couldn't be friendlier, and, of course, the rooms still have those killer views, but it's sad to see such a marvelous gem of a truly budget hotel change forever.

Across the lake in Menaggio, more sad news: The husband at tiny, homey, and utterly cheap Albergo-Ristorante Il Vapore passed away in 2002. While his widow and family are keeping the hotel running, they have, for now, closed down the excellent restaurant he ran. For more information on the Lakes, see chapter 8.

PIEDMONT & THE VALLE D'AOSTA

Turin Though this hasn't yet started affecting the city as we go to press, over the lifetime of this edition, Turin will be gearing up to host the 2006 Winter Olympic games, so expect some changes to come as they spruce up in preparation for worldwide attention. For more info, check out www.torino2006.org.

Meanwhile, in the center of town, the Palazzo Madama—Museo Civico di Arte Antica (Civic Museum of Ancient Art) is still partially closed: The long, ongoing renovations are now slated to end in 2006, but the good news is that the grand entrance hall and staircase designed by Juvarra is open once again, and it's free (they used to charge admission).

Courmayeur-Entrèves The tunnel under Mont Blanc connecting Italy with France—the longest in the world—reopened to traffic in 2002, 3 years after a massive fire.

You can read more information about Piedmont and the Valle d'Aosta in chapter 9.

LIGURIA & THE ITALIAN RIV- IERA Genoa The Palazzo Bianco (White Palace) will remain closed for renovations until late 2004. For more on Liguria & the Italian Riviera, see chapter 10.

1

The Best of Northern Italy

Northern Italy's riches are vast, varied, and yours to discover, from art-packed museums and mosaicked cathedrals to Roman ruins and hill towns amid vineyards that produce some of Europe's best wines. You can dine at refined restaurants that casually flaunt their Michelin star ratings, or chow down with the town priest and police chief at *osterie* (small local eateries) that have spent generations perfecting traditional recipes. You can spend the night in a sumptuous Renaissance villa on Lake Como in the Alpine foothills where Napoléon once stayed (the Villa d'Este), or in a converted 17th-century Venetian palazzo where the room opens directly onto the Grand Canal but costs a mere $109 (the Hotel Galleria). Here's a short list of the best of what northern Italy has to offer.

1 The Best Travel Experiences

- **Gondola Ride in Venice:** Yes, it's hokey. Yes, it's way overpriced. But when it comes down to it, there's nothing quite so romantic after a long Venetian dinner as a ride on one of these long black skiffs, settling back into the plush seats with that special someone and a bottle of wine and sliding through the waters of Venice's back canals guided by the expert oar of a gondolier. See p. 78.

- **A Day Among the Islands of the Venetian Lagoon:** Venice's ferry system extends outside the city proper to a series of other inhabited islands in the lagoon. First stop, Murano, a village where the famed local glassblowing industry began and where its largest factories and best artisans still reside. Not only can you tour a glass factory (complete with hard sell in the display room at the end), but you'll discover a pair of lovely churches, one hung with paintings by Giovanni Bellini, Veronese, and Tintoretto, the other a Byzantine-Romanesque masterpiece of decoration. The isle of Burano is a colorful fishing village with an ancient lace-making tradition and houses in a variety of super-saturated hues. Nearby, lonely Torcello may have been one of the first lagoon islands settled, but it's long been almost abandoned, home to a straggly vineyard, reed-banked canals, the fine Cipriani restaurant, and a stunning Byzantine cathedral swathed in mosaics (see "The Best Churches," below). Time it right and you'll be riding the last ferry back from Torcello into Venice proper as the sun sets and lights up the lagoon waters. See p. 151.

- **Cruising the Brenta Canal:** The lazy Brenta Canal, lacing its way into the Veneto from Venice's lagoon, has long been the Hamptons of Venice, where the city's nobility and merchant princes have kept summer villas. From the massive, palatial Villa Pisani, with its elaborate gardens, to the Villa Foscari, designed by Palladio himself, most of these villas span the 16th to 19th centuries and are open to visitors. In the past few years, a few have even been opened as elegant hotels. There are two ways to tour the Brenta: on a leisurely full-day cruise between Padua and Venice, stopping to tour several villas along the way with an optional fish lunch; or by driving yourself along the banks, which allows you to pop into the villas you are most interested in—plus you can pull over at any grassy embankment for a picnic lunch on the canal. See p. 168.

- **Driving the Great Dolomite Road:** From the Adige Valley outside Bozen (Bolzano) across to the ski resort of Cortina d'Ampezzo runs 110km (68 miles) of twisting, winding, switchbacked highway called the Great Dolomite Road, which wends its way around some of the most dramatic mountain scenery in Italy. The Dolomiti are craggier and sheerer than the Alps, and as this road crawls around the peaks and climbs over the passes, one breathtaking panorama after another opens before you, undulating to the distant Po plains to the south and to the mighty Swiss Alps to the north. See p. 232.

- **Riding the Cable Cars over Mont Blanc:** There are not many more dramatic trips in Europe than this one, where a series of cable cars and gondolas rise from Courmayeur in the Valle d'Aosta to the 3,300m (11,000-foot) Punta Helbronner from which the icy vistas spread over Mont Blanc's flank in one direction and across to Monte Cervina (the Matterhorn) in the other. It is here that the true thrill ride begins as you clamber into a four-seat enclosed gondola that

dangles from a trio of stout cables some 2.4km (1½ miles) above the deep fissures of the Vallée Blanche glacier. It takes half an hour to cross to Aiguille du Midi on French soil—the longest cable car ride in the world not supported by pylons. From here, you can take a jaunt down into France's charming Chamonix if you'd like, or turn around to head back into Italian territory, perhaps stopping at the Alpine Garden two-thirds of the way back to Courmayeur to sun yourself and admire the wildflowers. See p. 365.

- **Hiking the Cinque Terre:** At the southern end of the Italian Riviera lies a string of former pirate coves called the Cinque Terre. These five fishing villages are linked by a local train line; a meandering trail that clambers over headlands, plunges amid olive groves and vineyards, and skirts cliff edges above the glittering Ligurian Sea and hidden scraps of beach; and an excellent communal white wine. Though tourism is discovering this magical corner of Italy, there are as yet no big resort hotels or overdevelopment; just trattorie on the tiny harbors and houses and apartments converted into small family hotels and short-term rental units. It takes a full, long day to hike from one end to the other, or you can simply walk the stretches you prefer (conveniently, the trails get progressively easier from north to south) and use the cheap train to connect to the other towns. Pause as you like in the *osterie* and bars of each town to sample the dry Cinque Terre white wine and refresh yourself for the next stretch. See p. 410.

2 The Best Museums

- **Galleria dell'Accademia** (Venice): The single most important gallery of Venetian painting and one of Italy's top museums was founded in

1750 and gorgeously installed in this trio of Renaissance buildings by Napoléon himself in 1807. (Napoléon swelled the collections with altarpieces confiscated from churches and monasteries he suppressed.) The works, spanning the 14th through 18th centuries, include masterpieces by all the local, Northern Italian greats—the Bellini clan, Paolo Veneziano, Carpaccio, Giorgione, Mantegna, Piero della Francesca, Lorenzo Lotto, Palma il Vecchio, Paolo Veronese, Titian, Tintoretto, Tiepolo, and Canaletto. See p. 128.

- **Collezione Peggy Guggenheim** (Venice): The Guggenheim family was one of the 20th century's greatest art patrons. Peggy not only amassed a stunning collection of modern art, she even married Max Ernst. Her half-finished 18th-century palazzo on the Grand Canal is now installed with her collections, works by Picasso, Pollock (an artist Peggy "discovered"), Magritte, Dalí, Miró, Brancusi, Kandinsky, and Marini. See p. 128.

- **Museo Archeologico dell'Alto Adige** (Bozen): Bozen's major sight is a high-tech, modern museum crafted around one of the most important archaeological finds of the past 50 years. When hikers first discovered the body of Ötzi high in the Alps at the Austrian border, everyone thought it was a mountaineer who succumbed to the elements. It turned out to be a 5,300-year-old hunter whose body, clothing, and tools had been preserved intact by the ice in which he was frozen. The Ice Man has done more to give us glimpses into daily life in the Stone Age than any other find, and the museum does a great job of relaying all that scientists are still learning from him. See p. 216.

- **Pinacoteca di Brera** (Milan): One of Italy's finest collections of art, from medieval to modern, is housed in a 17th-century Milanese palazzo. Venice's Accademia may have a richer collection of Venetian art, but the Brera has a broader collection of masterpieces from across northern and central Italy. As with the Accademia, the Brera started as a warehouse for artworks Napoléon looted from churches, monasteries, and private collections. There are masterpieces from Mantegna, Raphael, Piero della Francesca, the Bellinis, Signorelli, Titian, Tintoretto, Reni, Caravaggio, Tiepolo, and Canaletto, and great works by 20th-century geniuses such as Umberto Boccioni, Gino Severini, Giorgio Morandi, and Giorgio de Chirico. They even throw in some works by Rembrandt, Goya, and Reynolds. See p. 265.

- **Museo Egizio & Galleria Sabauda** (Turin): The world's first real museum of Egyptian artifacts remains one of the most important outside Cairo and London's British Museum. The history between Italy and Egypt dates back to Julius Caesar and Cleopatra, though this collection of 30,000 pieces was largely amassed by the Piedmont Savoy kings. The exhibits range from a papyrus *Book of the Dead* to a full 15th-century B.C. temple to fascinating objects from everyday life. But Egypt isn't all; upstairs the Galleria Sabauda displays the Savoy's amazing collection of Flemish and Dutch paintings by Van Dyck, Van Eyck, Rembrandt, Hans Memling, and Van der Weyden. See p. 339.

3 The Best Churches

- **Basilica di San Marco** (Venice): No church in Europe is more lavishly decorated, more exquisitely mosaicked, more glittering with gold than Venice's San Marco. Built in the 11th century, the church has as its guiding architectural and decorative principles Byzantine style, but more than 6 centuries of expansion and decoration have left behind Romanesque and Gothic touches as well. The interior is encrusted with more than 40,000 square feet of gold-backed mosaics crafted between the 12th and 17th centuries, some based on cartoons by Tintoretto, Veronese, and Titian. The uneven floor is a mosaic of marble chips in swirling patterns; the Pala d'Oro altarpiece a gem-studded golden trophy from Constantinople. Stairs lead up to a view over the piazza from atop the atrium, where visitors get to see up close both the mosaics and the original *Triumphal Quadriga,* four massive bronze horses probably cast in the 2nd century A.D. See p. 120.

- **Santa Maria Gloriosa dei Frari** (Venice): "I Frari" is named for the Franciscan "brothers" who founded this Gothic giant in 1250, rebuilt it between 1330 and 1453, and made it one of the most art-bedecked churches in Venice, filled with works of art by Donatello, Titian, Giovanni Bellini, and Canova. See p. 136.

- **Cattedrale di Torcello** (Torcello, Venice): Venice's oldest church is pretty much all that remains of one of the lagoon's earliest settlements on the now all-but-abandoned island of Torcello, north of what is now the city of Venice. Santa Maria Assunta was begun in the 7th century, its interior slathered with glittering gold-backed Byzantine mosaics in the 11th and 12th centuries, precursors to those that would later decorate Venice's San Marco. The inside of the entrance wall is filled with a massive *Last Judgment.* This was a common device in medieval churches: placing a scene depicting the heavenly rewards that await the faithful and the horribly inventive, gruesome punishments for the damned in

hell above the door from which parishioners would exit—sort of a final sermon at the end of the service to remind everyone of what was at stake and keep them holy until the next Sunday. The bell tower offers a pretty panorama over the sparsely populated island and surrounding lagoon. See p. 152.

- **Basilica di Sant'Antonio** (Padua): Think of all the people of Italian descent you know or have heard of named Tony. You're starting to get an idea of how popular the 13th-century Portuguese-born St. Anthony is among Italians. The patron of the lost lived in Padua, and when he died in 1231, the citizenry quickly canonized the man and began building this huge church to honor his remains, and finished it in a remarkably short 76 years. The style in 13th-century Veneto was still largely Byzantine, so the brick basilica is topped by an octet of domes and twin minaret-style bell towers. Donatello, whose *Gattamelata* (the first large equestrian bronze cast since ancient Roman times) sits out front, even crafted the high altar, but that is virtually ignored by the flocks of faithful in favor of a chapel off the left aisle. This is where a constant stream of supplicants file past the saint's tomb to press their palms against it and leave flowers, small gifts, pictures, and written prayers asking for him to help them find everything from lost health to lost love to lost children (some even pray for material objects, but rarely). *Il Santo's* robes are also preserved here, as are the silver-tongued preacher's miraculously preserved jawbone, vocal chords, and tongue, all kept in a chapel behind the high altar. See p. 164.

- **Basilica San Zeno Maggiore** (Verona): Verona is home to perhaps the greatest Romanesque basilica in all of northern Italy, a stunning example of the early medieval sculptor's art. Between the 9th and 12th centuries, architects raised the church, crated the massive rose window *Wheel of Fortune* in the facade, and hired artists who revived the ancient art of casting in bronze to create magnificent doors set with 48 wonderfully minimalist panels telling stories from the Bible as well as the life of St. Zeno. The stone reliefs flanking them date to the 12th century. The 12th- to 14th-century frescoes inside lead up to Andrea Mantegna's 15th-century altarpiece. See p. 196.

- **Basilica** (Aquileia): Tiny Aquileia was a major town in Roman times, and wasted no time in building a church in A.D. 313 just as soon as Constantine the Great declared the religion legal in the empire. The town was a hotbed of early Christianity, hosting a theological conference in 381 attended by the likes of Jerome and Ambrose. Though the church was rebuilt and frescoed in the 11th and 12th centuries, the original flooring has been uncovered and is now on display, a marvelous and precious mosaic of complicated paleo-Christian and pagan iconography. A crypt retains more mosaics from the 4th century, plus even earlier ones from a pagan house dating to the early 1st century A.D. See p. 248.

- **Tempietto Longobardo** (Cividale): This fantastic 8th-century church hollowed out of the cliff face over Cividale's mighty gorge gives us a precious glimpse into true Lombard style, before the High Middle Ages began to mix and mingle the cultural groups of northern Italy. Flanking the entranceway are statues and decorations carved directly out of the native limestone in an early Lombard Romanesque style. See p. 254.

- **Duomo** (Milan): The greatest Gothic cathedral south of the Alps, a massive pile of pinnacles and buttresses, was begun in the 14th century and took 500 years to complete—but it remained true to its original, Gothic styling. It's the fourth-largest church in the world, its cavernous interior peppered with statues and monuments. The highlight, though, is the chance to climb up onto the eaves, weave your way through the statue-peaked buttresses, and clamber up onto the very rooftop to gaze out across the hazy city and beyond to the Alps rising from the lakes north of the Lombard plain. See p. 264.

- **Certosa** (Pavia, outside Milan): Though Milan's Sforza family completed this Carthusian monastery, called a charterhouse, it's really the late-14th-century brainchild of the Visconti clan. The massive building, rich with Lombardesque decorations and sculptures, was commissioned by Gian Galeazzo in 1396 as thanks that his second wife was delivered from illness and bore him heirs. It became the repository of funerary monuments to Milan's greatest rulers and despots—though the finest, to Ludovico il Moro and his wife Beatrice d'Este, neither houses worthy's remains, nor was it even ever supposed to be here (cash-poor Santa Maria della Grazie in Milan—the one with Leonardo's *The Last Supper*—sold it to the charterhouse). This is still a working monastery, now hosting a Cistercian community, and you can tour an example of the little houses they occupy (a far cry from the cramped cells one pictures monks enduring) and purchase their own beauty products and liqueurs. See p. 289.

• **Cappella Colleoni** (Bergamo): The mercenary commander Bartolomeo Colleoni, a son of Bergamo, fought so gloriously on behalf of Venice that he was actually given the generalship over the entire Venetian army (unheard of in such a suspicious republic formed of interlocking check-and-balance branches of power). They commissioned Verrocchio to erect a statue in his honor in Venice, and gave Colleoni control of his hometown. He was foresighted enough to commission his own tomb, which was created in the late 15th century as a separate chapel to the cathedral. Colleoni invited one of the great sculptors decorating the magnificent charterhouse at Pavia to carve on his tomb a complex series of panels and statues whose symbolisms interweave in medieval style grafted onto Renaissance architecture. In the 18th century, Tiepolo was brought in to fresco the ceiling. See p. 295.

• **Basilica di Superga** (Turin): Turin got a taste of the extravagant southern Italian baroque in the early 18th century when Sicilian architect Juvarra set up shop in town. After the Virgin saved the city from French troops, the Savoys dutifully erected a church in her honor, and hired Juvarra for the job. He married early neoclassical ideals of proportion with the theatricality of the baroque to build this magnificent balcony overlooking the Alps in the hills above Turin. Vittorio Amadeo II liked his results so much he decided to turn it into the Royal Tomb, wedging monuments to various Savoys into the chapels and the underground Crypt of Kings. See p. 341.

• **Sacra di San Michele** (outside Turin): Its stony bulk, elaborate carvings, and endless staircases, all towering over the valley from a Monte Pirchiriano perch, give this abbey a movie-set air. Its setting is more appropriate to a Tibetan monastery than a Christian abbey. The gravity-defying way it hangs halfway off the cliff face is all the more remarkable when you consider that the engineering is purely medieval—started in 983 and rebuilt in the 1100s. Before the Savoys were the bigwig kings they became, their early members were buried here, in rock-carved chapels under the partly frescoed main church interior and where today, free concerts are held April through September, with a range of offerings, from Gregorian chants and Celtic music to classical pieces and gospel hymns. See p. 347.

4 The Best Artistic Masterpieces

• **Scuola Grande di San Rocco** (Venice): When the Scuola di San Rocco (a sort of gentlemen's club/lay fraternity) held an art competition in 1564, the Renaissance master Tintoretto pulled a fast one on his rivals. Instead of preparing a sketch for the judges like everyone else, he went ahead and finished a painting, secretly installing it in the ceiling of the Sala dell'Albergo off the second-floor hall. The judges were suitably impressed, and Tintoretto got the job. Over the next 23 years, the artist filled the *scuola's* two floors with dozens of works. The *Rest on the Flight into Egypt* on the ground floor is superb, but his masterpiece hangs in that tiny Sala dell'Albergo, a huge *Crucifixion* that wraps around the walls and ranks among the greatest and most moving works in the history of Venetian art. The San Rocco baroque orchestra holds excellent regular chamber concerts in this fantastic setting; for info, contact ☎ 041-962-999 or www.musicinvenice.com. See p. 129.

- **Veronese's *Feast in the House of Levi*, Accademia** (Venice): Paolo Veronese was a master of human detail, often peopling his large canvases with a rogues' gallery of characters. When Veronese unveiled his *Last Supper,* puritanical church bigwigs nearly had a conniption. They threatened him with charges of blasphemy for portraying this holiest of moments as a rousing, drunken banquet that more resembled paintings of Roman orgies than the Last Supper. Veronese quickly retitled the work *Feast in the House of Levi,* a rather less holy subject at which Jesus and Apostles were also present, and the mollified censors let it pass. See p. 128.

- **Giotto's Scrovegni Chapel** (Padua): Padua's biggest sight by far is one of the two towering fresco cycles created by Giotto (the other one is in Assisi), the artist who did more than any other to lift painting from its static Byzantine stupor and set it on the naturalistic, expressive, dynamic Gothic road toward the Renaissance. From 1303 to 1306, Giotto covered the walls of this private chapel with a range of emotion, using foreshortening, modeled figures, and saturated colors, revolutionizing the concept of art and kicking off the modern era in painting. The chapel as a whole is breathtaking, depicting scenes from the life of Mary and Jesus in 38 panels, and has recently emerged from a 3-year cleaning. See p. 161.

- **Leonardo da Vinci's *The Last Supper*, Santa Maria delle Grazie** (Milan): This tempera fresco looks somehow more like a snapshot of a real dinner table than the staged holy event that Last Suppers usually appear to be—instead of a hovering halo, Jesus' holy nimbus is suggested by the window behind his head. Leonardo was as much a scientist and inventor as he was painter, and unfortunately for us he was wont to try new painting techniques directly on his major commissions rather than testing them fully first. When painting one fresco in Florence, he used wax in the pigments, but when it was drying too slowly he put heaters along the wall, and the whole thing simply melted. Well, whatever chemistry he was experimenting with in Milan when Ludovico Il Moro hired him to decorate the refectory (dining hall) of Santa Maria della Grazie with a *Last Supper,* it didn't work properly. The fresco began deteriorating almost as soon as he finished painting it, and it had to be touched up and painted over several times in the succeeding centuries. It also didn't help when Napoléon's troops moved in and used the wall for target practice, or when Allied World War II bombs tore the roof off the building, miraculously not damaging the fresco but still leaving it open to the elements for 3 years. A lengthy restoration has stripped away the centuries of grime and overpainting, so what we see now is more or less pure Leonardo, even if the result is extremely patchy and looks rather faded. See p. 266.

- **Michelangelo's *Rondanini Pietà*, Castello Sforzesco** (Milan): Michelangelo's first great sculptural triumph was a *Pietà* he carved for Rome's St. Peter's at age 19. During a lifetime in which he became the foremost artist of his age, acknowledged as a genius in painting, fresco, architecture, and engineering, he never lost his love for marble and chisel. At age 89, he was

the Middle Ages. The frescoed figures strolling about the balconies of its central courtyard spout cartoon balloon–like scrolls of speech that are a treasure trove for linguists unlocking the origins of the local dialect, which is founded largely in

a medieval variant on French. The furnishings, though all genuine castle antiques, were culled from sources throughout this area, Switzerland, and France to give the place that medieval lived-in look. See p. 360.

6 The Best Villas & Palazzi

- **Palazzo Ducale** (Venice): The Gothic palazzo from which the Venetian Republic was ruled for centuries offers two incredible experiences. One simply is to wander the gorgeous rooms and halls, which are decorated with frescoes and paintings (including the world's largest oil canvas) by all the Venetian School greats, from Titian, Tintoretto, and Veronese on down. The placards in each room are marvelously informative, not only about the art but also about the function of each room and its role in government or daily Venetian life. But to discover what really made the Byzantine Venetian political machine tick, take the "Secret Itineraries" tour, which lets you slip behind the camouflaged doors and enter the hidden world of the palace-within-the-palace, the chambers in which the real governing took place, all wedged into the massive space between the inner and outer walls of the palazzo. See the chamber where the powerful Council of Ten met, the tiny office where the doge's secretary kept track of all the machinations going on in high society, the tribunal where three judges condemned the guilty and hanged them from the rafters, and the cramped "leads" cells under the roof from which Casanova famously escaped. Then saunter across the storied Bridge of Sighs to explore the dank, dungeonlike prisons across the canal where lesser criminals served out

their miserable terms—lagoon floods and all. See p. 121.
- **Ca d'Oro** (Venice): Though no longer graced with the decorative facade that earned Venice's most beautiful palazzo its name "House of Gold," the 15th-century Ca d'Oro remains one of the most gorgeous palaces in Venice, outside (see the main facade from the Grand Canal) and in. The gallery of art, donated—along with the palace—to the state by Baron Giorgio Franchetti in 1916, includes paintings by Van Dyck, Giorgione, Titian, and Mantegna. There's also a small ceramics museum and fantastic canal views. See p. 137.
- **Ca' Rezzonico** (Venice): Even though Venice was in fact well past its heyday in the 18th century and technically in decline, this is nonetheless the era in which the city expressed its own unique character fully, the age of Casanova and costume balls, all the things we picture when we think of Venice. To this end, the Rezzonico, built in 1667 by the same architect who crafted the baroque Santa Maria della Salute and topped with an extra story in 1745 (and once owned by poet Robert Browning), was turned into a museum of the 18th century. The powers-that-be wanted the "museum" moniker to be taken lightly; in reality what the city has done is outfit this gracious palazzo as an actual house from the era as closely as possible, using

pieces culled from across the city. To add to the 200-year time warp are a series of scenes from daily Venetian life painted by Pietro Longhi plus several carnival frescoes that Giandomenico Tiepolo (son of the more famous Giovanni Battista Tiepolo) originally painted for his own house. See p. 133.

- **Villa Pisani** (Stra, Brenta Canal): Tiepolo frescoed the ballroom for this massive 18th-century villa built for the family of a Venetian doge, though Napoléon bought it in 1807. Its most notorious moment, though, came in 1934 when two European leaders met here for their very first summit: Benito Mussolini and Adolf Hitler. The rooms are sumptuous, and the gardens are extensive and include a quirky hedge maze. See p. 168.

- **Villa Barbaro** (outside Asolo): Though the villas right around Vicenza get more visitors, this 1560 Palladio-designed masterpiece outside Asolo is perhaps the most gorgeous to visit. That's because it matches the perfect Palladian architecture with stunning frescoes by Veronese, which carpet almost every inch of wall and ceiling inside. And to think it's still actually in private hands (with owners gracious enough to allow visitors in)! See p. 177.

- **Villa Rotonda** (outside Vicenza): If you've seen Monticello, the architecture of Washington, D.C., or Inigo Jones's buildings, you'll be prepared for La Rotonda—it was the model for them all. UNESCO has placed this pinnacle of Palladio's architectural theories on the same World Heritage List as the pyramids, a towering monument of human achievement and ingenuity. This is Palladio's strict neoclassical take on the Renaissance in all its textbook glory, an ancient temple rewritten as a home and

softened by Renaissance geometry of line. It was also one of his last, started in 1567 but largely executed by a faithful follower after the master's death. See p. 185.

- **Villa Valmarana** (outside Vicenza): Mattoni's 17th-century Palladian-style villa is nicknamed *ai Nani,* or "of the dwarves," because its walls are patrolled by an army of stone dwarves. The architecture isn't all that remarkable, but the 18th-century frescoes inside by Giambattista and Giandomenico Tiepolo certainly are. See p. 185.

- **Palazzo Patriarcale** (Udine): Until 1734 it was the bishops who ruled Udine as Patriarchs, and the final Patriarch had the foresight to invite Tiepolo to Udine to decorate their palace with scenes from the Old Testament that double as early-18th-century fashion shows. There's also a fine collection of locally carved wood sculptures spanning the 13th to 18th centuries. See p. 251.

- **Palazzo Te** (Mantua): Raphael's protégé Giulio Romano, hounded from Rome over a scandalous series of erotic engravings, was let loose to fill libidinous Frederico Gonzaga's Mannerist pleasure palace with racy frescoes. The place was built to look as if it were crumbling, from arch keystones to the illusionistic frescoes in the Room of Giants. See p. 300.

- **Il Vittoriale** (Gardone, Lake Garda): Gabriele D'Annunzio was a Romantic ideal made flesh, an Italian Hemingway-meets-Shelley, an adventurer, soldier, and poet who carried on a torrid affair with the greatest actress of his age, Eleonora Duse, who napped on a funeral bier covered in leopard skins, and who crafted every iota of his villa in meticulous Victorian detail. It's said that Mussolini himself gave D'Annunzio the property—either to honor his vociferous support of Fascism or simply to shut him up before he said something to get them all into trouble. D'Annunzio was a bit of a hothead, and not much of a team player. In 1918 he flew to Vienna just to drop leaflets on it and prove to what he saw as the wimpy Italian military command that he could penetrate that far. When the Adriatic town of Fiume, previously promised to Italy, ended up in Yugoslav hands, he led his own army to occupy the town and claim it—much to the chagrin of the Italian commanders, who had to talk him into giving it up and coming home (this is the "victory" after which the villa is named). With a whole villa to keep him occupied, D'Annunzio proceeded to remake it to his own image. The very route guests take upon entering is a subtle and intricate play on the structure of Dante's *Divine Comedy.* The sheer volume of bric-a-brac is enough to drive a maid with a feather duster nuts, but is redeemed by the fantastic anecdote or quirky explanation behind each one (hope for a chatty guide with a good command of English). Nestled in the extravagant gardens are a structure built as a ship, the actual boat D'Annunzio commanded during the Great War, his biplane, and his heroic hilltop tomb. See p. 308.

- **Palazzo Reale (Royal Palace)** (Turin): This was where the Savoy kings hung their crowns in all the sumptuous, overwrought, gilded glory that the 17th and 18th centuries could offer. From Gobelin tapestries to Oriental vases, from the royal armory to the elegant gardens laid out by master landscape architect Le Nôtre (who did the Versailles gardens and those of the Tuileries in Paris), this palace drips with royal frippery. See p. 340.

- **Palazzina di Caccia di Stupinigi** (outside Turin): Sicilian baroque genius Juvarra laid out this extravagant and palatial hunting lodge for the Savoys in 1729. To fill the numerous frescoed rooms and vast halls of its giant, sinuous X-shape, local authorities have collected furnishings, paintings, and other decorative elements from dozens of Savoy palaces to create here a sort of museum of 18th- and 19th-century interior decor. Napoléon liked it so much he set up housekeeping here for a time when he first conquered the region before pressing on. See p. 341.

- **Galleria Nazionale di Palazzo Spinola** (Genoa): The Spinola provides its collection of canvases (by Antonello da Messina, Guido Reni, Luca Giordano, Van Dyck, and Strozzi) with a stellar backdrop consisting of a Genovese palace of which the merchant/banking Spinola family lavishly frescoed and decorated each room. See p. 377.

7 The Best Festivals

- **Carnevale** (Venice): Every spring Venice brings back the glory days of the 18th century in all its silk and brocade, poof-sleeved, men-wearing-colored-hose, Casanova, ballroom-dancing glory. In most Catholic countries, the week before Lent begins has long been a time to let down your hair and party. It all culminates in Shrove Tuesday, the day of feasting before Ash Wednesday kicks off the sober Lenten period. This bash has earned the day the nickname Fat Tuesday—called *Martedì Grasso* in Italian, but better known by its

French name, Mardi Gras. Venice ranks with Rio and New Orleans as host of one of the most elaborate and famous Carnival celebrations anywhere. Rather than a Bacchanalian bash, Venice goes the genteel route, with concerts and masked costume balls filling performance spaces, churches, and frescoed palaces. Ten days leading up to Shrove Tuesday. See p. 140 and 142.

- **Venice International Film Festival:** This is one of the movie business's premier festivals, ranking just below Cannes in importance. The best films made over the past year from around the world are screened for audiences and judges at the Palazzo del Cinema, other movie houses, and sometimes even open-air piazzas. Unlike, say, the Oscars, which celebrates highly promoted Hollywood products, this is a chance for all movies— from would-be blockbusters to low-budget, unknown indies—to catch the attention of critics and distributors. Late August/early September. See p. 141.

- **Biennale d'Arte** (Venice): One of the most important art festivals in the world is hosted every 2 years by the city of Venice. Contemporary artists (both celebrated modern masters and talented unknowns), critics, and art aficionados from around the world fill the hotels to attend shows and peruse the works displayed in the gardens and Arsenale warehouses at the far end of the Castello district. June to early November, odd years. See p. 141.

- **Regata Storica** (Venice): Every Venetian must have an 18th-century outfit mothballed in a closet to break out for yearly fetes such as Carnevale and, of course, this "historical regatta"—less of a race than merely a parade of gorgeously bedecked gondolas and other boats laden with costumed gentry for a day cruising the Grand Canal. First Sunday in September. See chapter 3.

- **Partita a Scacchi** (Marostica): A living chess match may be a throwaway gag to Mel Brooks or special-effect sequence in a Harry Potter film, but it's the highlight of Marostica's calendar. This pretty little medieval hamlet, which barely fills the bottom third of the ring made by its ancient wall clambering up the hillside, would probably be overlooked if it weren't for the biennial festival that turns the checkerboard main piazza in front of the castle into a weird piece of yesteryear. After a parade of costumed gentlefolk and medieval-style entertainers (jugglers, fire-eaters, clowns), people dressed as chess pieces fill the piazza's board, the players sit atop a stage ready to call out their moves, and the match begins. Actually, it's technically not chess as we know it but rather a medieval variant, and it's not a proper match since they're in fact re-creating, move for move, a game played in the 15th century between two noblemen vying for the hand of a fair lady. Still, it's all great fun. Marostica has only a handful of hotels, so book a few months in advance. Second Sunday in September, even years. See p. 181.

- **Concerti in Villa** (Vicenza): The Veneto region around Vicenza opens up its villas or their grounds for a series of summertime concerts and performances. From famous masterpieces like Palladio's La Rotonda to little-known Renaissance villas, the settings are memorable and the music is sweet. June and July. See p. 182.

- **Opera in Arena** (Verona): La Scala and La Fenice may be more famous, but few opera stages in Italy have a more natural dramatic setting than Verona's ancient Roman amphitheater. Every season they put on *Aïda* as they have since 1913, surrounded by other operatic masterpieces by Giuseppe Verdi. For a huge 2,000-year-old sports stadium open to the sky, the Arena enjoys surprisingly good acoustics. Late June through August. See p. 193.

- **Festival Shakespeariano** (Verona): Verona mixes its two powerhouse attractions—ancient Roman heritage and Shakespearean fame—in a theater festival of Shakespeare's plays (along with ballets and concerts, from classical to jazz) put on in the garden-set ruins of the Teatro Romano ancient theater. Since 1998 they've invited the Royal Shakespeare Company to come and perform (naturally) *Romeo and Juliet* and *Two Gentlemen of Verona,* as well as other plays, in English. See p. 190.
- **Palio** (Asti): Medieval pageantry precedes a breakneck horse race on the piazza. The 2 weeks leading up to it comprise the **Douja d'Or,** a grape-and-wine festival and trade fair. Rival town **Alba** spoofs the event with a race of their own—riding asses—in their **Palio degli Asini** on the first Sunday in

October. Third Sunday in October. See p. 349.

- **Sanremo Festival** (San Remo): It's the Grammy Awards meets Sundance meets Star Search. Since 1950 Sanremo has been Italy's beloved festival of pop music, where faded Italian stars get to strut their stuff, major international rock stars and artists are invited to play, and scruffy teenage musicians from across Italy get the chance to play that carefully crafted song they just know would be a number-one hit if only they could sign a record contract (and many do). If you want to hear what will be belting out of boomboxes and Fiat speakers this summer at Italy's beaches and pumping in the discos, listen to the winning performances here. Late February or early March. See p. 386.
- **Sagra del Pesce** (Camogli): Take the world's largest frying pan (3.6m/12 ft. across) and place it on the wide, waterfront promenade of this tiny Riviera fishing town. Fill the pan with sizzling sardines and the town with hungry folks ready to party. There you have a *sagra,* or celebration of food, in this case of seafood, the town's traditional economic lynchpin. Second Sunday in May. See p. 397.

8 The Best Luxury Inns

- **Hotel Gritti Palace** (Venice): The grandest hotel on the Grand Canal, hosting the crème de la crème of whoever came and comes to visit Venice since Doge Andrea Gritti built the palace in the 16th century. Charles de Gaulle, Winston Churchill, Truman Capote, John Ruskin, Henry Ford, Mick Jagger, Giorgio Armani, Robert De Niro, Charlie Chaplin . . . the list goes on. This place is luxury-everything: hand-painted and inlaid antiques,

18th-century stuccoed ceilings, cutting-edge designer entertainment centers, and, of course, balconies overlooking the Grand Canal (well, from the top-notch rooms at least; everyone else gets to enjoy the water from the restaurant or piano bar, or can overlook a side canal). Because this is now a Westin property, you also get access (on a free hourly boat) to their Lido Westin Excelsior hotel and its facilities (see below). See p. 89.

- **Hotel Danieli** (Venice): Venice's *bacino* (the bay into which the Grand Canal spills) is lined with luxury hotels, but none beats the Danieli, a 14th-century doge's palace of pink plaster and elaborate marble windowsills that's been a hotel since 1822. The centerpiece is a four-story, sky-lit enclosed courtyard of Byzantine-Gothic arches, open stairwells, balustrades, and junglelike potted plants off of which open its luxurious salons. It's worth popping your head in just to see it even if you don't stay here. The rooms vary, but no matter what, insist upon a lagoon view— and try to stay in the original wing or, failing that, the larger rooms of the 19th-century palazzo next door (by all means avoid the bland, albeit cushy, 1940s wing). As with its Westin sister, Hotel Gritti Palace, you can enjoy the facilities at the chain's Excelsior on the Lido (see below). See p. 94.

- **Hotel Cipriani** (Venice): This is the last independent, locally owned luxury hotel in Venice, and quite possibly the best. It sits in splendid isolation at the tip of Giudecca, the only large island of central Venice not connected by a bridge (rather, it's a 10-min. boat ride to Piazza San Marco). Giuseppe Cipriani, the Venetian impresario behind Harry's Bar and the Locanda Cipriani on Torcello where Ernest Hemingway loved to hang out (he even made it into a Papa story), crafted this retreat out of several Renaissance palazzi in 1959, offering stylish accommodations, discreet service, and modern comfort. See p. 105.

- **Westin Excelsior** (Venice): The Lido might never have been developed as a bathing resort if not for the prescience of Nicolò Spada, who created the Excelsior's Moorish-style central structure in 1907.

As one of Venice's only custom-built luxury hotels, it didn't have to abide by all the historical considerations converted palazzi now have to take into account, so its architectural plans allowed for more spacious accommodations than those found in most Venetian hotels. Rooms overlook either the Adriatic (there's a private beach across the road) or the small, lush, Moorish garden. It also sports all the resort-type amenities: pool, fitness center, golf and tennis, sauna. See p. 106.

- **Villa Margherita** (Mira Porte, Brenta): This villa's role as a guesthouse hasn't changed much since it was built in the 17th century by Venice's Contarini family. It still looks much like a country-villa home (if your family happened to be Venetian and fabulously wealthy), with rooms overlooking the shady gardens, a restaurant across the street along the canal, and a similar sister property nearby with a swimming pool. See p. 170.

- **Hotel Villa Cipriani** (Asolo): In 1962 Giuseppe Cipriani branched out from his premium-grade Venice mini-empire to turn this 16th-century villa into a well-appointed hotel. Once the home of poets Robert and Elizabeth Barrett Browning, it enjoys a dreamlike setting: the medieval hill town of Asolo, famed for its vistas over the Veneto. See p. 176.

- **Hotel Greif** (Bozen): Boutique hotels have officially arrived in Italy—though so far only the Greif seems to have heard. The Staffler family has owned this 500-year-old hotel on the main square of Bozen—the Dolomiti's liveliest town—since 1796. But in 1999 and 2000, they decided to overhaul it completely in a minimalist, modern vein of burnished steel and original contemporary art mixed with 19th-century antiques and an Internet-equipped laptop in every room. See p. 218.

- **Four Seasons Hotel Milano** (Milan): In 1993 the Four Seasons opened and rewrote the rules on deluxe hotels in Milan. Seven years were spent restructuring and transforming a 1476 convent, a process that brought many of its Renaissance elements back to light, including a lovely cloister. The rooms are huge by Italian city standards and flush with amenities and small luxuries such as CD stereos and king-size beds. The bi-level suites with frescoed vaulting are particularly nice. See p. 276.

- **Grand Hotel et De Milan** (Milan): How do you define superior service? While resident guest Giuseppe Verdi, who lived for 30 years in the suite now named for him, lay dying in his bed, the hotel spread straw over the streets under his window every day to muffle the sounds of carriage wheels so as not to disturb the maestro's rest. They're constantly updating the luxury quotient here—even closing down from 1993 to 1995 for a complete overhaul (perhaps a response to the sudden competition from the Four Seasons)—to keep the 1863 hotel looking and feeling its best. This means marble and lush upholstery, thick curtains, and antique furnishings. Okay, so the opera music trickling lightly from hidden speakers may be overdoing it, but what did you expect from a hotel 3 blocks from La Scala that has played host to divas and tenors for decades? See p. 277.

- **Villa d'Este** (Cernobbio, Lake Como): On short lists of the world's greatest hotels, the Villa d'Este always ranks near the top. There's nothing reproduction or faux about this place. The villa is true Renaissance, the marble precious, the guestbook A-list, and the

Empire furnishings so genuine they actually date back to Napoléon's tenure when his aide-de-camp owned it. Add to all that several pools (one floating on the lake), a vast park that hides tennis courts, a fitness center that includes squash courts and a virtual driving range, and a trio of restaurants. See p. 317.

- **Grand Hôtel et des Iles Borromées** (Stresa, Lake Maggiore): Ernest Hemingway loved this retreat by the lake so much he set part of *A Farewell to Arms* at the hotel. Shell out $2,400 and you can stay in the suite named after him (two bedrooms with king-size beds and huge marble bathrooms in each, frescoed ceilings, lake-view terrace). Recent renovations have restored the decor to its original 1860s splendor and richness, regilding an old lily of the Italian hotel scene and restoring it to the ranks of Europe's most exclusive hotels. Rooms are sumptuously appointed in a variety of styles, from 19th-century inlaid wood to lavish Empire style to opulent Italianate rooms of lacquered furnishings and Murano chandeliers. See p. 328.

- **Hotel Splendido/Splendido Mare** (Portofino): Portofino is the fishing village chosen by the world's jet-set elite as their own little bit of Italy, its tiny cove harbor overshadowed by yachts, and the hillside Splendido hotel booked by the top names from Hollywood, European nobility registers, and CEO boardrooms. The villa itself is 19th century, though its foundation is a 16th-century monastery, set amid olive groves a 10-minute walk above the town. Suites come with antique furnishings and cutting-edge entertainment centers (DVD anyone?). Their sister hotel, Splendido Mare, sits right at the harborfront, stays open all year, and offers dining with a view of the boats. See p. 406.

- **Royal Hotel** (San Remo): With such a small town and such a major pop festival, once a year you'll find a concentration of rock stars here rarely seen outside of a major benefit concert. The rest of the year, with doubles starting at $228, almost all of us can enjoy its private beach across the road, its cushy accommodations, its stuccoed bar, and the wonderful pool styled as if it were carved out of rock. See p. 388.

9 The Best Moderate Hotels

- **Pensione Accademia** (Venice): If you ever wanted to live like Katharine Hepburn, here's your chance. Well, not exactly, though her character did live in this 16th-century Villa Maravege (Villa of Wonders) in the 1955 film *Summertime*. It sits in an enviable position, a flower-filled garden at the confluence of two canals emptying into the Grand Canal, and the rooms are done in a tasteful antique style that makes you feel as if you're staying in the home of your wealthy Venetian relative rather than in a hotel. See p. 100.

- **Hotel San Cassiano Ca' Favretto** (Venice): It's one of the cheapest hotels on the Grand Canal—plus the rooms and bar terrace overlook the prettiest stretch of the canal, with the Ca d'Oro directly across the waters. Even most non–Grand Canal rooms at least overlook a side canal. All that and the hotel in the 16th-century villa retains much of its 18th-century ambience (though room decor is vintage 1970s repro antiques). See p. 102.

- **Hotel Majestic Toscanelli** (Padua): The management of the Toscanelli is always reinvesting in this gem of a hotel three quiet shop- and osteria-lined blocks from the central Piazza delle Erbe. Its latest refurbishment came in 1999, with burnished cherry furnishings gracing the spacious rooms. The reception is warm and helpful, and the location excellent. See p. 166.

- **Hotel Aurora** (Verona): Situated right on the central piazza and overhauled in 1996 to freshen the furnishings and fixtures, the Aurora enjoys a combination of prime location, low prices, and perfect simple comfort that keep guests coming back. See p. 199.

- **Antica Locanda Solferino** (Milan): The most wonderfully eclectic hotel in Milan exudes character. It sits in the heart of the fashionable Brera neighborhood, its quirky amalgam of furnishings fitted into generally spacious rooms. With one of the friendliest managements in town under Sig. Gerardo Vitolo, it's no wonder this delightful place stays booked by regulars, who enjoy its creaky, homey atmosphere. See p. 277.

- **Agnello d'Oro** (Bergamo): Bergamo may not quite be the Alps, but you're high up enough in their foothills that this tall, narrow ochre building with its flower-box windows, patio fountain, and sloping roof looks perfectly appropriate, offering a bit of Italianate Alpine charm smack-dab in the center of the pedestrianized medieval quarter. Furnishings are simple and serviceable, but the price and location can't be beat. See p. 295.

- **Du Lac** (Bellagio, Lake Como): Of the hotels lining Bellagio's little lakefront piazza, the Du Lac is the friendliest by a long shot. For over a century and a half, it has offered comfort and genuine hospitality, from the panoramic dining room and rooftop sun terrace to the simple but fully stocked rooms and the bar tables tucked under the arcades of the sidewalk. They're also putting in a pool and tennis courts. See p. 319.

- **Verbano** (Stresa, Lake Maggiore): Why shell out hundreds of dollars for a hotel by the lake when you can have one *on* the lake for half the price? The dusty rose villa of the Verbano sits at the tip of Isola dei Pescatori, an island of colorful fishermen's houses in the midst of Lake Maggiore, with views over the landscaped Isola Bella, the lake, and the Alps beyond from most rooms and also from the gravelly terrace, where they serve excellent meals. See p. 328.

10 The Best Budget Gems

- **Hotel La Residenza** (Venice): Just off the highly fashionable Riva degli Schiavoni sits one of the great remaining cheap pensioni in Italy, a 15th-century palazzo converted into an inexpensive hotel. Hotels this cheap are hard to come by anywhere in Venice, let alone in such a prime location, and nowhere else with such remarkable decor and faded style. Its 15 rooms occupy the *piano nobile,* the high-ceilinged "noble floor" where the wealthy family once lived, so it sports 18th-century stuccoes over Venetian-style furnishings, 17th-century oil paintings, and Murano chandeliers. See p. 98.
- **Foresteria Valdese (Palazzo Cavagnis)** (Venice): If La Residenza (see above) is full, you may luck into even more decaying style (18th-century frescoes decorate the ceilings in several rooms) for less money at this 16th-century palazzo run as a hospice by the Waldesian and Methodist Church. The drawbacks are that it's a sort of hostel-type arrangement—many, but not all, of the accommodations are shared rooms—and the rooms lack amenities such as telephones and air-conditioning. The location isn't quite as sweet as that of La Residenza, but the rooms do have balconies over a lovely small side canal. See p. 96.
- **Hotel Galleria** (Venice): This place is remarkable: a 17th-century palazzo with double rooms for under $100, a half dozen of which open directly onto the Grand Canal, and it's next door to one of Venice's top sights, the Accademia Gallery. All that and you get breakfast (including freshly baked bread) in bed. See p. 99.
- **Pensione Guerrato** (Venice): This charming pensione is run by a pair of brothers-in-law in a converted 13th-century convent near the daily Rialto market. The furnishings are mismatched but lovely, a mix of antiques culled from markets over the years, and the breakfast is excellent. They also rent two great apartments at excellent prices near San Marco. See p. 101.
- **Hotel Bernardi-Semenzato** (Venice): The friendly Pepoli family runs this well-maintained palazzo hidden a block off the main drag about halfway between the train station and San Marco. It's surrounded by *osterie* and good restaurants patronized by locals, and the modernized rooms retain rough wood-beam ceilings and antique-style furnishings. They also rent simple but spacious rooms in two annexes nearby that make you feel as if you're staying in your own Venetian apartment; one room has a fireplace, another

overlooks a pair of side canals. See p. 104.

- **Due Mori** (Vicenza): Just off the central Piazza dei Signori lies this simple, no-frills, but comfortable hotel, the oldest in Vicenza, packed with genuine 19th-century antiques and a friendly reception. See p. 187.

- **Grifone** (Sirmione, Lake Garda): Would you believe a vine-covered hotel where the simple rooms enjoy views of the lake and access to a small beach for under $35 a person? Well that's what the Marcolini siblings offer at this gem of an inn around the corner from the little medieval castle. Book early. See p. 306.

- **Ostello La Primula** (Menaggio, Lake Como): If you don't mind hostel living (shared dorm rooms, bus your own table at dinner), you can get a bed overlooking the lake for $16 and some of the best fixed-price dinners in town for just $8. It's run by a family of ex–social workers, who also rent bikes and kayaks. See p. 325.

- **Fasce** (Santa Margherita Ligure): This little hotel a few blocks up from the harbor is now in its third generation of family management, which includes the incredibly helpful British-born Jane at the front desk. Not only are the bright guest rooms spacious and comfortable and the surroundings a lovely profusion of plants and flowers, but they pile on the extras, from free bicycles to Cinque Terre packets for guests who stay at least 3 nights (including a train ticket a day and all the info you need to explore the coast). See p. 401.

11 The Best Countryside Retreats

- **Cavallino d'Oro/Goldenes Rössl** (Kastelruth/Castelrotto, near Bozen): The village is a full-bore Tirolean mountain hamlet straight out of the Middle Ages, and this rambling hotel has sat at the cobblestoned center of town since the 1400s, its swinging shingle emblazoned with its Golden Horse moniker. It includes the corner bar where the locals hang out for lunch and a genuine, preserved 18th-century *Stuben* (beer nook) in the restaurant at back. It's a nice mix of new and old: The lounge has a widescreen TV with 300 digital channels set next to a picture window of the Alps; the rooms offer modern comforts amid hand-painted wood furnishings and four-poster beds. Best of all, the Urthaler family couldn't be more welcoming, and they happen to be Frommer's fans. See p. 220.

- **Hotel Castello Schloss Labers** (outside Merano): The road from town wends its way through vine-clad hills to the Stapf-Neubert family's 11th-century countryside castle, a hotel since 1885. The cozy hunting salons cluster around a magnificent central staircase that leads up to the eclectic collection of rooms tucked into towers, eaves, and high-ceilinged rooms. A statue-studded garden out back offers views across the valley to the surrounding peaks, and they also have a heated pool, tennis courts, and a Tirolean restaurant. See p. 226.

- **Villa Fiordaliso** (Gardone Riviera, Lake Garda): This Liberty-style villa was built in 1903 and immediately started attracting formidable owners, including poet Gabriele d'Annunzio and later Claretta Petacci, Mussolini's mistress (this is where they spent their final weeks in semi-hiding at the end of World War II before being hunted down and killed). Things have calmed down considerably since then, the villa transformed in 1990 into one of the most popular high-end restaurants in the lake region (it even has a Michelin star now), with seven elegant guest rooms upstairs. See p. 309.

- **Villa La Meridiana/Az. Agrituristica Reine** (near Alba): An *agriturismo* is a working farm whose family opens their home and hospitality to guests. The Pionzo family runs this gracious *agriturismo* above the Piedmont wine town of Alba, with rooms in the main house and converted from the former stalls, almost all overlooking the vineyards that produce their Barbera wine, the surrounding village-capped hills, and the peaks of the Alps in the distance. The ample breakfast may include apricot preserves from their own orchard and sheep's milk cheese from the neighbors. See p. 353.

- **La Cascina del Monastero** (outside La Morra): The di Grasso family runs an *agriturismo* similar to Villa La Meridiana (see above), another vineyard and fruit orchard farm outside a Piemontese village with large guest rooms and apartments filled with comfortable rustic furnishings and exposed wood beams. This place would be worth staying at if only for the sumptuous breakfast spread, the only drawback to which is that you may have to cancel lunch plans and head back to your room for a nap. See p. 356.

- **Milleluci** (outside Aosta): Four matrilineal generations of hoteliers have turned this family farm into one of the coziest, friendliest hotels in the whole of the Valle d'Aosta. A fire crackles in the large lounge downstairs, and the rooms are done in woodsy, Alpine style with canopy beds in suites, traditional wood furnishings, and hand-hewn ceilings. In true country tradition, the breakfast here is overwhelming, with freshly baked pies, cakes, and breads every morning accompanied by farm-fresh cheese, milk, and preserves. Unlike most countryside retreats, the Milleluci sports plenty of facilities a four-star hotel would be jealous of: a heated outdoor pool, tennis courts, exercise facilities, hot tub, and sauna. See p. 362.

- **La Grange** (Courmayeur-Entrèves): Entrèves may not properly be countryside, but this tiny collection of Alpine chalets below the Mont Blanc cable-car station is so small it barely qualifies as a village, and the atmosphere is fully rustic. The Berthold family converted this hotel from a barn by fitting the rooms with a mix of antiques and sturdy country furnishings. It makes a refreshing (and far less expensive) alternative to the resort hotels of Courmayeur just down the road. See p. 366.

12 The Best Restaurants

- **Do Forni** (Venice): Though the menu is vast, they seem to devote equal attention to every single dish, making this one of the best (if most eyebrow-raisingly expensive) restaurants in Venice. The bulk of the place is done in a vaguely rustic style, but the best room is the front one, fitted out like a car from the luxurious Orient Express. See p. 110.

- **La Cusina** (Venice): One of the new stars on the Venetian restaurant scene is also one of the few hotel dining rooms worth singling out. In warm weather this becomes one of the most romantic dinner settings in town, the tables set on terraces hanging over the Grand Canal. The location alone is worth booking ahead, but happily the cooking is as delicious as the view is stunning, offering an inventive take on Italian cuisine based on Venetian and Veneto traditions and using the freshest ingredients. See p. 111.

- **Le Bistrot de Venise** (Venice): The menu at this upscale bistro is split three ways to satisfy your appetite (or at least make your choice harder): Venetian/Italian, French, and ancient local recipes culled from historic cookbooks and documents. They attract hip artistic types by turning the back room into a coffeehouse-style performance space most nights, hosting poets, acoustic musicians, art exhibits, and cabarets. See p. 112.

- **Al Covo** (Venice): Texan Diane Rankin makes the pastries and chats with guests while husband-chef Cesare Benelli watches over the kitchen at this always-popular restaurant that mixes a warm welcome and excellent fresh seafood dishes with relatively reasonable prices (especially on the quality wine list). See p. 115.

- **La Milanese** (Milan): In a city with many fine restaurants whose stars rise and fall almost as soon as they make it onto the map, La Milanese is a stalwart survivor, a traditional trattoria that has never stopped offering typical Milanese dishes, smart service, and moderate prices, a formula that has kept it successful for almost 70 years now. See p. 282.

- **Antica Hosteria del Vino Buono** (Bergamo): This cozy restaurant is spread over two floors of a corner palazzo on the market square. The food is mountain-style, rib-sticking good, heavy on the game meats and thick polenta accompanied by hearty red wines. See p. 297.

- **Ochina Bianca** (Mantua): Mantuan cooking is somewhat more complex than most northern Italian cuisines, and the Venturinis put their own innovative spin on it at the "White Goose," marrying local ingredients with fresh fish from the Mincio and game in this elegant restaurant. See p. 303.

- **C'era Una Volta** (Turin): That you have to ring the bell and climb to the first floor gives this place a clubby air, but owner Piero Prete will instantly make you feel like a longtime member as he greets you warmly and comes back around to help you select your wine. The cooking is traditional Torinese, excellently prepared. See p. 344.

- **Lalibera** (Alba): Franco and Manuele reign over this stylish dining room on an alley off a pedestrian shopping street, with Marco in the kitchen crafting excellent variants on Piemontese cuisine by using only the freshest of ingredients, all locally produced, from the cheese to the fruit to the meats. See p. 354.

13 The Best Countryside Eateries

- **Al Camin** (outside of Cortina d'Ampezzo): This barnlike structure lies along the rushing Ru Bigontina mountain stream, 10 minutes outside of town, serving hearty Alpine food in a woodsy dining room around a stone fireplace. Some regional specialties that are hard to find elsewhere these days are staples on Al Camin's seasonal menus. See p. 237.

- **L'Osteria del Vignaiolo** (La Morra): This place is sophisticated rustic, simple rooms with pale-gold walls expanding to tables outside in summer. It's set amid the vineyards that produce its excellent wines and provide the excellent views. The cooking, in the hands of chef Luciano Marengo, samples from the varied bounty of Piemontese regional cuisines, accompanied by choice cheese platters and, of course, some of the best fine wines in Italy. See p. 356.

- **La Maison de Filippo** (Entrèves): This is the never-ending meal to beat all feasts. I honestly tried to keep track of the courses, but after the seventh appetizer I had to give it up. But it's not just quantity (two words: pace yourself): The food actually manages to be fantastic as well, and it's served in an archetypal rustic-countryside dining room of low wood ceilings, open kitchens, and sometimes even a dog under the table. Book here, then plan to spend much of the next day merely digesting. See p. 367.

14 The Best Down-Home Trattorie & Osterie

- **Vino Vino** (Venice): Antico Martini is a pricey but good restaurant near La Fenice opera house; Vino Vino is its worst-kept secret, an inexpensive *osteria* branch that serves simple but tasty dishes that come out of the same kitchen. You choose from the daily chalkboard menu, stake out a table, and then carry your meal to it along with a wine from their excellent and extensive shared wine cellar. See p. 114.

- **Ai Tre Spiedi** (Venice): This is where I take my buddies for a blow-out Venetian meal at remarkably low prices—not the cheapest in town, but perhaps the best value for your money. The owners are jolly, and the food is excellent, including the fish (which is often dicey at the more inexpensive places in Venice). See p. 114.

- **Cantina do Mori** (Venice): Notwithstanding the recent change in management (and a slight price hike), the Cantina do Mori has remained one of the best *bacari* in Venice, a wine bar that serves exquisite *cicchetti* (tapaslike snacks) to a crowd of regulars nightly under the low-beamed ceilings that seem unchanged since the joint opened in 1462. After all, this is the place where even Casanova supposedly came to tipple between affairs. See p. 118.

- **Toni del Spin** (Treviso): Seventy years of satisfying Trevisani diners has imparted a patina of reliability to this down-home trattoria of crisscrossing beams, swirling fans, and chalkboard menus. The choices are limited, but each dish is excellent, mixing local traditions with experimental cooking and some international dishes. The wine list is stellar—they also run the wine shop across the street. See p. 173.

- **La Taverna di Via Stella** (Verona): The Vantini brothers and their buddies have successfully started a brand-new, laid-back *osteria* that instantly feels as if it's been around for centuries. Here, the local volunteer fire squad shows up to hang out in uniform and hit on girls, and office workers troop in to unwind over traditional Veronese dishes and wine (of their some 180 bottles, 10 varieties are opened nightly so that you can sample by the glass). See p. 202.

- **Osteria del Duca** (Verona): The ladies bustling around this old fave of a trattoria know to doublecheck with foreign visitors who have inadvertently ordered one of the many traditional Veronese dishes involving horse or donkey meat. The setting is romantic in true Verona style: It's on the ground floor of a medieval palazzo that most likely belonged to the historical Montecchi family, immortalized by Shakespeare as the Montagues, whose son Romeo fell in love with Juliet of the enemy Capulet clan. See p. 202.

- **Vineria Cozzi** (Bergamo): Leonardo Vigorelli's wine bar is the turnstile around which Bergamo's upper city spins, a requisite stop for locals and visitors alike who enjoy his hospitality, good wine selection, and yummy panini, meat and cheese platters, and simple dishes. See p. 297.

2

Planning Your Trip to Northern Italy

Northern Italy ranges from the dreamy canals and Byzantine mosaics of Venice to the crowded streets and high-fashion boutiques of Milan, the fishing villages and chichi resorts along the Ligurian Riviera to chalet ski resorts in the Alps and Dolomites, and the Roman architecture and *Romeo and Juliet* memories of Verona to the vine-draped hills of Piedmont.

Sumptuous villas are strung along the shores of Como, Maggiore, and Garda, long lakes that start in the plains and run crookedly north to jut into the sheer peaks marking the Alpine boundary with Switzerland. Medieval castles outnumber towns in the valleys of Aosta and the Tirolean Upper Adige, where Italian is a foreign tongue and the lingua francas are ancient dialects of French and German, respectively.

Northern Italy offers a cornucopia of everything that makes Italy so seductive, from the grand old port cities of Genoa and Trieste to the Palladian architecture–graced art cities of the Veneto. This chapter will help make sense of it all, help you make the hard choices of which bits to visit, and get you on your way planning the details of your dream vacation.

1 The Regions in Brief

Italy as we know it was only united in the 1860s, and people still tend to identify themselves more as Milanese, Venetians, or Ligurians than as Italians. Regional dialects are so diverse and strong that for a Venetian to converse with a Milanese, he has to resort to the common "textbook Italian" learned in school. For many who reside in the upper reaches of the Alps, Dolomites, and South Tirol, Italian is actually a second language after their native Germanic or Frankish dialect.

Here's a quick description of the regions covered in this guide to help you decide where you want to go.

VENICE & THE VENETO

The Po River created the vast floodplain of the **Veneto** under the brow of pre-Venetian Alps to the north and the Dolomites in the west. What draws visitors to these agricultural flatlands are the art treasures of **Padua (Padova),** the Renaissance villas of Palladio in **Vicenza,** the ancient Roman and pseudo-Shakespearean sights of **Verona,** and—rising on pilings from a lagoon on the Adriatic coast—that most serene city of canals and year-round carnival, **Venice (Venezia).**

THE FRIULI-VENEZIA GIULIA

This forgotten northeast corner of Italy marks the border with Slovenia, a region of tame Alps, rolling hills, and Adriatic beaches. Its culture lies at the crossroads of Italy, Yugoslavia, and Austria—the Adriatic port city of **Trieste** was once the main port for Vienna and the Hapsburgs, and has the coffeehouses to prove it. The influence of the old neighboring sea power Venice is still strong in its staunch ally of **Udine,** while nearby **Cividale dei Friuli** preserves remnants of cultures from the Celts through the Lombards, with coastal **Aquiliea** weighing in with Roman ruins and mosaics.

THE DOLOMITES & SOUTH TIROL

The **Dolomites,** bordering Austria, cap the eastern stretches of the **South Tirol** region with sharp pinnacles straight out of a fairy tale, while the peaks of the Alps crown the west. This region is comprised of legendary resorts like **Cortina d'Ampezzo** and **Merano,** as well as cities such as **Trent (Trento)** and **Bozen (Bolzano**—home to a fascinating international scientific treasure, the prehistoric "Ice Man") that lie at the crossroads of the German and Italian worlds.

MILAN & LOMBARDY

Lombardy (Lombardia) is Italy's wealthiest province, an industrial, financial, and agricultural powerhouse named for the Lombards, a Germanic people who migrated south over the Alps in the early Dark Ages (they were part of the barbarian hordes that overran the Roman Empire). Beyond its Po Valley factories and cities, the scenic diversity of this prosperous region ranges from legendary lakes like **Como, Garda,** and **Maggiore** backed by Alpine peaks to the fertile plains of the Po River. The region's capital, **Milan (Milano)**—hotbed of high fashion, high finance, and avant-garde design— is a city of great art and architecture (Leonardo's *Last Supper* is but the beginning), and the region's Renaissance past is still much in evidence in mountain town **Bergamo,** merchant city **Mantua (Mantova),** musical **Cremona** (where Stradivarius once crafted his violins), and the other cities of the Lombard plains.

PIEDMONT & THE VALLE D'AOSTA

Piedmont (Piemonte) means "foot of the mountains," and the Alps are in sight from almost every parcel of Italy's northernmost province, which borders Switzerland and France. The flat plains of the Po River rise into rolling hills clad with orchards and vineyards. North of **Turin**—the historic baroque capital of the region and, with its wealth of auto factories, a cornerstone of Italy's "economic miracle"—the plains meet the Alps head-on in the **Valle d'Aosta,** with its craggy mountains, rugged mountain folk, and year-round skiing at resorts such as **Courmayeur** and **Entrèves** in the shadow of **Mont Blanc.**

LIGURIA: THE ITALIAN RIVIERA

The Italian Riviera follows the Ligurian Sea along a narrow coastal band backed by mountains. At the center of the rocky coast of **Liguria** is **Genoa (Genova),** the country's first port and still its most important—a fascinating city that greets visitors with a remarkable assemblage of Renaissance art and architecture. Some of Italy's most famous seaside retreats flank Genoa on either side, from the tony resort of **San Remo** on France's doorstep all the way down to the picturesque string of fishing villages known as the **Cinque Terre** that line the coast just above Tuscany.

2 Visitor Information

TOURIST OFFICES

For information before you go, contact the **Italian National Tourist Office (Ente Nazionale Italiano per il Turismo,** or ENIT). The Web address is **www.italiantourism.com.** You can also write directly (in English or Italian) to the provincial or local tourist boards of areas you plan to visit, but don't expect Swiss efficiency with a return response.

Canada Customs and Revenue Agency (© 800/461-9999 in Canada, or 204/983-3500; www.ccra-adrc.gc.ca).

For Australian Citizens A helpful brochure available from Australian consulates or Customs offices is *Know Before You Go.* For more information, call the **Australian Customs Service** at © **1300/363-263,** or log on to www.customs.gov.au.

For New Zealand Citizens Most questions can be answered in a free pamphlet available at New Zealand consulates and Customs offices: *New Zealand Customs Guide for Travellers, Notice no. 4.* For more information, contact **New Zealand Customs,** The Customhouse, 17–21 Whitmore St., Box 2218, Wellington (© **04/473-6099** or 0800/428-786; www.customs.govt.nz).

4 Money

Italy falls somewhere in the middle of pricing in Europe—not as expensive as, say, England, Switzerland, or Scandinavia, but not as cheap as Spain and Greece. Northern Italy, especially Venice and Milan, is one of the costliest regions of Italy to travel through, but the advice in this book should help guide you to the best options to fit any budget.

Luckily, ATMs (automated teller machines) are now to be found just about everywhere, even in the smallest towns, so cash is readily available, and as luck would have it, banks in Italy do not (as of yet) charge you a fee for using their bank—though your home bank probably will for using an out-of-network ATM, and these days often a premium for withdrawing foreign currency (for more, see "ATMs," below).

It's a good idea to exchange at least some money—just enough to cover airport incidentals and transportation to your hotel—before you leave home, so you can avoid lines at airport ATMs. You can exchange money at your local American Express or Thomas Cook office or your bank (often, though, only at the major branches). If you're far away from a bank with currency-exchange services, American Express offers traveler's checks and foreign currency, though with a $15 order fee and additional shipping costs, at www.american express.com or **800/807-6233.**

CURRENCY

In January 2002 Italy retired the lira and joined most of western Europe in switching to the euro. Coins are issued in denominations of .01€, .02€, .05€, .10€, .20€, and .50€ as well as 1€ and 2€; bills come in denominations of 5€, 10€, 20€, 50€, 100€, 200€, and 500€.

Exchange rates (see box below) are established daily and listed in most international newspapers. To get a transaction as close to this rate as possible, pay for as much as possible with credit cards and get cash out of ATMs. Traveler's checks, while still the safest way to carry money, are going the way of the dinosaur. The aggressive evolution of international computerized banking and consolidated ATM networks has led to the triumph of plastic throughout the Italian peninsula—even if cold cash is still the

---

Currency Converter

All the prices in this book were calculated at the rate of 1€ to $1.15. However, the exchange rate constantly fluctuates. The current rates are listed in the business and travel sections of most newspapers, and online at www.oanda.com.

Tips Dear Visa: I'm Off to Italy!

Some credit card companies recommend that you notify them of any impending trip abroad so that they don't become suspicious when the card is used numerous times in a foreign destination and block your charges. Even if you don't call your credit card company in advance, you can always call the card's toll-free emergency number if a charge is refused—a good reason to carry the phone number with you. But perhaps the most important lesson is to carry more than one card on your trip; if one card doesn't work for any number of reasons, you'll have a backup card just in case.

most trusted currency, especially in smaller towns or cheaper mom-and-pop joints, where credit cards may not be accepted.

You'll get the best rate if you **exchange money** at a bank or one of its ATMs. The rates at "Cambio/change/wechsel" exchange booths are invariably less favorable but still a good deal better than what you'd get exchanging money at a hotel or shop (a last-resort tactic only). The bill-to-bill changers you'll see in some touristy places exist solely to rip you off.

ATMS

The ability to access your personal checking account through the **Cirrus** (✆ **800/424-7787;** www.mastercard.com) or **PLUS** (✆ **800/843-7587;** www.visa.com) network of ATMs—or get a cash advance on an enabled Visa or MasterCard—has been growing by leaps and bounds in Italy in the last few years. It works just like at home. All you need do is search out a machine that has your network's symbol displayed (which these days is practically all of them), pop in your card, and punch in your PIN. It'll spit out local currency drawn directly from your home checking account (and at a more favorable rate than converting traveler's checks or cash). Also keep in mind that many banks impose a fee every time a card is used at a different bank's ATM, and that fee can be higher for international transactions (up to $5 or more) than

for domestic ones (where they're rarely more than $1.50). However, as I mentioned above, banks in Italy do not (at least yet) charge you a second fee to use their ATMs. To compare banks' ATM fees within the U.S., use www.bankrate.com. For international withdrawal fees, ask your bank.

An ATM in Italian is a *Bancomat* (though Bancomat is a private company, its name has become the generic word for ATMs). Increased internationalism has been slowly doing away with the old worry that your card's PIN, be it on a bank card or credit card, need be specially enabled to work abroad, but it always pays to check with the issuing bank to be sure. If at the ATM you get a message saying your card isn't valid for international transactions, it's likely the bank just can't make the phone connection to check it (occasionally this can be a citywide epidemic); try another ATM or another town.

When you withdraw money with your **bank card,** you technically get the interbank exchange rate—about 4% better than the "street rate" you'd get exchanging cash or traveler's checks. Note, however, that some U.S. banks are now charging a 1% to 3% "exchange fee" to convert the currency. (Ask your bank before you leave.)

Similarly, **Visa** has begun charging a standard 1% conversion fee for cash advances, and many credit card–issuing banks have begun tacking on an additional 1% to 3% (though as we go

0417

MONEY33

to press, Visa is currently being taken to court over this practice in a class-action lawsuit, so keep turned to the news to see what the future holds). Basically, they've gotten into the "commission" game, too. And, unlike with purchases, interest on a credit card cash advance starts accruing *immediately*, not when your statement cycles. Both methods are still a slightly better deal than converting traveler's checks or cash and considerably more convenient (no waiting in bank lines and pulling out your passport as ID). I use credit card advances only as an emergency option and get most of my euro with my bank card.

ATM withdrawals are often limited to 200€ ($230), or sometimes 300€ ($345) per transaction regardless of your cash advance allowance. **American Express** card cash advances are usually available only from the American Express offices in Milan and Venice (see the "Fast Facts" sections for those cities in chapters 7 and 3, respectively, for more information).

CREDIT CARDS

Visa and **MasterCard** are now almost universally accepted at most hotels, restaurants, and shops; the majority also accepts **American Express. Diners Club** is gaining some ground, especially in the bigger cities, at lake and seaside resorts, and in more expensive establishments throughout the region. However, you should never rely entirely on credit cards. Once you leave the larger or less-visited cities or patronize some of the smaller, family-run hotels and shops and trattorias, a cash-only policy still prevails.

If you arrange with your card issuer to enable the card's cash advance option (and get a PIN as well), you can also use them at ATMs (see "ATMs" above).

If you **lose your card,** call toll-free *in Italy:* **Visa** (© **800/819-014**), **Master-Card** (© **800/870-866**), or **American Express** (collect © **336/393-1111** from anywhere, or toll-free in Italy © **800/872-000**).

TRAVELER'S CHECKS

Traveler's checks are something of an anachronism from the days before the ATM made cash accessible at any time. Traveler's checks used to be the only sound alternative to traveling with dangerously large amounts of cash. They were as reliable as currency, but, unlike cash, could be replaced if lost or stolen.

These days, traveler's checks are less necessary because most cities have 24-hour ATMs that allow you to withdraw small amounts of cash as needed. However, keep in mind that you will likely be charged an ATM withdrawal fee if the bank is not your own, so if you're withdrawing money every day, you might be better off with traveler's checks—provided that you don't mind showing identification every time you want to cash one.

You can get traveler's checks at almost any bank. **American Express** offers denominations of $20, $50, $100, $500, and (for cardholders only) $1,000. You'll pay a service charge ranging from 1% to 4%. You can also get American Express traveler's checks over the phone by calling © **800/221-7282;** Amex gold and platinum cardholders who use this number are exempt from the 1% fee.

Tips **Small Change**

When you change money, ask for some small bills or loose change. Petty cash will come in handy for tipping and public transportation. Consider keeping the change separate from your larger bills, so that it's readily accessible and you'll be less of a target for theft.

The Euro, the U.S. Dollar & the U.K. Pound

At this writing, US$1=approximately .87€ (or 1€=$1.15)—the lowest the dollar has ever been (over the past 2 years, the two currencies were more on a par with each other). The rate fluctuates from day to day, depending on a complicated series of economic and political factors, and might not be the same when you travel to Italy.

Likewise, the ratio of the British pound to the euro fluctuates constantly. At press time, £1 = approximately 1.43€ (or 1€=70p).

These are the rates reflected in the table below, and the ones used to translate Euro amounts in ballpark dollar figures throughout this book, rounded to the nearest nickel for amounts under $5, to the nearest dollar for amounts $5 and above (though this table will be precise to the penny).

Euro	US$	UK£	Euro	US$	UK£
.50	.57	.35	30.00	34.50	21.00
1.00	1.15	.70	40.00	46.00	28.00
2.00	2.30	1.40	50.00	57.50	35.00
3.00	3.45	2.10	60.00	69.00	42.00
4.00	4.60	2.80	70.00	80.45	49.00
5.00	5.75	3.50	80.00	92.00	56.00
6.00	6.90	4.20	90.00	103.00	63.00
7.00	8.05	4.90	100.00	115.00	70.00
8.00	9.20	5.60	125.00	144.00	87.50
9.00	10.35	6.30	150.00	172.00	105.00
10.00	11.50	7.00	200.00	230.00	140.00
15.00	17.24	10.50	300.00	345.00	210.00
20.00	23.00	14.00	400.00	460.00	280.00
25.00	28.75	17.50	500.00	575.00	350.00

Visa offers traveler's checks at Citibank locations nationwide, as well as at several other banks. The service charge ranges between 1.5% and 2%; checks come in denominations of $20, $50, $100, $500, and $1,000. Call © **800/732-1322** for information. AAA members can obtain Visa checks without a fee at most AAA offices or by calling © **866/339-3378**. **MasterCard** also offers traveler's checks. Call © **800/ 223-9920** for a location near you.

If you choose to carry traveler's checks, be sure to keep a record of their serial numbers separate from your checks in the event that they are stolen or lost. You'll get a refund faster if you know the numbers. To report **lost or stolen traveler's checks,** call toll-free *in Italy:* **American Express** (© **800-872-000**), **Thomas Cook** (© **800-872-050**), **Visa** (© **800-874-155**), or **Citicorp** (© **813-623-1709** collect from anywhere).

5 When to Go

May to **June** and **September** and **October** are the most pleasant months for touring Italy—temperatures are usually mild and the hordes of tourists not so intense. But starting in mid-June, the summer rush really picks up, and from July to mid-September the country teems with visitors.

August (with July a close runner-up) is the worst month. Not only does it get uncomfortably hot, muggy, and crowded, but the entire country goes on vacation from at least August 15 to the end of the month—and a good percentage of Italians take off the entire month, leaving the cities to the tourists. Many hotels, restaurants, and shops are closed—except along the coast and on the islands, which is where most Italians head.

From **late October to Easter,** most sights have shorter winter hours or close for renovation periods, many hotels and restaurants take a month or two off between November and February, beach destinations become padlocked ghost towns, and it can get much colder than you'd expect (it may even snow). The crowds thin remarkably, especially outside Venice.

In **mountain towns and ski resorts,** high season is from mid-December through mid-March; low season is June, when many hotels are closed (which is a shame, for there's great hiking in the mountains during June's warming days).

High season on most airlines' routes to Milan usually stretches from June to the end of September plus Christmas/New Year's week. This is the most expensive and most crowded time to travel. **Shoulder season** is from the Easter season (usually late Mar or Apr) to May, late September to October, and December 15 to 24. **Low season** is generally January 6 to mid-March, November 1 to December 14, and December 25 to March 31.

Northern Italy's Average Daily Temperature & Monthly Rainfall

	Jan	Feb	Mar	Apr	May	June	July	Aug	Sept	Oct	Nov	Dec
Milan												
Temp. (°F)	35	39	47	56	63	72	77	75	69	57	47	37
Temp. (°C)	2	4	8	13	17	22	25	24	21	14	8	3
Rainfall (in.)	0.7	1.2	4.2	.8	3.3	.9	3.6	2.8	3.9	7.7	5.6	4.0

	Jan	Feb	Mar	Apr	May	June	July	Aug	Sept	Oct	Nov	Dec
Venice												
Temp. (°F)	38	41	48	56	64	71	74	74	70	58	48	42
Temp. (°C)	3	5	9	13	18	22	23	23	21	14	9	6
Rainfall (in.)	1.8	1.8	2	1.6	3.2	2.6	2.8	1.7	2.4	3.4	3.1	2.4

WEATHER

It's warm all over Italy in **summer,** especially inland. The high temperatures (measured in degrees Celsius) begin in May (sometimes later for the Alps), often lasting until some time in late September. July and August can be impossible, which explains why life in the cities slows down considerably (and life in the coastline resorts comes alive). Few budget hotels have air conditioning (and just a handful of hotels in all of Italy have discovered mosquito screens, so when you open the windows for some respite from the heat, you tend to invite dozens of tiny bloodsuckers in as well). The November rains kick off Venice's *acque alte,* when the lagoon backs up a few times each month, flooding the central city with 2 to 6 feet of water (no joke).

Winters in the north of Italy are cold with rain and snow, and December through February can often be unpleasant unless you're skiing in Cortina. Nights can be cold, and Italian hotels' heating systems can be, shall we say, frustrating. Purpose-built, modernized

Hot tickets

For major events where tickets should be procured well before arriving on the spot, check with **Global Tickets** in the United States at ℂ **800-223-6108** or www.globaltickets.com/GTS/INDEX.HTM. In Italy call ℂ **02-54-271.**

hotels in their own buildings often have independent heating/cooling systems you (or they) can control, but in older hotels and in small ones that take up only part of a building, the heat can often only be turned on for the winter on a pre-established date dictated by the local government, and only left on during certain hours of the day (just one of the many lovely laws still hanging on from the Fascist era).

For the most part, it's drier in Italy than in North America. Since the humidity is lower, high temperatures don't seem as bad; exceptions are cities known for their humidity factor, such as Venice. It's important to remember that this is not a country as smitten by the notion of air-conditioning and central heating as, say, the United States. And remember that the inexpensive hotels we list in this book are often the very places that will remind you of the pros and cons of ancient stone palazzi built with 3-foot-thick walls. Don't expect the comfort of the Ritz at cheaper inns.

HOLIDAYS

Offices and shops in Italy are closed on the following dates: **January 1** (New Year's Day), **January 6** (Epiphany, usually called *La Befana* after Italy's Christmas Witch, who used to bring the presents until Hollywood's version of Santa Claus moved the gift-giving to December 25 by popular kiddie demand, though a few presents are always held over for *La Befana*), **Easter Sunday, Easter Monday, April 25** (Liberation Day), **May 1** (Labor Day), **August 15** (Assumption of the Virgin—much of Italy takes its summer vacation **Aug 15–30**), **November 1**

(All Saints' Day), **December 8** (Feast of the Immaculate Conception), **December 25** (Christmas Day), and **December 26** (Santo Stefano); most Italians' **Christmas** holidays last from December 24 though January 6.

Closings are also observed in the following cities on feast days honoring patron saints: Venice, **April 25** (St. Mark); Genoa and Turin, **June 24** (St. John the Baptist); Bologna, **October 4** (St. Petronio); Trieste, **November 3** (San Giusto); and Milan, **December 7** (St. Ambrose).

NORTHERN ITALY CALENDAR OF EVENTS

For more details on each event below, contact the **tourist office** of the city or town where the festival is held (see the individual chapters).

January

Epiphany celebrations, nationwide. All cities, towns, and villages in Italy stage Roman Catholic Epiphany observances and Christmas Fairs. From Christmas to January 6.

Festival of Italian Popular Song, San Remo (Italian Riviera). A 3-day festival where major artists and up-and-comers perform the latest Italian pop songs and launch the newest hits. Late January.

Foire de Saint Ours, Aosta, Valle d'Aosta. Observing a tradition that's existed for 10 centuries, artisans from the mountain valleys come together to display their wares—often made of wood, lace, wool, or wrought iron—created during the long winter months. Late January.

February

Carnevale (Carnival), Venice. Venice's Carnival evokes the final theatrical 18th-century days of the Venetian Republic. Historical presentations, elaborate costumes, and music of all types in every piazza cap the festivities. The balls are by invitation, but the cultural events, piazza performances, and fireworks (Shrove Tuesday) are open to everyone. See chapter 3 for more information. From two Fridays before Shrove Tuesday to Shrove Tuesday.

April

Good Friday and Easter Week observances, nationwide. Processions and age-old ceremonies—some from pagan days, some from the Middle Ages—are staged. Beginning on the Thursday or Friday before Easter Sunday, usually in April.

May

Voga Longa, Venice. This 30km (19-mile) rowing "race" from San Marco to Burano and back again has been enthusiastically embraced since its inception in 1975, following the city's effort to keep alive the centuries-old heritage of the regatta. The event is colorful, and every local seems to have a relative or next-door neighbor competing. For details, call ✆ **041-521-0544.** A Sunday in mid-May.

June & Events That Last Throughout the Summer

Regatta of the Great Maritime Republics, Venice or Genoa. Every year, the four medieval maritime republics of Italy celebrate their glorious past with a boat race that rotates among Venice, Amalfi, Genoa, and Pisa. Call the tourist offices for details.

Biennale d'Arte, Venice. This is Europe's most prestigious—and controversial—International Exposition of Modern Art, taking place in odd-numbered years only. More than 50 nations take part, with art displayed in permanent pavilions in the Public Gardens and elsewhere about town. Many great modern artists have been discovered at this world-famous show. Contact the board at ✆ **041-521-8711** (www.labiennale.org) for more information. June to October.

Shakespearean Festival, Verona. Ballet, drama, and jazz performances are included in this festival of the Bard with a few performances in English. June to September.

Arena di Verona (Outdoor Opera Season in Verona), Verona. Culture buffs flock to the open-air, 20,000-seat Roman amphitheater, one of the world's best preserved. The season lasts from early July to August for awesome productions of *Aïda* and others.

July

Festa del Redentore (Feast of the Redeemer), Venice. This celebration marking the July 1576 lifting of a plague that had gripped the city is centered around the Palladio-designed Chiesa del Redentore on the island of Giudecca. A bridge of boats across the Giudecca Canal links the church with the banks of Le Zattere in Dorsoduro

---

⌒Tips Dog Days of August

Try to avoid traveling to Italy in August, as this is when most Italians take their vacations *(ferie)* and many shops and restaurants in the cities will be closed. Also keep in mind that many of the lodgings that will be open in August do not have air-conditioning.

and hundreds of boats of all shapes and sizes fill the Giudecca. It's one big floating *festa* until night descends and an awesome half-hour *spettacolo* of fireworks fills the sky. Third Saturday and Sunday in July.

August

Rossini Opera Festival, Pesaro. The world's top bel canto specialists perform Rossini's operas and choral works at this popular festival on the Italian Adriatic Riviera. Mid-August to late September.

Venice International Film Festival. Ranking after Cannes, this film festival brings together stars, directors, producers, and filmmakers from all over the world. Films are shown day and night to an international jury and to the public, at the Palazzo del Cinema, on the Lido, and other venues. Contact the tourist office or the Venice Film Festival (© 041-272-6501 or 041-524-1320; www.labiennale.org). Two weeks in late August to early September.

September

Regata Storica, Grand Canal, Venice. Just about every seaworthy gondola, richly decorated for the occasion and piloted by *gondolieri* in colorful livery, participates in the opening cavalcade. The aquatic parade is followed by three regattas that proceed along the Grand Canal. You can buy grandstand tickets through the tourist office or arrive early and pull up along a piece of embankment near the Rialto Bridge for the best seats in town. First Sunday in September.

Giostra del Saracino (Joust of the Saracen), Arezzo. A colorful procession in full historical regalia precedes the 13th-century–style tilting contest with knights in armor in the town's main piazza. First Sunday in September.

Partita a Scacchi con Personnagi Viventi (Living Chess Game), Marostica. This chess game is played in the town square by living pawns in period costume. The second Saturday and Sunday of September during even-numbered years.

October

Sagra del Tartufo, Alba, Piedmont. The truffle is the honoree in Alba, the truffle capital of Italy, with contests, truffle-hound competitions, and tastings of this ugly but precious and delectable (and expensive) fungus. Two weeks in mid-October.

Maratona (Marathon), Venice. The marathon starts at Villa Pisani on the mainland, runs alongside the Brenta Canal, and ends along the Zattere for a finish at the Basilica di Santa Maria della Salute on the tip of Dorsoduro. For details, call © 041-950-644. Usually the last Sunday of October.

November

Festa della Salute, Venice. For this festival, a pontoon bridge is erected across the Grand Canal to connect the churches of La Salute and Santa Maria del Giglio, commemorating another delivery from a plague in 1630 that wiped out a third of the lagoon's population; it's the only day La Salute opens its massive front doors (a secondary entrance is otherwise used). November 21.

December

La Scala Opera Season, Teatro alla Scala, Milan. At the most famous opera house of them all, the season opens on December 7, the feast day of Milan's patron St. Ambrogio, and runs into July. Though it's close to impossible to get opening-night tickets, it's worth a try; call © 02-860-787 or 02-860-775 for the box office, 02-7200-3744 for the information line (www.teatroallascala.org).

6 Travel Insurance

Check your existing insurance policies and credit-card coverage before you buy travel insurance. You may already be covered for lost luggage, canceled tickets, or medical expenses. The cost of travel insurance varies widely, depending on the cost and length of your trip, your age, health, and the type of trip you're taking.

TRIP-CANCELLATION INSUR-ANCE Trip-cancellation insurance helps you get your money back if you have to back out of a trip, if you have to go home early, or if your travel supplier goes bankrupt. Insurance policy details vary, so read the fine print—and especially make sure that your airline or cruise line is on the list of carriers covered in case of bankruptcy. For information, contact one of the following insurers: **Access America** (© 866/807-3982; www.accessamerica. com); **Travel Guard International** (© 800/826-4919; www.travelguard. com); **Travel Insured International** (© 800/243-3174; www.travelinsured. com); and **Travelex Insurance Services** (© 888/457-4602; www.travelex-insurance.com).

MEDICAL INSURANCE Most health insurance policies cover you if you get sick away from home—but check, particularly if you're insured by an HMO.

With the exception of certain HMOs and Medicare/Medicaid, your medical insurance should cover medical treatment—even hospital care—overseas. However, most out-of-country hospitals make you pay your bills up front, and send you a refund after you've returned home and filed the necessary paperwork. And in a worst-case scenario, there's the high cost of emergency evacuation. If you require additional medical insurance, try **MEDEX International** (© **800-527-0218** or 410-453-6300; www.medexassist. com) or **Travel Assistance International** (© **800-821-2828;** www.travel assistance.com; for general information on services, call the company's Worldwide Assistance Services, Inc., at © **800-777-8710**).

Again, most health insurance plans covering out-of-country illnesses and hospital stays require you to pay your local bills up front—your coverage takes the form of a refund after you've returned and filed the paperwork. However, **Blue Cross/Blue Shield members** (© **800-810-BLUE** or www. bluecares.com for a list of participating hospitals) can now use their plans and cards at select hospitals abroad as they would at home, which means much lower out-of-pocket costs. There are member hospitals in Bologna, Genoa, Milan (six of them), Modena, Padova, Turin, Venice, and Verona.

7 Health & Safety

STAYING HEALTHY

You'll encounter few health problems traveling in Italy. Aside from the occasional sign ACQUA NON POTABILE (water not drinkable), Italy's tap water is generally safe to drink (though, as it's often unfiltered and not subjected to the chemical "purification" barrage of U.S. tap water, it may taste different or appear milky—that's natural calcium).

Italy's milk is pasteurized, and its health services are excellent. In fact, with Italy's partially socialized medicine, you can usually stop by any hospital emergency room with an ailment, get swift and courteous service, be given a diagnosis and a prescription, and sent on your way with a wave and a smile—and not even a sheet of paperwork to fill out.

WHAT TO DO IF YOU GET SICK AWAY FROM HOME

In most cases, your existing health plan will provide the coverage you need. But double-check; you may want to buy **travel medical insurance** instead. (See the section on insurance, above.) Bring your insurance ID card with you when you travel.

If you suffer from a chronic illness, consult your doctor before your departure. For conditions like epilepsy, diabetes, or heart problems, wear a **Medic Alert Identification Tag** (© 800/825-3785; www.medicalert.org), which will immediately alert doctors to your condition and give them access to your records through Medic Alert's 24-hour hot line.

Pack **prescription medications** in your carry-on luggage, and carry prescription medications in their original containers, with pharmacy labels—otherwise they won't make it through airport security. Also bring along copies of your prescriptions in case you lose your pills or run out. Don't forget an extra pair of contact lenses or prescription glasses. Again, carry the generic name of prescription medicines, in case a local pharmacist is unfamiliar with the brand name.

Contact the **International Association for Medical Assistance to Travelers (IAMAT)** (© 716/754-4883 or, in Canada, 416/652-0137; www.iamat.org) for tips on travel and health concerns in the countries you're visiting, and lists of local, English-speaking doctors. The United States **Centers for Disease Control and Prevention** (© 800/311-3435; www.cdc.gov) provides up-to-date information on necessary vaccines and health hazards by region or country. Any foreign consulate can provide a list of area doctors who speak English. If you get sick, consider asking your hotel concierge to recommend a local doctor—even his or her own. You can also try the emergency room at a local hospital; many have walk-in clinics for emergency cases that are not life-threatening. You may not get immediate attention, but you won't pay the high price of an emergency room visit.

STAYING SAFE

Italy is a remarkably safe country. The worst threats you'll likely face are the pickpockets that sometimes frequent touristy areas and public buses; just keep your valuables in an under-the-clothes money belt and you should be fine. There are, of course, thieves in Italy as there are everywhere, so be smart; don't leave anything in your rental car overnight, and leave nothing visible in it at any time to avoid the temptation to a passing would-be thief.

8 Specialized Travel Resources

TRAVELERS WITH DISABILITIES

Italy certainly doesn't win any medals for being overly accessible, though a few of the top museums and churches are beginning at least to install ramps at the entrances, and a few hotels are converting first-floor rooms into accessible units by widening the doors and bathrooms.

Other than that, don't expect to find much of the landscape easy to tackle. Builders in the Middle Ages and renaissance didn't have wheelchairs or mobility impairments in mind when they built narrow doorways and spiral staircases, and preservation laws keep modern Italians from being able to do much about this.

That said, recent laws in Italy have compelled rail stations, airports, hotels, and most restaurants to follow a stricter set of regulations about **wheelchair accessibility** to restrooms, ticket counters, and so on. Many museums and other sightseeing attractions have conformed to these regulations, and even Venice has now installed wheelchair elevator platforms on many of the hundreds of bridges over the city's canals, effectively opening up well over half the historic center to mobility-impaired visitors (the tourist office map highlights the zones now accessible). **Alitalia,** as Italy's most visible airline, has made a special effort to make its planes, public areas, restrooms, and access ramps as wheelchair-friendly as possible.

Buses and trains can cause problems as well, with high, narrow doors and steep steps at entrances. There are, however, seats reserved on public transportation for travelers with disabilities.

Luckily, there's an endless list of organizations to help you plan your trip and offer specific advice before you go. Many travel agencies offer customized tours and itineraries for travelers with disabilities. **Flying Wheels Travel** (© 507/451-5005; www.flying wheelstravel.com) offers escorted tours and cruises that emphasize sports and private tours in minivans with lifts. **Accessible Journeys** (© 800/846-4537 or 610/521-0339; www.disability travel.com) caters specifically to slow walkers and wheelchair travelers and their families and friends.

Organizations that offer assistance to travelers with disabilities include **Moss-Rehab** (www.mossresourcenet.org), which provides a library of accessible-travel resources online; the **Society for Accessible Travel and Hospitality** (© 212/447-7284; www.sath.org; annual membership fees: $45 adults, $30 seniors and students), which offers a wealth of travel resources for all types of disabilities and informed recommendations on destinations, access guides, travel agents, tour operators, vehicle rentals, and companion services; and the **American Foundation for the Blind** (© 800/232-5463; www.afb. org), which provides information on traveling with Seeing Eye dogs.

For more information specifically targeted to travelers with disabilities, the community website **iCan** (www.ican online.net/channels/travel/index.cfm) has destination guides and several regular columns on accessible travel. Also check out the quarterly magazine *Emerging Horizons* ($14.95 per year, $19.95 outside the U.S.; www. emerginghorizons.com); **Twin Peaks Press** (© 360/694-2462; http:// disabilitybookshop.virtualave.net/ blist84.htm), offering travel-related books for travelers with special needs; and *Open World Magazine,* published by the Society for Accessible Travel and Hospitality (see above; subscription: $18 per year, $35 outside the U.S.).

Accessible Italy (www.tour-web. com/accitaly/index.html) concentrates on info pertinent to Rome, Florence, Venice, and Milan for the traveler with reduced mobility. This operator can help plan itineraries to a host of other Italian cities as well.

GAY & LESBIAN TRAVELERS

Since 1861 Italy has had liberal legislation regarding homosexuality, but that doesn't mean being gay is always looked on favorably in a Catholic country. Homosexuality is legal, and the age of consent is 16. Condoms are *profilatici* (pro-feel-*aht*-tee-chee).

Luckily, Italians are already more affectionate and physical than Americans in their general friendships, and even straight men regularly walk down the street with their arms around each other—however, kissing anywhere other than on the cheeks at greetings and goodbyes will certainly draw attention. As you might expect, smaller towns tend to be less permissive and accepting than cities. Homosexuality is much more accepted in the big cities and university towns, though in northern Italy only Milan has a significant gay community.

In fact, **Milan** considers itself the gay capital of Italy (though Bologna is

A Note for Families & Seniors

At most state-run museums, children under 18 and seniors get in free *but only if* they hail from one of the countries that has signed a reciprocal international cultural agreement to allow children and seniors this privilege. These countries include England, Canada, Ireland, Australia, New Zealand, and indeed much of the world—but *not* the United States. (However, many museum guards either don't ask for citizenship ID or wave kids and seniors on through anyway.) Children and seniors, no matter what their nationality, also get discounts on trains (see "Getting Around," later in this chapter).

---

a proud contender) and is the headquarters of **ARCI Gay** (www.gay.it), the country's leading gay organization, which has branches throughout Italy. A gay-operated, English-speaking travel agency in Rome, **Zipper Travel** (V. Francesco Carletti 8, Rome 00154, © 06/488-2730; fax 06/488-2729; www.zippertravel.it/) can help create itineraries in both large and small cities, as well as make reservations for travel and hotel.

The International Gay & Lesbian Travel Association (IGLTA) (© 800/448-8550 or 954/776-2626; www.iglta.org) is the trade association for the gay and lesbian travel industry, and offers an online directory of gay- and lesbian-friendly travel businesses; go to their website and click on "Members."

Many agencies offer tours and travel itineraries specifically for gay and lesbian travelers. **Above and Beyond Tours** (© 800/397-2681; www.abovebeyondtours.com) is the exclusive gay and lesbian tour operator for United Airlines. **Now, Voyager** (© 800/255-6951; www.nowvoyager.com) is a well-known San Francisco–based gay-owned and operated travel service.

The following travel guides are available at most travel bookstores and gay and lesbian bookstores, or you can order them from Giovanni's Room bookstore, 1145 Pine St., Philadelphia, PA 19107 (© 215/923-2960; www.giovannisroom.com): *Frommer's Gay & Lesbian Europe* (Wiley Publishing,

Inc.), an excellent travel resource; *Out and About* (© 800/929-2268 or 415-644-8044; www.outandabout.com), which offers guidebooks and a newsletter 10 times a year packed with solid information on the global gay and lesbian scene; *Spartacus International Gay Guide* (Bruno Gmunder Verlag) and *Odysseus: The International Gay Travel Planner* (Odysseus Enterprises Ltd.), both good, annual English-language guidebooks focused on gay men; the *Damron* guides (Damron Company), with separate, annual books for gay men and lesbians; and *Gay Travel A to Z: The World of Gay & Lesbian Travel Options at Your Fingertips* by Marianne Ferrari (Ferrari Publications; Box 35575, Phoenix, AZ 85069), a very good gay and lesbian guidebook series.

SENIOR TRAVEL

Italy is a multigenerational culture that doesn't tend to marginalize its seniors, and older people are treated with a great deal of respect and deference throughout Italy. But there are few specific programs, associations, or concessions made for them. The one exception is on admission prices for museums and sites, where those over 60 or 65 will often get in at a reduced rate or even free (see the "A Note for Families & Seniors" box). There are also special train passes and reductions on bus tickets and the like in various towns (see "Getting Around," later in this chapter). As a senior in Italy, you're *un anciano* (*una anciana* if you're a woman) or "ancient one"—look at it as a term of respect and let people know you're one if you think a discount may be in the works.

Members of **AARP** (formerly known as the American Association of Retired Persons), 601 E St. NW, Washington, DC 20049 (© **800/424-3410** or 202/434-2277; www.aarp.org), get discounts on hotels, airfares, and car rentals. AARP offers members a wide range of benefits, including *AARP: The Magazine* and a monthly newsletter. Anyone over 50 can join.

Sadly, most major **airlines** have in recent years canceled their discount programs for seniors, but you can always ask when booking. Of the big **car-rental** agencies, only National currently gives an AARP discount, but the many rental dealers that specialize in Europe—Auto Europe, Kemwel, Europe-by-Car—offer seniors 5% off their already low rates. In most European cities, people over 60 or 65 get reduced admission at theaters, museums, and other attractions, and they can often get discount fares or cards on public transportation and national rail systems. Carrying ID with proof of age can pay off in all these situations.

Many reliable agencies and organizations target the 50-plus market. **Elderhostel** (© **877/426-8056;** www.elderhostel.org) arranges study programs for those ages 55 and over (and a spouse or companion of any age) in the U.S. and in more than 80 countries around the world. Most courses last 5 to 7 days in the U.S. (2–4 weeks abroad), and many include airfare, accommodations in university dormitories or modest inns, meals, and tuition. **ElderTreks** (© **800/741-7956;** www.eldertreks.com) offers small-group tours to off-the-beaten-path or adventure-travel locations, restricted to travelers 50 and older.

Recommended publications offering travel resources and discounts for seniors include: the quarterly magazine *Travel 50 & Beyond* (www.travel50 andbeyond.com); *Travel Unlimited: Uncommon Adventures for the Mature Traveler* (Avalon); *101 Tips for Mature Travelers,* available from Grand Circle Travel (© **800/221-2610** or 617/350-7500; www.gct.com); *The 50+ Traveler's Guidebook* (St. Martin's Press); and *Unbelievably Good Deals and Great Adventures That You Absolutely Can't Get Unless You're Over 50* (McGraw-Hill).

WOMEN TRAVELERS

Women will feel remarkably welcome in Italy—sometimes a bit too welcome, actually. Yes, it sometimes seems every young Italian male is out to prove himself the most irresistible lover on the planet; remember, this is the land of Romeo and Casanova, so they have a lot to live up to.

From parading and preening like peacocks to wooing each passing female with words, whistles, and, if they can get close enough, the entirely inappropriate butt-pinch, these men and their attentiveness can range from charming and flattering to downright annoying and frustrating. The more exotic you look—statuesque blondes, ebony-skinned beauties, or simply an American accent—the more irresistible you become to these suitors.

And, as everyone around the world knows from watching Hollywood movies, American women are all uninhibited and passionate sex kittens. That this isn't actually true doesn't make much of a dent in Italian boys' fantasies.

Flirting back at these would-be Romeos, even mildly, only convinces them that you're ready to jump into bed. Heck, mere eye contact encourages them to redouble their efforts. Unless you want all this attention, take your cue from Italian women, who may wear tight skirts and fishnets but, you'll notice, usually ignore the men around them entirely unless it's someone they're already walking with.

If you find yourself moderately molested on a bus or other crowded place—mostly the infamous bottom-pinching and rather inappropriate rubbing—tell him to "*Smetti la!*" (stop it) and proceed to pinch, scratch, elbow, and so on to further discourage him or enlist the aid of the nearest convenient elderly Italian woman to noisily chastise the offender and perhaps whap him with her purse.

Note that all of this is kept to verbal flirtation and that occasional inappropriate touching that deserves a slap in the face. These men want to conquer you with their charm, not their muscles; rape is near unheard-of in Italy. Most women report feeling far safer wandering the deserted streets of an Italian city back to the their hotels at 2am than they do in their own neighborhoods back home, and that feeling is largely justified. You'll probably get tons of ride offers, though, from would-be chivalrous knights atop their Vespa or Fiat steeds.

Women Welcome Women World Wide (5W) (© **203/259-7832** in the U.S.; www.womenwelcomewomen. org.uk) works to foster international friendships by enabling women of different countries to visit one another (men can come along on the trips; they just can't join the club). It's a big, active organization, with more than 3,500 members from all walks of life in some 70 countries.

Check out the website **Journeywoman** (www.journeywoman.com), a lively travel resource, with "GirlTalk Guides" to destinations like New York, Hong Kong, and Toronto and a free e-mail newsletter; or the travel guide *Safety and Security for Women Who Travel* by Sheila Swan Laufer and Peter Laufer (Travelers' Tales, Inc.), offering common-sense advice and tips on safe travel.

9 Planning Your Trip Online

SURFING FOR AIRFARES

The "big three" online travel agencies, **Expedia.com, Travelocity.com,** and **Orbitz.com** sell most of the air tickets bought on the Internet. (Canadian travelers should try expedia.ca and Travelocity.ca; U.K. residents can go for expedia.co.uk and opodo.co.uk.) Each has different business deals with the airlines and may offer different fares on the same flights, so it's wise to shop around. Expedia and Travelocity will also send you **e-mail notification** when a cheap fare becomes available to your favorite destination. Of the smaller travel agency websites, **Side-Step** (www.sidestep.com) has gotten the best reviews from Frommer's authors. It's a browser add-on that purports to "search 140 sites at once," but in reality only beats competitors' fares as often as other sites do.

Also remember to check **airline websites**, especially those for low-fare carriers in Europe such as easyJet (www.easyjet.com) and Ryanair (www. ryanair.com), whose fares are often misreported or simply missing from travel agency websites. Even with major airlines, you can often shave a few bucks from a fare by booking directly through the airline and avoiding a travel agency's transaction fee. But you'll get these discounts only by **booking online:** Most airlines now offer online-only fares that even their phone agents know nothing about. For the websites of airlines that fly to and from your destination, go to "Getting There," below.

Great **last-minute deals** are available through free weekly e-mail services provided directly by the airlines. Most of these are announced on Tuesday or Wednesday and must be purchased online. Most are only valid for travel that weekend, but some can be booked weeks or months in advance. Sign up for weekly e-mail alerts at airline websites or check mega-sites that compile comprehensive lists of last-minute specials, such as **Smarter Living** (smarter living.com). For last-minute trips, **site 59.com** in the U.S. and **lastminute. com** in Europe often have better deals than the major-label sites.

If you're willing to give up some control over your flight details, use an **opaque fare service** like **Priceline** (www.priceline.com; www.priceline.co. uk for Europeans) or **Hotwire** (www. hotwire.com). Both offer rock-bottom prices in exchange for travel on a "mystery airline" at a mysterious time of day, often with a mysterious change of planes en route. The mystery airlines are all major, well-known carriers—and the possibility of being sent from Philadelphia to Italy via Japan is remote; the airlines' routing computers have gotten a lot better than they used to be. But your chances of getting a 6am or 11pm flight are pretty high. Hotwire tells you flight prices before you buy; Priceline usually has better deals than Hotwire, but you have to play their "name our price" game. If you're new at this, the helpful folks at **BiddingForTravel** (www. biddingfortravel.com) do a good job of demystifying Priceline's prices. Priceline and Hotwire are great for flights within North America and between the U.S. and Europe. But for flights to other parts of the world, consolidators will almost always beat their fares.

For much more about airfares and savvy air-travel tips and advice, pick up a copy of *Frommer's Fly Safe, Fly Smart* (Wiley Publishing, Inc.).

SURFING FOR HOTELS

Shopping online for hotels is much easier in the U.S., Canada, and certain parts of Europe than it is in the rest of the world. Also, many smaller hotels and B&Bs—especially outside the U.S.—don't show up on websites at all. Of the "big three" sites, **Expedia** may be the best choice, thanks to its long list of special deals. **Travelocity** runs a close second. Hotel specialist sites **hotels.com** and **hoteldiscounts. com** are also reliable. An excellent free program, **TravelAxe** (www.travelaxe. net), can help you search multiple hotel sites at once, even ones you may never have heard of.

Priceline and Hotwire are even better for hotels than for airfares; with both, you're allowed to pick the neighborhood and quality level of your hotel before offering up your money. Priceline's hotel product even covers Europe and Asia, though it's much better at getting five-star lodging for three-star prices than at finding anything at the bottom of the scale. *Note:* Hotwire overrates its hotels by one star—what Hotwire calls a four-star is a three-star anywhere else.

In Italy two long-established hotel booking engines—with far more choices than the big international ones listed above—are **www.venere.com** and **www.itwg.com**.

SURFING FOR RENTAL CARS

For booking rental cars online, the best deals are usually found at rental-car company websites, although all the major online travel agencies also offer rental-car reservations services. Priceline and Hotwire work well for rental cars, too; the only "mystery" is which major rental company you get, and for most travelers the difference between Hertz, Avis, and Budget is negligible.

The best prices on rentals in Europe are found at Auto Europe (www.auto europe.com), which acts as a sort of consolidator for rentals—you actually pick up your car at, say, the Avis or Hertz office in the destination, but you pay a rate below what those rental agencies charge the public. This company will also work out long-term

Online Traveler's Toolbox

Veteran travelers usually carry some essential items to make their trips easier. Following is a selection of online tools to bookmark and use.

- **Visa ATM Locator** (www.visa.com), for locations of Plus ATMs worldwide, or **MasterCard ATM Locator** (www.mastercard.com), for locations of Cirrus ATMs worldwide.
- **Foreign Languages for Travelers** (www.travlang.com). Learn basic terms in more than 70 languages and click on any underlined phrase to hear what it sounds like.
- **Intellicast** (www.intellicast.com) and **Weather.com** (www.weather.com). Provide weather forecasts for cities around the world.
- **Mapquest** (www.mapquest.com). This best of the mapping sites lets you choose a specific address or destination, and in seconds it will return a map and detailed directions.
- **Universal Currency Converter** (www.xe.com/ucc). See what your dollar or pound is worth in more than 100 other countries.

leases for periods longer than 17 days; it saves you lots over a rental, plus you get a brand-new car and *full* insurance coverage), as with Europe By Car (www.europebycar.com).

10 Getting There

BY PLANE

FROM NORTH AMERICA   From North America, direct flights are only available to Milan (and Rome, of course), though you can usually get a connecting flight to Venice or other major cities. **Flying time** to Milan from New York is 8 hours, from Chicago 9¼ hours, and from Los Angeles 11½ hours.

The Major Airlines   Italy's national airline, **Alitalia** (℃ 800-223-5730; www.alitalia.it), offers more flights daily to Italy than any other airline. It flies direct to both Rome and Milan from New York, Newark, Boston, Chicago, Los Angeles, and Miami. You can connect in Rome or Milan to any other Italian destination.

British Airways (℃ 800-247-9297; www.ba.com) flies direct from dozens of U.S. and Canadian cities to London, where you can get connecting flights to Milan. **Air Canada/Canadian Airlines**

(℃ 888-247-2262 or 800-361-8071 (TTY); www.aircanada.ca) flies daily from Toronto and Vancouver to Rome. **Continental** (℃ 800-231-0856; www.continental.com) doesn't fly to Italy itself, but it's partnered with Alitalia for the Newark-to-Rome and New York JFK-to-Milan flights, so if you're a Continental Frequent Flyer you can reserve through Continental and rack up the miles. **Delta** (℃ 800-241-4141; www.delta.com) flies daily out of New York JFK (you can connect from most major U.S. cities) to Rome and Milan.

Possibly less convenient alternatives are **American Airlines** (℃ 800-433-7300; www.aa.com), whose flights from the United States to Milan all go through Chicago; **United** (℃ 800-528-2929; www.ual.com), which flies once daily to Milan out of New York, Newark, and Washington, D.C. Dulles; or **US Airways** (℃ 800-622-1015; www.usairways.com), which offers one flight daily to Rome out of Philadelphia. (You can connect through Philly from most major U.S. cities.)

FROM GREAT BRITAIN and IRELAND   British Airways (℗ 0845-773-3377; www.ba.com) flies twice daily from London's Gatwick to Pisa. **Alitalia** (020-8745-8200; www.alitalia.it) has four daily flights from London to both Rome and Milan. **KLM UK** (formerly Air UK; ℗ 08705-074-074; www.klmuk.com) flies several times per week from London Heathrow to Milan (both airports) and Rome. In each case, there's a layover in Amsterdam.

No-frills upstart **Ryanair** (℗ 0871-246-0000 in the U.K.; www.ryanair.com) will fly you from London to Milan-Bergamo, Bologna, Genoa, Trieste, Turin, Venice-Treviso, and Venice-Brescia (as well as Alghero, Ancona, Palermo, Pescara, Pisa, and Rome). Its competitor **EasyJet** (www.easyjet.com) flies from London to Milan, Venice, and Bologna. Both usually charge less than £25 ($40) each way for such service. The East Midlands-based bmibaby (www.bmibaby.com) flies to Milan-Bergamo as well as Pisa.

The best and cheapest way to get to Italy from Ireland is to make your way first to London and fly from there (see above; to book through **British Airways** in Ireland, dial ℗ 800-626-747). **Aer Lingus** (℗ 0818-365-000 in Ireland; www.aerlingus.com) flies direct from Dublin to both Rome and Milan about 5 days a week. **Alitalia** (℗ 01-677-5171) puts you on a British Midland to get you to London, where you change to an Alitalia plane for the trip to Rome. For **RyanAir**, call ℗ 0818-303-030 in Ireland.

FROM AUSTRALIA & NEW ZEALAND   Alitalia (℗ 02-9922-1555; www.alitalia.it) has a flight from Sydney to Rome every Thursday and Saturday. **Qantas** (℗ 13-1313 in Australia, or 0649-357-8900 in Auckland, NZ; www.qantas.com) flies three times daily to Rome via Bangkok, leaving Australia from Sydney, Melbourne, Brisbane, or Cairns. Qantas will also book you through one of these Australian cities from Auckland, Wellington, or Christchurch in New Zealand. You can also look into flying first into London and connecting to Italy from there. (There are more flights, and it may work out to be cheaper.)

GETTING TO NORTHERN ITALY FROM ROME'S AIRPORTS

Most international flights to Rome will arrive at **Fiumicino Airport** (officially named **Leonardo da Vinci International Airport,** but few, including the airlines themselves, call it that). Some inter-European and transatlantic charter flights may land at the less convenient **Ciampino Airport.** You can connect to a plane at either to take you north, but it's often simpler, almost as fast in the long run, and cheaper to take the train.

Fiumicino (℗ 06-659-51; www.adr.it) is 30km (19 miles) from Rome's center. You can take the **express train** (8.80€/$10) from Fiumicino to Rome's central train station, Termini. A taxi to the station costs about 36€ ($41). From Termini, you can grab one of many daily trains headed north to Bologna, Milan, Genoa, Venice, or other points. If you happen to fly into **Ciampino Airport** (℗ 06-7934-0297), 15km (9¼ miles) south of the city, a none-too-frequent COTRAL bus will take you to the Anagnina metro station, where you can take the metro to Termini, the whole trip costing around 3€ ($3.45). A taxi to Rome's center from Ciampino should run about 25€ ($29).

Information on getting to most major Northern Italian cities from Rome **by train** is included under each destination throughout this book.

LANDING IN MILAN

Your flight may land at either **Linate Airport** (② 02-7485-2200; www. sea-aeroportimilano.it), about 8km (5 miles) southeast of the city, or **Malpensa Airport** (② 02-2680-0613; www.malpensa-airport.com), 45km (28 miles) from downtown—closer to Como than to Milan itself.

From **Malpensa,** a 40-minute express train heads half-hourly to the Cadorna train station in western Milan rather than the larger or more central Stazione Centrale from which most trains onward to other Northern Italian points leave (you'll have to take the Metro to get there). To grab a bus instead, which will take you directly to that central downtown rail station, your choices are Malpensa Express (② 02-9619-2301) which costs 5.05€ ($5.80), or the cheaper Malpensa Shuttle (② 02-5858-3185)—same service, different price: 4.50€ ($5.20)—two to three times per hour for the 50-minute ride to the east side of Milan's Stazione Centrale.

From **Linate,** STAM buses (② 02-717-100) make the 25-minute trip to Milan's Stazione Centrale, every 20 to 30 minutes daily from 7am to 11pm, costing 2€/$2.30 (buy on bus). The slightly slower city bus no. 73 leaves hourly for the S. Babila metro stop downtown (1€/$1.15 for a regular bus ticket bought from any news agent inside the airport, but no onboard purchases available).

GETTING THERE BY CAR

You'll get the **best rental rate** if you book your car from home instead of renting direct in Italy—in fact, if you decide to rent once you're over there, it's worth it to call home to have someone arrange it all from there. You must be over 25 to rent from most agencies (although some accept 21).

Though it once was smart shopping to see what rates Italian companies were offering, they're all now allied with the big agents in the States: **Avis** (② **800-230-4898;** in Italy toll-free 199-100-133; www.avis.com), **Budget** (② **800-527-0700;** www.budget. com), **Hertz** (② **800-654-3131** or 800-654-3001; www.hertz.com), and **National** (② **800-227-7368;** www. nationalcar.com).

You can usually get a better rate by going through one of the rental companies specializing in Europe: **Auto Europe** (② **888-223-5555;** www.auto europe.com), **Europe by Car** (② **800-223-1516,** or 212-581-3040 in New York City; www.europebycar.com), **Kemwell** (② **800-678-0678;** www. kemwell.com) and **Maiellano** (② **800-223-1616** or 718-727-0044). With constant price wars and special packages, it always pays to shop around among all the above.

When offered the choice between a compact car and a larger one, always choose the smaller car (unless you have a large group)—you'll need it for maneuvering the winding, steeply

---

Tips The Milan Connection

Note that if you find yourself flying into Milan, the domestic airport (Linate) is separate from the international one (Malpensa), and transferring planes to a connecting flight requires switching airports (an 8€/$9.20 bus connects the two airports), sometimes changing airlines, and an innate trust in the gods of luggage transfer. This isn't a problem for flights on Alitalia, however, which uses Milan's Malpensa airport for both international arrivals and domestic departures—a blatantly nationalistic protectionist scheme that has all other major airlines, European and American, up in arms.

graded Italian roads and the impossibly narrow alleyways of towns and cities. Likewise, if you can drive stick shift, order one; it'll help you better navigate the hilly terrain. It's also a good idea to opt for the **Collision Damage Wavier (CDW)** that for only $10 to $20 a day gives you the peace of mind and nerves of steel that driving in Italy requires; you can pay only $7 per day for this service if you buy it through a third party insurer such as Travel Guard (www.travelguard.com). Although the 19% IVA value-added tax is unavoidable, you can do away with the government airport pick-up tax of 10% by picking up your car at an office in town.

For more on driving in Italy, from road rule to maps to gasoline, see the "Getting Around" section below.

GETTING THERE BY TRAIN

Every day, up to 14 **Eurostar** trains (reservations in London ✆ **0875-186-186;** www.eurostar.com) zip from London to Paris's Gare du Nord via the **Chunnel** (Eurotunnel) in a bit over 4 hours. In Paris, you can transfer to the Paris Gare de Lyon station or Paris Bercy for one of three daily direct trains

to **Milan,** overnight to **Venice** (15 hr.), and a few other cities. Some of the Milan runs are high-speed TGV trains, a 6½-hour ride requiring a seat reservation. At least one will be an overnight Euronight (EN) train, with reservable sleeping couchettes; the Euronight leaves Paris around 10pm and gets into Milan around 8:45am.

The definitive 500-page book listing all official European train routes and schedules is the *Thomas Cook European Timetable,* available in the United States for $27.95 (plus $4.50 shipping and handling) from Forsyth Travel Library, P.O. Box 2975, Shawnee Mission, KS 66201 (✆ **800-367-7984**) or at travel specialty stores. You can also order the schedule online: **www.thomascooktimetables.com**.

If, you're traveling only in the regions covered by this guide or just in Italy, a European-wide rail pass will be a waste of money. Similarly, if you're merely coming straight to Italy by train from another point within Europe, it'll be cheaper to buy just a regular one-way ticket. For more information on trains and train passes in Italy, see "By Train" under "Getting Around," beginning on p. 55.

11 Packages for the Independent Traveler

Before you start your search for the lowest airfare, you may want to consider booking your flight as part of a travel package. Package tours are not the same thing as escorted tours. Package tours are simply a way to buy the airfare, accommodations, and other elements of your trip (such as car rentals, airport transfers, and sometimes even activities) at the same time and often at discounted prices—kind of like one-stop shopping. Packages are sold in bulk to tour operators—who resell them to the public at a cost that usually undercuts standard rates.

One good source of package deals is the airlines themselves. Most major airlines offer air/land packages. Several

big **online travel agencies**—Expedia, Travelocity, Orbitz, Site59, and Last minute.com—also do a brisk business in packages. If you're unsure about the pedigree of a smaller packager, check with the Better Business Bureau in the city where the company is based, or go online at www.bbb.org. If a packager won't tell you where it's based, don't fly with them.

The single best-priced packager to Europe, though, is **Go-Today.com** (www.go-today.com), offering packages throughout Italy. **Italiatours** (✆ **800-845-3365;** www.italiatourusa.com) is the tour operator branch of Alitalia airlines and offers package and escorted tours at extremely attractive prices.

TourCrafters (© 800-ITALY95 or 847-816-6510; www.tourcrafters.com) offers escorted, hosted, and independent tours throughout Italy. Far & Wide (© **866-FAR-WIDE**; www.farand wide.com) also has competitively priced deals, including one on the lakes of Lombardy.

Travel packages are also listed in the travel section of your local Sunday newspaper. Or check ads in the national travel magazines such as *Arthur Frommer's Budget Travel Magazine, Travel & Leisure, National Geographic Traveler,* and *Condé Nast Traveler.*

Package tours can vary by leaps and bounds. Some offer a better class of hotels than others. Some offer the same hotels for lower prices. Some offer flights on scheduled airlines, while others book charters. Some limit your choice of accommodations and travel days. You are often required to make a large payment up front. On the plus side, packages can save you money, offering group prices but allowing for independent travel. Some even let you add on a few guided excursions or escorted day trips (also at prices lower than if you booked them yourself) without booking an entirely escorted tour.

Before you invest in a package tour, get some answers. Ask about the **accommodations choices** and prices for each. Then look up the hotels' reviews in a Frommer's guide and check their rates for your specific dates of travel online. You'll also want to find out what **type of room** you get. If you need a certain type of room, ask for it; don't take whatever is thrown your way. Request a nonsmoking room, a quiet room, a room with a view, or whatever you fancy.

Finally, look for hidden expenses. Ask whether airport departure fees and taxes, for example, are included in the total cost. And, if you plan to travel alone, you'll need to know if a single supplement will be charged or if the company can match you up with a roommate.

12 Special-Interest Trips

PARLA ITALIANO?

Language courses are available at several centers around the Italian peninsula. You can contact any of the following for information about programs across Italy, varying in length, location (city versus rural), short- or long-term, and price: **Italian Cultural Institute** in New York (© 212-879-4242), **American Institute for Foreign Study** (© 800-727-AIFS; www.aifs.org), and **Institute of International Education** (© 800-445-0443 or 212-984-5413; www.iie.org).

BIKE TOURS

The Italian countryside has always been legendary for its beauty and architectural richness, and bicycle tours are a particularly memorable way to experience it.

Bike-it-yourselfers should arm themselves with a good map (see "Getting Around," below) and make use of the resources of the **Club Alpino Italiano,** 7 Via E. Fonseca Pimental, Milan 20127 (© **02-2614-1378**; fax 02-2614-1395; www.cai.it). You can rent a bike by the week or longer at outlets in most cities.

The best tour resource is the annual **Tourfinder** issue of *Bicycle USA.* A copy costs $15 from the League of American Bicyclists, 1612 K St. NW, Suite 401, Washington, DC 20006 (© **202/822-1333**; www.bikeleague.org). Membership is $30 per year and includes the Tourfinder and the annual almanac with information on European bicycling organizations.

Several companies specialize in bicycle tours, including Ciclismo

Tips **Prime Sightseeing Hours**

One mistake many people make when scheduling their hopping from hill town to hill town is getting up early in the mornings to travel to the next destination. Because many of Italy's sights are open only in the morning and almost all close for *riposo* (afternoon rest) from noonish to 3 or 4pm, this wastes valuable sightseeing time. I do my traveling just after noon, when everything is closing up. There's often a last train before *riposo* to wherever you're going or a country bus run (intended to shuttle school-children home for lunch). If you're driving, you can enjoy great country-side vistas under the noonday sun.

charge for this service if you're not a member. If you wish, you may join at the border as you're driving into Italy or online at **www.aci.it**.

RENTALS Many of Italy's most charming landscapes lie far away from the rail network. For that, and for sheer convenience, renting a car is usually the best way to explore the country. It's also the most expensive (Italy's rates have always been some of the highest in Europe) and is usually a consideration only for the budgeter traveling with one or more companions to split the cost. Also, note that it's much cheaper to book a rental car in your home country than it is once you get to Italy. If you're already in Italy, and you need a car immediately, have someone back home reserve one for you. The legalities and contractual obligations of renting a car in Italy (where accident and theft rates are very high) are more complicated than those in almost any other country in Europe. You must have nerves of steel, a sense of humor, a valid driver's license (with photo), a valid passport, and be over 25 (some places accept 21). Payment and paperwork are much easier if you present a valid credit card with your completed rental contract (many companies won't even consider a non–credit card payment). If that isn't possible, you'll likely be required to pay a substantial deposit, sometimes in cash. Insurance on all vehicles is compulsory, though what kind and how much is up to you and your credit card company: ask the right questions and check with your credit card company before leaving home. Also see "Surfing for Rental Cars" on p. 45.

DRIVING RULES Italian drivers aren't maniacs; they only appear to be. Actually, they tend to be very safe and alert drivers—if much more aggressive than Americans are used to. If someone races up behind you and flashes her lights, that's the signal for you to slow down so she can pass you quickly and safely. Stay in the right lane on highways; the left is only for passing and for cars with large engines and the pedal to the metal. If you see someone in your rearview mirror speeding up with his hazard lights blinking, get out of the way because it means his Mercedes is opened up full throttle. On a two-lane road, the idiot passing someone in the opposing traffic who has swerved into your lane expects you to veer obligingly over into the shoulder so three lanes of traffic can fit—he would do the same for you.

Autostrade are superhighways, denoted by green signs and a number prefaced with an A, like the famous A1 from Naples to Milan via Rome and Florence. Occasionally these aren't numbered and are simply called *raccordo,* a connecting road between two cities. On longer stretches, autostrade often become toll roads. **Strade Statale** are state roads, usually two lanes wide, indicated by blue signs. Their route numbers are prefaced with an SS or an S. On signs, however, these official route numbers are used infrequently. Usually, you'll just see blue signs listing destinations by name with arrows pointing off in the appropriate directions. Even if it's just a few miles down on the road, often the town you're looking for won't be mentioned on the sign at the appropriate turnoff. It's impossible to predict which of all the towns that lie along a road will be the ones chosen to list on a particular sign. Sometimes, the sign gives only the first miniscule village that lies past the turnoff; at other times it lists the first major town down that road, and some signs mention only the major city the road eventually leads to, even if its hundreds of miles away. It pays to study the map and fix in your mind the names of all three possibilities before coming to an intersection.

The **speed limit** on roads in built-up areas around towns and cities is 50kmph (31 mph). On rural roads and the highway it's 110kmph (68 mph), except on weekends when it's upped to 130 kmph (81 mph). Italians have an astounding disregard for these limits. However, police can ticket you and collect the fine on the spot. Although there's no official blood alcohol level at which you're "legally drunk," the police will throw you in jail if they pull you over and find you soused.

As far as **parcheggio** (**parking**) is concerned, on **streets** white lines indicate free public spaces and blue lines pay public spaces. Meters don't line the sidewalk; rather, there's one machine on the block where you punch in how long you want to park. The machine spits out a ticket that you leave on your dashboard. Sometimes streets will have an attendant who'll come around and give you your time ticket (pay him or her when you get ready to leave). If you park in an area marked PARCHEGGIO DISCO ORARIO, root around in your rental car's glove compartment for a cardboard parking disc (or buy one at a gas station). With this device, you dial up the hour of your arrival (it's the honor system) and display it on your dashboard. You're allowed *un ora* (1 hr.) or *due ore* (2 hr.), according to the sign. **Parking lots** have ticket dispensers but usually *not* manned booths as you exit. Take your ticket with you when you park; when you return to the lot to get your car and leave, first visit the office or automated payment machine to exchange your ticket for a paid receipt you then use to get through the automated exit.

ROAD SIGNS   Here's a brief rundown of the road signs you'll most frequently encounter. A **speed limit** sign is a black number inside a red circle on a white background. The **end of a speed zone** is just black and white, with a black slash through the number. A red circle with a white background, a black arrow pointing down, and a red arrow pointing up means **yield to oncoming traffic,** while a point-down red-and-white triangle means **yield ahead.** In town, a simple white circle with a red border or the words *zona pedonale* or *zona traffico limitato* denotes a **pedestrian zone** (you can drive through only to drop off baggage at your hotel); a white arrow on a blue background is used for Italy's many **one-way streets;** a mostly red circle with a horizontal white slash means **do not enter.** Any image in black on a white background surrounded by a red circle means that image is **not allowed** (for instance, if the image is two cars next to each other: no passing; a motorcycle means no Harleys permitted, and so on). A circular sign in blue with a red circle-slash means **no parking.**

GASOLINE   *Benzina* (gas or petrol) is even more expensive in Italy than in the rest of Europe. Even a small rental car guzzles between 30€ and 50€ ($35–$58) for a fill-up. There are many pull-in gas stations along major roads and on the outskirts of town, as well as 24-hour rest stops along the autostrada highways, but in towns most stations are small sidewalk gas stands where you parallel park to fill up. Almost all stations are closed for *riposo* and on Sundays, but the majority now have a pump fitted with a machine that accepts bills so you can self-service your tank at 3am. Unleaded gas is *senza piombo.*

BY TRAIN

Italy has one of the best train systems in Europe, and even traveling on a regional level, you'll find many destinations connected. Most lines are administered by the state-run **Ferrovie dello Stato** or **FS** (© **892-021** for national train info, 199-166-177 to buy tickets; or www.trenitalia.com), but private lines take up the slack in a few places. About the only difference you'll notice is that these private lines don't honor special discount cards or passes (see "Special Passes & Discounts," below).

Italian trains tend to be very clean and comfortable. Though increasingly trains are of the boring straight-through commuter variety, on long-haul runs especially you'll still be blessed with those old-fashioned cars made up of *couchette* compartments that seat only six or occasionally eight. (Try to find one full of nuns for a fighting chance at a smoke-free trip.) First class *(prima classe)* is usually only a shade better than second class *(seconda classe),* with four to six seats per couchette instead of six to eight. The only real benefit of first class comes if you're traveling overnight, in which case four berths per compartment are a lot more comfortable than six.

Few visitors are prepared for how **crowded** Italian trains can sometimes

get, though with the increase in automobile travel, they're not as crowded as they were in decades past. An Italian train is only full when the corridors are packed solid and there are more than eight people sitting on their luggage in the little vestibules by the doors. Overcrowding is usually only a problem on Friday evenings and weekends, especially in and out of big cities, and just after a strike. In summer the crowding escalates, and any train going toward a beach in August all but bulges like an overstuffed sausage.

Italian trains come in six varieties based on how often they stop. The **ETR/Pendolino** (P) is the "pendulum" train that zips back and forth between Rome and Milan, stopping at Florence and Bologna along the way. It's the fastest but most expensive option (first class only, a meal included); it has its own ticket window at the stations and *requires* a seat reservation. **Eurostar/ Eurocity** (ES/EC, EN if it runs overnight) trains connect Italian cities with cities outside the country; these are the speediest of the standard trains, offering both first and second class and always requiring a supplement (except for Eurailpass holders, though the conductors won't always believe you on this one); **Intercity** (IC) trains are similar to Eurocity trains in that they offer both first and second class and require a supplement, but they never cross an international border.

Of the regular trains that don't require supplements—often called *Regionale* (R) if they stay within a region (the Veneto) or *Interregionale* (IR) if they don't (the Veneto through Lombardy to Piemonte)—the **Espresso** stops at all the major and most of the secondary stations, the **Diretto** stops at virtually every station, and the snail-paced **Locale** (sometimes laughingly called *accelerato*) frequently stops between stations in the middle of the countryside for no apparent reason.

When buying a **regular ticket,** ask for either *andata* (one-way) or *andata e ritorno* (round-trip). If the train you plan to take is an ES/EC or IC, ask for the ticket *con supplemento rapido* (with speed supplement) to avoid on-train penalty charges. On a trip under 200km (124 miles), your ticket is good to leave within the next 6 hours; over 200km you have a full day. (This code isn't rigorously upheld by conductors, but don't push your luck.) On round-trip journeys of less than 250km (155 miles), the return ticket is valid only for 3 days. This mileage-time correlation continues, with an extra day added to your limit for each 200km above 250 (the maximum is 6 days). If you board a regular train without a ticket (or board an IC/EC without the supplement), you'll have to pay a hefty "tax" on top of the ticket or supplement the conductor will sell you. Most conductors also get extremely crabby if you forget to **stamp your ticket in the little yellow box** on the platform before boarding the train.

Schedules for all lines running through a given station are printed on posters tacked up on the station wall. *Binario (bin.)* means track. Useful schedules for all train lines are printed biannually in booklets (which are broken down into sections of the country—you want *nord e centro Italia,* north and central Italy, or simply *centro*) available at any newsstand. There are official FS-published booklets, but the better buy is the *Pozzorario,* which not only is cheaper but also lists private lines (and it's just as accurate). You can also get official schedules (and more train information, some even in English) on the web at **www.trenitalia.com**.

Stations tend to be well run and clean, with luggage storage facilities at all but the smallest and usually a good *bar* attached with surprisingly palatable food. If you pull into a dinky town with a shed-sized or nonexistent station, find the nearest *bar* or *tabacchi,* and the man behind the counter will most likely double as the "station master" to sell you tickets.

SPECIAL PASSES & DISCOUNTS

Note: The rates quoted below are for 2003, and will rise each year.

To buy the **Italy Flexi Railcard,** available only outside Italy, contact **Rail Europe** (www.raileurope.com). It works similarly to the Eurailpass, in that you have one month in which to use the train a set number of days; the base number of days is four, and you can add up to six more. For adults, the first class pass costs $239; adults traveling together can get the Saver version for $203 each. The second-class version costs $191 for adults ($163 on the Saver edition), or for youths under 26, the price is $160. Extra days cost $24 ($20 for Saver passes) in first class, $19 ($16 for Saver), and $16 for youths.

A 4-day **Trenitalia Pass** (good on all train runs in Italy) is 447€ ($514) in first class, 357€ ($411) in second; a 5-day pass is 492€ ($566) in first class, 393€ ($452) in second; a 6-day pass is 536€ ($616) in first class, 428€ ($492) in second; a 10-day pass is 716€ ($823) for first class and 570€ ($656) for second. The **Youth Pass** version (for ages 16 to 25 years) is available for second-class travel only. A 4-day pass is 229€ ($263); a 5-day pass is 329€ ($378). Each additional day (up to 10 days) is an additional 30€ ($34). A **Saver Pass** allows two to five people to ride the rails for four to ten days in either first or second class. A 4-day pass is 379€ ($436) in first class, 305€ ($351) in second class; a 5-day pass is 417€ ($480) in first and 335€ ($385) in second; a 10-day pass is 604€ ($695) for first class and 484€ ($557) for second class. Children ages 4 to 11 pay 50% of the adult fare.

There is also a **rail-and-drive** pass, which combines train and car travel

Travel Times Between the Major Cities

Cities	Distance	Air Travel Time	Train Travel Time	Driving Time
Florence to Milan	298km/185 miles	55 min.	2½ hr.	3½ hr.
Florence to Venice	281km/174 miles	2 hr. 5 min.	4 hr.	3 hr. 15 min.
Milan to Venice	267km/166 miles	50 min.	3½ hr.	3 hr. 10 min.
Milan to Rome	572km/355 miles	1 hr. 5 min.	5 hr.	6 hr. 30 min.
Venice to Rome	528km/327 miles	1 hr. 5 min.	5 hr. 15 min.	6 hr.
Genoa to Rome	501km/311 miles	1 hr.	6 hr.	5 hr. 45 min.
Torino to Rome	669km/415 miles	1 hr. 5 min.	9–11 hr.	7 hr. 45 min.

throughout Italy, allowing you to visit some of the smaller town—or anywhere else in Italy. The pass gives you, within 1 month, four days of 1st- or 2nd-class train travel within Italy and two days of car rental (and the possibility to add more car days cheaply). The pass is available from Rail Europe. Prices (per person 1 adult 1st class/ 1 adult 2nd class/2 adults 1st class/ 2 adults 2nd class) vary: $329/$279/ $249/$209 economy; $365/$319/ $269/$229 compact; $379/$335/ $275/$235 midsize. You may add as many as six rail days to the pass for $25/$21/$21/$17 per person per day. Additional car days are $45 economy, $65 compact, $75 midsize.

When it comes to regular tickets, if you're **under 26,** you can buy at any Italian train station a 26€ ($30) **Carta Verde** (Green Card) that gets you a 15% discount on all FS tickets for one year. Present it each time you go to buy a ticket. The same deal is available for anyone **over 60** with the **Carta d'Argento** (Silver Card). Children under 12 always ride half price (and can get the passes mentioned below at half price), and kids under 4 ride free.

BY BUS

Regional intertown buses are called *pullman,* though *autobus,* the term for a city bus, is also sometimes used. When you're getting down to the kind of small-town travel this guide describes, you'll probably need to use regional buses at some point. You can get just about anywhere through a network of dozens of local, provincial, and regional lines, but schedules aren't always easy to come by or to figure out—the local tourist office usually has a photocopy of the schedule, and in cities some companies have offices. Buses exist mainly to shuttle workers and schoolchildren, so the most runs are on weekdays, early in the morning and usually again around lunchtime. All too often, though, the only run of the day will be at 6am.

A town's bus stop is usually either the main piazza or, more often, a large square on the edge of town or the bend in the road just outside a small town's main city gate. You should always try to find the local ticket vendor—if there's no office, it's invariably the nearest newsstand or *tabacchi* (signaled by a sign with a white T), or occasionally a *bar*—but you can usually also buy tickets on the bus. You can also flag a bus down as it passes on a country road, but try to find an official stop (a small sign tacked onto a telephone pole). Tell the driver where you're going and ask him courteously if he'll let you know when you need to get off. When he says *"E la prossima fermata,"* that means yours is the next stop. *"Posso scendere?"* (*poh*-so *shen*-dair-ay?) is "May I please get off?"

14 Tips on Accommodations, Villa Rentals & Farm Stays

Alas, Italy is no longer the country of dirt-cheap *pensione,* with shared bathrooms and swaybacked beds. Most hotels have private bathrooms in the rooms now (if not, my reviews state this), regulations and standardization have become much stricter—which is all fine and well, the only problem is that prices have soared because of it, in most cases doubling and often tripling over just the past five years.

Many **bathrooms** are still dismal affairs—often a closet-size room with a sink, toilet, and bidet and just a shower head on the wall, a drain in the floor, and no curtain (rescue the toilet paper from a drenching before you turn on the water). Towels are often flat, pressed cotton sheets, though terry-cloth towels are coming into style. Soap isn't a given, but the water is safe to drink.

Italy and its regional boards now control the prices of its hotels, designating a minimum and a maximum rate for each category. Many hotels are opting to go with one year-round rate to avoid confusion (discounting during slow periods and off season); others maintain two (or multiple) separate high- and low-season tariffs, especially at seaside destinations. Prices can also vary based on a room's location, size, decor, and whether it offers a private or shared bathroom; however, if there is a range of rates listed for any hotel in this book, that range *always* implies a seasonal variation unless the review specifically says otherwise.

Italy's old *pensione* system no longer exists, and hotels are now **rated** by regional boards on a system of one to five stars. Prices aren't directly tied to the star system, but for the most part, the more stars a hotel has, the more expensive it'll be—but a four-star in a small town may be cheaper than a two-star in Milan . . . and probably even less expensive than a one-star in Venice.

The number of official stars awarded a hotel is based strictly on the amenities offered and not how clean, comfortable, or friendly a place is or whether it's a good value for the money overall. That is why you need this book! Also note that the stars I assign to hotels in this book have nothing to do with the official rating system; some fantastic little pensione with a government rating of one star might get three from me, while I might not assign any to some pricey inn officially rated five stars.

A few of the four- and five-star hotels have their own private **garages,** but most city inns have an accord with a local garage. In many small towns, a garage is unnecessary because public parking, both free and pay, is widely available and never too far from your hotel. Parking costs and procedures are indicated under each hotel, and the rates quoted are per day (overnight).

The **high season** throughout northern Italy runs from Easter to early September or October—peaking June through August—and from December 24 to January 6. Of course, in ski resorts such as Cortina or Courmayeur, the peak is from Christmastime through mid-March (and they can become ghost towns in June). You can almost always bargain for a cheaper rate if you're traveling in the shoulder season (early spring and late fall) or winter off season (not including Christmas). You can also often get a discount for stays of more than three days. Always ask.

Supposedly, Italian hotels must quote the price for **breakfast** separately from the room and can't force it on you if you don't want it. However, most hotels include breakfast automatically in the room rate hoping you won't notice, and many also argue that breakfast is required at their hotel. Whenever possible, I've tried to include the separate per-person breakfast price for each hotel throughout the book. With very few exceptions, Italian hotel breakfasts tend to consist of a roll or *cornetto* (croissant) and coffee, occasionally with juice and fresh fruit as well. It's rarely worth the 3€ to 15€ ($3.45–$17) charged for it, as you can get the same breakfast—and freshly made instead of packaged—for around 2€ ($2.30) at the *bar* down the block. Ask for your room quote with a *prezzo senza colazione* (pretz-zoh *sen*-zah coal-lat-zee-*oh*-nay), or price without breakfast.

The Italian term **albergo** is more and more commonly being replaced by the international word *hotel*. **Locanda** once meant a rustic inn or carriage stop, though it's now used sometimes to refer to a place quite charming or fancy. The **pensione** system of yesteryear has pretty much disappeared, and with it the obligation to share bathrooms and eat three meals a day prepared by the families that owned them. They are now one- and two-star hotels, with many of them retaining the word *pensione* in their names to connote a small, often family-run hotel of character or charm (not always the case!). In 2000, Italy also introduced *"il Bed and Breakfast"* classification to encourage more of the smaller *pensioni* or larger rental-room operations to stop hiding from the tax collector and officially incorporate as a business.

Single travelers stand to be the most disappointed: Rarely are single rooms anything to write home about (usually wedged into the space between the hall and the building's airshaft), and rarely is the rate charged actually half that of a double. Closet-size rooms are not uncommon; if it is a slow month, see if the hotel owner will consider renting a double room at a single-occupancy rate.

Reservations are always advised, even in the so-called slow months of November to March when you might find towns such as Verona (not to mention the large cities) booked solid with conventions and trade fairs. Travel to Italy peaks from May through October, when many of the best (or at least best-known) moderate and budget hotels are often filled up a few days to a few weeks in advance.

Italy's keeping-up-with-the-Jones's approaches to approval by its EU neighbors and government-imposed restrictions have done a tremendous amount to improve the status of its hotel situation—and it accounts for soaring prices. Many of the small guys have fallen between the cracks, however. The clean-as-a-whistle conditions that are a given in Switzerland or Germany's least expensive hostelries are not such a guarantee as you head south. All the more reason to rely on our suggestions

APARTMENTS, VILLAS & PALAZZI

Local tourist boards or the provincial tourist office in the city or town where you expect to stay will not be much help. Information on villas and apartments is available in daily newspapers or through local real-estate agents in Italy and some international travel publications. Millions of properties are put up for rent by their Italian owners—and to find them, you'll have to do your homework and legwork. Single travelers will find the option of rentals expensive, couples less so. Groups or families of four to six people (the more the merrier) may find villa or apartment rental an enjoyable savings. Everyone fantasizes about that dream villa amid the vineyards; but remember that photos do not always a thousand words tell. Research a potential rental thoroughly to make sure you're not getting a dump, or what looks like a gem but ends up being right next to the train tracks.

Each summer, thousands of visitors become temporary Italians by renting an old farmhouse or "villa," a marketing term used to inspire romantic images of manicured gardens, a

Renaissance mansion, and Barolo martinis, but in reality guaranteeing no more than four walls and most of a roof.

Actually, finding your countryside Eden isn't that simple, and if you want to ensure a romantic and memorable experience, brace yourself for a lot of research and legwork. Occasionally you can go through the property owners themselves, but the vast majority of villas are rented out via agencies (see below).

Shop around for a trustworthy agent or representative. Often several outfits will list the same property but charge radically different prices. At some you sign away any right to refunds if the place doesn't live up to your expectations. Expect to pay $10 to $25 for a copy of each company's catalog; most refund this expense if you rent through them. Make sure the agency is willing to work with you to find the right property. Try to work with someone who has personally visited the properties you're considering, and always ask to see lots of photos: Get the exterior from several angles to make sure the railroad doesn't pass by the back door, as well as pictures of the bedrooms, kitchen, and bathrooms, and photos of the views out each side of the house.

If you're traveling with several couples, ask to see a floor plan to make sure access to the bathroom isn't through one couple's bedroom. Find out if this is the only villa on the property—some people who rent the villa for the isolation find themselves living in a small enclave of foreigners all sharing the same small pool. Ask whether the villa is purely a rental unit or if, say, the family lives there during winter but lets it out during summer. Renting a lived-in place offers pretty good insurance that the lights, plumbing, heat, and so on will all be working.

These organizations rent villas or apartments, generally on the pricey side; stipulate your price range when inquiring. One of the best agencies to

call is **Renvillas.com** (formerly Rentals in Italy), 700 E. Main St., Ventura, CA 93001 (© **800-726-6702** or 805-641-1650; fax 805-641-1630; www.rentvillas.com). Its agents are very helpful in tracking down the perfect place to suit your needs. A United Kingdom agency—and one of the best all-around agents in Britain—is **International Chapters,** a division of Abercrombie & Kent, Sloane Square House, Holbein Place, London SW1W 8NS (© **08450-700-618;** www.villarentals.com). Marjorie Shaw's **Insider's Italy,** 41 Schermerhorn St., Brooklyn, NY 11201 (© **718-855-3878;** fax 718-855-3687; www.insidersitaly.com), is a small, upscale outfit run by a very personable agent who's thoroughly familiar with all of her properties and Italy in general.

Also in the United States, **Parker Company Ltd.,** Seaport Landing, 152 Lynnway, Lynn, MA 01902 (© **800-280-2811** or 781-596-8282; fax 781-596-3125; www.theparkercompany.com), handles overseas villa rentals.

For some of the top properties, call the local representative of the **Cottages to Castles** group. In the United Kingdom, contact **Cottages to Castles,** Tuscany House, 10 Tonbridge Rd., Maidstone, Kent ME16 8RP (© **1622-775-217;** fax 1622-775-278). In Australia and New Zealand, call **Italian Villa Holidays,** P.O. Box 2293, Wellington, 6015, New Zealand (© **800-125-555** in Australia, 800-4-TUSCANY in New Zealand; fax 64-4-479-0021). At press time, the organization was searching for a representative in the United States.

One of the most reasonably priced agencies is **Villas and Apartment Abroad, Ltd.,** 370 Lexington Ave., Suite 1401, New York, NY 10017 (© **212-897-5045;** fax 212-897-5039; www.vaanyc.com). **Homeabroad.com,** formerly Vacanze in Italia, 22 Railroad St., Great Barrington, MA 02130

(© **413-528-6610;** www.homeabroad. com), handles hundreds of rather upscale properties. A popular but *very* pricey agency is **Villas International,** 4340 Redwood Hwy., Suite D309, San Rafael, CA 94903 (© **800-221-2260** or 415-499-9490; fax 415-499-9491; www.villasintl.com).

AGRITURISMO—STAYING ON A FARM

Italy is at the forefront of the *agriturismo* movement, whereby a working farm or agricultural estate makes available accommodations for visitors who want to stay out in the countryside. The rural atmosphere is ensured by the fact that an operation can call itself *agriturismo* only if (a) it offers fewer than 30 beds total and (b) the agricultural component of the property brings in a larger economic share of profits than the hospitality part—in other words, the property has to remain a farm and not become a glorified hotel.

Agriturismi are generally a crapshoot. They're only loosely regulated, and the price, quality, and types of accommodation can vary dramatically. Some are sumptuous apartments or suites with hotel-like amenities; others are a straw's width away from sleeping in the barn on a haystack. Most, though, are mini-apartments, often furnished from secondhand dealers and usually rented out with a minimum stay of three days or a week. Sometimes you're invited to eat big country dinners at the table with the family; other times you cook for yourself. Rates can vary from 15€ ($17) for two per day all the way up to 250€ ($288)—as much as a four-star hotel in town—though most hover around the thoroughly reasonable rates of 50€ to 100€ ($58–$115) for a double. I've reviewed a few choice ones throughout this book, but there are hundreds more.

If you feel handy enough with Italian, you can avail yourself of the three independent national organizations that together represent all agriturismi (or, at least, all the reputable ones).

Go to the web site of **Terranostra** (www.terranostra.it) and click on "La tua vacanza," then "ricerche." This will pop you up a map of Italy. Mouse over the region you want, click, and you'll get hundreds of choices, arranged, unfortunately, alphabetically by name of the actual property (not by, say, town, which would make selecting one so much easier), with price categories of *basso* (low), *medio* (medium), and *alto* (high). When you click on the property name, you get a review with pictures and symbols (in Italian, but understandable enough) plus contact info and a link to the place's own website, if available.

At the site of **Turismo Verde** (www. turismoverde.it), click on "La guida agrituristica on-line." On the search page that pops up, you can choose to search by Regione (Lombardia, Veneto, Piemonte, etc.) or by Provincia (Como, Padova, Treviso, Asti, etc.), and the results pages that come up based on your criteria are pretty much like the ones at Terranostra, only this time it returns all the results on a single page (rather than by pages of 10 each), so it's a bit easier to quickly find, say, all the ones near Aosta. Again, click on a property name to learn much more about it and find a direct link.

The easiest to navigate—since, once you click on a region on the map or text list, the next page gives you the option of continuing in English—is **Agriturist** (www.agriturist.it), but the site fails after that: While you can, indeed, find hundreds upon hundreds of individual properties via its search engine, they do not provide each farm's own website (possibly because they want you to book via their own site), so tracking the *agriturismi* down is that much more difficult; plus the info provided about each is far skimpier than with the other resources.

In the States, a few agencies are popping up to help you track down a perfect *agriturismo* in Italy, including Ralph Levey's **Italy Farm Holidays,** 547 Martling Ave., Tarrytown, NY 10591 (© **914-631-7880;** fax 914-631-8831; www.italyfarmholidays.com), which represents many of the more upscale *agriturismo* properties.

15 Tips on Dining

For a quick bite, go to a *bar*—though it does serve alcohol, a *bar* in Italy functions mainly as a cafe. Prices at *bars* have a split personality: *al banco* is standing at the bar, while *à tavola* means sitting at a table where they'll wait on you and charge 2 to 4 times as much for the same cappuccino. In *bars* you can find *panini* sandwiches on various rolls and *tramezzini,* giant triangles of white-bread sandwiches with the crusts cut off. These run 1.50€ to 5€ ($1.75–$5.75) and are traditionally stuck in a kind of tiny pants press to flatten and toast them so the crust is crispy and the filling hot and gooey; microwaves have unfortunately invaded and are everywhere turning *panini* into something that resembles a very hot, soggy tissue.

Pizza à taglio or *pizza rustica* indicates a place where you can order pizza by the slice, though Venice is infamous for serving some of Italy's worst pizza this way. They fare somewhat better at *pizzerie,* casual sit-down restaurants that cook large, round pizzas with very thin crusts in wood-burning ovens. A *tavola calda* (literally "hot table") serves ready-made hot foods you can take away or eat at one of the few small tables often available. The food is usually very good, and you can get away with a full meal at a *tavola calda* for well under 15€ ($17). A *rosticceria* is the same type of place with some chickens roasting on a spit in the window. In Venice, you can often get *chichetti*—finger food, snack on sticks, pâtés on bread—at a number of bars in the early evening (5–7pm), each morsel costing a modest .50€ to 1€ (60¢–$1.15). Milan and Turin have the same thing, only they don't have a special name for it, and it almost always comes free—so long as you're drinking something.

Eating lunch *(pranzo)* or dinner *(cena)* in Italy can be a pretty elaborate affair, although the serious three-course lunch—*antipasto* (appetizer), *primo* (first course) of pasta, soup, or risotto, and *secondo* (second course) of meat or fish, possibly accompanied by a *contorno* (side dish) of veggies, finished off with *dolce* (dessert) and a *caffè* (espresso coffee)—is fast being reduced to the rushed American standard.

Full-fledged restaurants go by the names *osteria, trattoria,* or *ristorante.* Once upon a time, these terms meant something—*osterie* were basic places where you could get a plate of spaghetti and a glass of wine; *trattorie* were casual places serving simple full meals of filling peasant fare; and *ristoranti* were fancier places, with waiters in bow ties, printed menus, wine lists, and hefty prices. Nowadays, though, fancy restaurants often go by the name of *trattoria* to cash in on the associated charm factor, trendy spots use *osteria* to show they're hip, and simple inexpensive places sometimes tack on *ristorante* to ennoble their establishment.

The *pane e coperto* (bread and cover) is a cover charge of anywhere from .50€ to 15€ (60¢–$17) that you must pay at every Italian restaurant for the mere privilege of sitting at the table. Most Italians eat a full meal—appetizer and first (primo) and second (secondo) courses—at lunch and dinner and will expect you to do the same, or at least a first and second course. See "From the *Cucina Italiana:* Food and Wine" in appendix A for details of the meal and typical dishes to try. To request the bill, ask

Getting Your VAT Refund

Most purchases have a built-in **value added tax (IVA)** of 17.36%. Non-EU (European Union) citizens are entitled to a refund of this tax if they spend more than 155€ ($178), before tax, at any one store. To claim your refund, request an invoice from the cashier at the store and take it to the customs office *(dogana)* at the airport to have it stamped *before* you leave. **Note:** If you're going to another EU country before flying home, have it stamped at the airport customs office of the last EU country you'll be visiting (so if flying home via Britain, have your Italian invoices stamped in London).

Once back home, mail the stamped invoice back to the store within 90 days of the purchase, and they'll send you a refund check. Many shops are now part of the "Tax Free for Tourists" network. (Look for the sticker in the window.) Stores participating in this network issue a check along with your invoice at the time of purchase. After you have the invoice stamped at customs, you can redeem the check for cash directly at the tax-free booth in the airport, or mail it back in the envelope provided within 60 days. For more info, check out www.globalrefund.com.

"Il conto, per favore" (eel *con*-toh pore fah-*vohr*-ay). A tip of 15% is usually included in the bill these days, but if unsure ask "*è incluso il servizio?*" (ay een-*cloo*-soh eel sair-*vee*-tsoh?).

You'll find at many restaurants, especially larger ones and those in cities, a **menù turistico** (tourists' menu) costing from 10€ to 35€ ($12–$40). This set-price menu usually covers all meal incidentals, including table wine, cover charge, and a 15% service charge, along with a first and a second course. But it almost invariably offers an abbreviated selection of rather bland dishes: spaghetti in tomato sauce and slices of roast pork. Sometimes better is a **menù a prezzo fisso** (fixed-price menu), which usually doesn't include wine but sometimes covers the service and *coperto* and often has a wider selection of better dishes, occasionally including house specialties and local foods. Ordering a la carte, however, offers you the best chance for a memorable meal. Even better, forego the menu entirely and put yourself in the capable hands of your waiter.

Many restaurants that really care about their food—from *osterie* to classy *ristoranti*—will also offer a **menù degustazione (tasting menu),** allowing you to sample small portions of the kitchen's bounty, usually several antipasti, a few primi, and a secondo or two (and sometimes several local wines to taste by the glass). They're almost always highly recommendable and usually turn out to be a huge feast. Prices can vary wildly, anywhere from 20€ to 100€ ($23–$115). About 40€ to 50€ ($46–$58) is most common.

The **enoteca (wine bar)** is a growingly popular marriage of a wine bar and an osteria, where you sit and order from a host of local and regional wines by the glass while snacking on finger foods and simple primi. It's also possible to go into an **alimentari (general food store)** and have sandwiches prepared on the spot, or buy the makings for a picnic.

For more on Italy's food, see the "From the *Cucina Italiana:* Food & Wine" section of Appendix A, beginning on p. 440.

FAST FACTS: Northern Italy

The following list provides general information. You can find more specific information in the city-specific "Fast Facts" sections for Venice, Milan, Genoa, and Turin.

Banks They're open Monday through Friday from 8:30am to 1 or 1:30pm and 2 or 2:30 to 4pm and closed all day Saturday, Sunday, and national holidays. Hours change slightly from city to city.

Business Hours General open hours for **stores, offices,** and **churches** are from 9:30am to noon or 1pm and again from 3 or 3:30pm to 7:30pm. That early afternoon shutdown is the *riposo,* the Italian *siesta.* Most stores close all day Sunday and many also on Monday (morning only or all day). Some shops, especially grocery stores, also close Thursday afternoons. Some services and business offices are open to the public only in the morning. Traditionally, museums are closed Mondays, and though some of the biggest stay open all day long, many close for *riposo* or are only open in the morning (9am–2pm is popular). Some churches open earlier in the morning, but the largest often stay open all day. **Banks** tend to be open Monday through Friday from 8:30am to 1:30pm and 2:30 to 3:30pm or 3 to 4pm.

Drug Laws Penalties are severe and could lead to imprisonment or deportation. Selling drugs to minors is dealt with particularly harshly.

Drugstores You'll find **green neon crosses** above the entrances to most *farmacie* (pharmacies). You'll also find many *erborista* (herbalist) shops, which usually offer more traditional herbal remedies (some of which are marvelously effective) along with the standard pharmaceuticals. Most *farmacie* of any stripe keep everything behind the counter, so be prepared to point or pantomime. *Some help:* Most minor ailments start with the phrase *mal di* in Italian, so you can just say "Mahl dee" and point to your head, stomach, throat, or whatever. Pharmacies rotate which will stay open all night and on Sundays, and each store has a poster outside showing the month's rotation.

Electricity Italy operates on a 220 volts AC (50 cycles) system, as opposed to the United States' 110 volts AC (60 cycle) system. You'll need a simple adapter plug and, unless your appliance is dual-voltage (as some hair dryers and travel irons are), a currency converter.

Embassies/Consulates Embassies and their consulates (consulates are for citizens—lost passports and other services; embassies are mostly only for diplomats) are all located in Rome, though such other major cities as Milan often also have consular offices. Each major city chapter in this book has a Fast Facts section listing some local embassies/consulates and their open hours.

Emergencies Dial ℰ **113** for any emergency. You can also call ℰ **112** for the *carabinieri* (police), ℰ **118** for an ambulance, or ℰ **115** for the fire department. If your car breaks down, dial ℰ **116** for roadside aid courtesy of the Automotive Club of Italy. All of the above are free calls.

Hospitals The emergency ambulance number is ℰ **118**. Hospitals in Italy are partially socialized, and the care is efficient, very personalized, and of a high quality. There are also well-run private hospitals. Pharmacy staff also tends to be very competent health-care providers, so for less serious problems their advice will do fine. For non-life-threatening, but still concerning, ailments you can just walk into most hospitals and get taken care of speedily—no questions about insurance policies, no forms to fill out, and no fees to pay. Most hospitals will be able to find someone who speaks English.

Internet Access Cybercafes are in healthy supply in most Italian cities. In smaller towns you may have a bit of trouble, but, increasingly, hotels are setting up Internet points. In a pinch, hostels, local libraries, and, often, pubs will have a terminal for access. For getting online in Venice, Milan, Turin, or Genoa, see each city's own "Fast Facts" section.

Language Though Italian is the local language around these parts, English is a close second, especially amongst anyone below about age 40 since they all learned it in school. Anyone in the tourism industry will know the English they need to help smooth transactions with you. Besides, most Italians are delighted to help you learn a bit of their lingo as you go. To help, there is a short list of key phrases and useful terms in Appendix B.

Liquor Laws Driving drunk is illegal and not a smart idea on any road—never mind Italy's twisty, narrow roads. Legal drinking age in Italy is 16, but that's just on paper. Public drunkenness (aside from people getting noisily tipsy and flush at big dinners) is unusual except among some street people—usually among foreign vagabonds, not the Italian homeless.

Lost & Found Be sure to tell all of your credit card companies the minute you discover your wallet has been lost or stolen and file a report at the nearest police precinct. Your credit card company or insurer may require a police report number or record of the loss. Most credit card companies have an emergency toll-free number to call if your card is lost or stolen; they may be able to wire you a cash advance immediately or deliver an emergency credit card in a day or two. If you **lose your card,** call the following Italian toll-free numbers: **Visa** (© **800-819-014**), **MasterCard** (© **800-870-866**), or **American Express** (© **800-872-000**, or collect © **336-393-1111** from anywhere in the world). As a back-up, write down the phone numbers that appear on the back of each of your cards (Not the U.S. toll-free numbers—you can't dial those from abroad—but rather the number you can call collect from anywhere; if one does not appear, call the card company and ask).

   If you need emergency cash over the weekend when all banks and American Express offices are closed, you can have money wired to you via **Western Union** (© **800/325-6000**; www.westernunion.com).

Mail The Italian mail system is notoriously slow, and friends back home may not receive your postcards or aerograms for up to 8 weeks (sometimes longer). Postcards, aerograms, and letters, weighing up to 20 grams (.7 oz.) to North America cost .52€ (60¢), to the United Kingdom and Ireland .41€ (29p), and to Australia and New Zealand .52€ (AUS$.90).

Newspapers/Magazines The *International Herald Tribune* (published by the *New York Times* and with news catering to Americans abroad) and

USA Today are available at just about every newsstand, even in smaller towns. You can find the *Wall Street Journal Europe,* European editions of *Time* and *Newsweek*, and often the *London Times* at some of the larger kiosks. For events guides in English, see each individual city's "Visitor Information" listing.

Police For emergencies, call © **113**. Italy has several different police forces, but there are only two you'll most likely ever need to deal with. The first is the urban polizia, whose city headquarters is called the *questura* and can help with lost and stolen property. The most useful branch—the cops to go to for serious problems and crimes—is the *carabinieri* (© **112**), a national order-keeping, crime-fighting civilian police force.

Restrooms Public toilets are going out of fashion in northern Italy, but most *bars* will let you use their bathrooms without a scowl or forcing you to buy anything. Ask *"Posso usare il bagno?"* (*poh*-soh oo-*zar*-eh eel *ban*-yo). *Donne/signore* are women and *uomini/signori* men. Train stations usually have a bathroom, for a fee, often of the two-bricks-to-stand-on-and-a-hole-in-the-floor Turkish toilet variety. In many of the public toilets that remain, the little old lady with a basket has been replaced by a coin-op turnstile.

Safety Other than the inevitable pickpockets, especially in touristy areas, random violent crime is practically unheard of in Italy. You won't find quite as many **gypsy pickpocketing children** as in Rome, but they have started roving other major tourist cities. If you see a small group or pair of dirty children coming at you, often waving cardboard and jabbering in Ital-English, yell *"Va via!"* (go away) or simply "No!," or invoke the *polizia*. If they get close enough to touch you, push them away forcefully—don't hold back because they're kids—otherwise within a nanosecond you and your wallet will be permanently separated.

There are plenty of locals, of course, who prey on tourists as well, especially around tourist centers like the Piazza San Marco in Venice and the Piazza del Duomo in Milan. In general, just be smart. Keep your passport, traveler's checks, credit and ATM cards (if you feel the need to), and a photocopy of all your important documents under your clothes in a money belt or neck pouch. **For women:** There are occasional drive-by purse snatchings in cities by young moped-mounted thieves. Keep your purse on the wall side of the sidewalk and sling the strap across your chest. If your purse has a flap, keep the clasp side facing your body. **For men:** Keep your wallet in your front pocket and perhaps loop a rubber band around it. (The rubber catches on the fabric of your pocket and makes it harder for a thief to slip the wallet out easily.)

Taxes There's no sales tax added onto the price tag of your purchases, but there is a **value-added tax** (in Italy: IVA) automatically included in just about everything. For major purchases, you can get this refunded (see the, "Getting Your VAT Refund" box on p. 63). Some five-star and four-star hotels add a 13% "luxury tax" to the rack rates (others just include it in their quoted rates), so to avoid an unpleasant surprise upon check out, it's wise to ask when booking if the price includes all taxes.

Telephones The **country code** for Italy is **39**. In 1998, Italy incorporated what were once separate **city codes** (for example, Milan's was 02, Venice's was 041) into the numbers themselves. Therefore, you must dial the entire number, *including the initial zero,* when calling from *anywhere* outside or inside Italy and even within the same town. For those of you familiar with the old system, this means that now, to call Milan from the States, you must dial **011-39-02-xxx-xxxx.** Increasingly, you'll notice Milan numbers beginning with prefixes other than 02; these are usually cellphone numbers. Fixed-line phone numbers in Italy can range anywhere from 6 to 12 digits in length.

Local calls in Italy cost .10€ (12¢). There are three types of public pay phones: those that take coins only, those that take both coins and phone cards, and those that take only **phone cards** (*carta* or *scheda telefonica*). You can buy these prepaid phone cards at any *tabacchi* (tobacconists), most newsstands, and some bars in several denominations from 1€ to 7.50€. Break off the corner before inserting it; a digital display tracks how much money is left on the card as you talk. Don't forget to take the card with you when you leave!

For **operator-assisted international calls** (in English), dial toll-free ✆ **170**. Note, however, that you'll get better rates by calling a home operator for collect calls, as detailed here: To make **calling card calls,** insert a phone card or .10€ coin—it'll be refunded at the end of your call—and dial the local number for your service. For **Americans:** AT&T at ✆ **800-172-4444,** MCI at ✆ **172-1022,** or Sprint at ✆ **172-1877.** These numbers will connect you to an American operator, and you can use any one of them to place a **collect call** even if you don't carry that phone company's card. **Canadians** can reach Teleglobe at ✆ **172-1001. Brits** can call BT at ✆ **172-0044** or Mercury at ✆ **172-0544.** The **Irish** can get a home operator at ✆ **172-0353. Australians** can use Optus by calling ✆ **172-1161** or Telstra at ✆ **172-1061.** And **New Zealanders** can phone home at ✆ **172-1064.**

To **dial direct internationally from Italy,** dial ✆ **00,** then the country code, the area code, and the number. Country codes are as follows: the United States and Canada 1; the United Kingdom 44; Ireland 353; Australia 61; New Zealand 64. Make international calls from a public phone if possible because hotels charge ridiculously inflated rates for direct dial, but take along plenty of *schede* to feed the phone.

To call free national **telephone information** (in Italian) in Italy, dial ✆ **12.** International information for Europe is available at ✆ **176** but costs .60€ (70¢) a shot. For international information beyond Europe, dial ✆ **1790** for .50€ (60¢).

Time Zone Italy is 6 hours ahead of Eastern Standard Time in the United States. When it's noon in New York, it's 6pm in Florence.

Tipping In **hotels,** a service charge is usually included in your bill. In family-run operations, additional tips are unnecessary and sometimes considered rude. In fancier places with a hired staff, however, you may want to leave a .50€ (60¢) daily tip for the maid, pay the bellhop or porter 1€ ($1.15) per bag, and a helpful concierge 2€ ($2.30) for his or her troubles.

In **restaurants,** 10% to 15% is almost always included in the bill—to be sure, ask "*è incluso il servizio?*"—but you can leave up to an additional 10%, especially for good service. At **bars and cafes,** leave a .10€ (12¢) coin per drink on the counter for the barman; if you sit at a table, leave 10% to 15%. **Taxi** drivers expect 10% to 15%.

Water Although most Italians take mineral water with their meals, tap water is safe everywhere, as are any public drinking fountains you run across. Unsafe sources will be marked "*acqua non potabile.*" If tap water comes out cloudy, it's only the calcium or other minerals inherent in a water supply that often comes untreated from fresh springs.

Venice

Lord Byron called Venice (Venezia) "a fairy city of the heart." *La Serenissima,* "The Most Serene," is an improbable cityscape of stone palaces that seem to float on water, a place where cats nap in Oriental marble windowsills set in colorful plaster walls. Candy-stripe pylons stand sentry outside the tiny stone docks of palazzi whose front steps descend into the gently lapping waters of the canals that lace the city.

In Venice, cars are banned—every form of transportation floats, from water taxis and *vaporetti* (the public "bus" ferries) to ambulance speedboats and garbage scows. Venice is a place where locals stop at the *bacaro* (wine bar) to take *un ombra* (literally "a little bit of shade"; in practice, a glass of wine) and munch on *cicchetti* (tapaslike snacks) or linger over exquisite restaurant seafood dinners.

It is also a city of great art and grand old masters. Venetian painting enjoyed early masters such as the Bellini clan—Jacopo from the 1420s, sons Giovanni and Gentile from the 1460s. By the early 1500s Venice had taken the Renaissance torch from Florence and made it its own, lending the movement the new color and lighting schemes of such giants as Giorgione, Tiziano (Titian), Paolo Veronese, and Tintoretto.

So much for Venice the Serenissima. There's also Venice the insanely popular and overcrowded. Certainly, the tourists can seem inescapable, and prices can be double or triple here what they are elsewhere in Italy.

But visitors flock to this canalled wonder for very good reason: Venice is extraordinary, it is magical, and it is worth every cent. Its existence defies logic, but underneath its otherworldly beauty and sometimes-stifling tourism, Venice is a living, breathing, singular city that seems almost too exquisite to be genuine, too fragile to survive the never-ending stream of visitors who have been making the pilgrimage here for 1,500 years.

As barbarian hordes washed back and forth across the Alps during the decline of the Roman Empire (starting in the 4th c.), inhabitants of the Veneto flatlands grew tired of being routinely sacked and pillaged along the way. By the 6th century, many had begun moving out onto the mudflat islands of the marshy lagoon, created by what was in ancient times the Po River delta, to take up fishermen's lines or trading ships. When they saw that one barbarian horde, the Lombards, had stayed to settle the upper Po valley (still called Lombardy), these *Veneti* decided to remain on their new island homes and ally themselves instead with the eastern remnant of the old Roman Empire, Byzantium.

Oddly, what we now consider central Venice was the last area settled. After Attila the Hun rampaged through, citizens of the Roman town of Altino moved out onto Torcello and founded a tidy commercial empire under the control of the Byzantine emperor—ironic, since Torcello's star has long since fallen and it is now the least built-up of all of greater Venice's major inhabited islands. Townsfolk from Oderzo moved to Malamocco and made it the lagoon's political capital (the original site is now underwater, and the Malamocco that survives nearby is a fishing village on the southern stretch of the Lido, near the golf course). After barely defeating Charlemagne's son Pepin there in 810, the capital was moved to the more protected Rialto islands— now central Venice.

Greater Venice's oldest surviving structure is the cathedral on Torcello, founded in 639 but largely 9th and 10th century now. In fact, sparsely populated Torcello is one of the best glimpses into how early Venice must have looked—scattered buildings and canals banked by waving rushes and reeds, everything outlined by the dotted lines of wooden piles hammered down into the mud. This construction is what underlies all those stone palazzi of central Venice: a framework foundation of sunken tree trunks, hammered down into the *caranto* (a solid clay layer under the surface of mud and sand) and preserved in the anaerobic atmosphere of their muddy tomb, overlain with Istrian stone.

As its power began to peak in the early 13th century, Venice led the fourth and most successful Crusade, capturing Constantinople itself. It went on to conquer territories across what are today Turkey, the Greek isles, and Crete—and eventually became the capital of Italy's inland provinces, now the Veneto, Trentino, and Friuli. By 1300 it was one of the largest cities and the leading maritime republic of Europe and the Mediterranean. Although the Black Death carried off over half the population from 1347 to 1350, Venice bounced back and remained a maritime power until the 18th century, when trade through the new American colonies would increasingly steal much of the city's thunder.

By the end of the 18th century, Venice had run out of steam commercially, not to mention militarily after centuries spent fighting the Turks (who slowly regained most of Venice's Aegean and Greek territories). By the time Napoléon came along in 1797, the Venetian Republic offered little resistance. Napoléon gave control of Venice to Austria, under whose rule it remained for almost 70 years. Daniele Manin did stage an unsuccessful mini-revolution in 1848 and 1849, during which Venice was privileged to become the first city attacked from the air—from a fleet of hot-air balloons armed with long-fused time bombs. The *Risorgimento* (unification) movement and its king Vittorio Emanuele II defeated the Austrians, gained control of the Veneto, and made it a part of the newly minted state of Italy in 1866.

In its position at the crossroads of the Byzantine and Roman—later Eastern and Western—worlds, Venice over many centuries acquired a unique amalgamated heritage of art, architecture, and culture. And although hordes of traders and merchants no longer pass through as they once did, Venice nonetheless continues to find itself at a crossroads: an intersection in time between the uncontested period of maritime power that built it and the modern world that keeps it ever-so-gingerly afloat.

It is a great disservice to allot Venice the average stay of 2 nights and 3 days (it sometimes takes the better part of a day just to find your hotel). If you can, stay at least 3 nights and preferably longer—Venice has the potential to be the highlight of your travels through Italy. It is a city too special and unique on this globe to be rushed.

Leave your heels and excess luggage at home, and make sure to toss the map and this guide in your daypack for at least an afternoon, turn left when the signs to the sights point right, and get lost in the back *calli* (streets) and uncrowded *campi* (squares) where tourists seldom tread and you will encounter the true, living, breathing, gloriously decaying side of this most serene city.

1 Getting There

BY PLANE   You can fly into Venice from North America via Rome or Milan with Alitalia or a number of other airlines, or by connecting through a major European city with European carriers. No-frills carrier **Ryanair** (www.ryanair. com) flies direct from London much more cheaply than the major airlines, as does **EasyJet** (www.easyjet.com).

Flights land at the **Aeroporto Marco Polo,** 7km (4½ miles) north of the city on the mainland (© **041-260-9260** or 041-260-9250; www.veniceairport.it). There are two bus alternatives: The special **ATVO airport shuttle bus** (© **041-541-5180** or 041-520-5530; www.atvo.it) connects with Piazzale Roma not far from Venice's Santa Lucia train station (and the closest point to Venice's attractions accessible by land). Buses leave for/from the airport about every hour, cost 3€ ($3.45), and make the trip in about 20 minutes. The slightly less expensive, twice-hourly local public **ACTV bus no. 5** (© 041-541-5180) costs 1.50€ ($1.75) and takes 30 to 45 minutes. Buy tickets for either at the newsstand just inside the terminal from the signposted bus stop. With either bus, you'll have to walk to/from the final stop at Piazzale Roma to the nearby *vaporetto* (water buses) stop for the final connection to your hotel. It's rare to see porters around who'll help with luggage, so pack light.

A **land taxi** from the airport to the Piazzale Roma to pick up your *vaporetto* will run about 30€ ($34).

The most fashionable and traditional way to arrive in Piazza San Marco is by sea. For 10€ ($12), the **Cooperative San Marco/Alilaguna** (© **041-523-5775;** www.alilaguna.it) operates a large *motoscafo* (shuttle boat) service from the airport with two stops at Murano and the Lido before arriving after about 1 hour in Piazza San Marco. Call for the daily schedule of a dozen or so trips from about 6am to midnight; the schedule changes with the season and is coordinated with the principal arrival/departure of the major airlines (most hotels have the schedule). If your hotel isn't in the Piazza San Marco area, you'll have to make a connection at the *vaporetto* launches (your hotel can help you with the specifics if you booked before you left home).

A **private water taxi** (20–30 min. to/from the airport) is convenient but costly—a legal minimum of 55€ ($63) but usually closer to 75€ ($86) for two to four passengers with few bags. It's worth considering if you're pressed for time, have an early flight, are carrying a lot of luggage (a Venice no-no), or can split the cost with a friend or two. It may be able to drop you off at the front (or side) door of your hotel or as close as it can maneuver given your hotel's location (check with the hotel before arriving). Your taxi captain should be able to tell you before boarding just how close he can get you. Try the **Corsorzio Motoscafi Venezia** (© **041-522-2303;** www.motoscafivenezia.it) water taxis.

BY TRAIN   Trains from Rome (4½–7 hr.), Milan (2½–3½ hr.), Florence (3 hr.), and all over Europe arrive at the **Stazione Venezia–Santa Lucia** (© **848-888-088** or 147-888-088 toll-free from anywhere in Italy; www.fs-on-line.it). To get there, all must pass through (though not necessarily stop at) a station marked Venezia–Mestre. Don't be confused: Mestre is a charmless industrial city that's the last stop on the mainland. Occasionally trains end in Mestre, in which case you have to catch one of the frequent 10-minute shuttles connecting with Venice; it's inconvenient, so when you book your ticket, confirm that the final destination is Venezia–Stazione Santa Lucia.

Between the station's large front doors is a small, understaffed **tourist office** (℃ **041-529-8727** or 041-529-8740), with lines that can be discouraging and a strict "one person allowed in at a time" policy. It's open daily 8am to 7pm (closed Sun in winter). The railway info office, marked with a lowercase *i*, is also in the station's main hall, staffed daily from 8am to 8pm.

On exiting, you'll find the Grand Canal immediately in front of you, a sight that makes for a heart-stopping first impression. You'll find the docks for a number of *vaporetto* lines (the city's public ferries or "water buses") to your left and right. Head to the booths to your left, near the bridge, to catch either of the two lines plying the Canal Grande: the no. 82 express, which stops only at the station, S. Marcuola, Rialto Bridge, S. Tomà, S. Samuele, and Accademia before hitting San Marco (26 min. total); and the misnamed no. 1 *accellerato*, which is actually the local, making 14 stops between the station and San Marco (a 31-min. trip). Both leave every 10 minutes or so, but every other no. 82 stops short at Rialto, meaning you'll have to disembark and hop on the next no. 1 or 82 that comes along to continue to San Marco.

Note: The no. 82 goes in two directions from the train station: left down the Canal Grande toward San Marco—which is the (relatively) fast and scenic way—and right, which also eventually gets you to San Marco (at the San Zaccaria stop) but takes more than twice as long because it goes the long way around Dorsoduro (and serves mainly commuters). Make sure the no. 82 you get on is headed to "San Marco."

BY BUS   Though rail travel is more convenient and commonplace, Venice is serviced by long-distance buses from all over mainland Italy and some international cities. The final destination is Piazzale Roma, where you'll need to pick up *vaporetto* no. 82 or no. 1 (as described under "By Train," above) to connect you with stops in the heart of Venice and along the Grand Canal.

BY CAR   The only wheels you'll see in Venice are those attached to luggage. Venice is a city of canals and narrow alleys. No cars are allowed—even the police and ambulance services use boats. Arriving in Venice by car is problematic and expensive—and downright exasperating if it's high season and the parking facilities are full (they often are). You can drive across the Ponte della Libertà from Mestre to Venice, but you can go no farther than Piazzale Roma at the Venice end, where many garages eagerly await your euro. Do some research before choosing a garage—the rates vary widely, from 19€ ($22) per day for an average-size car at the communal **ASM garage** (℃ **041-272-7301;** www.asmvenezia.it) to 26€ ($30) per day at private outfits like **Garage San Marco** (℃ **041-523-2213;** www. garagesanmarco.it) both in Piazzale Roma. If you have reservations at a hotel, check before arriving: Most of them offer discount coupons for some of the parking facilities; just ask the hotel in which garage you need to park and pay for parking upon leaving the garage.

Vaporetto line nos. 1 and 82, described under "By Train," above, both stop at Piazzale Roma before continuing down the Canal Grande to the train station and, eventually, Piazza San Marco.

2 Orientation

VISITOR INFORMATION

TOURIST OFFICES   There's a small office in the train station (see "By Train," above), but the new main office is located right when you get off the

through the city like an inverted S is the **Canal Grande (Grand Canal),** the wide main artery of aquatic Venice.

The city is divided into six *sestieri* ("sixths" or "districts" or "wards"). **Cannaregio** stretches north and east, from the train station to the Jewish Ghetto and on to the vicinity of the Ca' d'Oro north of the Rialto Bridge. To the east beyond Cannaregio (and skirting the area north and east of Piazza San Marco) is **Castello,** whose ritzy canal-side esplanade, Riva degli Schiavoni, is lined with deluxe accommodations. The central **San Marco** shares this side of the Grand Canal with Castello and Cannaregio, anchored by the magnificent Piazza San Marco and St. Mark's Basilica to the south and the Rialto Bridge to the north; it's the city's commercial, religious, and political heart. On the other side of the Grand Canal, **San Polo** is north of the Rialto Bridge, stretching west to just beyond Campo dei Frari and Campo San Rocco. The residential **Santa Croce** is next, moving north and west, stretching all the way to Piazzale Roma. Finally, the residential **Dorsoduro** is on the opposite side of the Accademia Bridge from San Marco. It's the largest *sestiere* and something of an artists' haven, though escalating rents make it hardly bohemian these days.

Venice shares its lagoon with several other islands. Opposite Piazza San Marco and Dorsoduro is **La Giudecca,** a tranquil working-class place with mostly residential neighborhoods. The **Lido di Venezia** is the city's sandy beach; it's a popular summer destination and holds a concentration of seasonal hotels.

Murano, Burano, and **Torcello** are popular destinations northeast of the city and easily accessible by public transport *vaporetto.* Since the 13th century, Murano has exported its glass products worldwide; it's an interesting day trip for those with the time, but you can do just as well in "downtown" Venice's myriad glass stores. Colorful fishing-village–style Burano was and still is equally famous for its lace, an art now practiced by so few island women that its prices are generally unaffordable. Torcello is the most remote and least populated. The 40-minute boat ride is worthwhile for history and art buffs, who'll be awestruck by the Byzantine mosaics of the cathedral (some of Europe's finest outside Ravenna), whose foundation dates to the 7th century, making this the oldest Venetian monument in existence. **San Michele** is the cemetery island where such celebrities as Stravinsky and Diaghilev are buried.

Finally, the industrial city of **Mestre,** on the mainland, is the gateway to Venice and holds no reason for exploration. In a pinch, its host of inexpensive hotels are worth consideration when Venice's hotels are full, but that's about all.

The Scope of Venice

"Central Venice" refers to the built-up block of islands in the lagoon's center, including St. Mark's, the train station, and everything else in the six main *sestiere* that make up the bulk of the tourist city. "Greater Venice" includes all the inhabited islands of the lagoon—central Venice plus Murano, Burano, Torcello, and the Lido. The "Lagoon" comprises everything, from the city to the mud flats to the fish farms to the dozens of abandoned or uninhabited islets.

> **Tips   A Note on Addresses**
>
> Within each *sestiere* is a most original system of numbering the palazzi, using one continuous string of 6,000 or so numbers. The format for addresses in this chapter is the official mailing address: the *sestiere* name followed by the building number in that district, followed by the name of the street or *campo* on which you'll find that address—for example, San Marco 1471 (Salizzada San Moisè) means the mailing address is San Marco 1471, and you'll find it in the San Marco district on Salizzada San Moisè. Be aware that San Marco 1471 may not necessarily be found close to San Marco 1475 and that many buildings aren't numbered at all.

NEIGHBORHOODS IN BRIEF

Based on a tradition dating from the 12th century, for tax-related purposes, the city has officially been divided into six *sestieri* (literally "sixths," or wards) that have basically been the same since 1711. The *Canalazzo* or *Canale Grande* (Grand Canal) neatly divides them into three on each bank.

SAN MARCO   The central *sestiere* is anchored by the Piazza San Marco and the Basilica di San Marco to the south and the Rialto Bridge to the north. This is the most visited (and, as a result, the most expensive) of the *sestieri*. It's the commercial, religious, and political heart of the city and has been for more than a millennium (it was also its musical heart until a fire destroyed La Fenice Opera House in 1996; it now stands a hollow shell). Although you'll find glimpses and snippets of the real Venice here, ever-rising rents have nudged resident Venetians to look for housing in the outer neighborhoods: You'll be hard-pressed to find a grocery store or dry cleaner here. But if you're looking for Murano glass trinkets and mediocre restaurants, you'll find an embarrassment of choices. This area is a mecca of first-class hotels—but with direction from Frommer's, you can stay here in the heart of Venice without going broke.

CANNAREGIO   Sharing the same side of the Grand Canal with San Marco, Cannaregio stretches north and east from the train station to include the Jewish Ghetto and into the canal-hugging vicinity of the Ca' d'Oro and the Rialto Bridge. Its outer reaches are quiet, unspoiled, and residential (*what* high-season tourist crowds? you may wonder); one-third of Venice's ever-shrinking population of 20,000 is said to live here. Most of the city's one-star hotels are clustered about the train station—not a dangerous neighborhood, but not one known for its charm either. The gloss and dross of the tourist shop–lined Lista di Spagna strip continues as it morphs into the Strada Nuova in the direction of the Rialto Bridge.

CASTELLO   This quarter, whose tony "boulevard," Riva degli Schiavoni, follows the Bacino di San Marco (St. Mark's Basin), is lined with first-class and deluxe hotels. It begins just east of Piazza San Marco, skirting Venice's most congested area to absorb some of the crowds and better hotels and restaurants. But if you head farther east in the direction of the Arsenale or inland away from the *bacino,* the people traffic thins out, despite the presence of such major sights as Campo SS. Giovanni e Paolo and the Scuola di San Giorgio.

SAN POLO This mixed-bag *sestiere* of residential corners and tourist sites stretches northwest of the Rialto Bridge to the principal church of Santa Maria dei Frari and the Scuola di San Rocco. The hub of activity at the foot of the bridge is greatly due to the Rialto market that has taken place here for centuries—some of the city's best restaurants have flourished here for generations, alongside some of its worst tourist traps. The spacious Campo San Polo is the main piazza of Venice's smallest *sestiere.*

SANTA CROCE North and northwest of the San Polo district and across the Grand Canal from the train station, Santa Croce stretches all the way to Piazzale Roma. Its eastern section is generally one of the least-visited areas of Venice—making it all the more desirable for curious visitors. Less lively than San Polo, it is as authentic, and feels light-years away from San Marco. The quiet and lovely Campo San Giacomo dell'Orio is considered to be its heart.

DORSODURO You'll find the residential area of Dorsoduro on the opposite side of the Accademia

Bridge from San Marco. Known for the Accademia and Peggy Guggenheim museums, it is the largest of the *sestieri* and has been known as an artists' haven (hence the tireless comparison with New York's Greenwich Village—a far cry) until recent escalations of rents forced much of the community to relocate elsewhere. Good neighborhood restaurants, a charming gondola boatyard, the lively Campo Santa Margherita, and the sunny quay called le Zattere (a favorite promenade and gelato stop) all add to the character and color that make this one of the city's most-visited areas.

LA GIUDECCA Located opposite the Piazza San Marco and Dorsoduro, La Giudecca is a tranquil working-class residential area where you'll find a youth hostel and a handful of hotels (including the deluxe Cipriani, one of Europe's finest).

LIDO DI VENEZIA This slim, 11km (6¾-mile) long area is the city's beach; separating the lagoon from the open sea and permitting car traffic, its concentration of seasonal hotels (its landmark hotels serving as home base for the annual Venice Film Festival) makes it a popular summer destination, but it is also quite residential.

GETTING AROUND

Aside from boats, the only way to explore Venice is by walking—and getting lost repeatedly. You'll navigate many twisting streets whose names change constantly and don't appear on any map, and streets that may very well simply end in a blind alley or spill abruptly into a canal. You'll also cross dozens of footbridges. Treat getting bewilderingly lost in Venice as part of the fun, and budget more time than you'd ever think necessary to get wherever you're going.

STREET MAPS & SIGNAGE   The free map offered by the tourist office and most hotels has good intentions, but it doesn't even show—much less name or index—all the *calli* (streets) and pathways of Venice. For that, pick up a more detailed map (ask for a *pianta della città*) at news kiosks (especially those at the train station and around San Marco) or most bookstores.

The best (and most expensive) is the highly detailed **Touring Club Italiano map,** available in a variety of forms (folding or spiral-bound) and scales. Almost as good, and easier to carry, is the simple and cheap **1:6500 folding map** put

Cruising the Canals

A leisurely cruise along the **Grand Canal** ☆ from Piazza San Marco to the Ferrovia—or the reverse—is one of Venice's must-dos (p. 130). It's the world's most unusual Main Street, a watery boulevard whose palazzi have been converted into condos. Lower water-lapped floors are now deserted, but the higher floors are still coveted by the city's titled families, who have inhabited these glorious residences for centuries; others have become the summertime dream-homes-with-a-view of privileged expats, drawn here as irresistibly as the romantic Venetians-by-adoption who preceded them—Richard Wagner, Robert Browning, Lord Byron, and (more recently) Woody Allen.

As much a symbol of Venice as the winged lion, the **gondola** ☆☆☆ is one of Europe's great traditions, terribly expensive but truly as romantic as it looks (detractors who write it off as too touristy have most likely never tried it). Though it's often quoted in print at differing official rates, expect to pay 62€ ($71) for up to 50 minutes (77€/$89 between 8pm and 8am), with up to six passengers, and 31€ ($36) for another 25 minutes (39€/$45 at night). *Note:* At these ridiculously inflated prices, there is no need to tip the gondolier. Aim for late afternoon before sundown when the light does its magic on the canal reflections (and bring a bottle of *prosecco* [a champagnelike drink] and glasses). If the price is too high, ask visitors at your hotel or others lingering about at the gondola stations if they'd like to share it. Establish the cost, time, and route explanation (any of the back canals are preferable to the trafficked and often choppy Grand Canal) with the gondolier before setting off. They're regulated by the **Ente Gondola** (© **041-528-5075;** www.gondola venezia.it), so call if you have any questions or complaints.

And what of the serenading gondolier immortalized in film? Frankly, you're better off without. But if warbling is de rigueur for you, here's the scoop. An ensemble of accordion player and tenor is so expensive that it's shared among several gondolas traveling together. A number of travel agents around town book the evening serenades for around 30€ ($35) per person. The number of *gondolieri* willing to brave the winter cold and rain are minimal, though some come out of their wintertime hibernation for the Carnevale period.

There are 12 gondola stations around Venice, including Piazzale Roma, the train station, the Rialto Bridge, and Piazza San Marco. There are also a number of smaller stations, with gondoliers standing alongside their sleek 11m (36-ft.) black wonders looking for passengers. They all speak enough English to communicate the necessary details.

out by Storti Edizioni (its cover is white-edged with pink, which fades to blue at the bottom).

Still, Venice's confusing layout confounds even the best maps and navigators. You're often better off just stopping every couple of blocks and asking a local to point you in the right direction (always know the name of the *campo*/square or major site closest to the address you're looking for, and ask about that).

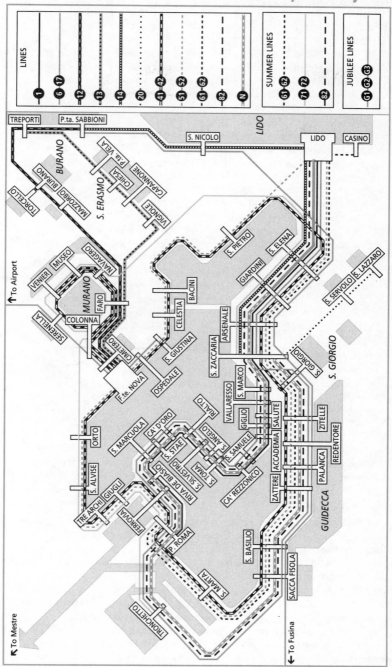

Venice *Vaporetto* System

Venetian Dialect

If, after a few days in Rome and Florence, you were just getting the hang of correlating your map to the reality of your new surroundings, you can put aside any short-term success upon your arrival in Venezia. Even the Italians (non-Venetian ones) look befuddled when trying to decipher street names and signs (given that you can ever find any).

Venice's colorful thousand-year history as a once-powerful maritime republic has everything to do with its local dialect, which absorbed nuances and vocabulary from far-flung outposts in the East and from the flourishing communities of foreign merchants who, for centuries, lived and traded in Venice. A linguist could gleefully spend a lifetime trying to make some sense of it all. It's been a successful one, though. From Venetian dialect we've inherited such words as *gondola* (naturally), *ciao, ghetto, lido,* and *arsenal.*

But for the Venice-bound traveler just trying to make sense of Venetian addresses, the following should give you the basics. (And don't even try to follow a conversation between two *gondolieri!*)

ca' The abbreviated use of the word "casa" is used for the noble *palazzi*, once private residences and now museums, lining the Grand Canal: Ca' d'Oro, Ca' Pesaro, and Ca' Rezzonico. There is only one palazzo, and it is the Palazzo Ducale, the former doge's residence. However, as time went on, some great houses gradually began to be called "palazzi," so today you'll also encounter the Palazzo Grassi or the Palazzo Labia.

Calle Taken from the Spanish (though pronounced as if Italian, i.e., *ca-*lay), this is the most commonplace word for street, known as "via" or "strada" elsewhere in Italy. There are numerous variations. "Ruga," from the French word "rue," once meant a Calle flanked with stores, a

As you wander, look for the ubiquitous yellow signs (well, *usually* yellow) whose destinations and arrows direct you toward five major landmarks: **Ferrovia** (the train station), **Piazzale Roma, Rialto** (the main bridge), **San Marco,** and the **Accademia** (also useful as the only other Grand Canal bridge below the train station).

BY BOAT   The various *sestieri* are linked by a comprehensive *vaporetto* (water bus/ferry) system of about a dozen lines operated by the **Azienda del Consorzio Trasporti Veneziano (ACTV),** Calle Fuseri 1810, off the Frezzeria in San Marco (*☎* **041-528-7886** for both offices; www.actv.it). Transit maps are available at the tourist office and most ACTV stations. It's easier to get around on foot; the *vaporetti* principally serve the Grand Canal (and can be crowded in summer), the outskirts, and the outer islands. The crisscross network of small canals is the province of delivery vessels, gondolas, and private boats.

A one-way ticket is a steep 3.50€ ($4.05). A round-trip ticket is 6€ ($7), while the 24-hour ticket at 11€ ($12) is a good buy if you'll be making more than three trips in a day. Most lines run every 10 to 15 minutes from 7am to midnight, then hourly until morning; most *vaporetto* docks (the only place you can buy tickets) have timetables posted. Note that not all stations sell tickets designation no longer valid. A "ramo" (literally "branch") is the offshoot of a street, and is often used interchangeably with "calle." "Salizzada" once meant a paved street, implying that all other, less important "calles" were once just dirt-packed alleyways. A "stretto" is a narrow passageway.

campo Elsewhere in Italy it's "piazza." In Venice the only piazza is the Piazza San Marco (and its two bordering "piazzette"); all other squares are "campi" or the diminutive, "campielli." Translated as "field" or "meadow," these were once small, unpaved grazing spots for the odd chicken or cow. Almost every one of Venice's campi carries the name of the church that dominates it (or once did) and most have wells, no longer used, in the center.

canale There are three wide, principal canals: the Canal Grande (affectionately called "il Canalazzo," the Canal), the Canale della Giudecca, and the Canale di Cannaregio. Each of the other 160-odd smaller canals is called a "rio." A "rio terrà" is a filled-in canal—wide and straight—now used as a street. A "piscina" is a filled-in basin, now acting as a campo or piazza.

fondamenta Referring to the foundations of the houses lining a canal, this is a walkway along the side of a rio (small canal). Promenades along the Grand Canal near the Piazza San Marco and the Rialto are called "riva" as in the Riva del Vin or Riva del Carbon, where cargo such as wine and coal were once unloaded.

ramo Literally "branch," a small side street.

salizzada The word originally meant "paved," so any street you see prefaced with "salizzada" was one of the first streets in Venice to be paved.

sottoportego An alley that ducks under a building.

after dark; if you haven't bought a pass or extra tickets beforehand, you'll have to settle up with the conductor onboard (you'll have to find him—he won't come looking for you) for an extra .50€ (60¢) per ticket or gamble on a 21€ ($24) fine, no excuses accepted. Also available are 72-hour tickets (22€/$25) and 7-day tickets (32€/$36).

Just three bridges span the Grand Canal. To fill in the gaps, *traghetti* skiffs (oversize gondolas rowed by two standing *gondolieri*) cross the Grand Canal at eight intermediate points. You'll find a station at the end of any street named Calle del Traghetto on your map and indicated by a yellow sign with the black gondola symbol. The fare is (.50€/60¢), which you hand to the gondolier when boarding. Most Venetians cross standing up. For the experience, try the "Santa Sofia" crossing that connects the Ca' d'Oro and the Pescheria fish market, opposite each other on the Grand Canal just north of the Rialto Bridge—the gondoliers expertly dodge water traffic at this point of the canal where it's the busiest and most heart-stopping.

BY WATER TAXI *Taxi acquei* (water taxis) charge high prices and aren't for visitors watching their euros. For (unlikely) journeys up to 7 minutes, the rate is 14€

($16); .25 € (30¢) click off for each 15 seconds thereafter. Each bag over 50 centimeters long costs 1.15€ ($1.35), plus there's a 4.40€ ($5) supplement for service from 10pm to 7am and a 4.65€ ($5.35) surcharge on Sunday and holidays (these last two charges, however, can't be applied simultaneously). If they have to come get you, tack on another 4.15€ ($4.80). Those rates cover up to four people; if any more squeeze in, it's another 1.60€ ($1.85) per extra passenger.

Six water-taxi stations serve key points in the city: the **Ferrovia** (© 041-716-286), **Piazzale Roma** (© 041-716-922), the **Rialto Bridge** (© 041-523-0575 or 041-723-112), **Piazza San Marco** (© 041-522-9750), the **Lido** (© 041-526-0059), and **Marco Polo Airport** (© 041-541-5084). **Radio Taxi** (© 041-522-2303 or 041-723-112) will come pick you up anyplace in the city.

BY GONDOLA   To come all the way to Venice and not indulge in a gondola ride could be one of your biggest regrets. Yes, it's touristy, and yes, it's expensive (see the "Cruising the Canals" box on p. 78), but only those with a heart of stone will be unmoved by the quintessential Venetian experience. Do not initiate your trip, however, until you have agreed upon a price and synchronized watches. Oh, and don't ask them to sing.

FAST FACTS: **Venice**

Acqua Alta   During the notorious tidal *acqua alta* (high water) floods, the lagoon backwashes into the city, leaving up to 5 or 6 feet of water in the lowest-lying streets (Piazza San Marco, as the lowest point in the city, goes first). These floods can start as early as late September or October, usually taking place November to March. As many as 50 a year have been recorded since they first started in the late 1700s. The waters usually recede after just a few hours and are often virtually gone by noon. Walkways are set up around town, but wet feet are a given, and the complex system of hydraulic dams being constructed out in the lagoon to cut off these high tides won't be operational until the end of this decade.

American Express   American Express is at San Marco 1471, 30124 Venezia, on Salizzada San Moisè just west of Piazza San Marco (© **041-520-0844**). In summer the office is open for banking Monday to Saturday 8am to 8pm (for all other services, 9am–5:30pm); in winter, hours are Monday to Friday 9am to 5:30pm and Saturday 9am to 12:30pm (for banking and other services).

Bookstores   See p. 144.

Business Hours   Standard hours for shops are 9am to 12:30pm and 3 to 7:30pm Monday to Saturday. In winter, shops are closed on Monday morning, while in summer it's usually Saturday afternoon. Most grocers are closed on Wednesday afternoon year-round. In Venice just about everything is closed on Sunday, though tourist shops in the tourist spots such as the San Marco area are permitted to stay open during high season. Restaurants are required to close at least 1 day a week, called *il giorno di riposo*, though the particular day varies from one trattoria to another. Many are open for Sunday lunch but close for Sunday dinner. Restaurants that specialize in fish and seafood also typically close Monday, when the fish market is closed. Restaurants will close for holidays, translated as *chiuso per ferie,* sometime in July or August, frequently over Christmas, and sometime in January before the Carnevale rush.

Climate May, June, September, and early October are the best months with respect to weather to visit (and the most crowded). July and August are hot—at times unbearably so. April and late October/early November are hit-and-miss; it can either be glorious or cool, rainy, and damp and only marginally less crowded. Also see "Acqua Alta," above.

Consulates The nearest **U.S. Consulate** is in Milan at Largo Donegani 1 (© 02-290-351). It's open Monday to Friday 9am to noon for visas only; from Monday to Friday it's also open for telephone service info 2 to 4pm. The **U.K. Consulate** in Venice is at Dorsoduro 1051 (© 041-522-7207), at the foot of the Accademia Bridge, just west of the museum in the Palazzo Querini; it's open Monday to Friday 9am to noon and 2 to 4pm. Like the U.S., **Canada, Australia,** and **New Zealand** have consulates in Milan, about 3 hours away by train (see chapter 7); all also maintain embassies in Rome.

Crime Be aware of petty crime like pickpocketing on the crowded *vaporetti,* particularly the tourist routes where passengers are more intent on the passing scenery than watching their bags. Venice's deserted back streets were once virtually crime-proof; occasional tales of theft are circulating only recently. Generally speaking, it's one of Italy's safest cities.

Dentists/Doctors For a short list, check with the consulate of the United Kingdom, the American Express office, or your hotel.

Drugstores Venice's pharmacies take turns staying open all night. To find out which one is on call in your area, ask at your hotel, check the rotational duty signs posted outside all drugstores, or dial © **041-523-0573.**

Emergencies In Venice and throughout Italy, dial © **113** to reach the **police.** Some Italians will recommend that you forgo the police and try the military-trained **Carabinieri** (© **112**). For an **ambulance,** phone © **523-0000.** To report a **fire,** dial © **115** or 041-520-0222 or 041-520-0223. For any **tourism-related complaint** (rip-offs, exceedingly shoddy service, and so on), dial the special agency **Venezia No Problem** toll-free at © **800-355-920.**

Fax From both the main post office and its Piazza San Marco branch (see "Mail," below) you can send faxes to almost any destination with the odd exception of the United States. For service to the United States, ask at your hotel; most will agree to do it for either a per-page or estimated-per-minute cost. Or look for SERVIZIO FAX signs in the windows of *cartolerie* (stationery stores).

Holidays Venice's patron saint, San Marco (St. Mark), is honored on April 25. For a list of official state holidays, see the "Holidays" section on p. 36.

Internet Access For checking e-mail, go to **Venetian Navigator,** Castello 5269 on Calle delle Bande between San Marco and Campo Santa Maria Formosa (© **041-522-6084;** www.venetiannavigator.com; *vaporetto*: San Marco, Zaccaria, Rialto), daily 10am to 10pm (Nov–Apr 10am–1pm and 2:30–8:30pm), which charges 6€ ($6.90) per hour. The **Internet Café,** 2967-2958 Campo Santo Stefano, San Marco (© **041-520-8128;** www.nethousecafes.com; *Vaporetto:* S. Samuele, Giglio), is a new spot open 24 hours daily that charges a steep 9€ ($10) per hour.

Laundry The self-service laundry most convenient to the train station is the **Lavaget** (✆ **041-715-976**), Cannaregio 1269, to the left as you cross Ponte alle Guglie from Lista di Spagna; the rate is about 9€ ($10) for up to 4.5 kilos (10 lb.). The most convenient laundry to San Marco is **Gabriella** (✆ **041-522-1758**), San Marco 985 on Rio Terrà Colonne (off Calle dei Fabbri), where they wash and dry your clothes for you within an hour or two for 14€ ($16) per load. They are open Monday to Friday 10am to 12:30pm and 2:30 to 7pm.

Lost & Found The central **Ufficio Oggetti Rinvenuti** (✆ **041-788-225**) is in the annex to the City Hall (Municipio), at San Marco 4134, on Calle Piscopia o Loredan, just off Riva del Carbon on the Grand Canal, near the Rialto Bridge (on the same side of the canal as the Rialto *vaporetto* station). Look for *scala* (stairway) "C"; the lost-and-found office is in the *Economato* section on the *mezzanino* level, one flight up. The office is ostensibly open only on Monday, Wednesday, and Friday from 9:30am to 12:30pm, but there's usually someone available weekdays from 9:30am until the building closes at 1:30pm.

There's also an **Ufficio Oggetti Smarriti** at the airport (✆ **041-260-6436**) and an **Ufficio Oggetti Rinvenuti** at the train station (✆ **041-785-238**), right at the head of Track 14; open Monday to Friday from 8am to 4pm.

Luggage Storage The *deposito bagagli* in the train station (✆ **041-785-531**) is open daily from 6am to midnight and charges for each bag 3€ ($3.45) for the first 12 hours, then 2€ ($2.30) for each additional 12-hour period.

Mail Venice's **Posta Centrale** is at San Marco 5554, 30124 Venezia, on the San Marco side of the Rialto Bridge at Rialto Fontego dei Tedeschi (✆ **041-271-7111** or 041-528-5813; *Vaporetto:* Rialto). This office sells stamps at Window 12 Monday to Saturday 8:30am to 6:30pm (for parcels, 8:10am–1:30pm). If you're at Piazza San Marco and need postal services, walk through Sottoportego San Geminian, the center portal at the opposite end of the piazza from the basilica on Calle Larga dell'Ascensione. Its usual hours are Monday to Friday 8:30am to 2pm and Saturday 8:30am to 1pm. You can buy *francobolli* (stamps) at any *tabacchi* (tobacconists). The limited mailboxes seen around town are red.

Police In an emergency, dial ✆ **112** or 113.

Taxes & Tipping See "Fast Facts: Northern Italy," in chapter 2, p. 67.

Telephone See "Fast Facts: Northern Italy," in chapter 2, p. 67.

Travel Agencies **Intras City Service** at Santa Croce 1303b (✆ **041-275-0783**) is centrally located, as is **Kele e Teo** on the Mercerie 4930 (✆ **041-520-8722**; fax 041-520-8913; www.keleteo.com). See also "American Express," above.

3 Where to Stay

Few cities boast as long a high season as that of Venice, beginning with the Easter period. May, June, and September are the best months weather-wise, and therefore the most crowded. July and August are hot—at times unbearably so (few of the one- and two-star hotels offer air-conditioning; when they do it usually costs extra). Like everything else, hotels are more expensive here than in any other Italian city, with no apparent upgrade in amenities. The least special of those below are clean and functional; at best, they're charming and thoroughly enjoyable with the serenade of a passing gondolier thrown in for good measure. Some may even provide you with your best stay in all of Europe.

I strongly suggest that you reserve in advance, even in the off season. If you haven't booked, arrive as early as you can, definitely before noon. The **Hotel Reservations booth** in the train station will book rooms for you, but the lines are long and the staff's patience is often (understandably) thin. For 1€ ($1.15), they'll try to find you a hotel in the price range of your choice; on confirmation from the hotel, they'll accept your deposit by credit card and issue you a voucher, and you pay the balance on your arrival at the hotel. There is a similar hotel reservations booth at the airport, but it charges a bit more.

Another alternative for reserving the same day as your arrival can be done through the **A.V.A.** (Venetian Hoteliers Association), toll-free from within Italy ✆ **800-843-006,** or 041-522-2264 from abroad, or online at www.veniceinfo.it. Simply state the price range you want to book and they'll confirm a hotel while you wait. There are offices at the train station, in Piazzale Roma garages, and in the airport. If you're looking to book on the Lido, contact their sister organization, **A.V.A.L.,** toll-free from within Italy ✆ **800-546-788** (www.venicehotels.com), or 041-595-2466 from abroad.

Recent state-imposed ordinances resulted in stringent deadlines for the updating of antiquated electrical, plumbing, and sewage systems—costly endeavors. To make up for this, small one- and two-star hotels raised their rates, often applying

Kids Family-Friendly Hotels

Albergo ai do Mori (p. 92)   Good news for weary legs: The larger, family-oriented rooms are on the lower floors in this elevator-challenged hotel just around the corner from San Marco. Can-do English-speaking Antonella has a solution for every problem.

Antica Locanda Sturion (p. 100)   Scottish-born Helen or her daughter Nicolette will settle you into any of the spacious rooms, two of which provide the special thrill of a Grand Canal view within sight of the famous Rialto Bridge. *One caveat:* The 69-step hike to the lobby may be a deterrent for little ones or for those who haven't mastered the art of traveling lightly.

Hotel Bernardi-Semenzato (p. 104)   Owner Maria Teresa moonlights as an English teacher on the side. As a mother of three, she's the perfect host for families, who will appreciate the renovated rooms that easily pass as triples or quads.

Pensione Guerrato (p. 101)   Young euro-conscious families will enjoy the inexpensive rates of this former convent, where an informal and casual atmosphere is nurtured by the upbeat brothers-in-law who run it as if it were their home. Kids should get a kick out of being in the middle of the market's hubbub right on the Grand Canal and within steps of the Rialto Bridge. Spacious rooms are an added plus.

Where to Stay in Venice

Albergo Adua **8**
Albergo ai do Mori **23**
Albergo al
   Gambero **25**
Albergo Santa Lucia **11**
Antica Locanda
   Sturion **17**
Foresteria Valdese
   (Palazzo Cavagnis) **18**
Hotel Ai Due Fanali **7**
Hotel Al Piave **19**
Hotel American **5**
Hotel Bauer/
   Bauer il Palazzo **32**
Hotel Bellini **9**
Hotel Bernardi-
   Semenzato **13**
Hotel Campiello **39**
Hotel Cipriani **44**
Hotel Concordia **22**
Hotel Danieli **38**
Hotel des Bains **44**
Hotel Do Pozzi **28**
Hotel Dolomiti **10**
Hotel Falier **1**
Hotel Flora **29**
Hotel Fontana **40**
Hotel Galleria **4**
Hotel Gallini **26**

Hotel Giorgione **15**
Hotel Gritti Palace **35**
Hotel La Fenice et
   Des Artistes **27**
Hotel La Residenza **43**
Hotel Messner **37**
Hotel Metropole **42**
Hotel Monaco
   & Grand Canal **34**
Hotel San Cassiano
   Ca'Favretto **15**
Hotel San Geremia **12**
Hotel Violino d'Oro **31**
Locanda Casa
   Verardo **20**
Locanda Fiorita **2**
Locanda Remedio—
   Dependance Hotel
   Colombina **21**
Londra Palace **41**
Luna Hotel Baglioni **33**
Pensione Accademia **3**
Pensione alla Salute **36**
Pensione Guerrato **16**
Pensione La Calcina **6**
Westin Excelsior **44**
Westin Hotel Europa
   & Regina **30**

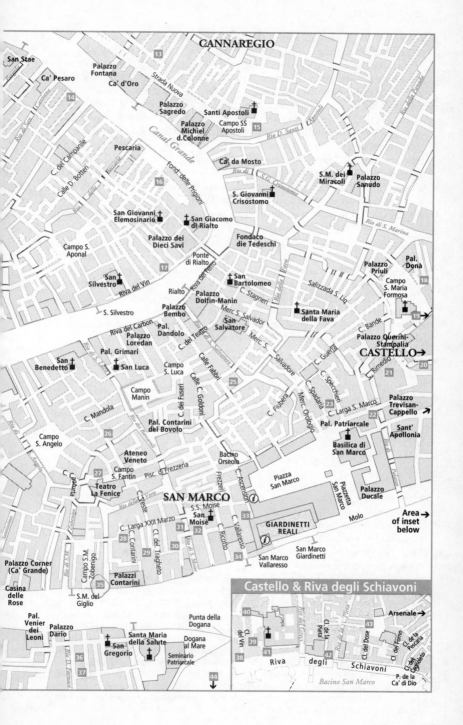

CANNAREGIO

San Stae
Ca' Pesaro

Palazzo Fontana
Ca' d'Oro

13

14

Palazzo Sagredo

Palazzo Michiel d.Colonne

Santi Apostoli
Campo SS Apostoli

15

Canal Grande

Pescaria

C. del Campanile

Calle D. Botteri

fond. delle Prigioni

16

Ca' da Mosto

Rio di S.C.G. Crisostomo

S.M. dei Miracoli
Palazzo Sanudo

San Giovanni Crisostomo

Rio di S. Marina

San Giovanni Elemosinario

San Giacomo di Rialto

Palazzo dei Dieci Savi

Fondaco die Tedeschi

Palazzo Priuli

Pal. Donà

Campo S. Aponal

Ponte di Rialto

17

Campo S. Maria Formosa

18

San Silvestro

Riva del Vin

San Bartolomeo

Salizzada S. Lio

C. Bande

19

S. Silvestro

Rialto

Palazzo Dolfin-Manin

C. Stagneri

Merc S. Salvador

Santa Maria della Fava

Palazzo Querini-Stampalia

Palazzo Bembo

San Salvatore

Merc S.

CASTELLO →

Riva del Carbon

Pal. Dandolo

C. del Teatro

Merc S. Salvador

C. Guerra

Rimedio

21

20

Palazzo Loredan

Campo S. Luca

Salvadore

C. Specchieri

22

Palazzo Trevisan-Cappello →

San Benedetto

Pal. Grimari

San Luca

Calle Fabbri

Calle C. Goldoni

23

C. Larga S. Marco

Sant' Apollonia

Campo Manin

C. dei Fuseri

C. Flubera

Merc. Orologio

Pal. Patriarcale

25

C. Mandola

26

Pal. Contarini del Bovolo

Campo S. Angelo

Bacino Orseolo

Basilica di San Marco

Ateneo Veneto

Campo S. Fantin

Pisc. di Frezzeria

Piazza San Marco

27

Teatro La Fenice

Frezzeria

Piazzetta San Marco

Palazzo Ducale

SAN MARCO

S.S. Moisè
San Moisè

C. Ascension

Area → of inset below

C. Larga XXII Marzo

31

32

33

GIARDINETTI REALI

Molo

28

Cl. del Traghetto

30

C. Vallaresso

San Marco Vallaresso

San Marco Giardinetti

Palazzo Corner (Ca' Grande)

Campo S.M. Zobenigo

29

C. Contarini

34

35

Palazzi Contarini

Casina delle Rose

S.M. del Giglio

Punta della Dogana

Pal. Venier dei Leoni

Palazzo Dario

Santa Maria della Salute

36

37

San Gregorio

Dogana al Mare

Seminario Patriarcale

44
↓

Castello & Riva degli Schiavoni

40

Arsenale →

43

Cl. del Vin

39

Cl. de la Pietà

Cl. del Dose

Cl. del Forno

Cl. de la Pescaria

38

41

42

Riva

degli

Schiavoni

P. de la Ca' di Dio

Bacino San Marco

for an upgrade in category for which they're now potentially eligible. Even more stuck TVs on the desks and hair dryers in the bathrooms to garner that extra star so they could inflate their rates during the Jubilee Year 2000. Then, of course, came the euro and prices jacked up yet again. The good news is that now you'll have accommodations of a better quality; the bad news is that yesteryear's affordable finds are slowly disappearing. The rates below were compiled in 2003. You can expect the usual increase of 4% to 8%, but you might be hit with an increase of as much as 20% if the hotel you pick is one that has been redone recently.

A few peculiarities about Venice hotels have everything to do with the fact that this city built on water does not consistently offer what you might take for granted: elevators, light, and spaciousness. Venice hotels often have tiny bathrooms. The rooms are generally smaller than elsewhere and can be dark, and canal views aren't half as prevalent as we'd like them to be. This doesn't mean that a welcoming family-run hotel in an atmospheric neighborhood can't offer a memorable stay—just don't expect the amenities of the Danieli or Grand Canal vistas.

SEASONAL CONSIDERATIONS   Most hotels observe high- and low-season rates, though many are gradually adopting a single year-round rate. Even where it's not indicated in the listings, be sure to ask when you book or when you arrive at a hotel whether off-season prices are in effect. High season in Venice is about March 15 to November 5, with a lull in July and August (when hotel discounts are often offered). Some small hotels close (sometimes without notice or to do renovation work) November or December until Carnevale, opening for about 2 weeks around Christmas and New Year's at high-season rates.

IN SAN MARCO
VERY EXPENSIVE
Hotel Bauer/Bauer il Palazzo ⍟   Don't let the modern lobby throw you. This inn, just a few blocks from Piazza San Marco, is one of the top deluxe hotels in town. In 1998 a massive hotel restructuring divided the hotel into two parts: the rather disappointing (especially at these prices) 1950s Hotel Bauer, with its standardized rooms and terrace on a side canal, and the Bauer il Palazzo. This 19th-century palace on the Grand Canal behind the modern wing enjoys views of Santa Maria della Salute across the way (arrive by water taxi for the best effect). The Palazzo is aiming for boutique-hotel status, with a more intimate reception area, a restaurant opening onto a terrace thrust over the Grand Canal, walk-in closets, and antique Venetian style (genuine 18th-century wherever possible). The higher the price, the classier the accommodations, up to the 3,410€ ($3,922) royal suites, with patterned chipped stone floors, elaborate stuccoed walls and ceilings, engraved mirrors, frescoed bedroom ceilings, and marble bathrooms.

San Marco 1459 (Campo San Moisè), 30124 Venezia. (℃) 041-520-7022. Fax 041-520-7557. www.bauervenezia. com. 192 units (75 in the Palazzo branch). At Hotel Bauer: 231€–550€ ($266–$633) superior double; 308€–660€ ($354–$759) deluxe double; 396€–770€ ($455–$886) jr. suite; 528€–1,045€ ($607–$1,202) suite. At Bauer Il Palazzo: 385€–754€ ($443–$867) palatial double; 517€–990€ ($595€$1,139) palatial double with view; 628€–1,194€ ($722–$1,373) jr. suite; 726€–1,254€ ($835–$1,442) deluxe suite; 869€–1,705€ ($999–$1,961) Grand Canal suite; from 794€–1,991€ ($913–$2,290) executive suite with view; 1,365€–2,277€ ($1,570–$2,619) presidential suite; 3,410€ ($3,922) royal suite. Buffet breakfast 33€ ($38). AE, DC, MC, V. *Vaporetto:* San Marco–Vallaresso (walk straight up Calle di Ca' Vallaresso then left on Salita S. Moisè into the *campo;* the hotel's on the left). **Amenities:** 2 Venetian/Mediterranean restaurants; 2 bars; spa; Jacuzzi; sauna; concierge; tour desk; car-rental desk; business center; salon (basic hairdresser); room service (24-hr.); massage; babysitting; laundry service; dry cleaning (same-day); nonsmoking rooms; executive-level rooms (the Palazzo suites). *In room:* A/C, TV, VCR (on request in Palazzo), fax (in suites), dataport, minibar, safe.

Hotel Gritti Palace ★★★   Although there are arguably more chichi hotels along the *bacino* off St. Mark's Square, if you're going for luxury status and the classiest hotel on the Grand Canal, the Gritti has been *it* for decades. It was the 16th-century palace of Doge Andrea Gritti, whose portrait graces one of the antiques-filled lounges, and everyone who is anyone has stayed here over the centuries, from international royalty to captains of industry, literary giants, and rock stars. Rooms have inlaid antique furnishings, gilt mirrors, ornate built-in dressers hand-painted in 18th-century Venetian style, tented curtains over the tall windows, and real box-spring beds set into curtained nooks. Many rooms have connecting doors so that families can share. Three of the suites on the *piano nobile* (with high, stuccoed ceilings, massive chandeliers, and 17th- and 18th-century furnishings mixed with overstuffed sofas and Bang & Olufson CD players and TVs) overlook the Grand Canal from small stone balconies; three more suites overlook the *campo*. Three junior suites open onto a side canal, with walk-in closets and one and a half bathrooms. The wood-beamed, elegantly clubby restaurant spills onto a Grand Canal terrace in warm weather, as does the bar, with its etched mirrors and evening piano music.

San Marco 2467 (Campo del Traghetto/Campo Santa Maria del Giglio), 30124 Venezia. ℂ 041-794-611. Fax 041-520-0942. www.luxurycollection.com/grittipalace. 91 units. 785€–868€ ($903–$998) double; 1,001€–1,107€ ($1,151–$1,273) double with Grand Canal view; 1,824€–2,002€ ($2,098–$2,302) jr. suite; 2,247€–2,470€ ($2,584–$2,840) suite with *campo* (square) view; 3,482€–3,838€ ($4,004–$4,414) suite with canal view. Buffet breakfast 55€ ($63). AE, DC, MC, V. *Vaporetto:* Santa Maria del Giglio (the hotel is right there). **Amenities:** Venetian/Mediterranean/international restaurant; bar; concierge; tour desk; car-rental desk; courtesy water taxi (free hourly boat to the Westin Excelsior on the Lido); salon; room service (24-hr.); massage (in-room); babysitting; laundry service; dry cleaning; nonsmoking rooms. *In room:* A/C, TV w/pay movies, VCR (in suites), fax (in suites), dataport, minibar, hair dryer, safe.

Westin Hotel Europa & Regina ★   A recent overhaul of one of Venice's venerable Grand Canal bastions put it back among the city's top hotels. Hidden down a tiny side alley just 2 minutes from Piazza San Marco, this hotel's Tiepolo and Regina wings sport eclectic early-20th-century European furnishings and modern fabrics. The Europa wing is decorated in traditional Venetian style. There's a cozy bar with tables right on the Grand Canal, elegant, airy salons, and professional service. The restaurant is so good I wrote a full review on p. 111. Room rates vary with season and view (Canale Grande rooms are priciest).

San Marco 2159 (off Via XXII Marzo), 30124 Venezia. ℂ 041-240-0001. Fax 041-523-1533. www.westin. com. 185 units. 667€–734€ ($767–$844) deluxe double; 696€–790€ ($800–$908) double with partial canal view; 795€–932€ ($914–$1,072) double with canal view; 889€ ($1,022) jr. suite on courtyard; 1,871€ ($2,152) suite with partial canal view; 2,443€ ($2,809) deluxe suite with canal view or panorama. Buffet breakfast 55€ ($63). AE, DC, MC, V. *Vaporetto:* San Marco (head west out of the southwest corner of Piazza San Marco down Saliz San Mose; cross the bridge to continue straight on Calle Larga XXII Marzo; you'll see hotel signs directing you down the alleyways to the left). **Amenities:** Excellent La Cusina restaurant (reviewed later in this chapter); terrace bar on the Grand Canal; use of pool at sister hotel on the Lido; golf course; tennis court; exercise room; sauna; watersports equipment; bike rental; children's center; concierge; tour desk; car-rental desk; courtesy water taxi (free hourly boat to the Westin Excelsior on the Lido); business center; room service (24-hr.); babysitting; laundry service; dry cleaning (same-day Mon–Fri); nonsmoking rooms. *In room:* A/C, TV w/pay movies, dataport, fax (on request), minibar, hair dryer, safe.

EXPENSIVE

Hotel Concordia ★   The big selling point here: It's the only hotel in Venice with rooms overlooking St. Mark's (technically, the Piazza San Marco, so what you see are the pinnacles and domes on the side of the cathedral). Most rooms are 18th-century Venetian period style, done in a floral motif, with ornate little writing desks, gilt mirrors, and Murano chandeliers. Some are done in a slightly scuffed Empire style, with a day bed in the little sitting area. Bathrooms are red marble, and though all rooms are perfectly nice, the Concordia really is all about those precious 15 rooms overlooking the Piazzetta and the Duomo. Of these, four sets of double rooms share a common door to the hallway, meaning they can be closed off and linked to make family suites. You have to tackle 27 steps before reaching the reception area and its elevator. If you ask, the hotel will provide you with a coupon for 10% off your bill at the parking garage in Piazzale Roma. The hotel restaurant, La Piazzetta, offers Venetian cuisine.

San Marco 367 (Calle Larga San Marco), 30124 Venezia. (✆ **041-520-6866.** Fax 041-520-6775. www.hotel concordia.it. 59 units. 185€–413€ ($213–$475) double; 211€–418€ ($243–$481) jr. suite; 237€–438€ ($273–$504) suite; extra bed 52€–83€ ($60–$95). Buffet breakfast included. AE, DC, MC, V. *Vaporetto:* San Marco-Giardinetti (walk to the right getting off the *vaporetto,* then left into Piazza San Marco; cross in front of the basilica and straight up the Merceria 1 brief block to take a right on Calle Larga San Marco). **Amenities:** Italian/regional restaurant; bar; concierge; tour desk; car-rental desk; room service (limited); babysitting; laundry service; dry cleaning (same-day); nonsmoking rooms. *In room:* A/C, TV, dataport, minibar, hair dryer, safe.

Hotel Monaco & Grand Canal ★★ You won't get a more choice location: right on the Grand Canal, across from Harry's Bar, 1 long block from St. Mark's Square, and all of it thoroughly renovated from 2001 to 2003. That said, only 10% of the rooms actually overlook the canal; these tend to be midsize with ornately painted headboards and closet doors and nicely done bathrooms with heated towel racks. Some good news: When they're not booked, the staff can block off the large sitting rooms of suites to turn them into canal-side doubles. Standard rooms without the view are more simply furnished but share the same tall ceilings and windows to let in that fine Venetian light. Several lounges feature windows on the canal, and the bar service, restaurant, and breakfast move out onto a canal-side terrace in warm weather (in winter, a piano bar operates in an inner lounge warmed by an open fire).

San Marco 1332 (right at the *vaporetto* stop, at the end of Calle Vallaresso off Salita San Moisè, the main road leading west out of Piazza San Marco), 30124 Venezia. (✆ **041-520-0211.** Fax 041-520-0501. www. hotelbook.com. 44 units. 393€ ($452) double; 506€ ($582) double with canal view; 620€ ($713) jr. suite with canal view; 671€ ($772) suite with canal view. Discounts (20%–25%) July–Aug. Rates include breakfast. AE, DC, MC, V. *Vaporetto:* San Marco–Vallaresso (hotel is right at the stop). **Amenities:** Venetian/Italian restaurant; bar; concierge; tour desk; car-rental desk; room service (limited); babysitting; laundry service; dry cleaning (same-day); nonsmoking rooms. *In room:* A/C, TV w/pay movies, dataport, minibar, hair dryer, safe.

Luna Hotel Baglioni ★★ Just around the corner from Piazza San Marco on the street leading down to Harry's Bar, this luxury hotel may be Venice's oldest inn, converted into a hotel from a convent in the 1200s. "Standard" rooms are situated on dreary air shafts but are otherwise very nice, midsize with more modish styling and walk-in closets (in some) than that of the pricier-category rooms. The more desirable "deluxe" rooms are richly carpeted, with ornate stucco around the wall fabrics, Murano chandeliers and sconces, watercolors and prints, and double sinks with golden fixtures set in the marble bathrooms. Some have half-testers over the beds, many sprout small balconies with a partial view of the little Royal Gardens at the Grand Canal. Junior suites are very large, with half-testers and huge bathrooms, though only no. 505 enjoys the views of the Bacino San Marco (into which the Grand Canal empties) enjoyed by full suites. Suites are spread across two rooms, and three have sizable terraces overlooking the *bacino*—all can sleep four or five if you convert the sitting room into a bedroom. The elegant breakfast room is covered with remarkable 18th-century frescoes and gilt-edged paintings. There's an airy, two-story lounge off the reception area, an Internet point (a computer terminal where you can go online), and salons strung along the canal across from the Giardinetti Reali.

San Marco 1243 (Calle di Ca'Vallaresso), 30124 Venezia. © **041-528-9840.** Fax 041-528-7160. www.baglioni hotels.com. 115 units. 270€–440€ ($310–$506) classic double; 320€–520€ ($368–$598) superior double; 370€–560€ ($426–$644) deluxe double; 430€–660€ ($495–$759) jr. suite; 570€–1,400€ ($656–$1,610) suite. Buffet breakfast included. AE, DC, MC, V. *Vaporetto:* San Marco–Vallaresso (it's on the street leading straight up from the *vaporetto* stop). **Amenities:** Italian/international restaurant; piano bar (music 2–3 times a week); concierge; tour desk; car-rental desk; room service (limited); babysitting; laundry service; dry cleaning (same-day); nonsmoking rooms. *In room:* A/C, TV, VCR (on request in suites), fax (in suites), dataport, minibar, hair dryer, safe.

MODERATE

Hotel Flora ⭑ The simple name of this small, charming hotel refers to its greatest attribute: a jewel-like patio garden immediately beyond the welcoming lobby. A delightful place to have breakfast, afternoon tea, or an aperitif, the garden is enclosed by climbing vines and ivy-covered walls, with an antique well, potted flowers, and blooming plants that create a cool green enclave, one of the hotel's many pleasant places to retreat. Seamlessly run by two generations of the highly professional Romanelli family and their friendly staff, the Flora has long been one of Venice's favorite spots and is ideally located just west of the American Express office on a tony shopping street. Despite rooms that can vary greatly (from small to standard in size, and rather plain to the nicest period-style ones overlooking the garden), and small bathrooms that could do with a face-lift, it is forever full of loyal devotees and romance-seekers. On the top floor, room no. 47 looks onto what is allegedly the palazzo of Desdemona (of Shakespeare's tragedy *Othello*), with the dome of La Salute church beyond. The owners of Hotel Flora recently opened a new hotel in the same area: **Locanda Novecento** (San Marco 2683–2684; © **041-241-3765;** fax 041-521-2145; www.locandanovecento.it) is a boutique hotel offering luxury accommodations in nine rooms, each decorated along the theme of "1900." Rooms have the same amenities as the Flora.

San Marco 2283a (off Calle Larga XXII Marzo, near Campo San Moisè), 30124 Venezia. © **041-520-5844.** Fax 041-522-8217. www.hotelflora.it. 44 units. 207€–230€ ($238–$265) double. Extra person 44€ ($51). Rates include continental breakfast. AE, DC, MC, V. Slow-period discounts of approximately 15%. *Vaporetto:* San Marco–Vallaresso (walk down Calle Vallaresso and turn left on to the V. XXII Marzo; after crossing the San Moisè Bridge and passing the Deutsche Bank, you'll see a sign on left side of street for the hotel, located down a narrow passageway off the V. XXII Marzo. **Amenities:** Bar; concierge; tour desk; room service (24-hr.); babysitting; laundry service; dry cleaning. *In room:* A/C, TV, dataport, hair dryer, safe.

Hotel Gallini Though the 1997 fire at La Fenice opera house doused this neighborhood's spark, it's now back to business as usual at the Gallini. The amiable Ceciliati brothers, Adriano and Gabriele, have been at the helm since 1952 and offer four floors (no elevator) of bright, spacious rooms and big, modern bathrooms (all rooms should have bathrooms by the time you get here). Ten rooms overlook narrow Rio della Verona, and a few have air-conditioning (for which there may be a small daily fee). Though there's nothing wrong with it in particular, the place is charmless, but it's the largest hotel I suggest in this area, and therefore a good moderately priced choice when the smaller options are full. The housekeeping staff seems to be forever cleaning, and rich-looking marble floors in green, red, or speckled black alternate with intricate parquet to lend an old-world air.

San Marco 3673 (on Calle della Verona), 30124 Venezia. © **041-520-4515.** Fax 041-520-9103. www.hotel gallini.it. 40 units, 35 with bathroom. 100€ ($115) double without bathroom; 130€ ($150) double with bathroom; 180€ ($207) triple with bathroom; 120€–227€ ($138–$261) suite. Off-season rates about 15% lower. Ask about special discount rates for Frommer's readers (varying with vacancy levels). Rates include continental breakfast. AE, DC, MC, V. Closed Nov 15 to Carnevale. *Vaporetto:* Sant'Angelo (follow zigzagging road south toward Campo Sant'Angelo; exit *campo* at northeast end by taking Calle della Mandola; turn right at the Ottica [optometrist] onto Calle dei Assasini, which becomes Calle della Verona) or Rialto. **Amenities:** Concierge; room service (limited). *In room:* A/C (some rooms), TV (some rooms), minibar (some rooms), hair dryer.

Hotel La Fenice et Des Artistes ⭐

The hallways are plastered with ornate little mirrors and tons of contemporary paintings and prints, and the location is great—around the corner from La Fenice opera house, halfway between San Marco and the Accademia. It's split into two early-19th-century palazzi on either side of a modern lobby entrance grafted into what was once an open courtyard, scraps of which survive off either side of the hall for breakfast alfresco. It's a perfectly nice, elegantly furnished hotel of modest luxury. Bathrooms were recently renovated, but the hotel unfortunately lacks random quality touches such as a decent air-conditioning system, and, most surprisingly, good beds—the mattresses rest on ancient, sway-backed cot springs. The string of homey lounges feel like comfy living rooms, scattered with assorted furnishings, card tables, a TV with VCR, and an Internet point (a computer terminal where you can go online) for guest use.

San Marco 1936 (Campiello della Fenice), 30124 Venezia. ℂ 041-523-2333. Fax 041-520-3721. www.fenice hotels.it. 70 units. 135€–230€ ($155–$265) double; 160€–270€ ($184–$311) superior double; 170€–265€ ($196–$305) triple; 200€–295€ ($230–$339) suite for 2 people; 205€–305€ ($236–$351) family suite. Rates include breakfast. AE, DC, MC, V. *Vaporetto:* Santa Maria del Giglio (walk up into Campo Santa Maria Zobenigo, turn right to cross the footbridge; the road on the other side makes a sharp turn left, then right to open into the wide Calle Larga/Via XXII Marzo; turn left up Calle delle Veste into Campo San Fantin; turn left to walk around the right flank of Teatro La Fenice, then make your 1st right down a narrow alley into the hotel's tiny *campiello*). **Amenities:** Bar; concierge; tour desk; car-rental desk; room service (limited); babysitting. *In room:* A/C, TV, dataport, minibar (in most; slowly adding to all), hair dryer, safe.

Hotel Violino d'Oro ⭐⭐

This small boutique hotel at a tiny *campiello* with a marble fountainhead on the main shopping drag from San Marco to the Accademia may be new, but the style is ever-popular 18th-century Venetian. The rooms, bathed in rich colors, are compact but graced with nice touches such as gold decoration on the marble-top desks, modest stuccoes and Murano chandeliers on the ceilings, very firm beds, and heated towel racks in the bathrooms. Six rooms even overlook Rio San Moisè canal. The low-season rates are incredible, and even high-season rates are (for Venice) decent for this level of comfort and style. The entire hotel is nonsmoking.

San Marco 2091 (Via XXII Marzo), 30124 Venezia. ℂ 041-277-0841. Fax 041-277-1001. www.violinodoro. com. 26 units. 60€–300€ ($69–$345) double; extra bed 50€ ($58). Ask about lower rates during low season. Rates include buffet breakfast. AE, DC, MC, V. *Vaporetto:* San Marco–Vallaresso (walk straight up Calle di Ca'-Vallaresso, left on Salita San Moisè; cross the wide footbridge and the hotel is just across the little *campiello* on the left). **Amenities:** Bar; concierge; room service (24-hr.); laundry service; dry cleaning; nonsmoking rooms (whole hotel). *In room:* A/C, TV, dataport, minibar, hair dryer.

INEXPENSIVE

Albergo ai do Mori ⭐ (Value) (Kids)

Antonella, the young hands-on owner/manager, creates an efficient yet comfortable ambience here, with special care given to Frommer's readers. The more accessible lower-floor rooms (there's no elevator and the hotel begins on the second floor) are slightly larger and offer rooftop views, but the top-floor rooms boast views of San Marco's cupolas and the Torre dell'Orologio, whose two bronze Moors ring the bells every hour (the large double-paned windows help to ensure quiet). A 1998 face-lift brought new tiled bathrooms (with hair dryers and heated towel racks), TVs, firm mattresses, and air-conditioning. Another renovation in 2001 gave every room but two a private bathroom and revealed the rest of the wood beams on the ceilings. The walls were painted bright colors and comfy new furnishings were added. Room nos. 4 (a small double) and 5 (a triple) share a bathroom and a small hallway and can be turned into a family suite. Additionally, Antonella has now opened a four-room annex nearby.

San Marco 658 (on Calle Larga San Marco), 30124 Venezia. ✆ 041-520-4817 or 041-528-9293. Fax 041-520-5328. www.hotelaidomori.com. 15 units. 70€–135€ ($81–$155) double; 180€–220€ ($207–$253) family suite (up to 5 people). Ask about lower off-season rates. MC, V. *Vaporetto:* San Marco (exit Piazza San Marco beneath Torre dell'Orologio; turn right at Max Mara store and hotel is on left, just before McDonald's). **Amenities:** Bar; concierge; nonsmoking rooms. *In room:* A/C, TV, hair dryer, safe.

Albergo al Gambero ★★ Midway along a main strip connecting Piazza San Marco and the Rialto Bridge, one of Venice's former budget hotels underwent a full makeover in 1998. Surrounded by striped damask-like bedspreads and curtains, you can slumber in one of the 14 canal-side rooms (five have bathrooms, including no. 203, which also has a small balcony). Rooms on the first two floors have higher ceilings, though upstairs rooms are the most freshly renovated (in 2002, when bathrooms were added to all). In 2003, management acquired an apartment in the adjacent building and planned to knock out the wall and turn this into five more rooms, which should be completed as this book goes to press. The entire hotel is nonsmoking. By Venice standards, the budget-level Gambero has all the trappings of a midscale hotel at moderate prices. Guests receive a 10% discount in the lively ground-floor Bistrot de Venise (p. 112).

San Marco 4687 (on Calle dei Fabbri), 30124 Venezia. ✆ 041-522-4384 or 041-520-1420. Fax 041-520-0431. www.locandaalgambero.com. 27 units, 15 with bathroom. 170€ ($196) double with bathroom; 150€–229€ ($173–$263) triple with bathroom; 170€–285€ ($196–$328) quad with bathroom. Rates include continental breakfast. MC, V. *Vaporetto:* Rialto (turn right along canal, cross small footbridge over Rio San Salvador, turn left onto Calle Bembo, which becomes Calle dei Fabbri; hotel about 5 blocks ahead on left). **Amenities:** Restaurant (Le Bistrot de Venise, p. 112); bar (in restaurant); concierge; tour desk; whole hotel nonsmoking. *In room:* A/C, TV, dataport, minibar, hair dryer, safe.

Hotel Do Pozzi ★ *Finds* Duck off bustling Calle Larga just 150m (500 ft.) from St. Mark's Square and you'll find a hidden little *campiello* whose namesake "two wells" flank the round tables where hotel guests take breakfast in warm weather. The quietest rooms overlook this tiny square from flower-fringed windows. All guest rooms were restructured in 1998 in a tidy, modern style with embroidered fabrics, a few 18th-century Venetian-style pieces, Murano chandeliers, wood floors, and glass mirrors on the closet doors to make the cozy quarters seem roomier. Nos. 20 and 40 get slivers of Grand Canal views down a short street; no. 47 opens onto the noisy shopping of Calle Larga, but it comes with frescoed ceilings and a small sitting room. Rooms in the seven-room annex **Dependance Favaro** around the corner are largely the same. Guests can receive a 10% discount off meals at the hotel restaurant Da Raffaele.

San Marco 2373 (off Calle Larga/Via XXII Marzo), 30124 Venezia. ✆ 041-520-7855. Fax 041-522-9413. www.hoteldopozzi.it. 30 units, plus 6 in Dependance Favaro. 130€–210€ ($150–$242) double; 40€–50€ ($46–$58) extra bed. AE, DC, MC, V. *Vaporetto:* Santa Maria del Giglio (walk straight up from *vaporetto* stop into Campo Santa Maria Zobenigo, turn right out of the *campo* and cross the bridge, doglegging slight left and right again onto broad Calle Larga; take the 1st right down a narrow alley to the hotel). **Amenities:** Venetian/Italian restaurant; concierge; tour desk; room service (breakfast and bar); babysitting; laundry service; dry cleaning (same-day); nonsmoking rooms. *In room:* A/C, TV, minibar, hair dryer.

Locanda Fiorita ★★ *Value* New owners have created a pretty little hotel in this Venetian red palazzo, parts of which date from the 1400s. In 1999 everything was renovated in 18th-century Venetian style. The wisteria vine partially covering the facade is at its glorious best in May or June, but the Fiorita is excellent year-round, as much for its simply furnished rooms boasting new bathrooms (now with hair dryers) as for its location on a *campiello* off the grand Campo Santo Stefano. Room nos. 1 and 10 have little terraces beneath the wisteria pergola and overlook the *campiello:* They can't be guaranteed on reserving, so ask when you arrive. Each of the two rooms without bathrooms has its own private facilities down the hall. Just a few meters away is **Ca' Morosini** ((C) **041-241-3800;** fax 041-522-8043; www. camorosini.com), the Fiorita's three-star annex. There you'll find more rooms with views of the *campo.*

San Marco 3457a (on Campiello Novo), 30124 Venezia. (C) 041-523-4754. Fax 041-522-8043. www.locanda fiorita.com. 10 units, 8 with bathroom, in main house; 6 units in annex. Main house: 90€–110€ ($104–$127) double without bathroom, 100€–130€ ($115–$150) double with bathroom. Annex: 140€–180€ ($161–$207) double with bathroom. Extra person 30% more at either. Rates include continental breakfast. AE, DC, MC, V. *Vaporetto:* S. Angelo (walk to the tall brick building, then turn right around its side; cross a small bridge and turn left down Calle del Pestrin; a bit farther down on your left is a small square 3 stairs above street level; hotel is against the back of it). **Amenities:** Concierge; tour desk; room service (limited); babysitting; nonsmoking rooms. *In room:* A/C, TV, dataport (annex only), minibar (annex only), hair dryer, safe (annex only).

Locanda Remedio—Dependance Hotel Colombina 🌟   In January 2003 the Remedio became the three-star annex of the four-star **Hotel Colombina** (Castello 4416, Calle del Remedio; (C) **041-277-0525;** fax 041-277-6044; info@hotelcolombina.it), so changes might be afoot. For now the hotel remains, by Venetian standards, a spot offering unusually large and quiet rooms with fine antiques (and good reproductions) in an ancient palazzo around the corner from one of St. Mark's busiest streets. Most rooms are on the second floor (no. 27 has lovely ceiling frescoes) off a ballroom-size corridor, and they feature modernized, if small, bathrooms, and TVs with VCRs (movies in English are available at the desk). The last significant renovation took place in 2001, but I should imagine the new owners will be making the place over themselves sometime during the shelf-life of this book.

San Marco 4412 (on Calle del Remedio), 30122 Venezia. (C) 041-520-6232. Fax 041-521-0485. 12 units. 120€–280€ ($138–$322) double; 160€–350€ ($184–$403) triple. Rates include breakfast. AE, DC, MC, V. *Vaporetto:* San Marco (exit Piazza San Marco under Torre dell'Orologio and turn right onto Calle Larga San Marco; at Ristorante All'Angelo, turn left onto Calle va al Ponte dell'Angelo and take 1st right onto Ramo del Anzolo; cross small footbridge onto Calle del Remedio). **Amenities:** Concierge; tour desk; in-room massage; nonsmoking rooms. *In room:* A/C, TV, minibar, hair dryer, safe.

IN CASTELLO
VERY EXPENSIVE
Hotel Danieli ★★★   Doge Dandolo built his glorious Venetian Gothic palace three doors down from the Palazzo Ducale in the 14th century, and it's been one of the most sumptuous hotels in Venice since 1822. It vies with the Gritti Palace (which is now in the same family) as the most desirable address in Venice proper (there are also luxurious properties on Giudecca and the Lido), and has been host to innumerable kings, celebrities, and other noted guests as far back as Dickens. This palatial accommodation's tone is set by the astounding four-story lobby of balustraded open balconies and stairwells, Venice's Oriental-tinged Gothic arches, and palm fronds. It's ornately decorated throughout, and the rooms vary in decor, size, and style but are all opulent, in rich fabrics, antique furnishings, Oriental rugs, and lavish accents from marble bathrooms or frescoes to oil paintings or stone fireplaces. It'd be a shame to miss out on that incredible lagoon view. Rooms in the original structure have the most atmos-phere but are smaller than the accommodations in the 19th-century wing.

Either is far preferable to the bleak 1940s wing next door—the rooms are fine there but lack that genteel, vintage touch.

Castello 4196 (Riva degli Schiavoni), 30122 Venezia. © **041-522-6480.** Fax 041-520-0208. www.luxury collection.com/danieli. 231 units. 667€–734€ ($767–$844) double; 795€–932€ ($914–$1,072) double with lagoon view; 889€ ($1,022) jr. suite; 1,126€ ($1,295) jr. suite with lagoon view; 2,443€ ($2,809) suite with lagoon view. Buffet breakfast 55€ ($63). AE, DC, MC, V. *Vaporetto:* S. Zaccaria (the hotel's right at the *vaporetto* launch). **Amenities:** Roof terrace Italian restaurant; 2 bars (1 with piano music); use of pool at sister hotel on the Lido; golf course; tennis court; exercise room; sauna; watersports equipment; bike rental; children's center; concierge; tour desk; car-rental desk; courtesy car; business center; room service (limited); babysitting; laundry service; dry cleaning (same-day); nonsmoking rooms. *In room:* A/C, TV w/pay movies, fax (in suite), dataport, minibar, hair dryer (in most), safe.

Londra Palace ✦   This 19th-century neo-Gothic palace is one of the best values on the prime real estate of the Riva degli Schiavoni. Tchaikovsky wrote his 4th Symphony in room no. 108. Accommodations are cushy, with lacquered furniture, and attic rooms are most romantic. With 100 windows overlooking the San Marco basin, you can enjoy watching people strolling below, as well as distant vistas of the lagoon, from the "deluxe" rooms. Quieter, cheaper "superior" rooms look out on the inner courtyard. The restaurant, Do Leoni, is one of the best hotel dining rooms in town. In 1999 the lobby and ground floor salons were overhauled by the same architect who does Versace boutiques.

Castello 4171 (Riva degli Schiavoni), 30122 Venezia. © **041-520-0533.** Fax 041-522-5032. www.hotelondra.it. 53 units. 275€–485€ ($316–$558) "superior" double without view; 380€–585€ ($437–$673) "superior" double with lagoon view; 485€–790€ ($558–$909) jr. suite; extra bed 100€ ($115); half pension 65€ ($75) per person. Continental breakfast included. AE, DC, MC, V. *Vaporetto:* San Zaccaria (on the canal right at the San Zaccaria *vaporetto* stop). **Amenities:** Excellent Venetian/international restaurant; bar; tennis (on Lido; special rate); golf (on Lido, special rate); concierge; tour desk; car-rental desk; room service (limited); massage; babysitting; laundry service; dry cleaning. *In room:* A/C, TV, dataport, minibar, hair dryer, safe.

EXPENSIVE

Hotel Metropole ✦✦   Vivaldi lived here from 1704 to 1738, when it was the chapter house of La Pietà church next door and he was its violin and concert master. The quirky palazzo that has evolved from that church building is now a member of the "Romantik" hotel association—and aptly so. The owner has tried to outfit his hotel as a Victorian-style home, packed with quirky collections of curios (fans, purses, bottle openers, crucifixes, cigarette cases), and its public salons are tucked with cozy bars and sitting niches. Personalized service is taken very seriously here; there are 67 staff members for 72 rooms. Accommodations vary widely in true Romantic style, though you may find such details as Burano glass lamps and Murano chandeliers, inlaid wood furnishings, marble tiled bathrooms, Romantic-era watercolors and prints, etched glass mirrors, or even twisty marble columns and frescoed putti behind the bed. Since every room is different, the true choice here is picking a room overlooking the Bacino San Marco, or at least the side canal where water taxis pull up, rather than the courtyard housing the lovely garden restaurant enlivened by nightly keyboard music. To the rates below, you'll have to add 104€ ($120) for that *bacino* view, but they make it up to you by offering free car parking (to everyone, not just lagoon-side renters) if you let them know you need it before 8pm the day you arrive.

Castello 4149 (Riva degli Schiavoni), 30122 Venezia. © **041-520-5044.** Fax 041-522-3679. www.hotel metropole.com. 72 units. 210€–465€ ($242–$535) double; 390€–620€ ($449–$713) jr. suite; 390€–725€ ($449–$834) suite. Buffet breakfast included. AE, DC, MC, V. *Vaporetto:* S. Zaccaria (walk right along Riva degli Schiavoni over 2 footbridges; the hotel is next to La Pietà church). **Amenities:** Venetian/Italian restaurant; bar; concierge; tour desk; car-rental desk; business center; room service (24-hr.); in-room massage; babysitting; laundry service; dry cleaning (same-day); nonsmoking rooms. *In room:* A/C, TV, minibar, hair dryer, safe.

Locanda Casa Verardo ★★ *Finds*   In 2000 Daniela and Francesco took over this one-star pensione and transformed it into a fine three-star hotel (and more than doubled its size), while still maintaining the feel of a Venetian palazzo romantically faded by time. The wood-paneled lobby is anchored by an ancient stone well. The rooms are done in chipped-stone floors, Murano chandeliers, and eclectic furnishings, from imposing armoires and 17th-century reproductions to pseudo Deco and modern functional; three have small terraces. The best accommodations come with stucco wall decorations and scraps of old ceiling frescoes—and tops are the six overlooking a little canal. The airy main hall doubles as a breakfast room. A 2001 renovation included the installation of "deluxe" rooms, the addition of minibars in guest rooms, and the conversion of two rooms for use by guests with disabilities.

Castello 4765 (at foot of Ponte Storto), 30122 Venezia. ℂ **041-528-6138** or 041-528-6127. Fax 041-523-2765. www.casaverardo.it. 26 units. 104€–165€ ($120–$190) double; 130€–206 ($150–$237) deluxe double; 156€–220€ ($179–$253) suite for 3–4; 197€–250€ ($227–$288) deluxe suite for 3–4. Rates include buffet breakfast. Prices much lower in off season; ask when you book. AE, MC, V. *Vaporetto:* San Zaccaria (walk straight ahead on Calle delle Rasse to Campo SS. Filippo e Giacomo; continue straight through the small *campo* to take Calle Chiesa to cross the 1st small bridge, Ponte Storto, to find the hotel on the left). **Amenities:** Bar; concierge; tour desk; room service (breakfast, drinks); babysitting, nonsmoking rooms. *In room:* A/C, TV, minibar, hair dryer (ask at desk), safe (only in 2).

INEXPENSIVE

Foresteria Valdese (Palazzo Cavagnis) ★ *Value*   Those lucky enough to get a room at this weathered, albeit elegant, 16th-century palazzo will find simple accommodations in a charming *foresteria,* the name given to religious institutions that traditionally provided lodging for pilgrims and guests. Affiliated with Italy's Waldesian and Methodist churches, the palazzo often fills the large dormitory-style rooms with visiting church groups, though everyone is warmly welcomed, and you'll find an international and inter-religious mix here. Each of the plainly furnished rooms in this once-noble residence opens onto a balcony overlooking a quiet canal. The 18th-century frescoes that grace the high ceilings in some doubles (including corner no. 10) and two of the dorms are by the same artist who decorated the Correr Civic Museum—and these rooms will cost you a few euros extra. The two apartments, complete with kitchen facilities, are the best budget choices in town for traveling families of four or five. (Be aware that guests staying in private rooms or apartments are required to stay at least 2 nights; those staying in dormitories can stay just 1.) A sweeping renovation begun in 1995 has finally been completed. The reception is open daily from 9am to 1pm and 6 to 8pm. The entire hotel is now nonsmoking.

Castello 5170 (at the end of Calle Lunga Santa Maria Formosa), 30122 Venezia. ℂ **041-528-6797.** Fax 041-241-6238. www.diaconiavaldese.org/venezia. 6 units with bathroom and TV (2–4 beds) often requiring a 2-night stay; 3 dorms (with 8, 11, or 16 beds), none with bathroom; 2 mini-apts (sleeping 4–5, minimum stay often required) with kitchen and bathroom. 56€ ($64) double without bathroom, 74€ ($85) double with bathroom; 102€ ($117) quad with bathroom; 102€ ($117) apt for 4; 115€ ($132) apt for 5; 20€ ($23) dorm bed (21€/$24 if you stay just 1 night). Rates include buffet breakfast, except in apts. DC, MC, V (but pay 3.5% more to use credit cards). Closed 2 weeks in Nov. *Vaporetto:* Rialto (Head southeast to the Campo Santa Maria Formosa; look for the Bar all'Orologio, just where Calle Lunga Santa Maria Formosa begins. The *campo* is just about equidistant from Piazza San Marco and the Rialto Bridge). **Amenities:** Nonsmoking rooms. *In room:* TV (except in dorms), dataport, kitchenette (in apts), no phone.

Hotel Al Piave ★★★ *Value*   The Puppin family's tasteful hotel is a steal: This level of attention coupled with the sophisticated *buon gusto* in decor and spirit is rare in this price category. You'll find orthopedic mattresses under ribbon candy–print or floral spreads, immaculate white-lace curtains, stained-glass windows, new bathrooms, and even (in a few rooms) tiny terraces. The family suites—with two bedrooms, minibars, and shared bathrooms—are particularly good deals, as are the small but stylishly rustic apartments with kitchenettes and washing machines (in the two smaller ones). A savvy international crowd has discovered this classy spot, so even with renovations that have expanded the hotel's size, you'll need to reserve far in advance.

Castello 4838–40 (on Ruga Giuffa), 30122 Venezia. ⓒ 041-528-5174. Fax 041-523-8512. www.hotelal piave.com. 13 units. 150€ double ($173); 150€–200€ ($173–$230) triple; 230€ ($265) family suite for 3; 260€ ($299) family suite for 4; 290€ ($334) family suite for 5. Often heavy discounts off season. Rates include continental breakfast. AE, DC, MC, V. Closed Jan 7 to Carnevale. *Vaporetto:* San Zaccaria (walk straight ahead on Calle delle Rasse to small Campo SS. Filippo e Giacomo, take right on Calle San Provolo, and cross over canal to Campo San Provolo; take a left, cross 1st small footbridge, and follow zigzagging street that becomes Ruga Giuffa). **Amenities:** Concierge; tour desk; babysitting. *In room:* A/C, TV, minibar, fridge (family suite), hair dryer, safe.

Hotel Campiello ⊛   At this gem on a tiny *campiello*, the atmosphere is airy and bright, and the relaxed hospitality and quality service are provided by the Bianchini sisters, Monica and Nicoletta. A 1998 renovation transformed the rooms' contemporary style into a more traditional decor—most are now done in authentic 18th-century and Art Nouveau antiques with inlaid *armadios* (armoire-like cabinets) and bas-reliefs on the headboards. The building's original 15th-century marble-mosaic pavement is still evident, a vestige of the days when the hotel was a convent under the patronage of the nearby San Zaccaria; you'll catch a glimpse of it in the lounge area opening onto a pleasant breakfast room. As we go to press, the owners have begun construction of an elevator and are renovating seven of the guest rooms.

Castello 4647 (on Campiello del Vin), 30122 Venezia. ⓒ 041-520-5764. Fax 041-520-5798. www. hcampiello.it. 16 units. 170€ ($196) double; 196€ ($225) triple; 227€ ($261) quad. Ask about discounts in low season. Rates include continental breakfast. AE, DC, MC, V. *Vaporetto:* 1, 51, or 82 to S. Zaccaria. **Amenities:** Bar; concierge; room service (24-hr.); babysitting; nonsmoking rooms. *In room:* A/C, TV, dataport, hair dryer, safe.

Hotel Fontana ⊛   Three generations of Stainers have been behind the front desk here since 1967 (for centuries prior to that, the Fontana was a convent for Austrian nuns), and their warmth seems to pour out of the lobby's leaded-glass windows. The four-story hotel offers a pensione-like family atmosphere coupled with a crisp, professional operation. Rooms have lovely antique furnishings but a decided lack of wattage in the overhead lights. The choice two on the upper floor have private terraces. There's no elevator, but those who brave the climb to the top floors are compensated by views of San Zaccaria's 15th-century facade.

Castello 4701 (on Campo San Provolo), 30122 Venezia. ⓒ 041-522-0579. Fax 041-523-1040. www.hotel fontana.it. 16 units. 80€–170€ ($92–$196) double; 145€–200€ ($167–$230) triple; 145€–230€ ($167–$265) quad. Rates include buffet breakfast. AE, DC, MC, V. *Vaporetto:* San Zaccaria (from Riva degli Schiavoni, take any narrow street north to Campiello SS. Filippo e Giacomo; exit this small *campo* from east side, in direction of Campo San Zaccaria, until reaching Campo San Provolo). **Amenities:** Concierge; tour desk; room service (limited). *In room:* TV, dataport, hair dryer (on request).

⟮*Tips*⟯ **Frommer's Discounts**

Traveling with Frommer's has its privileges. Many hotels recognize the name and will give readers a Frommer's discount. Just show the book when you check in. A lot of the prices listed in the book apply only to the likes of you and me—people who use this book.

Hotel La Residenza ★★ *Finds*   Feel like a doge; spend like a pauper. This is an excellent slice of old Venice at a fraction of the usual Venice cost. It's just a block up from the priciest real estate of the Riva degli Schiavoni, but you'd never know it. A few of the rooms at this pensione-style small hotel in a 15th-century palazzo overlook the very Venetian *campo* out front where kids play soccer and old ladies sit in the sun. Others open onto the surrounding quiet streets of a neighbor's garden. Stuccoes from the 1750s, 17th-century paintings, and a baby grand piano decorate the absolutely fabulous lobby/breakfast room. Though half the rooms still have carpeting, half were refurbished in 2001, and their polished wood floors support hand-painted 18th-century Venetian-style furnishings under Murano chandeliers. There's no elevator (it's 25 steps up to the reception). The whole hotel is now nonsmoking.

Castello 3608 (Campo Bandiera e Moro), 30122 Venezia. © **041-528-5315.** Fax 041-523-8859. www. venicelaresidenza.com. 15 units. 100€–155€ ($115–$178) double; 30€–35€ ($35–$40) extra bed. Breakfast included. AE, MC, V. *Vaporetto:* S. Zaccaria (from the *vaporetto*, turn left along Riva degli Schiavoni, cross 3 bridges, then take your 1st left into the *campo*) or Arsenale (from the *vaporetto* stop, turn left up Riva degli Schiavoni, over 1 bridge, left up Calle del Forno, and left on Calle va in Crosera, which spills into the *campo*). **Amenities:** Concierge; nonsmoking rooms (whole hotel). *In room:* A/C, TV, minibar, hair dryer (request one at the desk), safe.

IN DORSODURO
MODERATE

Hotel American ★★   Despite its potentially unromantic name (did you travel transatlantic for this?), the Hotel American is recommended for both its style and its substance. One of the nicest of Venice's moderate hotels, it has the perfect combination of old-fashioned charm and utility. This three-story hotel located near the Peggy Guggenheim Collection offers a dignified lobby and breakfast room liberally dressed with lovely Oriental carpets and marble flooring, polished woods, and leaded-glass windows and French doors. The best choices here are the larger corner rooms and the nine rooms overlooking a quiet canal; some even have small terraces. Every room is outfitted with traditional Venetian-style furnishings that usually include hand-painted furniture and Murano glass chandeliers. If it's late spring, don't miss a drink on the second-floor terrace beneath a wisteria arbor dripping with plump violet blossoms.

Dorsoduro 628 (on Fond. Bragadin), 30123 Venezia. © **041-520-4733.** Fax 041-520-4048. www.hotel american.com. 30 units. 130€–250€ ($150–$288) double; 180€–300€ ($207–$345) double with canal view. Rates include buffet breakfast. Extra person 60€ ($69). AE, MC, V. *Vaporetto:* Accademia (veer left around the Galleria dell'Accademia museum, taking the 1st left turn and walk straight ahead until you cross the 1st small footbridge. Turn right to follow the Fondamenta Bragadin that runs alongside the Rio di San Vio canal. The hotel is on your left). **Amenities:** Bar; concierge; tour desk; car-rental desk; room service (limited); babysitting; laundry service; nonsmoking rooms; Internet point. *In room:* A/C, TV, dataport, minibar, hair dryer, safe.

Pensione alla Salute (Da Cici) ★   An airy lobby with beamed ceilings and cool marble floors, a small but lovely terrace garden, and a cozy cocktail bar occupy the ground level of this converted 17th-century palazzo on Rio della Fornace. Upstairs, the comfortable guest rooms have high ceilings and huge windows (10 with canal views and 4 facing the garden), many of them large enough to accommodate families of four or even five at an additional charge (ask when booking). Breakfast is served in the garden in warm weather, and the entire hotel is now nonsmoking.

Dorsoduro 222 (on Fondamenta Ca' Balà), 30123 Venezia. © **041-523-5404.** Fax 041-522-2271. www.hotel salute.com. 58 units, 12 with shower only, some with bathroom. 70€–100€ ($81–$115) double without bathroom, 100€–135€ ($115–$155) double with bathroom; 140€–180€ ($161–$207) triple with bathroom. Ask about rooms sleeping 4–5 persons. Discounts given Mar and July–Aug. Rates include continental breakfast. No credit cards. Often closes in Jan or Feb for upkeep; call ahead. *Vaporetto:* Salute (facing La Salute, turn right and head to 1st small bridge; cross it and walk as straight ahead as possible to next narrow canal, then turn left, before crossing bridge, onto Fondamenta Ca' Balà). **Amenities:** Bar; nonsmoking rooms (whole hotel). *In room:* Hair dryer.

INEXPENSIVE

Hotel Falier ★ *Value* Owned by the same fellow who put the lovely Hotel American (see above) on Venice's map of moderately priced lodgings, the Falier is his savvy interpretation of less expensive accommodations, particularly worth booking when half-price low-season rates apply. Renovated in the early 1990s, it is a reliable good value at this price range, with standard-size rooms (and modern bathrooms) attractively decorated with white lace curtains and flowered bedspreads; some even have wood-beamed ceilings. The old-world lobby has potted ferns, Doric columns, and triangled, marble floors. Detractors may feel the need to be closer to Piazza San Marco, when in truth the Falier is much closer to the real Venice. It is situated in a lively area lined with stores and bars between the large Campo Santa Margherita, one of the city's most character-filled piazzas, and the much visited Frari Church.

Dorsoduro 130 (Salizzada San Pantalon), 30135 Venezia. ℂ **041-710-882** or 041-711-005. Fax 041-520-6554. www.hotelfalier.com. 19 units. 80€–180€ ($92–$207) double. Rates discounted 50% during low season. Rates include continental breakfast. AE, MC, V. *Vaporetto:* Ferrovia. If you've packed lightly, the walk from the train station is easy, easier yet from the Piazzale Roma. From the train station, cross the Scalzi Bridge, turn right along the Grand Canal for 45m (150 ft.), then left toward the Tolentini Church. Continue along the Salizzada San Pantalon in the general direction of Campo Santa Margherita. **Amenities:** Concierge; tour desk. *In room:* A/C, TV, hair dryer, safe.

Hotel Galleria ★★ *Value* If you've always dreamed of flinging open your hotel window to find the Grand Canal in front of you, choose this 17th-century palazzo. But reserve way in advance—these are the cheapest rooms on the canal and the most charming at these rates, thanks to new owners Luciano Benedetti and Stefano Franceschini. All rooms are done in a modestly sumptuous 17th- and 18th-century style, but this will soon change, as Luciano and Stefano are planning to overhaul the hotel—closing for renovations in November 2003 and reopening in February 2004. This work shouldn't influence prices for 2004. Six guest rooms overlook the canal; others have partial views that include the Ponte Accademia over an open-air bar/cafe (which can be annoying to anyone hoping to sleep before the bar closes). The bathrooms are small but should emerge nicely from the renovation. Breakfast, with oven-fresh bread, is served in your room.

Dorsoduro 878A (at foot of Accademia Bridge), 30123 Venezia. ℂ **041-523-2489.** Fax 041-520-4172. www.hotelgalleria.it. 10 units, 6 with bathroom. 95€–100€ ($109–$115) double without bathroom, 110€–145€ ($127–$167) double with bathroom. Extra bed 30% more. Rates include continental breakfast. AE, DC, MC, V. *Vaporetto:* Accademia (with Accademia Bridge behind you, hotel is just to your left, next to Totem Il Canale gallery). **Amenities:** Concierge; tour desk; room service (limited); babysitting. *In room:* Hair dryer.

Hotel Messner ★ Hotel Messner and the Pensione alla Salute (above) are the best choices in the Guggenheim area (the choice of those in the know looking for a quiet alternative to St. Mark's), at budget-embracing rates. The Messner is a two-part hotel: In the Casa Principale (Main House) are the handsome beamed-ceiling lobby and public rooms of a 14th-century palazzo and modernized guest rooms with comfortable modular furnishings and Murano chandeliers (three overlook picturesque Rio della Fornace). The 15th-century *dépendance* (annex) 18m (60 ft.) away doesn't show quite as much close attention to detail in the decor, but is perfectly nice. In summer you can take breakfast in a small garden. In 2002 the owners opened a new, six-room annex just 27m (90 ft.) away. Ask about the annex when booking.

Dorsoduro 216–217 (on Fondamenta Ca' Balà), 30123 Venezia. © 041-522-7443. Fax 041-522-7266. www. hotelmessner.it. Main House, 13 units; Annex, 20 units. Main House (ask about Frommer's discount in main house only): 145€–160€ ($167–$184) double; 165€–180€ ($190–$207) triple; 190€–200€ ($219–$230) quad. Annex: 115€ ($132) double; 145€ ($167) triple; 160€ ($184) quad. Ask about discounts such as Aug special: 4 nights for the price of 3. Rates include continental breakfast. AE, DC, MC, V. Closed Dec 1–27. *Vaporetto:* Salute (follow small canal immediately to right of La Salute; turn right onto 3rd bridge and walk straight until seeing white awning just before reaching Rio della Fornace). **Amenities:** Restaurant (traditional Italian cuisine); bar; concierge; room service (24-hr.); babysitting; nonsmoking rooms. *In room:* A/C (main house), TV (main house), dataport (main house), hair dryer, safe.

Pensione Accademia ★★   This *pensione* is beloved by Venice regulars. You'll have to reserve far in advance to get any room here, let alone one overlooking the breakfast garden, which is snuggled into the confluence of two canals. The 17th-century villa is fitted with period antiques in first-floor "superior" rooms, and the atmosphere is decidedly old-fashioned and elegant (Katharine Hepburn's character lived here in the 1955 classic *Summertime*). Formally and appropriately called the Villa Maravege (Villa of Wonders), it was built as a patrician villa in the 1600s and used as the Russian consulate until the 1930s. Its outdoor landscaping (the Venetian rarities of a flowering patio on the small Rio San Trovaso that spills into the Grand Canal and the grassy formal rose garden behind) and interior details (original pavement, wood-beamed and decoratively painted ceilings) still create the impression of being a privileged guest in an aristocratic Venetian home from another era.

Dorsoduro 1058 (Fondamenta Bollani, west of the Accademia Bridge), 30123 Venezia. © 041-521-0188 or 041-523-7846. Fax 041-523-9152. www.pensioneaccademia.it. 27 units. 128€–180€ ($147–$207) double; 170€–270€ ($196–$310) superior double. Off-season discounts available. AE, DC, MC, V. *Vaporetto:* Accademia (step off the *vaporetto* and turn right down Calle Gambara, which doglegs 1st left and then right; it becomes Calle Corfu, which ends at a side canal; walk left for a few feet to cross over the bridge, then head to the right back up toward the Grand Canal and the hotel). **Amenities:** Bar; concierge; tour desk; room service (limited); massage; babysitting; laundry service; dry cleaning. *In room:* A/C, TV, dataport, minibar, hair dryer, safe.

Pensione La Calcina ★   British author John Ruskin holed up here in 1876 when penning *The Stones of Venice* (you can request his room, no. 2, but good luck getting it), and this hotel on the sunny Zattere in the southern Dorsoduro has remained a quasi-sacred preference for writers, artists, and assorted bohemians. You can imagine their horror when a recent overhaul was announced. Luckily, it was executed quite sensitively, with the third-generation owners even refusing to add TVs. What *is* different are the rates, which have been creeping up. Half the unfussy but luminous rooms overlook the Giudecca Canal in the direction of Palladio's 16th-century Redentore. The outdoor floating terrace and the rooftop terrace are glorious places to begin or end the day. The three suites and two apartments were added in 2002.

Dorsoduro 780 (on Zattere al Gesuati), 30123 Venezia. © 041-520-6466. Fax 041-522-7045. www.la calcina.com. 28 units. 130€–145€ ($150–$167) double with bathroom but without canal view; 161€–182€ ($185–$209) double with bathroom and canal view; 150€–260€ ($173–$299) suite or apt. Rates include buffet breakfast. AE, DC, MC, V. *Vaporetto:* Zattere (follow le Zattere east; hotel is on water before 1st bridge). **Amenities:** Restaurant; concierge; room service (24-hr.); laundry service. *In room:* A/C, hair dryer, safe.

IN SAN POLO
MODERATE
Antica Locanda Sturion ★★ *Finds* *Kids*   Though there's been a *pensione* on this site since 1290, a recent gutting and rebuilding has made the Sturion into

a tastefully reincarnated moderate hotel managed by the charming Scottish-born Helen and co-owner Flavia. The hotel's reception area is perched four flights (and 69 challenging steps) above the Grand Canal (and, depending on the location of your room, there could be even more stairs involved). Unfortunately, only two rooms offer canal views of the Rialto Bridge (as does the delightful breakfast room—is there a better way to start your day?), and these command higher rates; they are spacious enough to accommodate families or groups of three, even four. The other rooms have charming views over the Rialto area rooftops. Throughout, the hotel is tastefully decorated with 18th-century–inspired Venetian furniture, parquet floors, red carpeting, and rich damasklike wallpaper. The hoteliers recently renovated two apartments nearby, each with a kitchen. The two-person apartment runs 100€ to 200€ ($115–$230); the four-person apartment is 150€ to 300€ ($173–$345). Both include breakfast at the hotel.

San Polo 679 (on Calle dello Sturion), 30125 Venezia. © 041-523-6243. Fax 041-522-8378. www.locanda sturion.com. 11 units. 120€–210€ ($138–$242) double without Grand Canal view; 210€–250€ ($242–$288) double with Grand Canal view; 170€–270€ ($196–$310) triple without Grand Canal view; 235€–310€ ($270–$357) triple with Grand Canal view; 210€–320€ ($242–$368) quad without Grand Canal view; 280€–360€ ($322–$414) quad with Grand Canal view. Special rates will be made for families. Rates include buffet breakfast. AE, MC, V. *Vaporetto:* Rialto (from the Rialto stop, cross the bridge, turn left at the other side, and walk along the Grand Canal; Calle d. Sturion will be the 4th narrow alleyway on the right, just before San Polo 740). **Amenities:** Bar; concierge; tour desk; room service (limited); babysitting; nonsmoking rooms (whole hotel). *In room:* A/C, TV, dataport, minibar, coffeemaker, hair dryer, safe.

INEXPENSIVE

Pensione Guerrato ★★★ *(Value)* *(Kids)*   The Guerrato is as reliable and clean a budget hotel as you're likely to find at these rates. Brothers-in-law Roberto and Piero own this former *pensione* in a 13th-century convent and manage to keep it almost always booked (mostly with Americans). The firm mattresses, good modernish bathrooms, and flea-market finds (hand-carved antique or Deco headboards and armoires) show their determination to run a top-notch budget hotel in pricey Venice. They don't exaggerate when they call their breakfast, accompanied by classical music, *buonissimo.* The Guerrato is in the Rialto's heart, so think of 7am noise before requesting a room overlooking the market-place (with a peek down the block to the Grand Canal and Ca d'Oro). Piero and Roberto have also renovated the building's top floor (great views; no elevator, 70 steps) to create five new rooms—with air-conditioning (for which you will pay slightly more).

Roberto also rents (2-night minimum) two lovely, fully equipped apartments between San Marco and the Rialto. The one-bedroom is 120€ to 130€ ($138–$150) for two or 180€ to 200€ ($207–$230) for four (though it would be cramped), while the much larger two-bedroom (on three levels) goes for 180€ to 200€ ($207–$230) for four.

San Polo 240A (on Calle Drio or Dietro la Scimia, near the Rialto Market), 30125 Venezia. © 041-522-7131. Fax 041-528-5927. www.pensioneguerrato.it. 20 units, 14 with bathroom. 80€–95€ ($92–$109) double without bathroom, 105€–115€ ($121–$132) double with bathroom; 120€–135€ ($138–$155) double with bathroom and A/C; 98€–110€ ($113–$127) triple without bathroom, 130€–140€ ($150–$161) triple with bathroom; 130€–150€ ($150–$173) triple with bathroom and A/C; 150€–165€ ($173–$190) quad with bathroom. Pay in cash, get 10% off. Rates include buffet breakfast. MC, V. Closed Dec 22–26 and Jan 10–31. *Vaporetto:* Rialto (from the north side of the Ponte Rialto, walk straight ahead through the stalls and market vendors; at the corner of Banca di Roma, go 1 more short block and turn right; the hotel is halfway down the narrow street). **Amenities:** Concierge; tour desk; babysitting; nonsmoking rooms. *In room:* A/C (top floor only), hair dryer.

IN SANTA CROCE
MODERATE
Hotel San Cassiano Ca'Favretto ★★ Call this place a moderate splurge choice, which gets two stars for its location and views. About half the rooms here look across the Grand Canal to the gorgeous Ca d'Oro (accounting for the highest rates listed below), and tend to be larger than the others, most of which open onto a side canal. Built into a 16th-century palace, the hotel is steeped in dusty old-world elegance, with Murano chandeliers (but no elevator). The rooms are outfitted in modest, dark-wood 1970s-style faux antiques. The breakfast room is done in 18th-century–style pastels and stuccoes—get down to breakfast early to snag one of the two tiny tables on the wide balcony overlooking the Grand Canal. There's also a wood-beamed bar and TV lounge with a canal-view window and a few small tables on the private boat launch where you can sip an *aperativo* in the evening, gaze at the Ca d'Oro, and just generally make other tourists on the passing *vaporetti* intensely jealous because they're booked elsewhere.

Santa Croce 2232 (Calle della Rosa), 30135 Venezia. ℂ **041-524-1768.** Fax 041-721-033. www.sancassiano.it. 35 units. 70€–325€ ($81–$374) double; 91€–423€ ($105–$486) triple. Rates include breakfast. AE, DC, MC, V. *Vaporetto:* San Stae (turn left to cross in front of the church, take the bridge over the side canal and turn right; then turn left, cross another canal and turn right, then left again; cross yet another canal and turn right, then immediately left and then left again toward the Grand Canal and the hotel). **Amenities:** Bar; concierge; tour desk; car-rental desk; room service (limited); massage (in-room); babysitting; laundry service; dry cleaning; non-smoking rooms. *In room:* A/C, TV, dataport, minibar, hair dryer, safe.

INEXPENSIVE
Hotel Ai Due Fanali ★★ *Finds* Ai Due Fanali's 16th-century altar-turned-reception-desk is your first clue that this is the hotel of choice for lovers of aesthetics with impeccable taste and restricted budgets. The hotel is located on a quiet square in the residential Santa Croce area, a 10-minute walk across the Grand Canal from the train station but a good 20-minute stroll from the Rialto Bridge. Signora Marina Stea and her daughter Stefania have beautifully restored a part of the 14th-century scuola of the Church of San Simeon Grando with their innate *buon gusto,* which is evident wall to wall, from the lobby furnished with period pieces to the third-floor breakfast terrace with a glimpse of the Grand Canal. Guest rooms boast headboards painted by local artisans, high-quality bed linens, chrome and gold bathroom fixtures, and good, fluffy towels. Prices drop considerably from November 8 through March 30 with the exception of Christmas week and Carnevale. Ask about the four equally classy waterfront apartments with a view (and kitchenette) near Vivaldi's Church (La Pietà) east of Piazza San Marco, sleeping four to five people at similar rates per person.

Santa Croce 946 (Campo San Simeone Profeta), 30125 Venezia. ℂ **041-718-490.** Fax 041-718-344. www. aiduefanali.com. 17 units. 98€–200€ ($113–$230) double; 110€–230€ ($127–$265) triple; 180€–380€ ($207–$437) apt. Rates include breakfast. AE, MC, V. Closed most of Jan. *Vaporetto:* a 10-min. walk from the train station or get off at the Riva di Biasio stop. **Amenities:** Bar; concierge; room service (limited); laundry service; dry cleaning. *In room:* A/C, TV, dataport, minibar, hair dryer, safe.

IN CANNAREGIO
Expect most (but not all) of the least expensive suggestions to be in or near the train station neighborhood, an area full of trinket shops and budget hotels. It's comparatively charmless (though safe), and in the high-season months is wall-to-wall with tourists who window-shop their way to Piazza San Marco, an easy half-hour-to-45-minute stroll away. *Vaporetto* connections from the train station are convenient.

EXPENSIVE

Hotel Bellini ⭐   By far the classiest hotel I'm listing near the train station, the Bellini is convenient if you have an early train. Though mere steps away from the station, it's well insulated from the neighborhood's bustle. Rooms are mid-size to large, with high ceilings (some stuccoed), done in a rich 19th-century decor with modern amenities. Several on the front have views of the Grand Canal, some from small balconies. Junior suites on the canal side are great for families—each comes with a loft with twin beds and its own bathroom and TV. Most "deluxe" rooms come with a view; those that do not are larger and nicer by way of compensation. Note that special offers can sometimes bring rates below even the lower prices listed below, depending on the time of year and availability.

Cannaregio 116A (Lista di Spagna), 30121 Venezia. 𝄢 041-524-2488. Fax 041-715-193. www.bellini. boscolohotels.com. 97 units. 276€–400€ ($317–$460) superior double; 312€–450€ ($259–$518) deluxe double; 298€–390€ ($343–$448) jr. suite. Buffet breakfast included. AE, DC, MC, V. *Vaporetto:* Ferrovia (turn left from the *vaporetto*—or right if you're exiting the train station—to walk down Lista di Spagna). **Amenities:** Bar; concierge; tour desk; car-rental desk; room service (limited); in-room massage; babysitting; laundry service; dry cleaning (same-day); nonsmoking rooms. *In room:* A/C, TV, minibar, hair dryer, safe.

MODERATE

Albergo Adua   It ain't too pretty, but it's cheap (for Venice), conveniently located near the station, clean, and very well run. The Adua family, in the low-end hotel business for more than 30 years, completed a welcome renovation in 1999, giving the largish rooms a unified summery look, with contemporary wood furnishings painted pale green. At an independent palazzo across the street, the six refurbished rooms (without bathroom, TV, or air-conditioning) costs 20% less.

Cannaregio 233A (on Lista di Spagna), 30121 Venezia. 𝄢 041-716-184. Fax 041-244-0162. 13 units, 9 with bathroom. 80€ ($92) double without bathroom, 120€ ($138) double with bathroom; 100€ ($115) triple without bathroom, 180€ ($207) triple with bathroom; 120€ ($138) quad without bathroom, 200€ ($230) quad with bathroom. Extra bed 50% more. Low-season rates 10%–15% less. Breakfast 8€ ($9). AE, DC, MC, V. *Vaporetto:* Ferrovia (exit train station and turn left onto Lista di Spagna). **Amenities:** Bar; concierge; tour desk; room service (limited). *In room:* A/C, TV, dataport, minibar, hair dryer.

Hotel Giorgione ⭐⭐ *Finds*   Original columns and huge wood beams decorate the salons off the reception area of this 16th-century palazzo. The best rooms overlook the private brick courtyard, a shaded breakfast nook with a small, decorative pool, a hushed oasis save for the splashing of the fountain. "Standard" rooms are carpeted, with small, bulging wood dressers and an early-19th-century style. In "superior" rooms, some beds have a small canopy curtain at the head, others are slightly lofted above the sitting area and flanked by twisting columns; some furnishings are 18th-century Venetian reproductions refreshingly done in brighter modern hues (in fact, each room follows its own, overwhelmingly strict, color scheme). Rooms on the second and third floors were renovated in 2002 and 2003. Suites, with midsize sitting rooms and bedrooms, are done in a vaguely romantic style—matching embroidered fabrics, half-testers, and the like. No. 105 has a great private flower-fringed terrace.

Cannaregio 4587 (Campo SS. Apostoli), 30131 Venezia. 𝄢 041-522-5810. Fax 041-523-9092. www.hotel giorgione.com. 76 units. 150€–265€ ($173–$305) "standard" double; 185€–310€ ($213–$357) "superior" double; 220€–360€ ($253–$414) jr. suite; 250€–400€ ($288–$460) suite; 40€–60€ ($46–$69) extra bed. Buffet breakfast included. AE, DC, MC, V. *Vaporetto:* Ca d'Oro (walk straight up Calle Ca d'Oro and turn right onto broad Strada Nuova, which ends in Campo SS. Apostoli just before a bridge). **Amenities:** Bar (from 6pm); concierge; tour desk; car-rental desk; room service (limited); babysitting; laundry service; dry cleaning; nonsmoking rooms (the 3rd floor); Internet point. *In room:* A/C, TV, minibar, hair dryer, safe.

INEXPENSIVE

Albergo Santa Lucia   Bordered by roses, oleander, and ivy, the flagstone patio/terrace of this contemporary building is a lovely place to enjoy breakfast, with coffee and tea brought to the table in sterling silver pots. The kindly owner, Emilia Gonzato, her son Gianangelo, and his wife, Alessandra, oversee everything with pride, and it shows: The large rooms are simple but bright and clean, with modular furnishings and a print or pastel to brighten things up.

Cannaregio 358 (on Calle della Misericordia), 30121 Venezia. © **041-715-180.** Fax 041-710-610. www.hotel slucia.com. 18 units, 12 with bathroom. 80€ ($92) double without bathroom, 100€ ($115) double with bathroom. Extra person 20€ ($23). Rates include continental breakfast. AE, DC, MC, V. Generally closed Dec 20–Feb 10. *Vaporetto:* Ferrovia (exit the train station, turn left onto Lista di Spagna, and take the 2nd left onto Calle della Misericordia). **Amenities:** Concierge; tour desk; room service (breakfast). *In room:* Hair dryer (ask at desk).

Hotel Bernardi-Semenzato ★★★ *Kids*   The exterior of this weather-worn palazzo belies its 1995 renovation, which left hand-hewn ceiling beams exposed, air-conditioned rooms outfitted with antique-style headboard/spread sets, and bathrooms modernized and brightly retiled. The enthusiastic young English-speaking owners, Maria Teresa and Leonardo Pepoli, offer three-star style at one-star rates (prices get even better off season). Upstairs rooms enjoy higher ceilings and more light. The recently renovated *dépendance* (annex) 3 blocks away offers the chance to feel as if you've rented an aristocratic apartment, with parquet floors and Murano chandeliers—room no. 5 is on a corner with a beamed ceiling and fireplace, no. 6 (a family-perfect two-room suite) looks out on the confluence of two canals, and no. 2 overlooks the lovely garden of a palazzo next door. About a month before we went to press, the Pepoli opened yet another annex nearby consisting of just four rooms, all done in a Venetian style, including one large family suite (two guest rooms, one of which can sleep four, sharing a common bathroom).

Cannaregio 4366 (on Calle de l'Oca), 30121 Venezia. © **041-522-7257.** Fax 041-522-2424. www.hotel bernardi.com. Hotel: 18 units, 11 with bathroom. Main annex: 7 units. New annex: 4 units. **For Frommer's readers:** 50€ ($58) double without bathroom, 80€ ($92) double with bathroom; 72€ ($83) triple without bathroom, 88€ ($101) triple with bathroom; 80€ ($92) quad without bathroom, 98€ ($113) quad with bathroom. Rates include continental breakfast. 10% less off season. AE, DC, MC, V. *Vaporetto:* Ca' d'Oro (walk straight ahead to Strada Nova, turn right toward Campo SS. Apostoli, and look for Cannaregio 4309, a stationery/toy store on your left; turn left on Calle Duca, then take 1st right onto Calle de l'Oca). **Amenities:** Concierge; tour desk; room service (limited). *In room:* A/C, TV, dataport, hair dryer, safe.

Hotel Dolomiti ★   For those who prefer to stay near the train station, this is an old-fashioned, reliable choice. Because it has large, clean but ordinary rooms spread over four floors (no elevator), your chances of finding availability are better here, one of the larger places I suggest. It's been in the Basardelli family for generations—the current head manager, Graziella, was even born in a second-floor room—and they and their efficient polyglot staff supply dining suggestions, umbrellas when necessary, and big smiles after a long day's sightseeing. Rooms without bathrooms always come with sinks. The Basardellis are slowly renovating the guest rooms; those that don't have air-conditioning now will soon.

Cannaregio 72–74 (on Calle Priuli ai Cavalletti), 30121 Venezia. © **041-715-113** or 041-719-983. Fax 041-716-635. www.hoteldolomiti-ve.it. 32 units, 22 with bathroom. 88€ ($101) double without bathroom, 125€ ($144) double with bathroom; 108€ ($124) triple without bathroom, 165€ ($190) triple with bathroom; 130€ ($150) quad without bathroom, 185€ ($213) quad with bathroom. Inquire about low-season discounts. Rates include continental breakfast. MC, V. Closed Nov 15–Jan 31. *Vaporetto:* Ferrovia (exit train station, turn left onto Lista di Spagna, and take 1st left onto Calle Priuli). **Amenities:** Bar; concierge; tour desk. *In room:* A/C (newest rooms), hair dryer (newest rooms).

Hotel San Geremia ★★ *(Finds)* Mention Frommer's when booking, show this guide when checking in, and you'll get the rates below. If this gem of a two-star hotel had an elevator and was in San Marco, it would cost twice as much and still be worth it. Consider yourself lucky to get one of the tastefully renovated rooms—ideally one of the seven overlooking the *campo* (better yet, one of three top-floor rooms with small terraces). The rooms have blond-wood paneling with built-in headboards and closets or whitewashed walls with deep-green or burnished rattan headboards and matching chairs. The small bathrooms offer hair dryers and heated towel racks, and rooms without bathrooms were recently renovated. Everything is overseen by an English-speaking staff and the owner/manager Claudio, who'll give you helpful tips and free passes to the winter Casino.

Cannaregio 290A (on Campo San Geremia), 30121 Venezia. ℂ **041-716-245.** Fax 041-524-2342. www.sangeremia.com (under construction at press time). 20 units, 14 with bathroom. **For Frommer's readers:** 77€ ($89) double without bathroom, 114€ ($131) double with bathroom. Ask about rates/availability for singles, triples, and quads and about off-season rates (about 20% cheaper). Rates include continental breakfast. AE, DC, MC, V. *Vaporetto:* Ferrovia (exit the train station, turn left onto Lista di Spagna, and continue to Campo San Geremia). **Amenities:** Concierge; tour desk; room service (breakfast); babysitting. *In room:* TV, hair dryer, safe.

ON GIUDECCA

You don't stay on Giudecca—the only one of Venice's main islands you must access by boat—for the atmosphere, sights, or the hotel scene (though it does host the official IYH Hostel, an utterly average hostel that's terribly inconvenient, especially with its curfew). You come for one reason only: the Cipriani.

VERY EXPENSIVE

Hotel Cipriani ★★★ Though the Gritti palace and Danieli might argue the point, the Cipriani is probably the top luxury hotel in Venice, a gorgeously elegant inn set into a string of Renaissance-era buildings on 1.2 hectares (3 acres) at the tip of Giudecca. Although by staying here you give up a central location and easy access to central Venice's sights, shops, and restaurants (it's a 10-min. boat ride to Piazza San Marco), that's the whole point: the Cipriani is a gilded retreat. The hotel was opened in 1959 by Giuseppe Cipriani, who also founded Harry's Bar and Torcello's Locanda Cipriani, and was such a good buddy to Ernest Hemingway that he appeared in one of the master's novels (*Across the River and into the Trees*). Room decor varies greatly, from full-bore 18th-century Venetian to discreetly contemporary, but all are among Venice's most stylish accommodations. The amenities-filled rooms overlook some combination of the gardens and Olympic-size pool, the lagoon, San Giorgio Maggiore, and St. Mark's Square across the wide mouth of the Grand Canal. The 15th-century Palazzo Vendramin annex, connected via a garden, is for guests who desire more privacy (not unusual given their celebrity guest list), a more homelike feel, and a private butler. It also stays open until mid-December. It has only junior and full suites, charging the highest rates listed below in each category.

Giudecca 10, 30133 Venezia. ℂ **041-520-7744.** Fax 041-520-3930. www.hotelcipriani.com. 96 units. **Hotel Cipriani:** 570€–813€ ($656–$935) standard double; 620€–1,102€ ($713–$1,267) superior double; 670€–1,248€ ($771–$1,435) deluxe double; 900€–1,683€ ($1,035–$1,935) superior jr. suite; 950€–1,887€ ($1,092–$2,170) deluxe jr. suite; 1,000€–2,118€ ($1,150–$2,436) special jr. suite; 1,400€–2,118€ ($1,610–$2,436) standard suite; 1,450€–2,437€ ($1,668–$2,803) superior suite; 1,500€–3,946€ ($1,725–$4,538) deluxe suite; 3rd person 175€ ($201); 3,946€–6,360€ ($4,538–$7,314) Palladio suite with 1 bedroom; 4,846€–8,043€ ($5,573–$9,249) Palladio suite with 2 bedrooms. **Palazzo Vendramin:** 853€–2,118€ ($981–$2,436) jr. suite; 1,364€–2,437€ ($1,569–$2,803) suite; 1,364€–3,946€ ($1,569–$4,538) suite Vendramin. Full American breakfast included. AE, DC, MC, V. Closed Nov 2–Apr 11. *Vaporetto:* Zitelle. **Amenities:** 3 restaurants (excellent Italian Cipriani with lagoon views; bar eatery, poolside lunch); 3 bars; Olympic-size outdoor pool; golf course; tennis courts (indoor); exercise room; spa; sauna; concierge; tour desk; car-rental desk; courtesy car (back and forth to Piazza San Marco 24-hr.); docking facilities; salon; room service (24-hr.); massage (in spa or in-room); babysitting; laundry service; dry cleaning. *In room:* A/C, TV, VCR (free movies), fax (on request), dataport, minibar, kitchenette (only in jr. suites and suites of the Palazzo Vendramin), hair dryer, safe.

ON THE LIDO

The Lido offers an entirely different Venice experience. The city is relatively close at hand, but you're really here to stay at an Italian beach resort and day-trip into the city for sightseeing. Although there are a few lower-end, moderately priced hotels here, they are entirely beside the point of the Lido and its jet-set reputation. So I'm just giving full write-ups of the biggies here.

If you are looking for a more reasonable option—and one that's open year-round—check out the modern **Hotel Belvedere,** Piazzale Santa Maria Elisabetta 4 ((C) **041-526-0115;** fax 041-526-1486; www.belvedere-venezia.com). It's right across from the *vaporetto* stop, has been in the same family for nearly 150 years, and sports a pretty good restaurant and a free beach cabana. It charges 44€ to 229€ ($51–$263) per double.

VERY EXPENSIVE

Westin Excelsior ★★★   The Excelsior is the first place most celebs phone for film festival or Biennale accommodations. The hotel was the first successful attempt to turn the grassy wilds between the Lido's fishing villages into a bathing resort. Its core was built a century ago in a faux-Moorish style, with horseshoe arches peeking out all over, lots of huge, ornate salons and banqueting halls, and a fountain-studded Arabian-style garden. As a purpose-built hotel, the rooms were free to be cut quite large, with nice big bathrooms flush with toiletries by Bulgari. Standard rooms keep the Moorish look going, with latticework doors, richly patterned wall fabrics, flamboyant bentwood headboards, and tented ceilings. Even if you don't have a sea view from balustraded balconies, you might overlook the gorgeous garden or the private boat-launch canal out back. Even junior-level suites are huge, with sitting areas, an entrance hall, and double sinks. A modern bar spills onto a large terrace overlooking the beach.

Lungarno Marconi 41, 30126 Venezia Lido. ((C) **041-526-0201.** Fax 041-526-7276. www.westin.com. 195 units. 503€–759€ ($578–$873) double; 582€–879€ ($669–$1,011) double with sea or lagoon view; 1,246€–1,549€ ($1,433–$1,781) jr. suite; 1,637€–2,542€ ($1,883–$2,923) suite. Buffet breakfast included. AE, DC, MC, V. Closed mid-Oct to mid-Mar. *Vaporetto:* Lido, then bus A. **Amenities:** 3 restaurants (Venetian/international terrace restaurant for dinner, lunch restaurants poolside and at beach); 2 bars; outdoor pool; special rates at nearby golf course; outdoor lit tennis courts; exercise room (at sister Hotel des Bains, nearby); watersports equipment; bike rental; children's program (July–Aug "Kid Club"); concierge; tour desk; car-rental desk; courtesy boat (from airport and from central Venice); business center; shopping arcade; salon; room service (24-hr.); massage (in-room); babysitting; laundry service; dry cleaning (same-day); nonsmoking rooms; executive-level rooms; video games in room. *In room:* A/C, TV w/pay movies, VCR (on request), fax (on request), dataport, minibar, hair dryer, safe.

EXPENSIVE

Hotel des Bains ★★★   Its sister Excelsior (above) may be the last word in luxury on Lido, but the Belle Epoque Hotel des Bains beats it for sheer style, with its creaky, polished wood floors and high, airy salons scattered with Oriental rugs. Not for nothing did Des Bains habitué Thomas Mann set his dreamy, decadent *Death in Venice* (and Visconti filmed it) here. The large rooms are fitted with the original, discreetly elegant, but getting worn, furnishings. Definitely ask for a sea-view room, since that's what the Lido is all about, though there's nothing wrong with pool- or park-view rooms. When the wood-paneled, two-story banqueting room is not being used for a conference, you can take tea there or out on the broad

to imitate an *Orient Express* car. The food is purely Venetian, with a huge menu that promises all the bounty of the sea, along with select specialties from world cooking. It's not cheap, though. Do Forni keeps busy, and the bustling sometimes detracts from the posh atmosphere.

Calle dei Specchieri. ☎ 041-523-2148. www.doforni.it. Reservations required. Primi 13€–23€ ($15–$26); secondi 20€–25€ ($23–$29). AE, DC, MC, V. Daily noon–3pm and 7–11pm. *Vaporetto:* San Marco (walk through Piazza San Marco and around the left flank of the basilica into Piazzetta dei Leoncini; take the 3rd left and continue straight across Calle Larga San Marco).

La Cusina ★★ VENETIAN/INVENTIVE Excepting maybe the Cipriani, newcomer La Cusina is the only hotel restaurant in Venice that deserves singling out on its own. The service is stellar, the kitchen is open (always a sign of quality), and the seating is in that most sought-after of spots: a terrace right on the Grand Canal overlooking floodlit Santa Maria della Salute across the water. They reserve a page in the menu for dishes made fresh from what the chef found that morning at the market. You may find ravioli stuffed with sea bass in a light cream sauce with wild fennel; *maltalgiati* noodles in a duck and truffle ragù; or rabbit saddle with sun-dried tomatoes and grilled leeks.

San Marco 2159 (In the Westin Hotel Europa & Regina off Via XXII Marzo). ☎ 041-240-0001. Primi 21€–23€ ($24–$26); secondi 23€–34€ ($26–$39). AE, DC, MC, V. Daily 7:30–11:30pm. *Vaporetto:* San Marco (head west out of the southwest corner of Piazza San Marco down Saliz San Mose; cross the bridge to continue straight on Calle Larga XXII Marzo; you'll see hotel signs directing you down the alleyways to the left).

Quadri ★ VENETIAN Dine by candlelight with a view across St. Mark's Square. That's the selling point of this restaurant, which is almost kitschily romantic—a single red rose, silver dish lids removed with a flourish, threadbare velvet benches, pop ballads by Andrea Bocelli, silk wall coverings, and painted wood ceilings all in dusty rose shades. The cooking is good, if generally uninspired, and service can be a little sour and short. But the place has got history: In 1725 Giorgio Quadri from Corfu and his wife bought this spot and started serving "khava," a dark, caffeinated Turkish drink served hot. As such "cafes" became popular—the restaurant sits above an elegant, still-functioning cafe— Austrian officers made the Quadri their hangout; Italians preferred the Florian across the way. Definitely call ahead, if possible a few days in advance, to get one of the few tables next to a window so you can get that view; otherwise, it's really not worth the prices.

Piazza San Marco 120. ☎ 041-522-2105 or 041-528-9299. www.quadrivenice.com. Reservations very highly recommended. www.quadrivenice.com. Primi 19€–23€ ($22–$26); secondi 23€–45€ ($26–$52). AE, DC, MC, V. Tues–Sun 7–10:30pm. *Vaporetto:* San Marco (it's on the north side of the square).

Vini da Arturo ★★ *Finds* VENETIAN This narrow dining room has long been one of my favorite hidden gems in Venice, even if prices have tripled in the past few years. Aside from the friendly service (the owner usually comes out to sit and chat with the last few diners at the end of the evening) and excellent cooking, this place sells itself on being perhaps the only restaurant in Venice with no seafood. Primi are pretty limited and sound standard—spaghetti with tomatoes and artichokes, or *alla siciliana* with mozzarella, eggplant, and tomatoes—but they are perfectly prepared. Secondi include *stracetti di filetto alla rucola* (beef strips tossed with torn arugula), *filetto al pepe verde* (steak in a green-peppercorn sauce), and veal scaloppine. It's got fewer than 10 tables, so booking is almost required.

San Marco 3656A (Calle degli Assassini). ☎ 041-528-6974. Reservations highly recommended. Primi 12€– 17€ ($14–$20); secondi 15€–31€ ($17–$36). No credit cards. Mon–Sat noon–3pm and 7–10:30pm. *Vaporetto:* Sant-Angelo, Rialto.

EXPENSIVE

Le Bistrot de Venise ★★★ VENETIAN/FRENCH   This relaxed spot offers indoor (with a nonsmoking section) and outdoor seating, young English-speaking waiters, and a varied, eclectic menu. It's a popular meeting spot for Venetians and young artists, and you're made to feel welcome to sit and write postcards over a cappuccino, enjoy a simple lunch of risotto and salad, or dine when most of Venice is shutting down. Linger over an elaborate meal that may include local favorites like *figa' de vedelo a la venexiana* (Venetian calves' liver) or the odd *morete a la caorlotta* (tagliolini made with cocoa, topped with a festival of crustaceans), or unique dishes made from historic 15th-century Venetian recipes or a classic French cookbook. Peek in the back room (or check out the website) to see what's going on in the evening—the place hosts art exhibits, cabarets, live music, and poetry readings.

San Marco 4687 (on Calle dei Fabbri), below the Albergo al Gambero. © 041-523-6651. www.bistrotde venise.com. Primi 8€–15€ ($9–$17); secondi 14€–22€ ($16–$25); classic Venetian tasting menu 35€ ($40); historical Venetian menu 45€ ($52). AE, MC, V. Daily noon–1am. *Vaporetto:* Rialto (turn right along canal, cross small footbridge over Rio San Salvador, turn left onto Calle Bembo, which becomes Calle dei Fabbri; Bistrot is about 5 blocks ahead in the direction of St. Mark's Sq.). Closed Dec 10–25.

Trattoria da Fiore ★★ VENETIAN   Don't confuse this laid-back trattoria with the expensive Osteria da Fiore. You might not eat better here, but it'll seem that way when your relatively modest bill arrives. Start with the house specialty, the *pennette alla Fiore* for two (with olive oil, garlic, and seven in-season vegetables), and you may be happy to call it a night. Or try the *frittura mista*, over a dozen varieties of fresh fish and seafood. The bouillabaisse-like *zuppa di pesce alla chef* is stocked with mussels, crab, clams, shrimp, and tuna—at only 13€ ($15), it doesn't get any better and is a meal in itself. You might want to come back some afternoon: This is a great place to snack or make a light lunch out of *cicchetti* at the Bar Fiore next door (10:30am–10:30pm).

San Marco 3461 (on Calle delle Botteghe). © 041-523-5310. Reservations suggested. Primi 7.80€–16€ ($9–$18); secondi 13€–21€ ($15–$24). AE, MC, V. Wed–Mon noon–3pm and 7–10pm. *Vaporetto:* Accademia (cross bridge to San Marco side and walk straight ahead to Campo Santo Stefano; exit *campo* at northern end, take a left at Bar/Gelateria Paolin onto Calle delle Botteghe). Closed 2 weeks in Jan and 2 weeks in Aug.

MODERATE

Rosticceria San Bartolomeo ★ *Kids* ITALIAN/TAVOLA CALDA   With long hours and a central location, this refurbished old-timer is Venice's most popular *rosticceria* (and for good reason), so the continuous turnover guarantees fresh food. With a dozen pasta dishes and as many fish, seafood, and meat entrees, this place can satisfy any combination of culinary desires. Since the ready-made food is displayed under a glass counter, you don't have to worry about mistranslations—you'll know exactly what you're ordering. There's no *coperto* (cover charge) if you take your meal standing up or seated at the stools in the aroma-filled ground-floor eating area. For those who prefer to linger, head to the dining hall upstairs, even though it costs more and, frankly, for the money you can do much better elsewhere than in this institutional setting.

San Marco 5424 (on Calle della Bissa). © 041-522-3569. Pizza and primi 3.35€–8€ ($3.85–$9); secondi 7€–12€ ($8–$14); *menù turistico* 8€–23€ ($9–$26). Prices are about 20%–30% higher upstairs. AE, MC, V. Daily 9:30am–10pm (until 3:30pm Mon). *Vaporetto:* Rialto (with bridge at your back on San Marco side of canal, walk straight ahead to Campo San Bartolomeo; take underpass slightly to your left marked SOTTOPORTEGO DELLA BISSA; you'll come across the rosticceria at 1st corner on your right; look for GISLON [its old name] above entrance).

Rosticceria Teatro Goldoni ITALIAN/INTERNATIONAL/FAST FOOD
Bright and modern (though it has been here for over 50 years), this showcase of

Venetian-style fast food tries to be everything: bar, cafe, *rosticceria,* and *tavola calda* (hot foods deli) on the ground floor and pizzeria upstairs. A variety of sandwiches and pastries beckons from a downstairs display counter, and another offers prepared foods (eggplant *parmigiana,* roast chicken, *pasta e fagioli,* lasagna) that'll be reheated when ordered; there are also a dozen pasta choices. A number of combination salads are a welcome concession to the American set and are freshest and most varied for lunch. This won't be your most memorable meal in Venice, but you won't walk away hungry or broke.

San Marco 4747 (at the corner of Calle dei Fabbri). ℂ 041-522-2446. Pizza and primi 6€–15€ ($7–$17); secondi 8€–20€ ($9–$23); *menù turistico* 14€ ($16). AE, DC, V. Daily 9am–9:30pm. *Vaporetto:* Rialto (walk from San Marco side of bridge to Campo San Bartolomeo and exit it to your right in direction of Campo San Luca).

INEXPENSIVE

Osteria alle Botteghe ⭐ PIZZERIA/ITALIAN   Casual, easy on the palate, easy on the wallet, and even easy to find (if you've made it to Campo Santo Stefano), this is a great choice for pizza, a light snack, or an elaborate meal. You can have stand-up *cicchetti* and fresh sandwiches at the bar or window-side counter, while more serious diners head to the tables in back to enjoy the dozen pizzas, pastas, or *tavola calda,* a glass counter–enclosed buffet of prepared dishes like eggplant *parmigiana,* lasagna, and fresh-cooked vegetables in season, reheated when you order.

San Marco 3454 (on Calle delle Botteghe, off Campo Santo Stefano). ℂ 041-522-8181. Primi 4.15€ ($4.75); secondi 7€–8€ ($8-$9); *menù turistico* 8.80€ ($10). DC, MC, V. Mon–Sat 11am–4pm and 7–10pm. *Vaporetto:*

(Kids) Family-Friendly Restaurants

Rosticceria San Bartolomeo (p. 112)   There's not much that isn't served at this big, efficient, and bustling fast-food *emporio* in the Rialto Bridge area. Much of it is displayed in glass cases to pique the fussy appetite, and you won't raise any eyebrows if you eat too little, too much, or at hours when the natives have either finished or haven't yet started.

Pizzeria ae Oche (p. 119)   If they're hankering for home and you (rightly) refuse to set foot in a McDonald's, this place not only serves great pizza and pumps rock music through the speakers, it even looks vaguely American—or at least trattoria-meets–Cracker Barrel.

Ai Tre Spiedi (p. 114)   There's nothing in particular that flags this as kid-friendly, but its genial atmosphere, friendly service, and good cookin' make it ideal and welcoming for families.

Pizzeria/Trattoria al Vecio Canton (p. 116)   This spot offers plenty of seating, a good location near San Marco, low prices, and an extensive menu of both pastas and some of the best pizzas in Venice.

Taverna San Trovaso (p. 117)   Here you'll find a bustling atmosphere, good-natured waiters, and a lengthy menu that covers all sorts of dishes and pizzas to please finicky youngsters and more adventurous palates alike. Good value-priced menus, too.

Da Sandro (p. 118)   This place offers good pizza and pasta, seating outdoors, and low prices. What more can you ask for?

Accademia or Sant'Angelo (find your way to Campo Santo Stefano by following stream of people or asking; take narrow Calle delle Botteghe at Gelateria Paolin [in northwest corner] across from Santo Stefano).

Vino Vino ★★★ *Value* WINE BAR/ITALIAN   Vino Vino is an informal wine-bar archetype serving simple, well-prepared food, but its biggest pull is the impressive selection of local and European wines sold by the bottle or glass (check out the website). The Venetian specialties are written on a chalkboard but are also usually displayed at the glass counter. After placing your order, settle into one of about a dozen wooden tables squeezed into two storefront-style rooms. Credit the high-quality food to the fact that Vino Vino shares a kitchen (and an owner) with the eminent and expensive Antico Martini restaurant a few doors down. It's also a great spot for a leisurely self-styled wine tasting (1€–3€/$1.15–$3.45 per glass), with great *cicchetti* bar food. At dinner the food often runs out around 10:30pm, so don't come too late.

San Marco 2007 (on Ponte delle Veste near La Fenice). © **041-523-7027.** www.vinovino.co.it. Primi 5€–9€ ($6–$10); secondi 10€–12€ ($12–$14). AE, DC, MC, V. Wed–Mon noon–3:30pm and 7–11pm. *Vaporetto:* San Marco (with your back to basilica, exit Piazza San Marco through arcade on far left side; keep walking straight, pass American Express, cross over canal, and, before street jags left, turn right onto Calle delle Veste).

IN CANNAREGIO
VERY EXPENSIVE
Fiaschetteria Toscana ★★ VENETIAN   One hundred years ago this was a Tuscan wine outlet and social center of the neighborhood, so the Busatto family couldn't very well change the name even if their cuisine is strictly traditional Venetian and fish based. Albino heads up the dining room, wife Mariuccia makes desserts, and son Stefano mans the kitchen. They care about quality here, draping choice San Daniele prosciutto over slices of ripe melon or figs, stuffing ravioli with seafood and coating it with a light parsley sauce, or tossing zucchini flowers with the scampi and homemade *tagliolini*. The *frittura della serenissima* mixes a fry of seafood, sole, zucchini, artichokes, shrimp, baby squid, and octopus.

Cannaregio 5719 (Salizzada San Giovanni). © **041-528-5281.** www.fiaschetteriatoscana.it. Reservations recommended. Primi 10€–20€ ($12–$23); secondi 13€–33€ ($15–$37). AE, DC, MC, V. Wed–Sun 12:30–2:30pm; Wed–Mon 7:30–10:30pm. *Vaporetto:* Rialto (from the *vaporetto* launch, walk left to the bridge, then right down Salita Pio X to Campo San Bartolomeo; hang a left, past the post office and over a bridge, and the street becomes Salizzada San Giovanni).

INEXPENSIVE
Ai Tre Spiedi ★★★ *Finds* *Kids* VENETIAN   Venetians bring their visiting friends here to make a *bella figura* (good impression) without breaking the bank, then swear them to secrecy. Rarely will you find as pleasant a setting and appetizing a meal as in this small, casually elegant trattoria with reasonably priced fresh-fish dining—and plenty to keep meat eaters happy as well. The *spaghetti O.P.A.* (with parsley, peperoncino, garlic, and olive oil) is excellent, and the *spaghetti al pesto* is the best this side of Liguria. Follow it up with the traditional *bisato in umido con polenta* (braised eel). This and Trattoria da Fiore (above) are the most reasonable choices for an authentic Venetian dinner of fresh fish; careful ordering needn't mean much of a splurge either—though inexplicably, prices have risen dramatically in the past 2 years.

Cannaregio 5906 (on Salizzada San Cazian). © **041-520-8035.** Reservations not accepted. Primi 4.50€–12€ ($5–$13); secondi 9.50€–18€ ($11–$20); *menù turistico* 15€–20€ ($17–$22). AE, MC, V. Tues–Sat noon–3pm; Tues–Sun 7–10pm. *Vaporetto:* Rialto (on San Marco side of bridge, walk straight ahead to Campo San Bartolomeo and take a left, passing post office, Coin department store, and San Crisostomo; cross 1st bridge after church, turn right at toy store onto Salizzada San Cazian). Closed July 20–Aug 10.

IN CASTELLO
EXPENSIVE

Al Covo ★★★ VENETIAN/SEAFOOD   For years this lovely restaurant has been consistently (and deservingly) popular with American food writers, putting it on the short list of every food-loving American tourist. There are nights when it seems you hear nothing but English spoken here. But this has never compromised the dining at this warm and welcoming spot, where the preparation of superfresh fish and an excellent selection of moderately priced wines is as commendable today—perhaps more so—as it was in its nascent days of pre-trendiness. Much of the tourist-friendly atmosphere can be credited to the naturally hospitable Diane Rankin, the co-owner and dessert whiz who hails from Texas. She will eagerly talk you through a wondrous fish-studded menu. Her husband, Cesare Benelli, is known for his infallible talent in the kitchen. Together they share an admirable dedication to their charming gem of a restaurant—the quality of an evening at Al Covo is tough to top in this town.

Castello 3968 (Campiello della Pescheria, east of Chiesa della Pietà in the Arsenale neighborhood). 🕿 041-522-3812. Reservations required. Primi 10€–17€ ($12–$20); secondi 25€ ($29); 3-course fixed-price lunch 33€ ($38). No credit cards. Fri–Tues 12:45–2pm and 7:30–10pm. *Vaporetto:* Arsenale (walk a short way back in the direction of Piazza San Marco, turning right at the Bar/cafe il Gabbiano; the restaurant is on your left; otherwise, it is an enjoyable 20-min. stroll along the waterfront Riva degli Schiavoni from Piazza San Marco, past the Chiesa della Pietà and the Metropole Hotel). Closed Dec 20–Jan 20 and 2 weeks in Aug.

Arcimboldo ★ VENETIAN/ITALIAN   Always popular, Arcimboldo is fast becoming one of Venice's leading restaurants. In summer it's a crime not to try to snag one of the outdoor tables overlooking the canal. The restaurant serves up meticulously prepared Venetian cuisine, but if you're tired of seafood and liver, cuisines from the rest of Italy are also represented. The ingredients are bought fresh daily, and the wines are heavenly.

Calle dei Furlani (a little street leading east from San Giorgio degli Schiavoni; when you reserve, ask about their boat service from San Marco). 🕿 041-528-6569. www.arcimboldovenice.com. Reservations recommended. Primi 5€–12€ ($6–$14); secondi 14€–27€ ($16–$31). AE, DC, MC, V. Wed–Mon noon–3pm and 7–10:30pm. *Vaporetto:* Arsenale or San Zaccaria.

Da Aciugheta ★ VENETIAN/WINE BAR/PIZZERIA   A long block north of the chic Riva degli Schiavoni hotels lies one of Venice's best wine bars, expanded to include an elbow-to-elbow trattoria/pizzeria in back. Its name refers to the toothpick-speared marinated anchovies that join other *cicchetti* lining the popular front bar of this friendly *bacaro,* where you can enjoy an excellent selection of dozens of Veneto and Italian wines by the glass. The staff is relaxed about those not ordering full multicourse meals—a pasta and glass of wine or pizza and beer will keep anyone happy. There's an unusually long list of half-bottles of wine, and an even more unusual nonsmoking room. Tables move out onto the small piazza when the warm weather moves in.

Castello 4357 (in Campo SS. Filippo e Giacomo east of Piazza San Marco). 🕿 041-522-4292. Primi 6€–17€ ($7–$20); secondi 6€–17€ ($7–$20). AE, MC, V. Daily 8am–midnight (closed Wed Nov–Mar). *Vaporetto:* San Zaccaria (walk north on Calle delle Rasse to Campo SS. Filippo e Giacomo).

Osteria alle Testiere ★★ VENETIAN/ITALIAN   The limited seating for just 24 savvy (and lucky) patrons at butcher paper–covered tables, the relaxed young staff, and the upbeat tavernlike atmosphere belie the seriousness of this informal *osteria.* Having already persisted beyond the usual 15 minutes of culinary fame, this is your guaranteed choice if you are of the foodie genre, curious to experience the increasingly interesting Venetian culinary scene without going broke. Start with the carefully chosen wine list; any of the 90 labels can be ordered by the half-bottle. The delicious homemade *gnocchetti ai calamaretti* (with baby squid) makes a frequent appearance, as does the traditional "secondo" specialty *scampi alla busara,* in a "secret" recipe some of whose identifiable ingredients include tomato, cinnamon, and a dash of hot pepper. Cheese is a rarity in these parts, except for Alle Testiere's exceptional cheese platter.

Castello 5801 (on Calle del Mondo Novo off Salizzada San Lio). ℂ **041-522-7220.** Reservations required for each of 2 seatings. Primi 13€ ($15); secondi 15€–25€ ($17–$29). MC, V. Mon–Sat 2 seatings at 7 and 9:15pm. *Vaporetto:* Equidistant from either the Rialto or San Marco stops. Find the store-lined Salizzada San Lio (west of the Campo Santa Maria Formosa) and from there ask where to turn off on the Calle del Mondo Novo.

Ristorante Corte Sconta ★★ VENETIAN SEAFOOD   The bare, simple decor doesn't hint at the trendiness of this out-of-the-way trattoria, nor at the high quality of its strictly seafood cuisine. The emphasis is on freshness here; they put the shrimp live on the grill. Seafood fans will want to make reservations here on their very first night to hang with the foodies, artists, and writers who patronize this hidden gem. There's seafood-studded spaghetti, risotti with scampi, and a great *frittura mista all'Adriatico* (mixed Adriatic seafood fry). In nice weather you can dine under a canopy of grapevines in the courtyard.

Calle del Pestrin 3886. ℂ **041-522-7024.** Reservations recommended. Primi 12€–16€ ($14–$18); secondi 12€–20€ ($14–$23). MC, V. Tues–Sat 12:30–2pm and 7:15–10pm. *Vaporetto:* Arsenale (walk west along Riva degli Schiavoni and over the footbridge; turn right up Calle del Forno, then as its crosses Calle va in Crosera, veer right up Calle del Pestrin where it branches to the left). Closed Jan 7–Feb 7 and July 15–Aug 15.

MODERATE

Pizzeria/Trattoria al Vecio Canton *Kids* ITALIAN/PIZZA   Good pizza is hard to find in Venice, and I mean that in the literal sense. Tucked away in a northeast corner behind Piazza San Marco on a well-trafficked route connecting it with Campo Santa Maria Formosa, the Canton's wood-paneled tavernalike atmosphere and great pizzas are worth the time you'll spend looking for the place. There is a full trattoria menu as well, with a number of pasta and side dishes *(contorni)* of vegetables providing a palatable alternative.

Castello 4738a (at the corner of Ruga Giuffa). ℂ **041-528-5176.** www.alveciocanton.com. Reservations not accepted. Primi and pizza 6€–9€ ($7–$10); secondi 11€–18€ ($13–$21). AE, DC, MC. Wed 7–10:30pm; Thurs–Mon noon–2:30pm and 7–10:30pm. *Vaporetto:* San Zaccaria (from the Riva degli Schiavoni waterfront, walk straight ahead to Campo SS. Filippo e Giacomo then turn right and continue east to the small Campo San Provolo; take a left heading north on the Salizzada San Provolo, cross the 1st footbridge and you'll find the pizzeria on the 1st corner on the left).

Trattoria alla Rivetta ★★ SEAFOOD/VENETIAN   Lively and frequented by gondoliers (always a clue of quality dining for the right price), merchants, and visitors drawn to its bonhomie and bustling popularity, this is one of the safer bets for genuine Venetian cuisine and company in the touristy San Marco area, a 10-minute walk east of the piazza. All sorts of fish—the specialty—decorate the window of this brightly lit place. Another good indicator: There's usually a short wait, even in the off season.

Castello 4625 (on Salizzada San Provolo). ℂ **041-528-7302.** Primi 6€–10€ ($7–$12); secondi 10€–15€ ($12–$17). AE, MC, V. Tues–Sun noon–2:30pm and 7–10pm. *Vaporetto:* San Zaccaria (with your back to water and facing Hotel Savoia e Jolanda, walk straight ahead to Campo SS. Filippo e Giacomo; trattoria is tucked away next to a bridge off the right side of *campo*).

INEXPENSIVE

Trattoria da Remigio ★★ *Value* ITALIAN/VENETIAN   Famous for its straightforward renditions of Adriatic classics, Remigio is the kind of place where you can order simple *gnocchi alla pescatora* (homemade gnocchi in tomato-based seafood sauce) or *frittura mista* (a cornucopia of seafood fried in clean oil for a flavorful but light secondo) and know that it will be memorable. It bucks current Venetian trends by continuing to offer exquisite food and excellent service at reasonable prices. The English-speaking headwaiter, Pino, will talk you through the day's perfectly prepared fish dishes (John Dory, sole, monkfish, cuttlefish). You'll even find a dozen meat choices. Dine in one of two pleasant but smallish rooms. Remigio's—less abuzz and more sedate than Alla Madonna (see below)—is well known though not as easy to find; just ask a local for directions.

Castello 3416 (on Calle Bosello near Scuola San Giorgio dei Greci). ℂ 041-523-0089. Reservations required. Primi 3.50€–6€ ($4.05–$7); secondi 5€–14€ ($6–$16). AE, DC, MC, V. Wed–Mon 1–3pm; Wed–Sun 7–11pm. *Vaporetto:* San Zaccaria (follow Riva degli Schiavoni east until you come to white Chiesa della Pietà; turn left onto Calle della Pietà, which jags left into Calle Bosello).

IN DORSODURO
MODERATE

Taverna San Trovaso ⚜ *Kids* VENETIAN   Wine bottles line the wood-paneled walls, and low vaulted brick ceilings augment the sense of character in this canal-side tavern, always packed with locals and visitors. The *menù turistico* includes wine, an ample *frittura mista* (assortment of fried seafood), and dessert. The gnocchi is homemade; the local specialty of calves' liver and onions is great, and the simply grilled fish is the taverna's claim to fame. There's also a variety of pizzas. For a special occasion that'll test your budget but not bankrupt you, consider the four-course menu: It starts with a fresh antipasto of seafood followed by pasta and a fish entree (changing with the day's catch) and includes side dishes, dessert, and wine.

Dorsoduro 1016 (on Fondamenta Priuli). ℂ 041-520-3703. Reservations recommended. Pizza and primi 6€–10€ ($7–$12); secondi 8€–16€ ($9–$18); *menù turistico* 17€ ($20). AE, DC, MC, V. Tues–Sun noon–2:30pm and 7–9:30pm. *Vaporetto:* Rialto (walk to right around Accademia and take a right onto Calle Gambara; when this street ends at small Rio di San Trovaso, turn left onto Fondamenta Priuli).

Trattoria ai Cugnai ⚜⚜ *Finds* VENETIAN   The unassuming storefront of this longtime favorite does little to announce that herein lies some of the neighborhood's best dining. The name refers to the brothers-in-law of the three women chefs, all sisters, who serve classic *cucina veneziana,* like the reliably good *spaghetti alle vongole verace* (with clams) or *fegato alla veneziana.* The homemade gnocchi and lasagna would meet any Italian grandmother's approval (you won't go wrong with any of the menu's *fatta in casa* choices of daily homemade specialties either). Equidistant from the Accademia and the Guggenheim, Ai Cugnai is the perfect place to recharge after an art overload.

Dorsoduro 857 (on Calle Nuova Sant'Agnese). ℂ 041-528-9238. Primi 5€–9€ ($6–$10); secondi 5€–17€ ($6–$19). AE, MC, V. Tues–Sun 12:30–3pm and 7–10:30pm. *Vaporetto:* Accademia (head east of bridge and Accademia in direction of Guggenheim Collection; on straight street connecting 2 museums, restaurant is on your right).

IN SAN POLO
MODERATE

A Le Do Spade ⚜⚜ WINE BAR/VENETIAN   Since 1415, workers, fishmongers, and shoppers from the nearby Mercato della Pescheria have flocked to this characterful wine bar. There's bonhomie galore here among the locals for their daily *ombra* (glass of wine)—a large number of excellent Veneto and Friuli wines are available by the glass. A counter is filled with *cicchetti* (potato croquettes, fried calamari, polenta squares, cheeses) and a special *picante* panino whose secret mix of superhot spices will sear your taste buds. Unlike at most *bacari,* this quintessentially Venetian cantina has added a number of tables and introduced a sit-down menu, accounting for my star here over its competitor, Cantina do Mori (below), which is a better choice for stand-up bar food.

San Polo 860 (on Sottoportego do Spade). ℭ 041-521-0574. www.dospadevenezia.it. Primi 6€–10€ ($7–$12); secondi 7€–10€ ($8–$12); *menù fisso* (fixed menu) 13€–18€ ($15–$21). AE, MC, V. Mon–Wed and Fri–Sat 11:30am–3pm and 6–11:30pm; Thurs 9am–3pm. *Vaporetto:* Rialto or San Silvestro (at San Polo side of Rialto Bridge, walk away from bridge and through open-air market until you see covered fish market on your right; take a left and then take 2nd right onto Sottoportego do Spade). Closed Jan 7–20.

Alla Madonna *(Overrated)* ITALIAN/VENETIAN   This bright and busy trattoria is a classic, and has been packing them in for more than 50 years. This Venetian institution has a convenient location near the Rialto Bridge, five large dining rooms to accommodate the demand (though this is to the detriment of individual customer attention), an encouraging mix of loyal local regulars and foreign patrons, a characteristic decor of high-beamed ceilings and walls frame-to-frame with local artists' work, and decent fresh fish and seafood. With all of this, and (by Venetian standards) moderate prices to boot, it's no surprise that this place is always jumping. Don't expect the waiter to smile if you linger too long over dessert, though. Most of the first courses are prepared with seafood, such as the spaghetti or risotto with *frutti di mare* (seafood) or pasta with *sepie* (cuttlefish), blackened from its own natural ink. Most of the day's special fish selections are best simply and deliciously prepared *alla griglia* (grilled). Despite the good food and reasonable prices for Venice, I marked this restaurant as overrated since you'll be rushed through your meal and made to feel like you're part of an assembly line, with waiters caring more about the money you're going to leave on the table than what a nice meal you might have had.

San Polo 594 (Calle d. Madonna) ℭ 041-522-3824. www.ristoranteallamadonna.com. Reservations not accepted for tables of fewer than 8. Primi 9€–11€ ($10–$13); secondi 9€–15€ ($10–$17). AE, DC, MC, V. Thurs–Tues noon–3pm and 7–10pm. Closed 2 weeks in Aug and all of Jan. *Vaporetto:* Rialto (from the foot of the Rialto Bridge on the San Polo side of the Grand Canal, turn left and follow the Riva d. Vin along the Grand Canal; Calle d. Madonna [also called Sottoportego d. Madonna] will be the 2nd calle on your right [look for the big yellow sign]; the restaurant is on your left).

Da Sandro *(★) (Kids)* ITALIAN/PIZZERIA   Like most pizzerie/trattorie, Sandro offers dozens of varieties of pizza (his specialty) as well as a full trattoria menu of pastas and entrees. If you're looking for a 9€ ($10) pizza-and-beer meal, this is a reliably good spot on the main drag linking the Rialto to Campo San Polo. Italians like to carb out, and you won't raise any eyebrows if you order a pasta and pizza and pass on the meat or fish. There's communal seating at a few wooden picnic tables placed outdoors, with just a handful of small tables stuffed into the two dining rooms—which, unusually, are on opposite sides of the street.

San Polo 1473 (Campiello dei Meloni). ℭ 041-523-4894. Primi and pizza 5.50€–16€ ($6–$18); secondi 6€–18€ ($7–$21); fixed-price menus 14€–17€ ($16–$20). AE, MC, V. Sat–Thurs 11:30am–11:30pm. *Vaporetto:* San Silvestro (with your back to Grand Canal, walk straight to store-lined Ruga Vecchia San Giovanni and take a left; head toward Campo San Polo until you come on Campiello dei Meloni).

INEXPENSIVE

Cantina do Mori *(★★★) (Value)* WINE BAR/SANDWICHES   Since 1462 this has been the local watering hole of choice in the market area; legend even pegs Casanova as a habitué. *Tramezzini* are the fuel of Venice—sample them here where you're guaranteed fresh combinations of thinly sliced meats, tuna, cheeses, and vegetables, along with tapaslike *cicchetti.* They're traditionally washed down with an *ombra*. Venetians stop to snack and socialize before and after meals, but if you don't mind standing (there are no tables), for a light lunch this is one of the best of the old-time *bacari* left. And now that it serves a limited number of first courses like *melanzane alla parmigiana* (eggplant Parmesan) and *fondi di carciofi saltati* (lightly fried artichoke hearts), my obligatory stop here is more fulfilling than ever.

San Polo 429 (entrances on Calle Galiazza and Calle Do Mori). © 041-522-5401. Sandwiches and *cicchetti* bar food 1€–2€ ($1.15–$2.30) per serving. No credit cards. Mon–Sat 8:30am–9:30pm. *Vaporetto:* Rialto (cross Rialto Bridge to San Polo side, walk to end of market stalls, turn left, then immediately right, and look for small wooden cantina sign on left).

IN SANTA CROCE
INEXPENSIVE

Pizzeria ae Oche ★★ *(Kids)* PIZZERIA   Whenever I just want to hole up with a pizza in a relaxed setting, I head for the Baskin-Robbins of Venice's pizzerias, an American-style tavern restaurant of wood beams and booths decorated with classic 1950s Coca-Cola signs and the like. Italians are zealously unapologetic about tucking into a good-size pizza and a pint of beer (with more than 20 here from which to choose); the walk to and from this slightly peripherally located hangout (with outside eating during warm weather) allays thoughts of calorie counts. Count 'em: 85 varieties of imaginative pizza fill the menu, including a dozen of the tomato-sauce-free "white" variety *(pizza bianca)*. The clientele is a mixed bag of young and old, students and not, Venetians and visitors.

Santa Croce 1552 (on Calle del Tintor south of Campo San Giacomo dell'Orio). © 041-52-41-161. Reservations recommended for weekends. Pizza 4.30€–7.40€ ($4.95–$9); primi 5.20€–6.30€ ($6–$7); secondi 5.80€–7.50€ ($7–$9). MC, V. Tues–Sun noon–midnight (in summer open daily). *Vaporetto:* equidistant from Rio San Biasio and San Stae. You can walk here in 10 min. from the nearby train station; otherwise, from the *vaporetto* station find your way to the Campo San Giacomo dell'Orio and exit the *campo* south on to the well-trammeled Calle del Tintor.

PICNICKING
You don't have to eat in a fancy restaurant to have a good time in Venice. Prepare a picnic, and while you eat alfresco, you can observe the life of the city's few open piazzas or the aquatic parade on its main thoroughfare, the Grand Canal. And you can still indulge in a late dinner *alla Veneziana*. Plus, doing your own shopping for food can be an interesting experience—the city has very few supermarkets as we know them, and small *alimentari* (food shops) in the highly visited neighborhoods (where few Venetians live) are scarce.

MERCATO RIALTO   Venice's principal open-air market is a sight to see, even for nonshoppers. It has two parts, beginning with the produce section, whose many stalls, alternating with that of souvenir vendors, unfold north on the San Polo side of the Rialto Bridge (behind these stalls are a few permanent food stores that sell delicious cheese, cold cuts, and bread selections). The vendors are here Monday to Saturday 7am to 1pm, with a number who stay on in the afternoon.

At the market's farthest point, you'll find the covered **fresh-fish market,** with its carnival atmosphere, picturesquely located on the Grand Canal opposite the magnificent Ca' d'Oro and still redolent of the days when it was one of the Mediterranean's great fish markets. The area is filled with a number of small *bacari* bars frequented by market vendors and shoppers where you can join in and ask for your morning's first glass of *prosecco* with a *cicchetto* pick-me-up. The fish merchants take Monday off (which explains why so many restaurants are closed on Mon; those that are open are selling Saturday's goods—beware!) and work mornings only.

CAMPO SANTA MARGHERITA On this spacious *campo,* Tuesday through Saturday from 8:30am to 1 or 2pm, a number of open-air stalls set up shop, selling fresh fruit and vegetables. You should have no trouble filling out your picnic spread with the fixings available at the various shops lining the sides of the *campo,* including an exceptional *panetteria* (bakery), Rizzo Pane, at no. 2772, a fine *salumeria* (deli) at no. 2844, and a good shop for wine, sweets, and other picnic accessories next door. There's even a conventional supermarket, Merlini, just off the *campo* in the direction of the quasi-adjacent *campo* San Barnabà at no. 3019. This is also the area where you'll find Venice's heavily photographed **floating market** operating from a boat moored just off San Barnabà at the Ponte dei Pugni. This market is open daily from 8am to 1pm and 3:30 to 7:30pm, except Wednesday afternoon and Sunday. You're almost better off just buying a few freshly prepared sandwiches (panini when made with rolls, *tramezzini* when made with white bread).

THE BEST PICNIC SPOTS Alas, to stay behind and picnic in Venice means you won't have much in the way of green space (it's not worth the boat ride to the Giardini Publici past the Arsenale, Venice's only green park). An enjoyable alternative is to find some of the larger piazzas or *campi* that have park benches, and in some cases even a tree or two to shade them, such as Campo San Giacomo dell'Orio (in the quiet *sestiere* of Santa Croce). The two most central are **Campo Santa Margherita** (*sestiere* of Dorsoduro) and **Campo San Polo** (*sestiere* of San Polo). For a picnic with a view, scout out the **Punta della Dogana area (Customs House)** near La Salute Church for a prime viewing site at the mouth of the Grand Canal. It's located directly across from the Piazza San Marco and the Palazzo Ducale—pull up on a piece of the embankment here and watch the flutter of water activity against a canvaslike backdrop deserving of the Accademia Museum. In this same area, the small **Campo San Vio** near the Guggenheim is directly on the Grand Canal (not many *campi* are) and even boasts a bench or two.

If you want to create a real Venice picnic, you'll have to take the no. 12 boat out to the near-deserted island of **Torcello,** with a hamper full of bread, cheese, and wine, and reenact the romantic scene between Katharine Hepburn and Rossano Brazzi from the 1950s film *Summertime.*

But perhaps the best picnic site of all is in a **patch of sun on the marble steps** leading down to the water of the Grand Canal, at the foot of the Rialto Bridge on the San Polo side. There is no better ringside seat for the Canalazzo's passing parade.

5 Exploring Venice

Venice is notorious for changing and extending the opening hours of its museums and, to a lesser degree, its churches. Before you begin your exploration of Venice's sights, ask at the tourist office for the season's list of museum and church hours. During the peak months, you can enjoy extended museum hours—some places stay open until 7 or even 10pm. Unfortunately, these hours are not released until approximately Easter of every year. Even then, little is done to publicize the information, so you'll have to do your own research.

IN PIAZZA SAN MARCO

Basilica di San Marco (St. Mark's Basilica) ★★★ Venice for centuries was Europe's principal gateway between the Orient and the West, so it should come

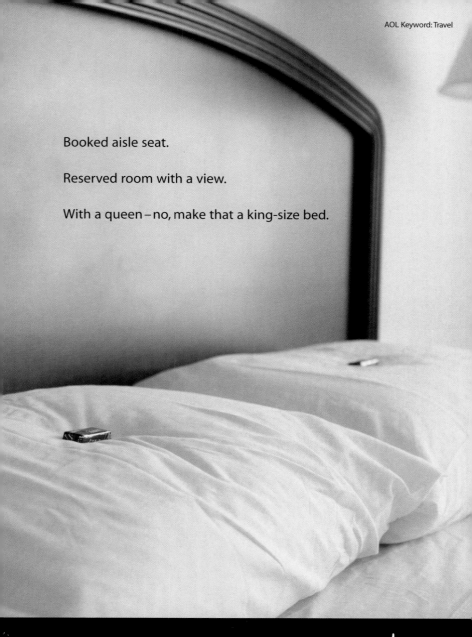

Booked aisle seat.

Reserved room with a view.

With a queen – no, make that a king-size bed.

With Travelocity, you can book your flights and hotels together, so you can get even better deals than if you booked them separately. You'll save time and money without compromising the quality of your trip. Choose your airline seat, search for alternate airports, pick your hotel room type, even choose the neighborhood you'd like to stay in.

Travelocity

**Visit www.travelocity.com
or call 1-888-TRAVELOCITY**

Travelocity® Travelocity.com® and the Travelocity airline logo are trademarks and/or service marks of Travelocity.com L.P. © 2003 Travelocity.com L.P. All rights reserved.

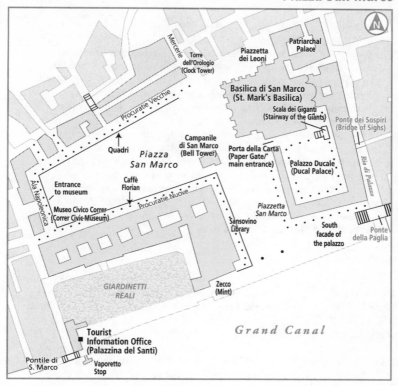

Unless you can tag along with an English-speaking tour group, you may otherwise miss out on the importance of much of what you're seeing.

The first room you'll come to is the spacious **Sala delle Quattro Porte (Hall of the Four Doors),** whose ceiling is by Tintoretto. The **Sala del Anti-Collegio** (adjacent to the College Chamber, whose ceiling is decorated by Tintoretto), the next main room, is where foreign ambassadors waited to be received (and thus the rich embellishment of its canvases, which served as self-aggrandizement) by this committee of 25 members: It is decorated with works by Tintoretto, and Veronese's *Rape of Europe,* considered one of the palazzo's finest. It steals some of the thunder of Tintoretto's *Three Graces,* and *Bacchus and Ariadne*—the latter considered one of his best by some critics. A right turn from this room leads into one of the most impressive of the spectacular interior rooms, the richly adorned **Sala del Senato (Senate Chamber),** with Tintoretto's ceiling painting, *The Triumph of Venice.* Here laws were passed by the Senate, a select group of 200 chosen from the Great Council. The latter was originally an elected body, but from the 13th century onward, it was an aristocratic stronghold that could number as many as 1,700. After passing again through the Sala delle Quattro Porte, you'll come to the Veronese-decorated **Stanza del Consiglio dei Dieci (Room of the Council of Ten,** the republic's dreaded security police), of particular historical interest. It was in this room that justice was dispensed (and decapitations ordered). Formed in the 14th century to deal with emergency situations, the Ten

An Insider's Look at the Palazzo Ducale

I cannot recommend the **"Itinerari Segreti" (Secret Itineraries)** ★★★ guided tours highly enough. The tours offer an unparalleled look into the world of Venetian politics over the centuries and are the only way to access the otherwise restricted quarters and hidden passageways of this enormous palace, such as the doges' private chambers and the torture chambers where prisoners were interrogated. The story of Giacomo Casanova's imprisonment in, and famous escape from, the palace's prisons is the tour highlight (though a few of the less-inspired guides harp on this aspect a bit too much). I strongly recommend you reserve in advance, by phone if possible—tours are often sold out at least a few days ahead, especially from spring through fall—or in person at the ticket desk. Tours are at 10:30am Thursday through Tuesday (by reservation only), and cost 13€ ($14) for adults, 7€ ($8) for students, and 4€ ($5) for children 6 to 14.

were frequently considered more powerful than the Senate, and feared by all. Just outside the adjacent chamber, in the **Sala della Bussola (The Compass Chamber),** notice the **Bocca dei Leoni ("lion's mouth"),** a slit in the wall into which secret denunciations and accusations of alleged enemies of the state were placed for quick action by the much-feared Council.

The main sight on the next level down—indeed in the entire palace—is the **Sala del Maggior Consiglio (Great Council Hall).** This enormous space is made special by Tintoretto's huge *Paradiso* at the far end of the hall above the doge's seat (the painter was in his seventies when he undertook the project with the help of his son; he died 6 years later). Measuring 7m by 23m (23 ft. by 75 ft.), it is said to be the world's largest oil painting; together with Veronese's gorgeous *Il Trionfo di Venezia* (*The Triumph of Venice*) in the oval panel on the ceiling, it affirms the power emanating from the council sessions held here. Tintoretto also did the portraits of the 76 doges encircling the top of this chamber; note that the picture of the Doge Marin Falier, who was convicted of treason and beheaded in 1355, has been blacked out—Venice has never forgiven him. Although elected for life since sometime in the 7th century, over time *il doge* became nothing but a figurehead (they were never allowed to meet with foreign ambassadors alone); the power rested in the Great Council. Exit the Great Council Hall via the tiny doorway on the opposite side of Tintoretto's *Paradiso* to find the enclosed **Ponte dei Sospiri (Bridge of Sighs),** which connects the Ducal Palace with the grim **Palazzo delle Prigioni (Prisons).** The bridge took its current name only in the 19th century, when visiting northern European poets romantically envisioned the prisoners' final breath of resignation upon viewing the outside world one last time before being locked in their fetid cells awaiting the quick justice of the Terrible Ten. Some attribute the name to Casanova, who, following his arrest in 1755 (he was accused of being a Freemason and spreading antireligious propaganda), crossed this very bridge. He was one of the rare few to escape 15 months after his imprisonment, alive, returning to Venice 20 years later. Some of the stone cells still have the original graffiti of past prisoners, many of them locked up interminably for petty crimes.

San Marco, Piazza San Marco. © **041-271-5911**. Admission on San Marco cumulative ticket (see "Venice Discounts" on p. 130) or 11€ ($13) adults, 5.50€ ($6) students ages 15–29, 3€ ($3.45) ages 6–14 (includes cumulative ticket, free under 5). For "Itinerari Segreti" guided tour in English, see "An Insider's Look at the Palazzo Ducale" box, below. Apr–Oct daily 9am–7pm; Nov–Mar daily 9am–5pm (ticket office closes 1 hr. earlier). *Vaporetto:* San Marco.

Campanile di San Marco (Bell Tower) ★★
It's an easy elevator ride up to the top of this 97m (324-ft.) bell tower for a breathtaking view of the cupolas of St. Mark's. It is the highest structure in the city, offering a pigeon's-eye view that includes the lagoon, its neighboring islands, and the red rooftops and church domes and bell towers of Venice—and, oddly, not a single canal. On a clear day you may even see the outline of the distant snowcapped Dolomite Mountains. Originally built in the 9th century, the bell tower was then rebuilt in the 12th, 14th, and 16th centuries, when the pretty marble loggia at its base was added by Jacopo Sansovino. It collapsed unexpectedly in 1902, miraculously hurting no one except a cat. It was rebuilt exactly as before, using most of the same materials, even rescuing one of the five historical bells that it still uses today (each bell was rung for a different purpose, such as war, the death of a doge, religious holidays, and so on).

San Marco, Piazza San Marco. © **041-522-4064**. Admission 6€ ($7). Apr–June 9:30am–5pm; July–Sept 9:45am–8pm. *Vaporetto:* San Marco.

Torre dell'Orologio (Clock Tower)
Unfortunately, the Clock Tower has been closed for a number of years despite plans to open it in time for the 500-year anniversary of its construction (long since passed). As you enter the magnificent Piazza San Marco, it is one of the first things you see, standing on the north side, next to and towering above the Procuratie Vecchie (the ancient administration buildings for the republic). The Renaissance tower was built in 1496, and the clock mechanism of that same period still keeps perfect time but is currently getting a cleaning by Piaget. The two bronze figures, known as "Moors" because of the dark color of the bronze, pivot to strike the hour. The base of the tower has always been a favorite *punto di incontro* ("meet me at the tower") for Venetians, and is the entranceway to the ancient Mercerie (from the word for merchandise), the principal souklike retail street of both high-end boutiques and trinket shops that zigzags its way to the Rialto Bridge. Visits to the top, stopped in the late 1980s, will resume upon the tower's reopening.

San Marco, Piazza San Marco. No phone. Scheduled to reopen in 2004, but this may change (many other "scheduled" reopening dates have come and gone over the past 7 years). Admission set to be 9€ ($10). Daily 9am–3:30pm. *Vaporetto:* San Marco.

Museo Civico Correr (Correr Civic Museum) ★
This museum, which you enter through an arcade at the west end of Piazza San Marco opposite the basilica, is no match for the Accademia but does include some interesting paintings of Venetian life, and a fine collection of artifacts, such as coins, costumes, the doges' ceremonial robes and hats, and an incredible pair of 15-inch platform shoes, that gives an interesting feel for aspects of the day-to-day life in La Serenissima in the heyday of its glory. Bequeathed to the city by the aristocratic Correr family in 1830, the museum is divided into three sections: the **Painting Section,** the **History Section,** and the **Museum of the Risorgimento** (1797–1866). The latter two aren't worth much mention. Of the painting collection from the 13th to 18th centuries, Vittorio Carpaccio's *Le Cortigiane (The Courtesans),* in room no. 15 on the upper floor, is one of the museum's most famous paintings (are they courtesans or the respected elite?), as are the star-attraction paintings by the Bellini

family, father Jacopo and sons Gentile and Giovanni. For a lesson in just how little this city has changed in the last several hundred years, head to room no. 22 and its anonymous 17th-century bird's-eye view of Venice. Most of the rooms have a sign with a few paragraphs in English explaining the significance of the contents.

San Marco, west end of Piazza San Marco. 📞 041-271-5911. Admission on San Marco cumulative ticket (see "Venice Discounts" on p. 130). Daily 9am–7pm (winter hours may be shorter; last entrance 1 hr. before closing). *Vaporetto:* San Marco.

TOP ATTRACTIONS BEYOND SAN MARCO

Galleria dell'Accademia (Academy Gallery) ★★★ The glory that was Venice lives on in the Accademia, the definitive treasure house of Venetian painting and one of Europe's great museums. Exhibited chronologically from the 13th through the 18th centuries, the collection features no one hallmark masterpiece in this collection; rather, this is an outstanding and comprehensive showcase of works by all the great master painters of Venice, the largest such collection in the world.

It includes Paolo and Lorenzo Veneziano from the 14th century; Gentile and Giovanni Bellini (and Giovanni's brother-in-law Andrea Mantegna from Padua) and Vittore Carpaccio from the 15th century; Giorgione (whose *Tempest* is one of the gallery's most famous highlights), Tintoretto, Veronese (see his *Feast in the House of Levi* here), and Titian from the 16th century; and from the 17th and 18th centuries, Canaletto, Piazzetta, Longhi, and Tiepolo, among others.

Most of all, though, the works open a window onto the Venice of 500 years ago. Indeed, the canvases reveal how little Venice has changed over the centuries. Housed in a deconsecrated church and its adjoining *scuola,* the church's confraternity hall, it is Venice's principal picture gallery, and one of the most important in Italy. Because of fire regulations, admission is limited, and lines can be daunting (check for extended evening hours in the peak months), but put up with the wait and don't miss it.

Dorsoduro, at foot of Accademia Bridge. 📞 041-522-2247. www.gallerieaccademia.org. Admission 6.50€ ($7) adults, 3.25€ ($3.75) children 12–18, free for children under 12. Mon 8:15am–2pm; Tues–Sun 8:15am–7:15pm; last admission 30 min. before close (winter hours may be shorter). *Vaporetto:* Accademia.

Collezione Peggy Guggenheim (Peggy Guggenheim Collection) ★★★ Considered to be one of the most comprehensive and important collections of modern art in the world and one of the most visited attractions in Venice, this collection of painting and sculpture was assembled by the eccentric and eclectic American expatriate Peggy Guggenheim. She did an excellent job of it, with particular strengths in Cubism, European Abstraction, Surrealism, and Abstract Expressionism since about 1910. Max Ernst was one of her early favorites (she even married him), as was Jackson Pollock.

Among the major works here are Magritte's *Empire of Light,* Picasso's *La Baignade,* Kandinsky's *Landscape with Church (with Red Spot),* Metzinger's *The Racing Cyclist,* and Pollock's *Alchemy.* The museum is also home to several haunting canvases by Ernst, Giacometti's unique figures, Brancusi's fluid sculptures, and numerous works by Braque, Dalí, Léger, Mondrian, Chagall, and Miró.

Directly on the Grand Canal, the elegant 18th-century Palazzo Venier dei Leoni (never finished; thus its unusual one-story structure) was purchased by Peggy Guggenheim in 1949 and was her home in Venice until her death in 1979. The year 1998 was marked by special exhibits to celebrate the centennial of her birth. The graves of her canine companions share the lovely interior garden with several prominent works of the Nasher Sculpture Garden, while the canal-side patio watched over by Marino Marini's *Angel of the Citadel* is one of the best spots to simply linger and watch the canal life. A new and interesting book and gift shop and cafe/bistro (recommended but not inexpensive) has opened in a separate wing across the inside courtyard where temporary exhibits are often housed.

Check the tourist office for an update on museum hours; it is often open when many others are closed and sometimes offers a few hours a week of free admission. Don't be shy about speaking English with the young staff working here on internship; most of them are American. They offer free tours in English of the permanent collection on Saturdays at 7pm.

Dorsoduro 701 (on Calle San Cristoforo). (© 041-240-5411. www.guggenheim-venice.it. Admission 8€ ($9) adults, 5€ ($6) students. Wed–Mon 10am–6pm; Apr–Oct open Sat until 10pm. *Vaporetto:* Accademia (walk around left side of Accademia, take 1st left, and walk straight ahead following signs—you'll cross a canal, then walk alongside another, until turning left when necessary).

Scuola Grande di San Rocco (Confraternity of St. Roch) ★★★   This museum is a dazzling monument to the work of Tintoretto—it holds the largest collection of his work anywhere. The series of the more than 50 dark and dramatic works took the artist more than 20 years to complete, making this the richest of the many confraternity guilds or *scuole* that once flourished in Venice.

Jacopo Robusti (1518–94), called Tintoretto because his father was a dyer, was a devout, unworldly man who only traveled once beyond Venice. His epic canvasses are filled with phantasmagoric light and intense, mystical spirituality.

Begin upstairs in the Sala dell'Albergo, where the most notable of the enormous, powerful canvases is the moving *La Crocifissione (The Crucifixion).* In the center of the gilt ceiling of the great hall, also upstairs, is *Il Serpente di Bronzo (The Bronze Snake).* Among the eight huge, sweeping paintings downstairs, each depicting a scene from the New Testament, *La Strage degli Innocenti (The Slaughter of the Innocents)* is the most noteworthy, so full of dramatic urgency and energy that the figures seem almost to tumble out of the frame. As you enter the room, it's on the opposite wall at the far end of the room.

There's a useful guide to the paintings posted inside on the wall just before the entrance to the museum. There are a few Tiepolos among the paintings, as well as a solitary work by Titian. Note that the works on or near the staircase are not by Tintoretto.

Venice's second most important and richly decorated *scuola,* or confraternity, is that of San Giorgio degli Schiavoni (also called San Giorgio dei Greci); see below.

For Church Fans

The **Associazione Chiese di Venezia** (© 041-275-0462; www.chorus-ve.org) now curates most of Venice's top churches. A visit to one of the association's churches costs 2€ ($2.30) and (with a few exceptions) is open Monday to Saturday 10am to 5pm and Sunday 1 to 5pm. The churches are closed Sundays in July and August. If you plan to visit more than four churches, buy the 8€ ($9) ticket (valid for 1 year), which allows you to visit all of the following churches: **Santa Maria del Giglio, Santo Stefano, Santa Maria Formosa, Santa Maria dei Miracoli, Santa Maria Gloriosa dei Frari** (reviewed here), **San Polo, San Giacomo dell'Orio, San Stae, Alvise, Madonna dell'Orto, San Pietro di Castello, Il Redentore** (reviewed here), **San Sebastiano** (reviewed here), and **San Marco cathedral's treasury.** The association also has audio guides available at some of the churches for .50€ (60¢).

Venice Discounts

The **Biglietto d'Ingresso Unificato** (Piazza San Marco cumulative ticket) grants admission to all the piazza's museums—the Palazzo Ducale, Museo Civico Correr, Museo Archeologico Nazionale, Museo Fortuny, and Biblioteca Nazionale Marciana—as well as to the Museo di Palazzo Mocenigo (Costume Museum), Museo del Vetro (Glass Museum) on Murano, and Museo di Merletto (Lace Museum) on Burano. It's available at any of the participating museums except Museo Fortuny for 16€ ($18) for adults, 10€ ($12) for children 6 to 14.

Venice, so delicate it cannot handle the hordes of visitors it receives every year, has been toying with the idea of charging admission to get into the very city itself. Slightly calmer heads seem to have prevailed, though, and as we go to press, the mayor's office has just instituted a **Venice Card** (*(C)* 899-909-090 in Italy or 041-271-4747 outside of Italy; www.venicecard.it). The **"blu"** version will get you free passage on buses and *vaporetti*, usage of public toilets, and a reduced daily rate of 6.70€ ($7.70), along with a reserved spot, at the public ASM parking garage, and a price of 5€ ($5.75) rather than 8€ ($9.20) for the Churches pass (see the "For Church Fans" box on p. 129). The **"orange"** version adds to these services admission to all the sights covered under the expanded version of the **Biglietto d'Ingresso Unificato** (Piazza San Marco cumulative ticket) (see above) plus the Ca' Rezzonico, plus the card lets you bypass the often long lines. There are versions that also include a ride into town from the airport, but that doesn't actually save you any money in the long run so skip it. (They're working on arranging reserved, timed entries, the logic being that so many people will

---

San Polo 3058 (on Campo San Rocco adjacent to Campo dei Frari). *(C)* 041-523-4864. www.sanrocco.it. Admission 5.50€ ($6) adults, 4€ ($4.60) students. Daily 9am–5:30pm (winter hours may be shorter). *Vaporetto:* San Tomà (walk straight ahead on Calle del Traghetto and turn right and immediately left across Campo San Tomà; walk as straight ahead as you can, on Ramo Mandoler, Calle Larga Prima, and Salizzada San Rocco, which leads into *campo* of the same name—look for crimson sign behind Frari Church).

Canal Grande (Grand Canal) ★★★   A leisurely cruise along the "Canalazzo" from Piazza San Marco to the Ferrovia (train station), or the reverse, is one of Venice's (and life's) must-do experiences. Hop on the no. 1 *vaporetto* in the late afternoon (try to get one of the coveted outdoor seats in the prow), when the weather-worn colors of the former homes of Venice's merchant elite are warmed by the soft light and reflected in the canal's rippling waters, and the busy traffic of delivery boats, *vaporetti*, and gondolas that fills the city's main thoroughfare has eased somewhat. The sheer number and opulence of the 200-odd palazzi, churches, and imposing republican buildings dating from the 14th to the 18th centuries is enough to make any boat-going visitor's head swim. Many of the largest are now converted into imposing international banks, government or university buildings, art galleries, and dignified consulates. They unfold along this singular 3.2km (2-mile) ribbon of water that loops through the city like an inverted S, crossed by only three bridges (the Rialto spans it at midpoint) and dividing the city into three *sestieri* neighborhoods to the left, three to the right.

have this card, the main sights will be effectively booked-up thus discouraging visitors who arrive without the card.) They're also encouraging various merchants to jump on the bandwagon in some way. *Note:* Since this card is new, there may be changes or tweaks to what it offers and how it works as time goes on.

For adults, the "blu" card costs 14€ ($16) for 1 day, 29€ ($33) for 3 days, or 51€ ($59) for 7 days; for ages 4 to 29, the "blu" card costs 9€ ($10) for 1 day, 22€ ($25) for 3 days, or 49€ ($56) for 7 days. For adults, the "orange" card costs 28€ ($32) for 1 day, 47€ ($54) for 3 days, or 68€ ($78) for 7 days; for ages 4 to 29, the "orange" card costs 18€ ($21) for 1 day, 35€ ($40) for 3 days, or 61€ ($70) for 7 days. You can order it in advance by phone or online, and they'll tell you where to pick it up.

Anyone between 16 and 29 is eligible for the terrific **Rolling Venice pass,** which gives discounts in museums, restaurants, stores, language courses, hotels, and bars across the city (it comes with a thick booklet listing everywhere it entitles you to get discounts). It's valid for 1 year and costs 2.60€ ($3). Year-round, you can pick one up at the **Informagiovani Assessorato alla Gioventù,** Corte Contarina 1529, off the Frezzeria west of St. Mark's Square (© **041-274-7645** or 041-274-7650), which is open Monday to Friday 9:30am to 1pm, plus Tuesday and Thursday 3 to 5pm. July to September you can stop by the special Rolling Venice office set up in the train station daily 8am to 8pm; in winter you can get the pass at the Transalpino travel agency just outside the station's front doors and to the right, at the top of the steps, open Monday to Friday 8:30am to 12:30pm and 3 to 7pm and Saturday 8:30am to 12:30pm.

Some of the waterfront palazzi have been converted into condominiums whose lower water-lapped floors are now deserted, but the higher floors are still the coveted domain of the city's titled families; others have become the summertime homes of privileged expatriates.

2 most popular stations located at Piazzale Roma/Ferrovia (train station); and at Piazza San Marco. *Vaporetto:* 1; ticket 3.50€ ($4.05).

IN SAN MARCO

Rialto ★★   This graceful arch over the Grand Canal is lined with overpriced boutiques and is teeming with tourists and overflow from the daily market along Riga degli Orefici on the S. Polo side. Until the 19th century, it was the only bridge across the Grand Canal, originally built as a pontoon bridge at the canal's narrowest point. Wooden versions of the bridge followed; the 1444 one was the first to include shops, interrupted by a drawbridge in the center. In 1592 this graceful stone span was finished to the designs of Antonio da Ponte, who beat out Sansovino, Palladio, and Michelangelo with his plans that called for a single, vast, 28m (92-ft.) wide arch in the center to allow trading ships to pass. Ponte del Rialto.

Chiesa di San Salvador ★   The interior is classic Renaissance, built by Giorgio Spavento, Tullio Lombardo, and Sansovino between 1508 and 1534; the facade is 1663 baroque. Between the second and third altars on the right aisle sits a polychrome marble monument to Doge Francesco Venier (1556). It includes a pair of sculptures (*Charity* and *Hope*) by an elderly Jacopo Sansovino, who may also have designed the third altar, which supports one of the church's treasures, Titian's *Annunciation* (1556). Titian also painted the *Transfiguration* (1560) on the high altar. Ask the sacristan to lower the painting so that you can see the ornate 14th-century silver reredos (ornamental partition) hidden behind. In the right transept rests Bernardino Contino's tomb for Caterina Cornaro (d. 1510), the one-time queen of Cyprus who abdicated her throne to Venice and ended up with Asolo (see chapter 4) as a consolation prize.

Campo San Salvador (just south from the Rialto bridge on Via 2 Aprile). ℂ **041-523-6717** or 041-270-2464. Free admission. Daily 9am–noon and 3–6pm. *Vaporetto:* Rialto.

IN CASTELLO

SS. Giovanni e Paolo ✦   This massive Gothic church was built by the Dominican order from the 13th to the 15th century and, together with the Frari Church in San Polo, is second in size only to the Basilica di San Marco. An unofficial Pantheon where 25 doges are buried (a number of tombs are part of the unfinished facade), the church, commonly known as Zanipolo in Venetian dialect, is also home to a number of artistic treasures.

Visit the **Cappella del Rosario** ✦ through a glass door off the left transept to see the three recently restored ceiling canvases by Paolo Veronese, particularly *The Assumption of the Madonna.* Also recently restored is the brilliantly colored *Polyptych of St. Vincent Ferrer* (ca. 1465) attributed to a young Giovanni Bellini, in the right aisle. You'll also see the foot of St. Catherine of Siena encased in glass. Adjacent to the church is the old **Scuola di San Marco,** an old confraternity-like association now run as a civic hospital, most noteworthy for its beautiful 15th-century Renaissance facade.

Anchoring the large and impressive *campo,* a popular crossroads for this area of Castello, is the **statue of Bartolomeo Colleoni** ✦✦, the Renaissance condottiere who defended Venice's interests at the height of its power and until his death in 1475. The 15th-century work is by the Florentine Andrea Verrocchio; it is considered one of the world's great equestrian monuments and Verrocchio's best.

Castello 6363 (on Campo Santi Giovanni e Paolo). ℂ **041-523-7510** or 041-235-5913. Admission 2€ ($2.30). Mon–Sat 8:30am–12:30pm and 3:30–7pm. *Vaporetto:* Rialto.

Chiesa di San Zaccaria (Church of St. Zacchary) ✦   Behind (east of) St. Mark's Basilica is a 9th-century Gothic church with its original 13th-century campanile and a splendid Renaissance facade designed by the Venetian architect Mario Codussi in the late 15th century. Of the interior's many artworks is the important *Madonna Enthroned with Four Saints,* painted by Giovanni Bellini in 1505. Recently restored, it can be found above the second altar in the left aisle; art historians have long held this as one of Bellini's finer Madonnas. Apply to the sacristan to see the Sisters' Choir, with works by Tintoretto, Titian, Il Vecchio, Anthony Van Dyck, and Bassano. The paintings aren't labeled, but the sacristan will point out the names of the artists. In the fan vaults of the Chapel of San Tarasio are the faded ceiling frescoes of the Florentine-born artist Andrea del Castagno, who was the first to bring the spirit of the Renaissance to Venice.

Castello, Campo San Zaccaria. ℂ **041-522-1257.** Free admission. Mon–Sat 10am–noon; daily 4–6pm. *Vaporetto:* San Zaccaria.

Museo Storico Navale and Arsenale (Naval History Museum and the Arsenal) ★★   The Naval History Museum's most fascinating exhibit is its collection of model ships. It was once common practice for vessels to be built not from blueprints, but from the precise scale models that you see here. The prize of the collection is a model of the legendary Bucintoro, the lavish ceremonial barge of the doges. Another section of the museum contains an array of historic vessels. Walk along the canal as it branches off from the museum to the Ships' Pavilion, where the historic vessels are displayed.

To reach the arsenal from the museum, walk up the Arsenale Canal and cross the wooden bridge to the Campo del'Arsenale, where you will soon reach the land gate of the Arsenale, not open to the public. Occupying one-fifth of the city's total acreage, the arsenal was once the very source of the republic's maritime power. It is now used as a military zone and is as closed as Fort Knox to the curious. The marble-columned Renaissance gate with the republic's winged lion above is flanked by four ancient lions, booty brought at various times from Greece and points farther east. It was founded in 1104, and at the height of Venice's power in the 15th century, it employed 16,000 workers who turned out merchant and wartime galley after galley on an early version of massive assembly lines at speeds and in volume unknown until modern times.

Castello 2148 (Campo San Biasio). ✆ **041-520-0276.** Admission 3€ ($3.45). Tues–Sun 9:30am–12:30pm; Tues–Sat 3:30–6:30pm. *Vaporetto:* Arsenale.

Scuola di San Giorgio degli Schiavoni ★   At the St. Antonino Bridge (Fondamenta dei Furlani) is the second-most important guild house to visit in Venice. The Schiavoni were an important and wealthy trading colony of Dalmatian merchants who built their own *scuola,* or confraternity (the coast of Dalmatia—the former Yugoslavia—was once ruled by the Greeks and therefore the *scuola's* alternative name of San Giorgio dei Greci).

Between 1502 and 1509, Vittore Carpaccio (himself of Dalmatian descent) painted a pictorial cycle of nine masterpieces illustrating episodes from the lives of St. George (patron saint of the *scuola*) and St. Jerome, the Dalmatian patron saints. These appealing pictures freeze in time moments in the lives of the saints: St. George charges his ferocious dragon on a field littered with half-eaten bodies and skulls (a horror story with a happy ending); St. Jerome leads his lion into a monastery, frightening the friars; St. Augustine has just taken up his pen to reply to a letter from St. Jerome when he and his little dog are transfixed by a miraculous light, and a voice telling them of St. Jerome's death.

Castello 3259, Calle Furlani. ✆ **041-522-8828.** Admission 3€ ($3.45). Tues–Sun 9:30am–12:30pm; Tues–Sat 3:30–6:30pm. *Vaporetto:* San Zaccaria.

IN DORSODURO

The Accademia and the Peggy Guggenheim museums are the top two sights in this neighborhood, and as such are both covered earlier in this chapter.

Ca' Rezzonico (Museo del '700 Veneziano; Museum of 18th-Century Venice) ★★   This museum, in a handsome palazzo on the Grand Canal, reopened after a complete restoration in late 2001. It offers an intriguing look into what living in a grand Venetian home was like in the final years of the Venetian Republic.

Begun by Baldassare Longhena, 17th-century architect of La Salute Church, the Rezzonico home is a sumptuous backdrop for this collection of period paintings (most important, works by Venetian artists Tiepolo and Guardi, and a special room dedicated to the dozens of works by Longhi), furniture, tapestries, and artifacts. This museum is one of the best windows into the sometimes frivolous life of Venice of 200 years ago, as seen through the tastes and fashions of the wealthy Rezzonico family of merchants—the lavishly frescoed ballroom alone will evoke the lifestyle of the idle Venetian rich. The English poet Robert Browning, after the death of his wife Elizabeth Barrett Browning, made this his last home; he died here in 1889.

Dorsoduro (on the Grand Canal on Fondamenta Rezzonico). ℂ 041-241-0100 or 041-520-4036. Admission 6.50€ ($7) adults, 4.50€ ($5) students. Wed–Mon 10am–6pm. *Vaporetto:* Ca' Rezzonico (walk straight ahead to Campo San Barnabà, turn right at the piazza and go over 1 bridge, then take an immediate right for the museum entrance).

Santa Maria della Salute (Church of the Virgin Mary of Good Health) ⭐
Generally referred to as "La Salute," this crown jewel of 17th-century baroque architecture proudly reigns at a commercially and aesthetically important point, almost directly across from the Piazza San Marco, where the Grand Canal empties into the lagoon.

The first stone was laid in 1631 after the Senate decided to honor the Virgin Mary of Good Health for delivering Venice from a plague (and after the completion of the neighboring Chiesa di San Giorgio: Along with the Piazza San Marco, city elders were looking to create an ensemble of awe-inspiring structures to impress those arriving in Venice for the 1st time). They accepted the revolutionary plans of a young, relatively unknown architect, Baldassare Longhena (who would go on to design, among other projects, the Ca' Rezzonico). He dedicated the next 50 years of his life to overseeing its progress (he would die 1 year after its inauguration but 5 years before its completion).

The only great baroque monument built in Italy outside of Rome, the octagonal Salute is recognized for its exuberant exterior of volutes, scrolls, and more than 125 statues and rather sober interior, though one highlighted by a small gallery of important works in the sacristy. (You have to pay to enter the sacristy; the entrance is through a small door to the left of the main altar.) A number of ceiling paintings and portraits of the Evangelists and church doctors are all by Titian. On the right wall is Tintoretto's *Marriage at Cana,* often considered one of his best.

Dorsoduro (on Campo della Salute). ℂ 041-522-5558. Church, free admission; sacristy, 1.50€ ($1.75). Daily 9am–noon and 3–5:30pm. *Vaporetto:* Salute.

Dogana da Mar ⭐⭐ *(Moments*
The eastern tip of Dorsoduro is covered by the triangular 15th-century (restructured with a new facade in 1676–82) customs house that once controlled all boats entering the Grand Canal. It's topped by a statue of Fortune holding aloft a golden ball. Now it makes for remarkable, sweeping views across the *bacino* San Marco, from the last leg of the Grand Canal past Piazzetta San Marco and the Ducal Palace, over the nearby isle of San Giorgio Maggiore, La Giudecca, and out into the lagoon itself.

Fondamenta Dogana alla Salute. *Vaporetto:* Salute.

I Gesuati (Santa Maria del Rosario) ⭐
Built from 1724 to 1736 to mirror the Redentore across the wide Canale della Giudecca, the Jesuits' church counters the Palladian sobriety of the Redentore with rococo flair. The interior is graced by airy 1737–39 ceiling frescoes (some of the 1st in Venice) by Giambattista Tiepolo celebrating Donenticna scenes. Tiepolo also did the *Virgin in Glory with Saints Rosa, Catherine of Siena, and Agnes of Montepulciano* on the first altar on the right. The third altar has a Tintoretto *Crucifixion.*

Fondamenta Zattere ai Gesuati. ℂ **041-275-0462.** www.chorus-ve.org. Admission 2€ ($2.30) adults, free for children under 5, or 8€ ($9) on cumulative ticket (see "For Church Fans," above). Mon–Sat 10am–5pm; Sun 1–5pm.

Squero di San Trovaso ★★ *(Finds)*   One of the most interesting (and photographed) sights you'll see in Venice is this small *squero* (boatyard), which first opened in the 17th century. Just north of the Zattere (the wide, sunny walkway that runs alongside the Giudecca Canal in Dorsoduro), the boatyard lies next to the Church of San Trovaso on the narrow Rio San Trovaso (not far from the Accademia Bridge). It is surrounded by Tyrolian-looking wooden structures (a true rarity in this city of stone built on water) that are home to the multigenerational owners and original workshops for traditional Venetian boats (see "The Art of the Gondola," below). Aware that they have become a tourist site themselves, the gondoliers don't mind if you watch them at work from across the narrow Rio di San Trovaso, but don't try to invite yourself in. It's the perfect midway photo op after a visit to the Gallerie dell'Accademia and a trip to the well-known gelateria, Da Nico (Zattere 922), whose chocolate *gianduiotto* is not to be missed.

Dorsoduro 1097 (on the Rio San Trovaso, southwest of the Accademia Gallery). No phone. Free admission.

San Sebastiano   Way out in the boondocks of Dorsoduro rises a 16th-century church for Paolo Veronese fans. Veronese, who lived nearby, scattered it with

---

The Art of the Gondola

Putting together one of the sleek black boats is a fascinatingly exact science that is still done in the revered traditional manner at boatyards such as the **Squero di San Trovaso** (see above). The boats have been painted black since a 16th-century sumptuary law—one of many passed by the local legislators as excess and extravagance spiraled out of control. Whether regarding boats or baubles, laws were passed to restrict the gaudy outlandishness that, at the time, was commonly used to outdo the Joneses.

Propelled by the strength of a single *gondoliere,* these boats, unique to Venice, have no modern equipment. They move with no great speed but with unrivaled grace. The right side of the gondola is lower because the *gondoliere* always stands in the back of the boat on the left. Although the San Trovaso *squero,* or boatyard, is the city's oldest and one of only three remaining (the other two are immeasurably more difficult to find), its predominant focus is on maintenance and repair. They will occasionally build a new gondola (which takes some 40–45 working days), carefully crafting it from the seven types of wood—mahogany, cherry, fir, walnut, oak, elm, and lime—necessary to give the shallow and asymmetrical boat its various characteristics. After all the pieces are put together, the painting, the *ferro* (the iron symbol of the city affixed to the bow), and the wood-carving that secures the oar are commissioned out to various local artisans.

Although some 10,000 of these elegant boats floated on the canals of Venice in the 16th century, today there are only 350. But the job of *gondoliere* remains a coveted profession, passed down from father to son over the centuries.

paintings from 1555 to 1570 and is buried in the majolica-floored chapel left of the high altar. The colorful Renaissance master provided the ceiling with paintings on the *Story of Esther,* the choir with a bevy of St. Sebastian–themed works, the organ with painted panels, the sacristy's ceiling with his earliest commissions, the nun's choir with St. Sebastian frescoes, and the third altar on the left with a *Madonna with Saints.* Titian makes a guest appearance with a late *St. Nicholas* (1563) on the first altar on the right.

Fondamenta di San Sebastiano. ℂ **041-275-0462.** 2€ ($2.30) or 8€ ($9) on cumulative ticket (see "For Church Fans," above). Mon–Sat 10am–5pm. *Vaporetto:* San Basilio.

IN SAN POLO & SANTA CROCE

Santa Maria Gloriosa dei Frari (Church of the Frari) ★★   Known simply as "i Frari," this immense 13th- to 14th-century Gothic church is easily found around the corner from the Scuola Grande di San Rocco—make sure you visit both when you're in this area. Built by the Franciscans (*frari* is a dialectal distortion of "frati," or brothers), it is the largest church in Venice after the Basilica of San Marco. The Frari has long been considered something of a memorial to the ancient glories of Venice. Since St. Francis and the order he founded emphasized prayer and poverty, it is not surprising that the church is austere both inside and out. Yet it houses a number of important works, including two Titian masterpieces. The more striking is his *Assumption of the Virgin* over the main altar, painted when the artist was only in his late 20s. His *Virgin of the Pesaro Family* is in the left nave; Titian's wife posed for the figure of Mary (and then died soon afterward in childbirth) for this work commissioned by one of Venice's most powerful families.

The church's other masterwork is Giovanni Bellini's important triptych on wood, the *Madonna and Child,* displayed in the sacristy (take the door on the right as you face the altar); it is one of his finest portraits of the Madonna. There is also an almost primitive-looking wood carving by Donatello of St. John the Baptist. The grandiose tombs of two famous Venetians are also here: Canova (d. 1822), the Italian sculptor who led the revival of classicism, and Titian, who died in 1576 during a deadly plague.

Free tours in English are sometimes offered by church volunteers during the high-season months; check at the church.

San Polo 3072 (on Campo dei Frari). ℂ **041-522-2637.** Admission 2€ ($2.30) or 8€ ($9) on cumulative ticket (see "For Church Fans," above). Mon–Sat 9am–6pm; Sun 1–6pm. *Vaporetto:* San Tomà (walk straight ahead on Calle del Traghetto, then turn right and left across Campo San Tomà; walk as straight ahead as you can, on Ramo Mandoler, then Calle Larga Prima, and turn right when you reach beginning of Salizzada San Rocco).

Ca' Pesaro   Tired of Venice's one-two punch of baroque and Byzantine? Check out the two museums housed in this late Renaissance palazzo on the Grand Canal. The first collection is the **Museo d'Arte Moderna (Museum of Modern Art),** largely closed in recent years for palace restoration and rearrangement, but the ground floor temporarily houses several works—most of them bought during Venice's own Biennale over the years—by the likes of Chagall, Kandinsky, Klimt, Miró, Henry Moore, Umberto Boccioni, Morandi, and Filippo De Pisis.

Up on the top level, also partially closed, is the **Museo d'Arte Orentale,** a collection of mostly Japanese artifacts, but also Chinese, Javanese, Siamese (Thai), Cambodian, and Indonesian pieces. There are rumors that this collection may eventually move to the Palazzo Marcello.

Santa Croce 2076 (Fondamenta Ca' Pesaro). ℂ **041-524-1173.** 5.50€ ($6), free for children under 12. Tues–Sun 10am–6pm. *Vaporetto:* S. Stae.

Another Cumulative Ticket

A cumulative ticket covers entrance to the **Ca' d'Oro** and the **Ca Pesaro** for 5.50€ ($6); add in the **Accademia** for 11€ ($13).

IN CANNAREGIO

Ca' d'Oro (Galleria Giorgio Franchetti) ★★   The 15th-century Ca' d'Oro is one of the best preserved and most impressive of the hundreds of patrician palazzi lining the Grand Canal. After the Palazzo Ducale, it's the city's finest example of Venetian Gothic architecture. A restoration of its delicate pink-and-white facade (its name, the Golden Palace, refers to the gilt-covered facade that faded long ago) was completed in 1995. Inside, the ornate beamed ceilings and palatial trappings provide an attention-grabbing backdrop for the private collection of former owner Baron Franchetti, who bequeathed his palazzo and artworks to the city during World War I.

The core collection, expanded over the years, now includes sculptures, furniture, 16th-century Flemish tapestries, an impressive collection of bronzes (12th–16th c.), and a gallery whose most important canvases are Andrea Mantegna's *San Sebastiano* and Titian's *Venus at the Mirror,* as well as lesser paintings by Tintoretto, Carpaccio, Van Dyck, Giorgione, and Jan Steen. For a delightful break, step out onto the palazzo's loggia, overlooking the Grand Canal, for a view up and down the waterway and across to the Pescheria, a timeless vignette of an unchanged city. Off the loggia is a small but worthy ceramics collection, open 10am to noon.

Cannaregio between 3931 and 3932 (on Calle Ca' d'Oro north of Rialto Bridge). ℰ 041-523-8790. Admission 5€ ($6), free for children under 12. Mon 8:15am–2pm; Tues–Sat 8:15am–7:15pm (winter hours may be shorter). *Vaporetto:* Ca' d'Oro.

Chiesa Santa Maria dei Miracoli   At a charming canal crossing hidden in a quiet corner of the residential section of Cannaregio northeast of the Rialto Bridge, the small 15th-century "Miracoli" is once again open to the public after a laborious 10-year renovation. It is one of the most attractive religious buildings in Europe, with one side of the precious polychrome-marbled facade running alongside a canal, creating colorful and shimmering reflections. The architect, Pietro Lombardo (a local artisan whose background in monuments and tombs is obvious) would go on to become one of the founding fathers of the Venetian Renaissance.

The less romantic are inclined to compare it to a large tomb with a dome, but the untold couples who have made this perfectly proportioned jewel-like church their choice for weddings will dispel such insensitivity. The small square in front is the perfect place for gondolas to drop off and pick up the newly betrothed. The inside is intricately decorated with early Renaissance marble reliefs, its pastel palette of pink, gray, and white marble making an appropriately elegant venue for all those weddings. In the 1470s an image of the Virgin Mary was responsible for a series of miracles (including bringing back to life someone who spent half an hour at the bottom of the Giudecca Canal) that led pilgrims to leave gifts and, eventually, enough donations to have this church built. Look for the icon now displayed over the main altar.

Cannaregio, Rio d. Miracoli. No phone. Admission 2€ ($2.30) or 8€ ($9) on cumulative ticket (see "For Church Fans" on p. 129). Mon–Sat 10am–5pm; Sun 3–5pm. *Vaporetto:* Rialto (located midway between the Rialto Bridge and the Campo SS. Giovanni e Paolo).

Il Ghetto (the Jewish Ghetto) ★★ Venice's relationship with its longtime Jewish community fluctuated over time from acceptance to borderline tolerance, attitudes often influenced by the fear that Jewish moneylenders and merchants would infiltrate other sectors of the republic's commerce under a government that thrived on secrecy and control. In 1516, 700 Jews were forced to move to this then-remote northwestern corner of Venice, to an abandoned site of a 14th-century foundry (*ghetto* is old Venetian dialect for "foundry," a word that would soon be used throughout Europe and the world to depict isolated minority groups).

As was commonplace with most of the hundreds of islands that make up Venice, this *ghetto* neighborhood was totally surrounded by water. Its two access points were controlled at night and early morning by heavy gates manned by Christian guards (paid for by the Jews), both protecting and segregating its inhabitants. Within one century, the community grew to more than 5,000, representing many languages and cultures. Although the original Ghetto Nuovo (New Ghetto) was expanded to include the Ghetto Vecchio (Old Ghetto; the names are confusing, but remember that "ghetto" meant foundry, so when the Jews moved into the area occupied by its ruins, it was rightly called the "old foundry," or *ghetto vecchio*), and later the Ghetto Nuovissimo (Newest Ghetto), land was limited and quarters always cramped. In 1797 when Napoléon rolled into town, the *ghetto* as an institution was disbanded and Jews were free to move elsewhere. Still, it remains the center of Venice's ever-diminishing community of Jewish families; although accounts vary widely, it's said that anywhere from 500 to 2,000 Jews live in all of Venice and Mestre.

Aside from its historic interest, this is also one of the less touristy neighborhoods in Venice (though it is becoming somewhat of a nightspot), and makes for a pleasant and scenic place to stroll.

Venice's first kosher restaurant, **Gam Gam,** recently opened on Fondamenta di Cannaregio 1122 (ⓒ **041-715-284**) near the entrance to the Jewish Ghetto and close to the Guglie *vaporetto* stop. Owned and run by Orthodox Jews from New York, it serves lunch and dinner Sunday through Friday, with an early Friday closing after lunch.

Cannaregio (Campo del Ghetto Nuovo). *Vaporetto:* Guglie or San Marcuola (from either of the 2 *vaporetto* stops, or if walking from the train station area, locate the Ponte delle Guglie; walking away from the Grand Canal along the Fondamenta di Cannaregio, look for a doorway on your right with Hebrew etched across the threshold; this is the entrance to the Calle del Ghetto Vecchio that leads to the Campo del Ghetto Nuovo).

Museo Communità Ebraica ★ The only way to visit any of the area's five 16th-century synagogues is through one of the Museo Communità Ebraica's frequent organized tours conducted in English. Your guide will elaborate on the commercial and political climate of those times, the unique "skyscraper" architecture (overcrowding resulted in many buildings having as many as seven low-ceilinged stories with no elevators), and the daily lifestyle of the Jewish community until the arrival of Napoléon in 1797, who declared the Jews free citizens. You'll get to visit historic temples dedicated to the rites of all three major Jewish groups who called Venice home: Italian (Scola Italiana), Sephardic (Scola Levantina), and Ashkenazi (Scola Canton).

Cannaregio 2902b (on Campo del Ghetto Nuovo). ⓒ **041-715-359**. Museum admission 3€ ($3.45) adults, 2€ ($2.30) children; museum and synagogue tour 8€ ($9) adults, 6.50€ ($7) children. Museum Apr–Sept Sun–Fri 10am–7pm, Oct–Mar Sun–Fri daily 10am–6pm; Synagogue tours hourly 10:30am–4:30pm (5pm Apr–Sept). Closed on Jewish holidays. *Vaporetto:* Guglie.

ON GIUDECCA & SAN GIORGIO

Chiesa di San Giorgio Maggiore ★★ *(Moments*   This church sits on the little island of San Giorgio Maggiore. It is one of the masterpieces of Andrea Palladio, the great Renaissance architect from nearby Vicenza. Most known for his country villas built for Venice's wealthy merchant families, Palladio was commissioned to build two churches (the other is the Redentore on the neighboring island of Giudecca), beginning with San Giorgio, designed in 1565 and completed in 1610. To impose a classical facade on the traditional church structure, Palladio designed two interlocking facades, with repeating triangles, rectangles, and columns that are carefully and harmoniously proportioned. Founded as early as the 10th century, the interior of the church was reinterpreted by Palladio with whitewashed surfaces, stark but majestic, and unadorned but harmonious space. The main altar is flanked by two epic paintings by an elderly Tintoretto, *The Fall of Manna* to the left and the more noteworthy *Last Supper* to the right, famous for its chiaroscuro. Through the doorway to the right of the choir leading to the Cappella dei Morti (Chapel of the Dead), you will find Tintoretto's *Deposition.*

To the left of the choir is an elevator that you can take to the top of the campanile, for a charge of 3€ ($3.45), to experience an unforgettable view of the island, the lagoon, and the Palazzo Ducale and Piazza San Marco across the way.

A handful of remaining Benedictine monks gather for Sunday Mass at 11am, sung in Gregorian chant.

On the island of San Giorgio Maggiore, across St. Mark's Basin from Piazzetta San Marco. ℂ 041-522-7827. Free admission. Mon–Sat 9:30am–12:30pm; daily 2–6pm. Transportation: Take the Giudecca-bound *vaporetto* (no. 82) on Riva degli Schiavoni and get off at the 1st stop, the island of San Giorgio Maggiore.

Il Redentore ★   Perhaps the masterpiece among Palladio's churches, Il Redentore was commissioned by Venice to give thanks for being delivered from the great plague (1575–77), which claimed over a quarter of the population (some 46,000 people). The doge established a tradition of visiting this church by crossing a long pontoon bridge made up of boats from the Dorsoduro's Zattere on the third Sunday of each July, a tradition that survived the demise of the doges and remains one of Venice's most popular festivals.

The interior is done in grand, austere, painstakingly classical Palladian style. The artworks tend to be workshop pieces (from the studios or schools, but not the actual brushes, of Tintoretto and Veronese), but there is a fine *Baptism of Christ* by Veronese himself in the sacristy, which also contains Alvise Vivarini's good *Adoration* and *Angels* alongside works by Jacopo da Bassano and Palma il Giovane, who also did the *Deposition* over the right aisle's third chapel. Recent renovations to the interior have now been completed, and the sacristy is to be next.

Campo del Redentore, La Giudecca. ℂ 041-523-1415. Admission 2€ ($2.30) or 8€ ($9) on cumulative ticket (see "For Church Fans," above). Mon–Sat 10am–5pm; Sun 1–5pm. *Vaporetto:* Redentore.

ESPECIALLY FOR KIDS

It goes without saying that a **gondola ride** will be the thrill of a lifetime for any child or adult. If that's too expensive, consider the convenient and far less expensive alternative: a **ride on the no. 1 *vaporetto.*** They offer two entirely different experiences: The gondola gives you the chance to see Venice through the back door (and ride past Marco Polo's house); the *vaporetto* provides a utilitarian—but no less gorgeous—journey down Venice's aquatic Main Street, the Grand Canal. Look for the ambulance boat, the garbage boat, the firefighters' boat, the funeral boat, even the Coca-Cola delivery boat. Best sightings are the special gondolas filled with flowers and rowed by *gondolieri* in livery delivering a happy bride and groom from the church.

Judging from the squeals of delight, **feeding the pigeons in Piazza San Marco** (purchase a bag of corn and you'll be draped in pigeons in a nanosecond; these birds have radar) could be the epitome of your child's visit to Venice, and it's the ultimate photo op. Be sure your child won't be startled by all the fluttering and flapping; when I was 11, my parents had me do it; all I remember is the scrabbly little feet of the pigeons.

A jaunt to the neighboring **island of Murano** can be as educational as it is recreational—follow the signs to any *fornace,* where a glassblowing performance of the island's thousand-year-old art is free entertainment. But be ready for the guaranteed sales pitch that follows.

Before you leave town, take the elevator to the **top of the Campanile di San Marco** (the highest structure in the city) for a pigeon's-eye view of Venice's rooftops and church cupolas, or get up close and personal to the four bronze horses on the facade of the Basilica San Marco. Its **outdoor loggia** with a view holds the copies of the famous *quadriga* (you can see the real ones in the Basilica's Museo Marciano), but the view from here is something you and your children won't forget.

Some children enjoy the **Museo Navale & Arsenale,** with its ship models and old vessels, and the many historic artifacts in the **Museo Civico Correr (Correr Civic Museum),** tangible vestiges of a time when Venice was a world unto itself.

The **winged lion,** said to have been a kind of good-luck mascot to St. Mark, patron saint of Venice, was the very symbol of the Serene Republic and to this day appears on everything from cafe napkins to T-shirts. Who can spot the most flying lions? They appear on facades, atop columns, over doorways, as pavement mosaics, government stamps, and on the local flag.

6 Organized Tours

Most of the central travel agencies will have posters in their windows advertising half- and full-day walking tours of the city's sights. Most of these tours are piggybacked onto those organized by American Express (see "Fast Facts: Venice," earlier in this chapter for the contact information for American Express) and should cost the same: about 21€ ($24) for a 2-hour tour and 34€ ($39) for a full day, per person.

Organized 3- to 4-hour visits to "The Islands of the Venetian Lagoon" include brief stops on Murano, Burano, and Torcello. See "Exploring Venice's Islands," later in this chapter.

7 Festivals & Special Events

Venice's most special event is the yearly pre-Lenten **Carnevale** ★★★ (© 041-241-0570; www.venice-carnival.com), a 2-week theatrical resuscitation of the 18th-century bacchanalia that drew tourists during the final heyday of the Serene Republic. Most of today's Carnevale-related events, masked balls, and costumes evoke that time. Many of the concerts around town are free, when baroque to samba to gospel to Dixieland jazz music fills the piazze and byways; check with the tourist office for a list of events.

The masked balls are often private; those where (exorbitantly priced) tickets are available are sumptuous, with candlelit banquets calling for extravagant costumes you can rent by the day from special shops. If you can score tickets, splurge 260€

($299) per person on the **Ballo del Doge,** or **Doge's Ball** (© 041-523-3851; www.ballodeldoge.com). They throw a real jet-set party (accessible to all) in the 16th-century Palazzo Pisani-Moretta on the Grand Canal (between the Rialto and the Foscari), sumptuously outfitted with Tiepolo frescoes and all the other accouterments of 18th-century Venetian style. Different ballrooms feature minuets, waltzes, baroque chamber orchestras—there's even a modern disco (acoustically self-contained)—all catered by posh Do Forni restaurant. Those not invited to any ball will be just as happy having their face painted and watching the ongoing street theater from a ringside cafe. There's a **daily market of Carnival masks and costumes** on Campo Santo Stefano (10am–10pm).

Carnevale builds for 10 days until the big blowout, **Shrove Tuesday** (Fat Tuesday or Mardi Gras), when fireworks illuminate the Grand Canal, and Piazza San Marco is turned into a giant open-air ballroom for the masses. Book your hotel months ahead, especially for the 2 weekends prior to Shrove Tuesday. See "Carnevale à Venezia," below, for more info.

The **Voga Longa** ✿ (literally "long row"), a 30km (19-mile) rowing "race" from San Marco to Burano and back again, has been enthusiastically embraced since its inception in 1975, following the city's effort to keep alive the centuries-old heritage of the regatta. It takes place on a Sunday in mid-May; for exact dates, consult the tourist office. It's a colorful event and a great excuse to party, plus every local seems to have a relative or next-door neighbor competing.

Stupendous fireworks light the night sky during the **Festa del Redentore** ✿, on the third Saturday and Sunday in July. This celebration marking the July 1576 lifting of a plague that had gripped the city is centered around the Palladio-designed Chiesa del Redentore (Church of the Redeemer) on the island of Giudecca. A bridge of boats across the Giudecca Canal links the church with the banks of Le Zattere in Dorsoduro, and hundreds of boats of all shapes and sizes fill the Giudecca. It's one big floating *festa* until night descends and an awesome half-hour *spettacolo* of fireworks fills the sky.

The **Venice International Film Festival** ✿✿✿, in late August and early September, is the most respected celebration of celluloid in Europe after Cannes. Films from all over the world are shown in the Palazzo del Cinema on the Lido as well as at various venues—and occasionally in some of the *campi.* Ticket prices vary, but those for the less sought-after films are usually modest. Check with the tourist office for listings.

Venice hosts the latest in modern and contemporary painting and sculpture from dozens of countries during the prestigious **Biennale d'Arte** ✿✿✿ (© 041-521-8846 or 041-271-9005; www.labiennale.org), one of the world's top international modern-art shows. It fills the pavilions of the public gardens at the east end of Castello and in the Arsenale from late May to October every odd-numbered year. Many great modern artists have been discovered at this world-famous show. In the past, awards have gone to Jackson Pollock, Henri Matisse, Alexander Calder, and Federico Fellini, among others. Tickets (10€/$12) can be reserved online or by calling © 199-199-100 in Italy.

The **Regata Storica** ✿✿ that takes place on the Grand Canal on the first Sunday in September is an extravagant seagoing parade in historic costume as well as a genuine regatta. Just about every seaworthy gondola, richly decorated for the occasion and piloted by *gondolieri* in colorful livery, participates in the opening cavalcade. The aquatic parade is followed by three regattas proceeding along the Grand Canal. You can buy grandstand tickets through the tourist office or

Carnevale à Venezia

Venetians once more are taking to the open piazzas and streets for the pre-Lenten holiday of Carnevale. The festival traditionally was the unbridled celebration that preceded Lent, the period of penitence and abstinence prior to Easter, and its name is derived from the Latin *carnem levare*, meaning "to take meat away."

Today Carnevale lasts no more than 5 to 10 days and culminates in the Friday to Tuesday before Ash Wednesday. In the 18th-century heyday of Carnevale in La Serenissima Republic, well-heeled revelers came from all over Europe to take part in festivities that began months prior to Lent and crescendoed until their raucous culmination at midnight on Shrove Tuesday. As the Venetian economy declined, and its colonies and trading posts fell to other powers, the Republic of Venice in its swan song turned to fantasy and escapism. The faster its decline, the longer, and more licentious, became its anything-goes merrymaking. Masks became ubiquitous, affording anonymity and the pardoning of a thousand sins. Masks permitted the fishmonger to attend the ball and dance with the baroness, the properly married to carry on as if they were not. The doges condemned it and the popes denounced it, but nothing could dampen the Venetian Carnevale spirit until Napoléon arrived in 1797 and put an end to the festivities.

Resuscitated in 1980 by local tourism powers to fill the empty winter months when tourism comes to a screeching halt, Carnevale is calmer nowadays, though just barely. The born-again festival got off to a shaky start, met at first with indifference and skepticism, but in the years since has grown in popularity and been embraced by the locals. In the 1980s Carnevale attracted an onslaught of what was seemingly the entire student population of Europe, backpacking young people who slept in the piazzas and train station. Politicians and city officials adopted a middle-of-the-road policy that helped establish Carnevale's image as neither a backpacker's free-for-all outdoor party nor a continuation of the exclusive private balls in the Grand Canal palazzi available to a very few.

Carnevale has returned to its dazzling best, a harlequin patchwork of musical and cultural events, many of them free of charge, that appeal to

come early and find a piece of embankment near the Rialto Bridge for the best seats in town.

Other notable events include **Festa della Salute** ✪ on November 21, when a pontoon bridge is erected across the Grand Canal to connect the churches of La Salute and Santa Maria del Giglio, commemorating delivery from another plague in 1630 that wiped out a third of the lagoon's population; it is the only day the Salute Church opens its massive front doors (a secondary entrance is otherwise used). The Festa della Sensa, on the Sunday following Ascension Day in May, reenacts the ancient ceremony when the doge would wed Venice to the sea. April 25 is a local holiday, the **feast day of Saint Mark,** beloved patron saint of Venice and of the ancient republic. A special High Mass is celebrated in the Basilica of San Marco, and Venetians exchange roses with those they love.

all ages, tastes, nationalities, and budgets. At any given moment, musical events are staged in any of the city's dozens of piazzas—from reggae and zydeco to jazz to baroque and chamber music. Special art exhibits are mounted at numerous museums and galleries. The recent involvement of international corporate commercial sponsors has met with a mixed reception, although it seems to be the direction of the future.

Carnevale is not for those who dislike crowds. Indeed, the crowds are what it's all about. All of Venice becomes a stage, and all its men and women players. Whether you spend months creating an extravagant costume, or grab one from the countless stands set up about the town, Carnevale is about giving in to the spontaneity of magic and surprise around every corner, the mystery behind every mask. Masks and costumes are everywhere, though you won't see anything along the lines of Teletubbies or Zorro. Emphasis is on the historical, for Venice's Carnevale is the chance to relive the glory days of the 1700s when Venetian life was at its most extravagant. Groups travel in coordinated getups that range from a contemporary passel of Felliniesque clowns to the court of the Sun King in all its wigged-out, over-the-top, drag-queen glory. There are the three musketeers riding the *vaporetto;* your waiter appears dressed as a nun; sitting alone on the church steps is a Romeo waiting for his Juliet; late at night crossing a small, deserted *campo,* a young, laughing couple appear out of a gray mist in a cloud of crinoline and sparkles, and then disappear down a small alley. The places to be seen in costume (only appropriate costumes need apply) are the historical cafes lining the Piazza San Marco, the **Florian** being the unquestioned command post. Don't expect to be seated in full view at a window seat unless your costume is straight off the stage of the local opera house.

The city is the quintessential set, the perfect venue; Hollywood could not create a more evocative location. This is a celebration about history, art, theater, and drama, as one would expect to find in Italy, the land that gave us the Renaissance and Zeffirelli—and Venice, an ancient and wealthy republic that gave us Casanova and Vivaldi. Venice and Carnevale were made for each other.

Finally, the ultimate anomaly: Venice's annual **October Maratona (Marathon),** starting at Villa Pisani on the mainland and ending up along the Zattere for a finish at the Basilica di Santa Maria della Salute on the tip of Dorsoduro. It's usually held the last Sunday of October.

8 Shopping

A mix of low-end trinket stores and middle-market–to-upscale boutiques line the narrow zigzagging **Mercerie** running north between Piazza San Marco and the Rialto Bridge. More expensive clothing and gift boutiques make for great window-shopping on **Calle Larga XXII Marzo,** the wide street that begins west of Piazza San Marco and wends its way to the expansive Campo Santo Stefano near the

> **Tips** **Venice Shopping Strategies**
>
> There are two rules of thumb for shopping in Venice: If you have the good fortune of continuing on to Florence or Rome, shop for clothing, leather goods, and accessories with prudence in Venice, because most items are more expensive here. If, however, you happen on something that strikes you, consider it twice on the spot (not back at your hotel), then buy it. In this web of alleys you may never find that shop again.

Accademia. The narrow **Frezzeria,** also west of the piazza and not far from Piazza San Marco, offers a grab bag of bars, souvenir shops, and tony clothing stores.

In a city that for centuries has thrived almost exclusively on tourism, remember this: **Where you buy cheap, you get cheap.** There are few bargains to be had, and there's nothing to compare with Florence's outdoor San Lorenzo Market; the nonproduce part of the Rialto Market is as good as it gets, where you'll find cheap T-shirts, glow-in-the-dark plastic gondolas, and tawdry glass trinkets. Venetians, centuries-old merchants, aren't known for bargaining. You'll stand a better chance of getting a bargain if you pay in cash or buy more than one.

Venice is uniquely famous for several local crafts that have been produced here for centuries and are hard to get elsewhere: the **glassware** from the island of Murano, the **delicate lace** from Burano, and the *cartapesta* (**papier-mâché**) **Carnevale masks** you'll find in endless *botteghe,* where you can watch artisans paint amid their wares.

Now here's the bad news: There's such an overwhelming sea of cheap glass gewgaws that buying Venetian glass can become something of a turn-off (shipping and insurance costs make most things unaffordable; the alternative is to hand-carry anything fragile). There are so few women left on Burano willing to spend countless tedious hours keeping alive the art of lace making that the few pieces you'll see not produced by machine in Hong Kong are sold at stratospheric prices; ditto the truly high-quality glass (though trinkets can be cheap and fun). Still, exceptions are to be found in all of the above, and when you find them you'll know. A discerning eye can cut through the dreck to find some lovely mementos.

ANTIQUES

The interesting **Mercatino dell'Antiquariato (Antiques Fair)** takes place three times annually in the charming Campo San Maurizio between Piazza San Marco and Campo Santo Stefano. Dates change yearly for the 3-day weekend market but generally fall the first weekend of April, mid-September, and the weekend before Christmas. More than 100 vendors sell everything from the sublime piece of Murano glass to quirky dust-collectors. Early birds might find reasonably priced finds such as Murano candy dishes from the 1950s, Venetian-pearl glass beads older still, vintage Italian posters advertising Campari-sponsored regattas, or antique postcards of Venice that could be from the 1930s or the 1830s—things change so little here. Those for whom price is less an issue might pick up antique lace by the yard, or a singular museum-quality piece of handblown glass from a local master.

BOOKS

Libreria Studium, San Marco 337 (© **041-522-2382**), carries lots of travel guides and maps as well as books in English. Another good choice is **Libreria al**

Ponte, Calle della Mandola, 3717D (© **041-522-4030**), which stocks travel guides and English-language books. Two other centrally located bookstores that carry a line of softcover and hardcover books in English are the **Libreria Sansovino** in the Bacino Orseolo 84, immediately north of the Piazza San Marco (© **041-522-2623**), and the **Libreria San Giorgio,** Calle Larga XXII Marzo 2087 (© **041-523-8451**), beyond the American Express Office toward Campo Santo Stefano. Both carry a selection of books about Venetian art, history, and literature.

For art books and other colorful hardbacks on history and Italian sights to hold down your coffee table at 40% to 50% off, head to **Libreria Bertoni Mario,** San Marco 3637B (Rio Terra dei Assassini; © **041-522-9583**), or **Libreria Beronti Alberto,** San Marco 4718 (Calle dei Fabbri; © **041-522-4615**).

CRAFTS

The **Murano Art Shop,** at San Marco 1232 (on the store-lined Frezzeria, parallel to the western border of, and close to, the Piazza San Marco; © **041-523-3851**), is a cultural experience. At this small, precious shop, every inch of wall space is draped with the whimsical crafts of the city's most creative artisans. Fusing the timeless with the contemporary—with a nod to the magic and romance of Venice past—the store offers a dramatic and ever-evolving collection of masks, puppets, music boxes, marionettes, costume jewelry, and the like. It's all expensive, but this rivals a visit to the Doge's Palace.

When it seems as if every gift-store window is awash with collectible bisque-faced dolls in elaborate pinafores and headdresses, head to **Bambole di Trilly** at Castello 4974 (Fondamenta dell'Osmarin, off the Campo San Provolo on your way east out of Piazza San Marco in the direction of the Church of San Zaccaria; © **041-521-2579;** www.trillyvenice.com), where the hand-sewn wardrobes of rich Venetian fabrics and painstakingly painted faces are particularly exquisite. The perfect souvenir starts at 20€ ($23) in this well-stocked workspace north of Campo San Zaccaria.

FOODSTUFFS

Food lovers will find charmingly packaged food products for themselves or friends at the well-known pasta manufacturer **Giacomo Rizzo** near the major Coin department store (but on the opposite side of the narrow street), northeast of the Rialto Bridge at Cannaregio 5778 at Calle San Giovanni Grisostomo (© **041-522-2824**). You'll find pasta made in the shape of gondolas, colorful carnival hats, and dozens of other imaginatively shaped possibilities (colored and flavored with squash, beet, and spinach).

Those with a sweet tooth should head in the opposite direction, to Giancarlo Vio's **Pasticceria Marchini,** just before Campo Santo Stefano (San Marco 2769 at Ponte San Maurizio; © **041-522-9109**), where the selection of traditional cookies are beautifully prepackaged for traveling—delicate *baicoli,* cornmeal raisin *zaleti,* and the S-shaped *buranelli.*

GLASS

If you're going to go all out, look no further than **Venini,** Piazzetta dei Leoni 314 (© **041-522-4045**), since 1921 one of the most respected and innovative glass-makers in all of Venice. Their products are really more works of art than merely blown glass. So renowned are they for their quality, Versace's own line of glass *objets d'art* are done by Venini. Their **workshop** on Murano is at Fondamenta Vetrai 50 (© **041-273-7211**). Cheap they are not, but no one else has such a lovely or original representation of handblown Murano glassware.

You should also visit the spacious emporium of quality glass items at **Marco Polo** (San Marco 1644; ✆ **041-522-9295**) just west of the Piazza San Marco. The front half of the first floor offers a variety of small gift ideas (candy dishes, glass-topped medicine boxes, paperweights).

Glass beads are called "Venetian pearls," and an abundance of exquisite antique and reproduced baubles are the draw at **Anticlea,** at Castello 4719 (on the Campo San Provolo in the direction of the Church of San Zaccaria; ✆ **041-528-6946**). Once used for trading in Venice's far-flung colonies, they now fill the coffers of this small shop east of Piazza San Marco, sold singly or already strung. The open-air stall of **Susie and Andrea** (Riva degli Schiavoni, near Pensione Wildner; just ask) has handcrafted beads that are new, well made and strung, and moderately priced. The stall operates from February through November.

JEWELRY

Chimento, San Marco 1460 (Campo S. Moisè; ✆ **041-523-6010;** www. chimento.it), carries gold and silver jewelry of their own manufacture as well as items from top international designers, including Faberge.

Tiny **Antichità Zaggia,** Dorsoduro 1195 (Calle della Toletta; ✆ **041-522-3159**), specializes in genuine antique jewelry (and glassware) of the highest quality and beautiful designs.

The jewelers at **Esperienze,** Cannaregio 326B (Ponte delle Guglie; ✆ **041-721-866**), marry their own art with the local glassblowing traditions to create unique pins, necklaces, and other jewelry.

LEATHER & SHOES

One usually thinks of Florence when thinking of Italian leather goods. But the plethora of mediocre-to-refined shoe stores in Venice is testimony to the tradition of small shoe factories along the nearby Brenta canal that supply most of Italy and much of the world with made-in-Italy footwear. Venice has plenty of fine shoe stores—including **Bruno Magli,** San Marco 1302 (Calle dell'Ascensione; ✆ **041-522-7210**), and **Mori e Bozzi,** Cannaregio 2367 (Rio Terrà della Madonna; ✆ **041-715-261**)—but one store deserves singling out for sheer oddness. Even if you're not in the market for shoes, stop by **Rolando Segalin,** San Marco 4365 (Calle dei Fuseri; ✆ **041-522-2115**), for fantastical footwear in an acid-trip of colors and shapes, including curly-toed creations; many are intended for Carnevale costumes.

If you're not going on to Florence and are in the market for a handbag or small leather goods, the two-storied **Marforio shop** very near the Rialto Bridge (on the Merceria 2 Aprile 5033; ✆ **041-25-734**) stocks small leather goods and accessories on the street level, and bags according to color and style (evening, casual, shoulder-strapped, backpack style) on the floors above. It's not a good place just to browse, but it's a great spot if you know what you're looking for. There are some designer labels, but less expensive lines are abundant and the selection is probably the largest in Venice.

LINENS & LACE

A doge's ransom will buy you an elaborately worked tablecloth at **Jesurum,** at Cannaregio 3219 (✆ **041-524-2540**), with another shop at Piazza San Marco 60–61 (✆ **041-520-6177;** www.jesurum.it), but some of the small items make gorgeous, affordable gifts for discerning friends for under 10€ ($11): small drawstring pouches for your baubles, hand-embroidered linen cocktail napkins in different colors, or hand-finished lace doilies and linen coasters.

Frette, San Marco 2070A (Calle Larga/Via XXII Marzo; ✆ **041-522-4914;** www.frette.com), is another long-respected place to head for classy linens, bedclothes, and silk jammies. They'll even do custom work for you.

For hand-tatted lace from the only school still teaching it in Venice, ride out to Burano to visit the **Scuola dei Merletti,** Piazza B. Galuppi (✆ **041-730-034**), founded in 1872, closed in 1972, and reopened in 1981.

MASKS

A shortage of mask *bottegas* in Venice is not your problem; the challenge is ferreting out the few exceptionally talented artists producing one-of-a-kind theatrical pieces.

Only the quality-conscious should shop at **La Bottega dei Mascareri** (San Polo 80—at the northern end of the Rialto Bridge amid the tourist booths; ✆ **041-522-3857**), where the charming Boldrin brothers' least elaborate masks begin under 20€ ($23). Anyone who thinks a mask is a mask is a mask should come here first for a look-see.

Not only does **Il Canovaccio,** Castello 5369–70 (Calle delle Bande; ✆ **041-521-0393**), produce high-quality artisan work, but it's undeniably cool. Rolling Stone guitarist Ron Wood has shopped here, and the shop provided the masks and costumes for the orgy scene in Stanley Kubrick's *Eyes Wide Shut.*

MUSIC

If you attended any of the many marvelous concerts in Venice's churches and *scuole,* you'll want to bring some of the musical magic home with you. **Nalesso** (San Marco 2765, on your left just before Campo Santo Stefano if you're arriving from the Piazza San Marco area; ✆ **041-520-3329**) specializes in classical-music recordings, particularly the entire works of Vivaldi and 18th-century Venetian music, and carries the widest selection in town. You can also pick up tickets here to most of the concerts around town.

PAPER PRODUCTS

Biblos, with shops in San Marco at 739 (Mercerie S. Zulian), 2087 (Via XXII Marzo), and 221 (Mercerie de l'Orolorgio; ✆ **041-521-0714** or 041-521-908; www.veneziart.com/biblos.htm), carries leather-bound blank books and journals, marbleized paper, enameled pill boxes, watercolor etchings, and fountain pens.

If you're a real fan of marbleizing, the tiny workshop of **Ebrû di Federica Novello,** San Marco 1920 (Calle della Fenince; ✆ **041-528-6302**), applies the technique to silk ties and scarves as well as paper.

WINE

For a broad selection of wines from the Veneto and across Italy at truly decent prices, head to **Bottiglieria Colonna,** Castello 5595 (Calle della Fava; ✆ **041-528-5137**), which will put together gift packets of wines in packs of six, and also handles liqueurs from around the world. There's a more down-to-earth cantina called **Nave de Oro,** Cannaregio 4657 (Rio Terrà dei SS. Apostoli; ✆ **041-522-7872**), where locals bring empty bottles to have them filled with a variety of Veneto table wines at low, low prices—around 2€ ($2.30) per liter.

9 Venice After Dark

Visit one of the tourist information centers for current English-language schedules of the month's special events. The monthly *Ospite di Venezia* is distributed free or online at **www.unospitedivenezia.it,** and is extremely helpful but usually available only in the more expensive hotels. If you're looking for serious nocturnal action, you're in the wrong town. Your best bet is to sit in the moonlit Piazza San Marco and listen to the cafes' outdoor orchestras, with the illuminated basilica before you—the perfect opera set.

THE PERFORMING ARTS

Venice has a long and rich tradition of classical music, and there's always a concert going on somewhere. Several churches regularly host classical-music concerts (with an emphasis on the baroque) by local and international artists. This was, after all, the home of Vivaldi, and the **Chiesa di Vivaldi** 🌟🌟 (officially the Chiesa Santa Maria della Pietà) is the most popular venue for the music of Vivaldi and his contemporaries. A number of other churches and confraternities (such as San Stefano, San Stae, the Scuola di San Giovanni Evangelista, and the Scuola di San Rocco) also host concerts, but the Vivaldi Church, where the red priest was the choral director, offers perhaps the highest quality ensembles (with tickets slightly more expensive). If you're lucky, they'll be performing *Le Quattro Staggioni (The Four Seasons)*. Tickets are sold at the church's box office (℗ **041-917-257** or 041-522-6405; www.vivaldi.it) on Riva degli Schiavoni, at the front desk of the Metropole Hotel next door, or at many of the hotels around town; they're usually 25€ ($29) for adults and 15€ ($17) for students. Information and schedules are available from the tourist office; tickets for most concerts should be bought in advance, though the frequency of concerts means that they rarely sell out.

The city stood still in shock as the famous **Teatro La Fenice** 🌟🌟🌟 (San Marco 1965, on Campo San Fantin; ℗ **041-786-562;** www.teatrolafenice.it), went up in flames in January 1996. For centuries it was Venice's principal stage for world-class opera, music, theater, and ballet. Carpenters and artisans were on standby to begin working around the clock to re-create the *teatro* (built in 1836) according to archival designs; however, for years little progress was made due to political factions' bickering. Finally, on December 14, 2003, La Fenice (which means "the Phoenix") arose from the ashes as Ricardo Muti conducted the Orchestra and Chorus of La Fenice in an inaugural concert in a completely renovated hall. Then, after a few other performances, on December 21, it closed its doors again! Work is not really quite finished yet, and most performances—orchestral, choral, and operatic—will continue to take place in a substitute venue: a year-round tent-like structure called the **PalaFenice** (℗ **041-521-0161**) in the unlikely area of the Tronchetto parking facilities near Piazzale Roma, convenient to many *vaporetto* lines. To say it ain't the same is something of an understatement. La Fenice itself will return to the limelight in November 2004 with a performance of *La Traviata*. In the meantime, decent tickets for the PalaFenice start at about 20€ ($23); at 10€ ($12) for those "partially obstructed view" seats), and the box office is open Monday to Friday from 9am to 6pm.

CAFES

Venice is a quiet town in the evening and offers very little in the way of nightlife. For tourists and locals alike, Venetian nightlife mainly centers around the many cafe/bars in one of the world's most remarkable piazzas: Piazza San Marco; even Napoléon called it the most beautiful drawing room of the world. It is also the most expensive and touristed place to linger over a Campari or cappuccino, but a splurge that should not be dismissed too readily.

The nostalgic 18th-century **Caffè Florian** 🌟🌟 (San Marco 56A–59A; ℗ **041-520-5641**) on the south side of the piazza, is the most famous (closed Wed in winter) and most theatrical inside; have a Bellini (*prosecco* and fresh peach nectar) at the back bar for half what you'd pay at an indoor table; alfresco seating is even more expensive when the band plays on, but it's worth every cent for the million-dollar scenario. It's said that when Casanova escaped from the prisons in the Doge's Palace, he stopped here for a coffee before fleeing Venice.

On the opposite side of the square at San Marco 133–134 is the old-world **Caffè Lavena** (© 041-522-4070; closed Tues in winter) and at no. 120 is **cafe Quadri** ⚝ (© 041-522-2105; www.quadrivenice.com; closed Mon in winter), the first to introduce coffee to Venice, with a restaurant upstairs that sports Piazza San Marco views. See p. 111 for more on cafe Quadri. At all spots, a cappuccino, tea, or Coca-Cola at a table will set you back about 5€ ($6). But no one will rush you, and if the sun is warm and the orchestras are playing, I can think of no more beautiful public open-air salon in the world. Around the corner (no. 11) and in front of the pink-and-white marble Palazzo Ducale with the lagoon on your right is the best deal, **Caffè Chioggia** ⚝⚝⚝ (© 041-528-5011; closed Sun). Come here at midnight and watch the Moors strike the hour atop the Clock Tower from your outside table, while the quartet or pianist plays everything from quality jazz to pop until the wee hours (and without taking a break every 6 min.; they also take requests).

If the weather is chilly or inclement, or for no other reason than to revel in the history and drama of Venice's grand-dame hotel, dress up, look confident, and stroll into the landmark lobby of the Danieli hotel and **Bar Dandolo** (© 041-522-6480; Castello 4196 on Riva degli Schiavoni, east of Piazza San Marco). Tea or coffee will only set you back 5€ ($6) and you can sit forever, taking in what once was the former residential palazzo of a 15th-century doge. A pianist plays from 7 to 9pm and from 10pm to 12:30am. Drinks are far more expensive; ask to see the price list before ordering.

CLUBS, BIRRERIE & GELATERIE

Although Venice boasts an old and prominent university, clubs and discos barely enjoy their 15 minutes of popularity before changing hands or closing down (some are only open in the summer months). Young Venetians tend to go to the Lido or mainland Mestre.

For just plain hanging out in the late afternoon and early evening, popular squares that serve as meeting points include **Campo San Bartolomeo,** at the foot of the Rialto Bridge, and nearby **Campo San Luca;** you'll see Venetians of all ages milling about engaged in animated conversation, particularly from 5pm till dinnertime. In late-night hours, for low prices and a low level of pretension, I'm fond of the **Campo Santa Margherita,** a huge open *campo* about halfway between the train station and Ca' Rezzonico. Look for the popular **Green Pub** (no. 3053; closed Thurs), **Bareto Rosso** (no. 2963; closed Sun) and **Bar Salus** (no. 3112). **Campo Santo Stefano** is also worth a visit, namely to sit and sample the goods at the **Bar/Gelateria Paolin** (no. 2962; closed Fri), one of the city's best ice-cream sources. Its runner-up, **Gelateria Nico,** is on the Zattere in Dorsoduro 922, south of the Gallerie dell'Accademia. For occasional evenings of live music, cabaret, or just a relaxed late-night hangout for a drink and a bite, consider the ever popular **Le Bistrot de Venise** (p. 112).

Note: Most bars are open Monday to Saturday from 8pm to midnight.

The **Devil's Forest Pub** ⚝, San Marco 5185, on Calle Stagneri (© 041-520-0623; *vaporetto:* San Marco), offers the outsider an authentic chance to take in the convivial atmosphere and find out where Venetians do hang out. It's popular for lunch with the neighborhood merchants and shop owners and ideal for relaxed socializing over a beer and a host of games like backgammon, chess, and Trivial Pursuit. A variety of simple pasta dishes and fresh sandwiches run from 3€ to 6€ ($3.45–$7). It's open daily 10am to 1am.

Bácaro Jazz ★★ (✆ **041-285-249;** *vaporetto:* Rialto) is a happening cocktail bar (the Bellinis are great) with restaurant seating in the back (tasty Venetian cuisine from 6.50€/$7) across from the Rialto post office at San Marco 5546, just north of Campo San Bartolomeo (the San Marco side of Rialto Bridge). It's a mix of jazzy music (a bit too loud), rough plank walls, industrial-steel tables, and a corrugated aluminum ceiling. It's open Thursday to Tuesday 11am to 2am (happy hour 2–7:30pm).

With a half-dozen beers on tap, **El Moro Pub** ★, at Castello 4531 (Calle delle Rasse; ✆ **041-528-2573**), is the biggest draw in town. The crowd can be a bit older here, where post-university types congregate at the bar. TVs sometimes transmit national soccer or tennis matches, and the management welcomes those who linger, but sensitive nonsmokers won't want to.

Good food at reasonable prices would be enough to regularly pack **Paradiso Perduto** ★★, Cannaregio 2540, on Fondamenta della Misericordia (✆ **041-720-581;** *vaporetto:* Ferrovie), but its biggest draw is the live jazz performed on a small stage several nights a week. Popular with Americans and other foreigners living in Venice, this bar was once largely devoid of tourists, primarily because of its hard-to-find location, but lately it looks as if the word is out. The good selection of well-prepared pizzas and pastas goes for under 8€ ($9); arrive early for a table. It's open Thursday to Tuesday 7pm to 1 and sometimes 2am.

The party spills well out from the plate-glass windows of **Torino@Notte,** San Marco 459 (Campo San Luca; ✆ **041-522-3914**), a bar that has brought this square to life after dark with live jazz many nights, unusual beer from Lapland, and good panini. It's open Tuesday to Sunday 10pm to 2am.

In 1932 famed restaurateur and hotelier Giuseppe Cipriani opened **Harry's Bar** ★★ right at the San Marco–Vallaresso Vaporetto stop, San Marco 1323 (Calle Vallaresso; ✆ **041-528-5777**). Named for his son Arrigo (Italian for Harry), it has been a preferred, if overpriced, retreat for everyone from Hemingway—when he didn't want a Bloody Mary, he mixed his own drink: 15 parts gin, 1 martini—to Woody Allen. Regulars prefer the close and elegant front room to the upstairs dining room (decent cooking, and they invented *carpaccio,* a dish of thinly sliced raw beef now served throughout Italy). Harry's is most famous for inventing the Bellini, a mix of champagne and peach juice. Prices—for both drinks and the fancy cuisine—are rather extravagant.

DANCE CLUBS

Venice is a quiet town at night and offers little in the line of dance clubs. Evenings are best spent lingering over a late dinner, having a pint in a *birrerie,* or nursing a glass of *prosecco* in one of Piazza San Marco's tony outdoor cafes. Dance clubs barely enjoy their 15 minutes of popularity before changing hands or closing; some of those that have survived are open only in summer.

University-age Venetians tend to frequent the Lido or mainland Mestre, but if you really need that disco fix, you're best off at **Piccolo Mondo** ★, Dorsoduro 1056, near the Accademia (✆ **041-520-0371;** *vaporetto:* Accademia). Billed as a disco/pub, it serves sandwiches during lunch to the sounds of America's latest dance music and offers a happy hour in the late afternoon in winter, and often features live music. But the only reason you'd want to come is if you want a disco night (summer only); the club is frequented mostly by curious foreigners and the young to not-so-young Venetians who seek them out. It's open daily from 10pm to 4am in summer, and 10am to 4pm and 5 to 8pm in winter.

Another dance club that seems to be surviving is **Casanova** (✆ **041-275-0199** or 041-534-7479), near the train station on Lista di Spoagna 158a. The bar and restaurant open at 6pm, but at 10pm the bar becomes a disco open until 4am (the restaurant stays open until around midnight). Admission is often free (if you arrive before midnight), though sometimes there's a 5€ ($6) or higher cover that includes the first drink. Wednesday is salsa night; Thursday is rock, pop, alternative, and indie; Friday is dance music; and Saturday brings in house and progressive DJ music.

THE CASINO

From May to October, **Casino Municipale di Venezia,** located at Palazzo Vendramin Calergi, Cannaregio 2040 (Fondamenta Vendramin; *vaporetto:* Marcuola; ✆ **041-529-7111;** www.casino-venezia.com), moves to its nondescript summer location on the Lido, where a visit is not as strongly recommended as during the winter months when it is housed in this handsome 15th-century palazzo on the Grand Canal. Venice's tradition of gambling goes back to the glory days of the republic and lives on in this august Renaissance palace built by Mauro Codussi. Though not of the caliber of Monte Carlo, and on a midweek winter's night, occasionally slow, this is one of only four casinos on Italian territory—and what a remarkable stage setting it is! Richard Wagner lived and died in a wing of this palazzo in 1883.

Check with your hotel before setting forth; some offer free passes for their guests. Otherwise, if you're not a gambler or a curiosity seeker, it may not be worth the admission cost of 5€ ($6) to get in. *Tip:* If you pay a higher 10€ ($11) admission fee, the casino will provide you with a 10€ ($15) credit for gambling, so your admission could actually be free—and perhaps, if you're lucky, better than free. *Note:* A passport and jacket are required for entrance, and the casino is open daily from 3pm (11am for the slots) to 3am.

10 Exploring Venice's Islands

Venice shares its lagoon with three other principal islands: Murano, Burano, and Torcello. Guided tours of the three are operated by a dozen agencies with docks on Riva degli Schiavoni/Piazzetta San Marco (all interchangeable). The 3- and 4-hour tours run 13€ to 21€ ($15–$24), usually include a visit to a Murano glass factory (you can easily do that on your own, with less of a hard sell), and leave daily around 9:30am and 2:30pm (times change; check in advance).

You can also visit the islands on your own conveniently and easily using the *vaporetti.* Line nos. 12, 13, 14, 41, and 42 make the journey to Murano from Fondamente Nove (on the north side of Castello), and line no. 12 continues on to Burano and Torcello. You can get a special 7.75€ ($9) Laguna Nord day ticket to cover the entire journey. The islands are small and easy to navigate, but check the schedule for the next island-to-island departure (usually hourly) and your return so that you don't spend most of your day waiting for connections.

MURANO & ITS GLASS

The island of **Murano** ★★ has long been famous throughout the world for the products of its glass factories, but there's little here in variety or prices that you won't find in Venice. A visit to the **Museo del Vetro (Museum of Glass),** Fondamenta Giustinian 8 (✆ **041-739-586**), will put the island's centuries-old legacy into perspective and is recommended for those considering major buys. Hours are Thursday to Tuesday 10am to 5pm (to 4pm Nov–Mar), and admission is 4€ ($4.60) for adults and 2.50€ ($2.90) for students, or free with the cumulative San Marco ticket (see "Venice Discounts" on p. 130).

Dozens of *fornaci* (furnaces) offer free shows of mouth-blown glassmaking almost invariably hitched to a hard-sell ("No obligation! Really!") tour of the factory outlet. These retail showrooms of delicate glassware can be enlightening or boring, depending on your frame of mind. Almost all the places ship, often doubling the price. On the other hand, these pieces are instant heirlooms.

Murano also has two worthy churches: **San Pietro Martire** ★, with its altarpieces by Tintoretto, Veronese, and Giovanni Bellini, and the ancient **Santa Maria e Donato** ★, with an intricate Byzantine exterior apse and a 6th-century pulpit and columns inside resting on a fantastic 12th-century inlaid floor.

BURANO & ITS LACE

Lace is the claim to fame of tiny colorful **Burano** ★★★, a craft kept alive for centuries by the wives of fishermen waiting for their husbands to return from sea. It's still worth a trip if you have time to stroll the island's "opera-set-like" back streets whose canals are lined with the brightly colored simple homes of the *buranesi* fisherman. The local government continues its attempt to keep its centuries-old lace legacy alive with subsidized classes.

Visit the **Museo del Merletto (Museum of Lace Making),** Piazza Galuppi (© 041-730-034), to understand why something so exquisite should not be left to fade into extinction. It's open Wednesday to Monday 10am to 5pm (to 4pm Nov–Mar), and admission is 4€ ($4.60) adults and 2.50€ ($2.90) children, or free with the cumulative San Marco ticket (see "Venice Discounts" on p. 130).

TORCELLO

Nearby **Torcello** ★ is perhaps the most charming of the islands. It was the first of the lagoon islands to be called home by the mainland population fleeing persecution (from here they eventually moved to join the growing area around what is now Rialto Bridge), but today it consists of little more than one long canal leading from the *vaporetto* landing past sad-sack vineyards to a clump of buildings at its center.

Torcello boasts the oldest Venetian monument, the **Cattedrale di Torcello (Santa Maria Assunta)** ★★★, whose foundation dates from the 7th century (© 041-270-2464 or 041-730-084). It's famous for its outstanding 11th- to 12-century Byzantine mosaics—a *Madonna and Child* in the apse and *Last Judgment* on the west wall—rivaling those of Ravenna's and St. Mark's Basilica. The cathedral is open daily 10:30am to 6pm (shorter hours in winter), and admission is 3€ ($3.45). You can climb the bell tower for a panorama for 2€ ($2.30). Also of interest is the adjacent **11th-century church** dedicated to St. Fosca and a **small archaeological museum;** the church's hours are the same as the cathedral's, and the museum is open Tuesday to Sunday 10am to 12:30pm and 2 to 4pm. Museum admission is 2€ ($2.30). A combined ticket for all three sights is 6€ ($7).

Peaceful Torcello is uninhabited except for a handful of land-working families and is a favorite picnic spot (you'll have to bring the food from Venice—there are no stores on the island and only one bar/trattoria and one rather expensive restaurant, the Cipriani, of Hemingway fame). Once the tour groups have left, it offers a very special moment of solitude and escape when St. Mark's bottleneck becomes oppressive.

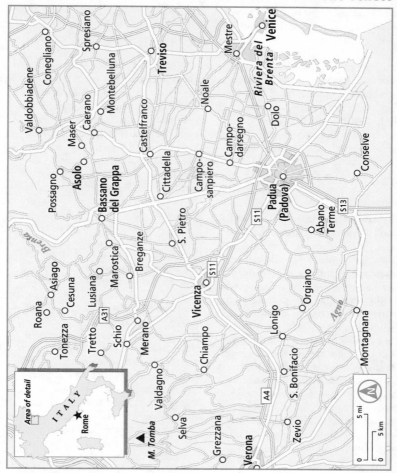

the agricultural wealth that has been the Veneto's sustenance.

The Veneto's three major cities, **Padua, Vicenza,** and **Verona,** not only hold the most historical and artistic interest in the region, but they are also extremely accessible by public transportation. Trains between these cities run on the Milan–Venice line and hence are inexpensive, frequent, and user-friendly. In fact, the distances between them are so small that you could very well stay put in Venice and tool into Verona—the most distant of the three—for an easy day trip. But

this would be a great shame, indeed, as each of the cities warrants the time it takes to explore it slowly.

Enjoy the Veneto in the late afternoon and early evening hours when the day-trippers have gone and the cities are left to their own—sip an *aperitivo* or take a leisurely *passeggiata,* window-shopping along streets lined with tony boutiques that represent the well-to-do status of the *Veneti.* End your day with a moderately priced meal of home-cooked regional specialties in a characteristic wine tavern amid much bonhomie and *brio* (vivacity), followed by a good night's rest in a small, friendly hotel located just off the postcard-perfect main square.

Spend time in the region's lesser-explored cities and small towns such as **Treviso, Bassano del Grappa,** and **Asolo.** All offer a host of excursions into the real countryside, where you only need a car or the slightest sense of adventure to jump on a local bus and enjoy the back roads and backwaters of the Veneto. Top it off with a leisurely cruise down the Brenta Canal to return to Venice and hop back on the well-trodden tourist path.

REGIONAL CUISINE The Veneto's food products are as diverse as its geography. From the mountains and their foothills come a proliferation of **mushrooms** and **game.** The northerly reaches around Treviso produce wild **white asparagus** and cherries in the spring, and in the late fall **radicchio,** a red chicory that was renowned in ancient Roman times. Much of the cuisine is based on the rice and corn grown here; **polenta** frequently appears on most menus, sauced with a hearty game stew with hints of Austrian influence. Rice is commonly served as **risotto,** a first course along with the season's vegetables or, more characteristically, offerings from the Adriatic on the east.

The ubiquitous use of olive oil from Tuscany throughout the south is seen only minimally here—it is not unusual to see the use of **butter,** so commonly associated with Emilian food. But above all it is the Adriatic that dictates even the landlocked cuisines of the Veneto.

The proliferation of desserts is a throwback to the two times in history that Veneto was ceded to Austria, sweet reminders of which are evident in many pastry shops. The now universal favorite, **tiramisù** (lady fingers soaked in espresso and liqueur, layered with sweetened mascarpone cheese and dusted with cacao), is said to have originated in the Veneto and remains a favorite finale at Italian restaurants the world over.

The Veneto—and Verona especially—plays an all-important role in the production and exportation of wines: **Soave, Bardolino,** and **Valpolicello** are world-recognized labels that originate in these acclaimed vineyards. No other region in Italy produces as many DOC (*Denominazione di Origine Controllata,* zones of controlled name and origin) red wines as the Veneto. The rich volcanic earth of the Colli Euganei produces a good number of these, while a light and fizzy *prosecco* hails from the hills around Asolo. Wine is an integral element in any meal; it is no compromise to limit yourself to the local regional wines that are some of Europe's finest.

For more information on the Veneto, check out this good region-wide website: **www.venetonet.com**.

1 Padua (Padova)

42km (26 miles) W of Venice, 81km (50 miles) E of Verona, 32km (20 miles) E of Vicenza, 234km (145 miles) E of Milan

The University of Bologna had already grown to 10,000 students by the time Padua (Padova) founded its university in 1222. Padua was long the academic heartbeat of the powerful Venetian Republic—and far before that, an ancient Roman stronghold—and for this reason one of the most important medieval and Renaissance cities in Italy. Dante and Copernicus studied here, Petrarch and Galileo taught here. When you wander the narrow, cobbled, arcaded side streets in the timeless neighborhoods surrounding the "Bo" (named after a 15th-century inn that once stood on the present-day site of the university), you will be transported back to those earlier times.

Paying Homage to the Original "Tony"

Giotto's frescoes draw art lovers and the city's university students, but pilgrims of another ilk have long secured Padua's place on the map. For more than 700 years, the enormous **Basilica di Sant'Antonio** has drawn millions from around the world. A mendicant Franciscan monk born in Lisbon, Antonio spent his last years in Padua. He died here in 1231, was canonized almost immediately, and the basilica—a fantastic mingling of Romanesque, Byzantine, and Gothic styles—was begun within a year.

St. Anthony is one of the Roman Catholic Church's most beloved saints—and one of Italy's most popular namesakes—universally known for his powers to locate the lost. Countless handwritten messages left on his tomb within the great domed church call upon this power to help find everything from lost love to lost limbs. Both the church and the miracle worker are simply referred to as "il Santo," and the church warrants a visit for its artistic treasures and architectural importance as well as its religious significance; for centuries it has been one of Europe's principal destinations of pilgrimage.

Padua is a vital city, with a young university population that gets about by bicycle and keeps the city's piazzas and cafes alive. The historical hub of town is still very evocative of the days when the city and its university flourished in the late Middle Ages and Renaissance as a center of learning and art.

Most visitors bypass Padua in their rush to get to nearby Venice. During peak season some even stay here when Venice's hotels are full, but see nothing outside the train station. You can spend a few hours or a few days in Padua, depending on your schedule. Its most important sites for those with limited time are Giotto's magnificent, not-to-be-missed **frescoes** in the Scrovegni Chapel (fully restored between 1999 and 2001) and the revered pilgrimage site of the eight-domed **Basilica of Sant'Antonio di Padova,** whose important **equestrian statue** by Donatello stands in the piazza before it.

FESTIVALS & MARKETS   The beloved Sant'Antonio (see "Paying Homage to the Original 'Tony,'" above) is celebrated with a **feast day** on June 13, when his relics are carried about town in an elaborate procession joined in by the thousands of pilgrims who come from all over the world.

The **outdoor markets** (Mon–Sat) in the twin Piazza delle Erbe (for fresh produce) and Piazza della Frutta (dry goods) that flank the enormous Palazzo della Ragione are some of Italy's best. The third Sunday of every month sees the area of the Prato delle Valle inundated by more than 200 antiques and collectibles dealers, one of the largest **antiques and collectibles fairs** in the region. Only early birds will beat the large number of local dealers to the worm.

Antiques lovers with a car might want to visit Italy's second-largest **Mercato dell'Antiquariato** at the 18th-century Villa Contarini (in Piazzola sul Brenta, a lovely 30-min. drive that can be combined with visiting some of the other Palladian and Palladian-inspired country villas along the Brenta Canal; see "Day Trips from Padua," later in this chapter), held the last Sunday of every month. There, an estimated 350 vendors hawk their wares; the villa is open for visits during those hours.

Padua (Padova)

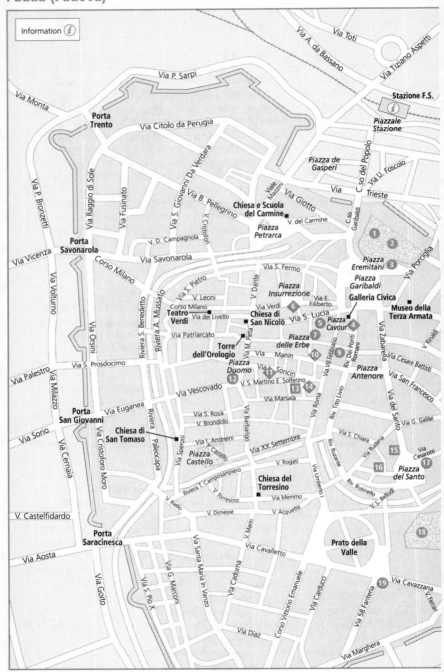

Information (i)

Via Toti

Via A. da Bassano

Via Tiziano Aspetti

Via P. Sarpi

Via Monta

Stazione F.S.

Porta Trento

Via Citolo da Perugia

Piazzale Stazione

Via Raggio di Sole

Via S. Giovanni Da Verdara

Via B. Pellegrino

V. Cristofori

Piazza de Gasperi

C.so del Popolo

Via U. Foscolo

Via P. Bronzetti

Via Fusinato

Viale Mazzini

Via Giotto

Via

Via

Trieste

Porta Savonarola

V. D. Campagnola

Via Savonarola

Chiesa e Scuola del Carmine

V. del Carmine

Piazza Petrarca

C.so Garibaldi

Via Porciglia

Via Vicenza

Corso Milano

Via S. Fermo

Piazza Eremitani

1
2
3

Via Volturno

Via S. Pietro

Via Dante

Piazza Insurrezione

Piazza Garibaldi

Via E. Filiberto

Galleria Civica

Museo della Terza Armata

Riviera S. Benedetto

Riviera A. Mussato

V. Leoni

Corso Milano

Via Verdi

6

Via S. Lucia

Piazza Cavour

5

4

V. Rinaldi

Via Orsini

Teatro Verdi

Via del Livello

Chiesa di San Nicolò

7

Via M. Pietà

Piazza delle Erbe

10

Via VIII Febbraio

Riv. Dei Ponti Romani

9

Via Zabarella

Via Cesare Battisti

Via S. Prosdocimo

Via Patriarcato

Torre dell'Orologio

Via Manin

Piazza Antenore

Via San Francesco

Via Palestro

Via Milazzo

Piazza Duomo

12

Via Soncin

11

V. S. Martino E. Solferino

13 **14**

Via Roma

Via Marsala

Riv. Tito Livio

Piazza Castello

Via del Santo

Via G. Galilei

Via S. Prosdocimo

Via Euganea

Via Vescovado

Via S. Rosa

V. Brondolo

Via Barbarigo

Via XX Settembre

Riv. Ruzante

Via S. Chiara

Via Rudena

15

Via Cesarotti

Porta San Giovanni

Via Sorio

Via Cernaia

Riviera T. Camposanpiero

Via Cristoforo Moro

Riviera Paleocapa

Via Sperone

Chiesa di San Tomaso

V. I. Andreini

V. Castello

V. Rogati

Via Umberto I

Riv. Businello

16

17

Piazza del Santo

V. Castelfidardo

V. Riello

V. Torresino

Chiesa del Torresino

Via Memmo

V. I. Balludi

18

Porta Saracinesca

Via Aosta

Via Giotto

V. S. Pio X

Via G. Marconi

Via Santa Maria In Vanzo

V. Dimesse

V. Marin

V. Acquette

Via Cavalletto

Via Cadorna

Corso Vittorio Emanuele

Via Carducci

Prato della Valle

Via 58 Fanteria

Via Cavazzana

V. Ferrari

19

Via Diaz

Via Marghera

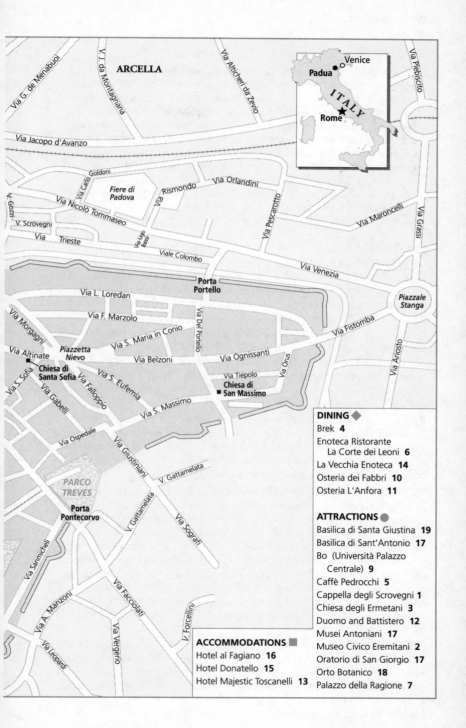

DINING ◆
Brek **4**
Enoteca Ristorante
La Corte dei Leoni **6**
La Vecchia Enoteca **14**
Osteria dei Fabbri **10**
Osteria L'Anfora **11**

ATTRACTIONS ●
Basilica di Santa Giustina **19**
Basilica di Sant'Antonio **17**
Bo (Università Palazzo
Centrale) **9**
Caffè Pedrocchi **5**
Cappella degli Scrovegni **1**
Chiesa degli Ermetani **3**
Duomo and Battistero **12**
Musei Antoniani **17**
Museo Civico Eremitani **2**
Oratorio di San Giorgio **17**
Orto Botanico **18**
Palazzo della Ragione **7**

ACCOMMODATIONS ■
Hotel al Fagiano **16**
Hotel Donatello **15**
Hotel Majestic Toscanelli **13**

> **Finds** Shoes & Spoons
>
> A less important street market is the weekly **Saturday outdoor market of nonantique goods** (selling clothes, pet food, household goods—nothing fascinating, but an interesting peek into local life and a good place to pick up kitchen items to re-create your own *cucina italiana* back home) in the Prato della Valle. It has a large number of (inexpensive) shoe stands hawking goods from the many shoe factories for which the nearby Brenta Canal area has long been renowned. Both the monthly antiques fair (listed above) and this weekly market will give you a reason to visit the 18th-century **Prato della Valle,** said to be one of the largest piazzas in Europe. Located just southwest of the Basilica di Sant'Antonio, it is ringed by a canal and populated by more than 80 statues.

ESSENTIALS

GETTING THERE   By Train   The main train station is at Piazza Stazione (© **049-875-1800;** www.trenitalia.it), in the northern part of town, just outside the 16th-century walls. Padua is well connected by frequent train service to points directly west and east: Verona (1 hr.), Venice (30 min.), Vicenza (25 min.), Milan (2½ hr.).

By Bus   The main **ACAP bus station** is located behind (east of) the Scrovegni Chapel and Arena Gardens area on Via Trieste 40 (near Piazza Boschetti) (© **049-824-1111;** www.aps-online.it). Frequent bus service to Venice and Verona costs approximately the same as train tickets, though tourists and locals alike seem to use this station principally for the smaller outlying cities such as Bassano del Grappa.

By Car   Padua is located directly on the principal A4 autostrada that links Venice with Milan. All the points of interest listed below are located in the city's historical center, which is closed to traffic. When booking at your hotel, ask about the closest parking lot. Hotels usually have an agreement with their neighborhood parking lot and pass those savings along to hotel guests.

VISITOR INFORMATION   The **tourist office** is in the train station (© **049-875-2077;** fax 049-875-5008; www.padovanet.it or www.apt.padova.it). April to October it's open Monday to Saturday 9am to 7pm and Sunday 9am to noon; November to March, hours are Monday to Saturday 9:20am to 5:45pm and Sunday 9am to noon. From the train station, bus nos. 3 and 8 head downtown (as do nos. 12 and 18 Mon–Sat and no. 32 Sun). There's another **office** at the cathedral on Piazza del Santo (© **049-875-3087**). It's open daily: summer 10am to 1pm and 3 to 6pm and winter 10am to 1pm and 2 to 5pm. Another, more central office on Vicolo Pedrocchi is set to open "soon" (though they've been saying that for a few years now). You can also visit the **APT office** at Riviera Mugnai 8 (© **049-876-7911**) for information.

CITY LAYOUT   Pick up a map from the tourist office and plan your attack. The train station marks the city's northernmost point, and the Prato delle Valle and Basilica di Sant'Antonio mark the southernmost. The following sites of interest can be organized into three clusters and are all within walking distance of one other: the Cappella degli Scrovegni (also called the Arena Chapel) and the adjacent Museo Civico are across a small piazza from the Eremitani Church; the

Caffè Pedrocchi can be found near the Palazzo della Ragione in the Piazza Cavour area (the Piazza della Frutta sits to the north and Piazza delle Erbe just to the south of the palazzo, with the Piazza degli Signori bringing up the west); and the Basilica di Sant'Antonio caps the southern end of town with the enormous Piazza Prato delle Valle just beyond.

GETTING AROUND Hotels, restaurants, and major points of interest all fall inside the historical center and can be reached on foot. Public ACAP buses service much of the center's streets, which are otherwise limited to traffic (pick up a bus map from the tourist office). Single tickets cost .85€ ($1); a round-trip ticket is 1.50€ ($1.75).

WHAT TO SEE & DO

Cappella degli Scrovegni (Scrovegni Chapel or Arena Chapel) ★★★

This is the one uncontested must-see during your stay in Padua, so be prepared for lengthy lines in high season, a wait made even longer by the small numbers of controlled groups (25 people maximum) allowed to enter the chapel at any one time (scandalously brief 15-min. visits are the limit often imposed during peak periods; check when buying your ticket so you can plan accordingly). Once inside, art lovers armed with binoculars behold the scene in awe—the recently renovated cycle of **vibrant frescoes** by Giotto that revolutionized 14th-century painting is still considered among the most important early Renaissance art. While some experts have questioned whether the famed frescoes in Assisi are entirely by Giotto, here there is no equivocation: These are the master's works. A brilliant cobalt blue is the dominant color; the illustrations are in that typical easy-to-understand medieval comic-strip format, but here they take on an unprecedented degree of realism and emotion.

This cycle is even larger, more complete, and better preserved than the famed St. Francis frescoes in Assisi. Giotto worked from 1303 to 1306 to completely cover the ceiling and walls with 38 scenes illustrating the lives of the Virgin and of Christ from floor to ceiling. With your back to the front door, the three bands that cover the walls are: top right, *Life of Joachim;* top left, *Life of the Virgin;* right center, *The Childhood of Christ;* left center, *Christ's Public Life;* right bottom, *The Passion of Christ* (the third panel of Judas kissing Christ is the best known of the entire cycle); left bottom, *Christ's Death and Resurrection.* Above the entrance is the fresco of the *Last Judgment:* Christ, as judge, sits in the center, surrounded by the angels and apostles. Below him, to the right, are the blessed, while to the

---

Value Cumulative Tickets

If you plan on taking in all the sites of Padua during a short visit—or even if you plan on visiting the Scrovegni Chapel and only one other site—a **PadovaCard** is a worthy investment. In addition to free use of the city's buses and free parking in some areas, the 13€ ($15) card gets you admission to the Cappella degli Scrovegni (although you still must call to make reservations), Musei Civici Eremitani, the Palazzo della Ragione, and other sites in Padua and the province as well as a seat in Caffè Pedrocchi. The card is valid for 48 hours and one card can be shared by both an adult and a child younger than 12. You'll find the card for sale at tourist offices and at sites at which you can use the card.

Atoning for the Sins of the Father

The area around the ancient Roman Arena where the chapel now stands (and hence the chapel's alternative name) was purchased in 1300 by a wealthy Padovan, Enrico Scrovegni. He built an extravagant palazzo (destroyed in 1820), and the family chapel next door with a simple and unadorned exterior. The chapel is actually dedicated to Enrico's father, an unethical usurer so notorious in his time that he was actually refused a Christian burial. The son, hoping to atone for his father's ways, decided to commission for the decoration Tuscan-born Giotto, whose work he had seen in the Basilica di Sant'Antonio. Giotto felt obligated to include the unscrupulous father's portrait in the half of the *Last Judgment* containing the ranks of blessed souls. Giotto's fellow Florentine Dante felt otherwise, however, immortalizing the elder Scrovegni amid the usurers condemned to the inferno in his epic *Divine Comedy.*

left, Giotto created a terrible hell in which devils and humans are condemned to eternal punishment.

Note: Each online reservation—even for holders of the PadovaCard, which allows for free admission—incurs a 1€/$1.15 reservation fee. If you want to be assured that you will have more time in the chapel, consider visiting between 7 and 9:30pm on the 11€/$13 "Double Turn" ticket, which allows you 30 minutes in the chapel, though you must still book timed-entry tickets in advance.

Piazza Eremitani 8 (off Corso Garibaldi). © 049-201-0020 for required reservations (call center lines open Mon–Fri 9am–7pm, Sat 9am–1pm). www.cappelladegliscrovegni.it or www.comune.padova.it/museicivici. For reservations: musei.comune@padovanet.it. Admission (joint ticket with the Museo Eremitani; add 1€/$1.15 per ticket to reservations made online) 11€ ($13) adults (includes a 1€/$1.15 reservation fee), 4€ ($4.60) ages 6–17, free for children under 6 (although admission still requires a reservation); free with purchase of Padova-Card (see "Cumulative Tickets," above). MC, V (online reservations only). Daily 9am–7pm; until 9:30pm in summer. Entrance through the Museo Eremitani. Bus: 3, 5, 6, 8, 9, 10, 11, 12, 13, 15, 16, 18, 22, or 42.

Museo Civico Eremitani ⭐   These centuries-old cloisters that were once home to the monks (*eremitani* means "hermits") who officiated in the adjacent Scrovegni Chapel (officially part of the museum complex) have been handsomely renovated to provide an airy display space as the city's new civic museum. Its prodigious collection begins on the ground floor with the Archaeological Museum's division of Egyptian, Roman, and Etruscan artifacts and antiquities. The upstairs collection represents an impressive panorama of minor works from major Venetian artists from the early 15th century to the 19th century: You'll find works by Titian, Tiepolo, and Tintoretto, whose *Crucifixion* is the museum's finest work. Special mention is given to Giotto's unusual wooden crucifix and Bellini's *Portrait of a Young Senator.*

Piazza Eremitani 8 (off Corso Garibaldi and adjacent to the Cappella Scrovegni). © 049-820-4550 or 049-820-4551. www.padovanet.it/museicivici. Admission to **Musei Civico Eremitani** only: 10€ ($12) adults, 8€ ($9) 6–17, free for children under 6 and seniors over 65. **Joint ticket** with the Cappella Scrovegni (add 1€/$1.15 per ticket to reservations made online) 11€ ($13) adults (includes a 1€/$1.15 reservation fee), 4€ ($4.60) ages 6–17, free for children under 6 (although admission still requires a reservation); free with purchase of PadovaCard (see "Cumulative Tickets," above). MC, V (online reservations only). Feb–Oct Tues–Sun 9am–7pm; Nov–Jan Tues–Sun 9am–6pm. Bus: 3, 5, 6, 8, 9, 10, 11, 12, 13, 15, 16, 18, 22, or 42.

Chiesa degli Eremitani (Church of the Hermits) ⭐   Padua's worst tragedy was the complete destruction of this church by Nazi bombings in 1944; some art historians consider it the country's greatest artistic wartime loss. It has been remarkably restored to its original early-13th-century Romanesque style, but the magnificent cycles of frescoes by the 23-year-old Andrea Mantegna could not be salvaged, except for a corner of the Ovetari Chapel on the right of the chancel. Here you'll find enough fragments left in the rubble of the frescoes he painted from 1454 to 1457 to understand the loss of what was considered one of the great artistic treasures of Italy. Mantegna was born in Padua (1431–1506) and studied under the Florentine master Donatello, who lived here while completing his commissions for the Basilica di Sant'Antonio as well as the famous equestrian statue that now stands in the piazza before it. Classical music concerts occasionally are held in the church.

Piazza Eremitani (off Corso Garibaldi). ℂ 049-875-6410 or 049-876-1855. Free admission. Daily 8:30am–12:30pm and 4:30–7pm. Bus: 3, 8, 10, 12, 32, or 42.

Caffè Pedrocchi ★★   The Pedrocchi is a historic landmark, as beloved by the Padovans as "their" own St. Anthony (who actually hailed from Lisbon). When it first opened in 1831, it was the largest cafe in Europe. Famous literary and political characters and local luminaries made this their command post—French-born Henri Beyle, aka Stendhal, had it in mind when he wrote: "The best Italian cafe is almost as good as the Parisian ones." Countless others were less reserved, calling it arguably the most beautiful coffeehouse in the world. Heavily damaged during World War II, it has been completely rebuilt in its original neoclassical 19th-century stage-set splendor, and, after a laborious renovation and heralded December 1998 reopening that was, for Padua, the event of the year, it is again the social heartbeat of the city.

It has the nicest restrooms in town, for the use of cafe patrons. They're worth the cost of a coffee. In warm weather Pedrocchi opens wide its doors (and hence its curious description as a "doorless cafe") onto the pedestrian piazza; sit here for a while to absorb the Padovan spirit. As is always the case, drinks cost less when you're standing at the bar, but then you will have missed the *dolce far niente* (sweetness of doing nothing) experience for which Pedrocchi has always been known. A cappuccino, tea, beer, or glass of white *prosecco* wine will cost 2.50€ ($2.90) at your table (half that at the bar), and hunger can be held at bay with a plate of dainty teatime pastries or a grilled ham-and-cheese toast, each 2.50€ ($2.90).

Pedrocchi often hosts live music in the evenings; check their website for dates, or just stop by during your visit to sip the atmosphere.

Via VIII Febbraio 15 (at Piazza Cavour). ℂ 049-878-1231. www.caffepedrocchi.it. AE, DC, MC, V. Historical salon upstairs: daily 9:30am–12:30pm and 3:30–8pm. Bar: Sun–Wed 9am–9pm, Thurs–Sat 9am–midnight. Bus: 3, 8, 12, 16, 18, or 22. Closed 2 weeks in mid-Aug.

Bo (Università Palazzo Centrale)   Galileo's battered desk and podium where he taught from 1592 to 1610 is still on display in Italy's second-oldest university (after Bologna). His name joins a legendary honor roll of students and professors—Petrarch, Dante, the poet Tasso, Copernicus—who came here from all over Europe. The University of Padua was founded in 1222 and grew to become one of the most famous and ambitious learning centers in Europe, reaching its zenith in the 16th and 17th centuries. Today, a number of buildings are spread about town, but the Palazzo del Bo (named after the "Bo" or Ox Inn—a favorite student hangout that stood on this spot in the 15th century) is the university's main seat. Ongoing restoration keeps most of it off-limits, but the perfectly preserved **Teatro Anatomico** ★ is one of the few sites regularly open to visitors. Built in 1594, it was here that William Harvey most probably developed his theory of the circulation of blood while earning his degree in 1602.

Via VIII Febbraio (south of Piazza Cavour). © 049-827-5111. Admission 3€ ($3.45) by guided tour only, some in English. Ask at tourist office for status of an ongoing renovation and visitor hours.

Palazzo della Ragione (Law Courts) ✦ Located just south of the historic Caffè Pedrocchi, and a necessary and inevitable destination for those meandering about the historic center of town, the picturesque open-air markets of **Piazza delle Erbe (Square of the Herbs)** ✦✦ and **Piazza della Frutta (Square of Fruit)** frame this massive 13th-century palazzo at their center. Together they have stood as the town's political and commercial nucleus for centuries.

Before being distracted by the color, smells, and cacophony of the sprawling outdoor fruit and vegetable market stalls, turn your attention to the magnificent Palazzo della Ragione, whose interior is as impressive as its exterior. Food shops by the dozen fill its ground floor, and stand-up bars and outdoor cafes make this lunchtime central. The two-story loggia-lined "Palace of Reason" is topped with a distinctive sloped roof that resembles the inverted hull of a ship, the largest of its kind in the world. It was built in 1219 as the seat of Padua's parliament and was used as an assembly hall, courthouse, and administrative center to celebrate Padua's newly won independence as a republican city. Considered a masterpiece of civil medieval architecture, it was heavily damaged by a fire in 1420 that destroyed, among other things, an elaborate cycle of frescoes by Giotto and his students that adorned the **il Salone (the Great Hall).** The hall, 81m (270 ft.) long, was almost immediately rebuilt and is today the prime draw, both for its floor-to-ceiling 15th-century frescoes commissioned immediately after the fire, and a large wooden sculpture of a horse attributed to Donatello (although many art historians don't agree). The 15th-century frescoes are similar in style and astrological theme to those that had been painted by Giotto, and comprise one of the very few complete zodiac cycles to survive until modern times. Museum-quality exhibitions are often held here, which gives you another reason to visit, beyond just seeing the impressive building itself.

On the far (west) side of the adjoining piazzas' canvas-topped stalls, flanking the Palazzo della Ragione, is the **Piazza dei Signori,** most noteworthy for the 15th-century clock tower that dominates it, the first of its kind in Italy.

Piazza delle Erbe/Piazza della Frutta. © 049-820-5006. www.padovanet.it/museicivici. Admission to palazzo 6€ ($7) adults, 3€ ($3.45) children. Feb–Oct Tues–Sun 9am–7pm; Nov–Jan Tues–Sun 9am–6pm. Bus: 3, 5, 6, 8, 9, 10, 11, 12, 13, 15, 18, 22, or 42.

Basilica di Sant'Antonio ✦✦ This enormous basilica's imposing interior is richly frescoed and decorated, filled with a number of tombs, works of art, and inlaid checkerboard marble flooring. It's all there to honor one man, Padua's patron Saint Anthony (Sant'Antonio). Simply and commonly referred to as "il Santo," Anthony was born in Lisbon in 1195 and died just outside of Padua in

---

Tips **When Venice Overflows**

Padua is convenient to both Venice and Verona. There isn't a wide choice of desirable hotels in the *centro storico* (historic center), but you'll pay close to half the rates of comparable accommodations in Venice and find the commute, just 34km (21 miles), an easy and inexpensive one (and often a necessary one when Venice is fully booked).

1231. Work began on the church almost immediately but was not completed until 1307. Its eight domes bring to mind the Byzantine influence found in Venice's St. Mark's Basilica that predates Padua's Romanesque-Gothic construction by more than 2 centuries. A pair of octagonal, minaret-like bell towers enhance its Eastern appearance. The seven **bronze statues** and towering central *Crucifixion* (1444–48) that adorn the main altar are by Donatello and are the basilica's artistic highlight.

The faithful could care less about the architecture and art; they flock here year-round to caress the **tomb** 🏛 holding the saint's body (off the left aisle) and pray for his help in finding what they've lost. The tomb is always covered with flowers, photographs, and handwritten personal petitions left by devout pilgrims from every corner of the globe whose numbers have remained constant over the centuries. The saint is the patron of lost or mislaid objects, and the faithful who flock here look for everything from lost love to lost health. The series of nine bronze bas-reliefs of scenes from the saint's life are some of the finest works by 16th-century northern Italian sculptors.

In his lifetime, St. Anthony was known for his eloquent preaching, so interpret as you will the saint's perfectly (some say miraculously) preserved **tongue, vocal chords,** and **jawbone** on display in the Cappella del Tesoro in the back of the church directly behind the main altar. These treasured relics are carried through town in a traditional procession every June 13 to celebrate the feast day of *il Santo.* You'll also see one of the original tattered tunics of *il Santo* dating from 1231.

Standing out amid the smattering of stalls across the large piazza in front of the basilica selling St. Anthony–emblazoned everything, is Donatello's famous *Gattamelata* 🏛🏛 **equestrian statue.** The first of its size to be cast in Italy since Roman antiquity, it is important for its detail, proportion, and powerful contrast between rider (the inconsequential Venetian condottiere Erasmo da Narni, nicknamed the "Spotted Cat") and horse. It was to have a seminal effect on Renaissance sculpture and casting and restore the lost art of equestrian statuary.

Piazza d. Santo (east of Prato d. Valle). © **049-878-9722.** www.santantonio.org. Free admission. Summer daily 6:20am–7:45pm; winter daily 6:20am–7pm. Bus: 3, 8, 12, 18, 32, or 43.

WHERE TO STAY

When making reservations, note that low season is usually considered December and January, and July and August. Inquire about discounts if you'll be in Padua at this time of year.

Hotel al Fagiano 🏛   Although small and family run, this newly renovated hotel is a great value for your money. Located just a few steps off the expansive Piazza del Santo (its most appealing asset), it doesn't exactly ooze coziness and charm, but given the less-than-encouraging hotel situation in town, the Fagiano's clean, bright, modern rooms are still a standout choice. Bathrooms have been freshly redone and include such niceties as hair dryers and bright lighting. Also, you rarely find air-conditioning and TVs at these rates. Don't confuse this Fagiano with the recently renamed Hotel Buenos Aires, formerly known as the Fagiano and just a block away.

Via Locatelli 45 (west of Piazza del Santo), 35123 Padova. © **049-875-0073.** Fax 049-875-3396. www.al fagiano.it. 29 units. 75€–81€ ($86–$93) double; 85€–92€ ($98–$106) triple. Continental breakfast 6.50€ ($7). Rates slightly discounted off season. AE, DC, MC, V. Private parking 10€ ($12). From train station: Bus no. 8, 12, 18, or 22. **Amenities:** Bar; concierge; bike rental. *In room:* A/C, TV, hair dryer.

Hotel Donatello 🏛   This is a modern hotel in an old building, flush with amenities and enjoying a great location right at the Basilica di Sant'Antonio.

More than half the rooms overlook the basilica, though those on the inner court-yard (some with hardwood flooring rather than carpets) are quieter. Guest quarters vary as the owners slowly refresh and update a few each year. Some feature plush modular furnishings, some retro-Empire style. Some of the older bathrooms have tubs with hand-held shower nozzles, but most are modernized. Apartments sleeping three to four come with two bedrooms and a common bathroom.

Via del Santo 102–104, 35123 Padova. ℂ 049-875-0634. Fax 049-875-0829. www.hoteldonatello.net. 45 units. 160€ ($184) double; 186€ ($214) triple; 186€ ($214) apt for 3; 250€ ($288) apt for 4. Breakfast 12€ ($14). AE, DC, MC, V. Parking 15€ ($17) in garage. **Amenities:** International restaurant; bar; concierge; tour desk; room service (limited); laundry service; dry cleaning. *In room:* A/C, TV w/pay movies, dataport, minibar, hair dryer, safe.

Hotel Majestic Toscanelli ★★ A four-star hotel this nice would cost a great deal more in nearby Venice, which is why the Toscanelli often finds itself with guests who make this their home base while they visit neighboring cities and the surrounding area. A 1992 redo has kept the hotel's old-world charm fresh and handsome, with rooms tastefully done in classic decor with coordinated pastel themes, burnished cherrywood furniture, and large, bright bathrooms with white ceramic and marble tiles. Work in 1999 freshened up the lobby, transforming it with highlights of gold leaf that hint of the Venetian rococo era. Off the lobby, a bright and attractive breakfast room serves a good buffet breakfast. This quiet, historic neighborhood is entirely closed to traffic, with porticoed alleyways lined with antiques shops and wine bars. From here it's an easy walk to the Via Roma and the Piazza delle Erbe.

The same management owns the excellent Hotel Leon Biano, a century-old palazzo smack in the heartbeat of town on Piazzetta Pedrocchi, but closed it down in late 2002 for a much-needed overhaul of the entire structure. They don't expect it to be ready until perhaps the end of 2004, so I can't say much about how it may look, but it's something to check into if you happen to roll into town toward the end of this edition's shelf life and find the other inn open.

Via dell'Arco 2 (2 blocks west of Via Roma and south of the Piazza d. Erbe), 35122 Padova. ℂ 049-663-244. Fax 049-876-0025. www.toscanelli.com. 34 units. 150€ ($173) double. Rates include buffet breakfast. Rates discounted mid-July to Aug. AE, DC, MC, V. Valet garage parking 19€ ($22). **Amenities:** Bar; concierge; tour desk; courtesy car; room service (limited); babysitting; laundry service; dry cleaning; nonsmoking rooms. *In room:* A/C, TV w/pay movies, fax (on request), dataport, kitchenette (in 2 units), minibar, hair dryer, safe.

WHERE TO DINE

Brek ⓥalue ITALIAN CAFETERIA Brek is self-service *all'italiana,* a home-grown northern Italian chain of upscale cafeterias that make concessions to the time-pressed modern world without sacrificing old-world quality. Put your language problems and calorie-counting aside as you help yourself to pastas that are made up fresh while you wait and topped with the sauce of your choice. There's a counter just for omelets made express, another for entrees and pizza. The dessert cart groans under an array of cheeses, fresh fruits, fruit salads, and fruit-topped tarts and cobblers. Join the thoroughly local eat-on-the-run lunch crowd from the university and surrounding shops, and save your day's budget for dinner.

Piazza Cavour 20. ℂ 049-875-3788. www.brek.it. Reservations not accepted. Primi and pizza 3€–6€ ($3.45–$7); secondi 3.60€–8€ ($4.15–$9). AE, DC, MC, V. Sat–Thurs 11:30am–3pm and 6–10pm.

Enoteca Ristorante La Corte dei Leoni ★ ⓕinds WINE BAR/PADOVANA
After a heady wander among the sights, sounds, and smells of Padua's open-air marketplace, one of Italy's most colorful and authentic, head for a respite at this

new *enoteca*. Your head need spin no longer, despite the 700 labels with which it stocks its well-respected wine cellar (at least 30 are available to sample by the glass at 2€–5€/$2.30–$6). A stylishly minimal decor in the cool white-and-moss-green interior is attractive, but the outdoor courtyard where centuries-old horse stables have been converted for modern-day grazers is the warm-weather draw. The interesting antipasti are as sophisticated as the setting: Look for the *mousse di fegato grasso d'oca tartufato,* a lighter-than-air foie gras heightened by the hint of truffles, or a platter of various Italian cheeses or *salumi,* each a perfect complement to the owner Leonardi's impressive selection of wines, including some interlopers from the Napa Valley. Only a handful of dishes are offered—and the menu changes weekly—but each is excellently prepared, such as *mezzelune* (a kind of ravioli) stuffed with ricotta and eggplant in a sauce of fresh mushrooms and mountain cheese, or a *petto d'anatra in salsa d'uva* (duck breast cooked with grapes that somehow escaped their fate as wine).

Via Pietro d'Abano 1 (on a side street just north of the Piazza della Frutta). **℃ 049-875-0083**. www.corte deileoni.com. Reservations suggested. Primi 7€–10€ ($8–$12); secondi 14€–19€ ($16–$22). AE, DC, MC, V. Tues–Sun 12:30–2:30pm; Tues–Sat 6:30pm–12:30am. Closed 1 week in Aug.

La Vecchia Enoteca ★★ PADOVANA   The sophistication of the Veneto's prodigious viticulture is shown off here in an appropriately refined venue that could easily fit into a less expensive category. Cozy, in a rustic and elegant kind of way, La Vecchia Enoteca is for that special evening of white linen and smooth service when you'd like the full-blown experience of Padovan cuisine and award-deserving wines. Prices are contained enough to encourage diners to leave caution at the door and indulge in a delicious menu and commendable selection of regional and Italian wines. The menu showcases the bounty-rich Veneto: The traditional polenta and risotto change with the season, as does the light, home-made gnocchi. Meat possibilities are numerous and tempting, while the influence of the Adriatic appears in such entrees as the favored *branzino in crosta di patate,* sea bass roasted in a light potato crust. This enoteca is another rarity in Italy: a nonsmoking restaurant.

Via S. Martino e Solferino 32 (just south of Piazza delle Erbe). **℃ 049-875-28-56**. Reservations recom-mended. Primi 7.50€–8€ ($8.65–$9.20); secondi 15€–18€ ($17–$21). MC, V. Tues–Sat 12:45–2pm; Mon–Sat 7:45–10pm. Closed 3 weeks in Aug.

Osteria Dei Fabbri ★ PADOVANA   Simple, well-prepared food is the great equalizer here. This rustic, old-fashioned tavern, or *osteria,* is a lively spot where intellectual types share tables with Zegna-suited bankers, and students stop by for a tipple or to find a quiet corner in which to pore over the newspaper (a pastime not encouraged during hours when meals are served). Some of the day's specials are displayed on the heavy oak bar—antipasti of grilled vegetables, rosemary potatoes, seafood salads—while hot dishes stream out of the kitchen. There's always at least one homemade pasta choice to start with, and osso buco, the specialty of the house, is especially memorable when accompanied by any of the local (and excellent) Venetian wines available by the bottle or glass. Stop by at least for the *dopo cena* (after-dinner drink) to top off your day in Padua. If this restaurant is full, head 2 blocks over to the reliable **Osteria L'Anfora** at Via del Soncin 13 (east of Piazza Duomo; **℃ 049-656-629**) for inexpensive wine and good food.

Via dei Fabbri 13 (on a side street south of Piazza delle Erbe). **℃ 049-650-336**. Reservations recommended. Primi 7.50€–8€ ($8.65–$9.20); secondi 12€–16€ ($14–$18). AE, DC, MC, V. Mon–Sat 12:30–3pm and 7:30–10:30pm. Closed Dec 25–Jan 4.

PADUA AFTER DARK

The classical music season usually runs from October to April at different venues around town. The historic **Teatro Verdi** at Via dei Livello 32 (℃ **049-877-7011** or 049-8777-0213; www.teatroverdipd.it) is the most impressive location. Programs are available at the tourist office. Look for posters advertising performances by the world-class Solisti Veneti, who are Padovans but spend most of the year, alas, traveling abroad.

As a university city, Padua has a large, very visible student population. You can network with the student crowd at any of the popular cafes along Via Cavour, or the *osterie,* wine bars, and beer dives in the porticoed medieval side streets encircling the Palazzo della Ragione (the area around the Bo) and its bookend Piazza delle Erbe and Piazza della Frutta.

DAY TRIPS FROM PADUA

The **Euganean Hills (Colli Euganei)** are at the center of the small but renowned wine industry of the Veneto, located southwest of Padua. You can pick up a *Strada dei Vini* wine route map from the tourist office. It also leads you to the small city of **Terme di Abano** (12km/7½ miles south of Padua), famous as a center for radioactive springs and mud treatments unique to this volcanic range.

THE FORGOTTEN RIVIERA

The navigable **Brenta Canal** ★★ links Padua with Venice in the east. Ambitiously called "the Forgotten Riviera" because of the dozens of historic summertime villas built here by Venice's aristocracy and wealthy merchants, it can be visited by car or by boat—you can even stay in a few of the villas (see "Where to Stay on the Brenta," below). Only one was designed by 16th-century master architect Palladio (the Villa Foscari), but many are Palladian-inspired (see "Vicenza," later in this chapter, for background on Palladio and how to visit his villas). The best way to see the villas is on a cruise down the Brenta (see below). Call the **Brenta Canal tourist office** at ℃ **041-424-973** for more information.

More than 30 villas can be viewed from the boats (some just partially or at a great distance), but only three are visited. The important 18th-century **Villa Pisani** ★★ (℃ **049-502-074**) in Stra was commissioned by the family of a Venetian doge and is famous for its ballroom frescoes by Tiepolo and its extensive gardens. The hedge maze here—something to engage youngsters bored with having to tour all these frescoed mansions—sprouts a tower at the center so that you can get a bird's-eye view of the trip back out; during the crowded summer season, a young man stands up here calling out instructions to maze-goers to hurry them along so the next group can get in. The villa is open Easter to September, Tuesday to Sunday 9am to 6pm (to 4pm in winter). Admission is 6€ ($7) for the villa, or 3€ ($3.45) for just the park and gardens. It's free for seniors over 60 and children under 18.

The other two biggies are in Mira, and fair warning: Both keep erratic hours (see notes after each). The 18th-century **Villa Valmarana** ★★ (℃ **041-426-6387** or 041-560-9350) is dramatically set amid weeping willows; it's open Tuesday to Sunday from April to October and costs 6€ ($7); free for children under 14. Tours leave every half-hour from 9:30am to noon and 2:30 to 5:30pm. (Note that sometimes they decide to open Sun only, and often in July–Aug, you can only visit as part of a large group, such as with the cruises detailed below.) The **Villa Foscari** (aka Villa Malcontenta, "The Unhappy Woman"; ℃ **041-547-0012** May–Oct, or ℃ 041-520-3966 Nov–Apr; www.lamalcontenta.com), is one of Palladio's finest works. It's open May to September, Tuesday to Friday 10am to 6pm, Saturday and Sunday 10am to 7pm; March, April, October, and November, Tuesday to Friday 10am to 5pm, Saturday and Sunday 10am to 6pm; requisite 7€ ($8) guided tours leave every hour from 10:15am on. (Some years, the villa opens only Tues and Sat 9am–noon.)

TOURING THE CANAL   The most popular Brenta cruise is **Il Burchiello,** now run by SITA, Via Orlandini 3 (© **049-877-4712;** www.ilburchiello.it). Be warned that in the past this outfit has proven to be quite disorganized, but new management installed just after I took my latest trip with them may have cleared that up by now. To whit: Last time I sailed with Il Burchiello, they lost my reservation, changed the hours without advising me or any of the other would-be passengers I ran into, and, once I finally did get on a boat, even managed to leave me behind not once, but at *two* different stops along the way. Luckily, large tour groups had booked several boats that day, and both times the capable guides managed to stick me on the next ship coming down the canal. The trip was worth the hassles, though. A similar outfit, with which I have no experience, is **I Battelli del Brenta,** Via Porciglia 34 (© **049-876-0233;** fax 049-876-3410; www.antoniana. it/bmain.html). Other companies come in and out of the market. For more info on plying the rivers, canals, and other watery byways of the region, check out the local river-craft consortium's website at www.padovanavigazione.it.

Il Burchiello leaves Padua at 8:15am Wednesday, Friday, and Sunday and takes you by bus from their office in Padua (on public bus terminus Piazzale Boschetti just northeast of the Eremitani) to the first stop, Stra and its Villa Pisani. After a tour of the villa, you board the boat, stop at the other two big villas and once for lunch, and arrive in Venice at 6:20pm. If you're doing the Brenta in the other direction, they leave from Venice's Pietà dock on Riva degli Schiavoni at 9am Tuesday, Thursday, and Saturday, arriving in Padua at 6:40pm. I Battelli del Brenta embarks in Padua from the Scalinata del Portello at 8:10am Saturday and Sunday, arriving in Venice at 7pm; from Venice's Riva degli Schiavoni dock in front of Caserma Cornolid, they leave Saturdays at 8:30am, finishing in Padua at 7pm.

Both charge 51€ to 62€ ($59–$71) for adults, 36€ ($41) for ages 6 to 17, for the trip, which includes admission to the Villa Malcontenta/Foscari and the Villa Valmarana, but not the Villa Pisani. The optional seafood lunch is another 24€ ($28), though it's nothing special and you'd do much better to buy your lunch in the morning before you leave or even the night before and bring it along to eat instead. The return trip is not included, so either catch a cheap, frequent train back, or ask about taking your luggage onboard so you can simply continue your trip from the end point.

If you want to do the tour yourself, the largest concentration of country villas can be found between Stra and Mira. A car tour does need some planning,

---

Moments   A Perfect Picnic Spot

The secondary road S11 runs alongside the canal in spots; it departs from the canal here and there but remains the best of any extant roadways for viewing the villas as it skirts the little canal-side villages. If you take a right-branching street through any of the towns, you'll come upon grassy verges leading down to the water—a perfect spot for a **Brenta picnic** ★ (though you might want to bring bug repellent).

as visiting hours and days differ from villa to villa and season to season. See the tourist office about a map. *Note:* If you want to try this by bus, know that difficult, erratic visiting hours and public bus connections may make this close to impossible for those without their own wheels.

WHERE TO STAY ON THE BRENTA

An excellent budget option to the admittedly pricey villa hotels below is the **Ostello di Mira,** Via Giare 169 (© **041-567-9203;** fax 041-567-6457; ostellomira.venezia@tin.it), a bare-bones hotel just outside Mira charging 13€ ($15) for a bed in an eight-bed dorm, or 16€ ($19) per person in a shared double. It's open March to September; the reception desk is open 7 to 10am and again from 3:30 to 11:30pm.

Villa Ducale ★★   This hotel occupies an 1884 villa built atop an older structure amid a lovely park of gravel paths, fountains, and flowering bushes under the shade of exotic palms, magnolias, and pines. The rooms feature marvelous inlaid wood floors scattered with Persian rugs and Murano chandeliers hanging from high, simply frescoed ceilings. The wrought-iron bedsteads are surrounded by (mostly) antiques, and the large marble bathrooms feature antique brass fittings. "Standard" rooms are smaller (some almost cramped—but those cost a bit less), with simpler parquet floors and smaller bathrooms. "King" rooms are larger and overlook the park from balconies or a small terrace. The breakfast room/restaurant is intimate—in fact, the Ducale has a generally classier setting (in its public areas, gardens, and salons) than the Margherita (below), but the Margherita tends to have classier rooms.

Riviera Martiri della Libertà 75, 30031 Dolo (Venezia). © 041-560-8020. Fax 041-560-8004. www.villa ducale.it. 11 units. 135€ ($155) small double; 150€ ($173) standard double; 180€ ($207) "king" double. Breakfast included. AE, DC, MC, V. Free parking. **Amenities:** Seafood restaurant; bar; bike rental; concierge; tour desk; car-rental desk; courtesy car; room service (24-hr.); in-room massage; babysitting; laundry service; dry cleaning. *In room:* A/C, TV, dataport, minibar, hair dryer, safe.

Villa Margherita ★★★   This 17th-century villa, expanded in the 19th century, once served as guest quarters for the noble Contarini family of Venice. Today it is run with refined gusto by the Dal Corso family, who provide fresh fruit and flowers in your room and a highly polished professional courtesy. All rooms overlook the large, pine-shaded lawn and are soundproofed against the noise of passing cars. "Standard" rooms, on the smaller side of medium, have rugs scattered over wood floors and tasteful built-in units. "Deluxe" rooms are larger (except for no. 218, which is a cozy lovers nook with a spacious terrace), with more interesting antiques and richer fabrics, and are more frequently blessed with balconies. "Junior suites" are larger still, and feature double sinks. The salons downstairs are appropriately furnished in the manner of a rich country villa, with chessboards fronting fireplaces and plush armchairs. In fine weather you can take breakfast on the brick terrace where the clipped grass of the lawn laps at its edges.

The Dal Corsos have finally opened their new Brenta hotel in Mira, about 5 minutes away. **Villa Franceschi** (Via Don Minzoni 28, Mira Porte, Venezia; © **041-426-6531;** fax 041-560-8996; www.villafranceschi.com), in the late-16th-century Villa Palladiana, features 27 guest rooms (mostly junior suites), lush gardens, a swimming pool, and an on-site restaurant. Grand doubles run 225€ ($259); deluxe superior doubles are 255€ ($293); junior suites cost 285€ ($328); and suites run 320€ ($368).

Via Nazionale 416–417 (on the Venice side of Mira), 30030 Mira Porte (Venezia). © **041-426-5800.** Fax 041-426-5838. www.villa-margherita.com. 19 units. 199€ ($229) standard double; 228€ ($262) deluxe double;

253€ ($291) jr. suite. Rates often discounted in slower periods and low season. Breakfast included. AE, DC, MC, V. Parking free. Public bus stop with half-hourly service to Venice, 15km (9¼ miles) away, is a 5-min. walk. **Amenities:** Frescoed Venetian/fish restaurant across the street; bar; bike rental; concierge; tour desk; room service (24-hr.); laundry service; nonsmoking rooms. *In room:* A/C, TV, dataport, minibar, hair dryer, safe.

2 Treviso

25km (16 miles) N of Mestre/Venice, 50km (31 miles) NE of Padua

Treviso is a bustling, prosperous small city and center in the northern Veneto. It seems to have changed little from its early days as a medieval market town and staunch ally to Venice. Much of the city had to be rebuilt after severe World War II damage, but it was done well. Treviso's medieval palazzi and houses with painted facades, churches frescoed by Giotto's follower Tomaso da Modena (1325–79), and pleasant streets cut across by pretty canals together make for a lovely, genuine-Italy break from the tourist beat of Padua–Vicenza–Verona.

FESTIVALS & MARKETS   Treviso leads up to the **Feast of the Assumption** with a week of street theater, dance, music competitions, and other performances (Aug 6–14). The daily **fish market** ★★ on the islets in the Cagnan canal is a picturesque slice of old Treviso (mornings are best). Treviso hosts an **antiques fair** the fourth Sunday of each month (except July) on Borgo Cavour (© 0422-419-195).

ESSENTIALS

GETTING THERE   By Train   There are trains two to four times an hour from Venice (25–35 min.). Fifteen runs daily (10 on Sun) come from Vicenza (40–80 min.).

By Bus   Ten buses (© 0422-577-311) run daily from Asolo (55 min.).

By Car   From Venice, the quick way is the A27 autostrada to the Treviso Sud exit, but the more direct route is the SS13 (though that can be slow-going at rush hour and midday). From Padua, take the A4 autostrada past Venice to the A27.

VISITOR INFORMATION   The **tourist office** is just behind the main Piazza dei Signori at Piazza Monte di Pietà 8 (© **0422-547-632;** fax 0422-419-092; www.sevenonline.it), and is open daily from 9am to 12:30pm, plus Tuesday to Friday 2:30 to 6:30pm and Saturday and Sunday 3:30 to 6pm. There's also a provincial **tourist office** at Via Turazza 7a (© **0422-541-052;** fax 0422-540-366; www.trevisotour.org), though it's mostly administrative.

WHAT TO SEE & DO

The center of town is **Piazza dei Signori,** lined with arcades that run under the retro-medieval **Palazzo del Podestà,** rebuilt in the 1870s with a tall battlemented clock tower, and spread into a loggia under the 13th-century brick council hall **Palazzo dei Trecento.**

Just beyond this square, on Piazza S. Vito, sits a pair of medieval churches: **Santa Lucia,** with Tomaso da Modena frescoes in the first alcove on the right,

---

Tips **Free Tours**

The tourist office offers free guided tours of the city, April 28 to December 29, on Saturdays, lasting from 10am to noon. The tours must be booked in advance at © **0422-547-632.**

and **San Vito,** with its rather faded Byzantine-style frescoes from the 12th or 13th century. Both are open daily 9am to noon and 4 to 6pm.

The overbearing facade of the **Duomo** 🏛 is from 1836, but it's flanked by Romanesque lions that, coupled with the seven green copper domes, speak to the cathedral's 12th-century origins in the Venetian-Byzantine style. The second pilaster features a late-1400s relief of the *Visitation* by Lorenzo Bregno. The chapel altarpiece at the end of the right aisle is an unusually bright and open *Annunciation* by Titian (the chapel's founder Broccardo Malchiostro was painted in later, crouching behind the classical building to peep at the scene). The crypt contains a forest of columns and fragments of 14th-century fresco and mosaic. It's open Monday to Saturday 7:30am to noon and 3:30 to 7pm, Sunday 7:30am to 1pm and 3:30 to 8pm.

Via Canoniche, next to the cathedral, runs past an ancient paleo-Christian mosaic of the 4th century to a Gothic priory housing the **Museo Diocesano d'Arte Sacra** (✆ **0422-416-707**). Inside are mid-13th-century frescoes, a Tomaso da Modena that used to decorate the bishop's palace, and plenty of medieval sculpture along with the usual vestments and holy silverware—though, frankly, if admission weren't free, it wouldn't be worth it. It's open Monday to Thursday 9am to noon, Saturday 9am to noon and 3 to 6pm.

More interesting—or at least it will be once it reopens—is the **Museo Civico,** Borgo Cavour 24 (✆ **0422-658-442** or 0422-591-337). On the ground floor is a remarkable collection of ancient bronze relics, including swords and ritualistic disks from the 5th century B.C., alongside Roman remains. Upstairs, the painting collection includes works, but no standouts, by Giovanni Bellini, Lorenzo Lotto, Titian, Jacopo Bassano, Cima da Conegliano, and both Giovanni Battista and Gian Domenico Tiepolo. At press time it had just closed for restorations and renovations, with no set date for reopening, but thankfully the best of the paintings are still being shown in Santa Caterina (below), where some of the museum's other collections may be moving on a permanent basis in the future as Treviso rethinks its civic museum scene. Though closed as we go to press, the old ticket price was 3€ ($3.45), and open hours were Tuesday to Saturday 9am to 12:30pm and 2:30 to 5pm, and Sunday 9am to noon.

Down in the southwest corner of town, the big brick 13th- to 14th-century Dominican church of **San Nicolò** 🏛 houses some good Gothic frescoes. Tomaso da Modena decorated the huge round columns with a series of saints; Antonio da Treviso did the absolutely gargantuan St. Christopher—his .9m (3-ft.) long feet strolling over biting fish—in 1410. On the right side of the apse, the tomb of Agostino d'Onigo from 1500 has courtly *Pages* frescoed by Lorenzo Lotto, who also did the altarpiece of the *Incredulity of St. Thomas with Apostles* in the chapel right of the altar. The late-14th-century Sienese School frescoes lining the walls include an *Adoration of the Magi,* complete with camels. It's open daily 8am to 12:30pm and 3:30 to 7pm. Next door to the (unused) front door of the church is the entrance to the adjoining seminary's **Sala del Capitolo,** Piazzetta Benedetto XI 2 (✆ **0422-3247**), frescoed in 1352 by Tomaso da Modena with 40 Dominicans busily studying and copying out manuscripts at their desks. It's open 8am to 6pm daily; admission is free (ring the bell if the door is shut).

On the other side of town—across the wide Cagnan canals, whose islands host a daily fish market (see above)—stands a (deconsecrated) church that's now well worth seeking out. The highlight of **Santa Caterina** (✆ **0422-591-337**) itself are frescoes by Tomaso da Modena, including a Madonna and (detached from a now-destroyed church and kept here) a series on the life of St. Ursula. The bonus is that a long restoration on the church complex was completed in summer 2003, and the city plans to transfer many of its treasures here to take up permanent display. The exact division of works between the (currently closed for its own restoration) Museo Civico and this space has yet to be decided, but in the meantime at least the city's painting collection is being kept here. Admission is now 3€ ($3.45) for adults, 2€ ($2.30) for students, and 1€ ($1.15) for kids under 10; it's open every Tuesday to Sunday from 9am to 12:30pm and 2:30 to 6pm.

WHERE TO STAY

Treviso doesn't have much of a hotel industry. If the places below are full, a lovely choice about a 10-minute drive north of the town walls is the **Hotel Scala** ✪, Viale Felissent (✆ **0422-307-600;** fax 0422-305-048; www.hotelscala.com), a suburban villa with 20 comfortable bedrooms—all with air-conditioning, TV, telephone, and minibar—and a good restaurant. Doubles go for 106€ ($122) including breakfast.

Albergo Campeol ✪   This simple but comfortable hotel sits smack in the center of town, on a little street off the main drag a half block from the Palazzo Podestà. Rooms vary in size and decor, with functional, pleasant-enough wood furnishings that match the step-gabled plank headboards. Three of the largest rooms come with three beds: no. 29 enjoys a small sitting area, no. 30 sits in the narrow end of the buildings with windows on three sides overlooking a canal, and the similar no. 34 lies directly above no. 30 on the top floor, so its windows feature views over two canals and the rooftops. Its location is far superior to that of the Continental (see below), though it's not as nicely appointed.

Piazza G. Ancilotto 4, 31100 Treviso. ✆ and fax **0422-56-601**. www.albergocampeol.it. 14 units. 83€ ($96) double. Breakfast 5€ ($6). AE, DC, MC, V. *In room:* TV, hair dryer.

Hotel Continental   The Continental is a large, modernized hotel 3 blocks from the train station at the city walls, a 10-minute walk from the central piazza. The modular furnishings are slightly worn but kept in good condition, the beds are firm, and there are parquet floors and some nice old touches such as ornate wood entablatures, chandeliers, or mirrored closet doors silk-screened with Oriental prints. A few rooms have small vestibule sitting areas, and corner units are larger and tend to be more nicely furnished. There is, however, a bit of street noise from the busy road below, and while some bathrooms are new, others are aging, and many have shower nozzles you have to hold and no shower curtains. By 2004 a restructuring should add a business center and nine suites on an executive level.

Via Roma 16, 31100 Treviso. ✆ **0422-411-216**. Fax 0422-55-054. www.hcontinental.it. 80 units. 120€ ($138) double. Breakfast included. AE, DC, MC, V. **Amenities:** Nearby restaurant; bar; concierge; tour desk; car rental; room service (breakfast and bar only); babysitting; laundry service; dry cleaning (same-day). *In room:* A/C, TV, dataport, hair dryer, safe.

WHERE TO DINE

In addition to the choices below, you can get classy, made-to-order cafeteria fare at the Treviso branch of the excellent **Brek** chain, Corso del Popolo 25 (✆ **0422-590-012**), open daily. For pizza and people-watching, **Da Pino,** Piazza dei Signori 23 (✆ **0422-56-426**), has tables set under the high, wood-coffered arcade of the main square; it's closed Tuesday.

Toni del Spin ✪✪ *Finds* TREVISIANA   Alfredo Sturlese has taken over for Toni, who opened this down-home joint more than 70 years ago. Blackboards with the daily list of dishes hang from the rough crossbeams below high, sloping wood ceilings. The kitchen prepares a carefully considered mix of simple but

> ## *Moments* Cappuccino on the Piazza
>
> Of the two spots for drinks and snacks at tables set under the loggia over-looking the main Piazza dei Signori, **Caffè Beltrame,** no. 27 (© **0422-540-789**), has a better position at the corner of the loggia, while **Biffi,** no. 28 (© **0422-540-784;** www.biffitv.it), serves better beer and sandwiches.

intriguing dishes such as *gazbacho andaluz* (cold tomato vegetable soup), *conchiglie con cavalfiori* (pasta shells with cauliflower), *panzerotti di funghi al burro* (fried mushroom pastries), *spiedino di carne misto alla griglia* (grilled shish kebob of mixed meats), and *faraona con polenta* (guinea fowl with polenta). The house wine is good, and they charge decent prices on a select list of regional bottles (the reds skewed toward popular new vintages using French grapes)—they even run a wine shop across the street.

Via Inferiore 7. © 0422-543-829. www.ristorantetonidelspin.com. Primi 4.50€–6.50€ ($5–$7); secondi 6€–14€ ($7–$16). AE, MC, V. Tues–Sat 12:30–2:30pm; Mon–Sat 7:30–10:30pm. Closed 3 weeks in July and 1 week in Aug.

Toulà-Da Alfredo ✮ TREVISANA/INTERNATIONAL   This chain of refined northern-cuisine restaurants, founded at the ski resort of Cortina about 2 hours north of Treviso in the Dolomites, is set in a modern series of rooms with odd murals and a ceiling trompe l'oeil frescoed with vines. Its longtime regular customers tend to be nearing (or beyond) retirement, but the cooking remains fresh, if solidly traditional and a bit overpriced. The specialty is *linguine verdi tradizione toulá* (green noodles in a cream and prosciutto sauce baked under *parmigiano*), though they also feature risotto with clams and wild asparagus, and chateaubriand in a béarnaise sauce.

Via Collalto 26. © 0422-540-275. www.toula.it. Reservations recommended. Primi 9€–14€ ($10–$16); secondi 16€–27€ ($18–$31). AE, DC, MC, V. Tues–Sun 12:30–2:30pm; Tues–Sat 7:30–11pm. Closed Aug 2–25. Bus: 1 or 7.

3 Asolo

73km (45 miles) N of Padua, 52km (32 miles) NE of Treviso, 16km (10 miles) E of Bassano del Grappa

Known as the "Town of a Hundred Horizons" because of its panoramic views, this nub of a medieval hill town (though it was founded during the twilight of Imperial Rome) has become the secret hideaway for true Veneto aficionados. It's a required stop for folks interested in meandering the backcountry or driving the wine roads, and it's a great place for those on bike tours to take a midday break.

Asolo was the Renaissance-era home of Caterina Cornaro of Venice, who was awarded the realm of Asolo for her help in (unsuccessfully) keeping the Turks out of Cyprus. Much of the 15th-century charm you see today is a result of her 12-year presence and patronage in the town. Other VIP residents were the English poet Robert Browning and Italy's early-20th-century grande dame of the stage, Eleonora Duse.

FESTIVALS & MARKETS   There's an **antiques market** the second Sunday of each month, with a special books and prints edition the third Sunday in October. The local **folk festival** is in honor of San Gottardo on May 5, with a market, procession, and the sale of traditional terra-cotta shepherd flutes. Asolo holds a **Palio race** the third Sunday of September, pitting the town's six *contrade* (neighborhoods) against each other to pull up the hill a Roman-style chariot bearing a local damsel dressed as Caterina Cornaro. There's also a **Festival of Chamber Music** in August and September.

ESSENTIALS

GETTING THERE   By Train   Since the nearest train station is in Cornuda, a 17-minute bus ride away, buses are a better bet. There are a dozen trains into Cornuda daily from Padua (40–60 min.). From Treviso there are only three direct trains (30 min.), at 8:23am, 12:33pm, and 5:28pm, but you can get 1 of 20 or so daily to Montebelluno (20–30 min.) and change to 1 of 14 on to Cornuda (a bit over 10 min.), though the wait may be anywhere from a few minutes to over an hour.

By Bus   A dozen **buses** (© 0423-493-464) run daily from Bassano del Grappa (25 min.), and about 10 daily from Treviso (© 0422-577-311; 55 min.). Buses stop at Asolo's Ca' Vescovo station on the main highway down in the valley, from which frequent shuttles climb up the long hill into the old town.

By Car   From Padua take SS47 north to Bassano di Grappa, then drive east to Asolo on SS248. From Treviso take the SS348 to Montebelluno, then the SS248 west.

VISITOR INFORMATION   The genuinely helpful **tourist office** is at Piazza Garibaldi 73 (© **0423-529-046;** fax 0423-524-137). Another can be found at Piazza Gabrielle d'Annunzio 3 (© **0423-55-045;** www.asolo.it or www.comune. asolo.tv.it; hours vary, so call ahead).

WHAT TO SEE & DO

Though the area's top sight is the **Villa Barbaro** outside town (see below), Asolo has a few diversions beyond merely strolling its streets and enjoying its "hundred horizons." Asolo was the seat of a bishopric until 969 and remained a countryside escape for rich Venetians thereafter, so it's no surprise that its cathedral, rebuilt in the 18th century, contains several artistic treasures. They apparently had a thing for paintings of the Assumption. There's one by Lorenzo Lotto (1506; on the left aisle), another by Jacopo "da Ponte" Bassano (1549; next to the last on the left aisle), and a bad 19th-century copy of a Titian version on the high altar. Breaking the theme is Lazzaro Bastiani's stiffly formal *St. Jerome* (1488), which features a pretty countryside in the background.

On the main square, the frescoed **Loggia del Capitano** houses a small museum that contains memorials to Robert Browning (whose son is buried in the local cemetery) and to Caterina Cornaro. Caterina was the Queen of Cyprus until her husband died and she abdicated. She sought refuge in the Republic of Venice, which gave her Asolo to rule from 1489 to her death in 1510. Her home was the medieval **Castello,** begun in the late 6th century (there's nothing special to see there now; it just has a cafe tucked against the inside of the old castle's towering wall), which became known as the "Queen's Palace."

Impressions

I assure you that, even though I have knowledge of and have seen with my own eyes the most beautiful panoramas in Italy and elsewhere, I have found nothing quite like the view one can enjoy from the tower of the Queen's Palace.

—Robert Browning

WHERE TO STAY

Hotel Duse The Hotel Duse, named for Italian actress Eleonora Duse, offers a perfect location at decent prices. This small, relatively inexpensive (for Asolo) hotel occupies a 16th-century house right on the corner of the main square. The rooms are smallish, but nicely furnished with modern pieces and a few art prints on the walls. Top-floor rooms have sloping plank ceilings and a cozy feel.

Via R. Browning 190, 31011 Asolo. ℭ **0423-55-241.** Fax 0423-950-404. www.hotelduse.com. 14 units. 95€–120€ ($109–$138) double; 115€–130€ ($132–$150) jr. suite. Extra bed 26€ ($30). Breakfast 6€ ($7). MC, V. Parking 3.10€ ($3.55). **Amenities:** Golf (nearby); concierge; tour desk; room service (limited); laundry service; nonsmoking rooms. *In room:* A/C, TV, dataport, minibar (in doubles), hair dryer (ask at desk).

Hotel Villa Cipriani ★★ One of the town's beautifully sited 16th-century villas, once owned by Robert and Elizabeth Barrett Browning, was turned into the area's most sought-after deluxe hotel in 1962 by Giuseppe Cipriani (owner of Venice's Harry's Bar). It retains that private villa feel, its main building wrapped around a lovely garden centered on a rose-trimmed well, with an 11-room annex and views spilling down a terraced private park and slopes of olive trees. "Superior" rooms—with worn Oriental carpets on parquet floors, stylish, subdued furnishings, and hand-painted Vietri tiles in the bathrooms—are slightly smaller than "Executive" accommodations, which often feature beamed ceilings, brass chandeliers, painted antiques mixed with discreetly modern TV chests, and a small sitting area of overstuffed easy chairs. Room nos. 101 and 102 enjoy large private terraces with valley views. Half board is 75€ ($86) per person per day.

Via Canova 298. ℭ **800/325-3535** in the U.S., or 0423-523-411 in Italy. Fax 0423-952-095. www.sheraton. com/villacipriani. 31 units. 345€ ($397) superior double; 405€ ($466) exclusive double without valley view; 455€ ($523) exclusive double with valley view; 505€ ($581) double with terrace. Extra bed 80€ ($92). Continental breakfast 20€ ($23); buffet breakfast 35€ ($40). AE, DC, MC, V. Parking 16€ ($18). **Amenities:** Restaurant; elegant bar; golf (nearby); bike rental; concierge; tour desk; car-rental desk; business center; room service (limited); in-room massage; babysitting; laundry service; dry cleaning (same day); nonsmoking rooms. *In room:* A/C, TV, dataport, minibar, hair dryer, safe.

WHERE TO DINE

Hosteria Ca' Derton ★★ VENEZIANA This haven of fine dining sits in a 17th-century palazzo on a quiet *piazzetta* just off the busy main square. The menu changes with the season and whim of chef-owner Nino Baggio, whose wife, Antoinetta, and grown children Guido, Enrico, and Cristina wait tables in the antiques-filled dining room with an easygoing professionalism. Nino looks to local culinary traditions and the freshest of ingredients to create such dishes as *bigoli al torchio con ragù d'anatra* (fat strands of handmade spaghetti in a duck ragù), *lasagnetta con zucchine e gamberoni* (delicate pasta casserole with zucchini and jumbo shrimp), *quagliette disossate e farcite arrosto* (roast stuffed quail), or simple *talgiata di manzo* (steak perfumed with rosemary). Secondi may look pricey, but unlike in most Italian restaurants, they come with a *contorno* (side dish) included—as

---

Moments A Glass of Wine

The best place in town to duck in for a glass of wine with the locals is **Antica Osteria Al Bacaro**, Via R. Browning 165 (ℭ **0423-55-150**), where townsfolk have gathered since 1892. Even if you're not staying at the **Hotel Villa Cipriani** (ℭ **0423-523-411**), you can still enjoy the same breathtaking views from the lovely terrace bar for the cost of an iced tea or cocktail.

Antoinetta explains it, "a vegetable Nino thinks appropriate . . . or sometimes just polenta!" The house merlot and Colli Asolani white are both excellent.

Piazza d'Annunzio 11. ⓒ **0423-529-648**. www.caderton.com. Reservations recommended. Primi 6€–9€ ($7–$10); secondi 13€–18€ ($14–$21). AE, DC, MC, V. Tues–Sun 12:30–2pm; Tues–Sat 7:30–9:45pm.

A VILLA OUTSIDE TOWN

The **Villa Barbaro** ⭐⭐ (ⓒ **0423-923-004;** www.villadimaser.it), also called Villa di Maser, is one of Palladio's most celebrated. It lies in the valley, east of Asolo outside the hamlet of Maser. Probably the most famous of the Palladian villas after Vicenza's Villa Rotonda and one of the most beautiful, the 1560 Barbaro is a standout for its gorgeous frescoes by Veronese (which La Rotonda lacks). It's privately owned by some very, very lucky folks who make you wear giant slippers to shuffle around and admire the frescoes on the ground floor. It's open March to October, Tuesday, Saturday, and Sunday 3 to 6pm; November to February, Saturday and Sunday 2:30 to 5pm; closed December 24 to January 6. Admission is 5€ ($6).

Ten to 15 daily **buses** (ⓒ **0422-577-311**) between Bassano (30 min.) and Treviso (50 min.), stopping also at Asolo (15–20 min.), stop in Maser. If you're coming by car from Asolo, drive down to the main road and turn left, then left when you see a pretty church squatting in the middle of the road.

4 Bassano del Grappa

35km (22miles) NE of Vicenza, 43km (27 miles) N of Padua, 16km (10 miles) W of Asolo, 47km (29 miles) W of Treviso

This picturesque town on the Brenta River is renowned for its centuries-old production of handcrafted ceramics and of grappa, Italy's national firewater of choice (see box below). Its Palladian covered wooden bridge is a highlight of the small *centro storico*. The city's arcaded homes, whose facades are painted in the traditional manner, and small squares make this a lovely break from the art-laden larger towns described in this chapter.

FESTIVALS In June, Bassano invites international street musicians and buskers to perform in a festival. Bassano's annual **Opera Estate Festival** ⭐ takes place from early July through August, with alfresco performances of opera, concerts, a mini jazz fest, and dance (ballet, modern, and folk). For information, contact the tourist office (Largo Corona d'Italia 35; ⓒ **0424-524-214;** fax 0424-525-138; www.comune.bassano.vi.it).

ESSENTIALS

VISITOR INFORMATION For information, call the **tourist office,** Lgo. Corona d'Italia 35 (ⓒ **0424-524-351;** fax 0424-525-301; www.comune. bassano.vi.it). It's open daily from 9am to 1pm and Monday to Saturday from 2 to 6pm.

GETTING THERE By Bus To get here from Vicenza, you can take one of two dozen daily **FTV buses** (ⓒ **0424-30-850;** www.ftv.vi.it) that make the 1-hour trip. Frequent buses from Padua take half the time, making fewer stops. There are also a dozen **buses** (ⓒ **0423-493-464** or 0423-529-966) daily from nearby Asolo (25 min.).

By Car From Asolo head west on the SS248; from Vicenza north on the SS248; from Padua north on the SS47. From Treviso the more scenic route follows the SS348 northwest to Montebelluno, where you pick up the smaller

SS248 west; the faster route is west along the SS53 toward Vicenza, turning north onto the SS47 at Cittadella.

WHAT TO SEE & DO

Bassano's historic center is just a half dozen or so blocks in either direction, its medieval buildings and baroque palazzi snuggled along the Brenta River. Andrea Palladio designed Bassano's lovely symbol, the wooden **Ponte degli Alpini** 👯 covered bridge, in 1569, and every time floods or disaster have struck, it has been rebuilt precisely along the original plan.

The stars of the **Museo Civico** 👯, Piazza Garibaldi (© **0424-522-235** or 0424-523-336; www.museobassano.it), are the Bassano family. Patriarch Jacopo was clearly the most talented, evident in his early *Flight into Egypt* and faded frescoes from local house facades to later works such as *St. John the Baptist* (1558) and *Pentecost* (1559), which are looser and show the influence of Titian. His sons Leandro and Francesco il Giovane (responsible for the nice *Lamentation*) had less success, as did their less talented sibling Gerolano, who stayed in Bassano to run the family workshop. There are also plaster casts and original sketches by neoclassical master Antonio Canova, and a fine collection of Attic and Apulian vases. Admission—which also covers the ceramics museum (see below)—is 4.50€ ($5) for adults, 3€ ($3.45) for children under 18 or seniors over 60. It's open Tuesday to Saturday from 9:30am to 6:30pm and Sunday from 3:30 to 6:30pm.

Palazzo Sturm (1765–66), overlooking the Brenta River on Via Schiavonetti, retains some original frescoes and stuccoes and houses a ceramics museum heavy on 18th- and 19th-century porcelains, with a contemporary collection downstairs. Admission is cumulative with the Museo Civico, above, and its hours are also the same.

WHERE TO STAY

Bonotto Hotel Belvedere 👯   It looks modern out front, but this has been Bassano's premier hotel since the 15th century. The Belvedere sits on the busy main road skirting the walls of the historic center, 4 blocks from the central Piazza Garibaldi, but the windows' double set of double panes cuts out most noise. Standard rooms in the 1985 wing have modular '80s-style units in baby blue or wood veneer and mirrors to make the midsize rooms feel larger. Superior accommodations are larger, with sturdy dark wood furnishings and Jacuzzi tubs. Junior suites are spruced up with 17th- and 18th-century Venetian-style antiques and double sinks, though some are furbished in a modern but still classy style, with embroidered sofas. The cozy rooms on the top floor have sloping beamed ceilings to match the chunky, slightly rustic furnishings.

Should the Belvedere be full, they may put you up in their modern, 66-room **Hotel Palladio,** around the corner at Via Gramsci 2 (© **0424-523-777;** fax 0424-524-050). There, a double runs from 78€ to 117€ ($90–$135).

Piazzale G. Giardino 14, 36061 Bassano del Grappa (VI). © **0424-529-845.** Fax 0424-529-849. www. bonotto.it. 87 units. 82€–137€ ($94–$158) double; 113€–158€ ($130–$182) superior double; 155€– 211€ ($178–$243) jr. suite. Breakfast included. AE, DC, MC, V. Parking 10€ ($12) in garage. **Amenities:** Excellent Veneta restaurant; bar; discount at golf course in nearby Asolo; exercise room and sauna at sister Hotel Palladio around the corner; free bikes; concierge; tour desk; car-rental desk (free Smart car with superior room or jr. suite); limited secretarial services; room service (limited); massage (in Palladio); babysitting; laundry service; dry cleaning (same-day); nonsmoking rooms. *In room:* A/C, TV w/pay movies, minibar, hair dryer, safe (in almost all).

WHERE TO DINE

Bassano has long been known for its white asparagus, green peas, and blend of Venetian and mountain cuisines. Unfortunately, few of Bassano's current crop of restaurants live up to its traditions. Along with the excellent restaurant at Bonotto Hotel Belvedere (see above), here are the best of what you will find.

Al Sole VENETA   This is one of the more refined restaurants in town, serving elegant local dishes based on seasonal fresh ingredients such as *bigoli al sugo d'anatra* (thick homemade pasta in a duck ragù), *risotto agli asparagi bianchi* (risotto made with the tender local white asparagus), or *baccalà con polenta* (salt cod served alongside creamy polenta).

Via Vittorelli 41–43. (C) 0424-523-206. Reservations recommended. Primi 6.50€–10€ ($7–$12); secondi 10€–17€ ($12–$20). AE, DC, MC, V. Tues–Sun noon–2:30pm and 7:30–10pm.

Birreria Ottone ⭐ AUSTRIAN/ITALIAN   This popular 1870 beer hall inhabits a 13th-century palazzo, which lent its stone walls to the elegant dining room. Bassano friends and families gather here sometimes just to drink in good company, sometimes for a full meal of grub that runs the gamut from traditional Italian dishes and local Veneto specialties to the best of Tirolean and Austrian cuisines.

Via Matteotti 48–50. (C) 0424-522-206. Reservations suggested on weekends. Primi 6€–7€ ($7–$8); secondi 7.50€–15€ ($9–$17). AE, DC, MC, V. Wed–Mon noon–3pm; Wed–Sun 7–11:30pm. Closed 2nd week of Aug.

A SIDE TRIP TO MAROSTICA

The delightful medieval walled village of Marostica, 30km (19 miles) north of Vicenza (7km/4½ miles west of Bassano), comes alive a la Brigadoon every other summer (in even years only), when the entire town dresses up to commemorate a true centuries-old chess game between two enamored knights for the hand of Lionora. The chivalric *Partita a Scacchi* ⭐⭐⭐ is re-enacted on the main piazza with real people as the pieces, dressed in full elaborate Renaissance costume, preceded by a flag-throwing procession. Everyone in town takes part, and the evocative torch-lit nighttime setting is gorgeous. For more information or to reserve tickets, visit www.marosticascacchi.it or call the tourist office at (C) 0424-72-127.

Performances are repeated over the course of the second weekend of September in even-numbered years (so, for example: Sept 10–12, 2004, hosts performances at 9pm each day, plus a 5pm "matinee" on Sun, Sept 12). A few of the worst seats are usually available each day of performance, but it's best to purchase tickets months in advance. **Tourist information** is at Piazza Castello 1 ((C) 0424-72-127; fax 0424-72-800; www.telemar.it/marostica.htm). Marostica's engaging *Sagra del Ciliege* (**Cherry Festival**) takes place in June. You can get here on one of two dozen daily buses from Vicenza in 40 minutes. Dozens of local buses do the short run daily from Bassano to Marostica. By car, head west on S248.

5 Vicenza

32km (20 miles) W of Padua, 74km (46 miles) W of Venice, 51km (32 miles) E of Verona, 204km (126 miles) E of Milan

Vicenza pays heartfelt homage to Andrea di Pietro della Gondola (born in Padua in 1508, died in Maser in 1580). He came to Vicenza at the age of 16, and lived out his life and dreams here under the name Palladio at a time when Vicenza was under the sway of the still-powerful Venice Republic. Although not highly innovative, he was the most important architect of the High Renaissance, one whose living monuments have inspired and influenced architecture in the Western world over the centuries to this very day.

Vicenza and its surroundings are a mecca for the architecture lover, a living museum of Palladian and Palladian-inspired monuments—and consequently one designated a protected UNESCO World Heritage Site in 1994. But even if you've never heard of Palladio, you'll find an evening stroll through illuminated piazzas and along boutique-lined streets plenty enjoyable. Plan on taking home a wealth of knowledge about architecture—a day in Vicenza is worth a semester back in school.

Today Vicenza is one of the wealthiest cities in Italy, thanks in part to the recent burgeoning of the local computer-component industry (Federico Faggin, inventor of the silicon chip, was born here). It is also the traditional center of the country's gold manufacturing industry (one-third of Italy's gold is made here, and each year three prestigious international gold fairs make finding a hotel in these parts impossible) and is one of Europe's largest producers of textiles. The average Vicentino is well-off, and it shows; join the entire town for the daily *passeggiata* and pick up on the palpable attitude.

FESTIVALS   The well-established summertime series of **Concerti in Villa** ★ (© **0444-399-104**) takes place in June and July; a few concerts are held outdoors at Vicenza's famed Villa la Rotonda, for others you will need a car. The tourist office will have the schedule and availability of seats; tickets usually cost around 15€ to 20€ ($17–$23). The stage of the delightful **Teatro Olimpico** (© **0444-222-101** or 0444-222-154; www.olimpico.vicenza.it) now hosts shows again in September and October, mainly classical plays (this year was the *Oedipus* cycle) or Shakespeare (*Henry V* and *Hamlet* are sort of strange in Italian). Tickets start at 15€ ($17).

ESSENTIALS

GETTING THERE   By Train   The **train station** is in Piazza Stazione, also called Campo Marzio (© **0444-325-046;** www.ftv.vi.it), at the southern end of Viale Roma. There's frequent service (2–3 per hour) connecting Vicenza with Venice (52–67 min.), Padua (20 min.), and Verona (30 min.).

By Bus   The **FTV bus station** (© **0444-223-115** or 0444-223-127) is located on Viale Milano, just to the west (left) of the train station. Buses leave frequently for all the major cities in the Veneto and to Milan; prices are comparable to train travel.

By Car   Vicenza is on the A4 autostrada that links Venice to the east with Milan to the west. Coming from Venice (about 1 hr.), you'll bypass Padua before arriving in Vicenza.

VISITOR INFORMATION   The **tourist information office** is at Piazza Matteotti 12 (© **0444-320-854;** fax 0444-994-779; www.ascom.vi.it/aptvicenza or www.comune.vicenza.it), next to the Teatro Olimpico. The office is open daily from 9am to 1pm and Monday to Saturday from 2:30 to 6pm. Mid-October to mid-March, closing time is 5:30pm. During summer an office at the train station is open Monday to Saturday 9am to 2pm and Sunday 1 to 6pm. The largely administrative APT tourism office is at Piazza Duomo 5 (© **0444-544-122;** fax 0444-325-001).

CITY LAYOUT   The city's layout is quite straightforward and easy to navigate on foot. The train station lies at its southernmost point. From here head straight ahead on Viale Roma; it ends at a turnabout with gated gardens beyond. Head right (east) into the *centro storico,* marked by the **Piazza Castello,** from which the main thoroughfare starts, the **Corso Palladio.** Lined with shops, offices and

Value Seeing Vicenza by Cumulative Ticket

Two cumulative admission tickets are available: The regular "Card Musei" costs 7€ ($8) for adults, 4€ ($4.60) for students, and includes admission to the **Teatro Olimpico, Museo Civico,** and **Museo Naturalistico Archaeologico.** The other, more inclusive "Card Musei" adds the frankly uninteresting **Museo del Risorgimento e della Resistenza** and costs 8€ ($9) for adults and 4.50€ ($5) students. Children under 14 get into every museum for free.

banks, the arrow-straight Corso cuts through town, running southwest (from Piazza Castello) to northeast (Piazza Matteotti), site of the Teatro Olimpico. Along the Corso you'll find urban palazzi by Palladio and his students; midway, the **Piazza dei Signori** (and its Basilica Palladiana) will be found on your right (south). Perpendicular to the Corso is the important **Contrà Porti,** a lovely palazzo-studded street, on your left (north).

GETTING AROUND   There is limited traffic (for taxis, buses, and residents) once you enter the Piazza del Castello and the *centro storico.* Everything of interest can be easily reached on foot; pick up a map at the tourist office. Even the two villas just outside town (see "Villas & A Basilica Nearby," below) can be reached by foot (not suggested in the heat of high season) or bike, as well as by bus or car.

PIAZZA DEI SIGNORI

South of Corso Palladio on the site of the ancient Roman Forum and still the town hub, this central square should be your first introduction to the city and Palladio, its local boy wonder.

The magnificent bigger-than-life **Basilica Palladiana** ★★ is not a church at all and was only partially designed by Palladio. Beneath it stood a Gothic-style Palazzo della Ragione (Law Courts and Assembly Hall) that Palladio was commissioned to convert to a High Renaissance style befitting a flourishing late-16th-century city under Venice's benevolent patronage. It was Palladio's first public work and secured his favor and reputation with the local authorities. He created two superimposed galleries, the lower with Doric pillars, the upper with Ionic. The roof was destroyed by World War II bombing but has since been rebuilt in its original style. It's open April to September, Tuesday to Saturday from 9:30am to noon and from 2 to 7pm; Sunday from 9:30am to 12:30pm and from 2 to 7pm. Off season, it's closed Sunday afternoon; free admission.

The 12th-century **Torre Bissara** (or **Torre di Piazza**) bell tower belonged to the original church and stands near two columns in the piazza's east end (the Piazza Blade), one topped by the winged lion of Venice's Serene Republic, the other by the *Redentore* (Redeemer). Of note elsewhere in the piazza are the Loggia del Capitaniato (1570), begun but never finished according to plans by Palladio except for the four massive redbrick columns (on the north side of piazza alongside the well-known Gran Caffè Garibaldi). Behind the basilica (to the south) is the **Piazza delle Erbe** ★, site of the daily produce market.

CORSO ANDREA PALLADIO

This is Vicenza's main street, and what a grand one it is, lined with the magnificent palazzi of Palladio and his students (and *their* students who, centuries later, were still influenced by the mastery of Palladio's work), today converted into cafes, swank shops, and imposing banks. The first one of note, starting from its southwest cap near the Piazza Castello, is the **Palazzo Valmarana** at no. 16, begun by Palladio in 1566. On the right (behind which stands the Piazza dei Signori and the Basilica Palladiana) is the **Palazzo del Comunale,** the Town Hall built in 1592 by Scamozzi (1552–1616), a native of Vicenza and Palladio's protégé and star pupil. This is said to be Scamozzi's greatest work.

From the Corso Palladio and heading northeast, take a left onto the Contrà Porti, the second most important street for its Palladian and Gothic palazzi. The two designed by Palladio are the **Palazzo Barbarano Porto** at no. 11, and (opposite) **Palazzo Thiene** at no.12 (now the headquarters of a bank); **Gothic palazzi** of particular note can be found at nos. 6 to 10, 14, 16, 17, and 19. Parallel, on Corso Fogazzaro, look for no. 16, **Palazzo Valmarana,** perhaps the most eccentric of Palladio's works.

Returning to Corso Palladio, look for no. 145/147, the pre-Palladian **Ca d'Oro (Golden Palace),** named for the gold leaf used in the frescoes that once covered its facade. It was bombed in 1944 and rebuilt in 1950. The simple **16th-century palazzo** at no. 163 was Palladio's home.

Before reaching the Piazza Matteotti and the end of the Corso Palladio, you'll see signs for the **Church of Santa Corona** ⭐, set back on the left on the Via Santa Corona 2 (open daily 8:30am–noon and 2:30–6pm). An unremarkable 13th-century Gothic church, it shelters two masterpieces (and Vicenza's most important church paintings) that make this worth a visit: Giovanni Bellini's *Baptism of Christ* (5th altar on left) and Veronese's *Adoration of the Magi* (3rd chapel on right). This is Vicenza's most interesting church, far more so than the cavernous Duomo southwest of the Piazza dei Signori, but worth seeking out only if you've got the extra time. At the end of the Corso Palladio at its northeastern end is Palladio's world-renowned **Teatro Olimpico** and, across the street, the **Museo Civico** in the Palazzo Chiericati.

Teatro Olimpico and Museo Civico ⭐⭐⭐   The splendid Teatro Olimpico was Palladio's greatest urban work, and one of his last. He began the project in 1580, the year of his death at the age of 72; it would be completed 5 years later by his student Vicenzo Scamozzi. It was the first covered theater in Europe, inspired by the theaters of antiquity. The seating area, in the shape of a half-moon as in the old arenas, seats 1,000. The stage seems profoundly deeper than its actual 4.2m (14 ft.), thanks to the permanent stage "curtain" and Scamozzi's clever use of trompe l'oeil added after Palladio's death. The stage scene represents the ancient streets of Thebes, while the faux clouds and sky covering the dome further the impression of being in an outdoor Roman amphitheater. Drama, music, and dance performances are still held here year-round; check with the tourist office.

Across the Piazza Matteotti is another Palladian opus, the **Palazzo Chiericati,** which houses the Museo Civico (Municipal Museum). Looking more like one of the country villas for which Palladio was equally famous, this major work is considered one of his finest and is visited as much for its two-tiered, statue-topped facade as for the collection of Venetian paintings it houses on the first floor. Venetian masters you'll recognize include Tiepolo, Tintoretto, and Veronese, while the lesser-known include works from the Vicenzan (founded by Bartolomeo Montagna) and Bassano schools of painting.

Piazza Matteotti (at Corso Palladio). ℂ **0444-222-800.** Admission for each is 4€ ($4.60) or 7€ ($8) with cumulative ticket (see "Seeing Vicenza by Cumulative Ticket," above). Apr–Sept Tues–Sun 9am–7pm; Oct–Mar Tues–Sun 9am–5pm. Bus: 1, 2, 5, or 7.

VILLAS & A BASILICA NEARBY

To reach the two important villas in the immediate environs of Vicenza, south-east of the train station, you can walk, bike, or take the no. 8 bus. First stop by the tourist office for a map, and check on visiting hours, which tend to change from year to year. The following two villas are generally open from mid-March to early November.

The **Villa Rotonda** ✹✹✹ (© **0444-321-793;** fax 0444-879-1380), alterna-tively referred to as Villa Capra Valmarana after its owners, is considered one of the most perfect buildings ever constructed and has been added to the World Heritage List by UNESCO; it is a particularly important must-do excursion for students and lovers of architecture. Most authorities refer to it as Palladio's finest work. Obviously inspired by ancient Greek and Roman designs, Palladio began this perfectly proportioned square building topped by a dome in 1567; it was completed between 1580 and 1592 by Scamozzi after Palladio's death. It is worth a visit if only to view it from the outside (in fact, you can really see much of it from the gate). Admission to enter the grounds for outside viewing is 3€ ($3.45); admission to visit the lavishly decorated interior is 6€ ($7). The grounds are open March 15 to November 4, Tuesday to Sunday 10am to noon and 3 to 6pm, the interior only Wednesday and Saturday during the same hours.

From here it is only a 10-minute walk to the **Villa Valmarana** ✹✹ (© **0444-543-976**), also called *ai Nani* (dwarves) after the statues that line the garden wall. Built in the 17th century by Mattoni, an admirer and follower of Palladio, it is an almost commonplace structure whose reason to visit is an interior covered with remarkable 18th-century frescoes by Giambattista Tiepolo and his son Gian-domenico. Admission is 5€ ($6), 7€ ($8) if you want to visit outside regular hours, which are complicated. It's open mornings as follows: March 15 to Novem-ber 5, Wednesday, Thursday, Saturday, and Sunday 10am to noon. It's open after-noons Tuesday to Sunday, as follows: March 15 through April, 2:30 to 5:30pm; May through September, 3 to 6pm; and October to November 5, 2 to 5pm.

Also in this area is the **Santuario di Monte Berico** ✹ (© **0444-320-999**), built in 1668 by a Bolognese architect. If you've already visited the Villa Rotonda, you will understand where the architect got his inspiration. The interior's most important work is in a chapel to the right of the main altar, *Lamentation* by Bor-tolomeo Montagna (1500), founder of the local school of painting and one of the Veneto's most famous artists. The terrace in front of the church affords beau-tiful views of Vicenza, the Monti Berici, and the distinct outline of the nearby Alps. The basilica is open in summer months Monday to Saturday from 6am to 12:30pm and 2:30 to 7:30pm, Sunday 6am to 8pm; closes earlier in winter months; free admission.

ORGANIZED TOURS

Each summer brings a different sort of guided tour of the city by the local tourism authorities, often free of charge—well, technically they're free, but only

---

(*Fun Fact* A Model for Monticello

Villa Rotonda may seem vaguely familiar, for it is the model that inspired Thomas Jefferson's home Monticello, the Chiswick House near London, myriad plantation homes in America's Deep South, and countless other noble homes and government buildings in the United States and Europe.

Touring the Villas

In addition to visiting the two villas located in the immediate out-skirts of Vicenza, a tour of the dozens of country *ville venete* farther afield is the most compelling outing from Vicenza. Check at the tourist office for availability of organized tours, something that has been on-again (and more frequently), off-again for the last few years. You most probably will have to do it yourself (this means hav-ing access to wheels). Many of the villas are still privately owned and inhabited, and each has its own hours and restrictions (not all the vil-las can be visited; others permit only visits to the grounds but not the interiors, and so forth). The tourist office can help you plan your trip around these restrictions, and it also has maps and a host of varied itineraries outlining the most important villas (not all of which are 16th-century Palladian designs), many of which are UNESCO-pro-tected sites. Public transportation for these visits is close to nonexist-ent. If you do have access to a car, ask about the summer concert series in June and July, Concerti in Villa (see "Festivals," above), which has drawn some first-class talent in the classical-music world.

if you buy the "Card Musei" (see "Seeing Vicenza by Cumulative Ticket," above). Check with the tourist office upon your arrival in town, or in advance by visiting its website (see "Visitor Information," above). Die-hard architecture buffs may want to splurge for the services of any of the accredited multilingual tour guides through their association **Guide Turistiche Autorizzate** (*C* and fax **0444-283-774;** www.vicenzatourguide.it). Rates are around 90€ ($104) for a half day, up to 30 people.

WHERE TO STAY

Unlike Padua, which gets the overflow when Venice is full, or the tourism-mag-net Verona, Vicenza can be very quiet in high season, August, or winter months when trade fairs are not in town; some hotels close without notice for a few weeks if there's little demand. Make sure you call in advance; the number of hotels in the city is limited.

Due Mori ✯   This fresh, bright, inexpensive hotel choice was fully renovated in 1996. Add to that the Due Mori's history as the oldest family-run hotel in Vicenza and its convenient location on a quiet side street just west of the sprawl-ing Piazza dei Signori, and you have the (deservedly) most popular spot in town for the budget-minded. Which is to say: Book early. In a modernized shell of a centuries-old palazzo, tasteful and authentic 19th-century pieces distinguish otherwise plain rooms whose amenities are kept at a minimum, but then, so are the prices. Recent renovations have increased the number of rooms with bath-rooms. This is as good as it gets in the very center of Palladio's hometown.

Via Do Rode 24 (1 block west of Piazza d. Signori), 36100 Vicenza. *C* **0444-321-886.** Fax 0444-326-127. hotelduemori@inwind.it. 30 units, 27 with bathroom. 50€ ($58) double without bathroom, 75€ ($86) dou-ble with bathroom; 84€ ($97) triple with bathroom. Breakfast 5€ ($6). Free parking. AE, MC, V. **Amenities:** Bar. *In room:* Dataport, hair dryer (ask at desk).

Hotel Cristina   Located west of the Piazza Castello and the green Giardino Salvi, this recently refurbished hotel is within easy walking distance of the historic center's principal sites. It's a good choice for those with wheels and a few extra dollars. A contemporary approach with occasional exposed beams and marble and parquet flooring results in a handsome, well-maintained lodging and makes this one of Vicenza's preferred three-star properties. An internal courtyard provides welcome parking space, and guests have access to bicycles for touring the traffic-free center of town as well as the nearby villas just southeast of the train station. After all that cycling, coast back to the hotel and into its Finnish sauna.

Corso San Felice 32 (west of Salvi Gardens), 36100 Vicenza. ℂ **0444-323-751** or 0444-324-297. Fax 0444-543-656. www.paginegialle.it/hotelcristinavicenza. 33 units. 100€–120€ ($115–$138) double. Rates include buffet breakfast. Discounts possible in low season. AE, DC, MC, V. Parking 7€ ($8). **Amenities:** Bar; sauna; bike rental; concierge; tour desk; room service (limited); laundry service; dry cleaning; nonsmoking rooms. *In room:* A/C, TV, dataport, minibar, hair dryer, safe (in some).

Palladio   A popular two-star choice spread over three floors (no elevator), the Palladio is the friendliest of the city's few hotels worth mentioning. Just a 2-minute walk from the Piazza dei Signori (and equidistant from the Piazza Matteotti and the Teatro Olimpico), this family-run hotel offers small, no-frills but efficient rooms in a quiet neighborhood. The beds may be cots, but they're underpinned by a board to ensure a good night's sleep. Most rooms on the back and along a side courtyard have balconies; top-floor room no. 32 even has a small terrace.

Via Oratorio dei Servi 25 (east of the Piazza della Signori), 36100 Vicenza ℂ **0444-321-072.** Fax 0444-547-328. 24 units, 15 with bathroom. 55€ ($63) double without bathroom (only 1; the other bathless ones are singles), 65€–72€ ($75–$83) double with bathroom. Breakfast included. AE, MC, DC, V. Bus from station: 1, 2 5, or 7. **Amenities:** Bar; laundry service. *In room:* TV, dataport, hair dryer.

WHERE TO DINE

Antica Casa della Malvasia ⭑ VICENTINO   This ever-lively, taverna-like *osteria* sits on a quiet, characteristic side street that links the principal Corso Palladio with the Piazza dei Signori. Service comes with a smile and is informal, the cooking homemade and regional. The food is reliably good, but it's just an excuse to accompany the selection of wines (80), whiskies (100), grappas (150), and teas (over 150). No wonder this place always buzzes. Even if you don't eat here, at least stop in for a late-night toddy, Vicentino-style—it's a favorite spot for locals and visitors alike, and there's often live music on Tuesday and Thursday evenings.

Contrà delle Morette 5 (off Corso Palladio). ℂ **0444-543-704.** Reservations suggested during high season. Primi 4€–6€ ($4.60–$7); secondi 5€–10€ ($6–$12). AE, MC, V. Tues–Sun noon–3pm and 7pm–midnight (sometimes later).

Gran Caffè Garibaldi CAFE   If it's a lovely day, set up camp here in the shade of a table with an umbrella that overlooks Vicenza's grand piazza. The most historically significant cafe in Palladio's city is as stage-set impressive inside as you would imagine. The upstairs restaurant is too expensive for what it offers, but the outside terrace gives you the chance to sit and gaze upon the wonders of the whale-size basilica, yet another Palladian masterpiece. A chef's salad or panino makes a great lunch, or just nurse a cappuccino or *aperitivo* for the same money at your outside table; prices are slightly less at the bar, but go for the front-row seats and the theater-in-the-round that the city's beautiful Piazza dei Signori offers.

Piazza d. Signori 5. ℂ **0444-542-455.** www.baccalaallavicentina.com. Panini from 3€ ($3.45); salads from 6€ ($7). MC, V. Wed–Mon noon–2:30pm and 7–10:30pm.

Righetti *Value* VICENTINO/ITALIAN   For a self-service operation, this place is a triple surprise: The diners are all local (and loyal); the food is reliably good—of the home-cooked generous-portions kind—and the interior is rustic, welcoming, and pleasant considering its inexpensive profile. But it's the opportunity to sit outdoors in the quiet, traffic-free Piazza Duomo that's the biggest draw. First stake out a table by setting your place, then order your food at the counter (prepared fresh on the spot), and when you're finished eating, just tell the cashier what you had and he'll add up the bill. There are three or four first courses to choose from (Tues and Fri are risotto days) and as many entrees. Evenings offer the added option of grilled meats (which makes eating indoors in the cold winter months more enjoyable), though this is the perfect relaxed place to revel in a simple lunch of pasta and a vegetable side, opting for a more special dinner venue.

Piazza Duomo 3/4. (€) **0444-543-135.** Primi 2.50€–3€ ($2.90–$3.45); secondi 4€–6€ ($4.60–$7). No credit cards. Mon–Fri noon–2:30pm and 7–10pm.

Trattoria Tre Visi ★★ VICENTINO/ITALIAN   Operating since the early 1600s around the corner until a 1997 change of address, this Vicentino institution is now located on this important palazzo-studded street in a setting somewhat less dramatic than the previous 15th-century palazzo (though here there is an alfresco courtyard). The menu has stayed unchanged, however, and this is good: Ignore items that concede to foreign requests and concentrate on the regional dishes they know how to prepare best. Almost all the pasta is made fresh daily, including the house specialty, *bigoli con anitra,* a fat spaghetti-like pasta served with duck ragout. The region's signature dish, *baccalà alla Vicentina* (a poor man's dish that, when prepared properly, is delicious) is a tender salt codfish simmered in a stew of onions, herbs, anchovies, garlic, and *parmigiano* for 8 hours before arriving at your table in perfection. Ask your kind waiter for help in selecting from Veneto's wide spectrum of very fine wines: It will enhance your bill but also the memories you'll bring home.

Corso Palladio 25 (near Piazza Castello). (€) **0444-324-868.** www.trevisi.vicenza.com. Reservations suggested. Primi 6€–10€ ($7–$12); secondi 12€–15€ ($14–$17). AE, DC, MC, V. Tues–Sun 12:30–2:30pm;Tues–Sat 7:30–10pm. Closed July.

6 Verona

114km (71 miles) W of Venice, 80km (50 miles) W of Padua, 61km (38 miles) W of Vicenza, 157km (97 miles) E of Milan

Suspend all disbelief regarding the real-life existence of Romeo and Juliet, and your stay in Verona can be magical. After Venice, this is the Veneto's most-visited city. Verona reached a cultural and artistic peak during the 13th and 14th centuries under the puissant and often cruel and sometimes quirky della Scala, or Scaligeri, dynasty that took up rule in the late 1200s. In 1405 it surrendered to Venice, which remained in charge until the invasion of Napoléon in 1797.

During the time of Venetian rule, Verona became a prestigious urban capital and controlled much of the Veneto and as far south as Tuscany. You'll see the emblem of the *scala* (ladder) around town, heraldic symbol of the Scaligeri dynasty. The city has a locked-in-time character that recalls its medieval and Renaissance heyday, and the magnificent medieval palazzi, towers, churches, and stagelike piazzas you see today are picture-perfect testimony to its centuries-old influence and wealth.

For some reason, visitors spend remarkably little time in this beautiful medieval city. While it has a short list of attractions, it is a handsome town to

schedule (℡ **045-807-7500** or 045-806-6485 or with the tourist office: www. estateteatraleveronese.it). Last-minute tickets go on sale at the Teatro Romano box office at 8:15pm (most performances start at 9pm). Tickets range from 13€ to 26€ ($15–$30) plus booking charges.

During Verona's summer-long festival of the arts, see what's happening in the Piazza dei Signori, where frequent **free concerts** (jazz, tango, classical) keep everyone out until the wee hours. And for something truly unique, check out *Sognando Shakespeare* (**Dreaming Shakespeare**): Follow this *teatro itinerante* (traveling theater) of young, talented actors in costume as they wander about the medieval corners of Verona from site to site, reciting *Romeo e Giulietta* (in Italian only) in situ, as Shakespeare would have loved it to be. For information, contact the tourist office. For information about performances July through September, call ℡ **045-800-0065.**

Other important events are the famous 4-day **horse fair,** Fieracavalli, in early November, and the important 5-day **VinItaly wine fair** (that overlaps with the equally important Olive Oil Fair) in mid-April. (Verona's schedule of fairs is long and varied; while few may be of interest to those outside the trades involved, their frequency can create problems for tourists in regard to hotel availability.) The Piazza San Zeno hosts a **traveling antiques market** the third Saturday of every month; come early.

ESSENTIALS

GETTING THERE   By Train   Verona is easily accessed on the west–east Milan–Venice line as well as the north–south Brennero–Rome line. At least 30 trains daily run west from Venice (86 min. to 2 hr.). Even more arrive from Milan (85 min. to 2 hr.). Trains also connect Verona with Vicenza (30–50 min.); Padua (35–50 min.); and Bologna (40 min. to 2 hr.).

The **Stazione Porta Nuova train station** (℡ **045-590-688**) is located rather far south of the Piazza Brà (and Arena) area and is serviced by at least half a dozen local bus lines. The bus network within the historical center is limited, so if you have luggage, you'll most probably want a taxi to get to your hotel.

To get downtown from the train station, walk straight out to the bus island marked MARCIAPIEDE F (parallel to the station) to catch minibus no. 72 or 73 (tickets on sale at the newsstand in the station or the AMT booth on MARCIAPIEDE A). Get off on Via Stella at Via Cappello for the center. Alternatively, over half the buses from the station stop at Piazza Brà, so just peruse the posted route signs.

By Bus   The bus station, **A.P.T.** (Azienda Provinciale Trasporti) is at Piazza XXV Aprile (℡ **045-887-1111;** www.amt.it), directly across from the train station. Buses leave from here for all regional destinations, including Largo di Garda. Although there is bus service to Vicenza, Padua, and Venice (only the summertime departures for Venice are direct; in other months there's a change), it is generally easier to travel by train.

By Car   The Serenissima autostrada (A4) links Venice and Milan; the exit for downtown Verona is Verona Sud. Coming from the north or south, use the A22 autostrada, taking exit Verona Nord.

VISITOR INFORMATION   A **central tourist office** is at Piazza Chiesa 34 (℡ and fax **045-705-0088**)—where summer hours are Monday to Saturday 9am to 8pm and Sunday 10am to 1pm and 4 to 7pm (winter hours are usually shorter, and it's closed Sun). Another **tourist office** is at Via degli Alpini 9, adjacent to the Arena off Piazza Brà (℡ **045-806-8680;** fax 045-801-0682), open Monday to

Will the Fat Lady Sing?

Verona's renowned **opera season** ★★★ begins in late June and extends through August in Verona's Arena, the ancient amphitheater. It began in 1913 with a staging of *Aïda* to commemorate the 100th anniversary of Verdi's birth, and *Aïda* in all of its extravagant glory has been performed yearly ever since; when I last attended, in 2000, modern dance and minimalist scenery were incorporated to great effect. Expect to see other Verdi works such as *Un Ballo in Maschera*, *Nabucco*, *La Traviata*, and *Rigoletto*.

Those seated on the least-expensive, unreserved stone steps costing 20€ ($22) Friday and Saturday and 22€ ($25) otherwise, enjoy fresh air, excellent acoustics, and a view over the Arena's top to the city and surrounding hills beyond. The rub is that Jose Carreras will only appear to be 1 inch high. Numbered seats below cost from 70€ ($81) to 154€ ($177); all tickets are subject to an advance booking fee of 2.50€–20€ ($2.90–$23)—worth it, unless you're willing to tough it out by lining up at 4 or 5pm for the 6pm opening of the gates for unreserved seating (and the show doesn't even start until 9pm).

The **box office** is located on Via Dietro Anfiteatro 6b; credit card purchase accepted by phone or online (© **045-800-5151**; fax 045-801-3287; www.arena.it). You pick up tickets the night of the performance. If you hope to find tickets upon arrival, remember that *Aïda* is everyone's most requested performance; weekend performances are usually sold out. As a last-minute resort, be nice to your hotel manager or concierge—everyone has a connection, or a relative with a connection. And even on the most coveted nights (weekend performances by top names), scalpers abound.

Saturday 9am to 6pm. A **small office** at the train station (© **045-800-0861**) is open Tuesday to Saturday 8am to 7:30pm and Sunday and Monday 10am to 4pm. Visit their website at www.tourism.verona.it.

Guided Tours　An air-conditioned *bus turistico* departs thrice daily for a 1½-hour Giro Turistico tour of the city's historical center every day except Monday from June 1 until September 28. The cost is 15€ ($17) for adults and 7€ ($8) for children under 18 for a recorded spiel in four languages, and you can buy your ticket on the bus. It leaves from the Gran Guardia in the Piazza Brà. The Saturday afternoon tour leaves at 3:30pm with a real live tour guide that ups the cost to 20€ ($23). I think you'll do just as well (if not better) with this guidebook, however.

CITY LAYOUT　The city lies alongside the banks of the S-shaped Adige River. As far as the average visitor is concerned, everything of interest—with the exception of the Teatro Romano—is found in the *centro storico* on the south side of the river's loop; there's no site that cannot be easily and enjoyably reached by foot.

The massive and impressive ancient Roman amphitheater, the **Arena,** sits at the southern end of the city's hub in the airy cafe-ringed **Piazza Brà**. The piazza is linked by the popular **Via Mazzini** pedestrian thoroughfare to the **Piazza delle Erbe** and its adjacent **Piazza dei Signori.** The grid of pedestrian-only streets between are lined with handsome shops and cafes and make up the principal strolling and window-shopping destinations in town.

Slightly out of this loop (though still an easy walk) is the **Basilica San Zeno Maggiore,** west of the Arena, and **Juliet's Tomb,** southeast of the Arena (only die-hard Juliet fans will appreciate the trek here). Both the **train station** and the **Fiera di Verona conference center** are located in the southern part of town beyond the Porta Nuova.

GETTING AROUND   Verona lends itself to walking and strolling, and most sites are concentrated within a few history-steeped blocks of each other. Venture off the store-lined treadmill and seek out the narrow, cobblestoned side streets that are evocative of eras past. Little to no traffic is permitted in town, so upon arrival stash your car in a parking area suggested by your hotel (where they'll most likely have a special arrangement), and let your feet do the transporting.

WHAT TO SEE & DO

If you're in town the first Sunday of any month, note that entrance is free for the following sites: Castelvecchio Museum, the Roman Theater, and Juliet's Tomb.

Because there are so many churches in Verona, an admission charge has been imposed in an attempt to cover custodian charges and offer longer hours.

TOP ATTRACTIONS

Arena di Verona ★★★   The best-preserved Roman amphitheater in the world and the best known in Italy after Rome's Colosseum, the elliptical Arena was built in a slightly pinkish marble around the year A.D. 100 and stands in the very middle of town with the Piazza Brà on its southern flank. Built to accommodate more than 20,000 people (outdone by Rome's contender that could seat more than twice that), it is in remarkable shape today (despite a 12th-century earthquake that left only four arches of the outer ring standing), beloved testimony to the pride and wealth of Verona and its populace.

Its acoustics (astoundingly good for an open-air venue) have survived the millennia and make it one of the wonders of the ancient world and one of the most fascinating venues for live performances today, conducted without microphones. If you're in town during the summer opera performances in July and August, do everything possible to procure a ticket (see "Will the Fat Lady Sing?," above) for any of the outdoor evening performances. Even opera-challenged audience members will take home the memory of a lifetime. Other events, such as orchestral concerts, are also staged here whenever the weather permits. Check with the tourist office for more information.

The cluster of outdoor cafes and trattorias/pizzerias on the western side of the Piazza Brà line a wide marble esplanade called Il Liston; they stay open long after the opera performances end. Enjoy some serious after-opera people-watching here.

Value **Verona by Cumulative Ticket**

The **VeronaCard,** a *biglietto cumulativo* (cumulative ticket) will help you visit several of the city's sites for just one fee. Two versions of the card are available. The 8€ ($9) card, valid for just 1 day, allows you to ride the city's buses and enter its museums, monuments, and churches. The 12€ ($14) card offers the same places, but allows you 3 days rather than one. You'll find the VeronaCard for sale at the sites below, or call ℂ 045-807-7503.

Piazza Brà. ✆ **045-800-3204.** Admission 3.10€ ($3.55). Mon 1:45–7:30pm; Tues–Sun 8:30am–7:30pm. (Last admission 45 min. before close.) During the July–Aug summer opera season 9am–3:30pm.

Piazza delle Erbe ★★ This bustling marketplace—the palazzi-flanked Square of the Herbs—sits on the former site of the Roman Forum where chariot races once took place. The herbs, spices, coffee beans, and bolts of silks and damasks that came through Verona after landing in Venice from faraway Cathay have given way to the fresh and aromatic produce of one of Italy's wealthiest agricultural regions—offset by the inevitable ever-growing presence of T-shirt and french-fry vendors, as the piazza has become something of a tourist trap. But the perfume of fennel and vegetables fresh from the earth still assaults your senses in the early morning, mixing with the cacophony of vendors touting plump tomatoes, dozens of different variations of salad greens, and picture-perfect fruits that can't possibly taste as good as they look, but do. Add to this the canary lady, the farmer's son who has brought in a half a dozen puppies to unload, and the furtive pickpocket who can spot a tourist at 50 paces—and you have one of Italy's loveliest little outdoor markets. Take a rest on one of the steps leading up to the small, 14th-century fountain in the piazza's center and a Roman statue dubbed *The Virgin of Verona.*

Between Via Mazzini and Corso Porta Borsari. Open-air produce and flower market Mon–Sat 8am–7pm.

Piazza dei Signori (Piazza Dante) ★ To reach the Piazza dei Signori from the Piazza delle Erbe, exit under the Arco della Costa (see "Liar, Liar," below). The perfect antidote to the color and bustle of the Piazza delle Erbe, the serene and elegant Piazza dei Signori is a slightly somber square, one of Verona's innermost chambers of calm. Its center is anchored by a large 19th-century statue of the "divine poet" Dante, who found political exile from Florence in Verona as a guest of Cangrande I and his Scaligeri family (in appreciation, Dante wrote of his patron in his poem, *Paradiso*).

If entering from the Archway, you'll be facing the Scaligeri's 13th-century crenellated residence before it was taken over by the governing Venetians. Left of that, behind Dante's back, is the Loggia del Consiglio (Portico of the Counsel), a 15th-century masterpiece of Venetian Renaissance style. Opposite that and facing Dante is the 12th-century Romanesque Palazzo della Ragione, whose courtyard and fine Gothic staircase should be visited. This piazza is Verona's finest microcosm, a balanced and refined assemblage of historical architecture. Secure an outdoor table at the square's legendary command post, the Antico Caffè Dante, and take it all in over a late-afternoon Campari and soda.

Piazza dei Signori, adjacent to Piazza delle Erbe.

Museo Castelvecchio ★★ A 5-minute walk west of the Arena amphitheater on the Via Roma and nestled on the banks of the swift-flowing Adige River, the

---

Fun Fact **Liar, Liar**

You'll be able to spot the Arco della Costa (Arch of the Rib) by the enormous whalebone hanging overhead. It was placed here 1,000 years ago when it was said to have been unearthed during excavations on this spot, indicating this area was once underwater. Local legend goes that the rib will fall on the first person to pass beneath it who has never told a lie—thus explaining the nonchalance with which every Veronese passes under it.

"Old Castle" is a crenellated fairy-tale pile of brick towers and turrets, protecting the bridge behind it. It was commissioned in 1354 by the Scaligeri warlord Cangrande II to serve the dual role of residential palace and military stronghold. It survived centuries of occupation by the Visconti family, the Serene Republic of Venice, and then Napoléon, only to be destroyed by the Germans during World War II bombing. Its painstaking restoration was initiated in 1958 by the acclaimed Venetian architect Carlos Scarpa, and it reopened in 1964. It is now a fascinating home to some 400 works of art.

The ground-floor rooms, displaying statues and carvings of the Middle Ages, lead to alleyways, vaulted halls, multileveled floors, and stairs, all as architecturally arresting as the Venetian masterworks from the 14th to 18th centuries—notably those by Tintoretto, Tiepolo, Veronese, Bellini, and the Verona-born Pisanello—found throughout. Don't miss the large courtyard with the equestrian statue of the warlord Cangrande I (a copy can be seen at the family cemetery at the Arche Scaligeri) with a peculiar dragon's head affixed to his back (actually his armor's helmet, removed from his head and resting behind him).

A stroll across the pedestrian bridge behind the castle affords you a fine view of the castle, the **Ponte Scaligeri** (built in 1355 and also destroyed during World War II; it was reconstructed using the original materials), and the river's banks.

Corso Castelvecchio 2 (at Via Roma, on the Adige River). © 045-594-734 or 045-800-5817. www.comune. verona.it/Castelvecchio/cvsito. Admission 3.10€ ($3.55). Free 1st Sun of each month. Mon 1:45–7:30pm; Tues–Sun 8:30am–7:30pm. (Last admission 45 min. before close.)

Casa di Giulietta (Juliet's House) ★★   There is no proof that a Capuleti (Capulet) family ever lived here (or if they did, that a young girl named Juliet ever existed), and it wasn't until 1905 that the city bought what was an abandoned, overgrown garden and decided its future. Rumor is, this was once actually a whorehouse.

So powerful is the legend of Juliet that over half a million tourists flock here every year to visit the simple courtyard and home that are considerably less affluent-looking than the sumptuous Franco Zeffirelli version as you may remember it (the movie was filmed in Tuscany). Many are those who leave behind layer upon layer of graffiti along the lines of *"Laura, ti amo!,"* or who engage in the peculiar tradition (whose origin no one can seem to explain) of rubbing the right breast (now buffed to a bright gold) of the 20th-century bronze statue of a forever nubile Juliet.

The curious might want to fork over the entrance fee to see the spartan interior of the 13th-century home, restored in 1996. Ceramics and furniture on display are authentic of the era but did not belong to Juliet's family—if there ever was a Juliet at all.

Stop by just before closing time, when the courtyard is relatively empty of tourists and it is easiest to imagine Romeo uttering, "But Soft! What light through yonder window breaks? It is the east, and Juliet is the sun!" No one is willing to confirm (or deny) that the balcony was added to the palazzo as recently as 1928 (doesn't stop many a young tourist lass from posing on it, staring dreamily at the sky).

La Tomba di Giulietta (Juliet's Tomb) (© **045-800-0361**) is about a 15-minute walk south of here (near the Adige River on Via delle Pontiere 5; admission 2.60€/$3; 1.50€/$1.75 children, and free first Sun of each month; Tues–Sun 9am–7pm). The would-be site of the star-crossed lovers' suicide is found within the graceful medieval cloisters of the Capuchin monastery of San Francesco al

Corso. Die-hard romantics may find this tomb with its surely posed "sarcophagus" rather more evocative than the crowded scene at Juliet's House and worth the trip. Others will find it overrated and shouldn't bother. The adjacent church is where their secret marriage was said to have taken place. A small museum of frescoes is also adjacent.

Via Cappello 23 (southeast of Piazza delle Erbe). ℂ **045-803-4303.** Admission (to building only; courtyard is free) 3.10€ ($3.55) adults, 2.10€ ($2.40) children. Mon 1:30–7:30pm; Tues–Sun 8:30am–7:30pm. (Last admission 45 min. before close.)

MORE ATTRACTIONS

Arche Scaligeri (Scaligeri Tombs) ★   Exit the Piazza dei Signori opposite the Arch of the Rib and immediately on your right, at the corner of Via delle Arche Scaligeri, are some of the most elaborate Gothic funerary monuments in Italy—the raised outdoor tombs of the canine-obsessed Scaligeri family (seen behind the original decorative grillwork), powerful and often ruthless rulers of Verona.

The most important are those by the peculiar names of Mastino I (Mastiff the First, founder of the dynasty, date of death unknown), Mastino II (Mastiff the Second, d. 1351), and Cansignorio (Head Dog, d. 1375). The most interesting is found over the side door of the family's private chapel Santa Maria Antica—the tomb of Cangrande I (Big Dog, d. 1329), with *cani* (dogs) holding up a *scala* (ladder), both elements that figure in the Scaligeri coat of arms. That's Cangrande I—patron of the arts and protector of Dante—and his steed you see above (the original can be seen in the Museo Castelvecchio). Recently restored, these tombs are considered one of the country's greatest medieval monuments. Entry is only to the neighboring Torre dei Lamberti; the tomb area itself is closed to visitors.

Around the corner on V. d. Arche Scaligeri 2 is the alleged 13th-century home of Juliet's significant other, **Romeo Montecchi** (Montague, in Shakespearian), which incorporates the popular Osteria del Duca (See "Where to Dine," below).

Via Arche Scaligeri. ℂ **045-803-2726.** 2.60€ ($3) to go up the tower in an elevator, 2.10€ ($2.40) on foot. Mon 1:45–7:30pm; Tues–Sun 9:30am–7:30pm. (Last admission 30 min. before close.)

Basilica San Zeno Maggiore ★★   This is one of the finest examples of Romanesque architecture in northern Italy, built between the 9th and 12th centuries. Slightly out of the old city's hub but still easily reached by foot, San Zeno (as it's often referred to), dedicated to the city's patron saint, is Verona's most visited church. Spend a moment outside to appreciate the fine, sober facade, highlighted by the immense 12th-century rose window, the *Ruota della Fortuna* **(Wheel of Fortune).**

This pales in importance compared to the **facade** ★★ below—two pillars supported by marble lions and massive doors whose 48 bronze panels were sculpted from the 9th to the 11th centuries and are believed to have been some of the first castings in bronze since Roman antiquity. They are among the city's most cherished artistic treasures and are worth the trip here even if the church is closed. Not yet as sophisticated as those that would adorn the Baptistery doors of Florence's Duomo in the centuries to come, these are like a naive illustration from a children's book and were meant to educate the illiterate masses with scenes from the Old and New Testaments and the life of San Zeno. They are complemented by the stone bas-reliefs found on either side of the doors, the 12th-century work of Niccolo, who was also responsible for the Duomo's portal. The 14th-century **tower** on the left belonged to the former abbey, while the freestanding slender **campanile** on the right was begun in 1045.

Tips **A Church Tip**

Verona's churches have banded together as the **Associazione Chiese Vive** (*(C)* **045-592-813;** www.veronatuttintorno.it/chiesevive/1000anni.htm). Admission to any one church is 2€ ($2.45), or you can buy a cumulative ticket for 5€ ($6) for adults, 4€ ($4.60) for seniors over 65 and students, granting admission to Sant'Anastasia, San Zeno, San Lorenzo, San Fermo, and the Duomo complex (the last only between noon and 4pm on this cumulative ticket). *Note:* If you're *only* going to visit Verona's churches, this is the deal for you. Otherwise, if you want to see all or most of the city's attractions, stick with the **VeronaCard** (see the "Verona by Cumulative Ticket" box on p. 193.)

The massive **interior** ☆ is filled with 12th- to 14th-century frescoes and crowned by the nave's ceiling, designed as a wooden ship's keel. But the interior's singular highlight is the famous triptych of the *Madonna and Child Enthroned with Saints* by Andrea Mantegna (1459), behind the main altar. Napoléon absconded with the beautiful centerpiece—a showcase for the Padua-born Mantegna's sophisticated sense of perspective and architectural detail—which was eventually returned to Verona, although two side panels stayed behind in the Louvre and in Tours. Look in the small apse to the left of the altar for the colored marble statue of a smiling San Zeno, much loved by the local Veronesi, in an act of blessing.

Piazza San Zeno. *(C)* **045-800-6120.** www.veronatuttintorno.it/chiesevive/sanzeno.htm. Admission 3€ ($3.45). Mar–Oct Tues–Sat 8am–1pm, Tues–Sun 1:30–6pm; Nov–Feb Tues–Sat 8am–1pm, Tues–Sun 1:30–5pm.

Basilica di Sant'Anastasia   Built between 1290 and 1481, this is Verona's largest church, considered the city's finest example of Gothic architecture, even though the facade remains unfinished. A lovely 14th-century campanile bell tower is adorned with frescoes and sculptures. The church's interior is typically Gothic in design, highlighted by two famous *gobbi* (hunchbacks) that support the holy-water fonts, an impressive patterned pavement, and 16 side chapels containing a number of noteworthy paintings and frescoes from the 15th and 16th centuries.

Most important is Verona-born Pisanello's *St. George Freeing the Princess of Trebisonda* (1433). After several relocations and now back in its original spot way up above the terra-cotta–filled Cappella Pellegrini in the right transept, it is considered one of his best paintings and is of the armed-knight-and-damsel-in-distress genre—with the large white rump of St. George's steed as one of its focal points. Also worth scouting out are the earlier 14th-century frescoes by the Giotto-inspired Altichiero in the Cavalli Chapel next door.

Piazza Anastasia at Corso Anastasia. *(C)* **045-592-813.** www.veronatuttintorno.it/chiesevive/sant anastasia.htm. Admission 2€ ($2.30). Mar–Oct Mon–Sat 9am–6pm, Sun 1–6pm; Nov–Feb Tues–Sat 10am–4pm, Sun 1–4pm.

Teatro Romano (Roman Theater) and the Museo Archeologico (Archaeological Museum) ☆   The oldest extant Roman monument in Verona dates from the time of Augustus when the Arena was built and Verona was a strong Roman outpost at the crossroads of the Empire's ancient north/south, east/west highways. There is something almost surreal about attending an open-air

---

Moments Beautiful Views

The view of Verona from the Roman Theater is beautiful any time of day, but particularly during the evening performances—the ancient Romans knew a thing or two about dramatic settings. For other views, you can take a rickety elevator to the 10th-century Church of Santa Libera above the theater, or to the former monastery and cloisters of San Girolamo, which now houses a small archaeological museum. Above this is the Castel San Pietro, whose foundations go back to the times of the Romans and whose terraces offer the best view in town.

---

performance of Shakespeare's *Two Gentlemen of Verona* or *Romeo and Juliet* here—even if you can't understand a word (see "Festivals & Markets," earlier in this section). Classical concerts and ballet and jazz performances are also given here, with evocative views of the city beyond. A small archaeological museum (same hours as the site itself) housed above in a lovely old monastery is included in the admission ticket. On Sundays (only), the promenade is open to the public.

Via Rigaste Redentore (over the Ponte Pietra bridge behind the Duomo, on the north banks of the river Adige). ☎ **045-800-0360.** Admission 2.60€ ($3); free 1st Sun of each month. Mon 1:30pm–6:45pm; Tues–Sun 8:30am–6:45pm; during theater season 9am–3pm. Bus: 31, 32, 33, or 73.

The Duomo ⚜   Begun in the 12th century and not finished until the 17th century, the city's main church still boasts its original main doors and portal, magnificently covered with low reliefs in the Lombard Romanesque style that are attributed to Niccolo, whose work can be seen at the Basilica of San Zeno Maggiore. You enter, however, way around to the right. The church was built upon the ruins of an even more ancient paleo-Christian church dating from the late Roman Empire. Visit the **Cappella Nichesola,** the first chapel on the left, where Titian's serene but boldly colorful *Assumption of the Virgin* is the cathedral's principal treasure, with an architectural frame by Sansovino (who also designed the choir). Also of interest is the semicircular screen that separates the altar from the rest of the church, attributed to Sanmicheli. To its right rises the 14th-century tomb of Saint Agatha.

The excavations of S. Elena church, also in the Duomo complex, reveal a bit of 6th-century mosaic floor; the Baptistery contains a Romanesque font carved with scenes from the Nativity cycle.

Don't leave the area without walking behind the Duomo to the river: Here you'll find the 13th-century Torre di Alberto della Scala tower and nearby Ponte della Pietra bridge, the oldest Roman monument in Verona (1st century B.C.; rebuilt in the 14th c.). There has been a crossing at this point of the river since Verona's days as a 1st-century Roman stronghold when the Teatro Romano was built on the river's northern banks and the Arena at its hub.

Piazza Duomo (at Via del Duomo). ☎ **045-592-813.** www.veronatuttintorno.it/chiesevive/duomo.htm. Single admission 2€ ($2.30). Mar–Oct Mon–Sat 9:30am–6pm, Sun 1–6pm; Nov–Feb Mon–Sat 10am–4pm, Sun 1:30–4pm.

GARDENS

Close to the Castel San Pietro is the well-known, multitiered **Giardino Giusti** gardens (☎ **045-803-4029**), whose formal 16th-century layout and geometrical designs of terraces, fountains, statuary, and staircases inspired, among many, Mozart and Goethe. The gardens are open daily from 9am to dusk; admission is 5€ ($6).

SHOPPING

Unlike in Venice, most of the people walking Verona's boutique-lined pedestrian streets are locals, not tourists. Come to Verona to spend some time doing what the locals do, shopping and stopping in any of the myriad cafes and *pasticcerie*. Despite Verona's acknowledgement of the tourism that supplements its economy (unlike Venice, Verona does not live for tourism alone and it shows), there are only the most predictable souvenirs to be found in the tourist trinket market. Shopping is mostly for the Veronesi, and upscale clothing and accessories boutiques line the two most fashionable shopping streets, **Via Mazzini** (connecting the Arena and the Piazza delle Erbe) and **Via Cappello,** heading southeast from the piazza and past Juliet's House. There's also **Corso Borsari** to check out, and **Corso Sant'Anastasia** (heading west and east, respectively, out of the Piazza delle Erbe), the latter having a concentration of interesting antiques stores.

WHERE TO STAY

Although the following prices reflect peak-season rates, expect inflated prices during the July/August opera season (when Venice is offering low-season discounts) or when one of the major trade fairs are in town. With this exception, low season is November through mid-March. The **C.A.V.** (Cooperativa Albergatori Veronesi), at Via Patuzzi 5, is an organization of dozens of hotels that will help you with bookings for a fee determined by your choice of hotel category (© **045-800-9844;** fax 045-800-9372; www.cav.vr.it).

Due Torri Hotel Baglioni ★★ *Overrated*   Verona's top hotel occupies a 14th-century palazzo that was reopened in the 1950s. It's where rock stars and opera singers stay when they play in town, picking up where Mozart, Goethe, and Garibaldi left off—perhaps because they're among the few who can afford it. The airy lobby looks like a stage set, with original 1370s columns and carvings and contemporary frescoes of medieval scenes, the ceilings set with oil paintings. The room furnishings range from Louis XIV to Biedermeier, and even standard rooms are luxurious, with patterned wall coverings, Murano chandeliers, and large, marble-sheathed bathrooms with double sinks. Windows are double-paned, so even on the piazza things are quiet. More recently, a roof terrace was installed—the hotel is up in the narrow end of Verona formed by the tight river bend, so many rooms, especially on the third floor, have great views over rooftops to the hills beyond.

Piazza S. Anastasia 4, 37121 Verona. © **045-595-044.** Fax 045-800-4130. www.baglionihotels.com. 90 units. 390€–407€ ($449–$468) standard double; 440€–495€ ($506–$569) deluxe double; 671€–770€ ($772–$886) jr. suite. Breakfast included. AE, DC, MC, V. **Amenities:** Veronese/international restaurant; bar; concierge; tour desk; car-rental desk; courtesy car on request; business center; babysitting; laundry service; dry cleaning (same-day); nonsmoking rooms. *In room:* A/C, TV, VCR, dataport, minibar, hair dryer, safe.

Hotel Aurora ★   Until now it was location, location, location that had loyal guests returning to the Aurora. But after a refurbishing of all guest rooms and ensuite bathrooms, it is the updated decor that brings them in as well. Six doubles are blessed with views of one of the world's great squares, the Piazza delle Erbe and the white-umbrella stalls that make up the daily marketplace. Consider yourself blessed if you snag the top-floor double (there is an elevator!) with a small balcony. There's another terrace overlooking the *mercato* (market) for the guests' use on the second floor, just above the breakfast room where the hotel's free daily ample buffet is served.

Piazza delle Erbe 2 (southwest side of piazza), 37121 Verona. © **045-594-717** or 045-597-834. Fax 045-801-0860. www.hotelaurora.biz. 19 units, 16 with bathroom. 98€–130€ ($113–$150) double; 124€–158€

($143–$182) suite. Rates include buffet breakfast. Prices discounted 10% off season. AE, DC, MC, V. Parking 10€ ($12). Bus: 72 or 73. **Amenities:** Bar; concierge. *In room:* A/C, TV, hair dryer.

Hotel Gabbia d'Oro ★★   One wall dates to 1320 at this cozy hotel of stone-trimmed doorways, rustic beams, and smart liveried service around the corner from the main piazza, but most of the palazzo is 18th century. The atmosphere hovers between medieval and eclectic, vaguely 19th-century Victorian romantic. It's all a bit put on—falsified fresco fragments, half-testers, and collectibles in little glass cases on wall brackets—but the result is more or less effective. Most rooms are terribly snug, but artfully placed mirrors help open up the space. Careful touches abound, from comfy couches in the sitting areas to extra-large shower heads and stone reliefs set in the tubs. A few rooms have small Romeo-o-Romeo balconies. The lovely winter garden is half enclosed and half open for nice weather.

Corso Porta Borsari 4a, 37121 Verona. ☎ 045-800-3060. Fax 045-590-293. www.hotelgabbiadoro.it. 27 units. 235€–351€ ($270–$404) double; 285€–520€ ($328–$598) superior suite; 415€–830€ ($477–$955) deluxe suite. Breakfast included, except during opera season (June 29–Sept 2), when it's 23€ ($26). AE, DC, MC, V. Valet parking 26€ ($30). Bus: 72 or 73. **Amenities:** Bar; bike rental; concierge; tour desk; car-rental desk; courtesy car on request; room service (14-hr.; bar only); in-room massage; babysitting; laundry service; dry cleaning (same-day). *In room:* A/C, TV, VCR, dataport, minibar, hair dryer, safe.

Hotel Giulietta & Romeo ★★   A block from the Arena is this handsomely refurbished palazzo-hotel recommended for its upscale ambience, cordial can-do staff, and its location in the heart of the *centro storico*. Brightly lit rooms are warmed by burnished cherrywood furnishings, and the large marble-tiled bathrooms are those you imagine finding in tony first-class hotels at less reasonable rates. The hotel takes its name seriously; sure enough, there are two small marble balconies a la Juliet on the facade (and some more prosaic ones at the back), but their view is unremarkable. The hotel is located on a narrow side street that is quiet and convenient to everything.

Vicolo Tre Marchetti 3 (south of Via Mazzini, 1 block east of the Arena), 37121 Verona ☎ **045-800-3554.** Fax 045-801-0862. www.giuliettaeromeo.com. 30 units. 115€–170€ ($132–$196) double; 125€–210€ ($144–$242) triple. Rates include buffet breakfast. Mention Frommer's when booking and show book upon arrival for a 10% discount. Add approximately 30% to all above rates during the opera season and major trade fairs. AE, DC, MC, V. Parking nearby 10€–15€ ($12–$17). From train station: all buses going to Piazza Brà. **Amenities:** Bar; bike rental; concierge; tour desk (summertime only); room service (24-hr.); babysitting; laundry service; dry cleaning; nonsmoking rooms. *In room:* A/C, TV, dataport, minibar, hair dryer, safe.

Hotel Torcolo ★   Lifelong friends Signoras Silvia and Diana are much of the reason behind the deserving success of this small, comfortable hotel just one peaceful block off the lively Piazza Brà. Bright and homey, it is inviting for its unfussy but tasteful decor. Each guest room is individually done, one lovely for its wrought-iron bed, another for the intricate parquet floor, another still in 19th-century furnishings. Room no. 31 is a country-style sunny top-floor room (the hotel has an elevator) with exposed ceiling beams; nos. 16 (a triple), 18, 21, and 34 are done with original Liberty-style furnishings. They truly care about your comfort here: Rooms are equipped with orthopedic mattresses on stiff springs, double-paned windows (though it's quiet already), extra air-conditioners on the top floor, and extra-wide single beds. They even keep different typical national travel tastes in consideration: They accept pets in a nod to Swiss travel habits, have a few rooms with tubs for Japanese, and offer some softer beds for the French. You can take the rather expensive breakfast outdoors on the small patio if the weather is pleasant, in a breakfast nook, or in your room.

Vicolo Listone 3 (just 1 block off the Piazza Brà), 37121 Verona. ☎ **045-800-7512** or 045-800-3871. Fax 045-800-4058. www.hoteltorcolo.it. 19 units. 60€–104€ ($69–$120) double. Breakfast 7€–10€ ($8–$12).

Above rates are in effect during the peak July/Aug opera season. Inquire about other rates during regular and low season. MC, V. Parking nearby 8€–10€ ($9–$12). Closed Jan 5–31. From train station: All buses to Piazza Brà. **Amenities:** Concierge; tour desk; room service (limited); babysitting; laundry service; nonsmoking rooms. *In room:* A/C, TV, minibar, hair dryer, safe.

Locanda Catullo *(Value)*   It's a three-floor hike to this homey pensione-like place that has been run by the affable Pollini family for more than 25 years, but it's ultra-central and the rooms are spacious and clean, the bathrooms nice and bright. The prices attract the 20- and 30-something euro-counters who make up the majority of the hotel's clientele. With impressive details and touches such as decorative plaster molding, French doors, and marble or parquet floors, the superfluous hanging tapestries and dried flower arrangements become almost too much. Single rooms are large and come equipped with a sink; solo travelers feel comfortable in the prevailing family atmosphere. There's no breakfast service available, but the bar downstairs couldn't be more convenient.

Via Catullo 1 (just north of the Via Mazzini; entrance from the alleyway Vicolo Catullo), 37121 Verona. ① **045-800-2786.** locandacatullo@tiscali.it. 21 units, 5 with bathroom. 55€ ($63) double without bathroom, 65€ ($75) double with bathroom; 81€ ($93) triple without bathroom, 96€ ($110) triple with bathroom; 125€ ($144) mini apt (2 doubles, I bathroom). No credit cards. Parking 10€ ($12). From train station: any bus going to Piazza Brà. **Amenities:** Bar. *In room:* No phone.

WHERE TO DINE

Bottega del Vino ✦ VERONESE/WINE BAR   Oenophiles can push an evening's meal here into the stratosphere if they succumb to the wine cellar's unmatched 80,000-bottle selection, the largest in Verona. This atmospheric *bottega* first opened in 1890, and the old-timers who spend hours in animated conversation seem to have been here since then. The ambience and conviviality are reason enough to come by for a tipple at the well-known bar, where five dozen good-to-excellent wines are for sale by the glass for 2€ to 10€ ($2.30–$12). There's no mistaking Verona's prominence in the wine industry here. At mealtimes the regulars head home, and the next shift arrives: Journalists and local merchants fill the few wooden tables ordering simple but excellent dishes where the Veneto's wines have infiltrated the kitchen, such as the *risotto al Amarone,* sauced with Verona's most dignified red.

Via Scudo di Francia 3 (off Via Mazzini), Verona. ① **045-800-4535.** www.bottegavini.com. Reservations necessary for dinner. Primi 7€–15€ ($8–$17); secondi 8€–22€ ($9–$25). AE, DC, MC, V. Wed–Mon noon–3pm (bar 10:30am–3pm) and 7pm–midnight (bar 6pm–midnight).

Brek *(Value)* PIZZERIA/CAFETERIA   The Veronesi (and Italians in general; Brek is part of a northern Italian restaurant chain) are forever dismissing this place as a mediocre tourist spot. But then who are all these Italian-speaking, local-looking patrons with their trays piled high, cutting in front of me in line at the pizza station and clamoring for all the best tables outside with a brilliant view of the sun-kissed Arena? This strip of the Piazza Brà is lined with pleasant alfresco alternatives such as the more serious Olivo and Tre Corone, but Brek is an informal, inexpensive preference of mine for a casual lunch where you can splurge (a lot) and walk away satisfied and solvent. Yes, this is fastfood *alla Veronese*—but do the Italians ever really go wrong in the culinary department? Inside it's a food fest, with various pastas and fresh vegetables made up as you wait, and some self-service where fruit salads and mixed green salads are displayed.

Piazza Brà 20. ① **045-800-4561.** www.brek.it. No reservations accepted. Primi and pizzas 2.60€–6€ ($3–$7); secondi 3.60€–9€ ($4.15–$10). AE, MC, V. Daily 11:30am–3pm and 6:30–10pm.

Il Desco ⭐ CREATIVE VERONESE   Il Desco offers highly creative cuisine made with a variety of the best ingredients the Veneto has to offer, with warm fresh-baked rolls and odd *amuse-bouches* such as olive-oil gelato with a tomato coulis. They tend to serve all meat dishes—from venison with pearl onions to salmon on a bed of lentils—extremely rare, so order it *ben cotto* (well done) if you want it cooked beyond merely flame-kissed. Some recent examples of the kitchen's rich creations include papardelle with sea snails, pork ravioli soup with shrimp, and stuffed pigeon and salt cod. Desserts are stupendous. Though the service is refined and the food of the highest quality, the inflated prices keep me from recommending it beyond a single star.

Via Dietro S. Sebastiano 7. ℭ 045-595-358. Reservations highly recommended. Primi 26€–32€ ($30–$37); secondi 28€–36€ ($32–$41); tasting menu 105€ ($121). AE, DC, MC, V. Mon–Sat 12:40–2pm and 7:40–10:30pm. Closed Dec 25–Jan 10.

La Taverna di Via Stella *(Finds)* OSTERIA VERONESE   Though opened only a few years ago by the Vantini brothers and their two friends, this taverna already feels as though it's been a popular neighborhood *osteria* for decades. There are faux medieval "fresco fragments" on the walls and small wooden tables packed in to seat the locals (the whole fire squad stopped in one time I visited) who come for huge portions of Veronese cuisine. To go with their 180 labels in the wine cellar, try *gnocchi con pastise de' caval* (gnocchi pasta dumplings in the very Veronese horse ragù), *bigoli al torchio* with shredded duck, *coniglio alla veronese con pesto* (rabbit served in a crushed-basil-and-garlic pesto), or *pastise de' caval con polenta* (horse goulash with polenta). The owners will soon be installing an outdoor dining terrace.

Via Stella 5c. ℭ 045-800-8008. Reservations recommended. Primi 6.20€–7.30€ ($7–$8); secondi 9.20€–16€ ($11–$19); fixed-price menu 20€ ($23). AE, DC, MC, V. Tues–Sun noon–3pm and 7–11pm.

Osteria del Duca ⭐⭐ VERONESE   There are no written records to confirm that this 13th-century palazzo was once owned by the Montecchi (Montagues) family, and, thankfully, the discreet management never considered calling this place the "Ristorante Romeo." But here you are, nonetheless, dining in what is believed to be Romeo's house, a characteristic medieval palazzo, and enjoying one of the nicest meals in town amid a spirited and friendly neighborhood ambience. You might find *penne con pomodoro e melanzane* (fresh tomato sauce with eggplant) or a perfectly grilled chop or filet with rosemary-roasted potatoes. It will be simple, it will be delicious, you'll probably make friends with the people sitting next to you, and you will always remember your meal at Romeo's Restaurant. If you don't fancy yourself an adventurous palate, avoid anything on the menu that has *cavallo* or *asino* in it, unless you want to sample horsemeat, a local specialty.

Via Arche Scaligeri 2 (east of Piazza dei Signori). ℭ 045-594-474. Reservations not accepted. Primi 5€ ($6); secondi 8.50€–11€ ($10–$13); *menù turistico* 13€ ($15). MC, V. Mon–Sat 12:30–2:30pm and 7–10:30pm.

Pizzeria Impero *(Kids)* PIZZERIA/TRATTORIA   Location is not everything, but to sit with a pleasant lunch or moonlit dinner in this most elegant of piazze will be one of those Verona memories that stays with you. Impero makes a perfectly respectable pizza (with a full trattoria menu to boot), and any of the two dozen or so varieties will taste pretty heavenly if you're sharing an outdoor table with your Romeo or Juliet.

If Impero is full and the Arena area is more convenient to your day's itinerary, try the well-known and always busy **Pizzeria Liston,** a block off Piazza Brà at Via Dietro Listone 19 (ℭ **045-803-4003**), which also serves a full trattoria menu (all major credit cards accepted; closed Wed). Its pizzas are said to be better, but its side-street setting—even with outdoor tables—doesn't quite match that of the Impero.

Piazza dei Signori 8. ☎ 045-803-0160. Reservations not accepted. Primi and pizzas 6€–9€ ($7–$10); secondi 7€–16€ ($8–$18). DC, MC, V. Summer daily noon–2am; winter Thurs–Tues noon–3:30pm and 7pm–midnight.

CAFES, PASTRIES & WINE BARS

When all is said and done in Verona, one of the most important things to consider is where you'll stop to sip, recharge, socialize, nibble, and revel in this handsome and affluent town.

CAFES & PASTRIES   Verona's grande dame of the local cafe society is the **Antico Caffè Dante** ✪ in the beautiful Piazza dei Signori (no phone). Verona's oldest cafe, it is rather formal indoors (read: expensive) where meals are served. But it's most recommended for those who want to soak up the million-dollar view of one of Verona's loveliest ancient squares from the outdoor tables smack in the middle of it all. During the Arena summer season, this is the traditional après-opera spot to complete—and contemplate—the evening's experience. It's open from 9am to 4am.

The oldest of the cafe/bars lining Verona's market square is **Caffè Filippini** at Piazza delle Erbe 26 (☎ **045-800-4549**). Repeated renovations have left little of yesteryear's character or charm, but centuries-old habits die hard: It's still the command post of choice whether indoors or out (preferably out), a lovely spot to take in the cacophony and colorful chaos of the market. It's open daily from 8am to 1am (closed Wed in winter).

An old-world temple of caffeine, **Caffè Tubino** (Corso Porta Borsari 15/d, 1 block west of the Piazza delle Erbe; ☎ **045-803-2296**) is stocked with packaged blends of Tubino-brand teas and coffees displayed on racks lining parallel walls in a small space made even smaller by the imposing crystal chandelier. The brand is well known, nicely packaged, and makes a great gift. It's open daily from 7am to 11pm. On the same street is **Pasticceria Bar Flego** (Corso Porta Borsari 9; ☎ **045-803-2471**), a beloved institution with eight tiny tables-for-two. Accompany a frothy cappuccino with an unbridled sampling of their deservedly famous bite-size pastries by the piece at .65€ to 1€ (75¢–$1.15) each. A regional specialty are the *zaletti,* traditional cookies made with corn flour, raisins, and pine nuts—much better tried than described! It's closed on Monday.

One of Verona's oldest and most patronized *pasticcerie* is **Cordioli**, a moment's stroll from Juliet's House on Via Cappello 39 (☎ **045-800-3055**). There are no tables and it's often three-deep at the bar, but with coffee this good and pastries this fresh (made on the premises), it's obvious why the crowds come. Verona's perfect souvenir? How about homemade *baci di Giulietta* (vanilla meringues called Juliet's kisses) and *sospiri di Romeo* (Romeo's sighs, chocolate hazelnut cookies)? It's closed Sunday afternoon and Wednesday.

WINE BARS   Verona is the epicenter of the region's important viticulture (Veneto produces more DOC wine than any other region in Italy), but the old time wine bars are decreasing in number and atmosphere. Recapture the spirit of yesteryear at **Carro Armato,** in a 14th-century palazzo at Vicolo Gatto 2A/Vicolo San Piero Martire (1 block south of Piazza Sant'Anastasia; ☎ **045-803-0175**), a great choice for after-hours or any hour when you want to sit and sample some of 30 or so regional wines by the glass (1€–3€/$1.15–$3.45) and make an informal meal out of fresh, inexpensive bar food. Oldsters linger during the day playing cards or reading the paper at long wooden tables, while a younger crowd fills the place in the evening. A small but good selection of cheeses and cold cuts or sausages might be enough to take the edge off, but there is always an entree or two and a fresh vegetable side dish. It's open Monday to Friday from 10am to 2pm and 5pm to 2am, Saturday and Sunday nonstop hours.

The wonderfully characteristic old wine bar, **Enoteca dal Zovo,** on Vicolo San Marco in Foro 7/5 (off Corso Porta Borsari near the above-mentioned Caffè Tubino; © **045-803-4369**), is run by Oreste, who knows everyone in town, and they all stop by for his excellent selection of Veneto wines averaging 1.50€ ($1.75) a glass, or you can go for broke and start with the very best at 2€ ($2.30). Oreste's *simpatica* American-born wife, Beverly, can give you a crash course. Salami, olives, and finger foods will help keep you vertical, since the few stools are always occupied by senior gentlemen who are as much a part of the fixtures as the hundreds of dusty bottles of wines and grappa that line the walls. Open Tuesday to Sunday from 8am to 1pm and 2 to 8pm.

SIDE TRIPS FROM VERONA

The ancient Greeks called Italy *Enotria*—the land of wines. It produces more wine than any other country in the world, so the annual **VinItaly** ☆☆ wine fair held every April in Verona is an understandably prestigious event. The Veneto produces more DOC (*Denominazione di Origine Controllata,* zones of controlled name and origin) wines than anywhere else in Italy, particularly the Veronese trio of Bardolino and Valpolicella (reds) and soave (white).

The costly, dry Valpolicello wine known as Amarone comes from the vineyards outside of Verona. **Masi** ☆ is one of the most respected producers, one of many in the Verona hills, whose *cantine* are open to the public for wine-tasting stops. Visit Verona's tourist information office for a listing of wine estates open to the public. No organized tours are available and you'll need your own wheels, but oenologically minded visitors will want to taste some of Italy's finest wines at the point of their origin.

Trentino–Alto Adige:
The Dolomites & South Tirol

Mountains dominate much of this region, which stretches north along the Adige River valley from the intersection of Lombardy and the Veneto. The soaring landscape of the Alps and the Dolomites (Dolomiti) presides over a different Italy, one that often doesn't seem very Italian at all.

Most of the Dolomites and Südtirol (the South Tirol, which encompasses the Trentino and Alto Adige regions) belonged to Austria until it was handed over to Italy at the end of World War I. In fact, many residents, especially in and around Bozen, Merano, and Brixen, still prefer the ways of the north to those of the south. They eat Austrian food, go about life with Teutonic crispness, and, most noticeably, tend to avoid speaking Italian in favor of their native German-based dialect—to them, these towns are called Bozen, Meran, and Brixen. Some villages even speak Ladin, a vestigial Latin dialect related to Switzerland's Romansch. And they live amid mountain landscapes that are more suggestive of Austria than of Italy.

The eastern Alps that cut into the region are gentle and beautiful. A little farther to the east rise the Dolomites—dramatically craggy peaks that are really coral formations that only recently (in geological terms) reared up from ancient seabeds. Throughout Trentino–Alto Adige, towering peaks, highland meadows, and lush valleys provide a paradise for hikers, skiers, and rock climbers. Set amid these natural spectacles are pretty, interesting towns and castles to explore and a hybrid Teutonic-Latin culture to enjoy.

REGIONAL CUISINE   The cuisine of the Alto Adige is more or less Austrian, with a few Italian touches. *Canederli* (bread dumplings) often replace pasta or polenta and are found floating in rich broths infused with liver; *Speck* (smoked ham) replaces prosciutto; and Wiener schnitzel *Grostl* (a combination of potatoes, onions, and veal—the local version of corned beef hash), and pork roasts are among preferred *secondi* (second courses).

The Trentino has several good wines, both white (pinot grigio, pinot bianco, traminer, chardonnay) and red (cabernet, cabernet franc, pinot nero, and lighter local reds Vernatsch, Cadaro, Lagrein, and Casteller), and the Adige Valley has proved an up-and-comer in recent vintages. Forst, a personal favorite in the fairly lowly pantheon of Italian beers, has been brewed outside Merano since 1857.

1 Trent (Trento)

230km (143 miles) NW of Milan, 101km (63 miles) N of Verona, 57km (35 miles) S of Bozen

Surrounded by mountains, this beautiful little city, founded by the Romans on the banks of the Adige River, definitely has an Alpine flair. It spent most of its history, from the 10th century though 1813, as a German-Austrian bishopric

---

Tips **Trentino–Alto Adige on the Web**

In addition to the city websites listed under each town throughout this chapter, the Trentino province around Trent maintains its own site at **www. provincia.tn.it**. The South Tirol is represented by a few private sites such as **www.sudtirol.com, www.stol.it,** and **www.hallo.com**. The Dolomites can be researched at various sites claiming to be "the official" one (all are loaded with good information at any rate), including **www.dolomiti.it** and **www.altoadige.com.**

---

ruled by powerful princely bishops from their seat in the Castello del Buonconsiglio. In fact, the town's status as an Italian city at the crossroads of the Teutonic and Latin worlds, along with the bishop's dual role as subject both to the pope and to the German Emperor, made Trent the ideal compromise site for the Council of Trent called in the 16th century to address the Protestant Reformation (see "Europe Divided: Protestant Reformation & the Council of Trent," below).

Napoléon's imperial sweep through Italy sent the last prince-bishop packing in 1796, and by 1813 Trent came under a century of direct Austrian rule. Austria's hegemony was constantly challenged by the local pro-Italian "Irredentist" movement, which was delighted when the treaties ending World War I landed Trent on the Italian side of the border in 1918.

And indeed, unlike other towns up here in the far north, which tend to lean heavily on their Austrian heritage, Trent is essentially Italian. The piazze are broad and sunny, the palaces are ocher-colored and tile-roofed, Italian is the lingua franca, and pasta is still a staple on menus. With its pleasant streets and the remnants of its most famous event, the 16th-century Council of Trent, Trent is a nice place to stay for a night or to visit en route to Bozen (see section 2) and other places in the Trentino–Alto Adige.

FESTIVALS & MARKETS In May and June, churches around the city are the evocative settings of performances of the *Festivale di Musica Sacra* (Festival of Sacred Music). Its final performances coincide with **Festive Vigiliane,** a medieval pageant for which townspeople turn up in the Piazza del Duomo appropriately decked out. Call the tourist office (© **0461-839-000**) for performance dates.

An ambitious program aptly named **Superfestival** stages musical performances, historic dramas, and reenactments of medieval and Renaissance legends in castles surrounding Trent; it runs from late June through September.

A small daily **food market** covers the paving stones of Piazza Alessandro Vittorio every day from 8am to 1pm. A **larger market,** this one with clothing, crafts, and bric-a-brac as well, is held Thursday 8am to 1pm in Piazza Arogno near the Duomo; this same piazza hosts a **flea market** the third Sunday of every month.

ESSENTIALS

GETTING THERE **By Train** Strategically located on a main north–south rail line between Italy and Austria, Trent is served by some 21 trains a day to and from Verona (55–69 min.), a major transfer point for trains to Milan, Florence, Rome, Venice, Trieste, and all points south. There are about two dozen trains a day from Bozen (32–49 min.). To reach the center of town from the train station, follow the Via Pozzo through several name changes until it reaches the Piazza del Duomo as Via Cavour.

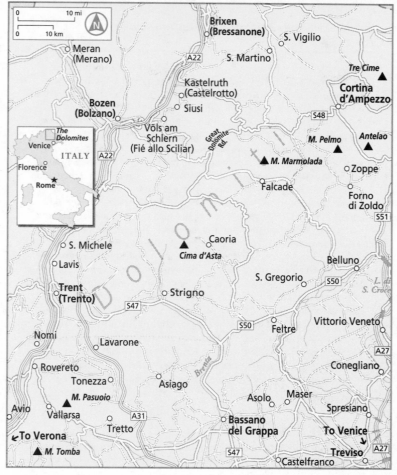

By Bus   Atesina buses (© **0461-821-000;** www.atesina.it), which leave from a terminal next to the train station, are the major links to outlying mountain towns. There's also hourly service to and from Riva del Garda on Lago di Garda (1 hr. 40 min.; see chapter 8, "The Lakes").

By Car   The A22 autostrada connects Trent with Verona in about an hour; from Verona you can connect with the A4 for Milan (total trip time between Milan and Trent is about 2½ hr.) and with A22 to Modena and from there A1 for Florence and Rome (Trent is a drive of about 3½ hr. from Florence and about 6½ hr. from Rome). A22 also runs north to Bozen, a little over half an hour away; the slower S12 also connects Trent and Bozen, and from it you can get on the scenic Strada di Vino.

VISITOR INFORMATION   The local **tourist office,** near the Duomo at Via Manci 2 (© **0461-983-880;** fax 0461-232-426; www.apt.trento.it), is open daily 9am to 7pm.

Europe Divided: Protestant Reformation & the Council of Trent

As you amble around this lovely town, you'll quickly learn that much of what is notable about it is in some way connected with the historic 16th-century Council of Trent, in which the Catholic church closed ranks against the waves of Protestant reform coming from the north.

Power in late medieval Europe was carefully balanced between the pope and the various kings and emperors. Power was consolidated through an intricate network wherein the secular alliances and post-feudal loyalties of princes, answerable to the Holy Roman Emperor, intersected with an overlying ecclesiastical structure of churches and monasteries, run by powerful bishoprics and answerable to the pope.

In short, by the 16th century the system had developed to the point where not only the Vatican's strength, but also that of the emperor and other kings, relied heavily on the power structure of the Catholic church. Therefore, the Protestant revolutions being fired in the north by Martin Luther and other reformers—who were distressed by the corruption on the part of the official church and its pope in regard to worldly interests—were seen as much more than a mere argument over style of worship: They threatened Europe's entire power base.

Germanic Holy Roman Emperor Charles V—who had brought that office to the heights of its power, ruling or controlling much of Europe—recognized this threat, both to Catholicism and to his domain. But he spent so much of his time and effort fighting wars with France and others that, despite holding his own diets to stamp out Luther's ideas, Protestantism kept growing in Germany. Charles eventually pressured the pope

WHAT TO SEE & DO

Castello di Buonconsiglio ★ Many Council of Trent sessions were held in this bishop's palace/fortress on the north edge of town, which you can reach by walking north from the Duomo along Via Belenzani, then east on Via Roma (though it's a bit of a trek from the rest of the center and the train station)—both streets, especially the former, are lined with the palaces, many with faded frescoes on their facades, built to house the church officials who came to Trent to attend the council sessions. The mazelike *castello* incorporates the 13th-century Castelvecchio, surrounded by medieval fortifications, and the elegant Magno Palazzo, a palace built for a prince-bishop in the 15th century.

Among the many small collections contained within the vast complex is the Museo Provincale d'Arte, where the pride of the collection is the ***Ciclo dei Mesi*** **(Cycle of the Months)** ★★, an enchanting fresco cycle painted around 1400. It presents a detailed look at life at court and in the countryside, showing amusements among the lords and ladies and much hard work among the peasants. It's housed in the Torre dell'Aquila, or Eagle's Tower; for admission, ask the guards at the Loggia del Romanino, an atrium named for the Renaissance artist who frescoed it.

You can also visit the cell where native son Cesare Battiste was held in 1916 for his part in the Irredentist movement, which sought to return Trent and other into instituting a great council to refute the reformers, and the Vatican called the council in 1536. But it took another 9 years to settle on Trent as the ideal compromise location in which to hold it, during which time Swiss reformer John Calvin introduced and perfected his own version of Protestantism. On and off for 18 years, from 1545 to 1563, the council held its debates and meetings, to which the Protestants were not really welcome and from which, probably wisely, they stayed away. The Great Council outlasted five popes, Martin Luther (who died in its second year), and Charles V himself (he died in 1556). Calvin passed on in 1564.

Far from taking Protestant complaints to heart, the council took a hard line, becoming more of a defensive strategy session. The Vatican dug in its heels and its doctrine, reorganizing church structure and policies to *tighten* control rather than loosen it. This became the Counter-Reformation, which, while not quite reaching the terrifying extremes of the Spanish Inquisition, brought the yardstick of conservatism down hard on the knuckles of Catholic Europe.

Still, it was all too late to stem the tide of Protestantism—and a general progressive slide away from the remnants of feudal power structures. The Germanic countries, soon to be followed by England, increasingly turned their backs on the Vatican. Charles V was the last German Emperor to be crowned by the Pope. The Papal States and the continent's secular kingdoms drifted apart, and the old power system gradually unraveled as Europe groped its way toward the system of nation-states we know today.

parts of the region to Italy—which indeed came to pass with the Treaty of Versailles in 1919, but not before Battiste was hanged in the moat that surrounds the Castelvecchio.

Via Bernardo Clesio 3. ✆ **0461-233-770** or 0461-492-840. www.buonconsiglio.it. Admission 5€ ($5.75) adults, 2.50€ ($2.90) children. Apr–Sept Tues–Sun 9am–noon and 2–5:30pm; Oct–Mar Tues–Sun 9am–noon and 2–5pm. Bus: 5, 7, 10, or B.

Duomo The outcomes of many Council of Trent sessions were announced in this 13th- to 16th-century cathedral, delightfully situated on the wide expanse of the cafe-filled Piazza Duomo. This square, with a statue of Neptune at its center, is referred to as the city's *salotto* (sitting room), so popular is it as a place to pass the time. More specifically, the decrees that came out of the council were read in the Duomo's Chapel of the Crucifix, beneath an enormous 15th-century cross. Beneath the altar of the main church is the crypt-cum-basilica Paleocristiana, a 6th-century church later used as a crypt for the city's powerful prince-bishops. A few scraps of mosaic and carvings remain.

Piazza Duomo. ✆ **0461-234-419**. Admission to the crypt 1€ ($1.15), or free with the Museo Diocesano ticket (see below). Mon–Sat 9:30am–12:30pm and 2:30–6pm; crypt 10am–noon and 2:30–6pm.

Museo Diocesano Tridentino The cathedral's museum is housed in the adjoining, heavily fortified palace of these bishops. The museum displays some fascinating paintings of council sessions that serve almost as news photos of the proceedings (one provides a seating plan for delegates), as well as 16th-century tapestries and statuary, objects from the Duomo's treasury, and a collection of medieval and Renaissance paintings. The latter often showcase local Saint Vigilio, Trent's 4th-century bishop and a literal iconoclast whose destruction of a Saturn idol earned him his martyrdom as enraged pagans beat him to death with their workmen's wooden shoes. By the Renaissance, these nail-studded sandals had inexplicably become the *zoccolo,* a silken slipper, which the hapless saint is always holding up in paintings as the symbol of his martyrdom.

Piazza Duomo 18. ℂ **0461-234-419.** www.museodiocesanotridentino.it. Admission (includes Duomo's crypt; see above) 3€ ($3.45) adults, .50€ (60¢) ages 14–18. Wed–Mon 9:30am–12:30pm and 2:30–6pm.

Santa Maria Maggiore   The pretty little church is a set piece of Lombard Renaissance architecture, designed and decorated almost entirely in the second quarter of the 16th century. Inside is an organ gallery ornately carved by Vincenzo Grandi in 1534. The church hosted several Council of Trent sessions, including the last ones.

Piazza Santa Maria Maggiore (between Via Rosimini and Via Cavour). ℂ **0461-239-888.** Free admission. Mon–Sat 9:30am–12:15pm and 3:30–7:30pm.

WHERE TO STAY

Trent, despite its history, has a pretty sorry hotel crop, with most of the nicer joints outside the center and focused mainly on conference centers and corporate rates. If you want a bit more class and a full complement of amenities in your hotel, you might check out the **Grand Hotel Trento,** Via Alfieri 1–3 (ℂ **0461-271-000;** fax 0461-271-001; www.grandtrento.boscolohotels.com), a large and somewhat bland business-oriented hotel near the bus and train station, a few blocks from the Duomo. Doubles go for 122€ to 165€ ($140–$190), and all major credit cards are accepted.

Accademia Hotel ★   This simple but nicely amenitied hotel is the best choice in the center, though prices are a bit steep. It's set in a restored medieval house on an alley about a block from the Duomo and Piazza Santa Maria Maggiore (whose bell tower some rooms overlook). The reception area's whitewashed vaulted ceilings and stone doorjambs don't really carry over into the rooms, which are a bit spartan, if well equipped, with modular or rattan furnishings, sometimes under nice sloping ceilings. Things would improve dramatically if the friendly staff would only replace the thin, stained carpet that covers every floor.

Trent on Two Wheels

You can rent a bike from **Moser Cicli,** a few blocks north from Piazza Duomo at Via Calepina 37–43 (ℂ **0461-230-327;** www.mosercicli.it), at 3€ ($3.45) per hour, 8.50€ ($10) for a half day, and 14€ ($16) for a full day. They're open daily 9am to noon and 3:15 to 7pm. You can tool along the Adige River, or set off on 1 of 20 marked trails at the city's periphery (ask the tourist office for details). In July and August the tourist office hosts Sunday morning bike tours of Trent. Each lasting 3 hours, the tours are limited to 20 people and depart from the tourist office at 9:30am (although they ask that you arrive 15 min. earlier). Call ℂ **0461-983-880** to see about reserving a space.

Getting a Lift Out of Town

For a breezy view of Trent and a heart-thumping aerial ride as well, take the **cable car** from Ponte di San Lorenzo near the train station up to Sardagna, a village on one of the mountainsides that enclose the city. You may want to provision yourself at the market and enjoy a picnic on one of the grassy meadows nearby. The cable car (⌀ **0461-822-075**) runs daily, every 30 minutes from 7am to 10:30pm (7:30pm on weekends) and the fare is .80€ (90¢) each way.

Vicolo Colico 4–6, 38100 Trento (off Via Cavour). ⌀ **0461-233-600.** Fax 0461-230-174. www.accademia hotel.it. 42 units. 120€–139€ ($138–$160) double; 161€–179€ ($185–$206) jr. suite; 212€–230€ ($244–$265) suite; extra bed 15€ ($17). Rates include buffet breakfast. Ask about lower rates for Fri–Sun stays. AE, DC, MC, V. **Amenities:** Restaurant; woodsy *enoteca* (wine bar); bike rental; concierge; tour desk; car-rental desk; 24-hr. room service (for bar; meal service only during restaurant hours); babysitting; laundry service; dry cleaning. *In room:* A/C, TV, minibar, hair dryer.

Hotel Aquila D'Oro ★   A recent renovation of an older hotel that in turn occupied a centuries-old palazzo has created some of the nicest rooms in Trent, with a wonderful location right around the corner from the Piazza Duomo. Decor throughout is stylishly contemporary, with a nice smattering of Oriental carpets, vaulted ceilings, and other interesting and cozy architectural touches in public rooms. The guest rooms are a little plainer, but have glossy, streamlined new furnishings and gleaming tile bathrooms, and more improvements are planned.

Via Belenzani 76, 38100 Trento. ⌀ and fax **0461-986-282.** www.aquiladoro.it. 19 units. 90€ ($104) double; 110€ ($127) triple. Rates include buffet breakfast. AE, DC, MC, V. **Amenities:** Bar; concierge; tour desk; car-rental desk; room service (limited); nonsmoking rooms. *In room:* A/C, TV, dataport, minibar, hair dryer.

Hotel Garni (aka Hotel Venezia)   This old hotel is rather less charming than its next-door neighbor Aquila D'Oro (see above), and its "amenities" consist entirely of toilet paper and one towel, but it's cheap. Marked by 1950s-style furnishings, the simple, high-ceiling rooms are a bit dowdy but offer solid, old-fashioned comfort (unfortunately, some beds still bear the sags left by generations of travelers). Its selling point: Those rooms in the front come with stunning views over the Piazza Duomo. Some of the younger members of the family who run the hotel speak English and are more than happy to dispense advice on what to see and do in town and the surrounding area. Some of the older ones are quite surly. No one mans the "reception" desk that sits just inside the official mailing address entrance on Via Belenzani; instead, walk around the corner to the "unofficial" entrance on Piazza Duomo to find someone to check you in. *Note:* Though the hotel's official name is now Hotel Garni, the website is still "venezia" and the signs and the name painted on the side of the building still say "Hotel Venezia" (since it's a historic landmark, they can't change the outside!).

Via Belenzani 70/Piazza Duomo 45, 38100 Trento. ⌀ and fax **0461-234-559.** www.hotelveneziatn.it. 48 units, 28 with bathroom. 50€ ($58) double without bathroom; 61€ ($70) double with bathroom; 66€ ($76) triple without bathroom; 79€ ($91) triple with bathroom. Rates include continental breakfast. MC, V. Free parking 200m/656 ft. from hotel. *In room:* Hair dryer, no phone.

WHERE TO DINE

It's almost a requirement to stroll down Trent's Renaissance streets with a gelato from **Torre Verde-Gelateria Zanella** on Via Suffragio 6 (⌀ **0461-232-039**). Many flavors are made from fresh, local fruits in season, while others make no such attempt at wholesomeness and incorporate the richest chocolate and cream.

Birreria Pedavena BEER HALL/PIZZERIA   It seems as if this dark, cavernous beer hall–style cafeteria can feed all of Trent, and it just might. It draws a big crowd for coffee and pastries in the morning and keeps serving a huge mix of pastas, *Würstel, canederli,* and pizza all day. You will probably be happiest if you order simply, maybe a plate of *Würstel* (essentially, hot dogs) or goulash or one of the excellent pizzas. Recently, the brewery was expanded, and Pedavena has begun producing its own beer. Additionally, this place keeps some of the latest hours in town, making Pedavena something of a late-evening spot in a town where the nightlife is scarce.

Piazza Fiera 13 at Via Santa Croce. ℂ 0461-986-255. www.birreriapedavena.com. Primi 3.50€–5.50€ ($4.05–$6); secondi 4.50€–10€ ($5–$12); pizza 3.25€–6€ ($3.75–$7). MC, V. Mon and Wed–Thurs 9am–12:30am; Fri–Sat 9am–1am; Sun 9am–midnight. Sometimes closed in July.

La Cantinota ITALIAN/TIROLEAN   With its white tablecloths, excellent service, and reasonably priced menu, La Cantinota may be the most popular restaurant in Trent. The color red is used with abandon, and a goose wanders among the tables in the atrium garden. The fare includes Italian and Tirolean dishes and is truly inspired, making use of fresh local ingredients: wonderful homemade gnocchi, *strangola preti* (spinach dumplings coated in melted butter), rich risottos with porcini mushrooms, grilled sausages with polenta, and *vitello barolo* (veal with a rich red-wine sauce). The adjoining piano bar is popular with local talent who tend to intersperse Frank Sinatra renditions with yodeling.

Via San Marco 24. ℂ 0461-238-527. Reservations recommended. Primi 6.50€–8€ ($7–$9); secondi 7.50€–13€ ($9–$15). AE, MC, V. Fri–Wed noon–3pm and 7–11pm (piano bar 10:30pm–2am).

Scrigno del Duomo ★★ *Finds* WINE BAR/ITALIAN   This stylish wine bar and restaurant is a surprisingly good value considering the quality of the creative cooking, immaculate service, and stellar location—from the front courtyard, with tables set under the frescoed facade, you can peek through the gate at the fountain splashing away on Trent's main piazza. The interiors mix the antique with postmodern: Renaissance painted beams or baroque stuccoed ceilings, designer CD changers, aluminum chairs, and sconces. There are more than 35 wines available by the glass (€2.60–€7.50/$3–$8.60). Dishes change constantly with the seasons and chef's whims. On my last visit, I sampled *lasagnette di asparagi con prosciutto corccante* (white asparagus lasagna in a béchamel sauce sprinkled with crunchy prosciutto bits) and a *trancio di salmone alle erbe con legume e salsa al jogurt* (salmon filet in a yogurt sauce with a side of steamed veggies).

Piazza Duomo 29. ℂ 0461-220-030. www.scrignodelduomo.com. Reservations recommended. Primi 6.50€–8€ ($7–$9); secondi 10€–13€ ($12–$15); tasting menu 47€ ($54) without wine. MC, V. Daily 11am–2:30pm and 6pm–midnight.

THE SOUTHERN TRENTINO: ROVERETO & CASTELLO SABBIONARA

ROVERETO   There are two main reasons to visit this noble, medieval town 24km (15 miles) south of Trent. One is simply to stroll through its winding streets and elegant, quiet piazze that lie in the shadow of the 15th-century **Castello di Rovereto** (ℂ 0464-438-100). This Venetian-built castle reminds its visitors that this is as far north as Venice got (by 1418) in its long battle with Austrian powers over control of the Tirol. By 1487 the Austrian factions had control again, but Italian hopes, and the native pro-Italy *Irrendentisti,* never truly disappeared. This brings us to the other reason to visit: to pay homage to the thousands of mostly Italian and Austrian soldiers who died in the surrounding hills during some of the fiercest fighting of World War I.

These soldiers are commemorated mainly by two sights: the daily sunset ringing of the **Campana della Pace,** or Bell of Peace (℗ **0464-434-412; open** Apr–July and Sept daily 9am–noon and 2–7pm, Aug 9am–7pm, Mar and Oct 9am–noon and 2–6pm, and Feb and Nov 9am–noon and 2–4pm; 1€/$1.15 adults, .30€/35¢ children), which perches atop the hillside near a neoclassical rotunda temple to the fallen; and the **Museo Storico Italiano della Guerra** (℗ **0464-438-100**). The latter occupies part of the castle, at Via Castelbarco 7, and displays photographs, weaponry, and other memorabilia associated with this and other battles. The museum is open March to June and October to November Tuesday to Sunday 8:30am to 12:30pm and 2 to 6pm; July to September Tuesday to Friday 10am to 6pm, and Saturday and Sunday 9:30am to 6:30pm; admission is 5.20€ ($6) adults, 1.60€ ($1.85) ages 6 to 12.

The third reason to come to Rovereto is to attend one of its much-heralded cultural events: The **Rovereto Festival** in early September features dance performances and a major exhibition of contemporary art; and the late-September **Festival Internazionale Mozart** (℗ **0464-439-988**) features world-renowned performances of the composer's work.

Rovereto is less than half an hour south of Trent via A22. About two buses an hour make the trip in 45 minutes; contact **Atesina** (℗ **0461-821-000;** www.atesina.it) for more information. The **APT tourist office,** at a park on the Leno Aiver at Corso Rosmini 6A (℗ **0464-430-363;** fax 0464-435-528; www.apt.rovereto.tn.it), is open Monday to Friday 8:30am to 12:15pm and 2:30 to 6pm, and Saturday (summer only) 8:30am to 12:15pm.

CASTELLO SABBIONARA   The first historical mention of the Castello Sabbionara (℗ **0464-684-453**), at the town of Avio 21km (13 miles) south of Rovereto, is from the 13th century, though the castle dates back at least to the 11th century. It was built on the ever-shifting battle line between the dominions of Austrian emperors and the Venetian Republic—so it's no surprise that, during a 13th-century period of Venetian control when the castle was enlarged, the Casa delle Guardie (Guard's House) was frescoed with marvelous medieval battle scenes featuring the castle in the background. Local folklore whispers that public executions were once carried out inside the imposing Picadòra tower, which defends the north side. The castle is open February to December 17 Tuesday to Sunday 10am to 1pm and 2 to 6pm (to 5pm Oct–Dec 17); admission is 3.50€ ($4.05) adults, 2.50€ ($2.90) ages 6 to 10.

EN ROUTE TO BOZEN: THE STRADA DI VINO

Some of Italy's finest wines are produced on the vines that cloak the hillsides between Trent and Bozen. (These local wines include many pinot grigios and pinot noirs among whites, and Vernatsch, the most common red of the region.) If you are traveling by car between the two cities, you can make the trip on the well-marked *Strada di Vino (Weinstrasse),* or Wine Road. Leave Trent on S12; 15km (9 miles) north you will come to the main turnoff for the village of Lavis; take this turnoff, and from here easy-to-follow yellow signs will lead you along a series of twisting roads past vineyards and around Lago di Caldaro to Bozen. Many of the vineyards have tasting rooms open to the public and sometimes offer cheese, sandwiches, and other refreshment as well.

The **Vini Josef Hofstätter** cantina on Piazza Municipio 5 in Termeno (℗ **0471-860-161**) welcomes drop-ins for free tastings, but for most vineyards you must book ahead; keep in mind that most are closed from around noon to 2pm. Check out **Georg Baron Widmann,** Via im Feld 1 in Cortaccia (✆ **0471-880-092**); **Alois Lageder** in Magrè (✆ **0471-809-500**; www.lageder.com); and **Castel Scwahburg** in Nalles (✆ **0471-678-622**). There's the small **Südtiroler Weinmuseum** (✆ **0471-963-168**) in the Caldaro village outside Termeno at Goldgasse 1, open Monday to Saturday 9:30am to noon and 2 to 6pm, Sunday 10am to noon. If you don't have your own wheels, the tourist offices in Trent and Bozen can provide lists of local tour companies that lead wine tours.

2 Bozen (Bolzano)

154km (92 miles) N of Verona, 118km (73 miles) S of Innsbruck, 57km (35 miles) NE of Trent

Without even crossing a border, by heading north from Trent into the Alto Adige region, you'll find yourself in a place that doesn't resemble Italy at all. During its long history, this pretty town at the confluence of the Talvera and Isarco rivers has been ruled by the bishops of Trent, the counts of Tirol, and the Hapsburgs, to name but a few of its lords. Bozen (Bolzano in Italian) has only been part of Italy since the end of World War I. As you explore the narrow streets and broad *Platzen* (piazze) and stroll through the parks that line the town's two rivers, you get the sense that, with its gabled, Tirolean-style houses and preference for Germanic dialect, the city is still more Teutonic than Italian.

Bozen's foundation dates back to the Iron Age—and now there's even a full-fledged, and famous, ice man cooling his 5,000-year-old heels in the excellent local archaeology museum. But Bozen didn't really pick up steam until the Middle Ages, when its situation at a river confluence just south of an Alpine pass made it an important small market town.

FESTIVALS & MARKETS   Bozen celebrates spring with **weekend concerts** throughout April and May in Piazza Walther, and adds a **flower show,** with more music, around the first of May. The city's most serious musical event is the **Concorso Internazionale Piantistico F. Busoni,** an international piano competition held the last 2 weeks of August. The **Festival del Teatro di Strada** draws wandering musicians, mimes, puppeteers, and other performers to the streets of the old city in October. One of the more colorful events in the region is the **Bartolomeo Horse Fair,** which brings together the region's most beautiful equines on the Renon plateau, which can be reached by funicular (see "Cable Cars" on p. 218).

One of the most enjoyable walks in the old city takes you through the stalls of the **fruit and vegetable market** in Piazza delle Erbe, which operates Monday through Saturday from 8am to 7pm. From November 28 to December 23, the city hosts a much-attended **Mercatino di Natale (Christkindlmarkt),** in which handmade ornaments, wooden toys, and other seasonal crafts, along with Christmas pastries and mulled wine, are sold from booths in a festively decorated Piazza Walther.

A **flea market** fills the Passeggiata del Talvera along the River Talvera (follow Via Museo from the center of town) the first Saturday of the month (except July–Aug), opening at 8am and closing at 5pm.

ESSENTIALS

GETTING THERE   **By Train**   Bozen is on the north–south rail line that links Verona with Innsbruck, Austria, via the Brenner Pass. There are some 17 trains daily from Verona (90 min.–1¾ hr.); twenty-five trains a day from Trent (32–45 min.). Hourly train service links Bozen with Merano (38 min.).

Free Bikes!
The best way to get about town—certainly out to the castles and to Gries—
is on one of the free bikes offered by the municipality. There's a stand on
the left side of Viale Stazione just before Piazza Walther, and another on
Piazza Gries. Just leave a 5€ ($5.75) deposit, have a passport or driver's
license handy (they write the number down), and bring the bike back by
7pm. Unfortunately, this initiative is only guaranteed from Easter through
October; in winter you may have to cough up a few euros to rent from **Velo
Sport,** Via Grappoli 56 (© **0471-977-719**).

By Bus   Bozen is the hub of the excellent **SAD bus** network, serving even the
most remote mountain villages (© **0471-450-111;** www.sad.it). There are
hourly buses to and from Merano (1 hr.), and Brixen (1 hr.). Two daily morning buses (currently 9:15 and 11:10am) make the trip to Cortina, with a change
in Dobbiaco (about 4 hr.). The extremely helpful staff at the bus station, the
round building 1 block up from the train station and on the left, will help you
make sense of the routing.

By Car   The A22 autostrada connects Bozen with Trent in a little over half an
hour and with Verona (where you can connect with the A4 for Milan and Rome)
in a little over an hour; and, farther south, Modena (where you can connect with
the A1 for Florence and Rome); A22 runs north to Innsbruck. Avoid parking in
the criminally expensive public garages; most hotels have arrangements for considerably less.

By Plane   Bozen's dinky **airport** (© **0471-254-070;** www.abd-airport.it), on
the south side of the Isarco River, a few minutes' taxi ride from the center, is the
Dolomite's official airport, and has daily flights from Rome and Frankfurt, as
well as service from Vienna.

VISITOR INFORMATION   The **city tourist office,** near the Duomo at Piazza
Walther 8 (© **0471-307-000;** fax 0471-980-128; www.bolzano-bozen.it), dispenses a wealth of information on Bozen and the South Tirol. It's open Monday
to Friday from 9am to 6:30pm and on Saturday from 9am to 12:30pm. The local
events calendar *BoBo* can also be found online at **www.bobo.it.**

A STROLL AROUND BOZEN
With its two rivers, surrounding hills, expansive greens, and medieval center,
Bozen is an extremely appealing city that seems to effortlessly meld urban sophistication with an appreciation for nature. The compact medieval old city is still the
heart of town, and at its center is **Piazza Walther,** honoring a 12th-century wandering minstrel. The piazza captures the mood of its lighthearted historical associations with a fringe of cafe tables to one side and the brightly tiled roof and lacy
spire of the **Duomo** on the other. The interior of this 12th- to 14th-century
edifice is far plainer, enlivened somewhat by some much-faded frescoes and an
intricately carved pulpit (© **0471-978-676;** open Mon–Fri 9:45am–noon and
2–5pm, Sat 9:45–noon; Sun for services only).

A far more enticing church is the **Chiesa dei Domenicani** (© **0471-973-
133**), just a few steps west of the Duomo. Inside the 13th-century church are
two sets of frescoes that comprise the city's greatest artistic treasures. One from

the 15th century, on the walls of the cloisters, depicts court life. The other, in the Capella di San Giovanni (under the arch behind the altar and to the right), is a 14th-century religious cycle attributed to the school of Giotto, including the *Triumph of Death*. In these rich frescoes you can see the beginnings of the use of such elements as perspective and foreshortening, suggesting the influence of the early Renaissance. It's open Monday to Saturday 9:30am to 6pm; Sunday for services only.

There is one more church to see in Bozen, but before you reach it, you will be distracted by the considerable worldly pleasures this city offers. If you walk north from Piazza Walther, you will soon come to the lively clamor of **Piazza dell'Erbe,** actually one long, wide street that winds past a statue of Neptune through the old town and is so called because it has hosted Bozen's **fruit and produce market** for centuries. The piazza is lined with shops selling bread, cheese, strudel, wine, and other comestibles, which spill into stalls along the pavement to create a cheerful, open-air supermarket. At the north end is Bozen's atmospheric main shopping street, **Via dei Portici,** also closed to traffic and lined with 15th-century houses whose porticoes overhang the sidewalk to create a cozy effect that is definitely more northern European than Italian.

The **Chiesa dei Francescani** (© 0471-977-293) is across Via dei Portici on Via Francescani. Inside there's a sumptuously carved **altar** ⭐ from 1500, one of the Gothic masterpieces of the Trentino–Alto Adige. The 14th-century cloisters are charming—intimate, frescoed on one side, gracefully vaulted, and beautifully planted—and are open Monday to Saturday 10am to noon and 2:30 to 6pm; Sunday for services only.

Bozen's newest and by far most popular sight is the thoroughly modernized **Museo Archeologico dell'Alto Adige** ⭐⭐, Via Museo at Via Cassa di Risparmio (© 0471-320-100; www.iceman.it), better known as "Ötzi's House" since it was remodeled in 1998 to house the famed 5,300-year-old "ice man." This mummy made headlines in 1991 when a pair of German hikers discovered him sticking out of a melting glacier high in the Tirol mountains—though whether he was of Alpine origin or merely trying to cross the Alps is still being debated. His equipment and one of his last meals seem to have come from lower-altitude valleys, nearer Verona.

Forensic analysis in 2001 brought the surprise revelation that, apparently, he was shot in the shoulder with an arrow shortly before he died. Just before we went to press with this addition, a new research team made even more stunning conclusions about the Ice Man's final moments. Further research published in 2003 (and based on blood samples, microscopic fibers, and re-creations of wound placements—real *CSI* kinda stuff) revealed that the Ice Man was killed in a battle or skirmish of some sort—shot in the back and then carried off by a companion who must have removed the arrow for him.

Along with the mummy were preserved remnants of clothing (including shoes and a bearskin hat), a flint dagger, a copper ax, and a quiver with flint-tipped arrows he was in the process of making. The museum is open Tuesday to Sunday 10am to 6pm (to 8pm Thurs). Admission is 8€ ($9) adults, 5.50€ ($6) students under 28 and seniors over 65, or 16€ ($18) for a family card (two adults plus kids under 14). The audio guides, which I highly recommend, are an extra 2€ ($2.30).

A walk across the **River Talvera** (follow Via Museo west across the Ponte Talvera) brings you into the newer "Italian" section of Bozen, constructed in the 1920s when the Mussolini government encouraged workers from other parts of

A Village Tipple

Gries has its own little communal **Kellerei/Cantina winery,** Grieserplatz 2 (© **0471-270-909**), descended from a monkish production that dates back nearly a thousand years. Of their two dozen varieties, the dark, earthy red "Südtiroler Grieser Lagrein Dunkel DOC Riserva" has won honorable mention at VinItaly, while the Slow Food organization has recommended the "Grieser Lagrein," rosé with fruity overtones, for its "drinkability." This *cantina sociale* welcomes visitors for tastings Monday to Friday 8am to noon and 2:30 to 6:30pm, Saturday 8am to noon.

Italy to settle here in the newly won territory. Those who bid the call were either inspired or intimidated by the imposing Fascist-era structures put up along Corso Libert (including the Monumento della Vittoria, a triumphal arch that is frequently the target of attacks by German-speaking groups that want the region to revert to Austrian rule).

In a few blocks, though, the Corso brings you into the pleasant confines of **Gries** ⓡ, once an outlying village and now a quaint, leafy neighborhood built around the Abbazia dei Benedettini di Gries, a Benedictine abbey (not usually open to the public) prettily surrounded by vineyards and gardens. Just beyond is the **Vecchia Parrochiale di Gries,** the village's parish church, whose treasures include a 12th-century crucifix and an elaborately carved 15th-century altar (© **0471-283-089;** open Mon–Fri 10:30am–noon and 2:30–4pm; closed Nov–Mar).

If you wish to continue walking or biking, Gries contains one end of the **Passeggiata del Guncina,** a beautifully maintained 8km (5-mile) long trail that leads through parklike forests planted with many botanical specimens to a belvedere and a waterfall before dumping you back into town. You wind up at the northerly end of the park stretched along the north bank of the Talvera River.

CASTLES   Of the many castles that surround Bozen, the closest to the center is the **Castel Mareccio,** just a short walk along the River Talvera (from the Piazza delle Erbe, follow the Via Museo west to the Ponte Talvera and from there the Lungo Talvera Bozen north for less than .5km/¼ mile). Though it is now used as a convention center and its five towers rise from a residential neighborhood of recent vintage, this 13th-century fortress is a stunning sight, all the more so because it is surrounded by a generous swath of vineyards that have been saved from urban encroachment, and backed by forested hills. You can step inside for a glimpse at the stone-walled medieval interior and enjoy a beverage at the bar; the castle is open to the public Wednesday through Monday, 9am to 6pm (hours vary when conferences are in session; © **0471-976-615**).

A longer walk of about 2km (just over a mile; or take the free bus from Piazza Walther, which only goes back and forth between the piazza and the castle) leads out of town north to the **Castel Roncolo** ⓡⓡ (© **800-210-003** or 0471-329-808; www.comune.bolzano.it/roncolo/ie), beautifully ensconced high above the town and beneath a massive, foreboding cliff face. The interior of this 13th-century castle is decorated with faded but fascinating frescoes from the 14th and 15th centuries that depict secular scenes from the story of *Tristan and Isolde* and other tales of romantic love and chivalry. These painted scenes are remarkably moving in their almost primitive craftsmanship that nonetheless reveals a certain worldliness. Admission is 8€ ($9) adults, 5.50€ ($6) students and seniors over 60, 13€ ($15) for a family card for four; hour-long guided tours in English cost an extra 2.70€ ($3.10) per person (minimum six people). The castle is open Tuesday to Sunday: October to June 10am to 6pm, July to September 10am to 8pm. To get here, follow the Via Castel Roncolo north from the Chiesa dei Francescani; you will pass one side of the Castel Mareccio, at which point sign posts will lead you along Via Beatro Arrigo and Via San Antonio for a gradual uphill climb to Castel Roncolo.

CABLE CARS   Several **cable cars** will whisk you right from the center of Bozen into the surrounding mountains. The most dramatic ride takes you from a terminal near the train station 900m (3,000 ft.) up to the **Altopiano del Renon** (www. renon.com), a pasture-covered plateau that provides dizzying views down to Bozen and up to higher Dolomite peaks. The ride deposits you in SopraBozen (Ober-bozen), where you can sip a beer and enjoy the view, then venture farther by footpath or an electric tram into a bizarre landscape of spindly rock spires—worn needle-thin by erosion, each seeming to balance a boulder on the top—that surrounds the village of Collabo. The cable car (© **0471-978-479**) makes the ascent in 15 minutes and operates daily from a terminus about 450m (1,500 ft.) east of the train station on Via Renon; it operates hourly from 7am to 8pm; the round-trip, 15 minutes each way, costs 5€ ($5.75) and includes tram fare between SopraBozen and Collabo (4€/$4.60 if you skip the tram).

The **Funivia di San Genesio** takes you up a forested hillside to the pretty village of San Genesio Atesino, surrounded by woods and mountain peaks. Cable cars (© **0471-978-436**) leave hourly from 7am to 7pm (from 8am on Sun) from a terminus on Via Sarentino on the northern outskirts of Bozen (take bus no. 12 or 14). The trip takes 15 minutes, and the round-trip fare is 3.50€ ($4.05). San Genesio's little **tourist office** (© **0471-354-196;** fax 0471-354-085; www. jenesien.net), at Schrann 7, is open Monday to Friday 9am to 1pm (July–Oct also 4–6pm). It can set you up with a 2-hour horseback ride across the high Alpine meadows for just 16€ ($18); it's best to call ahead.

WHERE TO STAY

Hotel Feichter   This charming little inn is one of the few hotels in the old city itself and, for the location and atmosphere it provides, is one of the city's better lodging values. On the main floor there's a Tirolean-style lobby and a bar and self-service restaurant that resemble a *Weinstube*. The rooms may not be full of mountain ambience (and the bathrooms are cramped), but they contain serviceable, modern, comfortable furnishings. The extremely firm beds are equipped with that wonderful local luxury: thick down quilts. There's also a narrow courtyard set with picnic tables and shaded by a grape arbor.

Via Grappoli 15, 39100 Bolzano. © **0471-978-768.** Fax 0471-974-803. www.paginegialle.it/feichter. 49 units. 80€ ($92) double; 95€ ($109) triple. Rates include breakfast. MC, V. Parking 6€ ($7) in garage (10 spots). Closed 3 weeks in Feb. **Amenities:** Tirolese restaurant; concierge; tour desk. *In room:* TV, hair dryer (ask at desk).

Hotel Greif ★★★   The boutique hotel is just now being discovered in Italy, and the Staffler family—who have owned this 500-year-old inn on the main square since 1796—have taken to the concept brilliantly. Since the Greif reopened in a newly minimalist steel-and-glass incarnation in January 2000, its motto "very personal" has shone through, from the laptop PC with free Internet access in every room to an extraordinary attention to detail (the silver umbrellas ranked by the doors match the burnished steel and glass of the entranceway). Each überstylish, modern room is unique, featuring an original work by a Tirolese artist (each key chain is a tiny catalog for that room's artist). Most accommodations are spacious, some with lofted bedrooms, others with Jacuzzi tubs and views over the main square. The furnishings are a mix of modern and late-19th-century antiques, including gorgeous inlaid wood dressers and desks. Room no. 211 is like a musician's studio apartment, with deep sloping ceilings, dormer windows onto Piazza Walther, and even a baby grand.

Piazza Walther, 39100 Bolzano. (C) **0471-318-000.** Fax 0471-318-148. www.greif.it. 33 units. 158€ ($182) comfort double; 195€ ($224) superior double; 235€ ($270) "De-luxe" double. 280€ ($322) jr. suite, 330€ ($380) jr. suite with sauna. Rates include buffet breakfast. AE, DC, MC, V. Parking 15€ ($17). **Amenities:** Restaurant; bar (at Parkhotel Laurin, see below); pool at Laurin; golf (nearby); children's center at Laurin; concierge; tour desk; car-rental desk; business center; shopping arcade; room service (limited); in-room massage; babysitting; laundry service; dry cleaning (same-day); nonsmoking rooms; executive-level rooms. *In room:* A/C, TV, VCR (in some rooms), free movies, fax (in some), dataport with laptop, minibar, hair dryer, safe; private sauna in two rooms.

Hotel Regina A. For pleasant and affordable lodgings in Bozen, you need look no further than this modern hotel across the street from the train station—a decent location, as you're still only 3 blocks from the main square, but the rate disparity below reflects the noisiness of the busy main street out front. *Families take note:* The bright rooms are unusually large, and there are several quads and one mansard quint on hand. Although accommodations are quite plain, they're nicely decorated with streamlined Scandinavian furnishings, and all offer a level of comfort and have amenities you would expect in a much more expensive hotel— including large bathrooms nicely equipped with stall showers. They also offer lower-ceilinged mansard rooms for 5€ ($5.75) less than the rates quoted below.

Via Renon 1, 39100 Bolzano. (C) **0471-972-195** or 0471-974-099. Fax 0471-978-944. www.hotelreginabz.it. 40 units. 83€–92€ ($95–$106) double; 105€–114€ ($121–$131) triple; 116€–124€ ($133–$143) quad; 130€ ($150) mansard quint. Rates include breakfast. MC, V. Free on-street parking. **Amenities:** Bar (24-hr.); concierge; tour desk; nonsmoking rooms. *In room:* TV, hair dryer (ask at desk).

Parkhotel Laurin ⭐ This early-20th-century Liberty-style edifice takes up an entire city block just a few hundred feet from both the train station and Piazza Walther. Though it's full of modern comforts, the quirky old structure gives it character and style (and plenty of windows), and rarely are any two rooms alike. The modern furnishings reinterpret antique styles, such as angular postmodern settees or exaggeratedly swooping Empire-style chairs lacquered black and red. All rooms are spacious, with walk-in closets featuring trouser presses and mottled gray marble bathrooms (except in suites). "Comfort" rooms are roughly the same as "superior," but are smaller and all face the street. About half the "superior" rooms overlook the garden (all of the larger "De-luxe" ones do), the other half the end of the building facing downtown. Suites are like mini-apartments with a hall off of which open the bedroom, a tiny sitting room (often with a balcony), and the bathroom (in brown marble with double sinks and separate tub and shower stalls); one even has its own sauna. The hotel's real selling point is its large, landscaped garden of flower-lined and tree-shaded gravel paths; the restaurant (recently remodeled) even moves out here in summer to a gravelly terrace shaded by a canopy. Children under 13 stay in their parent's room for free (though their breakfast costs another 15€/$17).

Via Laurin 4, 39100 Bolzano. (C) **0471-311-000.** Fax 0471-311-148. www.laurin.it. 96 units. 158€ ($182) comfort double; 195€ ($224) superior double; 225€ ($259) De-luxe double; 280€ ($322) jr. suite. Rates include breakfast. AE, DC, MC, V. Parking 13€ ($15). **Amenities:** Italian restaurant; period bar; outdoor heated pool; children's center and small playground; concierge; tour desk; car-rental desk; room service for a 5€ ($6) service fee; babysitting; laundry service; dry cleaning (same-day); nonsmoking rooms. *In room:* A/C, TV, dataport, minibar, hair dryer, safe.

Stadt Hotel Citta ★★ This modernized old hotel, with an attractive arcaded facade typical of this city's distinctive architecture, commands a sunny corner of Bozen's main piazza, and was massively overhauled by its new owners, the Hotel Alpi, in 2000 and 2001. The large and bright guest rooms have been done in a contemporary style, with nice touches such as extra-wide beds in many twins and singles and, where they could keep them, hardwood floors. The family suites consist either of two rooms and a bathroom off a common hall, or two rooms, each with its own bathroom, that connect. There's also a similar arrangement in a double-bedded studio suite (the couch in the second room can pull out). Top-floor rooms are cozier, with slope-edged singles. The bathrooms are spanking new. The best rooms overlook the square and the Duomo; Mussolini stayed in one of them (no. 303), a suite with a corner balcony. The ground-floor bar and cafe, which opens to the square, is a popular gathering spot, and the handsome paneled and terra-cotta–tiled lobby is also a much-used meeting place.

Piazza Walther 21, 39100 Bolzano. (℃ **0471-975-221.** Fax 0471-976-688. www.hotelcitta.info. 102 units. 110€–150€ ($127–$173) regular double; 135€–160€ ($155–$184) water bed double; 135€–180€ ($155–$207) triple; 165€–250€ ($190–$288) family apt for up to 5. Rates include breakfast. AE, DC, MC, V. Parking 13€ ($15) in garage. **Amenities:** Mediterranean/Tirolese restaurant; bar under the arcades of Piazza Walther; large sauna/baths complex in basement with Turkish baths and huge whirlpool tub; concierge; tour desk; car-rental desk; courtesy car from the airport; 24-hr. room service; in-room massage; babysitting; laundry service; dry cleaning; nonsmoking rooms. *In room:* A/C, TV, dataport, hair dryer.

MOUNTAIN HOTELS EN ROUTE TO BRIXEN

High on the eastern wall of the Adige valley, halfway up the Siusi Alps above the road from Bozen to Brixen, lies the **Schlern plateau** (Sciliar in Italian). Its summertime meadows and forest trails for hiking and mountain biking, modestly decent winter skiing, half-ruined castles, colorful folk festivals, and cute Tirolean villages draw a small clutch of devoted vacationers. It's also got some great hotel deals in a perfect Tirol setting that gets you away from it all, but is still just a half-hour from the large towns down in the valley.

Cavallino d'Oro/Goldenes Rössl ★★ This 15th-century inn right on the main square of its little village does an excellent job of marrying traditional and cozy Tirolean style with modern comforts—the parquet-floored lounge has a picture window overlooking the Alps in the backyard right next to a wide-screen TV with 300 channels. The nicest rooms have four-poster beds with carved wood canopies, some of the furnishings in a light local timber, others hand-painted in pale green with floral designs. Most accommodations are rather large, with space enough for a small sitting area; no. 24 is simply huge, featuring a four-poster and a small terrace. All rooms on the back have balconies with mountain vistas, while rooms on the front overlook the cobblestone main square and fountain. Off the excellent restaurant, with its mountain views, is a wood-paneled *Stuben* (beer nook) that's 18th century right down to the filament bulbs. For lighter fare, the corner bar is very popular with the locals (the mayor and town priest are regulars). The Urthalers' family reception is warm and friendly, and they love Frommer's (10 years ago, they made a 32-state U.S. odyssey using Frommer's guides).

Piazza Kraus, 39040 Castelrotto/Kastelruth (BZ). (℃ **0471-706-337.** Fax 0471-707-172. www.cavallino.it. 20 units. 98€–116€ ($113–$133) double with half board in summer (depending on month and type of room); 98€–154€ ($113–$177) double with half pension Dec 7–Mar 8. Add 12€ ($14) per person for full board. Add 25% if you stay fewer than 3 nights; subtract 20% if you just book bed and breakfast. AE, DC, MC, V.

Parking free. Closed Nov. **Amenities:** Old-fashioned tavern with food and a finer restaurant; sauna and tanning bed; bike rental; children's center nearby; concierge; tour desk; car-rental desk; room service (limited); in-room massage; babysitting; laundry service; nonsmoking rooms. *In room:* TV, hair dryer, safe.

Romantik Hotel Turm ★★   At the very top of this medieval hamlet and modest mountain resort lies the Turm, a series of buildings dating in part to the 13th century that have served time as a tribunal, a prison, and an *osteria.* During blizzards, the whole village would come to the *osteria* and shut themselves in together to feast, play cards, and wait out the storm. This tradition gave rise to its role as an inn, which Stefan Pramstrahler and his crew continue today in a mix of discreetly contemporary style (mod chairs and bathroom tiles) and Alpine tradition (varnished wood furnishings, four-poster beds with cheerful little curtains), all set in rooms with wood paneling or hand-plastered white vaults and curving walls. Accommodations in the main Turm structure vary considerably, from corner room no. 14, with views on two sides and a folding couch to sleep three, to suite no. 16, entered through a Gothic stone archway and featuring two midsize rooms, a four-poster, and mountain views. Rooms in the Kraiterhaus next door are done in a more modern country style. The owner has a sharp eye for modern art, and the hallways are hung with original oils, watercolors, and lithographs by Joseph Beuys, Otto Dix, Paul Kell, and Giorgio de Chirico. In 2002 the hoteliers installed a new gym and guest suites.

39050 Fié allo Sciliar/Völs am Schlern (BZ). ⓒ 0471-725-014. Fax 0471-725-474. www.hotelturm.it. 35 units. 120€–192€ ($138–$221) double without balcony, 138€–206€ ($159–$237) double with balcony; 182€–220€ ($209–$253) suite. Pension plans available. MC, V. Parking 4€ ($4.60). **Amenities:** Tirolean restaurant; *Stube* bar; an inside pool and an outside heated pool; tennis courts (in town); gym; Jacuzzi; sauna; 3 free bikes; concierge; tour desk (will also take you around in their old London Austin cab—when it's running); room service (limited); in-room massage; babysitting (book ahead); laundry service; dry cleaning. *In room:* TV, minibar, hair dryer, safe.

WHERE TO DINE

Some of the least expensive (and tasty) meals in town are supplied by the vendors who dispense a wide assortment of *Würstel* from carts in the Kornplatz and Piazza dell'Erbe.

Batzenhäusel TIROLEAN   The two floors of dining rooms here are charming and cozy, with dark carved Tirolean benches, hardwood floors, and heavily beamed ceilings; downstairs is primarily a *Weinstube,* a tavernlike room where you are welcome to linger over a beer and a plate of cheese. On both floors you can also order from a menu that, like those in many other restaurants in town, is typically Tirolean, which means mostly Austrian with some Italian touches. While an excellent minestrone is sometimes available, this is also the place to sample *leberknödelsuppe,* a thick broth with a liver dumpling floating in it. Pork loin, roast beef with potatoes, and other heavy northern fare dominate the entree choices.

Via Andreas Hofer/Andreas Hoferstrasse 30. ⓒ 0471-050-950. Primi 4.50€–6.50€ ($5–$7); secondi 8.80€–13€ ($10–$15). No credit cards. Wed–Mon 6:30pm–2am (Sun to 1am).

Cavallino Bianco TIROLEAN   This atmospheric *Stube* (beer hall) is darkly paneled and decorated with carved wooden furniture to create a cozy, typically Tirolean atmosphere. The restaurant opens early to operate as a cafe, dispensing coffee and pastry for breakfast, and remains open well into the night, sending out hearty lunches and dinners of local fare with only a slight Italian influence. Fried Camembert, herrings, and assorted salami are among the dozens of appetizers, while a pasta dish (and there are many to choose from) is likely to be followed by a main course of Wiener schnitzel or *Würstel.*

Via dei Bottai/Bindergasse 6. ✆ **0471-973-267**. Primi 3.50€–8€ ($4.05–$9); secondi 4€–15€ ($4.60–$17). No credit cards. Mon–Fri 8am–1am; Sat 8am–3pm.

Ristorante Hostaria Argentieri SEAFOOD   You'll feel like you've come back to Italy when you step into this attractive cream-colored, tile-floored room. There are several risottos and a grilled steak on the menu, but most of the offerings are fishy—unusual, and much in demand, up here in the Dolomiti. You can start with tasty *tagliolini al salmone, bigoli alla veneta* (homemade pasta with anchovies and capers), followed by grilled *branzino, rombo,* or *trancio di spada* (swordfish steak). In good weather there is dining on a tiny terrace in front of the restaurant, facing an attractive cobblestone street that is indeed Tyrolean in character.

Via Argentieri 14. ✆ **0471-981-718**. Reservations highly recommended. Primi and secondi 12€–20€ ($14–$23). DC, MC, V. Mon–Sat noon–2:30pm and 7–10:30pm.

Scheune TIROLEAN/PIZZA   This welcoming and cozy *Bierhalle* (beer hall) has expanded to full menu service since it opened in 1995. The remarkable rough-hewn beams and log-cabin look of the place is genuine—its name is Tirolese dialect for "hayloft," and the interior was lifted, intact, from an abandoned hayloft high up in the mountains. A cherry tree is planted in the middle of the bar, where Warsteiner beer flows from the taps. The tables in back wrap around a big, square rustic room-heater stove. Along with the 20-odd pasta dishes and typical Tirolean fare such as goulash and Wiener schnitzel, they have recently added decent pizzas.

Weintraubengasse 9. ✆ **0471-978-838**. Primi 5.50€–7€ ($6–$8); secondi 6.50€–15€ ($7–$17); fixed-price menu for singles (only) 9.50€ ($11) without wine. DC, MC, V. Daily 11am–11pm. Closed last 2 weeks of June.

Vogele TIROLEAN   If you ask someone in Bozen where to eat, there's a very good chance you will be sent to this attractive, always busy *Weinstube* and restaurant in the center of the old city just off Piazza Erbe. Like many such places in Bozen, it is open continuously all day and night, and some of the patrons seem to stop by for every meal and for coffee and a beer in between. One of the two long cross-vaulted rooms is set up as a cafe, and the other as a dining room (or you can eat under the arcade out front). Both have traditional, woody Tirolean furnishings, and wherever you sit you can order lightly, or relatively so, if you wish, from the long appetizer menu, maybe a platter of *speck* (ham) or *affumicato della casa* (smoked meats). First and second courses include many traditional favorites; a wonderful *zuppa di vino* (a soup with a white-wine–and-cream base) or different kinds of *canederli* (dumplings that here are laced with liver, bacon, or ham) are the ways to begin, followed by a *stinco di maiale* (roast pork shank) or other roast meat dish.

Via Goethe 3. ✆ **0471-973-938**. Primi 4€–8€ ($3–$9); secondi 8.50€–17€ ($10–$20). MC, V. Mon–Fri 9am–midnight; Sat 9am–3pm.

BARS & CAFES

Nightlife in Bozen—and daytime wine tasting—centers around the long curve of Piazza delle Erbe, and you'll find plenty more wine bars, pubs, *Stube,* and tiny live-music venues in addition to the following.

To sample the local wines (from 1€/$1.15 a glass), step into this tiny little stand-up bar at **Etti's Thekki** at Piazza Erbe 11 (✆ **0471-971-705**). **Hopfen & Co.,** Piazza Erbe 17 (✆ **0471-300-788**), is a tiny Tirolean pub serving its own brew to the crowded wooden tables inside and a few tiny round ones out on the sidewalk corner; they also serve up grub, mostly hearty local fare like *Würstel, bier goulasch,* and *speck canerdeli,* for 5€ to 11€ ($6–$13).

The chic **Exil** at Piazza del Grano/Kornplatz 2 (© **0471-971-814**) is filled with a young crowd night and day for whom it probably provides a welcome alternative to the many *Weinstubes* around town. Exil has the ambience of a coffeehouse (excellent coffee, pastries, and sandwiches are served) and a bar as well, with many kinds of beers from Italy and north of the Alps on tap. On weekend evenings, the elegant **Laurin Bar,** in the Parkhotel Laurin (recommended above) (© **0471-311-000**), turns its Art Nouveau lobby—a sumptuous room overlooking the hotel's private park—into a jazz club. An enthusiastic crowd turns out, making this one of the most popular places in town.

You won't find a more distinctive locale in Bozen to bend your elbow than **Fishbanke** at Via d. Streiter 26A (© **0471-971-714**); in fact, a stop at this outdoor wine bar is mandatory if your visit coincides with one of its seasonal openings. Wine, beer, and a few snacks (cheese and bruschetta) are served on the well-worn stone slabs of Bozen's centuries-old former fish market, an unusual experience that attracts a friendly crowd of regulars who, along with the animated proprietor, are always pleased to welcome strangers into their midst.

3 Meran (Merano)

86km (53 miles) N of Trent, 28km (17 miles) NW of Bozen

This well-heeled resort, tucked into a valley half an hour west of Bozen, sports Europe's northernmost palm trees—the product of a mild microclimate that ensures that summers are never too hot or humid and that winter temperatures remain above freezing even when the surrounding slopes fill with snow.

Austrian nobility and, in their wake, bourgeois vacationers from all over the continent have been descending on Merano since the 19th century for their famous grape cure (see "Taking the Cure," below). But the town flourished long before that. In fact, the counts of Venosta were lords of all of what would become Austria from here through much of the 13th and 14th centuries; the name "Tirol" came from the Castel Tirolo, just above Merano, from which they ruled. The capital of the vast territories that passed from the house of Venosta to the Hapsburgs wasn't moved from Merano to Innsbruck until 1420.

With its handsome, shop-lined streets, riverside promenades, and easy access to mountainous wilderness, Merano is a nice place to visit for a day or two of relaxation or hiking.

FESTIVALS & MARKETS   The Piazza del Duomo is the scene of Merano's civic life. A morning **fruit and produce market** is held here from 8am to 1pm Monday to Saturday. From late November through Christmas, the piazza fills with stalls selling carved ornaments and other seasonal paraphernalia during the town's **Christkindlmarkt.** From late August through September, the town hosts **Settimane Musicali Meranesi** in several concert halls and churches around town (© **0473-221-447;** www.meranofestival.com). On the second Sunday of October, enthusiasts of the grape take over the square for a **wine festival,** honoring the wines and grape juice yielded by local vineyards.

Merano on Two Wheels
From late May through September, the town provides free bikes at the main public parking lot (near the Terme, just across the river from the center) and at the train station.

ESSENTIALS
GETTING THERE **By Train** Hourly train service links Merano with Bozen (40 min.).

By Bus SAD buses (© 0472-801-075 or 800-846-047 in Italy; www.sad.it) arrive and depart from the train station and stop in the center of town, connecting Merano with Bozen hourly (1 hr.) and with villages throughout the region.

By Car Route S38, a pretty road that cuts through vineyards and mountain meadows, links Merano and Bozen in less than half an hour.

VISITOR INFORMATION The **tourist office,** Corso Libertà/Freiheistrasse 45 (© 0473-272-000; fax 0473-235-524; www.meraninfo.it), is open March through September, Monday to Friday 9am to 6:30pm, Saturday 9:30am to 6pm, Sunday 10am to 12:30pm; October through February, Monday to Friday 9am to 12:30pm and 2:30 to 6:30pm, Saturday 9:30am to 12:30pm. For events, pick up *MeMo* from the tourist office, or log on to **www.memopolis.com** or **memo.bobo.it**.

A good source of information on hiking the region is the local office of the **Club Alpino Italiano** at Via K. Wolf 15 (© 0473-448-944; www.cai.it). It's open Monday to Friday from 9am to 1pm, plus Thursday from 7 to 8:30pm.

WHAT TO SEE & DO
The charming old town that is a vestige of Merano's noble past clusters around the **Piazza del Duomo,** where the namesake 14th-century cathedral has a crenellated facade and heavy buttresses that make it look almost like a castle. Nearby, just to the west on Via Galilei, is a dollhouse-size castle—**Castello Principesco** or **Landesfürstliche Burg,** built by the counts of Tirol in 1470 and still filled with the austere furnishings they installed, along with a collection of armor and musical instruments. The castle (© 0473-250-329) is open Tuesday to Saturday 10am to 5pm, Sunday 10am to 1pm (July–Aug, Sun hours are 4–7pm only; closed Jan–Feb). Admission is 2€ ($2.30) adults, 1.50€ ($1.75) students and those over 60.

Merano's picturesque main shopping street, **Via Portici** (leading west from Piazza del Duomo) is lined with Tirolean-style houses whose porticoes extend over the sidewalk. The preferred places to stroll in Merano, though, are along any number of scenic promenades. Two follow the banks of the River Passer: the **Passeggiata d'Inverno** (Winter Walk, which faces south) and **Passeggiata d'Estate** (Summer Walk, which faces north).

The top of the Passeggiata is just below **Castel Tirolo** ⚜ (© 0473-220-221), which you can also reach by car or by walking along Via Monte San Zeno for 5km (3 miles) from Merano. Here, amid stony splendor, you can see the throne room from which the Counts of Tirol ruled much of present-day Austria and northern Italy, and a beautifully frescoed Romanesque chapel with a 1330 carved wood *Crucifix* (and enjoy a magnificent view that hasn't changed much since then). Unfortunately, much of the interior remains closed while a new museum on Tirolean history and culture is installed; once it's finished, admission rates will definitely go up (probably double), but hours may lengthen, and it will probably stay open in winter. Currently, the castle is open Easter through November, Tuesday to Sunday 10am to 5pm. Admission is 6€ ($7) adults, 3€ ($3.45) students under 28, and 12€ ($14) for a family ticket (2 adults with kids under 18). Occasional guided tours are available for a 2€ ($2.30) supplement. To get here without too much hoofing, you can take a half-hourly bus from

Taking the Cure

With its mild climate and mineral-rich springs bubbling up from beneath the town, Merano has long enjoyed a reputation as a spa town. To this day, one of Merano's most popular pastimes is taking the cure. You can take a complete treatment (mud bath, mineral wrap, hydrotherapy) at the **Terme di Merano** (© **0473-237-724;** www.termemerano.com), in the center of town but across the river at Via Piave 9, or just take a dip in the pool of mineral-rich water (7€/$8.05 with a hotel pass, 8€/$9.20 without); open daily 9am to 7pm—though expect hours to fluctuate as large-scale renovations slowly turn this place into a cutting-edge spa by 2005. A poor man's version of an elaborate spa regimen—but one you can follow only when grapes from the vineyards surrounding the town ripen in late September and early October—is Merano's famous *cura delle uva* (grape cure). One drastic form of the grape cure, which is allegedly beneficial for digestive disorders, requires eating 2 pounds of grapes a day. A more palatable approach calls for drinking several glasses a day of the delicious fresh *spermuta di uva fresca/traubensaft* (grape juice) that's available in cafes in the early fall.

Merano's train station or center to the village of Tirol, then finish the beautiful 15-minute walk along a trail amid grapevines and apple groves.

THE NATIONAL PARKS

For more strenuous excursions, Merano is the gateway to two national parks. The tourist office in town provides information on them, as does the Club Alpino Italiano (see "Visitor Information," above); both parks also have visitor centers within their boundaries.

PARCO NAZIONALE DELLA STELVIO   In this vast 520,000-hectare (1.3-million-acre) wilderness east of Merano, elk and chamois roam the mountainsides, and craggy, snowcapped peaks pierce the sky. A network of trails crisscross almost virgin wilderness, and some of Europe's largest glaciers provide year-round skiing. The official **park office** (© **0342-903-030**), in the center of the park, is open March to November daily 9am to 1pm and 4 to 6pm; in winter, call © **0342-903-300.** The office dispenses maps and lists of hiking trails and *rifugi* (huts where hikers can overnight) within the park; several buses a day travel from Merano to Silandro, at the park entrance, about 30km (18 miles) east via route S38.

PARCO NAZIONALE DI TESSA   This Alpine wonderland surrounds Merano with a pleasant terrain of meadows and gentle, forest-clad slopes. A relatively easy path, the southern route of the Meraner Hohenweg, allows even the most inexperienced hikers to cross the park effortlessly (in 2 days if you wish to follow the entire route) and is conveniently interspersed with restaurants and farmhouses offering rooms. The northern route is much more isolated, difficult, and scenic, with snack-bar–equipped *rifugi* conveniently placed every few hours or so along the route. The **park office** in Naturno, about 15km (9 miles) west on Route S44 (Via dei Campi 3; © **0473-668-201**), provides a wealth of information on hiking trails, meals, and accommodations. Hourly buses run between Merano and Naturno in about half an hour.

WHERE TO STAY

April, August through October, and the Christmas holidays constitute high sea-son in Merano, when rates are highest and rooms are scarce. The two hotels in the center of town are easy enough to find; for the Castel Rundegg and Hotel Castello Schloss Labers, follow the yellow arrows on *"alberghi"* road signs (Mer-ano has a complicated color-coded, geographical breakdown for all its hotels; just trust me and follow the yellow arrows) until a small brown-on-white sign for the hotels tells you otherwise.

Castel Rundegg ★   Unlike most Merano castle hotels, the Rundegg is barely outside town, offering the convenience of downtown with the atmosphere of a restored 1152 castle. It bills itself as a "Hotel & Beauty Farm," and many guests come to avail themselves of the spa and its programs, which make good use of the large exercise room, sauna, Turkish steam baths, various body treatments, Jacuzzi, tanning beds, and beauty center. Peter Castelforte, the owner, likes to say they'll take care of you from the top of your head (at the hairdresser) to the bottoms of your feet (the *knipfe* foot bath, where you walk against the current, a cure invented by a 19th-century German monk). As for the hotel part, the cross-vaulted reception halls and restaurant stuffed with painted wood statues set the tone. Even the "standard" rooms are large and perfectly nice, with rich tapestries upholstering the 18th-century–style chairs and bed frames (those that aren't in a more woodsy, Tirolean style), small, lofted sitting areas or nooks, and freshly tiled bathrooms with double sinks (though many have tubs with no place to hang the shower nozzle). Some "de luxe" rooms, such as no. 20, enjoy bal-conies over the courtyard with views of the mountains; a few even have small private gardens. A *molto particolari* (very unique) room might be no. 15, with tented windows on three sides and views over the valley and the hotel's own large park, where goldfish ponds and small lawns set with sunning chairs highlight the garden paths lined with a plethora of trees, plants, and flowers. This place would get a second star if the rates weren't so darn high.

Via Scena 2 (at the end of Via Cavour), 39012 Merano. ✆ **0473-234-100.** Fax 0473-237-200. www.rundegg. com. 30 units. 173€–217€ ($199–$250) "standard" double; 204€–248€ ($235–$285) "superior" double; 226€–270€ ($260–$311) "de Luxe" double; 246€–290€ ($283–$334) *molto particolari* double; 338€–404€ ($388–$464) suites. Rates include buffet breakfast. Half- and full-board option available. Discounts, but with half pension included, for stays of 3 days or more. Aug 4–25 and Dec 22–Jan 6, minimum stay 7 nights; Easter min-imum stay 5 nights. AE, DC, MC, V. Parking free in lot or 6€ ($7) in garage. Bus: 1, 3, 5. **Amenities:** Mediter-ranean restaurant; bar; indoor pool; 9-hole golf course 4km (2½ miles) away; nearby tennis courts; large health club and spa; bike rental; concierge; tour desk; car-rental desk; salon; room service (24-hr.); massage (in spa); babysitting; laundry service; dry cleaning (same-day). *In room:* TV, VCR (in some), minibar, hair dryer, safe.

Garni Domus Mea   Simple little bed-and-breakfasts are just about the only alternative to Merano's high-priced lodging, and this pleasant pensione in a modern multiuse building is one of the nicer of them. It is well located, on a major street about a 10-minute walk on the other side of Ponte Teatro from the center of town, and the prices never seem to go up. The friendly proprietor keeps the premises immaculate (cleanliness is her watchword) and welcoming, with cut flowers and freshly waxed floors. The rooms are basically but nicely fur-nished with wood dressers and armoires, and some have balconies overlooking the peaks. A small living room sports a TV. Places like this tend to fill up quickly, so be sure to reserve in advance.

Via Piave 8, 39012 Merano. ✆ **0473-236-777.** 13 units, all with bathroom. 41€–55€ ($47–$63) double. Rates include breakfast. No credit cards. Parking free in courtyard out back. **Amenities:** Room service (break-fast only). *In room:* Hair dryer (ask at desk).

Hotel Castello Schloss Labers ★★   The Stapf-Neubert family turned its pitch-roofed castle (begun in the 11th c.) into a remarkable hotel in 1885. The dark, airy hunting lodge–style salons, library, and billiards and dining rooms of the former residence have been seamlessly converted to guest use. Upper floors house distinctive and gracious accommodations, many with small terraces, no two of which are alike—in some, cozy conversation nooks are tucked into towers; others are luxurious garretlike arrangements under the eaves, and some are simply commodious, high-ceilinged, and elegantly appointed. The family has recently redone all the bathrooms and has added a "sauna Finlandia." The grounds wander down toward the surrounding grapevine-covered hillside, with a pleasant rose garden terrace overlooking the valley below and the peaks that hem it in. It's a good 10-minute drive high above downtown, so don't even consider it without a car.

Via Labers 25 (in Maia Alta, 3km/2miles east of town), 39012 Merano. © **0473-234-484.** Fax 0473-234-146. www.castellolabers.it or www.schlosslabers.it. 36 units, 25 with private bath. 168€ ($193) small double; 186€ ($214) regular double; 220€ ($253) double with terrace; 240€ ($276) superior double (corner or tower room); 300€ ($345) suite. Rates include breakfast. Subtract 11€ ($13) per person for days without half pension. For 3 nights or more, includes half-pension (meals available a la carte if your stay is fewer than 3 nights). MC, V. Free parking. Closed Nov 9–Apr 1. Bus: 1a. **Amenities:** Tirolean/Italian restaurant; bar; outdoor heated pool; tennis court; sauna; concierge; tour desk; courtesy car; room service (7am–11pm); babysitter; laundry service; dry cleaning; nonsmoking rooms; billiards room. *In room:* TV (on request), dataport (some rooms), minibar (ask at desk), hair dryer (ask at desk), safe (in some).

Hotel Europa Splendid ★   Conveniently located in the center of town a block off the Passer River, the Europa is an old-fashioned hotel that caters to guests who return year after year. The decor is charmingly faded, with an elegant, Regency-style salon and Tirolean-style bar downstairs. The large, bright guest rooms upstairs haven't been redecorated since the 1960s, but they're very comfortable, with handsome, sturdy furnishings and old but well-maintained bathrooms. A few accommodations are even Art Deco. Many of the rooms have small, flower-filled balconies, and a large, sunny hotel terrace is on the first floor. The rates reflect both season and room type (cheaper category "B" rooms suffer from less space, a poorer view, or more noise). Corner rooms (nos. 208, 308, and 408) are choice, with windows on two sides and small balconies. In November 2002 they closed for 3 months to overhaul the hotel—without changing the style.

Corso Liberta 178, 39012 Merano. © **0473-232-376.** Fax 0473-230-221. www.europa-splendid.com. 52 units, all with bathroom. 86€–113€ ($99–$130) standard double; 97€–124€ ($112–$143) comfort double; 108€–135€ ($124–$155) deluxe double. Rates include buffet breakfast. AE, DC, MC, V. Parking 9.50€ ($11). **Amenities:** Tirolese/Italian restaurant; bar; concierge; tour desk; car-rental desk; room service (24-hr.); laundry service; nonsmoking rooms. *In room:* TV, minibar, hair dryer, safe.

WHERE TO DINE

Yes, with all the grapes around, this region produces excellent, crisp wines. But be sure to set aside at least one *Prost!* (German for "cheers!") for a frosty glass of **Forst,** a rich and slightly bitter golden beer brewed here in Merano—the best beer in Italy, in my opinion.

Caffè Darling CAFE   The so-called "Winter Walk" along the banks of the Passer River is lined with cafes, and this one is especially pleasant. There's an awning out front, but the tables stretch much farther along the cobblestones to where they're practically hanging over the river. The comfortable interior room has a casual ambience that's not too common in this staid, refined resort area. You'll probably feel comfortable passing some time reading a book here while

Sampling the Local Grape in Wine Bars

Merano doesn't leave all its famous grapes unfermented for the cure, and you can sample local wine at *Weinstuben* (*enoteche* in Italian), or wine bars. **Rothaler Weinstube,** Via Portici 41 (no phone), is a cozy Tirolean tavern on Merano's arcaded main street, with a simple contemporary bar up front and a teensy, dimly lit back room half-paneled and heavily frescoed with images of grapes and vineyards. Cheese and meat platters run about 3.50€ to 6€ ($4.05–$7); closed Sunday and Saturday afternoon.

For less historical atmosphere but a larger choice, head to **Enoteca Claudia,** Piazza del Duomo 13 (② 0473-230-693; www.meranerkellerei. com), where over three dozen wines are available by the glass for 1.75€ to 5€ ($2–$6). There's a smattering of round tables outside in the shadow of the Duomo's bell tower and apse, plus more seating lined against the shelves upon shelves of wine inside. The various mixed platters of meats, cheeses with olives and artichokes, homemade sausages with vinegar-pickled veggies, and a sandwich or two, such as *speck,* cheese, tomatoes, and peppers, cost from 4€ to 9€ ($4.60–$10).

sipping a beer or a glass of the house grape juice. Pastries and light sandwiches are also available.

Passeggiata d'Inverno 5–9. ② 0473-237-221. Pastries from 1€ ($1.15); sandwiches from 2€ ($2.30). MC, V. Thurs–Tues 7:30am–1am.

Kavalier ITALIAN/TIROLEAN   Just a few steps off the river (you can hear it from the terrace) near Piazza Teatro, this informal restaurant, with a pleasant arbor-shaded terrace to one side, is a handy stop and can accommodate any level of hunger. A full menu of mostly Tirolean fare is served, featuring heaping platters of *speck,* a hearty beef goulash, the odd *Kavalierplatte* (Wiener schnitzel with pineapple, banana, rice, and mushrooms), and an amazingly filling pasta dish, *gnocchetti alla spinachi con prosciutto e panna* (little spinach gnocchi filled with ham in a cream sauce). You can also dine lightly on salads and omelets, or just stop by for a pizza.

Via Carducci 29. ② 0473-236-561. Primi 7€–8€ ($8–$9); secondi 10€–20€ ($12–$23); pizza 5€–9.75€ ($6–$11). MC, V. Thurs–Tues 11am–2:30pm and 5:30–9:30pm.

4 Brixen (Bressanone)

40km (24 miles) N of Bozen, 68km (41 miles) E of Merano

Tucked neatly in the Val d'Isarco between the Eisack and Rienz Rivers and surrounded by orchards and vineyards that climb the lower flanks of the surrounding peaks, Brixen is a gem of a Tirolean town with a hefty past that today's quaint, small-town atmosphere belies. From 1027 to 1803 Brixen was the center of a large ecclesiastical principality, and its bishop-princes ruled over much of the South Tirol. Their impressive monuments preside over the town's heavily gabled, pastel-colored houses and narrow cobblestone streets.

FESTIVALS & MARKETS   With its cozy, twisting medieval lanes and snug Tirolean-style houses, Brixen is especially well suited to Christmas celebrations.

The main holiday event is a **Christkindlmarkt (Christmas market)** from late November to Christmas Eve; stalls on and around Piazza Duomo sell hand-carved ornaments, crafts, holiday pastries, and other seasonal merchandise. A **fruit-and-vegetable market** enlivens Piazza Parrocchia near the Duomo Monday through Saturday from 8am to noon and 3 to about 6pm.

ESSENTIALS

GETTING THERE   By Train   Brixen lies on the same north–south rail line as Bozen and Verona, making connections between those cities extremely easy, with more than 18 trains a day from Bozen (25–35 min.). From Trent, trains run almost hourly (60–75 min.).

By Bus   STI buses (© 0472-801-075 or 800-846-047; www.sii.bz.it) leave from the front of the train station and connect Brixen and Bozen (1 hr.) and out-lying villages, including several daily (half-hourly in ski season) to Sant'Andrea, a good base for hiking and skiing (see below; 20 min.); service is augmented by a ski bus that is free for pass holders. There are also two daily buses to Cortina, with a change at Dobbiaco (about 2¾ hr.).

By Car   Brixen is about a half-hour drive north of Bozen on A22. It's easy to get around Brixen by foot—it's compact, and many of its streets are closed to cars. If you arrive by car, you will probably use the large parking lot south of the city on Via Dante (you will pass it as you drive into the city from the autostrada); the center is 5 minutes away up the Via Roma. From the train station, follow Viale Stazione for about 10 minutes to the center.

VISITOR INFORMATION   The **tourist office,** at the *centro storico* end of Via Stazione leading from the train station at no. 9 (© 0472-836-401; fax 0472-836-067; www.brixen.org), is open Monday to Friday 8:30am to 12:30pm and 2:30 to 6pm, Saturday 9am to 12:30pm. The provincial website, **www.provinz.bz.it**, has a section with tourism links.

WHAT TO SEE & DO

The center of town is the **Piazza Duomo,** a long, rectangular tree-shaded square with cafes on one side and the white facade of the Duomo on the other. A baroque renovation to the tall exterior, flanked by two bell towers, has masked much of the cathedral's original 13th-century architecture, which you'll see more of in the interior and in the crypt. The heavily frescoed cloisters (entered through a door to the right of the main one) are especially charming, even though the view of *Judgment Day* they portray is gloomy. Open daily 6am to noon and 3 to 6pm; there are guided tours (in Italian and German) Monday through Saturday at 10:30am and 3pm.

Just south of the Piazza del Duomo, on the adjoining Piazza Vescovile, stands the **palace of the prince-bishops,** whose power over the region—and the fragility of that power—is made clear by the surrounding moat and fortifying walls. The massive 14th-century palace now houses the **Museo Diocesano,** where more than 70 rooms display wooden statuary, somewhat unremarkable Renaissance paintings by local artists, and what is considered to be the museum's treasure and the objects most likely to capture your attention—an extensive and enchanting collection of antique Nativity scenes, filling eight rooms and one of the largest such assemblages anywhere. Frequent exhibits often double the admission price below. The museum (© 0472-830-505; www.dioezesanmuseum.bz.it) is open March 15 to October 31, Tuesday through Sunday 10am to 5pm; the Nativity-scene galleries are open only from December 1 to January 31, Tuesday through Sunday from 2 to 5pm

Hitting the Slopes

Brixen's major playground is Monte Plose, and the gateway to ski slopes and hiking trails alike is the outlying village of **Sant'Andrea** (see "By Bus," above). Skiing here is not as glamorous as it is in better-known resorts like Cortina, but it is excellent and much less expensive. A ski pass is 25€ to 28€ ($29–$32) a day, and can be purchased at one of the outlets near the **Sant'Andrea funicular** (✆ **0472-200-433**), which costs 9€ ($10) round-trip for adults and 7€ ($8) for children 8 to 14, and runs from July through September weekdays 9am to noon and 1 to 6pm, Saturday and Sunday 9am to 6pm; and December through May daily 9am to 4:30pm. (Winter schedules vary considerably with snow conditions; a summer ascent will take you to a network of Alpine trails near the stop at Valcroce.) The tourist board in Brixen provides maps, information on skiing, mountain refuges, and other details you need to know to enjoy this mountain wilderness.

(closed Dec 24–25); admission to the complete museum collection is 3.50€ ($4), to the Nativity scene exhibit alone, 2€ ($2.30).

WHERE TO STAY

Albergo Cremona   Like many of the other well-heeled resorts in this part of the world, Brixen offers few inexpensive beds. That's why this small, plain hotel near the train station and about a 10-minute walk to the center of town is a good find. The neighborhood is not as quaint as much of the rest of Brixen, but it's safe. The tiny reception area and rooms are more functional than charming. All but the two bathroomless singles are large, and the beds are firm and covered with the feather quilts that are standard issue in this part of the world.

Via Vittorio Veneto 26, 39042 Bressanone. ✆ **0472-835-602**. Fax 0472-200-794. 12 units, 10 with bathroom. 50€ ($58) double without bathroom, 56€ ($64) double with bathroom. Breakfast included. No credit cards. Closed early Jan to mid-Feb. *In room:* No phone.

Goldene Krone Vital Stadthotel   Everything about this amiable hotel at the edge of the old city suggests solid comfort, from the homey, wood-paneled lounge to the *Weinstube*-style bar to the breakfast room and restaurant, where booth tables are lit by pretty shaded lamps. There are two categories of guest rooms, and hence the range of prices. Those in the lower range are pleasant enough, with streamlined modern furnishings, and many have terraces. The more expensive rooms are really quite special, though, and well worth the extra expense. They're actually suites, with separate sitting and sleeping areas, equipped, respectively, with roomy couches and armchairs and king-size beds. The bathrooms are grand, with double sinks and large tubs equipped with Jacuzzi jets. A recent comprehensive remodeling preserved the hotel's style and added a small gym and sauna.

Via Fienili 4, 39042 Bressanone. ✆ **0472-835-154**. Fax 0472-835-014. www.goldenekrone.com. 35 units. 94€–103€ ($108–$118) double; 108€–175€ ($124–$201) suite. Rates include breakfast. Half board 15€ ($17) more per person. MC, V. Free parking. Closed Jan 6–Feb 6. **Amenities:** Italian/Tirolese restaurant; bar; gym; free bikes; children's program; concierge; tour desk; car-rental desk; room service (limited); babysitting; laundry service; dry cleaning; nonsmoking rooms. *In room:* TV, fax, dataport, minibar, hair dryer, safe.

Hotel Elephant   One of the Tirol's oldest and most famous inns (also some-times spelled the Hotel Elefant) is named for a 16th-century guest—an elephant accompanying Archduke Maximilian of Austria on the long trek from Genoa to Vienna, where the beast was to become part of the royal menagerie. During its 2-week stay, the pachyderm attracted onlookers from miles around, and the innkeeper renamed his establishment and commissioned a delightful elephant-themed fresco that still graces the front of the building. Today's hotel matches its provenance with excellent service and extraordinary environs that include dark-paneled hallways and grand staircases. The distinctive old rooms are full of nooks and crannies and furnished with heavy old Tirolean antiques and some tasteful modern pieces, including wonderfully solid beds. A generous buffet breakfast emphasizes delicious Austrian pastries. Among the hotel's nicest assets are a large garden and a pleasant swimming pool, and a recent remodeling included the addition of an elevator.

Via Rio Bianco 4, 39042 Bressanone. ☎ 0472-832-750. Fax 0472-836-579. www.hotelelephant.com. 44 units. 166€ ($191) comfort double; 186€ ($214) deluxe double; 217€ ($250) jr. suite. Half and full pension available. Ask about discounted rates for stays of more than 3 nights. Breakfast 13€ ($15). AE, DC, MC, V. Parking 6€ ($7). Closed Jan 7–Feb 28 and Nov 5–30. **Amenities:** Tirolese restaurant; bar; pool (heated and outside); tennis courts; small exercise room; 2 saunas; bike rental; concierge; tour desk; car-rental desk; cour-tesy car; small business center; room service; massage (in-room); babysitting; laundry service; dry cleaning. *In room:* TV, dataport, minibar, hair dryer.

WHERE TO DINE

Caffè Duomo CAFE   These minimalist, white-walled, smartly lit environs provide a contemporary version of the woody taverns that prevail in this part of the world (there are still little nooks off to one side for intimate conversation). No attempt is made at serious cuisine here, but there is a nice selection of panini made with local hams and mountain cheeses, as well as some sumptuous cakes and pastries. The coffee is excellent, and the wine-and-beer list extensive.

Piazza Parocchia 3. ☎ 0472-838-277. Sandwiches, snacks from 2€ ($2.30). Mon–Fri 8am–8pm; Sat 12:30–8pm.

Fink TIROLEAN   It only seems right that Brixen's charmingly arcaded main street should have a restaurant that looks like this, with paneling hung with antlers and oil paintings, while dishing out excellent local cuisine. Fink offers many mountain-style dishes that you are likely to encounter only within a close radius of Brixen, including a *piatto alla Val d'Isarco,* a platter of locally cured hams and salamis, and a *zuppa di vino,* a traditional Tirolean soup made with white wine and, here, crusty pieces of cinnamon toast. The *miale gratinato,* a pork roast topped with a cheese sauce, is surprisingly light and absolutely delicious, as are the local cheeses served for dessert. If in doubt about what to order, just ask—the English-speaking staff is extremely gracious. The upstairs dining room has a slightly more refined cuisine and atmosphere to go with the higher prices.

Via Portici Minori 4. ☎ 0472-834-883. Primi 3.65€–9.50€ ($4.20–$11) downstairs, 4€–11€ ($4.60–$13) upstairs; secondi 7€–12€ ($8–$13) downstairs, 11€–17 € ($13–$19) upstairs. AE, DC, MC, V. Thurs–Tues noon–2:30pm; Thurs–Mon 7–10pm. Closed July 1–14.

Finsterwirt WINE BAR   Occupying the same quarters as Oste Scuro restau-rant (see below) and run by the same family, this ground-floor tavern near the cathedral has the same dark paneling and leaded-window ambience. The fare and service, however, are much more casual, though excellent, and you are wel-come to settle into one of the nooklike tables for as long as you'd like to enjoy a beer or a glass of local wine (from 1€/$1.15) and a plate of fresh goat cheese or a platter of *speck* and salami. A lovely rear garden, candlelit at night, is open throughout the summer and well into chillier days when people from more southerly climes wouldn't think of sitting outdoors.

Vicolo Duomo 3. ℂ 0472-835-343. www.finsterwirt.com. Salads and light meals from 7€ ($8). AE, DC, MC, V. Tues–Sat 10am–midnight; Sun 10am–3pm. Closed Jan 10–Feb 2 and June 15–30.

Oste Scuro TIROLEAN   What may be Brixen's temple of gastronomy (Fink, above, is a close contender) occupies a welcoming series of intimate candlelit rooms above the Finsterwirt *Weinstube* (see above). The first of these rooms contains a standup bar where patrons stop by just to order one of the excellent wines by the glass. It would be a shame not to dine here, though, because the kitchen excels at simple but innovative preparations of the freshest local ingredients. A *terrina di formaggio di capra fresco* is a concoction of creamy cheese atop a bed of lightly sautéed spinach and greens; even if you have found the region's steady diet of *canederli* (dumplings) heavy, try them here where they are light and infused with fresh wild mushrooms. The kitchen excels at meat dishes, including an herb-infused veal roast. Fresh berries top off a meal in season, and the strudels are perfection.

Vicolo Duomo 3. ℂ 0472-835-343. www.finsterwirt.com. Reservations recommended. Primi 9€–11€ ($10–$13); secondi 15€–18€ ($17–$21). AE, DC, MC, V. Tues–Sun noon–2pm; Tues–Sat 7–9pm. Closed Jan 11–Feb 2 and June 21–July 5.

EN ROUTE TO CORTINA: THE STRADA DI DOLOMITI

The **Great Dolomite Road,** the scenic route between Bozen (follow signs to Eggental/Val d'Ega) and Cortina going east, S241 and S48, is 110km (68 miles) of stunning views. The road curves around some of the highest peaks in the Dolomites, including 3,000m (10,000-ft.) tall **Marmolda,** and goes through a scattering of mountain villages and ski resorts before dropping out of a high pass into Cortina. Some tour buses follow this route (the tourist offices in Bozen and Cortina can provide a list of tour operators; check with the bus station in Bozen), as do two daily buses of the **STI network** July through September (check with the bus station in Bozen or call ℂ 0471-450-111; www.sii.bz.it). You may want to rent a car, however, if only for a day, to make the spectacular round-trip, one of Europe's most scenic drives (allow at least 2½ hr. each way over the twists and turns of the passes). Keep in mind that the Strada di Dolomiti is often closed to vehicles because of heavy snow in the winter months, and you will often need to put chains on your tires between November and April.

5 Cortina d'Ampezzo

133km (82 miles) E of Bozen, 166km (103 miles) N of Venice

Italy's best-known mountain resort, put on the international map when it hosted the 1956 Winter Olympics, is often associated with wealth and sophistication. Long before the Olympics, though, Cortina was attracting European Alpine enthusiasts, who began coming here for stays in the town's first hotels as early as the 1860s. In 1902 Cortina hosted its first ski competitions, and in 1909 the completion of the first road in and out of the town, the magnificent Strada di Dolomiti (built by the Austro-Hungarian military), opened the slopes to more skiers.

Even without its 145km (90 miles) of ski runs and 50 cable cars and chairlifts that make the slopes easily accessible, Cortina would be one of Europe's most appealing Alpine towns. The surrounding Dolomite peaks are simply stunning. Eighteen of them rise more than 3,000m (10,000 ft.), ringing Cortina in an amphitheater of craggy stone. In full light the peaks are a soft bluish gray, and when they catch the rising and setting sun, they take on a welcoming rosy glow.

True to its reputation for glamour, Cortina can be expensive (especially in Aug and the high-ski-season months of Jan–Mar). Many well-to-do Italians have houses here, and a sense of privilege prevails. What's often forgotten, though, is that for all the town's fame, strict zoning has put a damper on development, and, as a result, Cortina is still a mountain town of white timbered houses, built aside a rushing stream and surrounded by forests, meadows, and, of course, stunning Dolomite peaks.

FESTIVALS & MARKETS   The **Piazza Italia** near the bus station doubles as Cortina's marketplace. Stalls sell produce, mountain cheeses, clothing, housewares, and other items on Tuesday and Friday mornings from 8:30am to 1pm. While chic Cortina concerns itself mostly with secular pursuits, the town turns out for a solemn religious procession down the main street, Corso Italia, on **Good Friday.**

ESSENTIALS

GETTING THERE   By Bus   Frequent **STI bus service** provides the only public transportation in and out of Cortina (© **800-846-047** in Italy; www.sii. bz.it). There are two daily buses each from Bozen (about 4 hr.), stopping in Brixen (about 2¾ hr.), that head to Cortina, but with a change in Dobbiaco. There is also one daily bus to and from Venice (© **035-237-641;** 4 hr. 20 min.) and a daily bus to and from Milan (© **02-801-161;** 6½ hr.). The bus station in Cortina is located in the former train station on Via Marconi.

By Train   The closest train station to Cortina is the one at **Calalzo di Cadore,** 30km (19 miles) south. From Calalzo, 30 daily buses connect with Cortina. There are 10 trains a day to Calalzo from Venice, but only two are direct (2 hr. 20 min.; with connections, allow 3–4 hr.). There are also six daily direct runs from Padua (3 hr.).

By Car   The spectacularly scenic Strada di Dolomiti (see above) links Bozen and Cortina, while S51 heads south toward Venice, connecting south of Belluno to Autostrada A27, for a total trip time of about 3 hours between Cortina and Venice.

VISITOR INFORMATION   The **APT tourist office,** Piazzetta San Francesco 8 (© **0436-3231;** fax 0436-3235; www.cortina.dolomiti.com, www.dolomiti. com, or www.dolomiti.org), is open daily 9am to 12:30pm and 4 to 7pm. In addition to a list of accommodations, the English-speaking staff will also provide a wealth of information on ski slopes, hiking trails, and bus schedules.

WHAT TO SEE & DO

The main in-town activity in Cortina appears to be walking up and down the main street, the pedestrian-only **Corso Italia,** in the most fashionable skiwear money can buy. Most of the buildings are new but pleasingly low-scale and Alpine in design, and at the town center is the pretty 18th-century church of **Santi Filippo e Giacomo,** with a charming bell tower eclipsed in height only by the majestic peaks. It is on these peaks that most visitors set their sights, enjoying an amazing array of outdoor activities on the slopes.

EXPLORING PEAKS   Skiers and nonskiers alike will enjoy the eye-popping scenery on a trip up the surrounding mountainsides on the funicular systems that leave right from town. The most spectacular trip is the ascent on the **Freccia nel**

Cielo (Arrow in the Sky), which departs from a terminus near the Stadio Olimpico del Ghiacchio (Olympic Ice Skating Stadium), about a 10-minute walk north and west of the town center. The top station is at **Tafano di Mezzo,** at 3,163m (10,543 ft.); the round-trip is 24€ ($28). It is a little less expensive (20€/$23)—and just as satisfying if mountain scenery and not high-Alpine skiing is your quest—to make the trip only as far as **Ra Valles,** the second stop, at 2,550m (8,500 ft.). The views over glaciers and the stony peaks are magnificent, and a bar serves sandwiches and other refreshments on an outdoor terrace. The funicular runs from mid-July to late September and mid-December to May 1, with departures every 20 minutes from 9am to 4 or 5pm, depending on the time of sunset; call ✆ **0436-5052** for information.

The **Funivia Faloria** (✆ **0436-2517**) arrives and departs from a terminus on the other side of town, about a 10-minute walk southeast of the town center. The ride is a little less dramatic than the one on the longer Freccia nel Cielo. Even so, the ascent over forests and meadows and then up a sheer cliff to the 2,100m (7,000-ft.) high ski station at Faloria is not without thrills, and the view from the terrace bar at Faloria, down to Cortina and to the curtain of high peaks to the north, is one you won't soon forget. Like the Freccia nel Cielo, the Funivia Faloria runs from mid July to late September and mid-December to May 1, with departures every 20 minutes from 9am to 4 or 5pm, depending on the time of sunset; round-trip fare is 13€ ($15).

Another trip for cable car enthusiasts is the one from the top of **Passo Falzarego,** 25km (15 miles) west of Cortina, to Lagazoul, a little skiing and hiking station at the 2,550m (8,364-ft.) level. In summer you can follow a network of trails at the top and scamper for miles across the dramatic, rocky terrain. The ride is a nearly vertical ascent up the rocky face of the mountain, and as an eerie alternative to the funicular, you can make the climb up or down through a series of tunnels dug into the cliff during World War I battles. Falzarego is the last pass through which you descend if you follow the Strada di Dolomiti into Cortina, so you may want to stop and board the funicular for a scenery-filled introduction to the region. If you are not driving, five buses a day make the 35-minute trip between Cortina and the funicular stop at the top of the Passo Falzarego; the fare is 1.50€ ($1.75) each way. The funivia runs from mid-July to late September and mid-December to May 1, with departures every 30 minutes; round-trip fare is 10€ ($12); call ✆ **0436-867-301** for information.

DOWNHILL SKIING   Cortina is Italy's leading ski resort, and it lives up to its reputation with eight exceptional ski areas that are easily accessible from town. Two of the best, **Tofana-Promedes** and **Faloria-Tondi,** are accessible by funiculars that lift off from the edges of town (see "Exploring Peaks," above), as are the novice slopes at **Mietres.** You can enjoy these facilities fairly economically with one of the comprehensive Dolomiti Superski passes that provide unlimited skiing (including all chairlift and funicular fees, as well as free shuttle bus service to and from Cortina and the ski areas) at all eight of Cortina's ski areas and those at 10 outlying resorts. You can get passes for any number of days up to 21; a few sample prices: during high season, December 21 to January 6 and February 1 to March 13, the cost is 34€ ($39) for 1 day, 95€ ($109) for 3 days, and 178€ ($205) for 7 days. Shave off about 4€ ($4.60) per day for low season, January 7 to 31 and March 13 to 27. For more information, contact the **tourist office** or **Dolomiti Superski,** Via d. Castello 33, 32043 Cortina (✆ **0436-862-171** or 0471-795-397; www.dolomitisuperski.com).

For **lessons,** contact the **Scuola di Sci Cortina,** Corso Italia (© **0436-2911;** www.scuolascicortina.it), which offers six consecutive mornings of group lessons for 195€ ($224) in high season, 160€ ($184) in low season. Private lessons cost 40€ ($46) per hour for one person (34€/$39 in low season), plus 12€ ($14) (9€/$10 in low season) each additional person.

You can **rent skis** at many outlets throughout town, including stands at the lower and upper stations of the Freccia nel Cielo cable car and other funiculars; rentals average 15€ to 25€ ($17–$29) for skis—plus 5€ to 10€ ($6–$11) for boots—or 20€ to 25€ ($23–$29) for snowboards.

HIKING & ROCK CLIMBING   In this mountainous terrain, these two activities are often synonymous. The tourist office can provide maps of hiking trails throughout the surrounding region. For high-altitude hiking, canyoning, and rock climbing, you may want to join one of the excursions led by **Gruppo Guide Alpine Cortina,** Corso Italia 69A (© **0463-868-505;** www.guidecortina.com), open daily 8am to noon and 4 to 8pm.

HORSEBACK RIDING   **Fattoria Meneguto,** in outlying Fraina (© **0463-860-441**), offers group and individual riding through the lovely valleys surrounding Cortina; the stables are open from late spring through late fall from 9am to noon and 3 to 7pm, and rides cost 9€ ($10) for 30 minutes and 17€ ($20) for an hour.

ICE SKATING   At the **Stadio Olimpico del Ghiaccio,** just to the northwest of the town center on Via del Stadio (© **0436-4380**), you can practice turns on the two recently refurbished rinks where Olympians tried for the gold in the 1956 games. Admission plus skate rental is 7€ ($8).

MOUNTAIN BIKING   The roads and tracks leading up to the peaks provide arduous biking terrain; cyclists from all over the world come to Cortina to practice for events. If you want to test your mettle, you can rent a bike from the **Mountain Bike Center,** Corso Italia 294 (© **0336-494-770**). Rentals are 12€ ($14) for 2 hours, 21€ ($24) for 4 hours, and 30€ ($35) for a day. The English-speaking staff will point you in the direction of routes that match your abilities.

RELAXING   Unwind after any of these activities in the indoor swimming pool at the **Piscina Coperta Comunale** (© **0436-860-581**), just north of town in outlying Guargne. It is open Monday to Friday from 5 to 8pm, until 10pm Tuesday and Thursday, Saturday and Sunday from 4 to 8pm. In high season, the pool is open daily from 3:30 to 8pm and until 9:30pm on Tuesdays and Thursdays. Admission is 6.50€ ($7).

You will find relief for sore muscles at **La Sauna di Cortina,** Via Stazione 18 (© **0436-866-784**); it's open daily from 9am to 9pm. Use of the facilities costs 22€ ($25), which includes Finnish saunas and Turkish baths.

WHERE TO STAY

Cortina is booked solid during the high season: August, Christmas, and late January through March. You should reserve well in advance. Rates are lowest in late spring and early fall. It's closed down tight in June. Keep in mind that many innkeepers prefer to give rooms to guests who will stay several days or longer and will take meals at the hotel. Given the scarcity of reasonably priced restaurants in town, you will probably be happy settling for a half- or full-board plan. The tourist board provides a list of private homes that take in guests, a way to keep costs down while enjoying the local hospitality, which is considerable.

Hotel Bellaria   The Majoni family, which owns this pleasant hotel a short walk from the center on the northern edge of town, did a complete refurbishing recently, and they chose to keep prices down for the benefit of the patrons who come here season after season. As a result, they still provide some of Cortina's most reasonably priced accommodations, and they house their guests in handsome, sunny rooms that overlook the mountains and have fresh Alpine-style pine furnishings, firm new beds, and crisp fabrics. All of the bathrooms have been redone and fitted out with heated towel racks. Downstairs, there's a lovely paneled lounge, a dining room, a pleasant terrace in front of the house, and a lawn out back.

Corso Italia 266, 32043 Cortina d'Ampezzo. © **0436-2505.** Fax 0436-5755. www.hbellaria.it. 22 units. 80€ ($92) double in low season; 100€–166€ ($115–$191) double with required half-board in high season. Rates include breakfast. Add 13€ ($15) per person for full board. DC, MC, V. Closed 1 month in fall or spring. **Amenities:** Tirolese/Italian restaurant; bar; concierge; tour desk; courtesy car; room service (limited); babysitting; laundry service; dry cleaning; nonsmoking rooms. *In room:* TV, dataport, hair dryer.

Hotel Menardi   One of the oldest and most charming hostelries in Cortina successfully combines the luxury and service of a fine hotel with the homelike comfort of a mountain inn. The Menardi family, which converted its farmhouse into a guesthouse in the 1920s, has over the years beautifully appointed the public rooms with antiques and comfortable furnishings, and done up the high-ceilinged, wood-floored guest rooms simply but tastefully with painted or pine armoires and bedsteads, down quilts, and attractive floral fabrics. Rooms in the rear of the house are especially quiet and pleasant, looking across the hotel's spacious lawns to the forests and peaks; some newer (but still panel-and-pine Alpine) rooms are located in an annex next door; many have large balconies with picnic tables. Most guests take half-board to avail themselves of the excellent meals in a dining room, which converted from the former stalls (in the early 20th century, they rented extra horses to carriages traveling the mountain roads), but it is also possible to make bed-and-breakfast arrangements when the hotel is not fully booked. A pretty, public foot trail leads from the back lawn into town in 15 minutes.

Via Majon 110, 32043 Cortina d'Ampezzo. © **0436-2400.** Fax 0436-862-183. www.hotelmenardi.it. 49 units. In winter 170€–256€ ($196–$294) double with half board. May 29–Sept 21 90€–236€ ($104–$271) double. Rates include breakfast. Add 20€–23€ ($23–$26) per person for half board; add 30€–32€ ($35–$37) per person for full board. DC, MC, V. Parking free or 8€ ($9) in garage. Closed Apr 10–June 15 and Sept 21–Dec 20. **Amenities:** International/Tirolese restaurant; bar; golf course (9 holes, 3km/1³⁄₄ miles away); bike rental; children's playground; concierge; tour desk; car-rental desk; courtesy car; room service (24-hr.); laundry service; dry cleaning. *In room:* TV, dataport, minibar, hair dryer, safe.

Hotel Montana ⭐   Right in the center of town, this hotel occupies a tall, pretty Alpine-style house and is run by the amiable Adriano and Roberta Lorenzi, who provide some of the resort's nicest lodgings for the price. Guest rooms are pleasant and cozy, with old-style armoires, hardwood floors, and down quilts on the beds, and many open onto balconies overlooking the peaks. Most of the doubles are quite large, and many are beautifully paneled and have separate sitting areas. Half the rooms here are singles, making this an ideal spot for solo travelers. There is no restaurant, but breakfast is served in a pleasant room where guests tend to linger through much of the morning.

Corso Italia 94, 32043 Cortina d'Ampezzo. © **0436-862-126.** Fax 0436-868-211. www.cortina-hotel.com. 30 units. 60€–118€ ($69–$136) double; 99€–142€ ($114–$163) triple. Rates include breakfast. AE, DC, MC, V. Free parking. Closed Nov and June. **Amenities:** Bike rental; concierge; tour desk; room service (limited); babysitting; laundry service; video arcade. *In room:* Satellite TV, dataport, hair dryer (ask at desk), safe.

Miramonti Majestic Grand Hotel   The top deluxe hotel in town since 1893, this enormous golden-age beauty of a hotel is set just outside and above the village, backed up against the pine woodland with sweeping views of the cut-glass peaks. Public spaces devoted to après-ski fun include a piano bar, billiards room, and even a small cinema, and it calls a (separately managed) golf course its next-door neighbor. The decor, if uninspired, is perfectly pleasant, where 19th century meets modern, classy lines, and rooms contain a full complement of amenities.

Loc. Peziè 103, 32043 Cortina d'Ampezzo. © **0436-4201**. Fax 0436-867-019. www.geturhotels.com. 105 units. 240€–688€ ($276–$791) double; 588€–1,290€ ($676–$1,484) suite. Rates include half pension. AE, DC, MC, V. Parking 8€ ($9) in garage. Closed Apr–June and Sept–Nov. **Amenities:** Regional and international restaurant; piano bar; indoor pool (heated); golf course; tennis courts (lit at night); exercise room; sauna; free bikes; children's center; concierge; tour desk; car-rental desk; courtesy car into town; business center; salon; room service (limited); massage; babysitting; laundry service; dry cleaning (same-day); nonsmoking rooms. *In room:* TV w/pay movies, VCR (in some), fax (in some), dataport, minibar, hair dryer, safe.

Villa Nevada   On a grassy hillside overlooking the town, valley, and mountains, the Villa Nevada is a low-slung Alpine building that has the appearance of a private home. The same ambience prevails inside, where an attractive, paneled lounge is grouped around a hearth and opens to a sunny terrace, inviting guests to linger as they might in a living room. The guest rooms are large and bright, and afford wonderful views over the Alpine landscape; they are nicely furnished with dark-stained pine pieces and thick rugs or carpeting, and all have large balconies. Located on the road to the outlying settlement of Ronco, this is probably a better option for those with a car than for those without—the center of Cortina is a pleasant 20-minute walk downhill, but it could be a long uphill trek home in bad weather or late at night.

Via Ronco 64, 32043 Cortina d'Ampezzo. © **0436-4778**. Fax 0436-4853. www.cortina.dolomiti.org/villanevada. 11 units. 46€–160€ ($53–$184) double. Rates include buffet breakfast. No credit cards. Closed first Sun Oct–Dec 1 and after Easter to mid-June. **Amenities:** Bar; room service (limited). *In room:* TV, safe.

WHERE TO DINE

Inexpensive meals are hard to come by in Cortina—even pizzerias are few and far between. For a low-cost meal, you might want to equip yourself for a picnic at **La Piazzetta,** Corso Italia 53, with a mouthwatering assortment of salamis, cheeses, breads, and other fare. Another source of supplies is the department store **La Cooperativa,** Corso Italia 40 (© **0436-861-245**), the largest, best-stocked supermarket for miles around.

Al Camin ALPINE   If you follow the Via Alverà along the Ru Bigontina, a rushing mountain stream, about 10 minutes east from the center of town, you'll come to this charming, rustic restaurant. The tables in the wood-paneled dining room are grouped around a large stone fireplace, and the menu includes many local favorites. Your meal may include what is known in this part of the region as *kenederli* (these dumplings flavored with liver are known as *canederli* outside of the immediate vicinity of Cortina) *in brodo* or *al formaggio,* as well as some dishes, many of them seasonal, that you may not encounter elsewhere—these include *radicchio di prato,* a mountain green that appears in early spring and is served dressed with hot lard, and in winter *formaggio fuso con funghi e polenta,* a lush combination of creamy melted mountain cheese and wild mushrooms served over polenta.

Via Alverà 99. © **0436-862-010**. www.alcamin.it. Reservations recommended. Primi 6€–9.50€ ($7–$11); secondi 7€–18€ ($8–$21). MC, V. Tues–Sun noon–3pm and 7–11:30pm.

Caffè Royal CAFE   The Corso Italia, Cortina's pedestrians-only main street, is the center of the town's social life. This cafe is one of several that occupy the ground floor of large hotels along the street, and it is one of the more pleasant. As soon as it's even remotely possible to sit outdoors, tables are set out front on a sunny terrace. At other times patrons are welcome to sit for hours over coffee, pastries, or light fare such as sandwiches in a pleasant room off the lobby of this hotel of the same name.

Corso Italia. ℂ **0436-867-045**. Sandwiches and other snacks from about 2€ ($2.30). MC, V. Wed–Mon 8am–9pm.

La Tavernetta ALPINE   A former barn, just steps from the Olympic ice-skating stadium, has been delightfully converted to a very stylish yet reasonably priced restaurant, with handsome paneled walls, timbered ceilings, and tile floors. The menu relies on local ingredients and typical dishes of the Alto Adige, and the rustic environs may inspire you to eat heartily. You might want to begin with a dish of polenta delicately infused with *asparagi selvatici* (the tips of fresh wild asparagus) or *gnocchi di spinachi* (filled with spinach and topped with a rich wild-game sauce), then move on to a robust *stinco di vitello con patate* (veal shank served with creamy potato) or *cervo in salsa di mirtilli* (venison with a sauce of myrtle berries with polenta).

Via d. Stadio 27 a/b. ℂ **0436-867-494**. Reservations recommended. Primi 6.50€–12€ ($7–$14); secondi 11€–20€ ($12–$23). AE, MC, V. Thurs–Tues noon–2:30pm and 7:30–11pm.

Ospitale ALPINE   A trip out to this roomy restaurant in a high-gabled house (about 8km/5 miles north of Cortina on the road to the village and lake of Dobbiaco) is a favorite outing for residents of Cortina. Many members of the Alvera family are on hand in the series of comfortable, wood-floored dining rooms and in the kitchen, preparing and serving local specialties as well as traditional Italian dishes. In season, fresh vegetables appear in such pasta dishes as *pappardelle ai porcini* (flat noodles with porcini mushrooms) and *casunziei rossi,* a short, local pasta mixed with beets, or *gnocchi di zucca con ricotta* (gnocchi made from squash and stuffed with ricotta). The *goulash con polenta* is one of any number of substantial main courses. If you don't have a car, you can take one of the hourly buses out here from the bus station in Cortina, but that is only an option at lunch.

Locale Ospitale. ℂ **0436/4585**. Primi 5€–7€ ($6–$8); secondi 8€–15€ ($9–$17). AE, MC. Tues–Sun noon–2:30pm and 7–10pm.

6

Friuli-Venezia Giulia

Trieste's Friuli region is a sliver of coastline across the Adriatic Sea from Venice. Any glance at a map will show you that it would probably be part of Slovenia today were it not for the border juggling that followed World War I. Though primarily known today for the shipping industry and naval yards around the Hapsburgs' old port city of **Trieste,** this region was actually a major center of both ancient Rome and the Dark Ages' Lombards.

In fact, there's an interesting inverse proportion between the size of the Friuli's most interesting centers and each one's era of domination over local affairs. Rule by the sprawling free port and current capital of Trieste dates back only through Austo-Hungarian control and the 16th century. The midsize city of **Udine** held the patriarchy and regional power from the 13th century until it came under Venetian control in the 15th century. Udine had wrested that patriarchal seat, and control, from what is today the oversize town of **Cividale,** where in the early Middle Ages the Lombards inaugurated their ruling system of duchies. Even the sleepy backwater town of **Aquileia,** with its ruins and early Christian mosaics, once held a position of power as the fourth-most important city of the Roman Empire.

Almost every town in the region has a museum or two devoted to the Risorgimento and/or World War I. Well worth a visit to help understand the history of this region (a history, unfortunately, rarely explained in English), these museums trace the Italian national movement from its mid-19th-century beginnings through the intense fighting that took place in Friuli's mountains to the border disputes involving the line separating Italy from Yugoslavia. Even then, these disputes were not always happily resolved. The treaty of Paris plopped the national boundary right through the town of **Gorzia.** It wasn't until later compromises in the 1970s that the line was finally moved over, so that only Gorzia's eastern suburbs, just beyond the medieval Castello's hill, remained Slovenian.

REGIONAL CUISINE   The cuisine of Friuli-Venezia Giulia ranges from the firmly Alpine mountain fare of the borderland **Tirol** (see chapter 5) to some exotic and hard-to-pronounce variations reflecting the region's mixed cultural heritage, coastal region, and Slovenian slant. Among these are *cevapcici,* Trieste's signature meatball dish; *jota,* minestrone with sauerkraut; and *brovada,* a secondo that combines turnips, grape skins, and pork sausage—a farmer's supper if ever there was one. The town of **San Daniele** produces what is widely acknowledged as the best prosciutto in all of Italy—no small claim.

Friuli wines (celebrated on the website www.friulidoc-vive.it) range from local varieties such as the common **Tocai,** sweeter **Verduzzo, Malvasia,** and beefier **Collio** to more international grapes such as merlot, cabernet and cabernet Franc, all the pinots, and chardonnay.

1 Trieste

158km (98 miles) E of Venice, 68km (42 miles) SE of Udine, 408km (253 miles) E of Milan

On a map, Trieste faces west, toward the rest of Italy, to which it is connected only by a strip of what would otherwise be Slovenian beachfront just a few miles wide. For many of its traditions—from the Slavic dialects you are likely to hear in the streets to the appearance of goulash and Viennese pastries on its menus—this handsome city of medieval, neoclassical, and modern buildings turns to other parts of Europe, and is more rightly considered a Hapsburgian Adriatic port, more closely tied to Vienna than to Venice.

Already a thriving port by the time it was absorbed into the Roman Empire in the second century A.D., Trieste competed with Venice for control of the seas from the 9th through the 15th centuries. For several centuries it thrived under the Hapsburgs; in the late 18th century, Maria Theresa, and later her heirs and successors, gave the city its grandiose neoclassical look. Trieste was the chief seaport of the Austro-Hungarian Empire until the end of World War I, when the Friuli was reunited with Italy. That changed again during World War II, when Trieste fell to the Nazis in 1943. At the end of the war, it was turned over to Yugoslavia, and then rejoined Italy in 1954.

Politics continue to shape this city—today you're likely to notice the recent influx of refugees from war-torn parts of the former Yugoslavia. You're also likely to notice that Trieste is a seagoing city. The traditional *passeggiata* here means a stroll along the waterfront to enjoy a sea breeze and watch the sun set over the Adriatic.

In the cafes that remain (thinner on the ground now than they were before World War I), you can experience the city's history as one of Europe's intellectual centers. James Joyce arrived in 1904 and stayed for more than a decade, teaching English and writing *Portrait of an Artist, Dubliners,* and at least part of *Ulysses* here; the poet Rainer Maria Rilke lived nearby; Sigmund Freud spent time here; and the city was home to Italo Svevo, one of Italy's greatest 20th-century novelists, and Umberto Saba, one of its greatest 20th-century poets.

FESTIVALS & MARKETS   The city celebrates summer with a **series of concerts and films,** many free and held in the outdoor theater in the Castello di San Giusto. If you are going to be in Trieste at this time, ask the tourist office for a copy of *Eventi Luglio-Agosto.* The **International Operetta Festival** presents three or four noted masterworks in the genre (and a new piece or two) from July to mid-August in the Teatro Lirico Giuseppe Verdi (© **040-672-2500;** www.teatroverdi-trieste.com). The **Barcolana Autumn Cup,** held in the Golfo di Trieste on the second Sunday in October, is the largest sailing regatta in the Mediterranean. The regatta celebrated its 35th anniversary in 2003. For more information, call © **040-411-664** or visit www.barcolana.it.

An **antiques market** fills the streets of the Old City the third Sunday of every month, while early November brings an important **antiques fair,** especially noted for Liberty (plus its Austrian cousin Jungendstil) and Biedermeier pieces, to the conference center of the Stazione Maritima (© **040-304-888**). Trieste's two **food markets** provide colorful surroundings and a chance to eye the makings of the local cuisine. The covered market, at the corner of Via Carducci and Via della Majolica, is open Monday from 8am to 2pm and Tuesday through Saturday from 8am to 7pm. The open-air market is on Ponte Ponterosso, alongside the canal that cuts into the center of the city from the harbor, and it operates Tuesday through Saturday from 8am to 5:30pm.

Mittewald

Drau

Gail

AUSTRIA

Weissensee

Millstatter See

Forni
Avoltri

Paluzza

Sappada

Vigo

Forni
di Sopra

Ampezzo

▲ M. Pramaggiore

S. Francesco

A23

SLOVENIA

Kobarid

S. Martino
di C.

Digliano

Udine

Cividale
del Friuli

S. Giorgio

Tagliamento

Pordenone

S13 Pozzuolo

A23

Gorzia

A28

A28

Palmanova

A4

Brugnera

Villalta

Annone

A4

Portogruaro

Monfalcone

Aquileia

Opicina

Ponte
di Piave

Livenza

Trieste

← To Venice

*Golfo di
Trieste*

Golfo di Venezia

SLOVENIA

CROATIA

Venice

*The
Friuli*

ITALY

Florence

★ Rome

Adriatic Sea

0   10 mi

0   10 km

N

ESSENTIALS

GETTING THERE   By Train   Trains arrive at and depart from **Stazione Centrale** on Piazza della Libertà (© **040-452-8111**), northwest of the historic center. There are on average two trains an hour to and from Venice (2½–3 hr.), where you can make connections to Milan and other Italian cities. There are also frequent, twice-hourly connections to and from Udine (60–96 min.). Two trains a day connect Trieste and Budapest, Hungary (11 hr.); three daily to Ljubljana, Slovenia (3 hr.).

By Bus   The **bus station** is on Corso Cavour, to the left of the train station (© **800-915-303;** www.saf.ud.it). Frequent buses (28 a day) link Trieste and Udine (1½ hr.), and many other towns throughout the region. There's also one bus Monday to Saturday (currently around 2pm) to Ljubljana, Slovenia (2 hr. 45 min.).

By Car   Trieste is a 2-hour trip from Venice along the Autostrada A4.

VISITOR INFORMATION   The **tourist office** is at Piazza dell'Unità d'Italia 4B near the waterfront (© **040-347-8312;** fax 040-437-8380; www.trieste tourism.it; open daily 9am–7pm). There's another office at Via S. Nicolò 20 (© **040-679-6111;** fax 040-679-6299).

CITY LAYOUT   The **center** of Trieste, which is snuggled between the hills and the sea, is compact and easy to get around on foot. The bus and train stations are at the northern end of the center, on the **Piazza della Libertà.** From there, follow the harbor south for about 10 minutes along Corso Cavour (you'll soon cross Trieste's Canal Grande) and its continuation, Riva III Novembre, to the **Piazza dell'Unità d'Italia.** This dramatic space—with Hapsburg-commissioned, neoclassical buildings on three sides, open to the sea on one side, and a fountain in its center—is the heart of old Trieste and the present-day city as well. **Via Carducci,** Trieste's main shopping street, cuts through the center of the orderly 19th-century city. It begins in Piazza Oberdan (a few blocks east of the train station on Via Ghega) and cuts a straight swath south to Piazza Goldoni; from there the Corso Italia leads west to Piazza dell'Unità d'Italia and the sea.

GETTING AROUND   Central Trieste is easily navigable on foot, but the footsore can use the extensive network of ACT buses and trams (© **040-425-001** or 800-016-675 in Italy; www.triestetrasporti.it) that run throughout the city. You can purchase tickets at any *tabacchi* (tobacconist) for .85€ ($1) for 60 minutes and 1€ ($1.15) for 75 minutes. One foot-saving route is the no. 24 line from the train station to the hilltop Castello di San Giusto and its adjoining cluster of remarkable buildings (see below), or call a taxi at © **040-54-533** or 040-307-730.

WHAT TO SEE & DO

The oldest part of Trieste climbs the **Capitoline Hill (Colle Capitolino),** just behind the grandiose **Piazza dell'Unità d'Italia** ✿. This is where many of the city's most interesting museums and monuments (including Roman remains) are located. A good way to approach the hill is to leave the southeastern end of Piazza dell'Unità d'Italia and step into Piazza Cavana.

In contrast to the assemblage of 18th- and 19th-century buildings on the main piazza, this part of Trieste, a warren of tiny streets climbing the hillside away from the sea, is medieval. From Piazza Cavana, follow Via Felice Veneziano to Piazza Barbacan, where you take a left to duck under the first-century A.D. **Arco di Riccardo,** then turn right up Via Cattedrale, and follow that for about

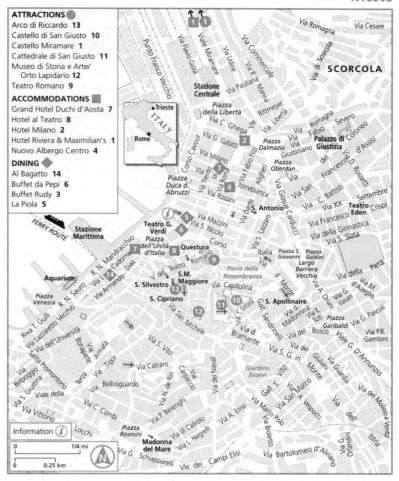

ATTRACTIONS ●
Arco di Riccardo **13**
Castello di San Giusto **10**
Castello Miramare **1**
Cattedrale di San Giusto **11**
Museo di Storia e Arte/
  Orto Lapidario **12**
Teatro Romano **9**

ACCOMMODATIONS ■
Grand Hotel Duchi d'Aosta **7**
Hotel al Teatro **8**
Hotel Milano **2**
Hotel Riviera & Maximilian's **1**
Nuovo Albergo Centro **4**

DINING ◆
Al Bagatto **14**
Buffet da Pepi **6**
Buffet Rudy **3**
La Piola **5**

10 minutes up the flanks of the Colle Capitolino to the **Cattedrale di San Giusto** (see below). Just above that is the **Castello di San Giusto** (see below), from which Trieste and the Adriatic unfold in an unforgettable view at your feet.

For a quicker descent, you can take the 265-step *Scala dei Giganti* **(Steps of the Giants)** back down the hill to Piazza Goldoni and Via Carducci, Trieste's main shopping street.

Cattedrale di San Giusto ✿   This hilltop basilica is one of several remarkable buildings atop the Capitoline Hill, which is littered with Roman ruins, evidence of the city's long history as an important port. In fact, the cathedral's squat, 14th-century **campanile** rises from the ruins of a first-century A.D. Roman temple. Pleasingly asymmetrical, the cathedral is dedicated to Saint Just, Trieste's patron. It incorporates two 5th-century Romanesque basilicas, one already dedicated to San Giusto, the other to Santa Maria Assunta. You'll see what remains of both as you step inside: The two right-hand aisles belong to the original San Giusto, the two left-hand aisles to Santa Maria Assuntà, and in the center is the 14th-century nave that was added to bring them together. The apse mosaics at the ends of the aisles are from the 13th century; those in the main apse date from 1932.

Piazza Cattedrale 3, Colle Capitolino. © **040-302-874** or 040-309-666. Free admission. Daily 8:30am–noon and 4–7pm. Bus: 24.

Castello di San Giusto ⭐ The tall walls of this bastion, built between 1470 and 1630, rise just behind the cathedral. Within the walls are an open-air theater, the **Cortile delle Milizie**, where a summer film-and-concert festival is held (see "Festivals & Markets," above), and a museum. But it's the walls that steal the show. A walk along them affords pleasant views over Trieste and the Adriatic, making this a popular spot just before its sunset closing time. The **Civic Museum** provides an interesting if not profound experience—among a series of period rooms is a "Venetian chamber" filled with antique chests, 17th-century Flemish tapestries, and other furnishings—as does the **Appartamento del Capitano,** the residence of the castle's 18th-century commander. A collection of antique weaponry is housed in the rooms of the castle watch.

Piazza Cattedrale, Colle Capitolino. © **040-309-362.** www.triestecultura.it. Castle ramparts 1€ ($1.15); Civico Museo del Castello 2€ ($2.30). For those under 14 and over 60, 1€ ($1.15) covers both. Castle Apr–Sept daily 9am–7pm; Oct–Mar daily 9am–5pm. Museum Tues–Sun 9am–1pm. Bus: 24.

Museo di Storia e Arte/Orto Lapidario This is Trieste's archaeological collection, and it includes prehistoric finds, exquisite Greek pieces (including some fine vases and a 4th-century B.C. silver Rhyton, a chalice shaped as a deer's head, from Taranto), and remnants of the city's Roman past. Most of the Roman architectural fragments, though, are scattered about the **Orto Lapidario (Lapidary Garden).** A few rooms of the museum house a growing Egyptian collection, including a female mummy.

Another outdoor remnant of Roman Trieste lies near the bottom of the Colle Capitolino. On Via Teatro Romano you'll find the **Teatro Romano (Roman Theater),** built in the 2nd century A.D. Only partially unearthed, the ruins can be glimpsed through a fence; let your imagination take you to the days when 6,000 spectators packed in for gladiatorial contests.

Piazza Cattedrale 1. © **040-310-500.** www.triestecultura.it. Admission 2€ ($2.30) adults, 1€ ($1.15) students under 25 and seniors over 65. Tues and Thurs–Sun 9am–1pm; Wed 9am–7pm. Bus: 24.

NEARBY SIGHTS

Castello di Miramare ⭐⭐ This vision of gleaming white turrets looms over the coast north of the city, 7km (4½ miles) from the center. Archduke Maximilian, brother of Austrian Emperor Franz Joseph, built this castle in the late 1850s when he was sent to Trieste to command the Austrian Navy. The interior reflects the somewhat insipid royal taste of the day, with room after room of gilt and velvet. Far more romantic are the adjoining gardens, where oaks, firs, and cypresses sway in sea breezes. Alluring, too, is the legend that those who sleep in the castle will meet a violent end, a belief to which history has given some credence—the same Maximilian went to Mexico in 1864 to assume the brief role of Emperor and was shot there in 1867; Archduke Ferdinand spent the night here before journeying to Sarajevo, where he was assassinated on the eve of World War I; and a later owner, Duke Amadeo of Austria, was also assassinated in 1938.

For sheer theatrics in such a theatrical setting, you can attend one of the campy sound-and-light shows in July and August; they depict Maximilian's final days in Mexico and are staged Tuesday, Thursday, and Sunday at 9:30 and 10:45pm; tickets begin at 10€ ($12).

Via Miramare, Grignano. (€ 040-224-143 or 040-224-7013. www.castello-miramare.it. Castle 4€ ($4.60) adults, 2€ ($2.30) ages 18–24, free for children under 18 and seniors over 65; grounds free. English-language tours available for 21€ ($24) for 1–10 people. Castle: Daily 9am–7pm; last admission 30 min. before close. Grounds: Apr–Sept daily 8am–7pm; Mar and Oct daily 8am–6pm; Nov–Feb daily 8am–5pm. Bus: 36 (catch at train station). Parking .50€ (60¢) per hour, or free along road and walk 5 min. Oct–Mar admission to the Castello after 5pm is from Viale dei Lecci only.

Grotto Gigante   The "Gigantic Cave" lives up to its name: 114m high, 924m long, and 64.5m wide (380 ft. by 924 ft. by 215 ft.), this single-chamber cave is the world's largest underground cavern open to the public. *Fair warning:* The requisite guided tours descend and ascend about 500 stairs total. Tours are in Italian, though if your group is mixed, they may play English and German recordings. The cave is about 15km (9¼ miles) north of the city near the community of Opicina. An exciting way to get here is via the rickety tram that climbs into the hills from Piazza Oberdan (just west of the train station) and ends at Opicina, where you can catch the no. 42 bus to the cave. The tram runs every 20 minutes from 7:30am to 8pm, and the fare is 1€ ($1.15).

Opicina. (€ 040-327-312. Admission 7.50€ ($9) adults, 5.50€ ($6) ages 6–12. Tues–Sun: tours every hour Nov–Feb 10am–noon and 2–4pm, Mar and Oct 10am–4pm; tours every half-hour Apr–Sept 10am–6pm. Bus: 42.

WHERE TO STAY

The **C.A.T.** (€ 040-452-8696; www.cat-trieste.com) office inside the train station will help you find a room if the choices below are full. Also, if you stay at one of their associate hotels (all of the ones listed below except the Hotel Riviera & Maximilian's and the Grand Hotel Duchi d'Aosta), you get a special shopping card good for the reduced price at most museums in town (and a reduction on the audio guide at Castello Miramare), plus 10% off at more than three dozen shops and restaurants.

One of my favorite Trieste hotels, the **Hotel al Teatro** (€ 040-366-220; fax 040-366-560), was closed at press time for a lengthy restoration with no set date for completion. I would have just cut the place out of the book entirely for the time being if this weren't—at least in its former incarnation—such a great place: a late-18th-century building full of character and old-fashioned comforts just steps away from the Piazza dell'Unità d'Italia. Prices in 2002, when it shut down, were 75€ ($86) double without bathroom, 100€ ($115) double with bathroom. Try calling before you go to see if it has reopened.

Grand Hotel Duchi d'Aosta ★   This is Trieste's best hotel, installed in one of the neoclassical buildings right on Piazza dell'Unità d'Italia. It's business-oriented and modernized, with snappy service and Jacuzzi box showers in the marble bathrooms, but retains plenty of class in the stylish wood furnishings and old-world charm of its reception and Harry's Grill restaurant, with tables out on the square.

Piazza dell'Unità d'Italia 2, 34121 Trieste. (€ 040-760-0011. Fax 040-366-092. www.magesta.com. 55 units. 285€ ($328) double; 358€ ($412) jr. suite; 576€ ($662) suite. AE, DC, MC, V. Parking 21€ ($24) in nearby garage. **Amenities:** International restaurant; bar; concierge; tour desk; car-rental desk; courtesy car; room service (limited); babysitting; laundry service; dry cleaning (same-day); nonsmoking rooms. *In room:* A/C, TV w/pay movies, VCR (on request), fax (on request), dataport, minibar, hair dryer.

Hotel Milano   Quiet and geared to business travelers as well as foreigners, this modern hotel is near the train station but within an easy walk to most of the sights in the city center. There's a spacious lounge and bar on the ground floor, as well as a breakfast room where a generous buffet, the only meal served, is laid out in the morning. The bright, cheerful guest rooms are decorated in contemporary style with wood-veneer furnishings to provide a comfortable ambience. The small bathrooms are completely up-to-date.

Via Ghega 17, 34132 Trieste. ℭ 040-369-680. Fax 040-369-727. www.hotel-milano.com. 44 units, all with bathroom. 118€ ($136) double; 155€ ($178) triple. Rates include breakfast. AE, DC, MC, V. Parking 8€ ($9) in garage. **Amenities:** Bar; concierge; tour desk; room service (limited); laundry service; dry cleaning. *In room:* A/C (in 26 rooms), TV, minibar, hair dryer, safe.

Hotel Riviera & Maximilian's ★★ This seaside retreat has been steadily expanded since it opened in 1910. Rooms in the older half have parquet floors, blue-tiled bathrooms, and carved wood furnishings with modern prints, and many neighboring doubles can be connected to make suites. No. 101 is already a family suite, though it is one of only three rooms without a sea view. In the new half, rooms have balconies but no air-conditioning as they are shaded by umbrella pines, cypress, and palms and cooled by Adriatic breezes. The furnishings are pleasant modular units in carpeted rooms with built-in closets. Those on the first floor have terraces opening directly onto the garden; those on the side have less of a sea view but more greenery. The Maximilian's branch is made up of 12 apartments with stylish, modern furnishings in burnished steel and light wood tones, minimalist and low to the ground for a vaguely Japanese-industrial look. In the single-bedroom apartments and in one of the bedrooms in the two- or three-room units, the bed folds away and an end table unfolds into a large desk. The kitchenettes are slipped behind pocket doors, so the rooms can be sold as doubles as well. The hotel's catwalk leads from the panoramic terrace with umbrella-shaded tables to an elevator tower down to two private beaches (the 2nd, which includes the pools, is a 5-min. walk along the coast).

Strada Costiera 22 (just north of Castello Miramare, 8km/5 miles from Trieste's center), 34010 Trieste. ℭ 040-224-551. Fax 040-224-300. www.hotelrivieraemaximilian.com. 70 units. 99€–178€ ($114–$205) double; 125€–280€ ($144–$322) suite; 388€–620€ ($446–$713) 1-room apt for 2 per week; 672€–956€ ($773–$1,099) 2-room apt for 2 per week. Breakfast included. AE, DC, MC, V. Free parking. **Amenities:** International/Italian terrace restaurant; beach buffet in summer; bar; outdoor pools (1 for adults, 1 for kids); golf course; tennis courts (10-min. walk away); watersports equipment; children's center at beach; concierge; tour desk; car-rental desk; room service (limited); massage (in room); babysitting; laundry service; dry cleaning; nonsmoking rooms. *In room:* A/C (in the half of the rooms that need it), TV w/pay movies, fax (on request), dataport, kitchenette (in apts), minibar, hair dryer.

Nuovo Albergo Centro New owners took over this formerly down-at-the-heels pensione in June of 2000 and immediately set to work overhauling the place, making it considerably more livable while maintaining the low prices and simple comforts. So now there's an Internet port for guest use and new in-room bathrooms. Next year they hope to add a bar and elevator, but for now, you will find firm, orthopedic beds, spanking-new modular furnishings, high ceilings, and linoleum-that-looks-like-wood floors. The shared bathrooms (four showers, six toilets) are of recent vintage, and a wide spot in the hall hosts a small sitting area with TV. The Centro occupies a floor of a large building about midway between the train station and the Piazza dell'Unità d'Italia, and it is less than a 10-minute walk from either. There's no elevator—you have to climb 34 steps to the first-floor reception.

Via Roma 13, 34132 Trieste. ℭ 040-347-8790. Fax 040-347-5258. www.hotelcentrotrieste.it. 17 units, 3 with bathroom. 49€ ($56) double without bathroom, 67€ ($77) double with bathroom; 66€ ($76) triple without bathroom, 90€ ($104) triple with bathroom; 83€ ($95) quad without bathroom, 114€ ($131) quad with bathroom. Rates include buffet breakfast. AE, DC, MC, V. Parking 8€ ($9) in garage. **Amenities:** Concierge; bike rental; tour desk; nonsmoking rooms. *In room:* TV, dataport, hair dryer.

WHERE TO DINE

Al Bagatto ★★ SEAFOOD   The best fish restaurant in Trieste occupies simply decorated quarters, overseen by a staff that seems to have been working the perpetually crowded dining room for decades. The emphasis is clearly on the freshest fish in simple but tasty preparations. *Risotto ai frutti di mare* is laden with tiny shrimp and squid from the Gulf of Trieste, and they also find their way into the *zuppa di pesce*. It would be a shame, though, to come this far and not join most of the other diners in ordering the house's *frittura mista*, a delicately fried sampling of the sea creatures that are fresh at the market that morning.

Via Felice Venezian 2/Via Cadoana. © 040-301-771. Reservations required. Primi 8€–11€ ($9–$13); secondi 11€–18€ ($12–$21). AE, DC, MC, V. Mon–Sat noon–2:30pm and 7pm–midnight. Closed Aug 15–30 and Dec 15–31.

Buffet da Pepi ★ TRIESTINO   Trieste has many such *tavola caldi* (hot foods deli) like this one, though none compare to century-old Pepi, a much-beloved institution and one of the most popular eateries in the city. You can get a panino (sandwich) of cold cuts or splurge on an 8€ ($9) platter of the house specialty, many varieties of boiled pork: spicy *cotechini* (pork sausages), *porchetta* (roast pork), *bollito di maiale* (a Trieste dish of boiled pork), and *prosciutto* (er, that's not boiled), all served with *crauti* (sauerkraut) and other vegetables.

Via della Cassa di Risparimio 3 (near Piazza d. Borsa, 1 block from the water and 2 blocks north of Piazza dell'Unità d'Italia). © 040-366-858. Sandwiches and dishes 2.50€–5€ ($2.90–$6). AE, DC, MC, V. Mon–Sat 9am–9pm. Closed July 15–Aug 7.

Buffet Rudy TRIESTINO/AUSTRIAN   Just because it's currently part of Italy doesn't mean you can't indulge in the cuisines of Trieste's former identities. This small Austrian/Bavarian *Bierhalle* serves Spaten beer on tap and sausages, wurst, and goulash alongside pastas, soups, and boiled meats. You can stand at the bar and choose nibblers from behind the glass—roast peppers, fried zucchini, rice croquettes, frankfurters in pastry—or grab a straw-bottomed chair at the little tables under Bavarian banners and pick from the chalkboard menu.

Via Valdirivo 32. © 040-639-428. Primi 3.50€–5€ ($4–$4.60); secondi 3€–11€ ($3.45–$13). No credit cards. Mon–Sat 11am–midnight.

La Piola ★ TRIESTINO   This animated trattoria in the center of town near Trieste's Greek Orthodox church of San Nicolò dei Greci is popular with workers from the surrounding offices. The *jota,* a soup of beans and cabbage, *cevapcici* (Trieste's special meatballs, with their unique spelling), and *gnocchi di patate* (potato gnocchi filled with cheese) and many other pastas are excellent, especially those topped with fresh porcini mushrooms. Main courses concentrate on meat, including *bistecche di cavallo* (horsemeat steak) or *costine di miale* (roast pork ribs), though fresh grilled Adriatic fish is often available.

Via San Nicolò 1B. © 040-366-354. Primi 8€ ($9); secondi 5€–14€ ($6–$16). DC, MC, V. Mon–Sat noon–3pm and 6–11pm. Closed July 15–Aug 7.

COFFEE & GELATO

Coffee is one of Trieste's most important products—Illy and many other major Italian brands are located here (in fact, an Illy family member has even served as the city's mayor). More to the point for travelers, drinking coffee is a local pastime, and the city's exquisite blends can be enjoyed in any number of august cafes.

Caffè degli Specchi at Piazza dell'Unità d'Italia 7 (© 040-365-777) enjoys a marvelous position on the city's main, seafront piazza, making its terrace a prime spot to linger. In bad weather a series of elegant rooms fill with shoppers and businesspeople. The pastries are excellent, as is the coffee. James Joyce spent much of his 12 years in Trieste at **Caffè-Pasticceria Pirona** ⭑, at the east end of Via Carducci at Largo Barriera Vecchia 12 (© **040-636-046**). It was here that he allegedly wrote part of *Ulysses*. With its photographs of old Trieste and gilded mirrors, the premises bear the mark of one of Europe's great remaining literary cafes. **Caffè San Marco** ⭑⭑, at Via Battisti 18 (© **040-371-373**), is one of Trieste's most elegant cafes; it dates from 1914, with a Liberty-style (as Art Nouveau is called in Italy) interior. A pianist puts the final touches on the ultimate cafe experience.

Gelateria Zampolli at Via Ghega 10 (© **040-364-868**) is reputed to be the best gelateria in Trieste. It's located near Stazione Centrale and the city center, serving more than 50 flavors, made on the premises daily. Another Zampolli, owned by a different member of the same family, is located on Piazza Cavana 6 (© **040-306-003**), just south of Piazza dell'Unità d'Italia.

AN ANCIENT DIVERSION EN ROUTE TO GORIZIA

Aquileia ⭑⭑ is one of those perfect Italian sites. This tiny village of just over 3,000 souls was once a major Roman city and early Christian stronghold, with a rich heritage that has left it littered with ruins and some of the best paleo-Christian mosaics in Europe. The Roman colony was founded in 181 B.C., and witnessed such momentous ancient events as Emperor Augustus's meeting with King Herod of Judea in A.D. 10, the murders of would-be Emperor Maximinus (by his own army) and Emperor Constantine II (by his brother), and the sacks of Attila the Hun in 452.

Remains of the **Roman colony** ⭑ are open sites (open 8:30am to an hour before sunset; free admission), some still being excavated, that lie scattered north of the current town. Just to the north of the main Piazza Capitolo, behind the tourist office, are a set of Roman houses and Christian oratories with excellent floor mosaics. From here walk right (east) a bit to turn north up Via Sacra alongside the river, which leads to the remains of the Roman harbor. Turn left on Via Gemina then left again on Via Giulia Augusta to pass, on the right, a stretch of ancient road and, on the left, a row of standing columns marking one edge of the **Forum** ⭑ (among the items displayed here, look for the Gorgon's head). The road forks at the **Grande Mausoleo**, a 1st-century-A.D. tomb hauled here from the edge of town. The right fork (Via XXIV Maggio) will lead you past the remaining scraps of the amphitheater and baths (still being excavated).

The left fork (really straight on down Via Giulio Augusto) takes you in a few blocks to Via Roma and the **Museo Archeologico** ⭑ (© **0431-91-016** or 0431-91-035), which houses some nice statuary, mosaics, bronzes, and glassware, plus the excellently preserved hull of a Roman ship. Admission to the museum is 4€ ($4.60) for adults, 2€ ($2.30) for ages 18 to 25, and free for those under 18 and over 65; it's open Monday 8:30am to 2pm, Tuesday to Sunday 8:30am to 7:30pm (open to 11pm on Sat June–Sept). The last admission is half an hour before closing.

Christianity is also ancient in Aquileia. A major church council called here in 381 was attended by such towering early theologians as Saints Jerome and Ambrose. The fabulously mosaicked **Basilica** ⭑⭑ on Piazza Capitolo (© **0431-91-067** or 0431-84-558) is precisely as old as the official church in Italy, founded in A.D. 313, the same year Emperor Constantine declared Christianity to be the state religion. In the early 20th century, the church's original 4th-century **mosaic floor** ⭑⭑⭑ was uncovered to reveal a colorful cornucopia of early Christian iconography mixed with pagan symbols and portraits of 4th-century congregants spreading over 7,500 square feet. The basilica was substantially rebuilt in the early 11th century, when the now-faded apse frescoes were painted. In the chapel to the left of the altar is a **bas-relief** ★ from 1170 of Christ with St. Peter and the freshly martyred St. Thomas of Canterbury. Later frescoes also litter the church, including some lovely Byzantine 12th-century ones in the **main crypt** ★★.

The **Cripta Affreschi** ★★ is entered next to the medieval reconstruction of the Holy Sepulchre at the entrance end of the basilica's left aisle. The mosaics here hail from three eras: Augustan ones from a Roman house (just to the left), an early-4th-century floor laid at the same time as the Basilica's (this was once a neighboring church), and later-4th-century ones as well. The Basilica is free; the Cripta charges a nominal fee (some years it is tied into the Museo Archeologico ticket); both are open daily from 8:30am to 12:30pm and 2:30 to 5:30pm. In summer they are open from 8:30am to 7pm. Admission is 2.60€ ($3) for adults and free for children under 10.

Aquileia lies on local road 352 (take the Palmanova exit from the A4) some 11km (7 miles) inland from Grado, a low-key Venice Lido–like semi-island resort where Aquileia's population, and fortunes, moved to escape Dark Ages barbarian raids by the likes of Huns and Lombards. The easiest way here without your own wheels is the bus from Udine to Grado, though you can also catch a bus here from the Cervignano del Friuli train station 8km (5 miles) to the north on the Trieste-Venice line.

Aquileia's **tourist office** is on the main Piazza Capitolo (© **0431-91-087** or 0431-919-491; www.aquileia.it, www.aptgrado.com, www.aquileia.net).

2 Udine

71km (44 miles) NW of Trieste, 127km (79 miles) N of Venice

Surrounded by the green, rolling plains of the Friuli, Udine is a delightful small city with a vibrant air, wonderful piazze (squares) and Gothic and Renaissance monuments, and some stunning artworks by the rococo painter Tiepolo. A possession of the Venetian Republic from the 14th century, Udine has enjoyed great prosperity as a major trading center and a crossroads for trade across the Alps, just to the north. The late 18th century saw an Austrian takeover, the 19th century saw unification with Italy, and the 20th century brought intense World War II bombings. Through it all, the city's landmarks and distinct character (reflecting Italian, Nordic, and central European influences) have remained intact.

FESTIVALS & MARKETS   **Udine d'Estate** is the city's major festival, running from July to mid-September with concerts and theatrical performances in churches and on Udine's beautiful piazze. An **outdoor food market** fills the atmospheric Piazza Matteotti daily from 8am to 1pm.

ESSENTIALS

GETTING THERE   **By Train**   From its train station on Viale Europa Unità, Udine runs about two trains hourly from Venice (1¾–2 hr.) and from Trieste (1–1½ hr.).

By Bus   The bus station is 1 block east of the train station on Viale Europa Unità. There is extensive service to other cities and towns in Friuli-Venezia Giulia, but little outside it, provided by **SAF** (© **800-915-303;** www.saf.ud.it). Hourly buses (more frequent between 7–9am and 4–7pm) make the hour-long trip to and from Trieste.

By Car Udine is an easy 2-hour drive north and west of Venice on A4 east to A23 and then north. From Trieste, it's a trip of a little under an hour west on A4, then north on A23. If you are driving from Cortina d'Ampezzo or another Dolomite resort, you will drop down from the mountains into Belluno on S51 as if you were going to Venice, but head east (toward Pordenone) instead on S13 at Vittorio Veneto. Allow about 3 hours for the drive.

VISITOR INFORMATION The **tourist office** is at Piazza I Maggio 7 (the other side of the Castello from Piazza della Libertà; ✆ **0432-295-972;** fax 0432-504-743; www.turismo.fvg.it), and is open Monday to Saturday 9am to 1pm and 3 to 6pm.

CITY LAYOUT Much of the center of Udine is closed to traffic and sur-rounded by ring roads. The train and bus stations are at the southern end of this ring network, on Viale Europa Unità. From there it is about a 15-minute walk into the center, following Via Aquileia and its continuation, Via Veneto, to Piazza della Libertà. Bus no. 1 makes the trip from the train station to the center (.85€/$1).

WHAT TO SEE & DO

In Udine's center, handsome streets open every few blocks or so onto another stunning piazza and sometimes even cross little streams. The effect is like walk-ing from one stage set to another. The heart of the city is the elegant **Piazza della Libertà** 𝕬𝕬, which bears the telltale marks of the Venetian presence in Udine: On one side is the **Loggia del Lionello,** the town hall, built in the mid–15th century in Venetian style with a pink-and-white-striped facade. Across the piazza is the Renaissance **Porticcato di San Giovanni** 𝕬𝕬, with a long portico supported by slender columns and, rising above it, a Venice-inspired clock tower emblazoned with the Venetian lion and topped with two Moors who strike the hours.

The great Renaissance architect Palladio designed the **Arco Bollani,** located to one side of the clock tower. Pass through it and make the short climb through verdant gardens to the somber 16th-century **Castello** 𝕬𝕬, which rises above the Piazza della Libertà on a hillock. Many Udinese come up here just to admire the view over the town and countryside, but you can also venture into the castle and visit the **Museo Civico.** While many of the galleries house an eclectic collection that includes coins, ancient pottery, and old photographs of Udine, the real treas-ures can be found in the **Galleria d'Arte Antica** 𝕬. Here you'll get a taste of the work of Giambattista Tiepolo, who came to Udine from Venice in 1726, when he was 30 and already regarded as a master of a rococo style that was the last great burst of Italian painting. His *Consilium in Arena* is pure Tiepolo, a swirl of lush skies and plump putti. The museum (✆ **0432-502-872**) is open Tuesday to Sat-urday 9:30am to 12:30pm and 3 to 6pm, Sunday 9:30am to 12:30pm; admis-sion is 2.50€ ($2.90) for adults, 1.75€ ($2) for students and those over 65, and free for children under 10; free for everyone Sunday mornings.

Many visitors come to Udine just to enjoy the Tiepolos that grace many of its buildings. To follow in their footsteps, descend again to Piazza della Libertà and follow Via Veneto south for a block or so to Piazza Duomo. The **Cathedral** 𝕬 (open daily 7am–noon and 4–8pm) dominates the square with its 14th-century Gothic facade, but the interior is theatrically baroque. The first, second, and fourth altars in the right nave are adorned with Tiepolo paintings; in the fourth chapel, his airy version of *Christ's Ascension* imparts lightness and a sense of exhil-aration at leaving earth (Tiepolo also did the frescoes here).

Tiepolo also frescoed the **Oratorio della Purità** ⚝ across the piazza (© 0432-506-830). In *Fall of the Angels,* the plummeting cherubs look like children who have just been scolded. An *Assumption,* appropriately adorning the ceiling, is so light that it seems to draw the viewer right off the floor. To enter, rustle up a sacristan in the Duomo (not on Sun) or try ringing the bell (mornings only).

Udine's largest collection of the artist's works adorn the **Palazzo Patriarcale** or **Palazzo Arcivescovile** ⚝⚝ (© 0432-25-003), just north of the Duomo on Piazza Patriarcato. This palace was once home to Udine's patriarchal bishops. One of the last (before the position was dissolved) was Dionisio Delfino (1699–1734), from a wealthy and influential Veneto family (they produced several Udine patriarchs; look for their "three dolphins on a blue field" coat of arms all over the palazzo). Delfino was the guy who brought Tiepolo to Udine to paint the second floor's airy frescoes, which depict Old Testament scenes full of familiar Biblical characters wearing fashionable 18th-century clothing. The most impressive room is the narrow **Galleria degli Ospiti,** though the balustraded *Biblioteca* **(library)** and double-decker *Sala del Trono* **(Throne Room)** are also notable. The Sala del Trono is plastered with portraits of the patriarchs, many redone by Tiepolo. Dionisio is the one on the bottom at the far left of the window wall. The palazzo, which also houses the Duomo's Museo Diocesano on the first floor containing Friuliana-School wood statues spanning the 13th to 18th centuries, is open Wednesday to Sunday 10am to noon and 3:30 to 6:30pm. Admission is 5€ ($6) for adults and 3€ ($3.45) for children under 10.

One more museum here deserves a visit, and that is the **Museo d'Arte Moderna** ⚝ (© 0432-295-891), on the other side of the city on Piazza Diacono (from Piazza della Libertà follow Via Mazzini and Via Anton Morro north to the edge of the old center). Here you will be shaken out of the reverie induced by Tiepolo's airy views of miracles and the afterlife—the galleries are filled, surprising in a small provincial city, with the works of 20th-century powerhouses such as Picasso and Giorgio de Chirico, as well as 1970s works by the likes of Lichtenstein and De Kooning. It's open Tuesday to Saturday 9:30am to 12:30pm and 3 to 6pm, Sunday 9:30am to 12:30pm. Admission is 2.60€ ($3) for adults, 1.80€ ($2.05) for those under 18 and over 65. Admission to the gallery is free on Sunday mornings.

WHERE TO STAY

Die-hard budgeters will want to check if the slightly dire **Al Vecchio Tram,** very centrally located at Via Brenari 32 (© 0432-502-516), has decided whether or not to keep renting its 10 exceedingly bare-bones, bathroomless rooms above the bar, which have been going for a mere 35€ ($40) per double. (Every year they talk like they're going to quit, but every year they seem to stay open just one season longer. And when I say "bare-bones," I mean it—a sway-backed cot and a bare bulb in the ceiling fixture.)

Astoria Hotel   This is a classy business hotel, smack in the center of town, that unfortunately charges expense-account rates. The rooms are smallish but not cramped, with firm enough beds and a mix of furnishings from cherry-veneer mod and 1980s vintage floral-print-on-black to restructured 18th- and 19th-century antiques. Oddly, the bathrooms are old-fashioned (some outright old and in need of renovation), with nowhere to hang the shower nozzle.

Piazza XX Settembre 24, 33100 Udine. © 0432-505-091. Fax 0432-509-070. www.hotelastoria.udine.it. 75 units. 98€–169€ ($113–$194) standard double; 112€–184€ ($129–$212) superior double; 158€–238€ ($182–$274) suite. Breakfast included. AE, DC, MC, V. Parking 16€ ($18) in garage. **Amenities:** Highly refined

Friuliana and international restaurant; bar; concierge; tour desk; car-rental desk; business center; room service (limited); babysitting; laundry service; dry cleaning (same-day). *In room:* A/C, TV, dataport, minibar, hair dryer, safe (in about half the rooms).

Hotel Clocchiatti ★★ The Clocchiatti have provided this hotel, installed in a Liberty-style 19th-century villa, with a wonderfully warm family reception since 1965. It's 10 minutes from the town center, close to the ring road, and offers a bit of quiet remove from Udine. The historic villa setting means guest quarters vary widely in size, shapes, and decor, though all enjoy rich fabrics and carpets. One of the nicest is suite no. 102, large and on a corner, with floor-to-ceiling windows and a sofa that can be replaced by a double or twin beds for families. Upper-floor rooms have low, vaguely rustic sloping plank ceilings. The only drawbacks are that there's no elevator and most bathrooms, while fully adequate, are quite cramped. A major renovation has added several new junior suites.

Via Cividale 29, 33100 Udine. ⓒ and fax 0432-505-047. www.hotelclocchiatti.it. 100€–120€ ($115–$138) double; 110€–130€ ($127–$150) triple; 136€ ($156) jr. suite. Rates include breakfast. AE, DC, MC, V. Parking free in little lot. Closed 2 weeks around Christmas. **Amenities:** Concierge; tour desk; room service (limited); massage (in room); laundry service; dry cleaning. *In room:* A/C, TV, dataport, minibar, hair dryer, safe.

Hotel Europa The blocks in front of Udine's train station comprise a pleasant residential neighborhood where many of the city's hotels are clustered. The Europa is one of the nicest, with the exception of a sometimes rude staff. A recent renovation, instead of rendering the premises banally modern, has combined style with comfort. The guest rooms are handsomely outfitted with sleek wood cabinetry and headboards, thick carpeting, and some nice touches that include brass wall lamps and framed reproductions. All of the bathrooms are new and equipped with generous basins and stall showers. The quietest rooms are those in the back, facing a sunny courtyard, but double-glazing on the front-room windows keeps noise there to a minimum as well. Additionally, the hoteliers have recently added air-conditioning.

Viale Europa Unità 47, 33100 Udine. ⓒ **0432-508-731** or 0432-294-446. Fax 0432-512-654. 44 units. 68€–88€ ($78–$101) double; 93€–123€ ($107–$141) triple. Breakfast included. AE, DC, MC, V. Parking 6€ ($7). **Amenities:** Regional restaurant next door; bar; concierge; car rental; tour desk; room service (bar service only). *In room:* A/C, TV, dataport, minibar, hair dryer.

WHERE TO DINE

Al Vecchio Stallo ★★ OSTERIA/UDINESE By the 1920s, this already served as a post station, offering refreshments and fresh horses to mounted mail carriers, so they decided to transform the old stalls into a full-fledged *osteria,* serving simple, filling, cheap traditional dishes along with lots of local wine. Things haven't changed much, though a token national Italian dish such as *penne amatriciana* is often added to the daily menu. Those in the know, however, recommend that you stick to local specialties like *orzo e fagioli* (barley-and-bean soup), *frico con polenta* (cheese melted over potatoes), *nervetti con cipolla* (cow leg tendons and veins tossed with onions—I think you have to be from Udine to appreciate them), or the ever-popular *polpettone con pure* (slices of giant meatball with mashed potatoes). Service is brisk, but jocular.

Via Viola 7 (off Viale Marco Volpe, near Piazza XXVI Luglio). ⓒ **0432-21-296.** Primi 4€–6€ ($4.60–$7); secondi 4.50€–9€ ($5–$10). No credit cards. Mon–Sat noon–3pm and 6pm–midnight.

Caffè Bistrot CAFE This welcoming cafe faces Udine's oldest square, which is surrounded by tall old houses with porticos and where a colorful morning produce market is held. You can take in these atmospheric surroundings from a table on the terrace, though the interior rooms, which spread across two floors, are inviting. Students, businesspeople, and neighborhood residents alike sit for hours chatting and reading over cups of coffee or one of the excellent local wines served by the glass. The delicious homemade pastries make this a popular breakfast spot. Sandwiches and a few other dishes, including an *insalata caprese* (with mozzarella, basil, and tomato) and crepes filled with ham and cheese, are also served throughout the day and night (after dark, in fact, this cafe often becomes a focal point of Old City nightlife; on some nights a DJ wedged in between the outdoor tables spins records while students dance on the flagstones of the raised square).

Piazza Matteotti. No phone. Sandwiches and snacks from 2.50€ ($2.90). MC, V. Tues–Fri 7:45am–2am; Sat 9am–2am.

Ristorante-Pizzeria Al Portici ✯ PIZZERIA/UDINESE   Udine has a large and energetic population of students, and they seem to spend much of their time in this large trattoria with red-checked tablecloths. The pizza oven turns out the most popular fare, but you can also dip into some of the city's simple, casual cuisine here, such as *cialzons,* as gnocchi are called here and often stuffed with smoked ricotta cheese, and *brovada* (a poor man's dish of turnips and pork sausage). Given the establishment's long open hours, you can stop by any time during the day for a coffee or beer, or a glass of some of the excellent Friuli wines.

Via Veneto 8. ✆ **0432-508-975.** Primi 5€–7€ ($6–$8); secondi 5€–16€ ($6–$18); pizza 3.50€–8€ ($4–$9). MC, V. Wed–Mon 9am–1am.

A DAY TRIP TO CIVIDALE DEL FRIULI

When the Lombards founded their first Italian duchy in the Dark Ages, it was centered on this pretty little city, so the entire region became known as *Friuli* after a corrupt elision of this Roman colony's original name, *Forum Iulii* (Caesar had modestly founded it as "Julius's Forum"). It later produced a few Lombard "Kings of Italy" from the 8th to 10th centuries, and until the Middle Ages was the seat of the local patriarch, after which its fortunes fell off. These days it's a largely medieval town perched on the lip of an impressive river gorge, where some of the best Lombard-era stone carving in Italy is preserved.

VISITOR INFORMATION   The **tourist office,** Corso Paolino d'Aquileia 10 (✆ **0432-731-398** or 0432-731-461; fax 0432-731-398; www.comune.cividale-del-friuli.ud.it), is open Monday to Friday 9am to 1pm and 3 to 7pm.

A STROLL THROUGH TOWN

From the train station, turn left on Viale Libertà to Via C. Alberto, where you can take a right and follow it (it becomes Corso Mazzini) into the heart of town, becoming Corso Paolino d'Aquileia after Piazza Duomo and then crossing the Ponte del Diavolo over the deep and seriously impressive limestone gorge carved by the Natisone River.

The current **Duomo** (backtrack from the bridge to the central Piazza Duomo) is largely of the 16th and 17th centuries, though its bare interior does house a fantastic silver altarpiece set with gold-backed enameled scenes from the 12th century. A small series of rooms opens on the right aisle, with detached frescoes and several gorgeously carved stone relief panels, including a cobbled-together 8th-century Baptistery, an 11th-century throne for the patriarch, and the **altar of the Duke of Ratchis** ✯✯ (A.D. 744–49), Duke of the Friuli and King of Italy, featuring gibbon-armed angels surrounding a beardless Christ, with side panels of the *Visitation* and *Adoration of the Magi.* The cathedral is open daily 9am to noon and 3 to 6pm (to 7pm Apr–Oct) and is closed Sunday morning.

Around the corner on Piazza Duomo sits the **Palazzo dei Provveditori Veneti,** designed by Andrea Palladio (but construction only began after his death in 1581; the building was finished in 1596). It now houses the **Museo Archeologico Nazionale** ⭐ (© 0432-700-700), whose treasures include ancient bronzes (look for the fragment of a toga-wearing man from the early 1st century A.D.), a Roman mosaic of Oceanus, and numerous early medieval pieces. Among the latter, standouts include the 6th-century Treasure of Duke Gisulfo (gold accouterments and a gem-studded cross, all found in his sarcophagus), and the Pace of Duke Ursus, an A.D. 800 ivory Crucifixion scene surrounded by a silver frame. Admission is 2€ ($2.30); open Tuesday to Sunday 8:30am to 7:30pm, Monday 9am to 2pm (in summer, Sat to 11pm).

Medieval streets behind the Palazzo dei Provveditori Veneti lead under the Romanesque Porta Patriarchale to Piazzetta San Biagio and the entrance to Cividale's top sight, the **Tempietto Longobardo** ⭐⭐⭐ (© 0432-700-867). The Lombards carved this cliff-side church directly into the limestone in the 8th century, decorating it with saintly high-relief statues and stuccoes. The stalls date to the 14th century. Admission is 2€ ($2.30) for adults, 1€ ($1.15) for students and seniors over 60. It's open daily: April to October 9am to 1pm and 3 to 6:30pm, November to March 10am to 1pm and 3:30 to 5pm.

For kicks, ask the guy at **Bar all'Ippogeo,** on Corso Paolino d'Aquileia at the corner with Via Monastero (Mon ask at the tourist office), for the *chiave all'Ippogeo Celtico* ("key to the Celtic Tomb"), an artificial grotto of uncertain date with a few highly worn carvings at Via Monastero 6 (© 0432-701-211). It's free, but relaxing with an espresso or Campari at the bar when you return the key never hurts!

WHERE TO DINE

For a quick bite or a sampler platter of meats and cheese near the Tempietto Longobardo, pop into the **Ostarie Bar Al Tempietto,** Via Michele della Torre 2 (© 0432-703-012; www.altempietto.it).

Osteria d'Italia/Enoteca de Feo ⭐⭐ FRIULIANA/SLIGHTLY CREATIVE ITALIAN   This wood-paneled modern joint has old-fashioned values. There's a wine-tasting bar down below and just five tables in the lofted dining nook (three more are squirreled away in the basement). Because this place is vino-driven, you can order a dozen each of red and white wine by the glass for 2€ to 5€ ($2.30–$6). The music is jazz, the service professional, and the food impeccable. Start off with a "salad" of prosciutto from San Daniele, *caprino* (soft goat cheese), and figs before moving on to a primo such as a *zuppa di orzo* (pasta soup with potatoes, asparagus, and summer vegetables) or *cannoli di crespelle alla ricotta di bufala* (pasta crepes stuffed with buffalo-milk ricotta). Secondi are hearty and come with side dishes: steak alongside oven-roasted potatoes, sea bass filets with steamed veggies.

Via A. Ristori 29. © 0432-732-033. www.enotecadefeo.com. Primi 8€–10€ ($9–$12); secondi 13€–18€ ($15–$21). AE, DC, MC, V. Mon–Sat 11am–3pm; Tues–Sat 6pm–midnight.

7

Milan & Lombardy

There is a lot more to Italy's most prosperous province than the factories that fuel its economy. Many of the attractions here are urban—in addition to Milan, a string of Renaissance cities dots the Lombardian plains, from Pavia to Mantua. To the north the region bumps up against craggy mountains and romantic lakes (see chapter 8, "The Lakes") and to the south Lombardy spreads out in fertile farmlands fed by the Po and other rivers. The Lombardians, originally one of the Germanic barbarian hordes who crossed the Alps during Rome's decline and ended up staying to settle down, have been ruled over the centuries by feudal dynasties, the Spanish, the Austrians, and the French. They tend to be a little more continental than their neighbors to the south, faster talking, and a little more fast-paced as well. They even dine a little differently, eschewing olive oil for butter and often forgoing pasta for polenta and risotto.

REGIONAL CUISINE   Polenta or risotto—a meal in Lombardy will probably start with one or the other, and both are served in variations that can sometimes stand in for an entire meal. *Polenta alla Bergamasca,* for one, is cooked with tomatoes, sausage, and cheese. Creamy risottos are often embellished with fish (in Mantua, perhaps with pikelike *luccio*) or any other ingredients an innovative chef might find at hand; one of the simplest and ever so common preparations here is *risotto alla Milanese,* infused with saffron. In Mantua you have a third choice of pasta—*tortelli,* little envelopes that are folded over and stuffed most commonly with *zucca* (pumpkin). Meat dishes tend to be plain and hearty. Best known and most typical of the region are *osso buco,* slowly braised veal shank served with *gremolada,* a sauce of lemon and parsley and *cotoletta alla milanese,* a veal cutlet that is breaded, dipped in egg, and sautéed in butter—not what would be considered a healthy dish, but so delicious it warrants a departure from a diet at least once during a stay in the region.

1 Milan (Milano)

552km (342 miles) NW of Rome, 288km (179 miles) NW of Florence, 257km (159 miles) W of Venice, 140km (87 miles) NE of Turin, 142km (88 miles) N of Genoa

True, Italy's financial center, business hub, fashion capital, and one of the world's most industrialized major cities is crowded, noisy, hot in the summer and damp and foggy in the winter, less easygoing and more expensive than other Italian places—in short, not as immediately appealing a stopover as Venice, Florence, or Rome.

Milan, though, reveals its long and event-filled history in a pride of monuments, museums, and churches. It sets one of the finest tables in Italy, features art by such towering geniuses as Michelangelo (his final sculpture) and Leonardo da Vinci *(Last Supper),* and supports a cultural scene that embraces La Scala, fashion shows, and nightlife. With its dazzling shop windows and sophisticated ways, Milan is a pleasure to get to know—and, despite all that's been said about the city's exorbitant prices, you needn't empty the bank account to do so.

FESTIVALS & MARKETS   Though it's overshadowed by the goings-on in Venice, Milan's pre-Lenten **Carnevale** is becoming increasingly popular, with costumed parades and an easygoing good time, much of it focusing around Piazza del Duomo beginning a week or so before Ash Wednesday. Just before the city shuts down in August, the city council stages a series of June and July **dance, theater, and music events** in theaters and open-air venues around the city; call ℭ **02-8646-4094** for more information.

In a city as well dressed as Milan, it only stands to reason that some great-looking castoffs are bound to turn up at **street markets.** Milan's largest street market is the one held on Via Papiniano in the Ticinese/Navigli district on Tuesday mornings from 8am to 1pm and on Saturdays from 9am to 7:30pm; many of the stalls sell designer seconds as well as barely used high-fashion ware (Metro: Sant'Agostino).

There's an **antiques market** on Via Fiori Chiari in the Brera district the third Saturday of each month, from 9am to about 7:30pm, but not in August (Metro: Moscova), and another the last Sunday of each month on the quays along the Canale Grande in the Navigli district, from 9am to about 7:30pm (ℭ **02-8940-9971;** Metro: Sant'Agostino).

Every Sunday morning there's a large **flea market,** with everything from books to clothing to appliances, at the San Donato metro stop. A fascinating array of handicrafts, from different regions of Italy and around the world, is on sale at the market around Viale Tunisia, Tuesday through Sunday from 9:30am to 1pm and 3 to 7:30pm (ℭ **02-2940-8057;** Metro: Porta Venezia).

The city's largest **food market** is the one at Piazza Wagner, just outside the city center due west of the church of Santa Maria delle Grazie (follow Corso Magenta and its extension, Corso Vercelli to Piazza Piemonte; the market is 1 block north); it's held Monday through Saturday from 8am to 1pm and Tuesday through Saturday from 4 to 7:30pm; the displays of mouthwatering foodstuffs fill an indoor market space and stalls that surround it (Metro: Piazza Wagner).

ESSENTIALS
GETTING THERE   By Train   Milan is one of Europe's busiest rail hubs, with connections to all major cities on the Continent. Trains arrive and depart about every half-hour to and from Venice (3 hr.), hourly to and from Rome (5 hr.), and hourly to and from Florence (3 hr.). **Stazione Centrale,** a vast structure of Fascist-era design, is about a half-hour walk northeast of the center, with easy connections to Piazza del Duomo by metro, tram, and bus. The station stop on the metro is Centrale F.S.; it is only 10 minutes (and 1€/$1.15) away from the Duomo stop, in the heart of the city. If you want to see something of the city en route, take the no. 60 bus from the station to Piazza del Duomo. If you decide to walk (a good half-hour), follow Via Pisani through the soulless district of high-rise office buildings that have sprung up around the station in the past several decades to the equally cheerless Piazza della Repubblica, and from there continue south on busy Via Turati and Via Manzoni to Piazza del Duomo.

Chances are you will arrive at Stazione Centrale, but some trains serve Milan's other train stations: **Stazione Nord** (with service to and from Como, among

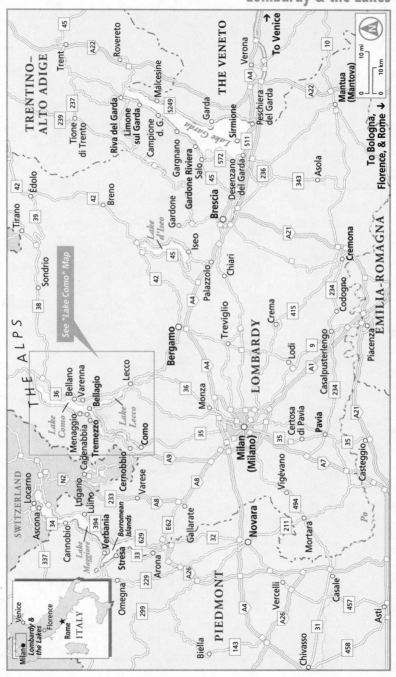

Milan (Milano)

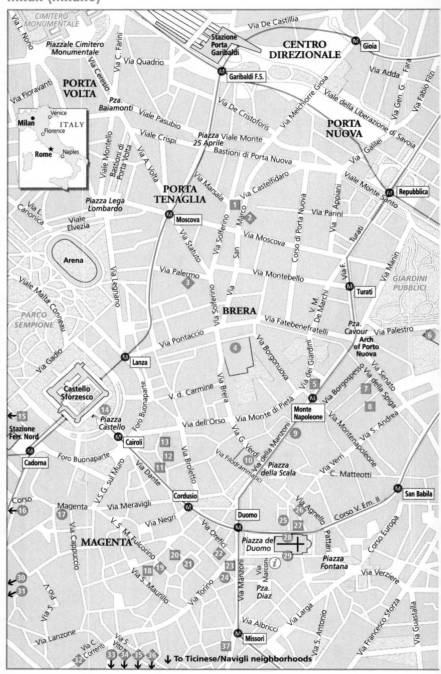

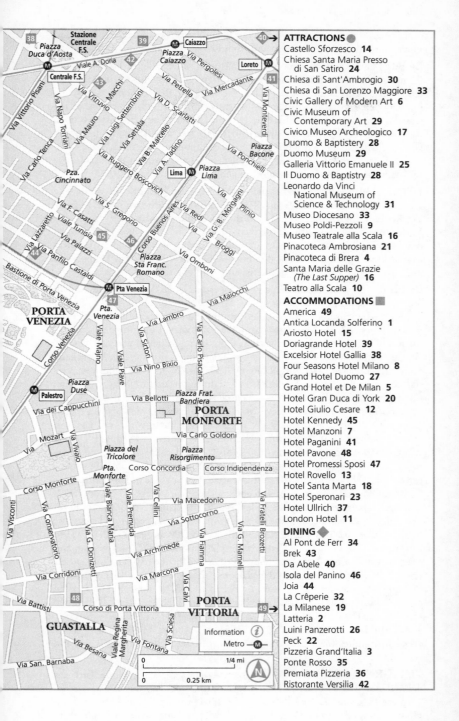

259

other cities), **Porta Genova** (with service to and from Alessandria and Asti), and **Porta Garibaldi** (with service to and from Lecco).

By Bus   Given Milan's excellent rail links with other cities in Lombardy and throughout Italy, it's usually unnecessary to travel by long-distance buses, which tend to take longer and cost more than the trains do. If you choose to travel by intercity bus, expect to arrive at and depart from Autostradale, in front of the Castello Sforzesco on Piazza Castello (Metro: Cairoli). The ticket office is open daily 6:30am to 9:30pm (✆ **166-845-010** is a special toll number for which you are charged .30€/35¢ a minute). A few common runs are the 12 daily buses to and from Turin (2½ hr.) and, for Milanese ski and outdoor enthusiasts, the two daily buses (more in the winter) to and from Aosta (allow 3½ hr.).

By Car   Milan is well served by Italy's superhighway (autostrada) system. The A1 links Milan with Florence and Rome (Florence is a little over 3 hr. away by car, Rome is a little under 6 hr.), and the A4 connects Milan with Verona and Venice to the east and Turin to the west (Venice is about 2½ hr. from Milan by car, Turin is a little over 1 hr.). Driving and parking in Milan are not experiences to be relished; in fact, much of the central city is closed to traffic. Many hotels make parking arrangements for guests; ask when you reserve a room.

By Plane   Both of Milan's airports are operated by **SEA** (✆ **02-7485-2200;** www.sea-aeroportimilano.it).

   Milan Malpensa, 45km (28 miles) west of the center, is Milan's new international airport. It has been crowned worst major airport in Europe by the continent's official oversight committee in terms of flight delays and convenience (it's far from the city, and the rail link wasn't ready until last year). For general information, call ✆ **02-7485-2200** or 02-7680-0613. A 40-minute express train heads half-hourly to Cadorna train station in western Milan rather than the larger and more central Stazione Centrale from which most trains onward to other northern Italian points leave (you'll have to take the Metro to get there). More convenient, perhaps, are the Malpensa shuttle buses, which will take you directly to that central downtown rail station. Your choices are Malpensa Express (✆ **02-9619-2301**), which costs 5.50€ ($6.35), or the cheaper Malpensa Shuttle (✆ **02-5858-3185**)—same service, different price: 4.50€ ($5.15)—two to three times per hour for the 50-minute ride to the east side of Milan's Stazione Centrale. The trip into town by taxi costs a whopping 60€ to 75€ ($69–$86).

   Milan Linate, only 7km (4¼ miles) east of the center, handles some European flights (which are increasingly being moved to Malpensa) and domestic flights. Call ✆ **02-7485-2200** for information. **STAM buses** (✆ **02-717-100**) run from Linate to Stazione Centrale every 20 minutes from 7am to 7pm and every half-hour from 7 to 9pm; allow 20 minutes for the trip. Purchase tickets (2€/$2.30) on the bus or from the Malpensa Shuttle terminal at the east end of Stazione Centrale. You can also take a city bus, no. 73, to and from Linate, from the southeast corner of Piazza San Babila, a few blocks east of the Duomo (1€/$1.15). The trip into town by taxi costs about 12€ to 18€ ($14–$21).

   Air Pullman buses (✆ **02-5858-3185**) also connect Malpensa and Linate every 90 minutes from 6am to 8pm. The trip takes 1 hour 15 minutes and costs 8€ ($9).

VISITOR INFORMATION   The main **Azienda di Promozione Turistica del Milanese (APT) tourist office** is in the Palazzo del Turismo at Via Marconi 1 on the Piazza del Duomo (✆ **02-7252-4301;** www.milanoinfotourist.com). Hours are Monday to Friday from 8:30am to 8pm, Saturday from 9am to 1pm

Bus Tours

Autostradale (✆ **02-3391-0794;** www.autostradale.com/altre/girocitt.htm) runs a 3-hour bus tour of Milan's major sights, including the *Last Supper* (admission is covered), which leaves daily at 9:30am from Piazza Duomo at the corner with Via Marconi. It costs 40€ ($46).

and 2 to 7pm, Sunday from 9am to 1pm and 2 to 5pm. There is also an **office in Stazione Centrale** (✆ **02-7252-4360**), open Monday to Friday 8am to 7pm, Saturday 9am to 6pm and Sunday 9am to 12:30pm and 1:30 to 6pm.

These offices issue maps, museum guides, hotel and restaurant listings, and a wealth of other useful information, but since they're now privately run, they charge nominal fees for most of the more useful pamphlets, including 1€ ($1.15) for *Milano: Where, When, How.* Monthly events brochure *Milano Mese,* and *Hello Milano* (www.hellomilano.it), both with extensive listings of museum exhibitions, performances, and other events, are still free.

CITY LAYOUT   Think of Milan as a series of concentric circles radiating from the Piazza del Duomo at the center. Within the inner circle, once enclosed by the city walls, are many of the churches, museums, and shops that will consume your visiting hours. For a general overview of the lay of the land, obtain one of the serviceable maps, with indices, that the tourist offices provide for free.

The city's major neighborhoods encircle the hub, **Piazza del Duomo.** Looking west from the Duomo, you can see the imposing **Castello Sforzesco** at one end of the well-heeled Magenta neighborhood. You can walk to the Castello in about 15 minutes by following Via Orefici to Piazza Cordusio and from there, Via Dante. The other major tourist draw in Magenta is the church of **Santa Maria delle Grazie;** to reach it, you'll leave Via Dante at Via Meravigli, which becomes Corso Magenta and leads to the church (total walking time from Piazza del Duomo to the church is about 20 min.).

Heading north from the Piazza del Duomo, walk through the city's glass-enclosed shopping center (the world's 1st), the **Galleria Vittorio Emanuele II.** Emerging from the northern end of the Galleria you'll be just steps away from **Piazza della Scala** and Milan's famous **opera house.** A walk northeast of about 5 minutes along Via Manzoni takes you to Via Montenapoleone and the city's **high-fashion shopping district,** the epicenter of Italian design. A walk of about 10 minutes north of Piazza della Scala along Via Brera brings you into the atmospheric **Brera neighborhood,** where cobblestone streets and old palazzos surround the city's major art collection, the **Pinacoteca di Brera.**

Another neighborhood to set your sights on is **Ticinese/Navigli,** usually referred to by the last word in that combination, which translates as "canals." Beyond the central city and due south of Piazza del Duomo, the Navigli's old quays follow what remains of an elaborate canal system, designed in part by Leonardo da Vinci, that once laced through the city. The moody charm of these waterways is not lost on prosperous young Milanese who are converting old lofts and moving into former quarters of the working classes. The attendant bars, shops, and restaurants on the ground floors have appeared to serve their needs, making this a great neighborhood to head to for dinner and then stay for the nightlife (it's also the only bit of town open through Aug, when cars are banned and all the eateries and bars move tables outside to fill the cobblestone quays). You can walk to the Navigli in about 30 minutes from Piazza del Duomo by following Via

Torino southwest to Corso Porta Ticinese, but a metro ride to Porta Genova will get you there more quickly.

Despite Milan's size and sprawl, many of its museums, churches, and other sights are within easy walking distance of one another in the vicinity of the Duomo and Castello Sforzesco.

GETTING AROUND   An extensive and efficient **subway system (Metropolitana Milanese), trams,** and **buses** make it very easy to move around Milan. The metro closes at midnight, though buses and trams run all night. Tickets good for one metro ride (or 75 min. of surface transportation) cost 1€ ($1.15). You can also purchase a ticket good for unlimited travel for 1 day (3€/$3.45) or 2 days (5.50€/$6). Tickets are available at metro stations and at newsstands. It's obligatory to stamp your ticket when you board a bus or tram—you can be slapped with a hefty fine if you don't. For information about Milan public transportation, visit the ATM information office in the Duomo metro stop, open Monday through Friday 8:30am to 8pm, weekends 9am to 1pm and 2 to 7pm (until 5pm Sun) (✆ **02-7252-4301** or 800-808-181; www.atm-mi.it).

FAST FACTS: **Milan**

American Express   The office is just north of La Scala and near the Pinacoteca di Brera at Via Brera 3, on the corner with Via dell'Orso (✆ **02-876-674**), and is open Monday to Friday from 9am to 5:30pm, Saturday from 9am to 5pm (Metro: Cairoli). Card members can arrange cash advances, receive mail (the postal code is 20121), and wire money.

Bookstores   Milan has two English-language bookshops. The **American Bookstore,** between the Duomo and Castello Sforzesco at Via Camperio 16 at the corner with Via Dante (✆ **02-878-920**), is open Monday 1 to 7pm, Tuesday to Saturday 10am to 7pm (Metro: Cardusio). The **English Bookshop,** Via Ariosto at Via Mascheroni 12 (✆ **02-469-4468**), is open Monday to Saturday 9am to 8pm. **Rizzoli,** the glamorous outlet of one of Italy's leading publishers, in the Galleria Vittorio Emanuele (✆ **02-8646-1071**), also has some English-language titles, as well as a sumptuous collection of art and photo books; open daily 8am to 8pm. For English-language newspapers and magazines, check out the **newsstands** in Stazione Centrale and around Piazza del Duomo.

Consulates   The **U.S. Consulate** is at Via Principe Amadeo 2/10, ✆ **02-290-351;** it's open Monday through Friday from 9 to 11am and 2 to 4pm (Metro: Turati). The **Canadian Consulate** at Via Pisani 19, ✆ **02-675-81,** is open Monday to Thursday 8:30am to 12:30pm and 1:15 to 5:30pm (Metro: F.S. Centrale or Repubblica); the **British Consulate,** Via San Paolo 7, ✆ **02-230-01,** is open Monday to Friday from 9:15am to 12:15pm and 2:30 to 4:30pm (Metro: Duomo); the **Australian Consulate** at Via Borgogna 2, ✆ **02-777-041,** is open Monday to Thursday 9am to noon and 2 to 4pm (Metro: San Babila); and the **New Zealand Consulate** at Via Arezzo 6, ✆ **02-4801-2544,** is open Monday to Friday from 9am to 11am (Metro: Pagano).

Crime   For police emergencies dial ✆ **113** (a free call); you can reach the English-speaking staff of the tourist police at ✆ **02-863-701.** There is a police station in Stazione Centrale and the main station, the **Questura,** is just west of the Giardini Pubblici at Via Fatebenefratelli 11, ✆ **02-622-61**

(Metro: Turati). Milan is generally safe, with some notable exceptions, especially at night, including the public gardens, Parco Sempione, and the area to the west of Stazione Centrale. The train station is notorious for pickpockets, whose favorite victims seems to be distracted passengers lining up for the airport buses at the east side of the building. You should likewise be vigilant for pickpockets on all public transportation and at street markets.

Drugstores Pharmacies rotate 24-hr. shifts; dial Ⓒ **192** to find pharmacies that are open around the clock on a given day or look for signs posted in most pharmacies announcing which shop is keeping a 24-hr. schedule. The **Farmacia Stazione Centrale** (Ⓒ **02-669-0935**), in the main train station, is open 24 hours daily and some of the staff speaks English.

Emergencies The general number for emergencies is Ⓒ **113.** For the police, call Ⓒ **112;** for first aid or an ambulance, dial Ⓒ **118.** These are all free calls.

Hospitals The **Ospedale Maggiore Policlinico,** Ⓒ **02-556-812,** is centrally located a 5-minute walk southeast of the Duomo at Via Francesco Sforza 35 (Metro: Duomo or Missori). Some of the medical personnel here speaks English.

Internet In August 2003, **easyInternetCafé** (www.easyinternetcafe.it) opened a shop with 60 PCs next to the Virgin Megastore bang in the center of town at Piazza Duomo 8. It's open daily from 10am to midnight, and while charges were still being worked out at press time, expect the costs to be as insanely cheap as at other franchises in this chain (on the order of 2€/$2.30 for a full-day pass).

Laundry A handy place to have your clothes laundered is **Minola,** south of the Duomo at Via San Vito 5 (follow Via Torino from the Piazza del Duomo for about 5 blocks where it intersects with Via San Vito), Ⓒ **02-5811-1271** (Metro: Missori). The staff will do your laundry (wash and dry) for 10€ ($12) per 5kg (11lb.) and dry cleaning for 12€ ($14) per 5kg (11lb.). Open Monday to Friday from 8am to 6pm and Saturday from 8am to noon.

Lost Property The lost baggage number for **Aeroporto della Malpensa** is Ⓒ **02-7485-4215.** For **Aeroporto Linate** the number is Ⓒ **02-7010-2094.** The English-speaking staff at these offices handle luggage that has gone astray on most airlines serving the airports, though a few airlines maintain their own lost baggage services. The **lost and found at Stazione Centrale** (located in the same office as the luggage storage) is open daily from 7am to 1pm and 2 to 8pm, Ⓒ **6371-2667.** The **city-run lost-and-found office** is just south of Piazza del Duomo at Via Friuli 30, Ⓒ **02-551 6141,** and is open Monday to Friday 8:30am to 12:45pm and 2:15 to 5pm (Metro: Duomo or Missori).

Luggage Storage The luggage storage office in Stazione Central is open daily from 5am to 4am; the fee is 2.60€ ($3) per piece of baggage for each 12-hour period.

Post Office The main post office, **Poste e Telecommunicazioni,** is just west of Piazza del Duomo at Via Cordusio 4, Ⓒ **02-805-6812** (Metro: Cardusio). Windows are open Monday to Friday 8:30am to 5:30pm and Saturday 8:30am to 1:50pm. Most branch offices are open Monday to Saturday 8:30am to 1:30pm. There is a post office in Stazione Centrale, open Monday through Friday 8:15am to 5:30pm and Saturday 8:15am to 3:30pm.

Taxis To find a taxi in Milan, walk to the nearest taxi stand, usually located near major piazzas and major Metro stops. In the center, there are taxi stands at Piazza Duomo and Piazza della Scala. Or, call a **radio taxi** at © **02-4040, 02-6767, 02-8585, 02-5353, or 02-8383** (the desk staff at many hotels will be happy to do this for you, even if you are not a guest). Cab meters start at 3.10€ ($3.55), and add a nighttime surcharge of 3.10€ ($3.55) and a Sunday surcharge of 1.55€ ($1.35).

Telephones You'll find public telephones throughout Milan. Local calls cost .10€ (12¢), and the phones accept coins or phone cards *(carta telefonica)*, which you can purchase at tobacco shops in denominations of 1€ ($1.15) to 7.50€ ($9). You can also make calls from the SIP/Telecom office in Stazione Centrale, open daily from 8am to 9:30pm, and the one in the Galleria Vittorio Emanuele, open daily from 8am to 9:30pm. Some phones in these offices also accept major credit cards, and you can buy Italian phone cards on the premises. The area code for Milan is © **02.**

Travel Services For budget travel options, including low-cost flights, contact **CIS,** in the Galleria Vittorio Emanuele (© **02-863-701**), open Monday through Friday from 9am to 7pm, Saturday from 9am to 1pm and 2 to 6pm. Students and those under 25 should try **CTS** (Centro Turistico Studentesco), Via S. Antonio 2 (© **02-5830-4121**), open Monday through Friday from 9:30am to 1pm and 2 to 6pm (no lunchtime closing June–Aug) and Saturday from 9:30am to noon.

WHAT TO SEE & DO
THE TOP SIGHTS

Duomo ★★★   When Milanese think something is taking too long, they refer to it as *la fabricca del duomo*—the making of the Duomo, a reference to the 5 centuries it took to complete the magnificent Gothic cathedral that rises from the center of the city. The last of Italy's great Gothic structures—begun by the ruling Visconti family in 1386—is the fourth-largest church in the world (after St. Peter's in Rome, Seville's cathedral, and a new one on the Ivory Coast), with 135 marble spires, a stunning triangular facade, and 3,400-some statues flanking the massive but airy, almost fanciful exterior.

The cavernous **interior,** lit by brilliant stained-glass windows, seats 40,000 but is unusually spartan and serene, divided into five aisles by a sea of 52 columns. The poet Shelley used to sit and read Dante here amid monuments that include a gruesomely graphic statue of *St. Bartholomew Flayed* ★ and the tombs of Giacomo de Medici, two Visconti, and many cardinals and archbishops. Another British visitor, Alfred, Lord Tennyson, rhapsodized about the **view** of the Alps from the **roof** ★★★ (elevators on the church's exterior northeast corner; stairs on the exterior north side), where you get to wander amidst the Gothic pinnacles, saintly statues, and flying buttresses. You are joined high above Milan by the spire-top gold statue of *Madonnina* (the little Madonna), the city's beloved protectress.

Back on terra firma, the **crypt** contains the remains of San Carlo Borromeo, one of the early cardinals of Milan. A far more interesting descent is the one down the staircase to the right of the main entrance to the **Battistero Paleocristiano,** the ruins of a 4th-century baptistery believed to be where Saint Ambrose baptized Saint Augustine.

Milan in a Day

For an excellent overview of the city, hop aboard **tram no. 20,** distinguished by CIAO MILANO emblazoned on its sides, for a tour with commentary in English and five other languages. The 1 hour and 45-minute tours run daily at 11am and 1pm (also 3pm in summer) and start at Piazza Castello (Metro: Cairoli); the cost is 20€ ($23). For more information, call ℂ **02-3391-0794.**

You can rent an **audio guide** wand that covers the interior and the crypt for 2.60€ ($3), or 2.05€ ($2.35) per person for two or more people.

The Duomo houses many of its treasures across the piazza from the right transept in the **Museo del Duomo** section of Milan's Palazzo Reale. Among the legions of statuary saints there is a gem of a painting by Jacopo Tintoretto, *Christ at the Temple,* and some riveting displays chronicling the construction of the cathedral. Adjoining this is the **Museo Civico d'Arte Contemporanea** (with works by living artists and such masters as De Chirico and Modigliani).

Piazza del Duomo. ℂ **02-860-358** or 02-8646-3456. Duomo: Free admission, daily 6:50am–7pm. Roof: Admission 3.50€ ($4.05), 5€ ($6) with elevator; daily 7am–7pm. Crypt: Admission 1.55€ ($1.75), daily 9am–noon and 2:30–6pm. Baptistery: Admission 1.55€ ($1.80), Tues–Sun 10am–noon and 3–5pm. Museum: Admission 6€ ($6.90) adults, 3€ ($3.45) children under 18 and seniors over 65; Combination ticket for museum and elevator to roof 7€ ($8.05); Tues–Sun 9:30am–12:30pm and 3–6pm. Metro: Duomo.

Galleria Vittorio Emanuele II ★★   Milan's late-19th-century version of a mall is this wonderful steel-and-glass-covered, cross-shaped arcade. The elegant Galleria is the prototype of the enclosed shopping malls that were to become the hallmark of 20th-century consumerism. It's safe to say that none of the imitators have come close to matching the Galleria for style and flair. The designer of this urban marvel, Giuseppe Mengoni, didn't live to see the Milanese embrace his creation: He tripped and fell from a girder a few days before the Galleria opened in 1878. His shopping mall par excellence provides a lovely route between the Duomo and La Scala and is a fine locale for watching the flocks of well-dressed Milanese—you'll understand why the Galleria is called *Il Salotto di Milano* (the drawing room of Milan).

Just off Piazza del Duomo and Piazza della Scala. Metro: Duomo.

Pinacoteca di Brera ★★★   This 17th-century palazzo houses one of Italy's finest collections of medieval and Renaissance art; it's inarguably the world's finest collection of northern Italian painting. The concentration of so many masterpieces here is the work of Napoléon, who used the palazzo as the repository for the art he confiscated from public and private holdings throughout northern Italy; fittingly, a bronze likeness of the emperor greets you upon entering the courtyard. Just as a sampling of what you'll encounter in these 40 or so rooms, three of Italy's greatest masterpieces hang here: Andrea Mantegna's amazingly foreshortened *Dead Christ* ★★★, Raphael's *Betrothal of the Virgin* ★★, and Piero della Francesca's *Madonna with Saints* (the *Montefeltro Altarpiece*) ★★. It is an indication of this museum's ability to overwhelm visitors that the last two absolute masterpieces hang near each other in a single room dedicated to works by Tuscan and Umbrian painters.

Paintings are continually being rearranged, but in the wake of a recently completed renovation, in the first rooms you will not encounter Napoleonic bounty but the museum's sizeable collection of 20th-century paintings. From there you enter several galleries of sumptuous Venetian works, including Jacopo Tintoretto's *Finding of the Body of St. Mark* ★, in which the dead saint eerily confronts appropriately startled grave robbers who come upon his corpse. Caravaggio (*Supper at Emmaus* ★★ is his masterpiece here) is surrounded by works of his followers, and just beyond is a room devoted to works by foreigners; among them Rembrandt's *Portrait of a Young Woman*. Given Napoléon's fondness for the Venetian schools, it is only just that the final rooms are again filled with works from that city, including Canaletto's *View of the Grand Canal*.

You can rent an audio guide for 3.50€ ($4.05), 5.50€ ($6) for two. Cheap guided tours are available weekdays if you book at least 2 to 3 days ahead (they'll do it even for just one person), Saturdays at 3pm and 5pm, Sundays at 10am, noon, 3pm, and 5pm.

Via Brera 28. (℣ **02-722-631** or 02-8942-1146 (for reservations). www.brera.beniculturali.it. Admission 6.20€ ($7.15). Tues–Sun 8:30am–7:30pm. Metro: Lanza or Montenapoleone. Tram: 1, 4, 8, 12, 14, or 27. Bus: 61 or 97.

Santa Maria delle Grazie/The *Last Supper* ★★   What draws so many visitors to Milan in the first place is the *Cenacolo Vinciano,* Leonardo da Vinci's *Last Supper.* From 1495 to 1497 Leonardo painted this poignant portrayal of confusion and betrayal for the far wall of the refectory when this was a Dominican convent. Aldous Huxley called this fresco the "saddest work of art in the world," a comment in part on the deterioration that set in even before the paint had dried on the moisture-ridden walls. The fresco got a lot of well-intentioned but poorly executed "touching up" in the 18th and 19th centuries, though a recent lengthy restoration has done away with these centuries of overpainting, as well as tried to undo the damage wrought by the clumsy patching and damage inflicted when Napoléon's troops used the wall for target practice, and from when Allied bombing during World War II tore off the room's roof, leaving the fresco exposed to the elements for 3 years.

In short, the *Last Supper* is a mere shadow of the work the artist intended it to be, but the work, which captures the moment when Christ told his Apostles that one of them would betray him, remains amazingly powerful and emotional nonetheless. Only 25 people are allowed to view the fresco at one time, and they must pass through a series of devices that remove pollutants from clothing. Accordingly, lines are long and tickets usually sold out days in advance. I'm serious: if you don't book ahead, you'll likely be turned away at the door, even in the dead of winter when you'd expect the place to be empty (tour bus groups swallow up inordinately large batches of tickets, leaving precious few for we poor do-it-yourself travelers).

Often overlooked are the other great treasures of the late-15th-century church itself, foremost among them the fine dome and other architectural innovations by one of the great architects of the high Renaissance, Donato Bramante (one of the 1st architects of St. Peter's in Rome). To one side of the apse, decorated in marble and terra cotta, is a lovely cloister.

Piazza Santa Maria delle Grazie. *Last Supper:* (℣ **02-8942-1146.** www.cenacolovinciano.it. Admission 6.50€ ($7.50) plus a booking fee of 1€ ($1.15). Tues–Sun 8am–7:30pm (may close at 1:45pm in winter). *Church:* (℣ **02-467-6111.** Free admission. Mon–Sat 7:30am–noon and 3–7pm, Sun 7:20am–12:15pm and 3:30–9pm (may close earlier in winter). Metro: Cardona or Conciliazione.

Castello Sforzesco ★★ *Value*   Though it's been clumsily restored many times, most recently at the end of the 19th century, this fortresslike castle continues to evoke Milan's two most powerful medieval and Renaissance families, the Visconti and the Sforza. The Visconti built the castle in the 14th century and the Sforza, who married into the Visconti clan and eclipsed them in power, reconstructed it in 1450. The most influential residents were Ludovico il Moro and Beatrice d'Este (he of the Sforza and she of the famous Este family of Ferrara). After ill-advisedly calling the French into Italy at the end of the 15th century, Ludovico died in the dungeons of a château in the Loire valley—but not before the couple made the Castello and Milan one of Italy's great centers of the Renaissance. It was they who commissioned the works by Bramante and Leonardo da Vinci, and these splendors can be viewed on a stroll through the miles of salons that surround the Castello's enormous courtyard.

The salons house a series of small city-administered museums known collectively as the Civici Musei Castello Sforzesco. They include a *pinacoteca* with works by Bellini, Correggio, and Magenta, and the extensive holdings of the Museo d'Arte Antica, filled with Egyptian funerary objects, prehistoric finds from Lombardy, and the last work of 89-year-old Michelangelo, his unfinished ***Rondanini Pietà*** 😖😖.

Piazza Castello. 📞 **02-6208-3940.** Free admission. Tues–Sun 9:30am–5:30pm. Metro: Cairoli, Cadorna, or Lanza.

MORE SIGHTS

Chiesa di San Lorenzo Maggiore 😖   The oldest church in Milan attests to the days when the city was the capital of the Western Roman Empire. This 4th-century early Christian structure has been rebuilt and altered many times over the centuries (its dome, the highest in Milan, is a 16th-century embellishment), but it still retains the flavor of its roots in its octagonal floor plan and a few surviving remnants. These include 5th-century mosaics (one depicting a beardless Christ) in the Cappella di Sant'Aquilino, which you enter from the atrium. A sarcophagus in the chapel is said to enshrine the remains of Galla Placidia, sister of Honorius, last emperor of Rome and wife of Ataulf, king of the Visigoths. Ironically, her mausoleum is one of the mosaic masterworks of Ravenna, and it is most likely she is buried in Rome, where she died. You'll be rewarded with a glimpse at even earlier history if you follow the stairs from behind the altar to a crypt-like room that contains what remains of a Roman amphitheater.

Corso di Porta Ticinese 39. No phone. www.sanlorenzomaggiore.com. Admission 2€ ($2.30) adults, 1€ ($1.15) children. Mon–Sat 8am–12:30pm and 2–6:30pm; Sun 10:30–11:15am and 3–5:30pm. Metro: Missori. Tram: 3. Bus: 94.

Chiesa di Sant'Ambrogio 😖   From the basilica that he constructed on this site in the 4th century A.D.—when he was bishop of Milan and the city, in turn, was briefly capital of the Western Roman Empire—Saint Ambrose had a profound effect on the development of the early church. Little remains of Ambrose's church, but the 11th-century structure built in its place, and renovated many times since, is remarkable. It has a striking atrium, lined with columned porticos and opening on the side to the brick facade, with two ranks of loggias and, on either side, a bell tower. Look carefully at the door on the left, where you'll see a relief of Saint Ambrose. Note the overall effect of this architectural assemblage, because the church of Sant'Ambrogio set a standard for Lombard Romanesque architecture that you'll see imitated many times on your travels through Lombardy.

On your wanderings through the three-aisled nave you'll come upon a gold altar from Charlemagne's days in Milan, and, in the right aisle, the all-too-scant remains of a Tiepolo fresco cycle, most of it blown into oblivion by World War II bombs. The little that remains of the original church is the Sacello di San Vittore in Ciel d'Oro, a little chapel in which the cupola glows with 5th-century mosaics of saints (enter from the right aisle). The skeletal remains of Ambrose himself are on view in the crypt. One of the "later" additions as you leave the main church from the left aisle is another work of the great architect Bramante—his Portico dell Canonica, lined with elegant columns, some of which are sculpted to resemble tree trunks.

Piazza Sant'Ambrogio 15. ⓒ 02-8645-0895. Church: Free admission. Sacello di San Vittore: 2€ ($2.30). Mon–Sat 9:30am–noon and 2:30–6pm. Metro: Sant'Ambrogio. Bus: 50, 58, or 94.

Chiesa Santa Maria Presso di San Satiro   What makes this beautiful church, just south of Piazza del Duomo, so exquisite is what it doesn't have— space. Stymied by not being able to expand the T-shaped apse to classical Renaissance, cross-shaped proportions, the architect Bramante created a marvelous relief behind the high altar. The effect of the trompe l'oeil columns and arches is not entirely convincing but nonetheless magical. Another gem lies to the rear of the left transept: the Cappella della Pietà, so called for the 15th-century terracotta *Pietà* it now houses but built in the 9th century to honor Saint Satiro, the brother of Saint Ambrose. The namesake statue is not the most alluring adornment in this charming little structure; it's the lovely Byzantine frescoes and Romanesque columns that will catch your eye. While this little-visited complex is now eclipsed by other, more famous Milan churches, it was an important pilgrimage site in the 13th and 14th centuries, after news spread through Christendom that an image of the Madonna here shed real blood when stabbed.

Via Torino (at Via Speronari). Free admission. Daily 9am–noon and 2:30–6pm. Metro: Duomo or Missori.

Civica Galleria d'Arte Moderna (Civic Gallery of Modern Art)   This sumptuous palazzo, where Napoléon and his stepson Eugene de Beauharnais lived, houses a collection that is "modern" in the true 19th-century sense. The salons are filled with works by Lombardians and other Italian painters who embraced trends from France. You'll probably be more familiar with the works by Cézanne, Gauguin, and other non-Italian modernists also included in the galleries (in a section housing the noted Grassi Collection), but it's fascinating to see the same dreamy landscapes and the flight from creeping industrialism reflected in the works of lesser-known Italian artists. The upper floors of the museum house the equestrian works of 20th-century sculptor Marino Marini.

In the Villa Reale. Via Palestro 16. ⓒ 02-7600-2819. Free admission. Daily 9:30am–5:30pm. Metro: Porta Venezia.

Civico Museo Archeologico ⭐ *Value*   The most fascinating finds in this sizable repository of civilizations past are the everyday items from Milan's Roman era— tools, eating utensils, jewelry, and some exquisite and remarkably well-preserved glassware. The exhibits, which seem to fill every corner of the 16th-century monastery in which the museum is housed, also include Greek, Etruscan, and Roman pieces from throughout Italy; there's even a section devoted to ancient remains from Ghandara, India. You can get a glimpse of Roman architecture in the garden, where two Roman towers and a section of a road, part of the walls enclosing the settlement of Mediolanum, once capital of the Western Roman Empire, remain on their original setting. Rarely in Italy do museums this good (even if the collections are relatively modest in size) come free, so take full advantage.

Corso Magenta 15. ⓒ 02-8645-0011. Free admission. Tues–Sun 9:30am–5:30pm. Metro: Cadorna.

Combo Ticket

There is a combination ticket for admission to the Pinacoteca Ambrosiana, Museo del Duomo, and the new Museo Diocesano that costs 12€ ($14). It can be purchased at any of the participating museums.

Museo Diocesano ★ *Finds*   This museum, set just inside the Parco delle Basiliche—a collection of grass-fringed paths, playgrounds, and volleyball courts created just after World War II on the site of Milan's ancient execution grounds—opened in November 2001. It brings together the best works from small church museums and treasuries across Milan and Lombardy, from the Church of Sant'Ambrogio on down, alongside works of religious significance donated from various private collections. Among the works from the now-defunct Museo di Sant'Ambrogio is an important 10th-century carved wooden tondo of *S. Ambrogio.*

The Crespi collections include many 14th- and early-15th-century Gothic works by such Tuscan-school masters as Bernardo Daddi, Sano di Pietro, Agnolo Gaddi, Taddeo di Bartolo, Bicci di Lorenzo, and Nardo di Cione. The giant, excellently preserved 1510 altarpiece of saints by Marco d'Oggiono came from the church of S. Stefano.

Other paintings include works by the prolific 16th-century Campi clan of Cremona, a Tintoretto *Christ and the Adulterer,* a luminous *Crucifixion with Mary Magdalene* by Francesco Hayez, many late-15th-century paintings by local boy Il Begognone, 17th- and 18th-century landscapes by Panini, Zuccarelli, and others, and Previati's important Via Crucis cycles from the 1880s. And what would a church museum be without a passel of 17th-century Flemish tapestries?

There are free audio guides in English, and lots of helpful multimedia panels scattered throughout the museum.

Corso di Porta Ticinese 95. (ℭ *02-8940-4714.* www.museodiocesano.it. Admission 6€ ($6.90) adults, 4€ ($4.60) ages 6–18 and over 60. Tues–Sun 10am–6pm (to 10pm Thurs). Metro: Missori or Sant'Ambrogio

Museo Nazionale della Scienza e delle Tecnica Leonardo da Vinci (Leonardo da Vinci National Museum of Science and Technology) ★ The heart and soul of this engaging museum are the **working scale models** ★★ of Leonardo's submarines, airplanes, and other engineering feats that, for the most part, the master only ever invented on paper (each exhibit includes a reproduction of the master's drawings and a model of his creations). This former Benedictine monastery and its beautiful cloisters are also filled with planes, trains, carriages, sewing machines, typewriters, optical devices, and other exhibits, including some enchanting recreations of workshops, that comprise one of the world's leading collections of mechanical and scientific wizardry.

Via San Vittore 21. (ℭ *02-485-551* or 02-4801-0016. www.museoscienza.org. Admission 6.20€ ($7.15) adults, 4.20€ ($4.85) under 18 and over 60. Tues–Fri 9:30am–5pm; Sat–Sun 9:30am–6:30pm. Metro: Sant'Ambrogio.

Museo Poldi-Pezzoli ★★   The pleasant effect of seeing the Bellinis, Botticellis, and Tiepolos amid these salons is reminiscent of a visit to other private collections, such as the Frick Collection in New York City and the Isabella Stewart Gardner Museum in Boston. This stunning treasure trove leans a bit toward Venetian painters (such as Francesco Guardi's elegantly moody *Grey Lagoon*), but also ventures widely throughout Italian painting and into the northern and Flemish schools. It was amassed by 19th-century collector Giacomo Poldi-Pezzoli, who donated his villa and its treasures to the city in 1881. Antonio Pollaiuolo's *Portrait of a Young Woman* is often likened to the *Mona Lisa,* in that it is a haunting image you will recognize immediately upon seeing it. The collections also include porcelain, watches, jewels, and many of the palazzo's original furnishings.

CD-ROM terminals let you explore bits of the collections not currently on display, especially arms and armor, the best of which is housed in an elaborate *pietra serena* room designed by Pomodoro. For now, the museum offers free audio guides (there may be a charge in the future). The admission ticket you buy here will include admission to the Museo Teatrale alla Scala.

Via Manzoni 12. (℃ **02-794-889.** www.museopoldipezzoli.it. Admission 6.20€ ($7.15) adults, 4€ ($4.60) for ages 11–18 and over 60. Tues–Sun 10am–6pm. Metro: Duomo or Montenapoleone. Tram: 2.

Pinacoteca Ambrosiana ★★ Much to the appreciation of art lovers who waited through the late 1990s for the museum to reopen, this exquisite collection is housed in newly restored galleries. The collection focuses on treasures from the 15th through 17th centuries: An *Adoration* by Titian, Raphael's cartoon for his *School of Athens* in the Vatican, Botticelli's *Madonna and Angels,* Caravaggio's *Basket of Fruit* (his only still life), and other stunning works hang in a series of intimate rooms. Notable (or infamous) among the paintings is *Portrait*

'Til the Fat Lady Sings . . . Again: The Restoration of La Scala

Arguably the single most important opera house in the world, Milan's **Teatro alla Scala** ★★ was built in the late 18th century on the site of a church of the same name in Piazza della Scala. La Scala is hallowed ground to lovers of Giuseppe Verdi (who was the house composer for decades), Maria Callas, Arturo Toscanini (conductor for much of the 20th c., a position held since 1970 by Riccardo Muti) and legions of other composers and singers who have hit the high notes of fame in the world's most revered opera house.

Although La Scala emerged from one renovation in 1999, the famed theater went under renovation wraps yet again in 2001, not to return to its duties and the traditional December 7 gala opening night until 2005 at the earliest. In the meantime, the show does go on, as shows must, in custom-built digs called the Teatro degli Arcimboldi (℃ **02-7200-3744;** www.teatroallascala.org) way the heck up in the northern suburb of Bicocca.

The **Museo Teatrale alla Scala,** which is normally part of the La Scala building, is being temporarily housed in a building just beyond the *Last Supper* at Corso Magenta 71 (℃ **02-805-3418**), where you can take a whiff of operatic nostalgia for days gone by amid such mementos as Toscanini's batons, a strand of Mozart's hair, a fine array of Callas postcards, original Verdi scores, a whole mess of historic gramophones and record players, and costumes designed by some of Milan's top fashion gurus and worn by the likes of Callas and Rudolf Nureyev on Las Scala's stage. The museum is open Tuesday to Sunday from 9am to 6pm; admission is 5€ ($5.75), though you can get in free if you have a ticket from the Museo Poldi-Pezzoli (see above).

of a Musician, attributed to Leonardo but, according to many scholars, of dubious provenance; if it is indeed a Leonardo, the haunting painting is the only portrait of his to hang in an Italian museum. The adjoining Biblioteca Ambrosiana, open to scholars only except for special exhibitions, houses a wealth of Renaissance literaria, including the letters of Lucrezia Borgia and a strand of her hair. The most notable holdings, though, are Leonardo's *Codice Atlantico,* 1,750 drawings and jottings the master did between 1478 and 1519. These and the library's other volumes, including a rich collection of medieval manuscripts, are frequently put on view to the public; at these times, an entrance fee of 9€ ($10) allows entrance to both the library and the art gallery.

Piazza Pio XI, 2. (℃ **02-809-921.** www.ambrosiana.it. Admission 7.50€ ($8.60) adults, 4.50€ ($5.20) children. Tues–Sun 10am–5pm. Metro: Cordusio, Duomo.

SHOPPING

The best fashion gazing is to be done along four adjoining streets north of the Duomo known collectively as the **Quadrilatero d'Oro (Golden Quadrilateral): Via Montenapoléone, Della Spiga, Via Borgospesso,** and **Via Sant'Andrea,** lined with Milan's most expensive high-fashion emporia. (To enter this hallowed precinct, follow Via Manzoni a few blocks north from Piazza della Scala; San Babila is the closest metro stop.) The main artery of this shopping heartland is Via Montenapoleone, lined with the chi-chi'est boutiques and most elegant fashion outlets, with parallel Via della Spiga running a close second.

For more down-home shopping with the Milanese, cruise wide Corso Buenos Aires (northeast of the center and just east of Stazione Centrale—follow Via Vitruvio from Piazza Duca d'Aosta in front of the station; Metro stops Lima and Loreto are the gateways to this bargain stretch), home to a little bit of everything from shops that hand-sew men's dress shirts to CD megastores. As it crosses Piazza Oberdan/Piazza Venezia heading south, it becomes Corso Venezia and the stores start moving up the scale.

HIGH FASHION—CLOTHING, ACCESSORIES & SHOES

Milan is home to the flagship stores of a litany of designers: Armani, Krizia, Versace, Ermenegildo Zenga, Missoni, Moschino, Mila Schön, and Trussardi.

With high fashion, chillingly expensive boutiques, and designer labels, it all comes down to personal taste, so I'll just let you know where to find the top names in town (but largely only Italian names—who comes to Milan to shop for Calvin Klein?) and you can steer your shopping cravings whither you will.

One store, though, deserves a visit whether you're into his über-trendy designs or not: The Grand Central of Italian fashion is the new flagship **Armani Megastore,** Via Manzoni 31, near La Scala (℃ **02-7231-8630;** www.armani-viamanzoni31.com; Metro: Montenapoleone). To celebrate 25 years in business in the summer of 2000, Giorgio opened this new flagship store (and offices) covering 8,000 square feet with outlets for his high-fashion creations, the Emporio Armani and Armani Jeans lines, plus the new Armani Casa selection of home furnishings as well as flower, book, and art shops; a high-tech Sony electronics boutique/play center in the basement; and an Emporio Café and branch of New York's Nobu sushi bar.

Other major labels also, of course, have Milan addresses. Here are some of the most popular. **Dolce e Gabbana** carries women's wear at Via della Spiga no. 2 (℃ **02-7600-1155;** www.dolcegabbana.it; Metro: San Babila), menswear nearby at Via della Spiga no. 26 (℃ **02-799-950;** Metro: Montenapoleone), and its youth-oriented fashions at Corso Venezia 7 (℃ **02-7600-4091;** Metro: Palestro).

Etro has its lines of clothing for men and women, along with accessories, at Via Montenapoleone 5 (© 02-7600-5450; www.etro.it; Metro: Montenapoleone), with a discount outlet at Via Spartaco 3.

Ermenegildo Zenga began as a textile house in 1910 (they still weave their own fabrics), and since the late 1960s has turned to making elegant, ready-to-wear men's suits that look custom-tailored, sold in Milan at Via P. Verri 3 (© 02-7600-6437; www.zegna.co.jp; Metro: Montenapoleone or San Babila).

Though in the past few years it is finally starting to go out of fashion, a fur coat has long, long been de rigueur for all Italian women heading out for an evening. Without a doubt, one of Italy's top purveyors of furs is **Fendi,** Via Sant'Andrea 16 (© 02-7602-1617; www.fendi.com; Metro: Montenapoleone or San Babila).

The firm that shod Hollywood's stars during its later golden era, **Ferragamo,** has an outlet for men's shoes at Via Montenapoleone 20 (© 02-7600-3117 or 02-7600-6660; www.ferragamo.it; Metro: Montenapoleone), and women's shoes at Via Montenapoleone 3 (© 02-7600-0054; Metro: Montenapoleone or San Babila).

Gianfranco Ferré sells women's wear and accessories at Via Sant'Andrea 15 (© 02-794-864; www.gianfrancoferre.com; Metro: Montenapoleone or San Babila); the men's lines are at Corso Venezia 6. Florentine leather specialist **Gucci** has a Milan outlet for bags, accessories, and clothing for men and women at Via Montenapoleone 27 (© 02-771-271; Metro: San Babila or Montenapoleone).

Several designer boutiques in Milan are devoted to women's wear, and women's wear only. They include **Krizia,** Via della Spiga 23 (© 02-7600-8429; www.krizia.it; Metro: Montenapoleone or San Babila); **Laura Biagiotti,** Via Borgospesso 19 (© 02-799-659; Metro: Montenapoleone or San Babila); and **Max Mara,** on Corso Vittorio Emanuele where it crosses Galleria de Cristoforis (© 02-7600-8849; Metro: San Babila).

Mila Schön's elegant clothing for women and men is displayed in a neoclassical palazzo, along with accessories, perfumes, and linens, at Via Manzoni 45 (© 02-781-190; www.milaschon.com; Metro: Montenapoleone or San Babila). **Miu Miu** carries women's wear and shoes at Corso Venezia 3 (© 02-7601-4448; www.miumiu.com; Metro: Palestro). **Missoni**'s colorful sweaters for men and women can be found at Via Sant'Andrea at Via Bagutta (© 02-7600-3555; www.missoni.com; Metro: Montenapoleone or San Babila). **Moschino** has men's and children's wear at Via Durini 14 (© 02-7600-4320; Metro: San Babila) and women's wear at Via Sant'Andrea 12 (© 02-7600-0832; www. moschino.com; Metro: Montenapoleone or San Babila).

Prada maintains several outlets across town for its minimalist red-stripe fashions, none of them cheap! There's a bit of everything (men's and women's wear, accessories, and jewelry) in their high-profile boutique at the crossing of the Galleria Vittorio Emanuele 63 (© 02-876-979; www.prada.com; Metro: San Babila); menswear, shoes, and accessories at Via Montenapoleone 8 (© 02-7602-0273; Metro: Montenapoleone or San Babila); women's wear and accessories at Via Sant'Andrea 21 (© 02-7600-1426; Metro: Montenapoleone or San Babila); bags, shoes, and accessories at Via della Spiga 1 (© 02-7600-8636; Metro: Montenapoleone or San Babila); and nearby even an underwear branch at Via della Spiga 5 (© 02-7601-4448; Metro: Montenapoleone or San Babila).

Trussardi sells men's and women's wear as well as accessories at Via Sant'Andrea 5 (© 02-781-878; www.trussardi.com; Metro: Montenapoleone or San Babila). **Ungaro**'s full line of men's and women's wear, accessories, bags, and shoes are at

Via Montenapoleone 27 (© **02-784-256;** www.ungaro.com; Metro: Monte-napoleone or San Babila). **Valentino** menswear is kept at Via Montenapoleone 20 (© **02-7602-0285;** www.valentino.it; Metro: Montenapoleone or San Babila); the women's wear is sold at Via Santo Spirito 3 (© **02-7600-6478;** Metro: Montenapoleone). **Versace** carries its men's and women's wear and accessories in its shop at Via Montenapoleone 11 (© **02-7600-1982;** www.versace.com; Metro: Montenapoleone or San Babila).

DESIGNER DISCOUNTS

If your fashion sense is greater than your credit line, don't despair: Even the most expensive clothing of the Armani ilk is usually less expensive in Italy than it is abroad, and citywide *saldi* (sales) run from early January into early February and again in late June and July.

Inspired by the window displays in the **Quadrilatero,** you can scour the racks of shops elsewhere for designer seconds, last year's fashions, imitations, and other bargains. The best place to begin is **Il Salvagente,** several blocks east of the Quadrilatero off Corso XXII Marzo at Via Fratelli Bronzetti 16 (© **02-7611-0328;** Metro: San Babila), where you can browse through an enormous collection of designer clothing for men, women, and children (mostly smaller sizes) at whole-sale prices. **DMagazine,** Via Montenapoleone 26 (© **02-7600-6027;** Metro: Montenapoleone), may sit on the boutique-lined main shopping drag, but its merchandise is pure discount overstock from big labels such as Armani (I saw slacks for 99€/$114), Prada (how about a sweater for 72€/$83?), and Fendi (designer scarves for 44€/$46 anyone?).

Another haven for bargain hunters is the **Navigli.** Women can shop at **Eliogabaldo,** Piazza Sant'Eustorgio 2 (© **02-837-8293;** Metro: San Agostino), where some of the offerings may be secondhand but only in the sense that a model donned them briefly for a show or shoot. **Biffi,** Corso Genova 6 (© **02-837-5170;** Metro: San Agostino), attracts fashion-conscious hordes of both sexes in search of designer labels and the store's own designs. One more Navigli stop, and again well stocked with designer ware for men and women—but especially dresses (no changing rooms, so come prepared)—is nearby **Floretta Coen Musil,** Via San Calocero 3 (© **02-5811-1708;** Metro: San Agostino), open Monday through Saturday, afternoons only from 3:30 to 7:30pm; no credit cards.

The other hunting ground for discount fashions is **Corso Buenos Aires,** northeast of the center and just east of Stazione Centrale (follow Via Vitruvio from Piazza Duca d'Aosta in front of the station; Metro stops Lima and Loreto are the gateways to this bargain stretch).

Men will want to stop at **Darsena,** Corso Buenos Aires 16 (© **02-2952-1535),** where you just might find an Armani suit or jacket at a rock-bottom price. **Il Drug Store,** Corso Buenos Aires 28 (© **02-2951-5592),** keeps Milanese of both sexes attired, affordably so, in chic clothing best worn by the young and the thin. **Calzaturificio di Parabiago,** Corso Buenos Aires 52 (© **02-2940-6851),** shods men and women fashionably at reasonable prices, with an enormous selection and a helpful staff. For designer shoes at a discount, look no further than **Rufus,** Via Vitruvio 35 (© **02-204-9648),** which carries men's and women's styles from lots of labels for under 80€/$92 (Metro: Centrale F.S. or Lima).

HOUSEWARES

The top name in Italian houseware design since 1921 has been **Alessi,** which just since the late 1980s has hired the likes of Michael Graves, Philippe Starck, Frank Ghery, and Ettore Sottsass to design the latest in tea kettles, bottle openers, and other housewares. They maintain a main showroom at Corso Matteotti 9 (© **02-795-726;** Metro: San Babila) and a sales outlet at Via Montenapoleone 19 (© **02-7602-1199;** www.alessi.com; Metro: Montenapoleone).

The 1980s was really part of a renaissance of Italian industrial design. This is the era when design team **Memphis** led by Ettore Sottsass virtually reinvented the art form, recruiting the best and brightest architects and designers to turn their talents to lighting fixtures, kitchen appliances, office supplies, even furnishings. Italian style has stayed at the very top of the designer housewares market (well, sharing popularity space with Scandinavian furniture) ever since. Part of the Memphis credo was to create the new modern, then bow out before they became establishment, so they self-destructed in 1988. You can still find their influential designs in many houseware shops, and in the showroom at Via della Moscova 27 (© **02-655-4731;** Metro: Turati).

For fine porcelains and ceramics, make a stop at **Richard-Ginori,** the renowned Florentine purveyor of fine china, at Corso Buenos Aires 1 (© **02-2951-6611;** www.richardginori1735.com; Metro: Lima or Loreto); the house's porcelain and crystal, as well as offerings from other manufacturers, is often available at discounted prices.

LINENS

For Milanese design with which to dress the bed and table and not the body, visit **Frette,** Via Visconti di Modrone (© **02-777-091;** www.frette.it; Metro: San Babila). This outlet branch of the high-fashion linen house offers the line of tablecloths, towels, robes, and bedding that it supplies to the world's top hotels at substantial discounts. They have other stores at Via Montenapoleone 21 (© **02-783-950;** Metro: Montenapoleone), Via Manzoni 11 (© **02-864-433;** Metro: Montenapoleone), Corso Buenos Aires 82 (© **02-2940-1072;** Metro: Lima), Corso Vercelli 23/25 (© **02-498-9756;** Metro: Conciliazione), and Via Torino 42 (© **02-8645-2281;** Metro: Duomo).

The elegant swirling paisleys of **Etro,** Via Montenapoleone 5 (© **02-7600-5049;** www.etro.it; Metro: Montenapoleone), have been decorating the walls, furniture covers, and accessories in some of Italy's richest and aristocratic homes since 1969. They've since expanded into full lines of clothing and leather goods, as well as perfumes and accessories (the latter are available at the branch on the corner of Via P. Verri and Via Bigli; © **02-7600-5450;** Metro: Montenapoleone).

Spacci Bassetti, Via Procaccini 32 (© **02-3450-125;** Metro: Garibaldi F.S., but closer on tram 33 or 94), is a discount outlet of the august Bassetti line of high-quality linen, and the huge space offers the luxurious towels and sheets at excellent prices. They have regular (nondiscount) stores at Corso Buenos Aires 52 (© **02-2940-0048;** Metro: Lima) and Via Botta 7A (© **02-5518-3191;** Metro: Porta Romana).

WHERE TO STAY

While you can pay more for a hotel room in Milan than you would almost anywhere else in Europe, there are also some decent accommodations at reasonable prices in good locations. It's difficult to find rooms in any price category when fashion shows and trade fairs are in full swing (often in Oct and Mar). Many hotels raise their prices at these times, too. August is low season, and hotels are often willing to bring prices down considerably, as they will sometimes on slow weekends. Rule of thumb: Always ask for the lowest possible rate when booking and be prepared to bargain.

Inveterate shoppers will want to stay in the Brera/Magenta neighborhood, avid sightseers near the Duomo; budgeters will find the most options near the central train station and along Corso Buenos Aires.

NEAR THE DUOMO
Very Expensive

Grand Hotel Duomo ★★   It's a luxury hotel right on Piazza del Duomo, and the whole point here is to book one of the suites—or one of the few doubles—that overlook the cathedral's pinnacled flank. Rooms are fairly large and comfortably furnished in a modern style. Duplex suites have rattan furnishings in the sitting area and built-in units in the bedroom upstairs. Two pairs of double rooms share common exterior doors so they can be turned into family suites. The hotel has been slowly expanding in the past few years, and there's a new wing of designer apartments and suites inspired by cinema and 20th-century art. Another oddity: The suites and even a few regular rooms come with a few pieces of fitness equipment (mostly an exercise bike; occasionally more).

Via San Raffaele 1/Piazza del Duomo, 20121 Milano. ✆ 02-8833. Fax 02-8645-0454 or 02-8646-2027. www.grandhotelduomo.com. 162 units. 340€–430€ ($391–$495) double; 460€–550€ ($529–$633) jr. suite; 530€–580€ ($610–$667) duplex suite; 740€–800€ ($851–$920) deluxe suite; 70€ ($81) extra bed. Rates include buffet breakfast. AE, DC, MC, V. Valet parking 52€ ($60). Metro: Duomo. **Amenities:** 3 restaurants (all Italian/international, 1 main dinner room, 1 for lunch and quick dishes, 1 intimate); bar; pool; exercise room, and sauna at nearby fitness club; concierge; tour desk; car-rental desk; secretarial services; room service (24-hr.); babysitting; laundry service; same-day dry cleaning; nonsmoking rooms (on 2 floors). *In room:* A/C, TV, VCR (on request), fax (in suites), dataport, minibar, hair dryer, safe.

Moderate

Hotel Gran Duca di York   This 19th-century palazzo was once used by the Duomo for housing visiting church officials. The midsize rooms are simple, with hideous 1970s built-in units, tile floors, and plush easy chairs—a few even get small terraces. The thin windows do not keep out all the traffic noise (not constant, but there). What it lacks in style, it makes up for in location—just off the main pedestrian drag leading from the cathedral to Castello Sforzesco.

Via Moneta 1a (a block off Piazza Edison), 20123 Milano. ✆ 02-874-863. Fax 02-869-0344. 33 units. 150€ ($173) double; 165€ ($190) triple. Rates include continental breakfast. AE, MC, V. Metro: Cordusio. **Amenities:** Bar; concierge; tour desk; car-rental desk; courtesy car (for a fee); room service (limited); babysitting; laundry service. *In room:* A/C, TV, dataport, hair dryer.

Hotel Santa Marta ★   The narrow Via Santa Marta is a slice of old Milan, cobblestoned and lined with charming old buildings, one of which houses the Santa Marta. It's also across the street from one of the city's most atmospheric restaurants (the Milanese), and a short walk from the Duomo and other sights. Recent modernizations have preserved the old-fashioned ambience while adding such modern comforts as air-conditioning. The tile-floored guest rooms are comfortable and decorated with a matter-of-fact fashion sense, some cramped, others quite large. Still, a recent drastic increase in prices seems to have been unjustified. If they're full, they'll send you to their sister hotel, the Hotel Rovello (see below).

Via Santa Marta 4, 20123 Milano. ✆ 02-804-567 or 02-804-621. Fax 02-8645-2661. 15 units. 160€–186€ ($184–$214) double; 190€–257€ ($219–$296) triple. Continental breakfast included. AE, DC, MC, V. Parking in nearby garage 15€ ($17). Closed 15 days in Aug. Metro: Cordusio or Duomo. Tram: 1, 2, 3, 4, 12, 14, 15, 19, 20, 24, or 27. **Amenities:** Bar; laundry service; nonsmoking rooms. *In room:* A/C, TV, hair dryer.

Hotel Speronari ★ *Finds*   This is a budget hotel in a deluxe location, tucked into a tiny pedestrian side street between Via Torino and Via Mazzini across from the church of Santa Maria Presso San Satiro. The staff is earnest, and the rooms are basic but done well: cool tile floors, functional furnishings, ceiling fans, brand-new cot springs, and fuzzy towels in the bathrooms. Even those without full bathroom have a sink and bidet, and all save a few of those without bathrooms have TVs. Rooms on the third and fourth floors are brighter, and those on the courtyard a tad quieter than rooms facing the street (there are terribly convenient trolleys a half block in either direction, but they come with a distant but noisy rumble for rooms on the street side).

Via Speronari 4, 20123 Milano. ✆ **02-8646-1125.** Fax 02-7200-3178. hotelsperonari@inwind.it. 33 units, 17 with bathroom. 73€ ($84) double without bathroom; 93€–104€ ($107–$120) double with bathroom; 98€ ($113) triple without bathroom, 140€ ($161) triple with bathroom; 155€ ($178) quad with bathroom. MC, V. Metro: Duomo or Missori. Tram: 1, 2, 3, 4, 12, 14, 15, 19, 20, 24, or 27. **Amenities:** Bar; concierge; tour desk. *In room:* TV, dataport, hair dryer (ask at desk), safe.

Inexpensive

Hotel Ullrich A 10-minute walk south of the Duomo, this attractive pensione offers a lot of comfort in addition to its good location. The management is friendly, and rooms are furnished with pleasant modern pieces and decent beds. Each has a tiny washroom with sink and bidet but no toilet; large, spanking-clean bathrooms are in the hallway. Rooms on the street side open to small balconies, but are noisier than those overlooking the *cortile* (courtyard). One of the bathrooms is equipped with a washing machine, and guests can do a load for 10€ ($12). The Ullrich books up quickly, so be sure to call ahead.

Corso Italia 6, 21023 Milano. ✆ **02-8645-0156** or 02-804-535. 7 units, none with bathroom. 70€–75€ ($81–$86) double; 90€–100€ ($104–$115) triple. Breakfast not offered. MC, V. Metro: Duomo. Tram: 15, 24, 65, or 94. *In room:* TV, hair dryer.

IN MAGENTA & BRERA
Very Expensive

Four Seasons Hotel Milano ★★★ Milan's top five-star deluxe hotel lies just off Via Montenapoleone, the city's swankiest shopping boulevard. Though lacking the antiques-drawn style of its competitor Grand Hotel et du Milan, it lays on more luxuries. Its central core retains many touches, including the lovely garden-planted cloisters, rediscovered during the 7-year restructuring that by 1993 had turned this 1476 convent into a hotel (the frescoes in the lobby hint that this room was once the convent's church). Rooms are terrifically spacious, with thick runs on modern parquet, designer chairs in comfy sitting areas, large marble-sheathed bathrooms with heated floors, CD stereos, and walk-in closets. "Superior" rooms are on the street (protected from noise by effective double-paned windows) rather than the cloisters, with queen-size beds rather than the king-size in the "deluxe" category. "Executive" suites have a midsize sitting area, and can be connected to deluxe doubles to form a family suite. Five bi-level suites on the ground floor of the cloisters have vaulted ceilings mostly re-frescoed (though one bit of the original painting remains), with a split-level sitting area and bedroom and the bathroom underneath, all overlooking a neighbor's quiet grassy garden. A new wing opened in 2001 in a *vecchia Milano* house with a central courtyard enclosed by a skylight and balcony running around each level, each of which hosts five rooms and suites. More recently, the hotel revamped the lobby and exercise room, and redid the Royal Suite.

Via Gesù 8, 20121 Milano. ✆ **800-332-3442** in the U.S., or 02-77-088 in Italy. Fax 02-7708-5000. www.fourseasons.com/milan. 118 units. 616€ ($708) superior double; 737€ ($848) deluxe double; 792€ ($911) jr. suite; 1,100€ ($1,265) executive suite; 1,650€ ($1,898) bilevel suite; 2,420€ ($2,783) cloister suite; 4,675€ ($5,376) Visconti or Royal suite. 28€ ($32) continental breakfast; 30€ ($35) buffet breakfast. AE, DC, MC, V. Valet parking 51€ ($59). Metro: Montenapoleone. Bus: 54, 64, 65, or 73. **Amenities:** 2 restaurants (elegant dinner restaurant under celebrity chef, casual restaurant overlooking cloisters open lunch and dinner); bar; small exercise room; bike rental; children's program and special menu; concierge; tour desk; car-rental desk; courtesy car (for a fee); business center; room service (24-hr.); massage; babysitting; laundry service; same-day dry cleaning; nonsmoking rooms; executive-level rooms. *In room:* A/C, TV, VCR, fax (on request), dataport, kitchenette (in Royal and Presidential suites), minibar, hair dryer, safe.

Grand Hotel et De Milan ★★★ Perhaps Milan's most intimate luxury hotel—an 1863 property so devoted to a complete overhaul it actually closed down from 1993 to 1995—the Grand Hotel et De Milan balances family management with refined service. It's perfectly positioned between La Scala (3 blocks away) and the shopping of Via Montenapoleone just up and across the street. The bathrooms are done in marble and the beds king-size in rooms with heavy curtains, chipped stone floors, elegant upholstered furnishings, and muted skylight domes. "Deluxe" rooms are larger than "classic" rooms, and have genuine antiques. The suites, divided into a good-size living room and separate bedroom, genuinely feel like small apartments rather than hotel rooms with their homelike arrangement of antiques and piped-in opera (perhaps something by Maria Callas, once a regular guest). The presidential Giuseppe Verdi suite has been preserved with the same furnishings as when the composer spent his last 30 years here (he even died in this room), including the desk upon which he composed many operas.

Via Manzoni 29, 20121 Milano. ✆ **02-723-141.** Fax 02-8646-0861. www.grandhoteletdemilan.it. 95 units. 448€ ($515) classic double; 520€ ($598) De luxe double; 605€ ($696) jr. suite; 840€–1,025€ ($966–$1,179) suite. Breakfast € 35 ($40). AE, DC, MC, V. Garage parking 43€ ($49). Metro: Montenapoleone. **Amenities:** 2 Italian/Milanese restaurants (the Don Carlo is popular even among nonguests); bar; large new exercise room open 24 hr.; bike rental; concierge; secretarial services; room service (limited); in-room massage; babysitting; laundry service; same-day dry cleaning. *In room:* A/C, TV w/pay movies, VCR (on request), fax (on request), dataport, minibar, hair dryer, safe.

Moderate

Antica Locanda Solferino ★★★ If this charming old hotel in the arty Brera neighborhood hadn't been discovered long ago by members of the fashion world and film stars (this was Marcello Mastroianni's preferred Milan hostelry), you would consider it a find. The rooms have more character than they do modern comforts, but, to the loyal guests, the eclectic smattering of country antiques and Art Nouveau pieces more than compensate for the absence of minibars. Nor do the repeat customers seem to mind that some of the bathrooms are miniscule (though modern), or that there is no lobby or breakfast room (coffee and rolls are delivered to your room). So be it—this is a delightful place to stay in one of Milan's most enticing neighborhoods, and reception manager Gerardo Vitolo is very friendly. New Jacuzzi baths and air-conditioning in some rooms only add to the experience. The rooms on the tiny courtyard are quieter, but those on the street have plant-filled balconies (the best is no. 10 on the corner, if you don't mind a tub rather than a shower).

Via Castelfidardo 2, 20121 Milano. ✆ **02-657-0129** or 02-659-2706. Fax 02-657-1361. www.anticalocanda solferino.it. 11 units. 155€–170€ ($178–$196) double; 200€–220€ ($230–$253) apt; 25€ ($29) extra bed. Rates include breakfast served in room. AE, DC, MC, V. Parking 20€–25€ ($23–$29) in nearby garage. Closed 2–3 weeks in mid-Aug. Metro: Moscova or Repubblica. Tram/Bus: 11, 29, 30, 33, 41, 43, or 94. **Amenities:** Concierge; tour desk; car-rental desk; laundry service; dry cleaning. *In room:* A/C (2 rooms), TV, hair dryer.

Ariosto Hotel ★★ Tucked away in a residential neighborhood of apartment houses and old villas near the Santa Maria delle Grazie church, the Ariosto is a refreshingly quiet retreat—all the more so because many of the newly refurbished rooms face a private garden, and some open onto balconies overlooking it. All the rooms are decorated with wood-and-wicker furnishings, shiny parquet floors, and hand-painted wallpaper. Most of the rooms are decently sized, but singles tend to be skinny. Many of the doubles have separate dressing areas off the tile or stone bathrooms, which are equipped with hair dryers and a few with Jacuzzis. There's free Internet access in the lobby, and satellite movie channels on the television.

Via Ariosto 22, 20145 Milano. ⓒ 02-481-7844. Fax 02-498-0516. www.hotelariosto.com. 53 units. 196€ ($225) double; 213€ ($245) triple. Those are the highest rates, applied during trade fairs, and may be discounted by as much as 45% during slower periods. Rates include breakfast. AE, DC, MC, V. Parking 20€–25€ ($23–$29) in garage. Closed 20 days in Aug. Metro: Conciliazione. Tram/Bus: 29, 30, 61, 67, or 68. **Amenities:** Restaurant (Italian); bar; bike rental; concierge; car-rental desk; room service (limited); laundry service; dry cleaning; nonsmoking rooms. *In room:* A/C, TV w/pay movies, dataport, minibar, hair dryer.

Hotel Giulio Cesare ★

A recent renovation has brought this old establishment thoroughly up-to-date, with a grandiose marble lobby and a handsome lounge and bar area with deep couches. Upstairs, the rooms are contemporary chic, but reflect the building's centuries-old heritage with their tall windows and high ceilings. Some are quirkily shaped, and a few singles are cramped, but the white tile floors and minimalist furnishings are starkly modern. The new bathrooms gleam and are equipped with stall showers and flat towels. Management can be a bit brusque. This is one of several similarly priced hotels on the block, a generally quiet street tucked away off Via Dante between the Duomo and La Scala in one direction and the Castello in the other. (See the London Hotel and Hotel Rovello listings below.)

Via Rovello 10, 20121 Milano. ⓒ 02-7200-3915. Fax 02-7200-2179. 25 units. 150€ ($173) double. Breakfast included. AE, MC, V. Metro: Cordusio. Tram/Bus: 1, 2, 3, 4, 12, 14, 18, 19, 20, 24, or 27. **Amenities:** Bar; room service (24-hr.). *In room:* A/C, TV, hair dryer.

Hotel Manzoni ★

This simple, midscale, laid-back hotel ain't particularly special, but it is relatively cheap for this high-rent neighborhood, perfect for those who want to stay in Milan's heart of the chichi shopping but not pay the prices at neighbors Four Seasons and Grand Hotel et De Milan. Historic photos and prints line the halls leading to good-size rooms outfitted with fairly standard '70s and '80s furnishings and glass-topped bamboo desks. The bathrooms are in good order, but some are still saddled with those shower nozzles you have to hold (others have stall showers). Suites include a small separate sitting area and separate tub and shower, and are a bit larger, but are otherwise no more luxurious than doubles, yet cost nearly 40% more.

Via Santo Spirito 20, 20121 Milano. ⓒ 02-7600-5700. Fax 02-784-212. www.hotelmanzoni.com. 52 units. 158€–176€ ($182–$202) double. Breakfast included. AE, DC, MC, V. Parking 30€ ($35) in garage. Metro: Montenapoleone. **Amenities:** Home-cooking restaurant; bar; concierge; tour desk; room service (limited); babysitting; laundry service; same-day dry cleaning. *In room:* A/C, TV, dataport, hair dryer.

Hotel Rovello ★

The Rovello is one of three hotels I recommend on this quiet street between the Duomo and the Castello and, like its neighbor the Hotel Giulio Cesare, it was thoroughly renovated in 1999 with striking results. The unusually large guest rooms occupy the first and second floors of a centuries-old building and incorporate many of the original architectural details, including exposed timbers and beamed ceilings. Handsome contemporary Italian furnishings are set off by gleaming hardwood floors, the tall casement windows are covered with attractive fabrics, and walls are painted in soothing green and gold tones. The orthopedic mattresses are covered with thick quilts for a homey feel. Many of the rooms have dressing areas in addition to the large new bathrooms. A breakfast of rolls and coffee is served in a sunny room off the lobby.

Via Rovello 18, 20121 Milano. ⓒ 02-8646-4654. Fax 02-7202-3656. www.hotel-rovello.it. 10 units. 100€–186€ ($115–$214) double. AE, DC, MC, V. Metro: Cordusio. Tram/Bus: 1, 2, 3, 4, 12, 14, 18, 19, 20, 24, or 27. **Amenities:** Bar; concierge; room service (limited); laundry service. *In room:* A/C, TV, dataport, hair dryer.

London Hotel ⭐ Unlike its neighbor the Hotel Giulio Cesare, the London sticks to its old-fashioned ways. The big fireplace and cozy green velvet furniture in the lobby say a lot about the comfort level and friendly atmosphere that bring many guests back time after time. Just beyond the lobby, there's a bar where beverages are available almost around the clock; guests can purchase cappuccino or a continental breakfast in the morning. Upstairs, the rooms look like they haven't been redecorated in a number of decades, but they're roomy and bright, and the heavy old furnishings lend a charm very much in keeping with the ambience of the hotel. Rooms on the first floor tend to be the largest, and they get smaller as you go up. Guests receive a 10% discount at the trattoria next door, the Opera Prima.

Via Rovello 3, 20121 Milano. ⓒ 02-7202-0166. Fax 02-8057-037. www.hotellondonmilano.com. 29 units. 140€ ($161) double; 180€ ($207) triple. Continental breakfast 8€ ($9). MC, V. Parking 25€ ($29) in nearby garage. Closed Aug and Christmas. Metro: Cordusio. Tram/Bus: 1, 2, 3, 4, 12, 14, 18, 19, 20, 24, or 27. **Amenities:** Bar; concierge; room service (limited); laundry service; same-day dry cleaning. *In room:* A/C, TV, dataport, hair dryer.

EAST OF THE DUOMO
Moderate

Hotel Pavone ⭐ The family-run Pavone is just off the Corso di Porta Vittoria, around the corner from the Palace of Justice, and about a 15-minute walk east of the Duomo. The surrounding neighborhood is more geared to business than to the tourist trade, but the friendly desk staff is eager to point out nearby restaurants and other conveniences, which are plentiful. Rooms are a bit sparse, with gray tile floors and no-nonsense Scandinavian-style furniture, but they have recently been spruced up with new linens and decor. Most are unusually large and cloaked in a silence unusual for big-city Milan, but for the quietest rest, check in to no. 12, 14, 16, or 18, all of which overlook a garden. The beds in most singles are extra wide. Many rooms are outfitted as triples and are large enough to accommodate an extra bed, making this a fine choice for families.

Via Dandolo 2 (off Corso di Porta Vittoria), 20122 Milano. ⓒ 02-5519-2133. Fax 02-5519-2421. www.hotel pavone.com. 24 units. 115€–170€ ($132–$196) double; 170€–230€ ($196–$265) triple. Continental breakfast 5€ ($6). AE, MC, V. Parking 10€ ($12). Tram: 12, 20, 23, 27, 60, or 73. **Amenities:** Bar; concierge; room service (24-hr.). *In room:* A/C, TV, dataport, hair dryer, safe.

Inexpensive

America Though this establishment is a bit off the beaten track in a middle-class neighborhood due east of Piazza del Duomo, the young owner and his family work overtime to make this pensione one of the best lower-priced lodgings in Milan. The newly refurbished rooms occupy the fourth floor of an apartment house. Several have private bathrooms, and all are bright and nicely decorated with streamlined, wood-veneer modern furnishings—many sporting a thematic stars-and-stripes color scheme. Guests are welcome to join the resident innkeepers in the living room and watch TV. All of the rooms without bathrooms have sinks, and two even have showers (but no toilet). The Rolling Stone music club, a venerable fixture on the Milan nightlife scene, is on the ground floor of the building, a good reason to ask for a room facing the quieter *giardino* (garden) courtyard (no. 10 even has a balcony). For more conventional sightseeing, the Duomo is about 20 minutes away by foot or 10 minutes by tram.

Corso XXII Marzo 32 (the block east of Piazza Emilia), 20135 Milano. © **02-738-1865.** Fax 02-738-1490. www.milanohotelamerica.com. 10 units, 2 with bathroom. 62€ ($71) double without bathroom, 68€ ($78) double with bathroom; 78€ ($90) triple with bathroom. No breakfast. AE, MC, V. Tram/Bus: 12, 27, 45, 60, 66, 73, or 92. *In room:* TV.

NEAR STAZIONE CENTRALE & CORSO BUENOS AIRES
Very Expensive
Excelsior Hotel Gallia ★   This 1937 bastion of Liberty-style luxury rises near the main train station—a thoroughly uninteresting area a 20-minute taxi ride from the center. It is convenient for late arrivals or early departures, and while the neighborhood is trafficky, the hotel is well soundproofed. It's oriented toward business clients and conferences, so it's flush with amenities, but also charges expense-account rates. The granite columns and murals in the salon lend the hotel an antique air balanced by the modern art in the hallways. Each floor is done in a different pastel color scheme. The spacious, comfortable rooms are done in modern parquet (some are carpeted) with classy antiques and the occasional quirky touch such as a TV atop a column stump or a ceiling frescoed with puffy clouds. Bathrooms are clad in a variety of marbles, with heated towel racks, large tubs, and double sinks in all but "superior" type rooms. Superior rooms are a bit smaller but only slightly less fashionable (they retain the old, fairly fussy, repro Deco look). Even singles are unusually large and have extra-wide beds.

Piazzale Duca d'Aosta 9, 20124 Milano. © **02-678-5716.** Fax 02-6698-6942. www.lemeridien-excelsior gallia.com. 237 units. 520€ ($598) standard double; 545€ ($627) superior double; 570€ ($656) De Luxe double; from 720€ ($828) suite; extra bed 80€ ($92). Continental breakfast 23€ ($26); buffet breakfast 33€ ($38). AE, DC, MC, V. Parking 15€ ($17) at hotel, or 31€ ($36) valet in garage. Metro: Centrale F.S. **Amenities:** Refined Italian restaurant; piano bar; small exercise room; Jacuzzi; sauna; bike rental; concierge; tour desk; car-rental desk; business center; small shopping arcade; salon; room service (24-hr.); massage; babysitting; laundry service; same-day dry cleaning; nonsmoking rooms. *In room:* A/C, TV w/pay movies, VCR (on request), fax, dataport, minibar, hair dryer, safe.

Expensive
Doriagrand Hotel ★   This luxury hotel offers enormously discounted weekend prices (the lower rates below, applied Fri–Sun nights) that makes it reasonable on weekends, most of August, and the Christmas/New Year's holiday (check for exact dates before booking; never applied during trade fairs). The Doriagrand is one of the large newer hotels that cluster around the station and is far more comfortable and stylish than most hotels in its luxury class. The good-size guest rooms are exquisitely appointed with handsome wood and marble-topped furniture, rich fabric wall coverings and draperies, and amenities such as linen sheets, ISDN jacks, satellite channels and pay-per-view, and bedroom slippers and bathrobes. The beautiful marble bathrooms are equipped with generous-size tubs, vanities, hair dryers, and a generous selection of toiletries. A sumptuous buffet breakfast is served in a stylishly decorated room on a level above the lobby (where they also serve 28€/$32 fixed menus at mealtimes), and Thursday and Friday evenings the piano bar becomes a jazz club.

Viale Andrea Doria 22, 20124 Milano. © **02-6741-1411.** Fax 02-669-6669. www.doriagrandhotel.it. 118 units, all with bathroom. 150€–360€ ($173–$414) double; 300€–450€ ($345–$518) suite. Rates include buffet breakfast. AE, DC, MC, V. Parking 30€ ($35) in garage. Metro: Loreto or Caiazzo. Tram: 1, 90, 91, or 92. **Amenities:** Restaurant; concierge; tour desk; car-rental desk; courtesy car; room service (limited); in-room massage; babysitting; laundry service; dry cleaning; nonsmoking rooms. *In room:* A/C, TV w/pay movies, dataport, minibar, hair dryer, safe.

Moderate
Hotel Promessi Sposi ★★   Travelers often find their way to this rambling hotel on the recommendation of former guests, many of them in the fashion

world, who tend to rave about the friendly service (Jerry at the desk lived in New York City until the age of 10), unusually pleasant accommodations, and excellent value. Downstairs, there's a cheerful lobby and bar area furnished with multi-colored couches that overlooks Piazza Oberdan and the public gardens through large windows. Upstairs, the spacious rooms are outfitted with comfortable rattan furniture painted burgundy and/or cream. Bathrooms are spacious and nicely maintained. Rooms in the back, overlooking a drab narrow alley between buildings, are considerably quieter (but less well-lit) than those on busy Corso Buenos Aires and Piazza Oberdan—double glazing helps, but can't entirely mask, the noise. However, I'd still ask for no. 222 or 332, which sit at the narrow end of the building and as such are quite large, with windows on three sides and small balconies. The name, which translates as "the Fiancées," is a reference to the 19th-century masterpiece by Lombardian novelist Alessandro Manzoni, a close second to Dante's *Inferno* on the required reading list in Italian high schools.

Piazza Oberdan 12, 20129 Milano. ⓒ 02-2951-3661. Fax 02-2940-4182. www.hotelpromessisposi.com. 40 units. 88€–139€ ($101–$160) double. 5% discount for stays of longer than 3 days (but not during trade fairs). Buffet breakfast included. AE, DC, MC, V. Parking 15€ ($17) in nearby garage, free on street. Metro: Porta Venezia. Tram: 9, 20, 29, or 30. **Amenities:** Bar. *In room:* A/C, TV w/pay movies, dataport, coffeemaker, hair dryer.

Inexpensive

Hotel Kennedy *(Value* The name reflects the English-speaking management's fondness for the late president, and the family is genuinely welcoming to the many Americans who find their way to their pensione a block off the southern end of Corso Buenos Aires. Their homey establishment on the sixth floor of an office-and-apartment building (there's an elevator) is sparkling clean and offers basic accommodations in large, tile-floored rooms. Room no. 13 has a terrace, while no. 15 has a small balcony that even glimpses the spires of the Duomo in the distance. Amenities include a bar in the reception area, where coffee and soft drinks are available, as is a light breakfast of brioche and coffee that doesn't cost much more than it would in a cafe.

Viale Tunisia 6 (6th floor), 20124 Milano. ⓒ 02-2940-0934. Fax 02-2940-1253. www.hotelkennedy.it. 12 units, 3 with shower, 5 with bathroom. 55€–70€ ($63–$81) double without bathroom; 75€–100€ ($86–$115) double with bathroom; 80€–120€ ($92–$138) triple with bathroom; 100€–140€ ($115–$161) quad with bathroom. Breakfast 3€ ($3.45). AE, DC, MC, V. Parking 15€–20€ ($17–$23) in nearby garage. Metro: Porta Venezia. Tram: 5 or 11. **Amenities:** Bar. *In room:* TV, dataport, hair dryer.

Hotel Paganini ⭐ *(Value* Occupying an old house on a quiet residential street off the north end of Corso Buenos Aires, the Paganini has minimal public areas (except for a reception area with a self-serve espresso machine), but the guest rooms are large, bright, and embellished with tile floors, high ceilings with elaborate moldings, solid beds, and banal modular furnishings of varying ages. The one room with a bathroom is just inside the entrance, with wood floors, a ceiling decorated with molded stuccoes, and plenty of elbowroom. The shared facilities are modern enough and kept spanking clean by the owners (one of whom lived in Brooklyn, NY for a number of years), who are happy to point their guests to restaurants and sights. The best rooms are in the rear, overlooking a huge private garden. There is much to be said for this location: The station is only a 10-minute walk way down Via Pergolsi, and if shopping is on your agenda, the nearby Corso Buenos Aires is one of the city's bargain fashion meccas.

Via Paganini 6, 20131 Milano. ⓒ 02-204-7443. www.paginegialle.it/hotelpaganini. 8 units, 1 with bathroom. 47€–52€ ($54–$60) double; 52€–62€ ($60–$71) triple. No breakfast. AE, DC, MC, V. Parking in garage across street 12€ ($14), free on street. Metro: Loreto. Tram/Bus: 33, 55, 55/, 56, 56/, 90, 91, or 93. **Amenities:** Concierge. *In room:* Hair dryer.

WHERE TO DINE

Geared to business, as the city is, Milanese are more willing than Italians elsewhere to break the sit-down-meal tradition and grab a sandwich or other light fare on the run. And with so many students and young professionals underfoot, Milan has no shortage of pizzerias and other low-cost eateries alongside its world-class dining options.

NEAR THE DUOMO

La Crêperie CREPERIE About a 10-minute walk southeast of Piazza Duomo (Via C. Corenti is an extension of Via Torino, one of the major aves. fanning out from the square), this busy creperie is an ideal stop for a light lunch or a snack while visiting the nearby church of Sant'Ambrogio or Museo Nazionale di Scienza e di Tecnica. The far-ranging offerings include meal-like crepes such as *prosciutto e formaggio* (ham and cheese) or more dessert-like options (the Nutella creamy chocolate ground nut spread is highly recommended). There are a few value menus: Before 3pm you can get one non-dessert crepe, one sweet one, and a drink for 5€ ($6); until 9pm you can get two "salty" ones, one dessert crepe, and a drink for 7.50€ ($9). (The Italians split food like this into two categories: "sweet" and "salty" (*dolci* versus *salati*). A "sweet" crepe might have Nutella in it, a "salty" one, ham and cheese. The menu at La Crêperie is divided accordingly.)

Via C. Corenti 21. ℘ 02-839-5913. Crepes 1.50€–4€ ($1.75–$4.60). Mon–Sat 11am–1am; Sun 4pm–midnight. Metro: Sant'Ambrogio.

Luini Panzerotti ★★ SNACKS A Milan institution since 1948, it's so good they've even opened a branch in London. At this stand-up counter near the Galleria, you'll have to elbow your way through a throng of well-dressed patrons to purchase the house specialty: *panzerotto*, a pocket of pizza crust stuffed with all sorts of ingredients, including the basic cheese-and-tomato. You'll also find many different kinds of panini here.

Via S. Radegonda 16. ℘ 02-8646-1917. www.luini.it. Panzerotto 2.10€ ($2.40). No credit cards. Mon 10am–3pm; Tues–Sat 10am–8pm. Closed Aug. Metro: Duomo.

MAGENTA & BRERA

La Milanese ★★★ MILANESE Giuseppe and Antonella Villa preside with a watchful eye over the centuries-old premises (a restaurant since 1933), tucked into a narrow lane in one of the oldest sections of Milan, just west of the Duomo. In the three-beamed dining room, Milanese families and other patrons share the long, crowded tables. Giuseppe, in the kitchen, prepares what many patrons consider to be some of the city's best traditional fare. The *risotto alla Milanese* with saffron and beef marrow, not surprisingly, is excellent, as is a minestrone that's served hot in the winter and at room temperature in the summer. The *costolette alla Milanese,* breaded and fried in butter, is all the better here because only the choicest veal chops are used and it's served with the bone in, and the osso buco is cooked to perfection. If you want to try their twin specialties without pigging out, the dish listed as *risotto e osso buco* buys you a half portion each of their *risotto alla Milanese* and the osso buco for just 18€ ($21). Polenta with rich Gorgonzola cheese is one of the few non-meat second courses. The attentive staff will help you choose an appropriate wine.

Via Santa Marta 11. ℘ 02-8645-1991. Reservations required. Primi 7€–10€ ($8–$12); secondi 6€–18€ ($7–$21); *menù turistico* 30€ ($35) without wine. AE, DC, MC, V. Wed–Mon noon–3pm and 7pm–1am. Metro: Cardusio.

Latteria ★★ MILANESE   The main business here at one time was dispensing milk and eggs to a press of neighborhood shoppers, but now the emphasis is on serving the La Brera neighborhood delicious, homemade fare in a room decorated with paintings and photographs of roses. The minestrone and other vegetable soups are delicious, as are the many variations of risotto, including some otherwise hard to find variations such as *riso al salto* and a delicious dish of leftover *risotto alla Milanese* that is fried with butter. The menu changes daily, and the friendly staff, including owners Arturo and Maria, won't mind explaining the different dishes. The place is tiny, and doesn't take bookings, so if you want to get one of the popular tables, arrive when it opens or wait until 8:30pm or later when a few will free up as the early-dining tourist clientele clears out and the locals take over.

Via San Marco 24. ☎ **02-659-7653**. Reservations not accepted (and it fills up fast). Primi 8€–9€ ($9–$10); secondi 7€–13€ ($8–$15). No credit cards. Mon–Fri 12:30–2:30pm and 7:30–10pm. Metro: Moscova.

Peck ★★ *Value* DELI   Milan's most famous food emporium offers a wonderful selection of roast veal, risottos, porchetta, salads, aspics, cheeses, pastries, and other fare from its exquisite larder in this natty snack bar around the corner from its shop. If you choose to eat here, you will do so at a stand-up bar where, especially around lunchtime, it can be hard to find elbowroom. This shouldn't discourage you, though, because the pleasure of having access to such a cornucopia of delicacies at a reasonable price will be a gourmand's vision of paradise. By the way, their full-fledged restaurant around the corner at Via Victor Hugò 4 (☎ **02-876-774**), recently remodeled and now called **Cracco-Peck,** serves high-test traditional and creative cuisine but charges such heart-stopping prices—their fixed-price tasting menus cost 88€ to 105€ ($101–$121)—we decided not to include a full write-up.

Via Spadari 9. ☎ **02-802-3161.** www.peck.it. Primi 3.50€–8€ ($4.05–$9); secondi 9€–13€ ($10–$15). AE, DC, MC, V. Mon–Sat 7:30am–9pm. Closed Jan 1–10 and July 1–20. Metro: Duomo.

Pizzeria Grand'Italia ★★ *Value* PIZZA/PASTA   One of Milan's most popular pizzerias—any time one of my Milanese friends says "Hey, let's go get pizza!" this is invariably where he or she takes me. Grand'Italia serves up a huge assortment of salads, pizzas, homemade pastas, and *focacce farcite* (focaccia bread stuffed with cheese, mushrooms, and other fillings), along with wine and oil from the Furfaro family's farm in Tuscany. Rather than get a whole pie, you get one thick-crusted megaslice topped however you like it. The late hours make this a prime nightspot, and part of the fun is watching the chic, young Milanese stopping by for a snack as they make the rounds of the nearby Brera-district bars and clubs.

Via Palermo 5. ☎ **02-877-759.** Pizza from 4€ ($4.60); salads from 6€ ($7). No credit cards. Daily noon–2:45pm and 7pm–1:30am. Metro: Moscova.

NEAR STAZIONE CENTRALE & CORSO BUENOS AIRES

Brek CAFETERIA   This outlet of Italy's popular cafeteria chain is not to be dismissed too quickly. Brek takes food, and its presentation, seriously. Pastas and risotto are made fresh; pork, veal, and chicken are roasted to order; and the large selection of cheeses would put many a formal restaurant to shame. Excellent wines and many kinds of beer are also available. Behind-the-counter service is friendly and helpful, and the country-style decor is quite attractive.

Via Lepetit 20. ☎ **02-670-5149.** www.brek.it. Primi and pizza 3€–6€ ($3.45–$7); secondi 3.50€–7€ ($4.05–$8). AE, MC, V. Mon–Sat 11:30am–3pm and 6:30–10:30pm. Metro: Stazione Centrale.

Da Abele ★ MILANESE   Once you get away from the sights and shops of the city center, you'll find yourself in some middle-class neighborhoods. Da Abele is tucked away in one, in a pleasant enclave of shops and apartment houses east of Stazione Centrale and north of the Corso Buenos Aires shopping strip (a few blocks north of Piazzale Loreto). This plain trattoria caters to local residents (hence its evening-only hours—they take reservations only before 8:30pm; afterward it's first-come, first-served) and serves a nice selection of soups (including a hearty seafood *zuppa di pesce*) and many kinds of risotto, including one with *frutti di mare* (a selection of fresh seafood) and others with fresh porcini in season. The amiable staff doesn't mind if you venture no further into the menu, but if you do, there is a nice selection of roast meats as well. Sadly, they joined that large percentage of shameful Italian businesses that used the arrival of the euro as an excuse to drastically inflate their prices.

Via Temperanza 5. ② 02-261-3855. Primi 7€–9€ ($8–$10); secondi 10€–12€ ($12–$14). MC, V. Tues–Sun 8–11:30pm. Closed July 20–Sept 1. Metro: Pasteur.

Isola del Panino SANDWICHES   This cafelike sandwich shop, in the midst of the bustle of the Corso Buenos Aires discount shops, sells some 50 different kinds of panini. You needn't feel you are foregoing an Italian experience in enjoying one of these sandwiches. In Milan, a panino is a very popular snack or lunch choice and is usually served warm; bread is stuffed with seafood, cheese, salami, vegetables, whatever, then grilled. You can eat the delicious creations here on the premises in an airy, chrome-and-tile dining area, or take them with you, perhaps for a picnic on the nearby public gardens.

Via Felice Casati 2. ② 02-2951-4925. Sandwiches from 2.40€ ($2.75). No credit cards. Tues–Sun 8am–midnight. Metro: Lima.

Joia ★★ VEGETARIAN   Milanese, who tend to be carnivorous, have embraced this refined vegetarian restaurant just north of the public gardens with great enthusiasm. Travelers may welcome the respite from northern Italy's orientation to red meat; those who have become accustomed to smoke-free environments back home will enjoy the *non fumatore* section of Joia's blonde-wood, neutral-toned dining rooms. Here, the innovative vegetarian creations of Swiss chef Pietro Lemman incorporate the freshest vegetables and herbs, which appear in many traditional pasta dishes, such as *lasagne con zucchine pomodoro* (layered with zucchini and fresh tomatoes and served at room temperature), *ravioli di melanzana* (stuffed with eggplant), or tagliolini with a simple tomato sauce. Any of these first courses can be ordered as a main course, and many of the main courses can be ordered as starters. These secondi (second courses) include some excellent fish choices, as well as elaborate vegetables-only creations such as *melanzani viola al vapore con finferli* (steamed eggplant with chanterelle mushrooms). There's also a wonderful assortment of cheeses and, likewise, a long wine list.

Via P. Castaldi 18. ② 02-204-9244. www.joia.it. Reservations highly recommended. Primi 14€–18€ ($16–$21); secondi 18€–21€ ($21–$24); tasting menus 42€–70€ ($48–$81). AE, DC, MC, V. Mon–Fri noon–2:30pm and 7:30–11:30pm. Closed Aug. Metro: Repubblica.

Ristorante Versilia ★ NORTHERN ITALIAN   The white tiles and high-tech lighting here suggest that this single room between the station and Corso Buenos Aires has more pretensions than it does. The modern environs are the result of a recent renovation to this friendly, family-run eatery that serves the surrounding neighborhood with excellent food and attentive service. The *risotti* are superb, including *alla pilota* with sausage. While the menu lists a *costoletta* *alla Milanese* and other meat dishes, daily specials often also include a wide selection of the freshest seafood.

Viale Andrea Doria 44. ℂ 02-670-4187. Primi 4€–6€ ($4.60–$7); secondi 5€–9€ ($6–$10). MC, V. Mon–Sat noon–2:30pm and 7–10pm. Metro: Loreto.

IN THE NAVIGLI

Al Pont de Ferr ★★ *Finds* PAN-ITALIAN   This is one of the more culinarily respectable of the dozens of restaurants around the Navigli, with tables set out on the flagstones overlooking the canal (regulars know to bring tiny cans of bug spray to battle the mosquitoes in summer). The *paste e fagioli* is livened up with bits of sausage, and the ricotta-stuffed ravioli inventively sauced with a pesto of *rucola* (arugula) and veggies. For a second course you can try the *tocchetti di coniglio* (oven-roasted rabbit with potatoes), *porchetta* (pork stuffed with spices), or the vegetable *cous-cous alla Trapanesi*—or just sack the whole idea of a secondo and order up a *tavolozza* selection of excellent cheeses. There's a surprisingly good selection of half-bottles of wine, but most full bottles start at 15€ ($17) and go senselessly higher. On the whole, portions could be a whole lot larger, but you gotta love a place whose menu opens with the quip "Good cooking is the friend of living well and the enemy of a hurried life."

Ripa di Porta Ticinese 55 (on the Naviglio Grande). ℂ 02-8940-6277. Primi 6€–11€ ($7–$13); secondi 14€–19€ ($16–$22). Mon–Sat 12:30–2:30pm and 8pm–1am. AE, MC, V. Tram: 3, 15, 29, 30, or 59.

Ponte Rosso ★ MILANESE/FRIULIANA   This is an old-fashioned trattoria on the canal, a long railroad room crowded with tiny tables and a short, simple menu of unfussy, hearty home cooking. The owner hails from Trieste originally (which explains the old Triestino photos on the walls), so kick a meal off with *salumi friuliani,* a mixed platter of cured meats from the region famous for producing the most delicate prosciutto in Italy. The *insalata di pasta* is a cold pasta salad with olives, capers, and mozzarella. They do a mean minestrone vegetable soup, Triestino *sarde in saor* (vinegar-kissed fried sardines), *manzo in salsa verde* (beef in an herb sauce), and *torta di verdure* (vegetable quiche).

Ripa di Porta Ticinese 23 (on the Naviglio Grande) ℂ 02-837-3132. Primi 6€ ($7); secondi 10€–12€ ($12–$14). AE, DC, MC, V. Mon–Sat noon–3pm; Mon–Tues and Thurs–Sat 7–11pm. Tram: 3, 15, 29, 30, or 59.

Premiata Pizzeria ★ PIZZA/PAN-ITALIAN   The most popular pizzeria in the Navigli stays packed from early dinnertime until the bar-hopping crowd stops by for late-night munchies. The restaurant rambles back forever, exposed copper pipes tracing across the ceilings of rooms wrapped around shaded outdoor terraces set with long, raucous tables. Seating is communal and service hurried, but the wood oven pizzas are excellent. If you're hungrier, there's a long menu of pastas and meat courses, while lighter appetites can enjoy a selection of salads or platters of cheese or *salumi* built for two.

Via Alzaia Naviglio Grande 2. ℂ 02-8940-0648. Reservations suggested. Primi 8€–10€ ($9–$12); secondi 12€–18€ ($14–$21); pizza 4.50€–12€ ($5–$14). MC, V. Wed–Mon noon–2:30pm; daily 7:30–11:30pm. Tram: 3, 15, 29, 30, or 59.

CAFES & GELATO

Bar Zucca/Caffè Miani, at the Duomo end of the Galleria Vittorio Emanuele II (ℂ 02-8646-4435; www.caffemiani.it; Metro: Duomo), is best known by its original name, "the Camparino." It's the most attractive and popular of the Galleria's many bars and holds the dubious distinction of having introduced Italy to what has become the country's ubiquitous red cordial, Campari, a viciously red liquid that tastes like hair tonic even when cut with soda water, as is traditional.

Strolling Through Milan

The prime spot for a *passeggiata* (stroll) is the Piazza Duomo and the adjoining Galleria, but many of the neighborhoods that fan out from the center are ideal for wandering and looking into the life of the Milanese. The **Golden Quadrilateral** (the city's center for high fashion), just north of the Piazza Duomo on and around Via Montenapoleone, is known for window-shopping; **Magenta** is an old residential quarter, filled with some of the city's most venerable churches, west of Piazza Duomo (follow Via Orifici and its extension, Via Dante, toward the Castello Sforzesco); the **Brera,** a parcel of old Milan now filled with bars and inexpensive restaurants along the streets clustered around the Pinacoteca Brera (follow Via Brera from the Teatro alla Scala); and the trendy **Navigli** neighborhood, at the southern edge of the center city, a series of narrow towpaths running alongside the remaining *navigli* (canals) that once laced the city, the former warehouse entrances along them now housing the hoppingest bars, *birrerie* (pubs), restaurants, and small clubs in the city (take the metro to Sant'Agostino). A stroll in Milan almost always includes a stop at a cafe or gelateria (see above).

You can sample one—along with a selection of light dishes to wipe the taste off your tongue (as you might gather, I'm not a fan of the popular Campari-soda)—while lingering at the tables set up in the Galleria with a bit of Duomo facade view, or in one of the Art Nouveau rooms inside.

You can find organic gelato at the **Gelateria Ecologica,** Corso di Porta Ticinese 40 (© **02-5810-1872;** Metro: Sant'Ambrogio or Missori), in the Ticinese/Navigli neighborhood. It's so popular, there's no need for a sign out front. Strollers in the atmospheric Brera neighborhood sooner or later stumble upon the **Gelateria Toldo,** Via Ponte Vetero 9 (© **02-8646-0863;** Metro: Cordusio or Lanza), where the gelato is wonderfully creamy and many of the *sorbetto* selections are so fruity and fresh they seem healthy.

The **Pasticceria Confetteria Cova,** Via Montenapoleone 8 (© **02-600-0578;** Metro: Montenapoleone), is nearing its 200th year in refined surroundings near the similarly atmospheric Museo Poldi-Pezzoli. It's usually filled with shoppers making the rounds in this high-fashion district. You can enjoy a quick coffee and a brioche at the long bar or take a seat in one of the elegant adjoining rooms.

The **Pasticceria Marchesi,** Via Santa Maria alla Porta 13 (© **02-862-770;** Metro: Cardusio), is a distinguished pastry shop with an adjoining wood-paneled tearoom. Since it's only steps from Santa Maria delle Grazie, you can enjoy the old-world ambience and a cup of excellent coffee (or one of the many teas and herbal infusions) as you dash off postcards of the *Last Supper.* Of course, you'll want to accompany your beverage with one of the elegant pastries, perhaps a slice of the *panettone* (cake laden with raisins and candied citron) that's a hallmark of Milan. No one prepares it better than they do at Marchesi. It's open Tuesday to Sunday 8am to 8pm.

MILAN AFTER DARK

On Wednesdays and Thursdays Milan's newspapers tend to devote a lot of ink to club schedules and cultural events. If you don't trust your command of Italian to plan your nightlife, check out the tourist office in Piazza Duomo—there are usually piles of fliers lying about that announce upcoming events. The tourist office also keeps visitors up-to-date with *Milano: Where, When, How,* a periodical it distributes for free with schedules of events, as well as listings of bars, clubs, and restaurants.

THE PERFORMING ARTS   For the low-down on the long-term renovations of Milan's premier opera house, **Teatro alla Scala** ★★★, and the new "temporary" (until 2005) venue for performances up in the northern 'burbs, see the "'Til the Fat Lady Sings . . . Again: The Restoration of La Scala" box on p. 270.

Milan's "Giuseppe Verdi" Symphony Orchestra, conducted by Riccardo Chailly, now plays at the **Auditorium di Milano,** a renovated 1930s movie house at Via S. Gottardo 42/Largo Gustav Mahler (© **02-8338-9222;** www.auditoriumdimilano.org; Metro: Duomo, then tram 3 or 15). Concerts run from late September through May, usually on Thursdays and Fridays at 8:30pm and Sundays at 4pm. There's a Sunday-morning (11am) early-matinee program that mixes chamber music and other smaller-scale performances. Kids get their own series of musical programs Saturdays at 3:30pm.

MOVIES   In Italy, English-language films are almost always dubbed into Italian, providing English speakers with an opportunity to bone up on their Italian but taking some of the fun out of a night at the movies. Fortunately, there are always a few theaters that screen English-language films in the original version 1 night a week: **Anteo,** Via Milazzo 9 (© **02-659-7732;** Metro: Moscova), on Monday; **Arcoboleno,** Vle. Tunisia 11 (© **02-2940-6054;** Metro: Porta Venezia), on Tuesday; and **Mexico,** Via Savona 57 (© **02-4895-1802;** Metro: Porta Genova), on Thursday.

PUBS   A publike atmosphere, induced in part by Guinness on tap, prevails at Liberty-style **Bar Magenta,** Via Carducci 13 at Corso Magenta (© **02-805-3808**), in the neighborhood from which it takes its name; open Tuesday to Sunday (Metro: Cadorna). One of the more popular La Brera hangouts, with a young following, is **El Tombon de San Marc,** Via San Marco 20 at Via Montebello (© **02-659-9507**), which, despite its name, is an English pub–style bar and restaurant open Monday to Saturday (Metro: Moscova).

If you're not quite young and up to partying with those who are, a pleasant alternative to Milan's youth-oriented venues is **Bar Margherita,** where there's jazz on the sound system (and sometimes live on stage) and a nice selection of wines and grappa; they also lay out a good selection of munchies-on-toothpicks (*crostini,* frittata wedges, and other canapés) around dinnertime. It's in La Brera at Via Moscova 25 (© **02-659-0833**); open Monday to Saturday 7am to 2am (Metro: Moscova).

Among the Navigli nightspots (growing in number all the time) is **El Brellin,** an intimate, canal-side piano bar (Sat) with its own mini-canal on Vicolo della Lavandaia, off Alzaia Naviglio Grande 14 (© **02-5810-1351**), open Monday through Saturday (Metro: Genova FS). **Birreria La Fontanella,** Alzaia Naviglio Pavese 6 (© **02-837-2391**), has canal-side tables outside and the oddest-shaped

---

Tips   Night Owls' Favorite Haunts

The Navigli/Ticinese neighborhood currently reigns as Milan's prime nighttime turf, though Brera retains its pull with night owls as well.

beer glasses around—that half-a-barbell kind everyone seems to order is called the "Cavalliere." It's open Tuesday to Sunday 7pm to 3am (Metro: Genova FS).

JAZZ CLUBS   Since Capolinea got ousted (*Warning:* the club's name is still there at Via Lodovico il Moro 119, but it's *not* the old jazz club where the greats came to play, rather it's some pathetic mimic of it slapped together by the next-door neighbors who forced the original owners out of this space), the best venue on the jazz club scene is **Le Scimmie,** which has its own bar-boat moored in the canal. It's in the Navigli at Via Ascanio Sforza 49 (© **02-8940-2874;** www.scimmie.it), and operates Wednesday to Monday (Metro: Porta Genova), with shows starting at 10:30pm.

MUSIC & DANCE CLUBS   The dance scene changes all the time in Milan, but at whatever club is popular (or in business) at the moment, expect to pay a cover of 10€ to 15€ ($12–$17)—sometimes more for big-name live acts. Models, actors, sports stars, and the attendant fashion set favor **Hollywood,** which is small, chic, and centrally located in La Brera at Corso Como 15 (© **02-655-5574** or 02-659-8996, or 02-679-8896 after 10:30pm); it closes Mondays and July 23 to September 7 (Metro: Moscova).

Grand Café Fashion, Corso di Porta Ticinese 60 at Via Vetere (© **02-8940-0709** or 0336-347-333), is a multipurpose nightspot halfway to the Navigli with a restaurant open from 9pm and a disco nightly from 11:30pm. It brings a beautiful crowd to the Ticinese neighborhood, where they dance the night away, sometimes to thematic evenings like Latino Mondays and, er, lap-dance Sundays (Metro: Porta Genova).

Milan's most venerable disco/live music club is **Rolling Stone,** Corso XXII Marzo 32 (© **02-733-172**), in business since the 1950s. Most of the performers these days are of a rock bent, and the club is as immensely popular as ever. Cover charges, which vary widely depending on who's performing, are less expensive for women than for men, and more expensive on weekends than on weekdays; closed Sundays and Mondays (Tram: 12, 27, 45, 60, 66, 73, or 92).

Note: There are no specific club hours in Milan. Opening and closing times seem to vary with the seasons and with the crowds, with openings anywhere from 7 to 11pm and closings anywhere from 1am to dawn, later on weekend nights, of course.

GAY CLUBS   Milan's largest gay club is **Nuovo Idea,** Via de Castillia 30 (© **02-6900-7859;** www.dinet.it/nuovaidea); it attracts a mostly male crowd of all ages and offers everything from disco to polkas, in a huge techno room. It's open Thursday to Sunday (Metro: Gioia). **Recycle,** Via Calabria 5 (© **02-376-1531**), is a women-only club Friday to Sunday 9pm to 2am, sometimes later (mixed crowd welcome Wed–Thurs nights).

Via Sammartini along the train station's left flank (Metro: Central FS) is a good street to hit. **Next Groove,** at no. 23 (© **02-6698-0450**), is a mixed gay and lesbian disco bar of the phone-on-the-table sort and thematic evenings; open daily. Next door at no. 25, **After Line Disco Pub** (© **02-669-2130**) is a bar-restaurant where a giant-screen TV and strobe light are switched on after dinner to turn it into a lesbian discotheque; open Tuesday to Sunday.

DAY TRIPS FROM MILAN
PAVIA & THE CERTOSA
At one time, the quiet and remarkably well preserved little city of **Pavia,** 35km (22 miles) south of Milan, was more powerful than Milan. It was the capital of

Lombardy in the 7th and 8th centuries, and by the early Renaissance, the Viscontis and later the Sforzas, the two families who so influenced the history of Milan and all of Lombardy, were wielding their power here. It was the Viscontis who built the city's imposing **Castello,** made Pavia one of Europe's great centers of learning (when they founded the university) in 1361, began construction on the **Duomo** (with the 3rd-largest dome in Italy) in 1488, and founded the city's most important monument and the one that brings most visitors to Pavia, the Certosa.

The **Certosa** ★★★ is 8km (5 miles) north of Pavia. One of the most unusual buildings in Lombardy, if not in Italy, this religious compound was commissioned by Gian Galeazzo Visconti in 1396 as a Carthusian monastery and a burial chapel for his family—officially as thanks for curing his second sickly wife (the 1st died) and granting him children and heirs. It was completed by the Sforzas. The facade of colored marbles, the frescoed interior, and the riot of funerary sculpture is evidence that this brood of often-tyrannical despots were also dedicated builders with grand schemes and large coffers. The finest and most acclaimed statuary monument here, that of Ludivico il Moro (buried in France, where he died a prisoner of war) and Beatrice d'Este (buried in Milan's Santa Maria delle Grazie), sits in the left transept of the massive church, beneath lapis lazuli–rich frescoes by Bergognone. Its presence here is a twist of fate—the monks at Milan's Chiesa di Santa Maria delle Grazie (which houses the *Last Supper*) sold the tomb to the Certosa to raise funds. In the right transept is the 15th-century tomb of Gian Galeazzo Visconti.

Across from the tomb is the entrance to the enormous cloister, lined with the monks' cells, each of which is actually a two-story cottage with its own garden plot. Most are now inhabited by a small community of Cistercian monks. It is possible to visit their refectory and an adjoining shop, where they sell their Chartreuse liqueur and herbal soaps and scents.

Admission to the Certosa (© 0382-925-613) is free; it's open Tuesday to Sunday 9am to 12:15pm and 2:30 to 6pm (until 4:30pm Nov–Feb and 5:30pm Sept–Oct and Mar–Apr).

GETTING THERE & TOURIST INFO   Half-hourly trains from **Milan** usually stop at the station near the Certosa, just before the main Pavia station (30 min.). To reach the Certosa from Pavia, take one of the half-hourly buses from the Autocorriere station (next to the train station); the trip takes about 15 minutes. By car, the Certosa is about half an hour south of Milan Via Autostrada A7 (follow exit signs).

The **tourist office** is near the train station at Via Fabio Filzi 2 (© 0382-22-156); it's open Monday to Saturday from 8:30am to 12:30pm and 2 to 6pm.

CREMONA

Violins have been drawing visitors to this little city on the river Po, 92km (57 miles) southeast of Milan, since the 17th century, when fine string instruments began emerging from the workshops of Nicolo Amati and his more famous protégé, Antonio Stradivari. The tradition continues: Cremona's Scuola di Luteria (Violin School) is world-renowned.

Cremona's charms extend far beyond the musical. Its central Piazza del Commune is one of the largest and most beautiful town squares in Italy, fronted by remarkable structures. Among these is the 12th-century **Duomo** (© 0372-26-707), clad in pink marble and overshadowed by Italy's tallest campanile; inside, it is covered with 16th-century frescoes (admission is free and hours are daily 7:30am–noon and 3:30–7pm).

The **Palazzo del Commune** rises gracefully above a Gothic arcade and is embellished with terra-cotta panels. Its **Raccolta dei Violini** 🖈🖈 displays a small collection of 17th- and 18th-century violins by Amati, the Guarneri, and one Stradt (𝄽 **0372-22-138**). A local maestro comes over every morning to play them, since a fine instrument needs to be played to remain in top form (for security reasons, you cannot attend these impromptu concerts). The **Museo Stradivariano** 🖈, in the Museo Civico alongside an unimportant *pinacoteca* collection of paintings at Via Palestro 17 (𝄽 **0372-461-886**), displays the finest violins ever made, including those by Amatis, Stradivari, and Guaneri.

Admission to the Museo Civico is 8€ ($9.20) and it's open Tuesday to Saturday 8:30am to 6:30pm, Sunday 10am to 6pm. Open hours for the Racolta dei Violini were not yet confirmed when we went to press on this edition (the collection's Palazzo del Comune home had been closed for renovations, and was to open one month after this book is printed and on the shelves). However, the admission price has already been set, at 6€ ($6.90) for admission alone, plus another 1.50€ ($1.75) if you want to hear the things being played (they are regularly bowed by local musicians to keep their coveted tones intact)—though for this honor, you must call the Comune at 𝄽 **0372-22-138** to find out when the next "concert" is and book a seat.

GETTING THERE & TOURIST INFO   Trains arrive almost hourly from **Milan** (65 min.). Hourly trains to **Brescia** (50 min.) also make it possible to combine an excursion from Milan to Cremona and Brescia (see below). If you are traveling by car, you can make the trip to Cremona by following A1 from Milan to Piacenza and A21 from Piacenza to Cremona.

The **tourist office** is near the Duomo at Piazza del Commune 5 (𝄽 **0372-23-233;** www.cremonaturismo.com); Monday to Saturday 9:30am to 12:30pm and 3 to 6pm, Sunday 10am to 1pm.

BRESCIA

Ringed by industrialized suburbs, Brescia (97km/60 miles from Milan) doesn't readily beckon travelers to stop. Those who do, however, have the pleasure of wandering through a centuries-old town center where Roman ruins, not one but two duomos, and medieval palazzi line winding streets and gracious piazzas.

The center of Brescia is Piazza Paolo VI, better known as Piazza del Duomo after its two duomos—the 17th- to 19th-century Duomo Nuovo (New Duomo), which is pretty bland, and the much more charming (on the outside, though it's nearly bare inside) 11th- to 12th-century **Duomo Vecchio (Old Duomo)** 🖈, also called Rotonda, for its shape. Year-round the New Duomo is open Monday to Saturday 7:30am to noon and 4 to 7:30pm and Sunday 8am to 1pm and 4 to 7:30pm. April to September the Old Duomo is open Wednesday to Monday 9am to noon and 3 to 7pm; October to March, hours are Saturday and Sunday 9am to noon and 3 to 6pm. Next to the New Duomo rises the Broletto, Brescia's medieval town hall.

Brescia's Roman past emerges if you leave the piazza on Via dei Musei and follow it to the **Capitolino** 🖈, a temple erected in A.D. 73. Jog up Vicolo del Fontanone to its right to see the remains of the Teatro Romano (Roman Theater). A few blocks farther down the street is the Monasterio di San Salvatore e Santa Giulia, where Charlemagne's ex-wife, Ermengarde, spent her last days. The monastery incorporates several churches and museums, together housing a rich collection of prehistoric, Roman, and medieval objects (lots of them high-quality pieces); everything is well documented and explained in Italian and English. This **Museo della Città** 🖈🖈 is at Via dei Musei 1b (𝄽 **800-762-811** or

030-297-7834). Admission is 8€ ($9) for adults, 6€ ($7) for students, and free for those under 17 and over 65. It's open Tuesday to Sunday June to September 10am to 6pm and October to May 9:30am to 5:30pm. Special exhibits raise the prices a tad and lengthen the hours.

If you leave Piazza del Duomo from the other direction, through the archways into Piazza Loggia, you come upon Brescia's most enchanting building, the Renaissance **Loggia** ★★, a two-story colonnade festooned with reliefs and statues and dating to the turn of the 16th century (the bottom half) and the mid-1550s through 1570s (the top half). As beautiful and renowned as the Loggia is, oddly enough, we don't know who designed it, though great names such as Jacopo Sansovino and Andrea Palladio have been suggested to have been involved. The Torre dell'Orologio, on the opposite side of the square, resembles the campanile on Piazza San Marco in Venice, bespeaking the days when Brescia was a Venetian stronghold.

Brescia's excellent painting collection, the **Pinacoteca Tosio-Matinengo** ★★, is at Piazza Moretto 4 (© **030-377-4999;** www.asm.brescia.it/musei). From Piazza Loggia, walk south into the ugly Fascist-era Piazza Vittorio and follow that south into Piazza dei Mercati; from there Corso Zanardelli and Corso Magenta lead west to Via Crispi, which leads south to the museum. Works by Moretto, Foppa, and other painters of the school of Brescia hang alongside Raphaels and Tintorettos in an old palazzo. Admission is 3€ ($3.45) for adults, 2€ ($2.30) for students, and free for children 16 and under and seniors over 65. It's open Tuesday to Friday June to September 10am to 5pm and October to May 9:30am to 1pm and 2:30 to 5pm.

GETTING THERE & TOURIST INFO   Trains arrive from Milan about every half-hour (45–65 min.). Brescia is linked to Milan by the A4, which continues east to Verona and Venice; the trip from Milan to Brescia takes a little under an hour. There's a **tourist info office** at Piazza Loggia 6 (© **030-240-0357**), open in summer Monday to Saturday 9am to 6:30pm and in winter Monday to Saturday 9:30am to 12:30pm and Monday to Friday 2 to 5pm.

The **APT tourist office** is at Corso Zanardelli 34 (© **030-43-418**); open Monday to Saturday 9am to 12:30pm and Monday to Friday 3 to 6pm. You can get more details on the web at www.bresciaholiday.com and www.comune.brescia.it.

2 Bergamo

47km (29 miles) NE of Milan, 52km (32 miles) NW of Brescia

Bergamo is two cities. Bergamo Bassa, the lower, a mostly 19th- and 20th-century city, concerns itself with everyday business. Bergamo Alta, a beautiful medieval/Renaissance town perched on a green hill, concerns itself these days with entertaining the visitors who come to admire its piazze, palazzi, and churches; enjoy the lovely vistas from its belvederes; and soak in a hushed beauty that inspired Italian poet Gabriel d'Annunzio to call old Bergamo "a city of muteness." The distinct characters of the two parts of this city go back to its founding as a Roman settlement, when the *civitas* (Latin for city) was on the hill and farms and suburban villas dotted the plains below.

ESSENTIALS

GETTING THERE   By Train   Trains arrive from and depart for Milan hourly (50 min.); service to and from Brescia is even more frequent, with half-hourly service during peak early-morning and early-evening travel times (50 min.). Given the frequency of train service, you can easily make a daylong sightseeing loop from Milan, arriving in Bergamo in the morning, moving on to Brescia in the afternoon, and returning to Milan from there. If you're coming from or going on to nearby Lake Como, there's hourly service between Bergamo and Lecco, on the southeast end of the lake (40 min.).

By Bus   An extensive bus network links Bergamo with many other towns in Lombardy. There are five to six buses a day to and from Como (2 hr.) run by **SPT** (© 031-247-247). Service to and from Milan by **Autostradale** (© 02-3391-0843) runs every half-hour (1 hr.). The bus station is next to the train station on Piazza Marconi.

By Car   Bergamo is linked directly to Milan via the A4, which continues east to Brescia, Verona, and Venice. The trip between Milan and Bergamo takes a little over half an hour. Parking in or near the Città Alta, most of which is closed to traffic, can be difficult. There is a parking lot on the northern end of the Città Alta near Porta Garibaldi (about 1€/$1.15 per hour) and street parking along Viale delle Mura, which loops around the outer flanks of the walls of the Città Alta.

VISITOR INFORMATION   The **Città Bassa tourist office,** Viale Vittorio Emanuele 20 (© **035-210-204;** fax 035-230-184; www.apt.bergamo.it), is 9 long blocks straight out from the train station; it's open Monday to Friday 9am to 12:30pm and 2 to 5:30pm. The **Città Alta office,** Vicola Aquila Nera 2 (© **035-232-730;** fax 035-242-994), is just off Piazza Vecchia, open daily the same hours.

FESTIVALS & MARKETS   Bergamo is a cultured city, and its celebrations include the May-to-June **Festivale Piantistico,** one of the world's major piano competitions. In September the city celebrates its native composer Gaetano Donizetti with **performances of his works,** most of them at the Teatro Donizetti in the Città Bassa (see below).

CITY LAYOUT   Piazza Vecchia, the Colleoni Chapel, and most of the other sights that bring visitors to Bergamo are in the **Città Alta**—the exception is the Accademia Carrara, which is in the Città Bassa but on the flanks of the hillside, so within easy walking distance of the upper-town sights. **Via Colleoni** cuts a swath through the medieval heart of the Città Alta, beginning at **Piazza Vecchia.** To reach this lovely square from the funicular station at **Piazza Mercato delle Scarpi,** walk along **Via Gombito** for about 5 minutes. Most of the Città Alta is closed to traffic, but it's compact and easy to navigate on foot. Down below, the main square known as the **Sentierone** is the center of the **Città Bassa.** It's about a 5-minute walk from the train station north along **Viale Papa Giovanni XXIII.**

GETTING AROUND   Bergamo has an extensive **bus system** that runs through the Città Bassa and to points outside the walls of the Città Alta; tickets are .90€ ($1.05) and are available from newsstands and tobacco shops. With the exception of the trip from the train or bus stations up to the Città Alta, you probably won't have much need of public transit, since most of the sights are within an easy walk of one another.

To reach the Città Alta from the train station, take bus no. 1 or 1A and make the free transfer to the **Funicolare Bergamo Alta,** connecting the upper and lower cities and running every 7 minutes from 6:30am to 12:30am. You can make the walk to the funicular easily in about 15 minutes (and see something of the pleasant new city en route) by following Viale Papa Giovanni XXIII and its continuations Viale Roma and Viale Vittorio Emanuele II straight through town to the funicular station.

If you're feeling hearty, a footpath next to the funicular winds up to Città Alta; the steep climb up (made easier by intermittent staircases) takes about 20 minutes. Bus no. 1A also continues up and around the Città Alta walls to end just outside Porta San Vigilio, and hence more convenient to hotels San Lorenzo and Gourmet.

EXPLORING THE CITTA BASSA

Most visitors scurry through Bergamo's lower, newer town on their way to the Città Alta, but you may want to pause long enough to enjoy a coffee along the **Sentierone,** the elongated piazza/street at the center of town. This spacious square graciously combines a mishmash of architectural styles (including 16th-century porticos on one side, the Mussolini-era Palazzo di Giustizia and two imitation Doric temples on another). Locals sit in its gardens, lounge in its cafes, and attend classical concerts at the **Teatro Donizetti.** This 19th-century theater is the center of Bergamo's lively culture scene, with a fall opera season and a winter-to-spring season of dramatic performances; for details, check with the tourist office or call the theater at © **035-416-0611** (http://teatro.gaetano-donizetti.com).

The main draw for most visitors down here, though, is the **Galleria dell' Accademia Carrara** ✷✷, Piazza Carrara 82a (© **035-399-640;** www.accademia carrara.bergamo.it). The city's exquisite art gallery is one of the finest in northern Italy, founded in 1795 when Napoléon's troops were busy rounding up the art treasures of their newly occupied northern Italian states. Many of these works ended up in Bergamo under the stewardship of Count Giacomo Carrara. The collection came into its own after World War I, when a young Bernard Berenson, the 20th century's most noted art connoisseur, took stock of what was here and classified the immense holdings, making sure "every Lotto [was] a Lotto." Lorenzo Lotto (1480–1556) was a Venetian who fled the stupefying society of his native city and spent 1513 to 1525 in Bergamo perfecting his highly emotive portraits. Many of his works from the Accademia recently toured the United States, but they're now back in place in the salons of this neoclassical palace alongside a staggering inventory with paintings by Bellini, Canaletto, Carpaccio, Guardi, Mantegna, and Tiepolo. Most of these masterworks are in the 17 third-floor galleries.

It's easy to become overwhelmed here, but among the paintings you may want to view first is Lotto's *Portrait of Lucina Brembrati,* in which you'll see the immense sensitivity with which the artist was able to imbue his subjects. Look carefully at the moon in the upper-left corner—it has the letters "ci" painted into it, a playful anagram of the sitter's first name; in Italian, *moon* is *luna,* and this one has a "ci" in the middle). Botticelli's much-reproduced *Portrait of Giuliano de Medici* hangs nearby, as does Raphael's sensual *St. Sebastian.* You can visit the Accademia on foot from the Città Alta by following Via Porta Dipinta halfway down the hill to the Porto Sant'Agostino and then a terraced, ramplike staircase to the doors of the museum. From the Città Bassa, the museum is about a 10-minute walk from the Sentierone—from the east end of the square, take a left on Largo Belloti, then a right on Via Giuseppe Verdi and follow that for several blocks to Via Pignolo and turn left to Via Tomaso, which takes you to Piazza Carrara (the route is well signposted). Admission is 2.60€ ($3), free for those under 18 and over 60, and free for all ages on Sunday. It's open Tuesday to Sunday 9:30am to 1pm and 2:30 to 6:45pm (Oct–Mar 10am–1pm and 2:30–5:45pm).

Across the street is the **Galleria d'Arte Moderna e Contemporanea** (© **035-399-527**), containing works by such 20th-century masters as Fattori, Boccioni,

De Chirico, Morandi, and Kandinsky. Admission is free, and it's open Tuesday to Saturday 10am to 1pm and 3 to 7pm and Sunday 10am to 7pm.

EXPLORING THE CITTA ALTA

The higher, older part of Bergamo owes its stone palazzos, proud monuments, and what remains of its extensive fortified walls to more than 3 centuries of Venetian rule, beginning in 1428, when soldiers of the Republic wrestled control of the city out of the hands of the Milan-based Visconti. The Venetians left their mark elegantly in the town's theatrically adjoining squares, **Piazza Vecchia** and **Piazza del Duomo,** which together create one of the most beautiful outdoor assemblages in Italy—actually, French writer Stendahl went so far as to call this heart of old Bergamo the "most beautiful place on earth."

On Piazza Vecchia you'll see traces of the Venetian presence in the 12th-century **Palazzo della Ragione (Courts of Justice),** which has been embellished with a graceful ground-floor arcade and the Lion of San Mark's, symbol of the Venetian Republic, above a 16th-century balcony reached by a covered staircase (the bells atop its adjoining tower, the **Torre Civico,** sound the hours sonorously). The interiors will remain closed over the next few years for renovations. Across the piazza, the **Biblioteca Civica** was modeled after the Sansovino Library in Venice. Piazza del Duomo, reached through one of the archways of the Palazzo della Ragione, is filled with an overpowering collection of religious structures that include the **Duomo** and the much more enticing **Cappella Colleoni** (see below), the **Baptistery,** and the **Basilica di Santa Maria Maggiore** (see below).

Bergamese strongman Colleoni (see the "Cappella Colleoni" entry below) lent his name to the upper town's delightful main street, cobblestoned and so narrow you can just about touch the buildings on either side when standing in the center. If you follow it to its far western end, you'll emerge into **Largo Colle Aperto,** refreshingly green and open to the Città Bassa and valleys below. For better views and a short excursion into the countryside, board the **Funicolare San Vigilio** for the ascent up the San Vigilio hill; the funicular runs daily every 12 minutes or so between 7am and midnight and costs .90€ ($1.05). The strategic importance of these heights was not lost on Bergamo's medieval residents, who erected a summit-top **Castello** (© **035-236-284**), now mostly in ruin. Its keep, still surrounded by the old walls, is a park in which every bench affords a far-reaching view. It's open daily: April to September 9am to 8pm, October and March 10am to 6pm, and November to February 10am to 4pm.

The Castello is a good place to begin a trek around the flanks of the Città Alta—go down the San Vigilio hill (or take the funicular) back into the Città Alta through the Porta San Alessandro. For a look at the old walls and some more good views, instead of following Via Colleoni back into the center of the town, turn left on Via della Mura and follow the 16th-century bastions for about .8km (half a mile) to the Porta Sant'Agostino on the other side of the town.

Basilica di Santa Maria Maggiore ✦ Behind the plain marble facade and a portico whose columns rise out of the backs of lions lies an overly baroque gilt-covered interior hung with Renaissance tapestries. **Gaetano Donizetti,** the wildly popular composer of frothy operas, who was born in Bergamo in 1797 (see "Museo Donizettiano," below) and returned here to die in 1848, is entombed in a **marble sarcophagus** that's as excessive as the rest of the church's decor. The finest works are the **choir stalls,** with rich wood inlays depicting landscapes and biblical scenes; they're the creation of Lorenzo Lotto, the Venetian who worked in Bergamo in the early 16th century and whose work you'll encounter at the

Accademia and elsewhere around the city. The stalls are usually kept under cloth to protect the sensitive hardwoods from light and pollutants, but they're unveiled for Lent. The octagonal **Baptistery** in the piazza outside the church was originally inside but removed, reconstructed, and much embellished in the 19th century.

Piazza del Duomo. ℭ 035-223-327. Free admission. May–Sept Mon–Sat 9am–noon and 3–6pm, Sun 8–10:30am and 3–6pm; Oct–Apr Mon–Sat 9am–noon and 3–4:30pm, Sun 8–10:30am and 3–4:30pm.

Cappella Colleoni ★★★ Bartolomeo Colleoni was a Bergamese *condottiere* who fought for Venice to maintain the Venetian stronghold on the city. In return for his labors, the much-honored soldier was given Bergamo to rule for the republic. If you've already visited Venice, you may have seen Signore Colleoni astride the Verrocchio equestrian bronze in Campo Santi Giovanni e Paolo. He rests for eternity in this elaborate funerary chapel designed by Amadeo, the great sculptor from nearby Pavia (where he completed his most famous work, the Certosa; see p. 289). The pink-and-white marble exterior, laced with finely sculpted columns and loggias, is airy and almost whimsical; inside, the soldier and his favorite daughter, Medea, lie beneath a ceiling frescoed by Tiepolo and surrounded by reliefs and statuary; here, Colleoni appears on horseback again atop his marble tomb.

Piazza del Duomo. ℭ 035-210-061. Free admission. Apr–Oct daily 9:30am–12:30pm and 2–6pm; Nov–Mar Tues–Sun 9:30am–12:30pm and 2–4:30pm.

Museo Donizettiano This charming little museum commemorates Gaetano Donizetti, who was born in Bergamo in 1797 and—little wonder, given the romance of his boyhood surroundings—became one of Italy's most acclaimed composers of opera. Fans can swoon over his sheet music, piano, and other memorabilia and see the deathbed where he succumbed to syphilis in 1848. Thus inspired, you can make the pilgrimage to the humble house where he claimed to have been born in a cellar, the **Casa Nateledi Gaetano Donizetti,** Via B. Canale 14 (ℭ 035-399-432), a rural street that descends the hillside from the Porta Sant'Alessandro on the western edge of the city. It's open Saturday and Sunday only 11am to 6:30pm (donations requested).

Via Arena 9. ℭ 035-247-116. www.museostoricobg.org. Admission 3€ ($3.45). June–Sept daily 9:30am–1pm and 2–5:30pm; Oct–May Tues–Fri 9:30am–1pm, Sat–Sun 9:30am–1pm and 2–5:30pm. Bus: 1 or 1a.

WHERE TO STAY

The charms of staying in the Città Alta are no secret. Rooms tend to fill up quickly, especially in summer and on weekends. Reserve well in advance. If they're out of room, or you prefer a huge, modern business hotel flush with all the amenities in the Città Bassa, call the charmless but comfortable 163-room **Excelsior San Marco,** Piazza Repubblica 6, a square off Viale Vittorio Emanuele halfway between Piazza Matteotti and the funicular up to the Città Alta (ℭ 035-366-111; fax 035-223-201; www.hotelsanmarco.com), where doubles go for from 140€ to 210€ ($161–$242).

Agnello d'Oro ★★ *Value* In keeping with its location a few steps from Piazza Vecchia, the Agnello d'Oro looks like it's right out of an old tourist brochure extolling the quaint charms of Italy. The tall, narrow ocher-colored building, with flower boxes at each of its tall windows, overlooks a small piazzetta where a fountain splashes next to potted greenery. The wood-paneled lounge and intimate dining room add to the charm quotient, which declines somewhat as you ascend in a tiny elevator to the rooms. These lean more toward serviceable comfort than luxury, but warm color schemes and old prints help compensate for the lack of space and amenities; the bathrooms are roomy and have been modernized. Front rooms (the ones to request) have narrow balconies overlooking the piazza. This is the most popular hostelry in the Città Alta (even though the friendliness level of the desk staff can vary wildly), so reservations are mandatory.

Via Gombito 22, 24129 Bergamo Alta. ⓒ 035-249-883. Fax 035-235-612. www.agnellodoro.it. 20 units. 92€ ($106) double. Continental breakfast 6€ ($7). AE, DC, MC, V. **Amenities:** Concierge; tour desk. *In room:* TV, dataport, hair dryer.

Gourmet ⚡ This pleasant hotel offers the best of both worlds—it's only steps away from the Città Alta (a few hundred feet outside the Porta Sant'Agostino on the road leading up to the Castello) but on a rural hillside, giving it the air of a country retreat. The villa-style building is set behind walls in a lush garden and enjoys wonderful views. A wide terrace on two sides makes the most of these views and the song of caged canaries. Many of the very large, bright rooms look across the hillside to the heavily developed valley, too. They're furnished in plain modern (or at least modern a few decades ago) fashion geared more to solid comfort than to style, with king-size beds. They also rent a large, two-floor apartment with a sitting area and kitchen downstairs and upstairs two bedrooms—a double and a twin, each with bathroom. There's a highly reputed restaurant on the premises, hence the name, with indoor and outdoor tables and midrange prices on Bergamasco and Lombard cuisine.

Via San Vigilio 1, 24129 Bergamo. ⓒ and fax **035-437-3004**. www.gourmet-bg.it. 11 units. 90€ ($104) double; 180€ ($207) apt for 4. Continental breakfast 10€ ($12). AE, DC, MC, V. Closed Dec 27–Jan 7. **Amenities:** International/Bergamasco restaurant; bar; room service (24-hr.). *In room:* A/C, TV, minibar, hair dryer.

San Lorenzo ⚡⚡ Bergamo Alta was blessed with some much-needed additional hotel rooms when this stylish place opened in 1998, in a former convent building of Santa Agata. The centuries-old setting is tailor-made for this unusually pleasant inn—most of the rooms face a courtyard and open through French doors to a balcony that wraps around it. Though the hotel is right in town, just a few steps off Via Colleoni, its hillside location provides views over the green slopes flowing down to the valley below. The rooms are small but comfortable, with striped silk draperies and bed coverings and cane-backed lounge chairs; the marble bathrooms come with hand-held shower massagers and hair dryers. A sumptuous buffet breakfast is served in the breakfast room. The discovery of Roman ruins put the brakes on construction of an underground parking facility, though the hotel provides a permit allowing you to park for free in the adjoining square.

Piazza Mascheroni 9A, 24129 Bergamo. ⓒ **035-237-383**. Fax 035-237-958. www.hotelsanlorenzobg.it. 25 units. 125€ ($144) double; 140€ ($161) triple. Rates include continental breakfast. AE, DC, MC, V. Parking free. **Amenities:** Bar; room service (limited); laundry service; dry cleaning; nonsmoking rooms. *In room:* A/C, TV, dataport, minibar, hair dryer, safe.

WHERE TO DINE

Your gambols through the Città Alta can be nicely interspersed with fortifying stops at the city's many pastry shops and stand-up eateries. **Forno Tresoldi,** Via Colleoni 13, sells excellent pizzas and focaccia breads by the slice topped with cheese, salami, and vegetables (from 2€/$2.30). It's open Tuesday to Sunday from 8am to 1:30pm and 4 to 10pm.

Al Donizetti ⚡ WINE BAR This charming restaurant faces the upper city's old covered market, which now serves no purpose other than to look medieval and romantic. In good weather, tables are set out under the market's arcaded loggia, and meals are also served in the two small vaulted-ceiling dining rooms.

The bulk of the menu is devoted to various kinds of salami, ham, and cheeses, though many dishes also rely on fresh vegetables—perhaps a light zucchini flan or *raddichio con gorgonzola* (the bitter red greens are lightly grilled and the creamy cheese is added at the last minute). More than 360 wines are available, including dozens by the glass, to accompany a meal, and the staff will help you choose the right one.

Via Gombito 17a. © **035-242-661.** www.donizetti.it. Panini from 2.60€ ($3); salads and platters of cheese and/or meats 8.30€–13€ ($9–$15). MC, V. Thurs–Mon noon–3pm and 6:30–10:30pm.

Antica Hosteria del Vino Buono ★★★ NORTHERN ITALIAN   At this

cozy trattoria tucked into smallish rooms in a corner house on Piazza Mercato delle Scarpe at the top of the funicular station, an enthusiastic young staff takes food and wine seriously. It's a pleasure to dine in the handsome surroundings of brick, tile work, and photos of old Bergamo. For an introduction to food from the region, try one of the several tasting menus. Polenta figures prominently and is served *alla bergamese* (with wild mushrooms) and sometimes with olive paste folded into it—you can even sample three with the *tris di polenta.* The main courses lean toward meat. A dish like roast quail or rabbit should be accompanied by a Valcalepio Rosso, a medium-strength red from local vineyards (avoid the house red, a harsh cabernet).

Via Donizetti 25. © **035-247-993.** Reservations recommended. Primi 6€–8€ ($7–$9); secondi 8€–11€ ($9–$13); *menù turistico* 13€ ($15). AE, DC, MC, V. Tues–Sun noon–2:30pm and 7–10:30pm.

Taverna del Colleoni & Dell'Angelo ★ CREATIVE NORTHERN ITALIAN

Pierangelo Cornaro and chef Odorico Pinato run one of Bergamo's top restaurants, right on the main square in a Renaissance palazzo—in summer the best tables are outside on the piazza; otherwise you're in a refined medieval-looking space of high vaulted ceilings. The ingredients are fresh and the recipes inspired by local tradition, but the menu is a more creative *cucina nuova* (nouvelle portions, nouvelle prices). The best part of the menu is the back page, where they list some of their more typical dishes such as *fiorade bergamesche ai porcini e mirtilli* (wide noodles with porcini and blueberries), *cannoli di farro al ragù di cinghiale, salsa di zucca e patate* (pasta tubes made of emmer flour stuffed with wild boar and served under a pumpkin-potato sauce), *stoccafisso gratinato alla moda dell'Angelo* (cod casserole with cheese and polenta), and *cous cous siciliano di gamberi allo zafferano* (couscous tinged with saffron and studded with shrimp). Desserts are good, too.

Piazza Vecchia 7. © **035-232-596.** www.colleonidellangelo.com. Reservations recommended. Primi 11€–15€ ($13–$17); secondi 12€–26€ ($14–$30); lunch menu 31€ ($36); dinner "gourmand" menu 60€ ($69), neither with wine. AE, DC, MC, V. Tues–Sun noon–2:30pm and 7:30–10:30pm.

Vineria Cozzi ★★ *Value* NORTHERN ITALIAN   Cozzi isn't just a wine bar

but a Bergamo institution. Its cane chairs are well worn with use by Bergamese and visitors who can't resist stopping in for a glass of wine while walking down Via Colleoni. Hundreds of bottles from throughout Italy line the walls and are served by the glass (from 1.55€/$1.80). Sandwiches are always available, as are several kinds of cheese, but the changing daily offerings usually include several pasta dishes and polenta with rich cheese folded into it, perhaps a torta stuffed with fresh vegetables and a main course or two—if the duck breast stuffed with cabbage is available, order it.

Via Colleoni 22. © **035-238-836.** www.vineriacozzi.it. Sandwiches from 4€ ($4.60); primi 8€–10€ ($9–$12); secondi 8€–11€ ($9–$13). AE, MC, V. Daily 11am–2am. Closed Wed in winter and closed Fri in summer. Also closed 10 days in Jan and 12 days in Aug.

CAFES

Caffè del Tasso ⚜, Piazza Vecchia 3, is a prime piece of real estate on the main square of the Città Alta. It began life as a tailor's shop 500 years ago, but it's been a cafe and bar since 1581. Legend has it that Garibaldi's Redshirts used to gather here (Bergamo was a stronghold of Italian independence, which explains why an edict from the 1850s on the wall of this cafe prohibits rebellion).

While the location of **Caffè della Funicolare** in the Piazza Mercato delle Scarpe, in the upper terminal of the funicular that climbs the hill from the Città Bassa to the Città Alta, doesn't suggest a memorable dining experience, the station dates from 1887 and has enough Belle Epoque flourishes and curlicues to make the surroundings interesting. Plus, the dining room and terrace look straight down the hill to the town and valley, providing some of the best tables with a view (accompanied by low-cost fare) in the upper town. Stop in for a coffee, 1 of the 50 kinds of beer on tap, a sandwich, or a salad.

3 Mantua (Mantova): A Gem of Lombardy

158km (98 miles) E of Milan, 62km (38 miles) N of Parma, 150km (93 miles) SW of Venice

One of Lombardy's finest cities is in the farthest reaches of the region, making it a logical addition to a trip to Venice or Parma as well as to Milan. Like its neighboring cities in Emilia-Romagna, Mantua (Mantova) owes its past greatness and its beautiful Renaissance monuments to one family, in this case the Gonzagas, who rose from peasant origins to conquer the city in 1328 and ruled benevolently until 1707. You'll encounter the Gonzagas—and, since they were avid collectors of art and ruled through the greatest centuries of Italian art, the treasures they collected—in the massive Palazzo Ducale that dominates much of the town center; in their refreshing suburban retreat, the Palazzo Te; and in the churches and piazze that grew up around their court.

One of Mantua's greatest charms is its location—on a meandering river, the Mincio, which widens here to envelop the city in a necklace of moodily romantic lakes. Often shrouded in mist and surrounded by flat, lonely plains, Mantua can seem almost melancholy. Aldous Huxley wrote of the city, "I have seen great cities dead or in decay—but over none, it seemed to me, did there brood so profound a melancholy as over Mantua." Since his visit in the 1930s, though, the Palazzo Ducale and other monuments have been restored, and what will probably strike you more is what a remarkable gem of a city Mantua is.

ESSENTIALS

GETTING THERE   By Train   Ten trains daily arrive from Milan (2 hr.). There are hourly runs from Verona, with connections to Venice (30–40 min.).

By Car   The speediest connections from Milan are via the autostradas, the A4 to Verona and the A22 from Verona to Mantua (the trip takes less than 2 hr.). From Mantua, it's also an easy drive south to Parma and other cities in Emilia-Romagna, on S420.

VISITOR INFORMATION   The **tourist office** is at Piazza Mantegna 6 (© **0376-328-253;** fax 0376-363-292; www.aptmantova.it), open Monday to Saturday from 8:30am to 12:30pm and 3 to 6pm and Sunday 9:30am to 12:30pm (closed most Sun Jan–Feb).

FESTIVALS & MARKETS   Mantua enlivens its steamy summer with a **jazz festival** the third weekend (Thurs–Sun) of July. Year-round, Piazza delle Erbe is the scene of a bustling **food market** Monday through Saturday from 8am to

1pm. On Thursday mornings, a **bigger market,** filled with clothing, housewares and more food, spills through Piazza Magenta and adjoining streets.

CITY LAYOUT   Mantua is tucked onto a point of land surrounded on three sides by the **Mincio River,** which widens here into a series of lakes, named prosaically **Lago Superiore, Lago di Mezzo,** and **Lago Inferiore.** Most of the sights are within an easy walk of one another within the compact center, which is only a 10-minute walk from the lakeside train station. Follow **Via Solferino** to **Via Marangoni,** turn right and follow that to **Piazza Cavallotti,** where a left turn on **Corso Umberto I** will bring you to **Piazza delle Erbe,** the first of the gracious piazze that flow through the city center to the palace of the Gonzagas. You can also make the trip on the no. 2 bus, which leaves from the front of the station.

EXPLORING THE CITY

As you wander around, you'll notice that Mantua's squares are handsomely proportioned spaces surrounded by medieval and Renaissance churches and palazzi. The piazze open one into another, creating the wonderful illusion that walkers in the city are strolling through a series of opera sets.

The southernmost of these squares, and the place to begin your explorations, is **Piazza delle Erbe (Square of the Herbs)** ✱, so named for the produce-and-food market that transpires in stalls to one side (see "Festivals & Markets," above). Mantua's civic might is clustered here in a series of late-medieval and early Renaissance structures that include the **Palazzo della Ragione (Courts of Justice)** and **Palazzo del Podestà (Mayor's Palace),** from the 12th and 13th centuries, and the **Torre dell'Orologio,** topped with a 14th-century astrological clock. Also on this square is Mantua's earliest religious structure, the **Rotunda di San Lorenzo** ✱, a miniature round church from the 11th century (summer daily 10am–noon and 2:30–4:30pm, winter daily 11am–noon, though hours may vary; free admission). The city's Renaissance masterpiece, **Sant'Andrea Basilica** (see below), is off to one side on Piazza Mantegna.

In the adjoining **Piazza Broletto** (just north as you work your way through the old city), the statue of Virgil commemorates the poet who was born near here in 70 B.C. and celebrated Mantua's river Mincio in his *Bucolics.* The next square, **Piazza Sordello,** is huge, rectangular, and somberly medieval, lined with crenellated palazzi. Most notably, though, the massive hulk of the **Palazzo Ducale** (see below) forms one wall of the piazza. To enjoy Mantua's soulful lakeside vistas, follow Via Accademia through Piazza Arche and the Lungolago Gonzaga.

Palazzo d'Arco   Mantua's aristocratic D'Arco family lived in this elegant Renaissance palazzo until 1973, when the last member of the family donated it to the city. Though most of the extant palazzo is neoclassical (1780s), the gardens shelter a wing from the 15th century; the highlight of the rooms is the Sala dello Zodiaco, brilliantly frescoed with astrological signs by Giovanni Falconetto in 1520.

Piazza d'Arco 4. 🕐 **0376-322-242.** www.museodarco.it. Admission 3€ ($3.45). Mar–Oct Tues–Sun 10am–12:30pm and 2:30–6pm; Nov–Feb Sat–Sun 10am–12:30pm and 2–5pm.

Palazzo Ducale ✱✱   Behind the walls of this massive fortress/palace lies the history of the Gonzagas, Mantua's most powerful family, and what remains of the treasure trove they amassed in a rule that began in 1328 and lasted into the early 18th century. Between their skills as warriors and their penchant for marrying into wealthier and more cultured houses, they managed to acquire power, money, and an artistic following that included Pisanello, Titian, and most notably Andrea Mantegna, their court painter, who spent most of his career working for his Mantua patrons.

The most fortunate of these unions was that of Francesco Gonzaga to Isabelle d'Este in 1490. This well-bred daughter of Ferrara's Este clan commissioned many of the art-filled frescoed apartments you see today, including the Camera degli Sposi in Isabella's apartments—the masterpiece, and only remaining fresco cycle, of Mantegna. It took the artist 9 years to complete the cycle, and in it, he included many of the visitors to the court; it's a fascinating account of late-15th-century court life.

Most of Mantegna's works for the palace, though, have been carted off to other collections; his famous *Parnassus,* which he painted for an intimate room known as the *studiolo,* is now in the Louvre, as are works that Perugino and Corregio painted for the same room (in one of the more compelling current stories from the art world, Mantua is demanding their return).

The Gonzagas expanded their palace by incorporating any structure that lay within reach, including the Duomo and the Castello di San Giorgio (1396–1406). As a result, it's now a small city of 500 rooms connected by a labyrinth of corridors, ramps, courtyards, and staircases, filled with Renaissance frescoes and ancient Roman sculpture. The Sala del Pisanello frescoes feature Arthurian legends (mostly Tristan and Isolde) painted by Pisanello between 1436 and 1444, which were discovered beneath layers of plaster only in 1969. The Salle degli Arazzi (Tapestry Rooms) are hung with copies—woven at the same time but by a different Flemish workshop—of the Vatican's tapestries designed by Raphael and his students (among them Giulio Romano). The Camera degli Sposi was frescoed by Mantegna (the trompe l'oeil oculus in the center of the ceiling is an icon of Renaissance art and a masterpiece of foreshortening).

Other highlights include the Galleria degli Specchi (Hall of Mirrors); the low-ceiling Appartemento dei Nani (Apartments of the Dwarfs), where a replica of the Holy Staircase in the Vatican is built to miniature scale (in keeping with noble custom of the time, dwarfs were part of Isabella's court); and the Galleria dei Mesi (Hall of the Months). Some of the mostly delightful chambers in the vast complex make up the Appartemento Estivale (Summer Apartment), which looks over a courtyard where hanging gardens provide the greenery.

Piazza Sordello. ✆ **0376-382-150.** www.mantovaducale.it. Admission 6.50€ ($7). Tues–Sun 8:45am–7:15pm.

Palazzo Te ⭐ Frederico Gonzaga, the pleasure-loving refined son of Isabella d'Este, built this splendid Mannerist palace as a retreat from court life. As soon as you enter the courtyard, you'll see that the purpose of this palace was to amuse—the keystone of the monumental archway is designed to look like it's falling out of place. Throughout the lovely whimsical interior, sexually frank frescoes (by Giulio Romano, who left a scandal behind him in Rome that arose over his licentious engravings) depict *Psyche* and other erotically charged subject matter and make unsubtle reference to one of Frederico's favorite pastimes (horses and astrology, Frederico's other passions, also figure prominently). The greatest and most playful achievement here, though, has to do with power: In the **Sala dei Giganti (Room of the Giants)** ⭐⭐, Titan is overthrown by the gods in a dizzying play of architectural proportion that gives the illusion that the ceiling is falling.

The palazzo is a 20-minute walk from the center of town along Via Mazzini. En route, at Via Acerbi 47, sits **Casa di Mantegna,** the house and studio of Andrea Mantegna. Admission is free, so devotees of Mantua's most famous painter may choose to stop by for a look. It's open Tuesday to Sunday 10am to 12:30pm and 3 to 6pm (© **0376-360-506;** hours may vary).

Viale Te. © **0376-323-266.** Admission 8€ ($9.20) adults, 2.50€ ($2.90) ages 12–18 and seniors over 65; free under 12. Mon 1–6pm; Tues–Sun 9am–6pm. Box office closes a half-hour earlier.

Sant'Andrea Basilica 🔍 A graceful Renaissance facade fronts this 15th-century church by Leon Battista Alberti, with an 18th-century dome by Juvarra. The simple arches seem to float beneath the classic pediment, and the unadorned elegance forms a sharp contrast to other Lombardy monuments, such as the Duomo in Milan, the Cappella Colleoni in Bergamo, and the Certosa in Pavia. Inside, the classically proportioned vast space is centered on a single aisle. The Gonzaga court painter Mantegna is buried in the first chapel on the left. The crypt houses a reliquary containing the blood of Christ (allegedly brought here by Longinus, the Roman soldier who thrust his spear into Jesus' side), which is carried through town on March 18, the feast of Mantua's patron, Sant'Anselmo.

Piazza Mantegna. Free admission. Daily 7:30am–noon and 3–7pm. Bus: 1.

WHERE TO STAY

If you're interested in the lowest-priced accommodations, the tourist office can provide details and make reservations for rooms at five hostel-like farmhouses in the surrounding countryside. Rates are about 20€ to 30€ ($23–$35) per person. Since several of the properties are within a few kilometers of town, you can reach them without too much trouble by bike or combination bus ride and trek.

ABC Moderno 🔍 The prices at this recently renovated hotel across from the train station are remarkably low, considering the pleasant surroundings and the amenities. A pleasant lounge area and breakfast room open onto a sunny terrace. Upstairs, the renovated rooms have bright tile floors, fresh plaster and paint, new modular furnishings, and modern bathrooms. Architectural details, such as stone walls and patches of old frescoes, have been uncovered to provide decorative touches. The management is extremely helpful, and their hospitality extends to lending out the three bikes they have on hand for free (first-come, first-served). If the Moderno is full, bypass the other nearby hotels, which tend to be dreary and overpriced.

Piazza Don Leoni 25, 46100 Mantova. © **0376-323-347.** Fax 0376-322-349. 31 units. 66€–110€ ($76–$127) double. Rates include buffet breakfast. MC, V. Parking 10€ ($12). **Amenities:** Restaurant (cafe); bar; bike lending; concierge; tour desk. *In room:* TV, dataport, hair dryer.

Broletto 🔍🔍 This atmospheric old hotel is in the center of the old city, only a few steps from the lake and the *castello*, making it a fine base for a late-night stroll through the moonlit piazze. The rooms have contemporary furnishings that are vaguely rustic in design, with orthopedic bed frames. Bright corner room no. 16 has balconies and windows on two sides. The most alluring feature of the decor, though, are the massive beams on the ceilings and other architectural details from the palazzo's 16th-century origins.

Via Accademia 1, 46100 Mantova. © **0376-326-784.** Fax 0376-221-297. http://space.tin.it/viaggi/fsmirnov. 16 units. 93€–115€ ($107–$132) double. Continental breakfast 6.50€ ($7). AE, DC, MC, V. Closed Dec 22–Jan 4. **Amenities:** Concierge; tour desk; car-rental desk; babysitting; laundry service. *In room:* A/C, TV, dataport, minibar, hair dryer.

Mantegna On a quiet side street just a few steps south of the *centro storico*, the Mantegna offers solid comfort in surroundings that are thoroughly modern. The cozy narrow singles resemble ships' cabins, but the doubles are unusually roomy. All have been renovated within the past few years and have new bathrooms; many face a sunny and quiet courtyard.

Via Fabio Filzi 10, 46100 Mantova. ℂ **0376-328-019.** Fax 0376-368-564. www.hotelmantegna.it. 42 units. 110€ ($127) double. Buffet breakfast 8€ ($9). AE, MC, V. Parking free in courtyard. Closed Dec 24–Jan 7 and 2 weeks in Aug. **Amenities:** Bar; concierge. *In room:* A/C, TV, dataport, minibar, hair dryer.

Rechigi Hotel   This is a modern hotel 1 block down and three over from the main piazza and Duomo. It's decorated with modern sculptures and paintings, with regular exhibits by contemporary artists filling the common spaces sheathed in tan marble panels for a minimalist look that permeates the hotel. It's got loads of amenities and a great location, but the rooms aren't all that outstanding. They're midsize to large, fitted with thin carpets, unimaginative built-in units, and hand-held nozzles in some tubs of the generous-size bathrooms. Some do come with king beds, though. There's a small patio for summer breakfasts alfresco.

Via Pier Fortunato Calvi 30, 46100 Mantova. ℂ **0376-320-781.** Fax 0376-220-291. www.rechigi.com. 59 units. 176€ ($202) double; 191€ ($220) triple; 202€ ($232) deluxe; 233€ ($268) suite. Breakfast included. AE, DC, MC, V. Garage parking 20€ ($23). **Amenities:** Bar; sauna; concierge; tour desk; car-rental desk; courtesy car; room service (24-hr.); laundry service; dry cleaning; nonsmoking rooms. *In room:* A/C, TV, dataport, minibar, hair dryer, safe.

San Lorenzo ⭐⭐   One of Italy's more gracious inns was fashioned out of a row of old houses just off Piazza delle Erbe. Oil paintings and oriental carpets grace the marble-floored salons. The guest rooms, no two of which are alike, are furnished with exquisite reproductions of 18th- and 19th-century antiques— plus at least one original piece in each room—and come with elegant touches like a bit of stucco work on ceilings as well as all the conveniences you'd expect from a luxury hotel. A panoramic roof terrace overlooks the towers and rooftops of the *centro storico,* and the lavish buffet breakfast is served in an elegant room overlooking the rotunda, with a series of sitting salons around a bar nearby.

Piazza Concordia 14, 46100 Mantova. ℂ **0376-220-500.** Fax 0376-327-194. www.hotelsanlorenzo.it. 32 units. 145€–220€ ($167–$253) double; 168€–280€ ($193–$322) room for 3 people; 196€–300 ($225–$345) room for 4 people; 160€–240€ ($184–$276) jr. suite. Rates include breakfast. Frequent promotions may lower the price up to 40% in slow periods (ask when you call). AE, DC, MC, V. Parking 20€ ($23) in garage. **Amenities:** Concierge; room service (24-hr.); babysitting; laundry service; same-day dry cleaning. *In room:* A/C, TV, VCR (on request), fax (on request), dataport, minibar, hair dryer, safe.

WHERE TO DINE

Mantovian cuisine is quite refined—an array of pastas stuffed with pumpkin and squash, a fine selection of fish from the surrounding lakes and rivers, and exquisite risotto dishes (rice has been cultivated here since the early 1500s; the tourist office even promotes a *strada del riso,* or "rice road," through the region modeling the "wine roads" of other regions, and showing how important rice is to the area).

Leoncino Rosso ⭐⭐ MANTOVANA   This fine old restaurant with an attractive rustic dining room, just off Piazza Broletto (on a parallel street) in the center of the old city, has been serving food since 1750. This is a good place to sample Mantua's distinctive cuisine. Topping the list is *tortelli di zucca,* a large ravioli pillow stuffed with pumpkin. If you want to continue to eat as the Mantovese do, move on to *stracotto Mantovano* (stewed donkey; that store next door is a horsemeat butcher). For more familiar fare from the barnyard, try the delicious *cotechino e fagioli* (pork sausage and beans). You can tell it's a local place by the TV in the corner (a bit loud, actually) that always manages to have a soccer game playing.

and sister Nicola and Christina Marcolini oversee the hotel and adjoining restaurant with a great deal of graciousness, carrying on several generations of a family business. The rooms are simple but pleasant, with tile floors and plain furnishings; top-floor rooms (nos. 36–42) have small balconies from which to survey the views. The tidy bathrooms have stall showers or curtainless tubs. The Grifone books up quickly, often with return guests, so reserve well in advance.

Via Bocchio 4, 25019 Sirmione (BS). © 030-916-014. Fax 030-916-548. 16 units. 55€ ($63) double; extra bed 19€ ($22). No credit cards. Free parking. Closed late Oct–Easter. **Amenities:** International-cuisine restaurant; bar. *In room:* Hair dryer (ask at desk).

Hotel Speranza   This modest hotel occupies the upper floors of an old building that arches across Sirmione's main street, providing a prime location near the castle and only a few steps in either direction from the lake. The emphasis here is on clean efficiency rather than luxury: Public rooms consist of a tiny lobby and breakfast room, and the bare-bones rooms are tidy and perfectly serviceable. In fact, the plain modern furnishings set against parquet floors and stark white walls make for a fairly chic look. Bathrooms are modernized (save for the flat waffle towels on heated racks), with box showers.

Via Castello 6, 25019 Sirmione (BS). © 030-916-116. Fax 030-916-403. 13 units. 70€ ($81) double. Rates include breakfast. AE, DC, MC, V. Closed mid-Nov to late Feb. **Amenities:** Concierge. *In room:* A/C, TV.

Olivi ★★   This pleasant modern hotel offers the chance to live the high life at reasonable rates. It's not directly on the lake, which you can see from most rooms and the sunny terrace, but instead commands a hilltop position near the Roman ruins amid pines and olive groves. The rooms are stunningly decorated in varying schemes of bold, handsome pastels, and earth tones. There are separate dressing areas off the bathrooms, and most have balconies. There's a pool in the garden and, to bring a lakeside feeling to the grounds, an artificial river that streams past the terrace and glass windows of the lobby and breakfast room.

Via San Pietro 5, 25019 Sirmione (BS). © 030-990-5365. Fax 030-916-472. www.gardalake.it/hotel-olivi. 58 units. 126€–194€ ($145–$223) double. Rates include breakfast. AE, MC, V. Closed Jan. **Amenities:** 2 restaurants; 2 bars; pool; concierge; tour desk; car-rental desk; courtesy car; room service (limited); massage; babysitting; laundry service; dry cleaning. *In-room:* A/C, TV, minibar, hairdryer, safe.

Palace Hotel Villa Cortine ★★★   This is clearly something special: You enter the gates, drive around a statue-lined lily pond lorded over by Neptune to a snaking, cypress-lined road that ends at a Palladian villa. Actually, it was only built in the early 20th century (the main hotel core behind it was added in 1957) by a German count who was forcibly repatriated back north of the Alps during World War I, but its neoclassical grandeur is none the less impressive for it. The small gravel parking lot is packed with luxury automobiles and limited-edition sports cars. There are views across the trees to the lake below, where there is a private beach with a motorboat launch. The staff prides itself on personalized service. The decor is a quirky mix of styles ranging from Renaissance and baroque to Empire and neoclassical, all of it terribly elegant and refined. Guests enjoy breezy meals on the colonnaded flagstone terrace and access to a landscaped 4.8-hectare (12-acre) park.

Via Grotte 6, 25019 Sirmione (BS). © 030-990-5890. Fax 030-916-390. www.hotelvillacortine.com. 54 units. 300€–400€ ($345–$460) double; 420€–550€ ($483–$633) deluxe double; 450€–600€ ($518–$690) jr. suite; 470€–650€ ($541–$748) suite. Half-board adds 15€ ($17) per person, and is required Easter week and June 20–Sept 21. Rates include continental breakfast. AE, DC, MC, V. Closed Oct 19–Apr 10. **Amenities:** 2 restaurants (international/Italian main dining room, on palm-shaded terrace in summer; BBQ lunch at the beach June–Sept); bar; heated outdoor pool; outdoor clay tennis courts (lighted); can arrange watersports equipment rental, bike rental; concierge; tour desk; car-rental desk; courtesy car (for a fee); room service (limited); in-room massage; babysitting; laundry service; dry cleaning; nonsmoking rooms. *In room:* A/C, TV, VCR (on request), fax (on request), dataport, minibar, hair dryer, safe.

WHERE TO DINE

In addition to the choices below, you can get a quick pizza with a view of the lake from the terrace at **L'Archimboldo,** Via Vittorio Emanuele 71 (© **030-916-409;** closed Tues).

La Roccia ITALIAN/PIZZA   This trattoria/pizza parlor caters to the flocks of tourists who stream through Sirmione, but it does so with excellent food and unusually pleasant surroundings. In good weather, the best seating is in the large garden to one side of the restaurant. The menu includes more than 20 excellent pizzas made in a wood-burning oven, plus plenty of traditional pastas, including lasagna and excellent cheese tortellini in a cream-and-prosciutto sauce. The fish (try the trout roasted or fried in butter and sage) and meat are excellent, and the best dishes are grilled over an open fire.

Via Piana 2. © **030-916-392.** Primi 5.50€–16€ ($6–$18); secondi 8€–15€ ($9–$17); pizza 5€–8€ ($6–$9). DC, MC, V. Fri–Wed 12:30–3pm and 7–10:30pm. Closed Nov–Mar.

Ristorante Al Progresso SEAFOOD/ITALIAN   This fan-cooled room on the main street of the old town is appealingly plain but has a touch of style. The pastas include excellent tortellini variations, and some come with shellfish from the not-too-distant Adriatic. Fresh lake trout is often on the menu—grilled or *al Sirmionese* (boiled with a house sauce of garlic, oil, capers, and anchovies)— as are some simple veal preparations, including a *vitello al limone,* made with fresh lemons that grow on the shores of the lake.

Via Vittorio Emanuele 18–20. © **030-916-108.** Primi 6.50€–9€ ($7–$10); secondi 8.50€–16€ ($10–$18). AE, DC, MC, V. Fri–Wed (daily in summer) noon–2:30pm and 6:30–10:30pm. Closed either Nov–Dec or Dec–Jan (depending on flow of tourism).

GARDONE RIVIERA

The little resort of Gardone Riviera, 47km (29 miles) south of Riva del Garda on the western shore of the lake, has two interesting attractions. Once Italy's most famous soldier/poet, Gabriele d'Annunzio is today remembered not for his lackluster verse but more for his adventures and grand lifestyle at **Il Vittoriale** (© **0365-296-511;** www.vittoriale.it), a hillside estate that is one of Lake Garda's major sites. He bought the estate (it's also alleged that Mussolini presented it to the poet as a way to coerce his sympathies) in 1921 and died here in 1936. The claustrophobic rooms of this ornately and bizarrely decorated villa are filled with bric-a-brac and artifacts from the poet's colorful life, including many mementos of his long affair with actress Eleanora Duse. Elsewhere on the grounds, which cascade down the hillside in a series of luxuriant gardens, are the patrol boat D'Annunzio commanded in World War I, a museum containing his biplane and photos, and his pompous hilltop tomb.

Admission is 6€ ($6.90) for adults and 4€ ($4.60) for children ages 7 to 12 and seniors over 60 to the grounds only; you pay 5€ ($5.75) (4€/$4.60 kids and seniors) additional to tour the villa, which you can visit only via a 25-minute guided tour (in Italian; even if you don't understand a word of the tour, it's worth taking it to look inside the villa). April to September the grounds are open daily 8:30am to 8pm and the villa Tuesday to Sunday 10am to 6pm; October to March the grounds are open daily 9am to 5pm and the villa Tuesday to Friday 9am to 1pm and 2 to 5pm and Saturday and Sunday 9am to 1pm and 2 to 5:30pm. The villa also hosts a July-to-August season of concerts and plays; call ℭ **0365-296-519** (www.teatrodelvittoriale.it) for more information.

Just down the hill on Via Roma is the **Giardino Botanica Hruska** (ℭ **0336-410-877**), a small but delightful bower planted a hundred years ago by the Swiss naturalist Arturo Hruska (a dentist whose clientele included European royalty). More than 2,000 species of exotic flora from around the world continue to thrive in the balmy microclimate around the lake here. Admission is 6€ ($6.90). March 15 to October 15 the garden is open daily from 9am to 7pm.

GETTING THERE For ferry connections with Riva del Garda and Sirmione, see those sections elsewhere in this chapter (from Limone sul Garda, prices are the same as from Riva del Garda, but the trip is 30 min. quicker by hydrofoil, 45 min. faster by ferry). You can also bus here from Riva del Garda in 65 minutes. From Sirmione, you have to transfer at Desenzano del Garda for one of six daily runs (1 hr. total). Hourly buses also make the 1-hour trip to and from Brescia, and two buses a day make the 3-hour trip to and from Milan.

VISITOR INFORMATION Gardone's **tourist office** is at Corso Repubblica 8 (ℭ/fax **0365-20-347**). April to October it's open Tuesday to Saturday 9am to 12:30pm and 4 to 7pm and Sunday 9am to 12:30pm; November to March, hours are Monday to Wednesday and Friday 9am to 12:30pm and 3 to 6pm and Thursday 9am to 12:30pm.

WHERE TO STAY & DINE

Grand Hotel Fasano ★★ Sig. Mayer, the owner of this lakeside retreat, exclaims, "We sell water and sun; everything else is just a frame around it." He and his brother must be doing something right to ensure a 90% return rate on their guests—all the more remarkable since their clientele is made up entirely of private tourists (lots of them German), as they refuse to take tour groups or agency bookings. Terraces and balconies overlook the palm- and willow-shaded garden right on the lake, where guests can take breakfast or dinner and swim off the small pier. The terraces above the gardens host the awning-shaded, fan-cooled restaurant and bar, which feature live piano music several times a week. Rooms at either end of the villa are larger, those in the long connecting wing smaller but with larger terraces. "Classic" rooms are fitted with simple, homey furnishings, but are very comfy, featuring modern bathrooms and paintings of putti. "Clima" rooms are larger, with a small curtained-off terrace/sitting area. Accommodations in the separate Villa Principe, set amid the trees at one end of the property, are slightly more exclusive, with larger rooms but similar furnishings. The Mayers are constantly reinvesting in the hotel, planning a small business center and a fitness center to debut in 2005.

25083 Gardone Riviera (BS). ℭ **0365-290-220.** Fax 0365-290-221. www.ghf.it. 75 units in main hotel, 12 in Villa Principe. 100€–120€ ($115–$138) standard double without lake view; 150€–180€ ($173–$207) classic double without lake view; 180€–210€ ($207–$242) "clima" double without lake view; 150€–180€ ($173–$207) standard double with lake view; 180€–210€ ($207–$242) classic double with lake view; 220€–250€ ($253–$288) "clima" double with lake view. Half-pension 30€ ($35) per person (minimum 3-night stay). Breakfast included. Credit cards to be accepted in 2004 (inquire). **Amenities:** Italian/international restaurant; bar; outdoor heated pool; nearby golf course; outdoor tennis courts; watersports equipment; bike rental; video arcade; concierge; tour desk; car-rental desk; courtesy car (for a fee); room service (24-hr.); in-room massage; babysitting; laundry service; dry cleaning. *In room:* A/C (in "clima" rooms), TV, dataport, mini-bar, hair dryer, safe (in most).

Villa Fiordaliso ★★★ This gorgeous villa is a mix of neoclassical and Liberty style, built in 1903 and later host to several very famous guests, including poet Gabriele d'Annunzio from 1921 to 1923, and Mussolini's mistress Claretta Petacci from 1943 to 1945. The dictator visited his lover frequently here, and they spent the final weeks of their lives at the villa. It's been a hotel since 1990. To choose your room, head to the villa's website, which features 360-degree panoramic photos of each one. The most requested is the "Claretta" suite, where the doomed woman spent her final years surrounded by elaborate ceilings and marble-clad bath fixtures. All rooms have lake views except the "Mimosa," which overlooks the garden from a small terrace. The "Gardenia" and the "Magnolia" below it have windows on three sides (lake view, garden view, and a view overlooking the road). Children under 12 are not allowed. The exquisite restaurant (closed Tues at lunch and Mon all day) has earned itself a Michelin star for its refined cuisine. In warm weather, meals are served on a broad terrace where the lake laps almost to the tables; in winter you dine in a series of rooms with inlaid wood floors, coffered and decorated ceilings, and bottle-bottom windows. There's also a piano bar, Torre San Marco, in a fanciful minicastle on the property that's built half out over the water. It opens at 10:30 every evening.

Via Zanardelli 150, 25083 Gardone Riviera (BS). © **0365-20-158.** Fax 0365-290-011. www.villafiordaliso.it. 7 units. 230€–400€ ($265–$460) double; 540€ ($621) "Claretta" suite. Rates include continental breakfast. AE, DC, MC, V. Free parking. Closed Jan–Feb 10. Children under 12 are not allowed. **Amenities:** Excellent restaurant; bar; watersports equipment; concierge; tour desk; room service (limited); laundry service; same-day dry cleaning. *In room:* A/C, TV, minibar, hair dryer.

RIVA DEL GARDA

The northernmost town on the lake is not just a resort but a real, prosperous Italian town, with medieval towers, a nice smattering of Renaissance churches and palazzi, and narrow cobblestone streets where everyday business proceeds in its alluring way.

ESSENTIALS

GETTING THERE **By Train** See "Getting There: By Train," under Sirmione, earlier in this chapter, for connections to Desenzano del Garda, from which you must take a bus (see below).

By Bus Six buses a day link Riva del Garda and Desenzano del Garda on the southern end of the lake, about a 2-hour trip. You can also travel between Sirmione and Riva del Garda by bus, though except for a 4:30pm direct run, you must transfer at Peschiera (2 hr.). From Limone sul Garda, there are 11 trips daily (18 min.). Twenty-five daily buses connect Riva del Garda and Trent (1 hr. 40 min.). From Verona there are 16 a day (2 hr.), and from Brescia five daily (2 hr.).

By Boat Navigazione Lago di Garda (see "Sirmione" earlier in this chapter for more information) runs the boats. Fifteen ferries and three hydrofoils per day connect Riva del Garda with Limone sul Garda (35–45 min. by ferry; 30 min. by hydrofoil). Two ferries and three hydrofoils per day connect Riva del Garda with Gardone (2 hr. 45 min. by ferry; 1 hr. 20 min. by hydrofoil), Sirmione (almost 4 hr. by ferry; 2 hr. 10 min. by hydrofoil), and Desenzano del Garda (4 hr. 15 min. by ferry; 2½ hr. by hydrofoil). Schedules vary with the season, with very limited service in the winter.

By Car The fastest link between Riva del Garda and points north and south is via the A22, which shoots up the east side of the lake (exit at Mori, 13km/8 miles east of Riva del Garda). A far more scenic drive is along the western shore, on the beautiful corniche between Riva del Garda and Salo that hugs cliffs and passes through mile after mile of tunnel. Depending on the route, by car Riva del Garda is about an hour from Verona and about 45 minutes from Sirmione.

VISITOR INFORMATION   The **tourist office,** which supplies information on hotels, restaurants, and activities in the area, is near the lakefront Giardini di Porta Orientale 8 (© **0464-554-444;** fax 0464-520-308; www.garda.com or www. gardatrentino.com). June 16 to September 15 it's open Monday to Saturday 9am to noon and 3 to 6:30pm and Sunday 10am to noon and 4 to 6:30pm; April to June 15 and September 16 to October, hours are Monday to Saturday 9am to noon and 3 to 6:15pm; November to March, hours are Monday to Friday 9am to noon and 2:30 to 5:15pm.

FESTIVALS & MARKETS   Riva del Garda becomes a cultural oasis in July, when the town hosts an **international festival of classical music.**

EXPLORING THE TOWN

Riva del Garda's Old Town is pleasant enough, though the only historic attractions of note are the 13th-century **Torre d'Apponale** (a picturesque medieval tower on the main square, which is sometimes open for climbing and sometimes not) and, nearby, the moated lakeside castle, **La Rocca.** Part of the castle interior now houses an unassuming collection of local arts and crafts (© **0464-573-869**). It's open Tuesday to Saturday 9:30am to 5:30pm and Sunday 9:30am to noon and 2 to 5:30pm; admission is 3€ ($3.45). The castle also occasionally hosts minor traveling exhibits.

The tourist office runs a few free guided tours (in many languages, including English). On weekends they do walking tours of the town; on Tuesdays and Fridays they offer walking tours of a few sights in the area. You must book in advance, by 5pm the previous day, at © **0464-554-444.** The sights aren't of staggering interest or importance (and that's being kind), but they're a good activity if you happen to be in town and your lazy vacationing by the lakeside is getting boring or you want something cultural to do between windsurfing lessons.

The main attraction here is the **lake itself,** which Riva del Garda takes advantage of with a waterside promenade stretching for several miles past parks and pebbly beaches. The water is warm enough for swimming May to October, and air currents fanned by the mountains make Garda popular for windsurfing year-round.

WATER & LAND SPORTS   A convenient point of embarkation for a lake outing is the beach next to the castle, where you can rent rowboats or pedal boats for about 6€ to 7€ ($6.90–$8.05) per hour (buy 2 hr., get a 3rd free); from March to October, the concession is open daily 8am to 8pm.

For a more adventurous outing, check out the **windsurfing** at the **Nautic Club Riva,** Via Rovereto 44 (© **0464-552-453;** www.nauticclubriva.com), where you can rent equipment for 39€ ($45) per day or 17€ ($20) for an hour, 24€ ($28) for 2 hours. Multiday and weekly packages, as well as lessons, are also available.

You can rent **bikes** from Superbike Girelli, Viale Damiano Chiesa 15 (© **0464-556-602;** www.girellibike.it) for 10€ ($12) per day (4€/$4.60 per hr.); or from Fori e Bike, Viale dei Tigli 24 (© **0464-551-830**), whose bikes cost about 8€ to 13€ ($9.20–$15) per day, depending on the type of bike (mountain bikes are on the more expensive end).

WHERE TO STAY

Montanara   It ain't fancy, but it's cheap. The Montanara is squirreled away above its cheap trattoria in a quiet part of the *centro storico.* The wood-floored midsize rooms occupy three stories of an old palazzo and are exceedingly basic—not to say a bit down at the heels—but are kept immaculate, with a picture or two framed on the whitewashed walls for relief from the spartan environs. Rooms without bathrooms at least have a sink. The two top-floor accommodations are the best for their general brightness and high ceilings.

Via Montanara 18–20, 38066 Riva del Garda (BS). ©/fax **0464-554-857.** 9 units, 6 with bathroom. 42€ ($48) double without bathroom, 46€ ($52) double with bathroom; 64€ ($73) triple with bathroom. Rates include breakfast. MC, V. Free parking. Closed Nov–Easter. **Amenities:** Restaurant; bar. *In room:* No phone.

Portici   The management pays much more attention to their ground-floor restaurant/bar under a portico of the main square than they do to the hotel, but perhaps that's because it's mainly booked by tour groups—keeping this central and surprisingly reasonable choice off the radar of more independent travelers. Sadly, its location in the upper leg of the piazza's L-shape deprives almost all rooms of a lake view—and the functional units are boringly modern to boot, done up in a monotonous blue tone. Still, for these prices, you can easily walk to a cafe to enjoy the view.

Piazza III Novembre 19, 38066 Riva del Garda (BS). © **0464-555-400.** Fax 0464-555-453. www.hotelportici.it. 45 units. 62€–92€ ($71–$106) double. Half-board available. MC, V. Closed Nov–Mar. **Amenities:** International-cuisine restaurant; bar. *In room:* TV, hair dryer.

Sole ★★   One of the finest hotels in town enjoys a wonderful location right on the lake at the main square. The management lavishes a great deal of attention on the public rooms and guest rooms and charges very fairly. The lobby is filled with rare Persian carpets and abstract art. The rooms reached via a sweeping circular staircase are warm and luxurious, with tasteful furnishings and marble-trimmed bathrooms; the best rooms have balconies hanging out over the lake. Lake-view rooms are outfitted in antique style; those overlooking the square and town are done in modern functional. Amenities include a formal restaurant, a casual cafe/bar extending onto a lakeside terrace, a rooftop solarium with sauna, and a nearby gated parking lot.

Piazza III Novembre 35, 38066 Riva del Garda (TN). © **0464-552-686.** Fax 0464-552-811. www.hotelsole.net. 81 units. 108€–168€ ($124–$193) double without lake view; 124€–184€ ($143–$212) double with lake view. Rates include half pension. Add 15€ ($17) per person for full pension. AE, DC, MC, V. Parking on street 3€ ($3.45), in garage 6€ ($6.90). Closed Nov to mid-Mar (except at Christmastime and during frequent trade fares). **Amenities:** International-cuisine restaurant; bar; small exercise room; sauna; free bikes; concierge; tour desk; room service (limited); laundry service. *In room:* A/C (in 30 rooms), TV, dataport (in some rooms), minibar, hair dryer, safe.

WHERE TO DINE

Birreria Spaten ITALIAN/TIROLEAN   This noisy indoor beer garden occupies the ground floor of an old palazzo and features a wide-ranging mix of food from the surrounding regions, so you can dine on the cuisine of Trent (Trento) or Lombardy or from the other side of the Alps. Many of the German and Austrian visitors who favor Riva del Garda opt for the schnitzel-sauerkraut-sauerbraten fare, but you can also enjoy a pasta like *strangolapreti* (spinach-and-ricotta dumplings in a butter sauce), one of 30 pizzas, or a simply grilled lake trout. If you can't decide, the *Piatto Spaten* is an ample 14€ ($16) sampler of their Tirolean specialties: *cotechino* (spicy sausage), wurstel, *canederli* (a giant bread dumpling), a ham steak, and sauerkraut.

Via Maffei 7. © **0464-553-670.** Primi 4.50€–8€ ($5–$9); secondi 5.50€–14€ ($6–$16); pizza 4.50€–7.50€ ($5–$9). MC, V. Thurs–Tues 11am–3pm and 5:30pm–midnight. Closed Nov–Feb.

Two-Wheeling Limone

Rent a mountain bike in Limone sul Garda at **Tombola Rent**, Via L. Einaudi 1B (© **0365-954-051**). Rates are 11€ ($12) for 5 hours, 17€ ($19) for a full day (6am–10pm). They also rent scooters starting at 21€ ($24) for 3 hours, 29€ ($33) for 5 hours, and 37€ ($43) for a full day.

LIMONE SUL GARDA

Limone sul Garda is a pretty resort wedged between the lake and mountains just 10km (6¼ miles) south of Riva del Garda on the lakeside corniche. For ferry connections with Riva del Garda and Sirmione, see those sections above. Despite the onslaught of tourists who come down through the mountains from Austria and Germany, it's a pleasant place to spend some time and offers more moderately priced lakeside hotels than those found in Riva del Garda. Romans planted lemon groves here (hence the name); the ruins of the protective structures that once covered the groves are still visible on the hills around the town, and lemons continue to thrive on every available parcel of land.

There's a small **IAT tourist info office** at Via Comboni 15 (© **0365-954 070;** fax 0365-954-689). From March to October it's open daily 9am to 12:30pm and Monday to Saturday 3:30 to 7pm; November to February, hours are Monday to Saturday 9am to 12:30pm and 4:30 to 6pm. Also try the private website **www.limone.com.**

WHERE TO STAY

Capo Reamol ★ *Kids*   This is a modern, family-run hotel set just below the road, with a terrace swimming pool above the lake; they even host their own windsurf school on a private pier. The best, type "A" rooms come with large terraces set with beach chairs so that you can gaze over the lake; modern, comfortable built-in furnishings; and nice bathrooms graced with heated towel racks. "B" category rooms are somewhat smaller, with balconies rather than terraces, though some have connecting doors to turn into family suites. Only four rooms, "C" type, overlook the garden rather than the lake. Rooms in the *dipendence* at the end of an olive-shaded terrace come with slightly older (but spick-and-span) bathrooms and lake views, but lack air-conditioning; some are large enough for four. The restaurant occupies a panoramic room with picture windows overlooking the water, with an antipasto buffet and choice of dishes.

Via IV Novembre 92, 25010 Limone sul Garda (BS). © 0365-954-040. Fax 0365-954-262. www.gardaresort.it. 58 units. 86€–140€ ($99–$161) "C" double without lake view or balcony; 104€–158€ ($120–$182) "B" double with lake view and balcony; 120€–176€ ($138–$202) "A" large double with lake view and terrace. All rates include required half-board. AE, DC, MC, V. Closed mid-Oct to Easter. **Amenities:** Italian restaurant; large modern bar; outdoor pool; outdoor tennis courts nearby; small exercise room; sauna; watersports equipment; free mountain bikes; children's playground; concierge; tour desk; car-rental desk; salon; room service (24-hr.); massage; babysitting. *In room:* A/C (in main building), TV, dataport, minibar, hair dryer, safe.

Le Palme ★★   This gracious hotel is one of the most pleasant places to stay on Garda. It's on the lake at one end of Limone sul Garda's narrow main street and surrounded by palm trees. Downstairs, a bar and reasonably priced restaurant flow onto a flowery terrace right on the lake. Upstairs, the large, pleasant rooms are furnished in Venetian-style antiques (some genuine, others reproduction), and all but a few face the lake; the three best have small balconies hanging out over the water (if your room doesn't have a balcony, you can enjoy the lake from the downstairs terrace or rooftop solarium). A small beach is just a few steps down the road, and the hotel has a small pool amid lemon-shaded terraces nearby. There's also a larger pool available at its sibling hotel, the hillside Splendid Palace, where they'll be happy to reserve a room for you if Le Palme is full.

Via Porto 36, 25010 Limone sul Garda (BS). ⓒ **0365-954-681** or 0365-954-612. Fax 0365-954-120. www. sunhotels.it. 28 units. 66€–138€ ($76–$159) double. Rates include breakfast. Add 16€ ($18) per person for half pension, 32€ ($37) per person for full pension. MC, V. Closed Nov–Easter. **Amenities:** International/ Italian restaurant; bar; pool; tennis courts nearby; children's games; concierge; tour desk; room service. *In room:* A/C, TV, hair dryer, safe.

WHERE TO DINE

Ristorante Gemma ITALIAN   In a town where many restaurants cater to tourists with bland fish and chips and bratwurst, Gemma remains an authentic, family-style trattoria. It also enjoys a pretty lakeside location, and the waves lap right up against the dining terrace. Gemma is the best place in town for grilled lake trout, which, like all entrees, can be accompanied by a fine *spaghetti alla mare* (with seafood) and other delicious pastas.

Piazza Garibaldi 12. ⓒ **0365-954-814** or 0365-940-145. Primi 4.50€–9€ ($5–$10); secondi 6€–20€ ($7–$23). MC, V. Thurs–Tues 11:30am–2:30pm and 6:30–10pm. Closed mid-Oct to Mar.

2 Lake Como (Lago di Como)

Como (town): 78km (48 miles) NE of Milan; Menaggio: 35km (22 miles) NE of Como and 85km (53 miles) N of Milan; Varenna: 50km (31 miles) NE of Como and 80km (50 miles) NE of Milan

The first sight of the dramatic expanse of azure-hued **Lake Como** ★★★, ringed by gardens and forests and backed by the snowcapped Alps, is likely to evoke strong emotions. Romance, soulfulness, even gentle melancholy—these are the stirrings that over the centuries the lake has inspired in poets (Lord Byron), novelists (Stendhal), composers (Verdi and Rossini), and plenty of other visitors, too—be they deposed queens, such as Caroline of Brunswick, whom George IV of England exiled here for her adulterous ways, well-heeled modern travelers who glide up and down these waters in the ubiquitous lake steamers, or these days the rich and über-famous (George Clooney recently bought a villa here).

Aside from its emotional pull, Como is also just an enjoyable place to spend time. Less than an hour from Milan by train or car, its deep waters and verdant shores provide a wonderful respite from modern life. Tellingly, Lake Como served as a backdrop for the romantic scenes in *Star Wars II: Attack of the Clones*—one of the very few settings in the film that was *not* created entirely by CGI computer programs. I guess even George Lucas realized that Como was a place of such unearthly beauty as to need little digital touching-up.

COMO

The largest and southernmost town on the lake isn't likely to charm you off the bat for its slight sprawl, but the historic center is lovely if you take the time to stroll it and pop into its little churches. Long a center of silk making, this city that traces its roots to the Gauls, and after them, the Romans, bustles with commerce and industry. You'll probably want to stay in one of the more peaceful settings farther up the lake, but Como amply rewards a day's visit with some fine Renaissance churches and palaces and a nice lakefront promenade.

ESSENTIALS

GETTING THERE   By Train   One to three trains hourly connect Milan and Como's Stazione San Giovanni on Piazzale San Gottardo (regional: from

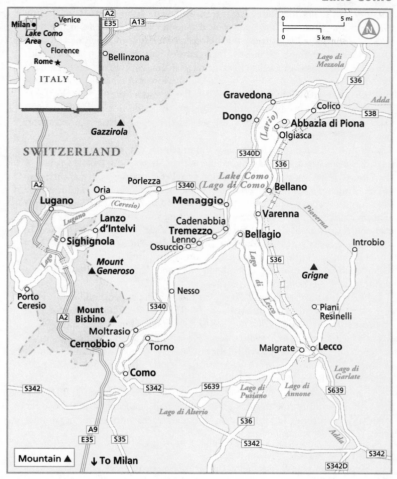

Milan's Piazza Garibaldi station, 55–60 min.; high-speed: from Milan's Stazione Centrale station, 40 min.).

VISITOR INFORMATION The **regional tourist office** dispenses a wealth of information on hotels, restaurants, and campgrounds around the lake from its offices at Piazza Cavour 17 (© **031-269-712** or 031-264-215; www.lakecomo. org). It's open daily 9am to 1pm and 2 to 5pm (sometimes closed Sun in winter). There is also a **city tourist office** in a little trailer that has moved around a bit since it opened in 2000, but stays near Piazza del Duomo, and seems to have settled on a spot along Via Maestri Comacini around the right side of the cathedral (© **031-337-1063**). It's open Monday to Friday 10am to 12:30pm and 2:30 to 6pm, Saturday and Sunday 10am to 6pm.

EXPLORING COMO

Part Gothic and part Renaissance, the **Duomo,** Piazza del Duomo, in the center of town just off the lake (© **031-265-244**), is festooned with exuberant masonry and sculpture. Statues of two of the town's famous native sons, Pliny the Elder and Pliny the Younger, flank the main entrance. Inside, beneath an 18th-century dome by Juvarra—the architect who designed much of Turin—is a lavish interior hung with mostly 16th-century paintings and tapestries, with lots of helpful leaflets in English to explain the major works of art. It's open daily 7:30am to noon and 3 to 7pm. The black-and-white-striped 13th-century **Broletto (Town Hall)** abuts the Duomo's left flank, and adjoining it is the **Torre del Comune.** As a study in contrasts, the starkly modernist and aptly named **Casa del Fascio,** built in 1936 as the seat of the region's Fascist government, rises just behind the Duomo.

Como's main street, **Corso Vittorio Emanuele II,** cuts through the medieval quarter, where wood-beamed houses line narrow streets. Just 2 blocks south of the Duomo, the five-sided 12th-century **San Fedele** stands above a charming square of the same name; parts of the church, including the altar, date from the 6th century. It's open daily 8am to noon and 3:30 to 7pm. To see Como's most alluring church, though, it's necessary to venture into the dull outlying neighborhood southwest of the center where, just off Viale Roosevelt, you'll come to the five-aisle heavily frescoed **Basilica of Sant'Abbondio** (✆ 631-338-8111), a Romanesque masterpiece from the 11th century with great 14th-century frescoes (bring coins so you can illuminate them). It's open daily 8am to 6pm (unless a wedding, which is popular here, is on).

Lakeside life revolves around Piazza Cavour and the adjoining Giardini Publici, where the circular **Tempio Voltano** (✆ 031-574-705) houses memorabilia on the life and experiments of native son and electricity pioneer Alessandro Volta. It was closed for renovations when we went to press, with no specific date yet set for reopening; its old hours were Tuesday to Sunday 10am to noon and 3 to 6pm (2–4pm Oct–Mar); admission seems to be set at 1.30€ ($1.50) for when it reopens—which is odd, since it used to cost 2€ ($2.30).

For a quick retreat and some stunning views, take the **funicular** (✆ 031-303-608) for a 7-minute ride up to the top of Brunate, the forested hill above the town (it leaves from the Lungo Lario Trieste every 15 min. or so, in summer every ½ hr.).

WHERE TO STAY

The Hotel Metropole Suisse (below) is actually a pretty good value—especially when you consider Como's sad, moderately priced hotel scene. But if you're really pinching pennies, you could do worse (not much worse, mind you) than the seven bare-bones rooms above the **Ristorante Sociale** (see below). Their big selling points are a prime location next-door to the Duomo, and that the double rooms go for just 38€ ($44) without private bathroom, 48€ ($55) with bathroom.

Hotel Metropole Suisse ✦ This massive 1892 hotel closes one side of Como's main square overlooking the lake. Accommodations vary; some rooms are carpeted and have very nice contemporary furnishings; others are older, with wood floors, brass beds, and embroidered upholstery. Many have been refurbished in the past year. Almost all rooms overlook the lake at least partially—some full-on (the best with small balconies), some askance over the cafes ringing the piazza, and others beyond the tree-lined promenade leading to the city park. The corner bar/lounge has picture windows for lake views, and the restaurant (under separate management) has tables out on the piazza.

Piazza Cavour 19, 22100 Como. ✆ 031-269-444. Fax 031-300-808. www.hotelmetropolesuisse.com. 71 units. 164€–194€ ($189–$223) double; 196€–216€ ($225–$248) triple; 189€–209€ ($217–$240) jr. suite.

Rates include buffet breakfast. AE, DC, MC, V. Parking 12€ ($14). **Amenities:** International-cuisine restaurant; bar; golf (nearby); sauna; concierge; tour desk; car-rental desk; room service (limited); babysitting; laundry service; same-day dry cleaning; nonsmoking rooms. *In room:* A/C, TV w/pay movies, minibar, hair dryer, safe.

WHERE TO DINE

Pasticceria Monti CAFE   Above all, the busy Monti on the main lakefront piazza is one of Como's favorite places to gather and watch passersby. You can enjoy some of the excellent gelato or a coffee or cocktail, plus tasty sandwiches and some other light fare, including some daily pasta dishes.

Piazza Cavour 21. (C) **031-301-165.** Gelato from 1€ ($1.15) for a single scoop; pastries from 1.50€ ($1.75); sandwiches from 2.50€ ($2.90). MC, V. Wed–Mon 7am–2am (to 1am in winter).

Ristorante Sociale *Value* LOMBARD   Here you'll find simple dishes at low prices. This trattoria tucked under an arcade next to the Duomo's right flank is where Comashci go after a play or concert at Como's Teatro Sociale (the walls are plastered with unsung heroes of the northern Italian stage and the yellowing posters of plays in which they appeared). It's where the local soccer team celebrates victories, where the equivalent of the ladies' auxiliary meets to have long, voluble conversations while enjoying one of the best-priced fixed menus on the lake. The fixed menus gives you your choice of four primi (first courses), four secondi (second courses), side dish, and water or wine (though they usually give you both at no extra charge). Just steer clear of the fish—it's frozen . . . rather scandalous for a place located just 2 blocks from the fishing boats bobbing in the lake harbor. They also rent rooms (see above).

Via Maestri Comacini 8. (C) **031-264-042.** Primi 4€–8€ ($4.60–$9); secondi 7€–14€ ($8–$16); fixed-price menu 16€ ($18) with wine. AE, DC, MC, V. Tues–Sun noon–2pm and 7:30–10:30pm.

A TOP HOTEL IN NEARBY CERNOBBIO

Villa d'Este ★★★   One of the most exclusive hotels in the world, this Renaissance villa is set amid 4 hectares (10 acres) of meticulously landscaped lakeside gardens. It has hosted everyone from Mark Twain to Joseph Heller, Clark Gable to Mel Gibson, Carreras to Madonna. Many guests arrive by helicopter or private boat (something which, incidentally, you can rent for yourself when you arrive). It's the sort of place that spares no expense, from the precious marbles in the spacious bathrooms and the genuine antique prints and oil paintings lining the halls and rooms, to the Como silk brocades covering the antiques and the Empire furnishings that actually date back to Napoléon's stay here (when it was still a private villa). The villa, in fact, is steeped in history. From 1815 to 1821 it was owned by Caroline, Princess of Wales and estranged queen to George IV, who had only married her for her dowry. Caroline spent her only happy years here, partying (or throwing orgies, according to vicious rumors of the day) and running up debts while her kingly husband tried to divorce her. The last owner before it became a hotel in 1873 was Russian Tsarina Maria Fedorowna. Service today is almost as discreet and personal as it was for those royal inhabitants. The Queen's Pavilion annex was built partially over the water at the boat tie-up in 1856 (named for Caroline, but built by the villa's then-owner, Napoléon's former aide-de-camp, Baron Ciani), its trompe l'oeil walls painted to mimic a Moorish-Venetian palazzo. No two rooms here are alike, but rest assured all are fit for a prince and princess. The main pool floats out on the lake itself; the indoor pool is banked by the indoor tennis and squash courts. Villa d'Este is a member of he Leading Hotels of the World.

Via Regina 40, 22012 Cernobbio, Lago di Como. (C) **031-3481** or 031-348-834. Fax 031-348-873. www.villa deste.it. 160 units. 450€–675€ ($518–$776) double; 715€–1,055€ ($822–$1,213) jr. suite; 995€–1,665€

($1,144–$1,915) 1-bedroom suite; call for rates on 2-bedroom suite. Buffet breakfast (or continental breakfast served in your room) included. AE, DC, MC, V. Free parking. Closed mid-Nov to Feb. **Amenities:** 3 restaurants (a formal, jacket-and-tie international-cuisine restaurant; casual dinner-only grill in Queen's Pavilion; Japanese dinner restaurant); 2 bars (1 elegant, with music, the other poolside); indoor and outdoor heated pools; 7 18-hole golf courses (14km/8¾ miles) away; virtual driving range at hotel; outdoor lighted and indoor tennis courts; spa; exercise room; Jacuzzi; sauna; watersports equipment; free bikes; concierge; tour desk; car-rental desk; courtesy car; salon; room service (limited); massage; babysitting; laundry service; same-day dry cleaning. *In room:* A/C, TV w/pay movies, VCR (on request), fax (on request), dataport, minibar, hair dryer, safe.

BELLAGIO & THE CENTRAL LAKE REGION

By far the loveliest spot on the lake (and where travelers should definitely set their sights) is the section known as the Centro Lago. Three towns—**Bellagio, Varenna,** and **Menaggio**—sit across the water from one another on three different shorelines.

ESSENTIALS

GETTING THERE & GETTING AROUND   By Train   The closest train station to Bellagio and the other Central Lake towns is in Como (see above); from there you can continue by bus or boat.

By Boat   From Como, boats stop first at Bellagio: by ferry 2 hours; by hydrofoil 35 to 45 minutes. They continue on to Menaggio: by ferry another 15 minutes; by hydrofoil, another 5 minutes. About half the boats then stop in Varenna as well (plus there are about two dozen short-haul ferries each from Bellagio and Menaggio to Varenna): by ferry another 10 minutes; by hydrofoil, another 5 minutes. You can also get day passes good for just the central lake or for the whole lake.

Many of the ferries carry cars for an additional fee. Schedules vary with the season, but from Easter through September a ferry or hydrofoil makes the trip from Como to Bellagio and other towns along the lake at least hourly. For more information, contact **Navigazione Lago di Como** (© **800-551-801** or 031-579-211); the office is on the lakefront in Como on Lungo Lario Trieste.

By Bus   One to three SPT buses (© **031-304-744**) per hour travel from Como to Bellagio (about 70 min.). Hourly buses to Menaggio take 65 minutes. Buses leave Como from in front of the main train station; get tickets at the bar inside.

By Car   Bellagio is connected to Como by a picturesque lakeshore road, S583, which can be very crowded in summer. The A9 links Como with Milan in about an hour. To reach Menaggio from Como, follow route S340 along the western shore of the lake. For Varenna, follow S342 to Nibionno, a speck of a town where it intersects with S36, which runs north through industrialized Lecco and thence along the lake's eastern shore. All of these roads tend to be crowded, especially on weekends and in summer, so allow at least an hour of traveling time.

BELLAGIO

Bellagio ★★★ is at the tip of the peninsula at a point where the lake forks into three distinct basins: One long leg sweeps north into the Alps, Como is at the southern end of the western leg, and Lecco is at the southern end of the eastern leg. Boats from Bellagio make it easy to visit the nearby shores of the Centro Lago—not that you'll be in a great hurry to leave this pretty old town, with its steep narrow streets, lakeside piazza, and beautiful gardens.

FESTIVALS & MARKETS   A pleasant way to spend a summer evening in Bellagio is at one of the concerts held in the Chiesa di Cappuccini on the grounds of the Rockefeller Foundation between June and July. Bellagio's outdoor market fills the waterfront every third Wednesday of the month.

Outdoor Adventures in Bellagio

The Bellagio region has a great outfitter who can treat you to some light adventurous exploration for decent prices. They run mountain bike treks, horseback rides through panoramic mountain passes, kayak excursions around the lake, canyoning (a combination of hiking, swimming, rappelling, and, well, jumping up and down a river gorge), and tandem paragliding lasting anywhere from an hour or 2 to 2 days, starting around 35€ ($40). Contact the **Cavalcalario Club,** Loc. Gallasco 1, Bellagio (✆ **031-984-814;** cellphone 339-538-138; www. bellagio-mountains.it) for more information.

VISITOR INFORMATION   The **Bellagio tourist office** is at Piazza d. Chiesa 14 (✆/fax **031-950-204;** www.fromitaly.net and www.bellagiolakecomo.com). Its hours are Monday and Wednesday to Saturday 9am to noon and 3 to 6pm, Tuesday and Sunday 10:30am to 12:30pm and 3:30 to 5:30pm.

Exploring the Town

Bellagio is often called one of the most beautiful towns in Italy. Nestled amid cypress groves and verdant gardens, its earth-toned old buildings climb from the lakefront promenade along stepped cobbled lanes. While Bellagio is a popular retreat for everyone from Milanese out for a day of relaxation to British and Americans who come to relax for a week or two, the town is for the most part unmarred by tourism.

One of Bellagio's famed gardens surrounds the **Villa Melzi** (✆ **031-951-281**), built by Francesco Melzi, a friend of Napoléon and an official of his Italian Republic. The villa was later the retreat of Franz Liszt and is now the home of a distinguished Lombardian family; they allow the public to stroll through their acres of manicured lawns and fountains and visit a pavilion where a collection of Egyptian sculpture is on display. It's open March 18 through October daily 9am to 6:30pm; admission is 5€ ($5.75).

Bellagio's other famous gardens are those of the **Villa Serbelloni,** occupying land once owned by Pliny the Younger and now in the hands of the Rockefeller Foundation. You can visit the gardens on twice-daily guided tours (reserve ahead), about 1½ hours long, in Italian and English (tours require 6 people minimum, 20 people maximum). From April to October, tours are Tuesday to Sunday at 11am and 4pm and cost 6.50€ ($7.50); for more information and to book a spot on the tour, call ✆ **031-951-555.** You meet at the little tower on the back side of Piazza della Chiesa, a steep block-and-a-half up from the port.

Where to Stay

For a wider selection of moderately priced hotels, you'd do best to head across the lake from Bellagio to Menaggio or Varenna (see below).

Du Lac 🌟🌟   The Leoni family ensures that an air of graciousness and old-fashioned comfort pervades its gracious 150-year-old hotel overlooking the lake from the main piazza. Downstairs, a bar spills onto the arcaded sidewalk in front and there are a series of pleasant sitting rooms. Meals are served in a nicely appointed dining room with panoramic views of the lake, and in the guest rooms, each of which is unique, cushy armchairs and a nice smattering of antiques and reproductions lend a great amount of charm. Many of the smallish rooms have balconies or terraces, and there's a rooftop sun terrace with sweeping lake views. In June 2002 they opened a sports center nearby with a pool, tennis courts, and a children's center, free for guests.

Piazza Mazzini 32, 22021 Bellagio. (C) 031-950-320. Fax 031-951-624. www.bellagiohoteldulac.com. 47 units. 160€ ($184) double without lake view; 170€ ($196) double with lake view; 190€ ($219) double with lake view and balcony. Rates include buffet breakfast. Half and full board available. MC, V. Closed early Nov to Easter. **Amenities:** Restaurant (Italian/international cuisine); bar; concierge; tour desk; car-rental desk; babysitting; laundry service; same-day dry cleaning. *In room:* A/C, TV, minibar, hairdryer, safe (in suites and superior rooms).

Giardinetto   The best lodging deal is at this little hotel at the top of town, reached from the lakefront by Bellagio's narrow stepped streets. A snug lobby, with a big fireplace, opens to a gravelly grapevine–covered terrace, where you're welcome to bring your own food for an alfresco meal. Most of the rooms also overlook the terrace (a flight and a half with no elevator). Most are quite large and bright, with big windows (those on the upper floors provide nice views from balconies over the town and lake beyond, especially nos. 18–20) and furnishings like solid old armoires and, in the better rooms, box-spring-and-mattress beds rather than Italy's usual cots. Some are on the airshaft, however, or come with no window whatsoever. The place is basic, but comfortable enough.

Piazza del Chiesa, 22021 Bellagio. (C) 031-950-168. 13 units, 11 with bathroom. 45€ ($52) double without bathroom, 52€ ($60) double with bathroom. Breakfast 6€ ($7). No credit cards. Closed Nov–Apr. *In room:* Hair dryer.

Grand Hotel Villa Serbelloni ★★   A grandiose 1850s villa lies at the core of this luxury hotel whose vast grounds expand from Bellagio's central square along the lake and up into the wooded hills. The tone is set by the high-ceilinged salons frescoed with *grotteschi* (fanciful stucco ornamentation) and blessed with lake views and live music on some evenings. Rooms vary widely in decor, with stuccoed ceilings in some, walnut furnishings in others, and oil paintings on the walls. Room categories boil down mostly to size, though almost all lake-view rooms are deluxe (not all deluxe rooms have the view, though), executive, or suite. They also run a health and beauty center with a large exercise room and full body treatments. In the back of the property, over the spa, is the **Residence Ulivo,** a series of apartments recommended separately below.

Via Roma/Piazza Mazzini, 22021 Bellagio. (C) 031-950-216. Fax 031-951-529. www.villaserbelloni.com. 83 units. 250€–310€ ($288–$357) classic double; 340€–420€ ($391–$483) deluxe double; 495€–620€ ($569–$713) executive double; 650€–800€ ($748–$920) senior suite. Half pension available. Breakfast included. AE, DC, MC, V. Closed Dec–Mar. **Amenities:** 2 Italian/international restaurants (1 jacket-and-tie terrace restaurant, 1 informal nautical-looking dinner-only restaurant); bar; indoor and outdoor heated pools; golf course (in Menaggio); outdoor tennis courts; exercise room; spa; sauna; watersports equipment; children's playground; concierge; tour desk; car-rental desk; courtesy car (on request); secretarial services; salon; room service (limited); massage; babysitting; laundry service; same-day dry cleaning. *In room:* A/C, TV, dataport, minibar, hair dryer, safe.

Suisse ★   The simple rooms above this restaurant in a 15th-century lakeside villa on the main square are currently at budget status in terms of decor (though the price has crept up), but they plan to renovate another level up soon. The parquet floors will remain, as will the stylish solid wood furnishings—with lovely details of inlay or carving. The bathrooms are plain, and there's no elevator, but you're right on the harbor, and the midpriced restaurant is quite good. It offers Italian fare year-round, with an inventive fusion flair in summer; the downstairs room looks very plain (though you can also sit out front under the arcades), but the upstairs dining room is understatedly elegant, with a stuccoed ceiling and a lake-view terrace. March to November the restaurant is open daily (closed Wed Oct–Feb).

Piazza Mazzini 23, 22021 Bellagio. © **031-950-335.** Fax 031-951-755. www.bellagio.co.nz/suisse. 10 units. 100€–154€ ($115–$177) double. Breakfast included. Half- and full-pension plans available. AE, DC, MC, V. Closed Dec–Feb. **Amenities:** Restaurant (international cuisine); bar; concierge; tour desk; room service (limited). *In room:* TV, hair dryer, no phone.

Apartment Stays

Residence Ulivo ★★ *Value*   The Villa Serbelloni (see above) is one of Italy's grandest hotels, surrounded by beautiful gardens and manicured lawns on the lakeshore. For those looking for less grandiose and expensive accommodations than those the main hotel provides (while still enjoying all the hotel's amenities, including its lovely lakeside pool, private beach, fitness club with sauna, game room, and frescoed salons), the Serbelloni has recently added these stylish apartments in an outbuilding on a hill above the lake. All have sitting areas and either separate bedrooms or alcove sleeping areas and are nicely decorated with terra-cotta floors and attractive rattan furniture. All have large kitchenettes; the best have partial views of the lake (no. 10 gets the best vistas, while no. 8 is larger and has some partial views, including from the bedroom). Although rentals are officially by the week, shorter stays can be arranged when space is available. Even when the main hotel is closed (mid-Nov–Mar) and the Residence stays open, there's always a section containing a covered grottolike pool, spa with massage and beauty treatments, and a lake-view restaurant open to residence guests.

Via Roma/Piazza Mazzini, 22021 Bellagio. © **031-956-434.** Fax 031-951-529. www.villaserbelloni.com. 13 apts. Weekly rates: 875€–1,197€ ($1,006–$1,377) small apt; 1,008€–1,253€ ($1,159–$1,441) medium apt; 1,400€–1,757€ ($1,610–$2,021) large apt. Rates are for 2 and vary with season. Buffet breakfast in main hotel (walk down a path to get there) 22€ ($25). AE, DC, MC. V. **Amenities:** Italian-international restaurant; bar; indoor and outdoor heated pools; golf course (in Menaggio); outdoor tennis courts; exercise room; spa; sauna; watersports equipment; children's playground; concierge; tour desk; car-rental desk; courtesy car (on request); secretarial services; salon; room service (limited); massage; babysitting; laundry service; same-day dry cleaning. *In room:* A/C, TV, kitchenette.

Where to Dine

Bar Café Rossi ★★ LIGHT FARE   One of the nicest of Bellagio's pleasant lakefront cafes is tucked under the arcades of the town's main square. You can dine at one of the few outside tables or in the delightful Art Nouveau dining room, with intricate tile work, carved wood cabinets, and stucco ceilings. Wine and the excellent house coffee are available all day, but a nice selection of pastries and sandwiches makes this a good stop for breakfast or lunch.

Piazza Mazzini 22/24. © **031-950-196.** Sandwiches 2.50€–4€ ($2.90–$4.60). AE, DC, MC, V. Fri–Wed 7:30am–10:30pm (open daily and to midnight Apr–Sept).

La Grotta ★ *Value* ITALIAN/PIZZERIA   Tucked away on a stepped street just off lakefront Piazza Manzini, this cozy, informal restaurant consists of a series of vaulted-ceiling dining rooms. The service is extremely friendly, and the

---

Drinking with Dante

Bellagio hosts a great bar called **Divina Commedia** ★★, Salita Mella 43–45 (© **031-951-680**; www.divinacommedia.com), modeled after Dante's epic poem: upstairs are frescoes with puffy clouds and cherubs as Paradise, the ground floor is Purgatory, and the tiny basement room is a fantastical black-lit Inferno cave of papier-mâché demons.

wide-ranging menu includes many pasta and meat dishes. Most of the regulars, though, come for the fish specials, including lake trout, or the delectable pizzas that are the best for miles around.

Salita Cernaia 14. (© 031-951-152. Primi 4.65€–6€ ($5.35–$7); secondi 4.65€–13€ ($5.35–$15); pizza 4.65€–10€ ($5.35–$12). AE, DC, MC, V (credit cards accepted only for bills totaling more than 21€/$24). Tues–Sun noon–2:30pm and 7pm–1am (daily July–Sept).

Ristorante Barchetta ★★ SEAFOOD/LOMBARDA One of Bellagio's best restaurants specializes in fresh lake fish and other seafood. In all but the coldest weather, food is served on a bamboo-enclosed heated terrace. (They have recently added a bar on the terrace.) Most of the pastas don't use seafood but are innovative variations on traditional recipes, such as *ravioli caprino* (with goat's cheese, topped with pear sauce) and savory risotto with hazelnuts and pistachios. For a main course, however, you should try one of the delicious preparations of local perch or angler fish; the meat entrees, including baby lamb chops with rosemary, are also excellent. You can enjoy a pasta dish, as well as a meat and a fish dish, on one of the set menus.

Salita Mella 13. (© 031-951-389. www.acena.it/labarchettadibellagio. Reservations highly recommended. Primi 9€–18€ ($10–$21); secondi 16€–21€ ($18–$24); tasting menu (for 2 only) 42€ ($48) not including wine. AE, DC, MC, V. Wed–Mon noon–2:30pm; Wed–Tues 7–10:30pm. Closed Nov–Mar.

VARENNA

You can happily spend some time clamoring up and down the steep steps that substitute for streets in this charming village (on the eastern shore of the lake, about 20 min. by ferry from Bellagio) that until not too long ago made its living by fishing. The main attractions, though, are outside of town.

The hilltop ruins of the **Castello di Vezio** (© **0341-831-000**) are about a 20-minute walk above the town on a gradually ascending path. The main reason for a visit is to enjoy the stunning views of the lake, its shoreline villages, and the backdrop of mountains at the northern end. May to June the castle is open daily 10am to 6pm, July to September 11am to 8pm; admission is 1€ ($1.15).

The **gardens of the Villa Monastero** (© **0341-830-129**) are more easily accessible, at the southern edge of town along Via 4 Novembre, and you can reach them by following the series of lakeside promenades through the Old Town from the ferry landing. This villa and the terraced gardens that rise up from the lakeshore were once a not-so-spartan monastery—until it was dissolved in the late 17th century when the nuns in residence began bearing living proof that they were on too-friendly terms with the priests across the way. If you find it hard to tear yourself from the bowers of citrus trees and rhododendrons clinging to terraces, you'll find equally enchanting surroundings in the adjoining gardens of the **Villa Cipressi** (© **0341-830-113**).

Both gardens are open daily March to October: Villa Monastero 10am to 7pm and Villa Cipressi 9am to 7pm. Admission is 2€ ($2.30) for adults (1.30€/$1.50 for kids under 10 and seniors over 60) to just one garden, 3.50€ ($4.05) (2.50€/$2.90 kids and seniors) to visit both. Call © **0341-830-113** for more details.

In season, **ferries** make the 20-minute run between Bellagio and Varenna about every half-hour (see above). There's a tiny **tourist office** at Piazza S. Giorgio/Via 4 Novembre (© **0341-830-367;** www.fromitaly.net/lakecomo/varenna), open Tuesday to Sunday 10am to 12:30pm and Tuesday to Saturday 3 to 6pm.

Where to Stay

Milano ★★ *Value* You'd have to look hard to find a more pleasant retreat by the lake. This old house hanging over Varenna's lakefront was taken over in 2002 by

Bettina and Egidio Mallone, a friendly young Italian-Swiss couple. Their plans are to renovate it into a boutique hotel but retain the family atmosphere, which has long been the Milano's hallmark, with the aid of two cats and their infant daughter Carlotta. Sadly, prices will rise slowly as they finish overhauling each room; they've already jumped up 30% from last edition's rates. First on the list of room renovations is to add safes and hair dryers. They've already redone the common area downstairs in a modern style, and installed a TV with satellite channels and a computer for free Internet access. The rooms were overhauled in 2003 with new beds and antique-style furnishings, each with its own color scheme. All have balconies and views—nos. 1 and 2 open onto a wide terrace, and nos. 5 and 6 both have full-on lake vistas; the other half overlook the neighbor's pretty garden with askance lake views. The furnishings are a pleasant mix of old and unobtrusive modern pieces, brightened up with small Persian rugs. In summer breakfast is served on the outdoor terrace. They have also started serving 25€ ($29) three-course dinners (but not on Sun or Tues) out on the terrace in nice weather. In addition, they have an apartment nearby (no views, though) that they'll rent out, preferably to families or groups of four, for 50€ ($58) per person, including breakfast, back at the hotel.

Via XX Settembre 29, 23829 Varenna. ©/fax **0341-830-298.** www.varenna.net. 8 units. 110€–120€ ($127–$138) double with lateral lake view; 120€–130€ ($138–$150) double with full lake view. Rates include buffet breakfast. 3-course dinner 25€ ($29) upon request. AE, DC, MC, V. Closed late Mar to Feb. **Amenities:** Bar; concierge; tour desk; room service (limited); massage; laundry service; dry cleaning; Internet terminal.

Villa Cipressi ★★ *(Finds* If you enjoyed your tour of Varenna's lush gardens (see above), there's no need to leave. This 16th-century villa and several outbuildings were converted to a hotel in the early 1800s; it's now geared to conferences but takes other guests as well, space permitting. Though the rooms have been renovated without any attempt to retain historic character, they're extremely large and attractive. Suites take advantage of the high ceilings and contain loft bedrooms, with sitting areas below that can easily fit a couple of single beds for families. Although not every room gets a lake view, all save a few small ones on the road side enjoy marvelous views over the gardens, which you can also enjoy on the delightful terraces. There are plans to add air-conditioning at some point. In June 2002 they opened up 10 new rooms on the top floor with lake views and high ceilings decorated with molded stuccoes—the best is the corner suite, with a coffered ceiling, alcove bed, four windows, and a nonworking fireplace. They're busily preparing five more accommodations in a 15th-century building on the property.

Via IV Novembre 18, 22050 Varenna. © **0341-830-113.** Fax 0341-830-401. villacipressi@libero.it. 32 units. 95€ ($109) double without lake view; 110€ ($127) double with lake view; 120€ ($138) "superior" double or regular suite with lake view; 180€ ($207) superior suite with lake view. Rates include buffet breakfast. AE, DC, MC, V. Usually closes late Oct to Mar, but some years open year-round. **Amenities:** Restaurant; bar; concierge; car-rental desk; courtesy car; babysitting. *In room:* A/C (in ⅔ of rooms), TV, dataport, hair dryer.

Where to Dine

Vecchia Varenna ★★ LOMBARD/SEAFOOD   One of your most memorable experiences in this region could be a meal at this romantic restaurant at the water's edge in Varenna's oldest section. Dining is in a beautiful stone-floored room with white stone walls or on a terrace on the water. The kitchen makes the most of local herbs and vegetables and, of course, the bounty of the lake—for starters, *quadrucci* (pasta pockets) are stuffed with trout, and one of the best of the many risottos combines wild mushrooms and *lavarello* (a white fish from the lake). Grilled lake trout stuffed with mountain herbs is a sublime main course, though many other kinds of lake fish are also available.

Via Scoscesa 10. © **031-830-793.** Reservations required. Primi 11€ ($13); secondi 15€ ($17). MC, V. Tues–Sun 12:30–2pm and 7:30–10pm. Closed Jan.

MENAGGIO

This lively resort town hugs the western shore of the lake, across from Bellagio on its peninsula and Varenna on the distant shore. Hikers should stop in at the **tourist office** on Piazza Garibaldi 8 (©/fax **0344-32-924;** www.menaggio.com), open Monday to Saturday 9am to noon and 3 to 6pm (July and Aug also Sun 7:30am–6:30pm). The very helpful staff distributes a booklet, *Hiking in the Area around Menaggio,* with descriptions of more than a dozen walks, accompanied by maps and instructions on what buses to take to trail heads. The town's bus stop is at Piazza Garibaldi (Sun on Via Mazzini); tickets are sold at Bar Centrale or the newsstand on Via Calvi at the piazza.

The major nearby attraction is about 2.5km (1½ miles) south of town: The **Villa Carlotta** (© **0344-40-405;** www.villacarlotta.it) is the most famous villa on the lake and was begun in 1643 for the Marquis Giorgio Clerici, who made his fortune supplying Napoléon's troops with uniforms; he spent much of it on this neoclassical villa and gardens. After a succession of owners, including Prussian royalty who lavished their funds and attention on the gardens, the villa is now in the hands of the Italian government. It's filled with romantic paintings, statues by Canova and his imitators, and Empire furnishings, but the gardens are the main attraction, with azaleas, orchids, banana trees, cacti, palms, and forests of ferns spreading in all directions. You can take the no. C10 bus from Menaggio or walk along the lake (about a 30–45 min. walk). The nearest ferry landing is at Cadenabbia, just north of the gardens, though ferries to Menaggio are more frequent. The villa and gardens are open daily: the months of March and October from 9 to 11:30am and 2 to 4:30pm, and April through September from 9am to 6pm. Admission is 6.50€ ($7) for adults and 3.25€ ($3.75) for seniors over 65 and students.

WATERSPORTS   The lido, at the north end of town, has an excellent **beach,** as well as a **pool,** and is open late June to mid-September daily 9am to 7pm. For information on water-skiing and other activities, contact **Centro Lago Service,** in the Grand Hotel Victoria along the lakeside Via Castelli (© **0344-320-03**). Also ask at the hostel (see below) about boat and bike rentals, which are available to nonguests during slow periods.

Where to Stay & Dine

Albergo-Ristorante Il Vapore ⭐   This very pleasant small restaurant/hotel faces a quiet square just off the lakefront. The rooms are comfortable, with rather nice modern furnishings (plus antiques in a few) and fuzzy towels in the cramped bathrooms. Six rooms open onto partial lake views: nos. 21 and 22 from tall windows; nos. 25 and 26 from small terraces; and nos. 28 and 29 (the biggest room, with windows on two sides for a breeze) from tiny balconies. They usually won't accept reservations for just 1 or 2 nights (but you can just stop by and ask). Sadly, the husband of this family-run affair passed away in 2002, and while they were still renting out rooms, the restaurant has been closed for the time being, its future uncertain. Meals of local specialties from the nearby mountain valleys were normally served beneath the wisteria-shaded arbor of the entranceway or in an attractive pale-blue dining room with paintings by local artists.

Piazza Grossi 3, 22017 Menaggio. ⓒ 0344-32-229. Fax 0304-34-850. www.italiaabc.com/a/ilvapore. 10 units. 45€ ($52) double without lake view; 50€ ($58) double with lake view. Breakfast 6.50€ ($7). No credit cards. Closed 20 days in Nov and late Feb to early Mar. **Amenities:** Bar. *In room:* No phone.

Grand Hotel Menaggio ★★
This 19th-century palazzo just down to the left from the ferry dock was refurbished in 1988 and 1995, but the owners were careful to retain the original stucco work and chandeliers in the main hall and salons. The spacious rooms are nicely furnished in a modern style. "Superior" ones are larger, have lake views, and come with Jacuzzi tubs in the bathrooms (some "standard" rooms have lake views, some mountain views). Three "superior" rooms even have small terraces rather than balconies; the three junior suites also come with nice terraces whose stone balustrades overlook the pool. The restaurant's picture windows open to the lawn and the lake, which shares its view with the pool and pier, overlooking Lake Como to the less-developed eastern shore.

Via IV Novembre 69, 22017 Menaggio (CO). ⓒ 0344-30-640. Fax 0344-30-619. www.grandhotelmenaggio. com. 97 units. 180€ ($207) standard double without lake view; 210€ ($242) standard double with lake view; 230€ ($265) superior double with lake view; 260€ ($299) superior double with lake view and balcony. Half pension available. Breakfast included. AE, MC, V. Closed Nov–Jan. **Amenities:** Italian/international restaurant; bar; outdoor heated pool; golf course 3km (1¾ miles) away; outdoor tennis courts; tiny exercise room; watersports equipment; concierge; tour desk; car-rental desk; courtesy car (on request); room service (limited); babysitting; laundry service; dry cleaning; nonsmoking rooms. *In room:* A/C, TV, VCR (on request), dataport, kitchenette (in 2 apts), minibar, hair dryer, safe.

Ostello La Primula (Value)
I don't particularly like hostels (didn't even when I was a student), so when I list one you know it's got something special. This delightful example is easily accessible from Bellagio and other towns on the Centro Lago by boat, and is frequented about evenly by frugal adults and back-packing students. The dorms are relatively cozy, with no more than six beds per room. Most of the rooms have a view of the lake—nos. 3, 4, and 5 on the first floor even share a balcony. Everyone enjoys the view from the large, sunny, communal terrace. *One drawback:* no luggage lockers. It's run by a couple of ex–social workers, and they serve an 8.50€ ($10) dinner that's so good it even attracts locals (you're expected to set your own table on the terrace, retrieve each course as it's called, and wash your own dishes).

You can explore the surrounding countryside on one of the bikes that are available or get onto the lake in one of the kayaks (rental of either for a full day is 11€/$12). Internet access is 3.50€ ($4.05) per 15 minutes; laundry is 3.50€ ($4.05) per load. The hostel offers special programs, such as 1-week cooking courses and an organized weeklong hike through the area. Curfew is 11:30pm.

Via IV Novembre 86 (on the south edge of town), 22017 Menaggio (CO). ⓒ and fax 0344-32-356. www. menaggiohostel.com. 35 beds. 14€ ($16) per person in dorm; 14€ ($16) per person in family suites (sleep 4–6 people) with private bathroom. Breakfast included. No credit cards. Open Mar 15 to 1st weekend in Nov. Office open 8–10am and 5–11:30pm. **Amenities:** Restaurant; bar; watersports equipment rental; bike rental; washer/dryer. *In room:* No phone.

3 Lake Maggiore (Lago Maggiore) & the Borromean Islands
Stresa: 80km (50 miles) NW of Milan

Anyone who reads Hemingway will know this lake and its forested shores from *A Farewell to Arms.* That's just the sort of place Lake Maggiore is—a pleasure ground that's steeped in associations with famous figures (Flaubert, Wagner, Goethe, and many of Europe's other great minds seem to have been inspired by the deep, moody waters, backed by the Alps) and not-so-famous wealthy visitors.

Fortunately, you need not be famous or wealthy to enjoy Maggiore, which is on the Swiss border to the east and north of Milan.

STRESA

The major town on the lake is a pretty, festive little place, with a long lakefront promenade, a lively and attractive commercial center, and a bevy of restaurants and hotels that range from the expensively splendid to the affordably comfortable.

ESSENTIALS

GETTING THERE   By Train   Stresa is linked with Milan by 20 trains a day (regional: 75 min.; high-speed: 58 min.).

By Boat   Boats arrive and depart from Piazza Marconi, connecting Stresa with the Borromean Islands (Isole Borromee) and with many other lakeside spots; most boats on the lake are operated by **Navigazione Sul Lago Maggiore** (© **800-551-801** or 0322-233-200; www.navlaghi.it).

By Car   A8 runs between Milan and Sesto, near the southern end of the lake; from there Route S33 follows the western shore to Stresa. The trip takes a little over an hour.

VISITOR INFORMATION   The **tourist office** has moved to the ferry dock (©/fax **0323-31-308**) and is open Monday to Saturday (daily Mar–Oct) 10am to 12:30pm and 3 to 6:30pm. You can also get info from private websites (try www.lagomaggiore.it and www.stresa.it). For hiking information, ask for the booklet *Percorsi Verdi.*

FESTIVALS & MARKETS   July to September, Stresa draws visitors from around the world for its *Settimane Musicali,* or Festival of Musical Weeks, a major gathering of classical musicians. The festival has an info office at Via Canonica 6 (© **0323-31-095;** www.stresa.net/settimanemusicali).

EXPLORING STRESA & THE ISLANDS

STRESA

Strolling and relaxing seem to be the main activities in Stresa. The action is at the lakeside promenade, running from the center of town north past the grand lakeside hotels, including the Iles des Borromees, where Hemingway set *A Farewell to Arms.* Sooner or later, though, most visitors climb into a boat for the short ride to the famed islands themselves, the Borromean Islands.

BORROMEAN ISLANDS (ISOLE BORROMEE)

These three islands, named for the Borromeo family, which has owned them since the 12th century, float in the misty waters off Stresa and entice visitors with their stunning beauty. Note that Isola Bella and Isola Superiore have villages you can hang out in for free, but Isola Madre consists solely of the admission-charging gardens.

Public **ferries** leave for the islands every half-hour from Stresa's Piazza Marconi; an 8€ ($9) **day pass** is the most economical way to visit all three—and if you buy your admission tickets for the *isole* sights at the Stresa ferry office along with your ferry tickets, you'll save 1€ ($1.15) off each—though the generally grumpy ticket agents will not advise you of this; you have to ask. Buy tickets only from the public Navigazione Lago Maggiore (© **800-551-801** or 0322-233-200; www.navlaghi.it), in the big building with triple arches. Private boats also make

Tips **Budgeting Your Time**

To squeeze as much of Stresa's sights in as you can in a day, note that the ferry back from the Isole Borromee stops first at the Mottarone cable car area before chugging down the coast to the center of Stresa and the main docks. You can hop off at this first stop to either ride the cable car up the mountain or simply to walk back into Stresa itself along a pretty lakeside promenade, past crumbling villas and impromptu sculpture gardens, in about 20 minutes.

the trip out to the island—at obscene rates; you'll see other ticket booths as well as hucksters dressed as sailors trying to lure you aboard (for large groups, the prices can be reasonable, but do your negotiating on the dock before you get on the boat). For more information, visit www.borromeoturismo.it.

ISOLA BELLA   Isola Bella (5 min. from Stresa) remains true to its name, with splendid 17th-century gardens that ascend from the shore in 10 luxuriantly planted terraces. The Borromeo palazzo provides a chance to explore opulently decorated rooms, including the one where Napoléon and Josephine once slept. It's open daily: March to September 9am to noon and 1:30 to 5:30pm (to 5pm Oct 1–24). Admission is 8.50€ ($10) for adults and 4€ ($4.60) for children 6 to 15. Audio tours help make sense of it all for 3.50€ ($4.05) each or 5€ ($6) to rent two sets of headphones. For more details, call © **0323-30-556.**

ISOLA SUPERIORE   Most of Isola Superiore, also known as Isola Pescatori (10 min. from Stresa), is occupied by a not-so-quaint old fishing village—every one of the tall houses on this tiny strip of land seems to harbor a souvenir shop or pizza stand, and there are hordes of visitors to keep them busy.

ISOLA MADRE   The largest and most peaceful of the islands is Isola Madre (30 min. from Stresa), every inch of which is covered with the exquisite flora and exotic, colorful birds of the 3.2-hectare (8-acre) **Orto Botanico** (© **0323-31-261**). The map they hand out at the entrance/ticket booth details all the flora; you're on your own to ID the various peacocks, game fowl, exotic birds, and funky chickens, and other avians that strut, flit, and roost amidst the lawns around the central villa (1518–85), filled with Borromeo family memorabilia and some interesting old puppet-show stages. The botanical garden is open daily: March 27 through September 9am to noon and 1:30 to 5:30pm, and October 1 to October 24 9:30am to 12:30pm and 1:30 to 5pm; admission is 8€ ($9) for adults and 4€ ($4.60) for children 6 to 15.

HIKING & BIKING IN THE AREA

The forested slopes above Stresa are prime hiking and mountain biking terrain. To reach a network of trails, take the funivia from near the lakefront at the north end of town up **Monte Mottarone;** the funivia (© **0323-30-399** or 0323-30-295; www.paginegialle.it/funistresa) runs every 20 minutes from roughly 9 to 11:40am and 12:40 to 5:30pm (hours vary with the season). It costs 9.20€ ($11) one-way to take the funivia along with a bike, which you can rent at the station for 21€ ($24) for a half day or 26€ ($30) for a full day. The **Alpina garden** halfway up is open Tuesday to Saturday 9am to 6pm and Sunday (and July–Aug) 9:30am to 6:30pm.

If you don't want to venture too far from the lake, there's a nice **beach** near the station.

WHERE TO STAY
Very Expensive
Grand Hôtel et des Iles Borromées ★★★   This is one of the grande dame hotels of the Italian lakes, a favorite of Ernest Hemingway, who set part of *A Farewell to Arms* in the hotel. Renovations over the past decade have restored the elegance to the decor—gilded stuccoes, mosaics lining the hall runners, giant Murano chandeliers—in the spirit and style of the 1860s era in which the hotel was built. Its Liberty-style facade is surrounded by well-manicured gardens of palms, flowers, ponds, fountains, and pools. Rooms come in various types. "Alla Stresa" means 19th-century-style furnishings in intricately inlaid wood, large, comfy beds, and marble bathrooms. "Al Impero" rooms are done in Empire style, with gilded Napoléon-type headboards and dressers, richly patterned carpets, *pietra dura* inlaid stone tabletops, and stucco decorations in the bathrooms. "Alla Baveno" rooms are mostly junior suites, some on the garden and some with lake views, with small tapestries, elegantly detailed lacquer furnishings, Murano chandeliers, and gilded and inlaid appointments. Suites are sumptuous and vary widely; the Hemingway suite in particular is out of this world (and at a cool 2,860€/$3,289 per night, a wee bit out of most people's price range), with two bedrooms of half-tester king beds, three bathrooms (two with Jacuzzi tubs built for two), frescoed ceilings, and a large terrace. The hotel cares for all its guests, though; in 2003 they even added balconies to the least expensive rooms, the ones on the back overlooking the mountains.

Corso Umberto I 67, 28838 Stresa. © **0323-938-938.** Fax 0323-32-405. www.borromees.it. 174 units. 277€ **($319)** double with garden view; 263€ ($302) double with lake view; 478€ ($550) jr. suite; 670€ ($771) jr. suite deluxe; 670€–2,860€ ($771–$3,289) suite. Breakfast included. AE, DC, MC, V. **Amenities:** 2 restaurants (1 elegant Italian, 1 poolside lunch bar); bar; 2 outdoor heated pools (1 for diving); indoor pool; golf course (7km/4¼ miles away); outdoor tennis courts; large exercise room and spa; Jacuzzi; sauna; concierge; tour desk; business center; salon; room service (limited); massage; babysitting; laundry service; same-day dry cleaning. *In room:* A/C, TV, VCR (on request), fax (on request), dataport, kitchenette (in residence), minibar, hair dryer, safe.

Expensive
La Palma ★★   The Palma is one of the nicest of Stresa's luxury hotels and, given the high-level comfort and the amenities, one of the most reasonably priced. Most of the large rooms, recently redone in rich floral fabrics and wood tones, open to balconies overlooking the lake, and 98% of the spacious marble bathrooms have Jacuzzis. There's a rooftop sun terrace and fitness center, with a hot tub sauna, but the most pleasant places to relax are in the flowery garden in front of the hotel and the terrace surrounding the lakeside pool.

Lungolago Umberto I, 33, 28838 Stresa. © **0323-933-906** or 0323-32-401. Fax 0323-933-930. www.hla palma.it. 128 units. 130€–205€ ($150–$236) double; 220€–260€ ($253–$299) triple/jr. suite. Rates include buffet breakfast. AE, DC, MC, V. Free parking. Closed mid-Nov to mid-Mar. **Amenities:** Restaurant; bar; pool; tennis courts; exercise room; Jacuzzi; sauna; bike rental; concierge; tour desk; car-rental desk; courtesy car; room service (24-hr.); babysitting; laundry service; dry cleaning; nonsmoking rooms. *In room:* A/C, TV, dataport, minibar, hair dryer, safe.

Moderate
Verbano ★★ *Finds*   This dusty-rose villa has one of the most envied positions on all of Lago Maggiore, sitting at the tip of the Isola dei Pescatori, overlooking the back side of Isola Bella. The flower-fringed terrace, with its excellent restaurant

(reviewed separately below), enjoys great lake views in three directions. Each room is named after the flower that drives the villa's color scheme; all feature parquet floors, big old wood furnishings, real beds with wrought-iron bedsteads, and large tiled bathrooms. Nos. 1 and 2, on the front of the villa with Isola Bella views, have working fireplaces; highly requested no. 2 on the corner has a balcony on the front and a shared terrace on the side. Rooms on the first floor share a large terrace overlooking Isola Madre and the Lombard, eastern shore of the lake.

Isola Superiore dei Pescatori, 28049 Stresa. (C) **0323-32-534.** Fax 0323-33-129. www.hotelverbano.it. 12 units. 140€ ($161) double; 160€ ($184) triple. Half pension 95€ ($109) per person. Breakfast included. AE, DC, MC, V. Closed Jan. **Amenities:** Excellent restaurant (see review below); bar; concierge; tour desk; courtesy boat from the mainland in the evenings after public ferry service ends; room service (breakfast only); babysitting; laundry service. In room: Hair dryer.

Inexpensive

Meeting ★ *Value*   The name comes from the proximity of Stresa's small conference center, where a much-attended music festival is held from July to early September (see "Festivals & Markets" above). Although the lakefront is a 5-minute walk away, the setting is quiet and leafy, though light sleepers on the back may notice the trains passing in the distance. The rooms, in Scandinavian modern, are big and bright, and many have terraces. There's a cozy bar and lounge downstairs, as well as a casual (but slightly impersonal) dining room. In 2000 they overhauled the exterior, adding balconies to all rooms lacking them (they plan to add air-conditioning soon as well—perhaps during the winter 2003–04 lull).

Via Bonghi 9, 28049 Stresa. (C) **0323-32-741.** Fax 0323-33-458. www.stresa.it. 27 units. 75€–105€ ($86–$121) double. Rates include breakfast. AE, DC, MC, V. Parking 7.50€ ($9). Closed Jan–Feb. **Amenities:** Restaurant (Italian cuisine); bar; bike rental; concierge; tour desk; car-rental desk; room service (24-hr.); laundry service; dry cleaning. In room: TV, dataport, hair dryer.

Mon Toc ★   Just uphill from the train station, this family-run hotel surrounded by a big private garden and lawn is convenient to the lake and town (a 10- to 15-min. walk) but enough removed to provide an almost countrylike atmosphere. With functional furniture, the rooms are unusually pleasant for a hotel in this price range and have tidy bathrooms (though a few are of the miniscule, molded, airplane variety). The friendly owner refuses, out of honesty, to call the sliver of lake visible over the rooftops from the second-floor rooms (no elevator) a "lake view."

Via Duchessa di Genova 67–69, 28049 Stresa. (C) **0323-30-282.** Fax 0323-933-860. www.hotelmontoc.com. 15 units, 12 with bathroom. 78€ ($90) double with bathroom; 95€ ($109) triple with bathroom (the 3 that share a bath are all singles). Buffet breakfast included. AE, DC, MC, V. Closed Jan or Nov. **Amenities:** Home-cooking restaurant; bar; concierge; tour desk; room service (breakfast only). In room: TV.

Primavera ★★   For much of the spring and summer, the street in front of this hotel is closed to traffic and filled with flowering plants and cafe tables. The relaxed air prevails throughout this bright little hotel, a block off the lake in the town center. A tiny lounge and bar are downstairs. Upstairs, the tile-floored rooms are furnished in functional walnut veneer; you can have a minifridge on request. Many rooms have balconies, just wide enough to accommodate a pair of chairs, with flower boxes overlooking the town. A few fourth-floor rooms get in a sliver of lake view around the apse and stone bell tower of the Duomo.

Via Cavour 30, 28049 Stresa. (C) **0323-31-286.** Fax 0323-33-458. www.stresa.it. 34 units. 75€–105€ ($86–$121) double. Rates include breakfast. AE, DC, MC, V. Parking 7.50€ ($9) at Hotel Meeting. Closed mid-Nov to Dec 20 and Jan 7–Feb. **Amenities:** Bar; bike rental; concierge; tour desk; car-rental desk; room service (24-hr.); laundry service; dry cleaning. *In room:* TV, dataport, minibar (on request), hair dryer, safe.

WHERE TO DINE

Hotel Ristorante Fiorentino *Value* ITALIAN   It's hard to find friendlier service or homier trattoria-type food in Stresa, especially at these prices. Everything that comes out of this family-run kitchen is made fresh daily, including cannelloni and other pastas. You can dine in a big cozy room or on a patio out back in good weather.

Via Bolongaro 9–11. ℂ 0323-30-254. Primi 4.50€–8€ ($5–$9); secondi 7€–13€ ($8–$15); *menù turistico* 14€ ($16) not including wine. AE, DC, MC, V. Mar–Oct daily 11am–3pm and 6–10pm. Closed Dec–Mar.

Osteria degli Amici *Finds* ITALIAN/PIZZERIA   This popular spot, beloved by locals and Italian vacationers alike, is tucked into a nook of a piazza with a tiny outdoor eating area shaded by vines. The rambling interior consists of tiny rooms with three to five tables each, so the overall effect is cozy. Pizzas come bubbling hot from a wood-fired oven, or you can try risotto enriched with porcini, *persico* (lake perch), or *rucola e gamberetti* (arugula and tiny shrimp). The *spaghetti montecarlo* puts on airs with its caviar and salmon cream sauce, while the *crespelle valdostane* comes back down to earth with a rib-sticking combo of ham and cheese wrapped in sheets of homemade pasta. Second courses are straightforward: *tagliata al rosmarino* (sirloin steak scented with rosemary), *filetto di persico alle mandorle* (broiled lake perch filet under almonds), or fresh grilled *sogliola* (sole) or *orata* (bream).

Via A. M. Bolongaro 33. ℂ 0323-30-453. Reservations highly recommended. Primi 5€–8€ ($6–$9); secondi 8.50€–14€ ($10–$16); pizza 4€–9.80€ ($4.60–$11). MC, V. Thurs–Tues noon–2:30pm and 7pm–midnight. Closed Jan and Nov.

Ristorante Pescatore *⭐* SEAFOOD   This small dining room in the center of town is where residents of Stresa come for a fish meal. The starters include a wonderful seafood salad, an appetizer of smoked salmon or tuna, or any number of pasta dishes served with clams or squid. The main courses include a paella—35€/$40 for two people—worthy of southern Spain (the owners and some of the cooks and waiters are Spanish) as well as *zarzuela de pescada,* a rich fish stew. Lake or ocean fish are always fresh and served grilled and topped with the simplest sauces.

Vicolo del Poncivo. ℂ 0323-31-986. Reservations recommended. Primi 7€–11€ ($8–$13); secondi 11€–21€ ($12–$24); fixed-price menu 14€ ($16) not including wine. DC, MC, V. Fri–Wed noon–2pm and 7–10pm. Closed Dec–Feb.

Taverna del Pappagallo *⭐* ITALIAN/PIZZERIA   Most of Stresa seems to congregate in this pleasant restaurant for the most popular pizza in town. But just about all the fare that comes out of this family-run kitchen is delicious, including delectable homemade gnocchi and dishes such as grilled sausage. Weather permitting, try to dine at one of the tables in the pleasant garden.

Via Principessa Margherita 46. ℂ 0323-30-411. Primi and pizza 4€–11€ ($4.60–$12); secondi 8€–12€ ($9–$14). No credit cards. Thurs–Mon 11:30am–2:30pm and 6:30–10:30pm (daily in summer).

Verbano *⭐⭐* ITALIAN   Verbano offers a fairy-tale location on the point of the "Fisherman's Isle," taking up the jasmine-fringed gravelly terrace next to the hotel (recommended above). The waters lap right up to the wall, and the views are over the back side of Isola Bella and the lake around you on three sides. The cooking needn't be anything special given its location in a prime tourist spot, but surprisingly it is almost as lovely as the setting. The *zuppa di verdure* vegetable soup is hearty with barley and grains; *paglia e fieno* ("hay and straw") is a mix of regular (yellow) and spinach (green) tagliatelle noodles in a ragù made of scorpion fish, carrots, and zucchini. The *crespelle con passato di melanzane e toma* are pasta sheets wrapped around a purée of eggplant and local cheese. For secondo, definitely try grilled lake trout, or the *luccio percia* (lake perch) filet in a smoked-salmon and poppy crust sided with rice stained black from squid ink. Landlubbers can dig into *faraona dissosata farcita con spinaci e ricotta* (guinea fowl done up like ravioli, and stuffed with ricotta cheese and spinach).

Isola Superiore dei Pescatori. (𝐶 0323-32-534. Reservations recommended. Primi 5€–10 ($6–$12); secondi 10€–21€ ($12–$24). AE, DC, MC, V. Daily noon–2:30pm and 7–10pm (closed Wed in winter). Closed Jan.

9

Piedmont & the Valle d'Aosta

Loosely translated, Piedmont (Piemonte) means "at the foot of the mountains." Those mountains, of course, are the Alps, which define the region and are part of Italy's northern and western borders. These dramatic peaks are visible in much of the province, most of which rises and rolls over fertile foothills that produce a bounty that is as rich as the region is green. Piedmont is a land of cheeses, truffles, plump fruit, and, of course, wine—among which are some of Italy's most powerful, complex, and delicious reds, including **Barolo** and **Barbaresco,** lighter reds **Barbera** and **Dolcetto,** and Italy's top sparkling white, **Asti Spumanti.**

Not that all of Piedmont is rural, of course. **Turin,** Italy's car town, is the region's capital. But within its ring of industrialized suburbs, rather than an Italian Detroit lies an elegant city of mannerly squares, baroque palaces, and stunning art collections. Torinese and their neighbors from other parts of Italy often retreat to the **Valle d'Aosta,** the smallest, northernmost, and most mountainous of Italian provinces.

REGIONAL CUISINE   Given such vast geographic diversity, it's not surprising that the region's cuisine varies according to the topography. In the southern stretches of Piedmont, the palate turns primarily to those magnificent red wines from the wine villages around Asti and Alba. Barbaresco, Barbera, Barolo, Dolcetto, Nebbiolo—the names are legendary, and they often appear on the table to accompany meat dishes stewed in red wine; one of the most favored of these is *brasato al barolo* (beef or veal braised in Barolo).

The way to begin a meal here, but usually available in winter only, is with *bagna cauda,* literally, "hot bath," a plate of raw vegetables that are dipped into a steaming sauce of olive oil, garlic, and anchovies. The Piemontese pasta is *tarajin,* and it is often topped with sauces made with walnuts or, for a special occasion, what is perhaps the region's greatest contribution to Italian cuisine, white truffles. As the land climbs higher toward the Valle d'Aosta, local mountain fare (a rib-sticking variant on Piemontese), called Valdostana, takes over—polenta is a popular *primo* (first course), stews are thick with beef and red wine (*carbonada* is the most common stew like this), and buttery fontina is the preferred cheese.

1 Turin

669km (415 miles) NW of Rome, 140km (87 miles) E of Milan

It's often said that Turin is the most French city in Italy or the most Italian city in France. The reason is partly historic and partly architectural. From the late 13th century to Italy's unification in 1861 (when the city served very briefly as capital), Turin was the capital of the **House of Savoy.** The Savoys were as French as they were Italian, and their holdings extended well into the present-day French regions of Savoy and the Côte d'Azur as well as Sardegna. The city's Francophile

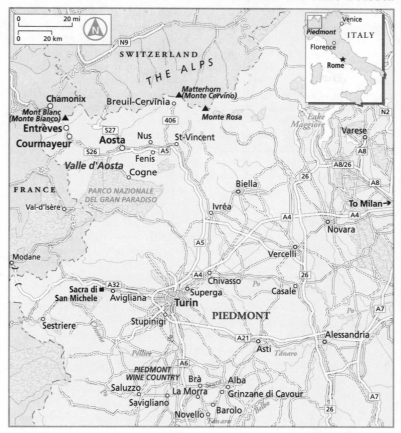

17th- and 18th-century architects, inspired by the tastes of the French court, laid out broad avenues and airy piazzas and lined them with low-slung neoclassical buildings.

After Napoléon's occupation, the city's intellectuals began percolating the ideas that would eventually blossom into the Risorgimento unification movement, with hometown king Vittorio Emanuele II of Savoy as its royal ruler. Italy's first prime minister was Torinese gentleman artist Massimo d'Azeglio, followed by the Risorgimento's political leader and another local hero, Camillo Cavour. Later, the Italian Communist Party was born here on the Fiat factory floor under the leadership of poet Antonio Gramsci, though that same factory floor also gave rise to the ultra-radical Red Brigades terrorist group in the 1970s.

Most visitors come to Turin with business in mind (often at the Fiat and Pirelli factories in the sprawling industrial suburbs). Those who take the time to look around the historic center, though, will find an elegant and sophisticated city that has changed little since more gracious centuries, with some fine museum collections and the charm of a place that, for all its Francophile leanings, is quintessentially Italian and perhaps the most pleasant big city in northern Italy.

FESTIVALS & MARKETS   Dance, opera, theater, and musical performances (mostly classical) are on the agenda in June and the first week of July, during the **Sere d'Estate festival,** when companies come from around the world to perform. September is the month to enjoy further classical music—more than 60 classical concerts are held on stages around the city during the month-long **Settembre Musica** festival (© 011-442-4703; www.settembremusica.it).

Bric-a-brac of all kinds, be it household utensils, books, or used clothing, fills the stalls of the **Mercato del Baton,** held every Saturday at Piazza della Republica. **Gran Baton** fills the piazza the second Sunday of every month and is a larger affair, with some genuine antiques and artworks included in the mix. **Mercato della Crocetta,** at Largo Cassini, sells clothing at very low prices. For a look at the bounty of the surrounding farmlands, wander through the extensive outdoor food market at Porta Palazzo, open Monday through Saturday from 6:30am to 1:30pm and Saturday from 3:30 to 7:30pm.

ESSENTIALS

GETTING THERE   By Plane   Domestic and international flights land at the **Caselle International Airport** (© 011-567-6361; www.turin-airport.com), 14km (9 miles) north of Turin. Buses run between the airport and the city's main bus terminal (Autostazione Terminal Bus) on Corso Inghilterra and Porto Nuova train station (Stazione Porta Nuova); the trip takes about 30 minutes. A **taxi** from the airport takes about 30 minutes and costs around 26€ ($30).

By Train   Turin's main train station is **Stazione di Porta Nuova** (© 011-561-3333; www.trenitalia.it), just south of the center on Piazza Carlo Felice, which marks the intersection of Turin's two major thoroughfares, Corso Vittorio Emanuele and Via Roma. From this station, there are two dozen trains a day to and from Milan—the trip takes 1¾ hours each way (many trains to and from Milan also stop at Turin's other station, Stazione di Porta Susa); 16 trains a day to and from Venice, 4½ to 5 hours; 17 trains a day to and from Genoa, 2 hours; 20 trains a day to and from Rome, 6 to 7 hours. **Stazione di Porta Susa,** west of the center on Piazza XVIII Dicembre, connects Turin with many outlying Piedmont towns; it is also the terminus for TGV service to and from Paris, with three trains a day making the trip in about 6 hours.

By Bus   Turin's main bus terminal is **Autostazione Terminal Bus,** Corso Inghilterra 3 (near Stazione di Porta Sousa) (© 011-300-0611; www.sadem.it). The ticket office is open daily from 7am to noon and 3 to 7pm. Buses connect Turin and Courmayeur (4 hr.), Aosta (3 hr.), Milan (2 hr.), Chamonix (3½ hr.), and many smaller towns in Piedmont.

By Car   Turin is at the hub of an extensive network of autostradas. A4 connects Turin with Milan, a little over an hour away; A6 connects Turin with the Ligurian coast (and from there, with Genoa via A10, with a total travel time between the two cities of about 1½ hr.); A5 connects Turin with Aosta, about an hour away; and A21 connects Turin with Asti and Piacenza, where you can connect with the A1 for Florence (about 3½ hr. from Turin) and Rome (about 6½ hr. from Turin).

VISITOR INFORMATION   Tourist offices are at **Piazza Castello** 161 (© 011-535-181; fax 011-530-070; www.turismotorino.org) and in the Porta Nuova train station (© 011-531-327). Both are open Monday through Saturday from 9:30am to 7pm and Sunday from 9:30am to 3pm and will book rooms for you up to 48 hours in advance. There's also an office in the airport (© 011-567-8124), open daily from 8:30am to 11pm.

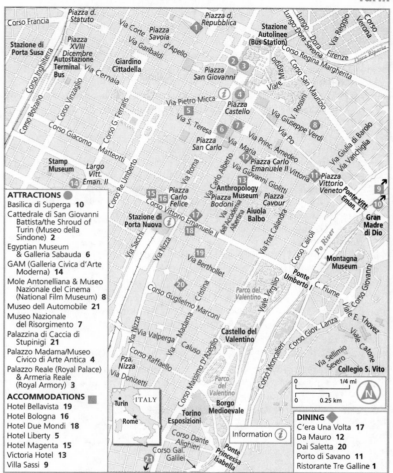

ATTRACTIONS

Basilica di Superga **10**
Cattedrale di San Giovanni Battista/the Shroud of Turin (Museo della Sindone) **2**
Egyptian Museum & Galleria Sabauda **6**
GAM (Galleria Civica d'Arte Moderna) **14**
Mole Antonelliana & Museo Nazionale del Cinema (National Film Museum) **8**
Museo dell'Automobile **21**
Museo Nazionale del Risorgimento **7**
Palazzina di Caccia di Stupinigi **21**
Palazzo Madama/Museo Civico di Arte Antica **4**
Palazzo Reale (Royal Palace) & Armeria Reale (Royal Armory) **3**

ACCOMMODATIONS

Hotel Bellavista **19**
Hotel Bologna **16**
Hotel Due Mondi **18**
Hotel Liberty **5**
Hotel Magenta **15**
Victoria Hotel **13**
Villa Sassi **9**

DINING

C'era Una Volta **17**
Da Mauro **12**
Dai Saletta **20**
Porto di Savano **11**
Ristorante Tre Galline **1**

GETTING AROUND   It's easy to get around central Turin **by foot.** There's also a vast network of ATM trams and buses (© **800-019-152** in Italy, or 011-57-641; www.atm.to.it, www.comune.torino.it/atm, or www.satti.it). Tickets on public transportation are available at newsstands for .90€ ($1.05). With the **Torino Card** (see "What to See & Do," below), you can ride the city's public transportation for free for 48 hours.

CITY LAYOUT   You will get a sense of Turin's refined air as soon as you step off the train into the mannerly 19th-century Stazione Porta Nuova. The stately arcaded Via Roma, lined with shops and cafes, proceeds from the front of the station through a series of piazzas toward the Piazza Castello and the center of the city, about a 15-minute walk.

Directly in front of the station, the circular **Piazza Carlo Felice** is built around a garden surrounded by outdoor cafes that invite even business-minded Torinese to linger. Walking farther along the street will lead you into the **Piazza San Carlo,** which is flanked by the twin churches of San Carlo and Santa Christina. At the end of Via Roma, the **Piazza Castello** is dominated by the **Palazzo Madama,** so named for its 17th-century inhabitant Marie Christine. Just off the piazza is the **Palazzo Reale,** residence of the Savoys from 1646 to 1865, whose gardens now provide a pleasant respite from traffic and paving stones.

From here, a walk east toward the river along Via Po takes you through Turin's university district to one of Italy's largest squares, the much-elongated Piazza Vittorio Veneto and, at the end of this elegant expanse, the Po River.

FAST FACTS: Turin

Bookstores **Libreria Internazionale Luxemburg,** Via C. Battisti 7 (✆ **011-561-3896**), has a large selection of British books and a helpful English-speaking staff; it is open Tuesday through Saturday from 9am to 7:30pm and Monday from 3 to 7:30pm. Another good bet for books in English is the chain **Libreria Feltrinelli,** Piazza Castello 19 (✆ **011-541-627**; www.feltrinelli.it). Turin has many stores specializing in rare books and old prints, and many of these shops sell their wares from the secondhand-book stalls along the Via Po, which runs between Piazza Castello and the river.

Consulates **British** subjects will find their consulate at Via Saluzzo 60 (✆ **011-650-9202**), open Monday through Friday from 9:15am to 12:15pm and 2:30 to 4:30pm. **Americans** will find their nearest consulate in Milan at Via Principe Amadeo 2/10 (✆ **02-290-351**); it is open Monday through Friday from 9 to 11am and 2 to 4pm.

Crime Turin is a relatively safe city, but use the same precautions you would exercise in any large city. Specifically, avoid the riverside streets along the Po at night, when they tend to be deserted. In an **emergency,** call ✆ **113,** which is a free call. The **central police station** is near Stazione di Porta Susa at Corso Vinzaglio 10 (✆ **011-558-81-112**).

Drugstores A convenient late-night pharmacy is **Farmacia Boniscontro,** Corso Vittorio Emanuele 66 (✆ **011-541-271**); it is open most of the day and night, closing only between 12:30 and 3pm.

Emergencies The general emergency number is ✆ **113**; for an ambulance, dial ✆ **118.** Both are free calls.

Internet For Internet access, the **Internet Train** (✆ **011-543-000**; www.internettrain.it), just down the street from the central Piazza Castello at Via Carlo Alberto 18, is open Monday to Friday from 9:30am to 10pm, Saturday from 9:30am to 8pm, and Sunday from 3 to 7pm.

Laundry **Speedy Wash,** east of the station at Via Principe Tommaso 12 (✆ **0338-589-8990**), charges 8€ ($9.20) for a wash-and-dry (soap included) of a small load, and though it's technically do-it-yourself, the staff is always around to throw it into the dryer for you, provided you pick up your things by the end of the day. It's open daily from 9am to 8:30pm, and offers do-it-yourself dry cleaning as well.

Lost Property To report lost property, contact the Ufficio Oggetti Smarriti at ✆ **011-665-3315.**

Luggage Storage Luggage storage is available at the Porta Nuova train station; 2.50€ ($2.90) per bag for each 12-hour period; the office is open daily from 4:30am to 2:30am.

Newspapers Your best bet for English-language newspapers is at the newsstands in Porta Nuova station.

Post Office Turin's main post office is just west of Piazza San Carlo at Via Alfieri 10 (© **011-546-800**); it is open Monday through Friday from 8:15am to 5:30pm and Saturday from 8:15am to 1pm. The postal code for Turin is 10100.

Taxis You can find taxis at cab stands; especially convenient in the central city are the stands in front of the train stations and around Piazza San Carlo and Piazza Castello. Dial © **011-5737,** 011-5730, or 011-3399 for a radio taxi.

WHAT TO SEE & DO

The tourist office sells a **Torino Card** for 15€ ($17), valid for one adult plus one child under 12. The card grants you 48 hours of free public transport within Turin, discounts on concerts and the like, and lets you pick two museums to enter for free, with discounts at other museums (though no reduction is available at the most popular museums, including Palazzo Reale/Armeria Reale, Galleria Sabuada, and the Museo Egizio). For 17€ ($20), your card is valid for 72 hours.

Cattedrale di San Giovanni Battista ★★ The controversial **Shroud of Turin (Santissima Sindone)** and the chapel in which it is sometimes enshrined, **Capella della Santa Sindone,** hold pride of place in this otherwise uninteresting, pompous 15th-century church. Even without the presence of one of Christianity's most precious relics (and it's only rarely on view in the silver casket elevated on an altar in the center of the room), the chapel is well worth a visit. Recently restored after a 1997 fire (one of many the shroud has miraculously survived, with an occasional singeing, over the centuries), the chapel is somberly clad in black marble. But, as if to suggest that better things await us in the heavens, it ascends to an airy, light-flooded six-tiered dome, one of the masterpieces of Italian baroque architecture.

The shroud, of course, is allegedly the one in which the body of Christ was wrapped when taken from the cross—and to which his image was miraculously affixed. The image is of a man 5 feet 7 inches tall, with bloodstains consistent with a crown of thorns, a cut in the ribcage, cuts in the wrists and ankles, and scourge marks on the back from flagellation. Recent carbon dating suggests that the shroud was manufactured sometime around the 13th or 14th centuries, but the mystery remains, at least in part, because no one can explain how the haunting image appeared on the cloth. Also, additional radio carbon dating has suggested that, since the shroud has been exposed to fire (thus affecting carbon readings), it could indeed date from around the time of the death of Christ. Regardless of scientific skepticism, the shroud continues to entice hordes of the faithful.

The shroud is usually tucked away out of sight at **Museo della Sindone (Holy Shroud Museum)** around the corner at Via San Domenico 28 (© **011-436-5832;** www.sindone.org), open daily from 9am to noon and 3 to 7pm; admission is 5.15€ ($5.95) for adults and 4.15€ ($4.75) for those under 14 and over 65. The shroud was last on view during Italy's Jubilee celebrations in 2000. Technically, it shouldn't be on display again until the next Jubilee, in 25 years, but it tends to pop up every 5 to 15 years for special occasions (and rumor has it that it may go on permanent display, either in the cathedral or in its own space; plus, the faithful flock here even if they can't see it, just to be near it). Otherwise, you'll have to content yourself with a series of dramatically backlit photos of the relic near the entrance to the Capella della Santa Sindone. The museum houses a plethora of information (including photos, X-rays, and history) relating to the shroud.

In front of the cathedral stand two landmarks of Roman Turin—the remains of a theater and the **Porta Palatina,** a Roman-era city gate, flanked by twin 16-sided towers.

Piazza San Giovanni. ℂ 011-436-1540. Free admission. Daily 7am–12:30pm and 3–7pm. Bus: 6, 11, 12, 27, 56, or 57.

GAM (Galleria Civica d'Arte Moderna e Contemporanea) ✫ Turin's
modern-art museum is one of the most important in Italy. It was founded in 1863, so its collections actually start with late-18th- and 19th-century neoclassical and Romantic works by Piemontese and other artists (Canova, Massimo d'Azeglio, Francesco Hayez)—in fact, the modern building itself makes a sharp point about our notions about art and its relevance with a glowing sign on the roof: "All art has been contemporary." The collections are largely arranged chronologically, with rooms focusing on specific movements or periods. Of the over 600 works on display, you'll see art by Modigliani, Giorgio de Chirico, Gino Severini, Otto Dix, Max Ernst, Paul Klee, and Andy Warhol. On the first Friday of each month, you can take a free guided tour of the museum. Call for times.

Via Magenta 31. ℂ 011-442-9518. www.gamtorino.it. Admission 5.50€ ($6) adults, 3€ ($3.45) ages 10–18 and seniors over 65. Tues–Sun 9am–7pm. Bus: 5, 52, 58, or 62. Tram: 1 or 10.

Mole Antonelliana & Museo Nazionale del Cinema (National Film
Museum) ✫✫ Turin's most peculiar building—in fact, one of the strangest structures anywhere—is comprised of a squat brick base, a steep conelike roof, which supports several layers of Greek temples piled one atop the other, topped in turn by a needlelike spire, all of it rising 166m (552 ft.) above the rooftops of the city center (a height that at one time made the Mole the world's tallest building). Begun in 1863 and designed as a synagogue, the Mole is now a monument to Italian unification and architectural hubris and home to Italy's **National Film Museum.**

The museum's first section tracks the development of moving pictures from shadow puppets to kinescopes. The rest is more of a tribute to film than a true museum, offering clips and stills to illustrate some of the major aspects of movie production, from *Empire Strikes Back* storyboards to the creepy steady-cam work in *The Shining.* Of memorabilia, masks from the original *Planet of the Apes, Satyricon,* and *Star Wars* hang together near *Lawrence of Arabia*'s robe, *Chaplin*'s bowler, and *What Ever Happened to Baby Jane*'s dress. Curiously, most of the clips (all in Italian-dubbed versions), as well as posters and other memorabilia, are heavily weighted toward American movies, with exceptions mainly for the major players of European/International cinema like Fellini, Bertolucci, Truffaut, and Wim Wenders.

Even if you skip the museum, you can still ascend to an observation platform at the top, an experience that affords two advantages—the view of Turin and the surrounding countryside, backed by the Alps, is stunning—and, echoing Guy de Maupassant's famous comment on the Eiffel Tower, it's the only place in Turin where you won't have to look at the damned thing.

Via Montebello 20. ℭ 011-812-5658. www.museonazionaledelcinema.org. Admission to museum 5.20€ ($6); observation platform 4.20€ ($4.85); both 6.80€ ($8). Tues–Fri and Sun 9am–8pm; Sat to 11pm. Bus 55, 56, 61, or 68.

Museo dell'Automobile (Automobile Museum)

As befits a city that is responsible for 80% of Italian car manufacturing, this shiny collection of mostly Italian automobiles, housed in a purpose-built, light-filled exhibition hall of classic 1960s design, draws car buffs from all over the world. Not too surprisingly, a century's worth of output from Fiat, which is headquartered in Turin, is well represented. The collection includes most of the cars that have done Italy proud over the years, including Lancias, Isotta Frashinis, and the Itala that came in first place in the 1907 Peking-to-Paris rally. Oddities include a roadster emblazoned with the initials ND that Gloria Swanson drove for her role as faded movie queen Norma Desmond in *Sunset Boulevard*.

Corso Unita d'Italia 40. ℭ 011-677-666. www.museoauto.org. Admission 5.50€ ($6) adults, 4€ ($4.60) ages under 15 or over 65. Tues–Sat 10am–6:30pm; Sun 10am–8:30pm. Bus: 1, 17, 18, 34, or 35.

Museo Egizio (Egyptian Museum) & Galleria Sabauda ★★★

Turin's magnificent **Egyptian collection** is one of the world's largest. This was in fact the world's first Egyptian museum, thanks to the fact that the Savoys ardently amassed artifacts through most of their reign, and the museum continued to mount collecting expeditions throughout the early 20th century. Of the 30,000 pieces on display, some of the more captivating exhibits are in the first rooms you enter on the ground floor. These include the **Rock Temple of Ellessiya,** from the 15th century B.C., which the Egyptian government presented to the museum in gratitude for Italian efforts to save monuments threatened by the Aswan Dam. The two statuary rooms nearby are staggering in the size and drama of the objects they house, most notably two sphinxes and a massive, richly painted statue of Ramses II. Smaller objects—mummies, funerary objects, and a papyrus Book of the Dead—fill the galleries on the next floor; the most enchanting exhibit here is the everyday paraphernalia, including eating utensils and shriveled foodstuffs, from the tomb of the 14th-century B.C. architect Khaie and his wife.

The Savoys other treasure trove, a magnificent collection of European paintings, fills the salons of the **Galleria Sabauda** above the Egyptian collection. The Savoys' royal taste ran heavily to painters of the Flemish and Dutch schools, and the works by Van Dyck, Van Eyck, Rembrandt, and Van der Weyden, among others, comprise one of Italy's largest collections of northern European paintings. In fact, two of Europe's most prized Flemish masterpieces are here, Jan Van Eyck's *Stigmata of St. Francis* and Hans Memling's *Passion of Christ.* Italian artists, including those from Piedmont, are also well represented; one of the first canvases you see upon entering the galleries is the work of a Tuscan, Fra'Angelico's sublime *Virgin and Child.*

Via Accademia delle Scienze 6. **Museo Egizio:** ℭ 011-561-7776. www.museoegizio.org. Admission 6.50€ ($7) adults, 3€ ($3.45) ages 18–25, free for under 18 and over 60. DC, MC, V. Tues–Sun 8:30am–7:30pm (to 11pm Sat in summer). **Galleria Sabauda:** ℭ 011-440-6903. Admission 4€ ($4.60) adults, 2€ ($2.30) ages 18–25, free for under 18 and over 65. Tues–Sun 8:30am–7:30pm (to 11pm Sat in summer). Bus: 4, 13, 18, 55, or 66.

Museo Nazionale del Risorgimento (National Museum of the Risorgimento)

Much of modern Italian history has been played out in Turin and much of it, fittingly, in this palazzo that was home to the first king of a unified

Italy, Vittorio Emanuele II, and the seat of its first parliament, in 1861. While any self-respecting town in Italy has a museum of the Risorgimento, the movement that launched Italian unification, this one is the best. Documents, paintings, and other paraphernalia recount the heady days when Vittorio Emanuele banded with Garibaldi and his Red Shirts to oust the Bourbons from Sicily and the Austrians from the north to create a unified Italy. The plaques summing up each room are in English, and will finally reveal to you just who those people are after whom half the major streets and piazzas in Italy are named—including Mazzini, Vittorio Emanuele II, Massimo d'Azeglio, Cavour, and Garibaldi. The last rooms house a fascinating collection that chronicles Italian Fascism and the resistance against it.

Via Accademia delle Scienze 5. ℂ **011-562-1147.** Admission 5€ ($6) adults; 3.50€ ($4.05) ages 10–18, students under 25, and seniors over 65. Tues–Sun 9am–7pm. Bus: 4, 13, 18, 55, or 66.

Palazzo Madama—Museo Civico di Arte Antica (Civic Museum of Ancient Art) ★   Don't be misled by the baroque facade, added by architect Filippo Juvarra in the 18th century. If you walk around the exterior of the palazzo (named for its most popular resident, Madama Reale, aka Marie Christine of France), you'll discover that the massive structure incorporates a medieval castle, a Roman gate, and several Renaissance additions. Juvarra also added a monumental marble staircase to the interior, most of which is given over to the far-reaching collections of the Museo Civico di Arte Antica. The holdings focus on the medieval and Renaissance periods, shown off against the castle's unaltered, stony medieval interior. One of Italy's largest collections of ceramics is here, as well as some stunning canvases, including Anotello da Messina's *Portrait of a Man.* The museum has been closed for nearly 15 years for an extensive renovation. While it's possible to visit the atrium and grand Juvarra staircase just inside, the other rooms and the museum itself won't be open in its entirety until 2006.

In the Palazzo Madama, Piazza Castello. ℂ **011-442-9911.** www.comune.torino.it/palazzomadama. Free admission. Tues–Sat 10am–8pm; Sun 10am–11pm. Confirm hours with the tourist board. Bus: 6, 11, 12, 27, 56, or 57.

Palazzo Reale (Royal Palace) & Armeria Reale (Royal Armory) ★   The residence of the House of Savoy, begun in 1645 and designed by the Francophile count of Castellamonte, reflects the ornately baroque tastes of European ruling families of the time—a fact that will not be lost on you as you pass from one opulently decorated, heavily gilded room to the next. (The Savoys had a keener eye for paintings than for decor, and most of the canvases they collected are in the nearby Galleria Sabauda). What are most notable here are some of the tapestries, including the Gobelins depicting the life of Don Quixote, in the Sala delle Virtu (Hall of Virtues), and the collection of Chinese and Japanese vases in the Sala dell'Alcova. One of the quirkier architectural innovations, an antidote to several monumental staircases, is a manually driven elevator from the 18th century.

One wing houses the **Armeria Reale,** one of the most important arms and armor collections in Europe, especially of weapons from the 16th and 17th centuries. Most rooms were reopened after extensive renovations in October 2003. The balance of the exhibition rooms should reopen in 2004. Behind the palace, and offering a refreshing change from its frippery, are the **Giardini Reali (Royal Gardens),** laid out by Le Nôtre, more famous for Paris's Tuileries park and the gardens at Versailles.

Piazza Castello (Armeria entrance at no. 191). **Palazzo:** ℂ **011-436-1455.** Admission 6.50€ ($7). Tues–Sun 8:30am–7:30pm (to 11pm Sat in summer). **Armeria:** ℂ **011-543-889.** Admission 2€ ($2.30)—though may go up to 4€ ($4.60) when all the rooms are reopened. Tues and Thurs–Sun 3:30–7:30pm; Wed and Fri 8am–2pm. Bus: 6, 11, 12, 27, 56, or 57.

PARKS & PIAZZAS

Piazza San Carlo, Turin's most beautiful square, is the city's outdoor living room, surrounded by arcaded sidewalks that house the terraces of the cafes for which Turin is famous (see below). In the center is an equestrian statue of Duke Emanuele Filiberto of Savoy, and facing each other at the northern end of the piazza are a pair of 17th-century churches, San Carlo and Santa Cristina. The overall effect is one of elegant harmony.

The **Parco del Valentino** (© **011-669-9372;** www.comune.torino.it/verde pubblico), a lush sweep of greenery along the Po south of Corso Vittorio Emanuele II, provides a wonderful retreat from Turin's well-mannered streets and piazzas. It is open daily from 8am to 8pm. Aside from riverfront promenades and extensive lawns and gardens, inside the park there's a collection of enchanting buildings. The **Borgo Medioevale** (© **011-443-1701**), built for Turin's 1884 world exposition, is a faithful reconstruction of a medieval village based on those in rural Piedmont and the Valle d'Aosta, with shops, taverns, houses, churches, and even a castle—but since Italy is home to literally thousands of bona-fide medieval villages, it's hard to imagine a good reason to pony up 3€ ($3.45) admission for a look. (Free guided tours are offered Sun between 11am and 4pm.) In winter it's open daily from 9am to 7pm. It's open until 8pm in summer.

The nearby **Castello del Valentino** is the real thing—a royal residence, begun in the 16th century but completed in the 17th century for Turin's beloved Marie Christine ("Madama Reale," wife of Savoy king Vittorio Amedeo) as a summer residence. It's a sign of Madama's Francophile leanings that, with its sloping roofs and forecourt, the castle resembles a French château. Used as a school of veterinary medicine, a military barracks, and currently as a university facility, the *castello* is continually undergoing renovations and much of it, including many frescoed salons, is open to the public only on special occasions.

NEARBY ATTRACTIONS

Basilica di Superga ★★ As thanksgiving to the Virgin Mary for Turin's deliverance from the French siege of 1706, Vittorio Amedeo II commissioned Juvarra, the Sicilian architect who did his greatest work in Turin, to build this baroque basilica on a hill high above the city. The exterior, with a beautiful neoclassic porch and lofty drum dome, is far more interesting than the gloomy interior, a vast circular chamber beneath the dome with six side chapels. The church more or less serves as a pantheon for the House of Savoy, whose tombs are scattered about, many in the so-called Crypt of Kings beneath the main chapel. There's a fine view of the Alps from the terrace in front. The trip up to the basilica on a narrow railway through verdant parkland is a favorite Torinese outing.

Strada della Basilica di Superga 73, about 6.5km (4 miles) northeast of the town center in Parco Naturale della Collina di Superga. © 011-898-0083. Free admission. Apr–Oct daily 9am–noon and 3–6pm; Nov–Mar daily 9am–noon and 3–5pm. Reached by rack railway with a terminus at Stazione Sassi on Piazza Gustavo Modena (follow Corso Casale on east side of the River Po). Tram: 15 from Via XX Settembre to Stazione Sassi.

Palazzina di Caccia di Stupinigi ★ The other great work of the architect Juvarra (see "Basilica di Superga," above) is this sumptuous, lavishly decorated hunting lodge that the Savoys commissioned in 1729. The main part of the lodge, to which the members of the House of Savoy retired for hunts in the royal forests that still surround it, is shaped like a Saint Andrew's cross (the lower arms extended and curved back inwards like giant pincers), fanning out from a circular, domed pavilion topped with a large bronze stag. The lavish interior is filled with furniture, paintings, and bric-a-brac assembled from the many Savoy residences, technically comprising a **Museo d'Arte e Ammobiliamento (Museum of Art and Furniture).** Stroll through the acres of excessively decorated apartments to understand why Napoléon chose this for his brief residency in the region. Outstanding among the many, many frescoes are the scenes of a deer hunt in the King's Apartment and the Triumph of Diana in the grand salon. The elegant gardens and surrounding forests provide lovely terrain for a jaunt.

Piazza Principe Amedeo 7, Stupinigi-Nichelino, 8.5km (5¼ miles) southwest of the city center. © 011-358-1220. www.mauriziano.it. Admission 6.20€ ($7) adults, 5.15€ ($6) ages 6–14. Tues–Sun 10am–6pm (to 5pm late Oct to late Mar). Bus: 63 from Porta Nuova train station to Piazza Caio Mario; change to bus 41.

WHERE TO STAY
VERY EXPENSIVE

Villa Sassi ★★   This early-17th-century villa is set in its own 20-hectare (50-acre) park east of town near the **Basilica di Superga.** Rooms on the first floor are larger, with Oriental rugs and semi-designer 1980s furnishings or antique dressers scattered across the parquet floors; a few open onto spacious terraces. Second-floor rooms are smaller, with terra-cotta tiled floors and sloping ceilings and better views over the surrounding forested hills. The bar opens onto a pleasant cobblestone terrace. Their restaurant (on the first floor, with large windows opening to tree views, and with the terrace to be enjoyed during the warmer weather) is highly regarded in the area, popular with Torinese for a breezy summer escape from the city.

Strada al Traforo di Pino 47 (about 4km/2½ miles from the center, near Superga), 10132 Torino. © 010-898-0556 or 011-898-0557. Fax 010-898-0095. www.villasassi.com. 16 units. 240€ ($276) double; 280€ ($322) suite. Continental breakfast included. AE, DC, MC, V. Free parking. Bus: 61 or tram 15, then a 3km (1¾-mile) walk (better to take a taxi). **Amenities:** Highly regarded Piemontese restaurant; bar; concierge; tour desk; car-rental desk; room service (24-hr.); massage; babysitting; laundry service; same-day dry cleaning; nonsmoking rooms. *In room:* A/C, TV, dataport, minibar, hair dryer, safe.

EXPENSIVE

Hotel Due Mondi   This is a modern hotel 2 blocks east of the train station, with comfortable beds and modern units. Rooms are a wee bit cramped, but retain some nice touches such as faded remnants of frescoes on some ceilings. It must be noted, though, that my A/C unit only blew room-temperature air, even though several employees swore it was working. The wildly varying room rates below change with the season, and those high prices really apply only during trade fairs.

Via Saluzzo 3, 10125 Torino. © **011-650-5084** or 011-669-8981. Fax 011-669-9383. www.hotelduemondi.it. 43 units. 66€–139€ ($76–$160) double; 92€–181€ ($106–$208) triple. Breakfast included. AE, DC, MC, V. **Amenities:** Italian restaurant; bar; concierge; tour desk; room service (24-hr.); laundry service; same-day dry cleaning; nonsmoking rooms (3rd and 4th floors). *In room:* A/C, TV w/pay movies, dataport, minibar, hair dryer, safe.

Victoria Hotel ★★   Step through the doors of this somewhat plain-looking building between the Via Roma and the river and you'll think you're in an English country house. That's the whole idea, and the Anglophile decor works splendidly. The lobby is decorated as a country house drawing room, with floral sofas, deep armchairs, and a view onto a garden; the room doubles as a bar and is an extremely pleasant place to enjoy a drink before setting out for one of the nearby restaurants. The glass-enclosed breakfast room, where a sumptuous buffet is served, resembles a conservatory. Accommodations are classified as deluxe or standard, depending on size and decor. "Standard" guest rooms are handsomely furnished in a chic style that soothingly combines contemporary and traditional styles, with mahogany bedsteads and writing desks, and rich fabric wall-coverings and draperies. "Deluxe" accommodations, each with its own distinctive look, are oversized and furnished with carefully chosen antiques and such flourishes as canopied beds and richly covered divans. A major ongoing renovation (expected to be completed in 2005) will add a new breakfast room, garden, garage, and swimming pool to the Victoria.

Via Nino Costa 4, 10123 Turin. © 011-561-1909. Fax 011-561-1806. www.hotelvictoria-torino.com. 90 units. 147€ ($169) standard double; 165€ ($190) deluxe double; 191€–235€ ($220–$270) jr. suite. Rates include breakfast. AE, DC, MC, V. **Amenities:** Bar; concierge; room service (limited); laundry service; dry cleaning; non-smoking rooms; free bikes; Internet connection. *In room:* A/C (some rooms), TV, dataport, minibar, hair dryer, safe.

MODERATE

Hotel Liberty ★★ *Finds* An excellent location a few blocks southwest of Piazza Castello puts the Liberty within easy walking distance of most of Turin's museums, other monuments and shops, and restaurants. What's most remarkable about this hotel, though, is its ambience. It occupies an early-20th-century mansion built in the Art Deco style, which in Italian is known as "Liberty." Many of the original features, such as ornately carved doorways and etched windows, remain, and the public rooms especially retain a great deal of grandeur with turn-of-the-20th-century furnishings and polished parquet floors. The guest rooms are large and nonfussily stylish, with some period pieces augmented by comfortable newer furnishings, including firm beds; the smallish bathrooms have been brought nicely up to date. However, things may look a bit different during your stay; renovations are planned for 2004. These surroundings seem all the more pleasant with the attentive presence of the Anfossi family, which has run this charming hotel for decades. There's also a small bar and restaurant off the lobby.

Via P. Micca 15, 10121 Turin. © 011-562-8801. Fax 011-562-8163. www.hotelliberty-torino.it. 35 units. 124€ ($143) double. 23€ ($26) extra bed. Ask about special weekend rates in summer. Rates include breakfast. AE, DC, MC, V. Parking 16€ ($18). Bus: 4, 11, 12, 13, 15, 56, 63, or 67. **Amenities:** Restaurant (Italian); bar; concierge; room service (limited); nonsmoking rooms. *In room:* A/C (in some rooms), TV w/pay movies, dataport, hair dryer.

INEXPENSIVE

Hotel Bellavista The neighborhood between the Porta Nuova railway station and Parco del Valentino is pleasant and residential, and this pensione occupies the sixth floor of an apartment house on a quiet street. What is likely to strike you immediately is just how pleasant the surroundings are—step off the elevator and you will find yourself in a sun-filled corridor that's a garden of houseplants and opens onto a wide terrace. There's also a pleasant bar area, where guests can buy rolls and coffee at breakfast. Rooms are airy and comfortable but a little less inspiring in decor, with banal, functional modern furnishings. Most, though, afford pleasant views over the surrounding rooftops—the best outlooks in the house are across the river toward the hills. What most rooms don't have is a private bathroom, though the several communal ones are well placed so most rooms are only a few steps away from a facility.

Via Galliari 15, 10125 Turin. © 011-669-8139. Fax 011-668-7989. 18 units, 7 with bathroom. 60€ ($69) double without bathroom, 70€ ($81) double with bathroom. Breakfast included. AE, MC, V. **Amenities:** Bar; nonsmoking rooms. *In room:* TV.

Hotel Bologna ★ *Value* This family-run hotel just across the street from the Porta Nuova train station offers location, affordable comfort, and a very attentive, English-speaking staff. Each of the 50 rooms, spread over several floors of a gracious 18th-century apartment house, is different. Some are quite grand, incorporating frescoes, fireplaces, and other original details (of these, rooms 52 and 64 are the largest and most elegant). Other rooms have been renovated in sleek modern style, with laminated, built-in cabinetry and neutral carpeting. Still others fall in between, with well-maintained 1970s-style furnishings and linoleum flooring. Whatever the vintage, all of the rooms are spotlessly clean and nicely maintained. In 2001 two small suites were added with separate sitting rooms, which go for the same rates as regular rooms.

Corso Vittorio Emanuele II 60, 10121 Turin. 🕿 011-562-0290 or 011-562-0193. Fax 011-562-0193. www. hotelbolognasrl.it. 50 units. 77€ ($89) double. Breakfast 3€ ($3.45) for 1, 5€ ($6) for 2. AE, MC, V. **Amenities:** Bar; Jacuzzi (in 3 rooms); concierge; tour desk; car-rental desk; room service. *In room:* A/C, TV, minibar (in some rooms), hair dryer, safe.

Hotel Magenta   Unlike the areas around train stations in most large cities, the Porta Nuova neighborhood is stylish and safe, and many of the city's hotels are here. The Magenta is one of the least expensive, and it is handily located just west of the station along one of the arcaded sidewalks that follow busy Corso Vittorio Emanuele. The surroundings of this pleasant pensione, which occupies a wing of the second floor of an apartment house, suggest that the premises have seen grander days. Ornate moldings and polished parquet floors and crystal chandeliers grace a long central hallway that is furnished with comfortable, upholstered easy chairs. With banal, standard-issue hotel furnishings, guest rooms are a bit less opulent, but they are spacious and high-ceilinged nonetheless and some have newly installed bathrooms. In the morning, you can enjoy an espresso and pastry at the little bar in the lobby.

Corso Vittorio Emanuele II 67, 10121 Turin. 🕿 **011-542-649.** Fax 011-544-755. 18 units, 10 with bathroom. 47€ ($54) double without bathroom, 67€ ($77) double with bathroom. Breakfast 3.50€ ($4.05). AE, MC, V. **Amenities:** Bar. *In room:* TV.

WHERE TO DINE

One of the great pleasures of being in Piedmont is sampling the cuisine that is unique to this region. Two new pastas you will encounter on menus are *agnolotti* (a thick tube often stuffed with an infusion of cheese and meat) and *tajarin,* a flat egg noodle that is often topped with porcini mushrooms. While chilly, foggy evenings call for grilled meat and game, truffles abound in the moist soil, and the farm gardens produce enough vegetables to make meatless meals a special occasion; one of the favorite preparations is *bagna cauda* (hot bath), in which raw vegetables are dipped into a heated preparation of oil, anchovies, and garlic. If you have a sweet tooth, you will soon discover that Turin and outlying towns can amply satisfy cravings for sweets, largely with pastries (remember, this region abuts France!). Additionally, with wines as good as the ones Piedmont produces (see "Visiting the Wine Villages," later in this chapter), even a carafe of the house red is likely to be excellent.

C'era Una Volta ★★★ TORINESE   To enter "Once Upon a Time," you must ring a bell at street level, then climb the stairs or take the elevator to a large, old-fashioned dining room filled with heavy old tables and chairs and dark credenzas. Until recently, they only offered the set-price tasting menu—and for most of us that was plenty (in fact, that was often more than plenty in that we didn't have to make plans to eat anything for the next 24 hr.). However, due to popular demand by eager diners who just couldn't handle those massive meals, the restaurant has now introduced prices a la carte—though they've rigorously refused to change anything else about this classic Torinese establishment. The food, delivered by a highly professional waitstaff that has been here for years, is authentically Torinese and never seems to stop coming. A typical menu, which changes daily, might include crepes with ham and cheese, risotto with artichokes, a carrot flan, rabbit stew, a slice of beef with polenta, and any number of other wonderfully prepared dishes. You will want to accompany your meal with a fine Barolo or other regional wine.

Corso Vittorio Emanuele II 42. (011-650-4589. Reservations recommended. Primi 7€–8.50€ ($8–$10); secondi 14€–16€ ($16–$18); tasting menu 24€ ($28). AE, MC, V. Mon–Sat 7–10:30pm. Closed Aug.

Dai Saletta ⭐ PIEMONTESE   One of the few kitchens in Turin that remains open into the wee hours turns out a nice selection of homey trattoria fare, served in a tiny, cramped dining room near the train station. Homemade pasta dishes are delicious and you may want to order some of them, such as *tortelloni alla salsiccia* (a large pasta shell stuffed with sausage) or *peposelle* (a thick pasta tossed with Gorgonzola and walnuts), as a main course. If you want to venture out, it may well be with such traditional favorites as tripe.

Via Belfiore 37. (011-668-7867. Primi 7€ ($8); secondi 8€ ($9). AE, DC, MC, V. Mon–Sat 12:30–2:30pm and 8–10:30pm. Closed Aug. Bus: 1 or 16.

Da Mauro ITALIAN   This simple, tile-floored room is more relaxed than many Torinese restaurants, and if the informal ambience and the menu remind you of regions to the south, you are quite right. The family that owns and runs the restaurant emphasizes Tuscan dishes, though the range seems to run the gamut of Italian cooking. There are a number of spicy pasta dishes, including a deftly prepared cannelloni, and the meat courses are indeed similar to those you would find in Tuscany—steak, lamb, sausages, and game birds are simply grilled or roasted.

Via Maria Vittoria 21. (011-817-0604. Primi 4€–6€ ($4.60–$7); secondi 5€–9€ ($6–$10). No credit cards. Tues–Sun 12:30–3pm and 7–10pm. Closed July. Bus: 4, 11, 12, 18, 27, 57, 63.

Porto di Savona ⭐⭐ *Value* PIEMONTESE   What is probably the most popular trattoria in Turin is tucked under the arcades along the city's largest piazza. Seating is family style, at long tables that crowd a series of rooms beneath old photos and mementos, and the typically Piemontese fare never fails to please (all the more so on Sun, when many other restaurants in central Turin are closed). Several variations of gnocchi are usually made fresh daily, as is the Piemontese flat noodle, *tajarin,* and *pasticcio,* a pasta casserole with meat and cream. Another way to start a meal is with some variation of porcini mushrooms, which are served in many different variations, perhaps best when simply sautéed. These starters can be nicely followed with a grilled meat dish—a house specialty.

Piazza Vittorio Veneto 2. (011-817-3500. www.portodisavona.com. Reservations recommended. Primi 3.50€–5€ ($4.05–$6); secondi 5€–12€ ($6–$14). MC, V. Tues 7:30–10:30pm; Wed–Sun 12:30–2:30pm and 7:30–10:30pm. Closed Jan 1–7. Bus: 30, 53, 55, 56, 61, or 70.

Ristorante Tre Galline ⭐ PIEMONTESE/TORINESE   As one of Turin's most popular eateries for over 3 centuries, this bright wood-paneled room has friendly, professional service and a good-value tasting menu. The *salumi* are hand-carved at your table for an appetizer, and the daily changing menu mixes Torinese and Piemontese specialties with slightly creative dishes using local ingredients. Some of their better creations include *agnolotti* (meat-filled pasta ringlets) in a pink ragù, risotto with basil and truffles, *carré d'agnello in crosta di erbette* (lamb cooked with herbs), and rabbit cooked in apple vinegar. One local dish that definitely takes some getting used to is the mix of zucchini, meatballs, a veal scallop, eggs, and a frog (an entire frog, not just the legs), all of it breaded and deep fried, soaked in vinegar, and served cold.

Via Gian Francesco Bellezia 37. ℂ 011-436-6553. Reservations highly recommended. Primi 7€–10€ ($8–$12); secondi 11€–15€ ($13–$17); tasting menu 31€ ($36) without wine. AE, DC, MC, V. Tues–Sat 12:30–2:30pm and 7:30–10:30pm; Mon 7:30–10:30pm. Bus: 3, 4, 16, or 57.

CAFES & DELICACY SHOPS

Cafe sitting is a centuries-old tradition in sophisticated Turin. Via Roma and the piazzas it widens into are lined with gracious salons that have been serving coffee to Torinese for decades, even centuries. Below are some of the city's classic cafes. While espresso and pastries are the mainstays of the menu at all of them, most also serve chocolates—including the mix of chocolate and hazelnuts known as *gianduiotti*—that are among the city's major contributions to culinary culture.

Turin has a sizable sweet tooth, satisfied by any number of pastry and candy shops. Perhaps the best chocolatier north of Perugia is **Pfatisch/Peyrano** ⍟, Corso Vittorio Emanuele II 76 (ℂ **011-538-765;** www.peyrano.com), open Monday through Saturday from 9am to 12:45pm and 4 to 7:30pm and Sunday from 9am to 1pm. A wide variety of chocolates and other sweets, including sumptuous meringues, have been dispensed since 1836 at **Fratelli Stratta,** Piazza San Carlo 191 (ℂ **011-547-920;** www.stratta1836.it), open Tuesday through Sunday from 9:30am to 1pm and daily from 3 to 7:30pm.

The surrounding region is known not only for its wines but also for vermouth—the famed **Cinzano,** for instance, is produced south of the city in the town of Santa Vittoria d'Alba. Come evening, a glass of vermouth is the preferred drink at many of the city's cafes. **Paissa,** at Piazza San Carlo 196 (ℂ **011-562-8462**), open Monday through Saturday from 9am to 1pm and 3:30 to 7:30pm (closed Wed afternoons), is an excellent place to purchase local vermouths by the bottle.

Caffè Confetteria al Bicerin ⍟ CAFE   What claims to be Turin's oldest cafe in continuous operation (since 1763) is famous for its illustrious clientele, which has included Nietzsche, Dumas, and Puccini, as well as its signature drink—the Bicerin (local dialect for "something delicious"). It's a heady combination of coffee, hot chocolate, and cream—to be accompanied by one the house's exquisite pastries.

Piazza della Consolata 5. ℂ 011-436-9325. www.bicerin.it. Sandwiches and pastries 1.80€ ($2.05). MC, V. Mon–Tues and Thurs–Fri 8:30am–9:30pm; Sat–Sun 8:30am–12:30pm and 3:30–7:30pm. Closed Aug.

Caffè-Pasticceria Baratti e Milano CAFE   No small part of the pleasure of sitting for a time in this stylish cafe, opened in 1875, is watching a clientele that includes auto executives, students from the nearby university, elegantly clad shoppers, and visitors to the nearby museums, all sipping espressos and munching on the delicious house pastries.

Piazza Castello 27. ℂ 011-561-3060 or 011-752-903. Sandwiches and pastries 1.50€–3€ ($1.75–$3.45). AE, DC, MC, V. Tues–Sun 8am–1am.

Caffè San Carlo ⍟ CAFE   One of the essential stops on any tour of Turin is this classic cafe. The San Carlo opened its doors in 1837 and ever since has been accommodating patrons beneath a huge chandelier of Murano glass in a salon that is a remarkable assemblage of gilt, mirrors, and marble. An adjoining, frescoed tearoom is quieter and only a little less grand.

Piazza San Carlo 156. ℂ 011-532-586 or 011-812-2090. Sandwiches, pastries, and dishes 2€–11€ ($2.30–$13). AE, DC, MC, V. Tues–Sun 7am–1am; Mon 7am–8pm.

Caffè Torino ★★ CAFE Although some of the mirrored and frescoed salons here serve full meals, we suggest you dine at another restaurant and here instead enjoy only a light refreshment (one of the pastries or chocolates handsomely displayed in the main room) while soaking in the ambience of this classic, century-old cafe. Many mirrors, smoky oil paintings, and acres of carved wood create just the ambience you would expect to find in one of the city's most beloved institutions. This place is great for a cheap, fast, light meal: At lunch and dinner, bar plates are loaded with bite-sized sandwiches, pizzas, stuffed olives, fried cheese and veggies, and other goodies—all yours for the gobbling with the purchase of a drink.

Piazza San Carlo 204. ✆ **011-547-356** or 011-546-690. Sandwiches, pastries, and dishes 1.50€–8.50€ ($1.75–$10). AE, DC, MC, V. Daily 7:30am–1am.

TURIN AFTER DARK

Turin has a lively classical-music and opera scene, and you can get info on these and other cultural events at the **Vetrina Infocultura** office at Piazza San Carlo 159 (✆ **800-015-475** or 011-443-9040), open Monday to Saturday 11am to 7pm. Aside from the city's much attended summer festivals (see "Festivals & Markets," earlier in this section), there are regular classical concerts by the National Symphonic Orchestra at **Auditorium della RAI,** Via Rossini 15 (✆ **011-810-4653;** www.orchestrasinfonica.rai.it). Other concerts, dance performances, and operas are staged at the city's venerable **Teatro Regio** (✆ **011-881-5241;** www.teatro regio.torino.it), in the center of the city on Piazza Castello.

DAY TRIPS FROM TURIN
SACRA DI SAN MICHELE ★★★

Perched high atop Monte Pirchiriano—part of it projecting over the precipice on an elaborate support system that was one of the engineering feats of the Middle Ages—this dramatically situated abbey dedicated to Saint Michael provides views and an astonishing look at medieval religious life. It may well remind you of Mont Saint-Michel in France (both are laced with endless flights of stairs; the famous Mont Saint-Michel monastery and tourist site off the Normandy coast of France was one of the 176 religious institutions that once fell under the jurisdiction of Italy's San Michele, which today is all but forgotten) or, with its dizzying views and scary drops, of the abbey in the novel and film *The Name of the Rose* (probably because author Umberto Eco based his fictional abbey on this one). It was started in 983, but the extant church dates to the abbey's 12th-century heyday. A vast staircase hewn out of rock and clinging to the abbey's buttresses (known as *Scalone dei Morti* [Stairs of Death] because corpses were once laid out here) leads to the massive carved doorway depicting the signs of the zodiac and the drafty Gothic and Romanesque church, decorated only with scraps of 16th-century frescoes by Secondo del Bosco. Another stairway leads down to three tiny chapels carved into the rock and containing tombs of some of the earliest members of the House of Savoy.

On Saturday evenings (and some Fri) from April to September, the atmospheric church hosts **free concerts** of everything from chant and liturgical music to Renaissance chamber pieces, gospel, and traditional Celtic airs; check the website for schedules.

Outside Aviglina, 15km (9¼ miles) west of Turin's ring road. ✆ **011-939-130.** www.sacradisanmichele.com. Admission 2.50€ ($2.90) adults, 1.50€ ($1.75) ages 6–14 and over 65 (Sun afternoon it's 3.50€/$4.05 adults, 2€/$2.30 youths and seniors, because they give tours leaving every 20 min. that cover even more of the complex). Mar 16–Oct 15 Tues–Sat 9:30am–12:30pm and 3–6pm, Sun 9:30am–noon and 2:40–6pm; Oct 16–Mar 17 closes 5pm.

GETTING THERE Take 1 of 15 trains a day from Turin to Sant'Ambrogio Torinese (30 min.); from there, it's a stiff 1½-hour trek up to the abbey. In summer only, call ahead to see about the once-daily bus that in past years has met trains from Torino at the Avigliana station (usually around 9am) to carry pilgrims up here. By car, follow the A32 from Turin's western ring highway toward Bardonecchia/Frejus. Get off at the Avigliana exit and follow brown signs to the Sacra; the trip takes about an hour.

SAVIGLIANO & SALUZZO

Savigliano ★★ is one of those towns everyone dreams of stumbling upon in Italy—it's filled with Renaissance riches, but it's still undiscovered. The town center is the broad expanse of the Piazza Santa Rosa, surrounded by arcades, overlooked by a medieval tower, and lined with many of the town's grand palaces, which once housed summering members of the Savoy clan. Unfortunately, these and another fine collection of palazzi along the Via Jerusalem are closed to the public, so you'll have to settle for a gander at their gorgeous facades.

The pride of **Saluzzo** ★ is its sleepy upper town, huddled beneath its Castello di Manta. Along the warren of narrow lanes, you'll find the 13th-century Chiesa di San Giovanni and the Casa Cavassa, which is worth a look, not for the musty civic museum it houses, but for its porticoed courtyard.

GETTING THERE Savigliano is 54km (33 miles) south of Turin, from which there are two to four trains per hour (35–50 min.). From there, hourly trains make the 13-minute run to Saluzzo. Saluzzo is also connected with Turin by 15 buses a day. The most direct driving route to Savigliano from Turin follows the A6 autostrada for 34km (21 miles) south to the exit near Brà; from the exit, follow S231 west for 9.5km (6 miles). Saluzzo is another 13km (8 miles) west on S231. If you are making the sweep through the wine country via Asti and Alba (see below), you can continue west from Alba for 34km (21 miles) on S231 to Savigliano.

2 The Piedmont Wine Country

Asti is 60km (37 miles) SE of Turin, 127km (79 miles) SW of Milan; Alba is 60km (37 miles) S of Turin, 155km (96 miles) SW of Milan

South of Turin, the Po valley rises into the rolling Langhe and Roero hills, flanked by orchards and vineyards. You'll recognize the region's place names from the labels of its excellent wines, among them **Asti Spumanti, Barbaresco,** and **Barolo.** Tasting these vintages at the source is one reason to visit the wine country, of course; another is to stroll through the medieval and Renaissance towns that rise from the vineyards and the picturesque villages that crown many a hilltop. And vines are not all that flourish in the fertile soil—truffles top the list of the region's gastronomic delights, which also include down-home country fare like rabbit and game dishes, excellent cheeses, and plump fruit.

ASTI

The Asti of sparkling-wine fame is a bustling city more concerned with everyday business than entertaining visitors, but there are many treasures to be found in the history-drenched old town—medieval towers (120 of them still stand), Renaissance palaces, and broad piazze provide the perfect setting in which to sample the town's famous product.

Horses & Donkeys

Asti and Alba, bitter rivals through much of the Middle Ages, each celebrate the autumnal harvest with equine celebrations that are horses of a very different color.

The **Palio** (© 0141-399-482), Asti's annual horse race, is run the third Sunday of September. Like the similar but more famous horse race that the Tuscan city of Siena mounts, Asti's Palio begins with a medieval pageant through the town and ends with a wild bareback ride around the Campo del Palio. The race coincides with Asti's other great revel, the **Douja d'Or** (www.doujador.it), a weeklong fair-cum-bacchanal celebrating the grape.

On the first Sunday of October, Alba pulls a spoof on Asti with the **Palio degli Asini (Race of the Asses)** (© 0173-362-806). The event, which coincides with Alba's annual truffle fair, is not as speedy as Asti's slicker, horseback Palio, but it's a lot more fun. Good-natured as the event is, though, it is rooted in some of the darkest days of Alba's history. In the 13th century, Asti, then one of the most powerful republics of northern Italy, besieged Alba and burned the surrounding vineyards. Then, to add insult to injury, the victors held their *palio* in Alba, just to put the humbled citizenry further in its place. Alba then staged a *palio* with asses, a not-so-subtle hint of what they thought of their victors and their pompous pageantry.

ESSENTIALS

GETTING THERE **By Train** One to four trains an hour link Asti with **Turin** (30–60 min.). There are 14 trains daily between Asti and Alba, some of which require that you change trains at Nizza Monferrato or occasionally at Castagnole delle Lanze (35 min.–1 hr.).

By Bus From Turin, **Arfea** (© 0144-322-023 or 0131-445-433; www.arfea. com) runs two buses per day, one morning and one midafternoon, on the hourlong ride to Asti. **Giachino** (© 0141-937-510; www.giachino.it) makes the hourlong trip to and from Alba, about once per hour.

By Car Asti, 73km (45 miles) east of Turin, can be reached from Turin in less than an hour via the A21 autostrada.

VISITOR INFORMATION The **APT tourist office** is near the train station at Piazza Alfieri 29 (© 0141-530-357; fax 0141-538-300; www.terredasti.it). May to September hours are Monday to Saturday 9am to 6:30pm and Sunday 10am to 1pm; October to April hours are Monday to Saturday 9am to 1pm and 2:30 to 6:30pm and Sunday 10am to 1pm. Among the office's offerings is a *Carta del Vini*, an annotated map that will point you to surrounding vineyards that provide wine tastings.

FESTIVALS & MARKETS In late June and early July, Asti stages **Astiteatro** (© 0141-399-111 or 0141-399-032), a theater festival with performances that incorporate dance as well as music. In 2003 Astiteatro celebrated its 25th anniversary. September, though, is the town's busy cultural month, with townsfolk and horses alike donning medieval garb for its famous **Palio** on the third Sunday (see the "Horses & Donkeys" box, above). Local wine producers converge on the town the 2 weeks before the Palio for the **Douja d'Or** (www.doujador.it), an exhibition of local vintages accompanied by tastings; this is an excellent way to sample the products of the many wineries in the hills surrounding Asti and nearby Alba. On the second Sunday of September, surrounding villages mount feasts (almost always accompanied by a communal meal) known collectively as the **Pjasan.**

Agricultural center that it is, Asti has two **food markets.** The larger is held Wednesdays and Saturdays from 7:30am to 1pm in the **Campo del Palio,** with stalls selling every foodstuff imaginable—seeds, herbs, flowers, farm implements, and no end of other merchandise spilling over to two adjoining piazzas, the Piazza della Liberta and Piazza Alfieri. Meanwhile, Asti's covered food market, the **Mercato Coperto,** is also located in this vicinity, on Piazza della Liberta, and is open Monday through Wednesday and Friday from 8am to 1pm and 3:30 to 7:30pm, Thursday from 8:30am to 1pm, and Saturday from 8am to 7:30pm. There's also a small **antiques fair** on the fourth Sunday of every month except August.

EXPLORING THE TOWN

If you take the train to Asti, you will step right into the heart of the action—the town's lively clothing-and-food **markets** occupy three adjoining piazzas just to the north of the station (Campo del Palio, Piazza Liberta, and Piazza Alfieri). If you're driving into Asti, you're most likely to find parking in one of the lots in this area as well.

Walk through the piazzas to **Corso Alfieri;** the town's Renaissance palaces are located on or just off this major thoroughfare, usually closed to traffic. This street and Asti's grandest piazza are named for the town's most famous native son, the 18th-century poet Vittorio Alfieri. His home, on the Corso at 375, houses a small, memento-filled museum.

Second to none in Asti is San Secondo, the town's patron saint. He was imprisoned at the western end of Corso Alfieri in the **Torre Rossa**—much of which dates to the 1st century (probably part of a Roman gate) with two levels tacked on in the 11th—then beheaded on the spot just south of Corso Alfieri where the church erected in his honor, the **Collegiata di San Secondo** (© 0141-530-066), now stands. Not only does this Romanesque-Gothic structure have the honor of housing the saint's remains in its eerie crypt, but it is also the permanent home of the coveted Palio Astigiano, the banner awarded to the horseman who wins the town's annual Palio (see the "Horses & Donkeys" box, above; Secondo is the patron saint of this event). The church is open daily from 10:45am to noon and 3:30 to 5:30pm (Sun morning for Mass only).

Asti's "other" church is its 14th-century, redbrick **Cattedrale** (© 0141-592-924), which you can reach by walking through Piazza Cairoli, at the western end of Corso Alfieri, into the nearby Piazza Cattedrale. Every inch of this brick church's cavernous interior is festooned with frescoes by late-18th-century artists, including Gandolfino d'Asti; trompe l'oeil vines climb many of the columns. The cathedral is open daily from 8:30am to noon and 3 to 5:30pm.

The most notable feature of the church of **San Pietro in Consavia** (© 0141-353-072), at the eastern end of Corso Alfieri, is its round, 10th-century baptistery; the 15th-century interior and adjoining cloisters house a one-room paleontology collection (open Tues–Sun 10am–12:30pm and 3–7pm).

WHERE TO STAY

Hotel Rainero ⭐ *Kids* Occupying a centuries-old house, the Rainero enjoys a wonderful location near the Campo del Palio and San Secondo. Not only is this setting convenient, but, since many of the surrounding streets are closed to traffic, the neighborhood is quiet. Rooms 301 to 303 have terraces (views only of surrounding modern buildings), and 153 and 155 have balconies looking onto a cobbled street; there's also a large roof terrace. Despite the provenance of the structure, renovations are tasteful but lean toward a clean modern look. As a result, the rooms are perfectly comfortable though a little bland. The modular furnishings vary and seem to represent each decade since the 1960s; the best have bent-tube bedsteads and granite-topped sinks with brass-plated fixtures. Room nos. 157 and 158 (which families can connect) open off a hanging walkway over a pretty pair of tiny courtyards and red-tile roofs; no. 158 is large enough to be a quad and has a table and chairs on the walkway out front. Large room no. 161 gets one of those plant-filled courtyards all to itself.

Via Cavour 85, 14100 Asti. © 0141-353-866. Fax 0141-594-985. www.hotelrainero.com. 55 units. 88€ ($101) double; 117€ ($135) suite. Breakfast 8€ ($9). AE, DC, MC, V. Parking 7.50€ ($9). Closed 1st week of Jan. **Amenities:** Bar; room service (24-hr.); laundry service; same-day dry cleaning. *In room:* A/C, TV, dataport, minibar, hair dryer.

Hotel Reale ★   This has been an inn on Asti's main piazza since 1793, with good-size rooms, modern furnishings, double sinks, and from some, views over the piazza. The floors are wood panel, the beds comfy, some rooms have couches that double as cots for kids, and the location can't be beat.

Piazza Alfieri 6, 14100 Asti. © 0141-530-240. Fax 0141-34-357. www.hotel-reale.com. 23 units. 110€–140€ ($127–$161) double. AE, DC, MC, V. Parking in nearby garage 12€ ($14). **Amenities:** Tour desk; room service (breakfast only); laundry service; dry cleaning. *In room:* A/C, TV, dataport (in some), minibar, hair dryer, safe.

WHERE TO DINE

Il Convivio ★★ PIEMONTESE   The decor of this double-height, pastel-colored dining room is straightforward, with a clean, contemporary look. These no-nonsense surroundings reflect the fact that the main business here is to serve excellently prepared food and accompany it with the region's best, but not necessarily most expensive, wines (these are dispensed from an extensive cave that you are welcome to visit, and you can also purchase wine by the bottle or case on the premises). Only a few starters, pasta dishes, and main courses are prepared daily. They always include some wonderful fresh-made pastas such as the lightest gnocchi in a sweet pepper sauce, a soup incorporating vegetables bought that morning from Asti's markets, and some serious meat dishes, such as a masterful *osso buco di vitello, brasato di cinghiale,* or *coniglio,* a rabbit that is often sautéed with olives and white wine. Desserts, including a heavenly *panna cotta al cioccolato,* are as memorable as the rest of the dining experience.

Via G. B. Giuliani 4–6. © 0141-594-188. Reservations recommended. Primi 5.50€–6€ ($6–$7); secondi 8.50€ ($10). AE, DC, MC, V. Mon–Sat noon–2:30pm and 8–10pm. Closed last 2 weeks of Aug.

L'Altra Campana ★ PIEMONTESE   As you pass through the large gate into the paved stone courtyard backed by this little building, you'll feel as if you've arrived at a country inn from a forgotten age—which, actually, it once was. The Natta family's medieval palazzo stood at the city walls, and was used as a prison from the 16th century through 1777, at which point it was converted into La Campana Inn. Only the restaurant part of the inn is still in operation, and it continues to offer fantastic Piemontese food. The menu changes so frequently that it's recited rather than printed up. Some delicious local dishes may include *agnolotti* in *ragù, taglierini* with truffles, *cinghiale* (stewed wild boar), *stracotta alla Barbera* (strip beef cooked in red wine), or *coniglio al vino bianco* (rabbit cooked in white wine). The wine list is extensive and well priced, and the only real detraction here is an often-curt waitstaff.

Via Q. Sella 2. ⓒ 0141-437-083. Reservations recommended. Primi 6€–8€ ($7–$9); secondi 7.50€–10€ ($9–$12). AE, MC, V. Wed–Mon noon–2pm and 7:30–10pm.

ALBA

Lovely old Alba retains a medieval flavor that's as mellow as the wines it produces. It's a pleasure to walk along the Via Vittorio Emanuele and the narrow streets of the Old Town, visit the 14th-century duomo, and peer into shop windows with lavish displays of Alba's wines, its other famous product, truffles, and its less noble but enticing *nocciola,* a decadent concoction of nuts and chocolate.

ESSENTIALS

GETTING THERE   By Train   Only one direct train (in the evening, after 6pm) runs between Turin and Alba (1 hr.); otherwise, there's one per hour requiring a change either in Brà or Cavallarmaggiore (80min.–2hr.). There are 11 trains daily between Alba and Asti (30min–1 hr.).

By Bus   Alba's Autostazione bus terminal (ⓒ **0173-362-949;** www.atibus.it) is on Piazza Medford. Hourly Satti (ⓒ **800-217-216;** www.satti.it) buses make the trip between Alba and Turin in about 1½ hours. **Giachino** (ⓒ **0141-937-510;** www.giachino.it [this site is entirely in Italian]) makes the hour-long trip to and from Asti, about once per hour.

By Car   The most direct way to reach Alba from Turin is to follow the A6 autostrada for 35km (22 miles) south to the exit near Brà, and from the autostrada exit S231 east for 24km (15 miles) to Alba. If you want to work Alba into a trip to Asti, take A21 to Asti and from there follow S231 southwest for 30km (18 miles) to Alba.

VISITOR INFORMATION   Alba has two **tourist offices.** The downtown branch is halfway along Corso Vittorio Emanuele at no. 19 (ⓒ/fax **0173-362-562;** www.comune.alba.cn.it), open daily from 9am to 1pm and 2 to 6pm (may close Sun in winter). A **regional info office** is at Piazza Medford 3, across from the bus station (ⓒ **0173-35-833** or 0173-362-807; fax 0173-363-878; www.langheroero.it), open Monday through Friday from 9am to 12:30pm and 2:30 to 6:30pm and Saturday from 9am to 12:30pm (afternoons, too, in Oct).

FESTIVALS & MARKETS   October is Alba's big month. Its annual **truffle festival** is held the first week, and this in turn climaxes in the **Palio degli Asini (Race of the Asses)** (ⓒ 0173-362-806), a humble version of neighboring Asti's equine palio (see "Horses & Donkeys" box, above). On Saturday and Sunday mornings from the second weekend in October through December, Alba hosts a **truffle market** where you may well be tempted to part with your hard-earned cash for one of the fragrant specimens (which could cost as much as $1,000 a pound).

EXPLORING THE TOWN

Alba's two major sights face the brick expanse of **Piazza Risorgimento,** at the northern end of its major thoroughfare, **Corso Vittorio Emanuele.** The 14th-century brick **Duomo** is flanked by a 13th-century bell tower. Most of the interior and paintings hail from the late 19th century, save the two late baroque lateral chapels and the **elaborately carved and inlaid choir stalls** ✦ from 1512.

The town's two art treasures hang in the council chamber of the **Palazzo Comunale** across the square (go through the right-hand door and up to the top of the stairs)—an early-16th-century portrait of the Virgin by Alba's greatest painter, Macrino d'Alba, and *Concertino,* by Mattia Preti, a follower of Caravaggio. It's open only during city office hours, Tuesday through Friday from 8:15am to 12:15pm, Saturday from 8:15am to noon.

From here, stroll the shopping promenade **Corso Vittorio** a few blocks to enjoy the low-key pace in the traffic-free heart of the town.

WHERE TO STAY

Hotel Savona ✯   Renovations have added a slick, modern look to this old hotel facing a shady little piazza at the south edge of the old town. In fact, the premises have more or less been denuded of character, but the hotel offers solid comfort and many more amenities than you would expect for the price. Downstairs is a slick breakfast room and a bar that is also popular with patrons from the town. Upstairs, the guest rooms are pleasantly decorated in pastel shades and have contemporary furnishings and shiny new bathrooms, most with bathtubs and many with Jacuzzis, especially in the modest split-level junior suites preferred by bigwigs like Pavarotti when they stay. Many open on to small terraces; the quietest face an interior courtyard. The TVs are interactive, allowing you to call up reams of information on Alba, its wines, and the surrounding area (or watch satellite channels and pay-per-view movies). The housekeeping staff seems to work overtime to keep the premises clean and running like clockwork.

Via Roma 1 (a block from Piazza Savona), 12051 Alba (CN). ✆ **0173-440-440.** Fax 0173-364-312. www.hotelsavona.com. 99 units. 93€ ($107) double; 125€ ($144) jr. suite. Breakfast included. AE, DC, MC, V. Parking 6€ ($7) in courtyard. **Amenities:** Restaurant (local cuisine); bar; concierge; room service; in-room massage; laundry service; same-day dry cleaning. *In room:* A/C, TV w/pay movies, dataport, minibar, hair dryer.

Villa La Meridiana/Az. Agrituristica Reine ✯✯✯ *Finds*   On a hillside outside Alba (about 2.5km/1 mile from the center of town), this sprawling, ivy-covered villa, the home of the Pionzo family, is a pleasant and convenient retreat. Most of the public areas are outdoors and include a flower-filled patio, covered terrace overlooking the town and countryside, a room with a billiards table and gym equipment, a patio with a barbecue and wood oven you can use, and (in summer) a swimming pool. A breakfast of homemade cakes and jams, accompanied by cheeses from local farms, is served in a brick-vaulted dining room. You'll find an array of accommodations in the main villa and its extension, formerly the stalls and peasant quarters. Some (nos. 3 and 4 or nos. 5 and 6) can be combined to create family suites, and the four mini-apartments come with kitchenettes (and no. 1 has two rooms and a large terrace—great for families). All are decorated in a pleasant mix of old country furnishings that have been passed down through the family; no. 6 even has a working fireplace. All save two cozy doubles (nos. 4 and 5, which have shady groves out the windows) provide airy views over the city and the surrounding hill towns with a snowy alpine backdrop, or of the family's Barbera vineyards, apricot orchard, and pine grove; some also have terraces.

To get here, from the Piazza Grassi in Alba, follow signs to Barbareso, which will take you into the hills on Via Nizza-Acqui; a sign to the villa is about 2.5km (a mile) outside of Alba; turn left and follow the unpaved road to its end, where there is a gated drive onto the property.

Località Altavilla 9, 12051 Alba (CN). ✆/fax **0173-440-112.** 9 units. 75€ ($86) double; 85€ ($98) mini-apts. Rates include breakfast. MC, V. **Amenities:** Outdoor pool; small exercise room; bike rental; concierge; tour desk; room service (breakfast only). *In room:* TV, kitchenette (apts only), fridge (apts only), coffeemaker (apts only), hair dryer.

WHERE TO DINE

Enoclub ✮ PIEMONTESE The evocatively chic brick-vaulted basement here is devoted to fine wine coupled with solid, slightly refined Piemontese cooking. The nice variety of rich pasta dishes includes *tarajin* (Piedmont's answer to tagliatelle) topped with a rich lamb sauce, and *fettucine di farro* (noodles made from the barleylike grain emmer rather than wheat) tossed with pesto and served with potatoes and beans. The *secondi* are meaty: veal steak with aromatic herbs, rabbit cooked in red wine, and duck breast in a black-olive paste.

Up on the ground floor is the busy **Umberto Notte** bar (open evenings only), one of Alba's few late-night scenes, dispensing wines by the glass, from 1€ ($1.15). This is a fine place to sample the produce of the local vineyards as well as wines from all over the world.

Piazza Savona 4. © 0173-33-994. Primi 6.50€–9€ ($7–$10); secondi 10€–13€ ($12–$15); tasting menu 30€ ($34) without wine. AE, MC, V. Tues–Sun noon–2:30pm and 7:30pm–midnight. Closed Aug.

Lalibera ✮✮ PIEMONTESE A careful eye to design permeates this stylish *osteria* in the center of town. The marble floors, blonde contemporary furnishings, and pale green walls provide a restful environment in which to enjoy the variations on traditional cuisine that the kitchen prepares. An *antipasto misto* is a nice way to sample the daily specialties, which are often lighter than most of the regional cuisine—it might include *insaltina de tacchino* (a salad of fresh greens and roast turkey breast), *vitello tonato* (the traditionally warm-weather Venetian dish of veal and tuna sauce), *fiori di zucca* (zucchini flowers stuffed with a trout mouse), or another truffle season specialty, the *raviolone* (one giant ricotta- and spinach-filled ravioli cupped around an egg yolk and showered with *parmigiano* and truffle shavings). Pasta dishes are equally innovative, and many of them, such as *agnolotti* (a large tubular pasta stuffed with cabbage and rice), often combine fresh vegetables.

Via E. Pertinace 24a. © 0173-293-155. Reservations recommended. Primi 6.50€–7.50€ ($7–$9); secondi 10€–13€ ($12–$15). AE, DC, MC, V. Tues–Sat noon–2pm; Mon–Sat 8–10pm. Closed 2 weeks in late Feb/ early Mar and last 2 weeks of Aug.

VISITING THE WINE VILLAGES

Just to the south of Alba lie some of the region's, and Italy's, most enchanting wine villages. As you set out to explore the wine country, consider three words: **Rent a car.** While it's quite easy to reach some of the major towns by train or bus from Turin, setting out from those centers for smaller places can be difficult (there are some buses, but they tend to be very few and far between). In Turin, contact **Avis,** Corso Turati 15 (© 011-500-852; www.avis.com), or **Hertz,** at Via Magellano 12 (© 011-502-080; www.hertz.it) and Via Ascoli 39 (© 011-437-8175). Before you head out on the labyrinth of small country roads, outfit yourself with a good map and list of vineyards from the tourist office in Alba or Asti.

THE WINES While the wines of Chianti and other Tuscan regions are on the top of the list for many oenologically minded travelers, the wines of Piedmont are often less heralded among non-Italians, and unjustifiably so. Most are of exceptional quality and usually made with grapes grown only in the Piedmont and often on tiny family plots, making the region a lovely patchwork of vineyards and small farms. Here are some wines you are likely to encounter again and again as you explore the area.

Barbaresco is refined, dry, and, with Barolo, one of the region's most exalted wines. **Barbera d'Alba** is smooth and rich, the product of many of the delightful villages south of Alba. **Barolo** is called the king of reds (and is considered one of

Italy's top two wines), the richest and heartiest of the Piedmont wines, and the one most likely to accompany game or meat. **Dolcetto** is dry, fruity, and mellow (not sweet, as its name leads many to assume). **Nebbiolo d'Alba** is rich, full, and dry (the best Nebbiolo grapes are used to make Barbaresco and Barolo).

Spumanti is the sparkling wine that has put Asti on the map for many travelers, and **Moscato d'Asti** is a floral dessert wine. You can taste and purchase these wines at cantinas and enotecas in almost all towns and villages throughout the region; several are noted below.

THE REGION   The central road through the region and running between Alba and Asti is S231, a heavily trafficked and unattractive highway that links many of the region's towns and cities; turn off this road whenever possible to explore the region's more rustic backwaters.

One of the loveliest drives takes you south of Alba to a string of wine villages in what are known as the **Langhe hills** (from Corso Europa, a ring road that encircles the Old City in Alba, follow signs out of town for Barolo). After 8km (5 miles), you'll come to the turnoff for **Grinzane di Cavour,** a hilltop village built around a castle housing an enoteca (© 0173-262-159), open February to December, Wednesday to Monday 9am to noon and 2 to 6pm (2:30–6:30pm in summer), where you can enjoy a fine sampling of local wines from their over 300 labels.

Continuing south another 4km (2½ miles), you'll come to the turnoff to **La Morra,** another hilltop village that affords stunning views over the rolling, vineyard-clad countryside from its central Piazza Castello (with parking). It has places to eat (see below) and taste the local wines. The **Cantina Comunale di La Morra** (© 0173-509-204), on the Piazza del Municipo, operates both as the local tourist office and as a representative for local growers, selling and offering tastings of Barolo, Nebbiolo, Barbara, and Dolcetto. You can also procure a map of hikes in the local countryside, many of which take you through the vineyards to the doors of local growers. It's open Wednesday to Monday 10am to 12:30 and 2:30 to 6:30pm.

Barolo, a romantic-looking place dominated by its 12th-century castle (about 5km/3 miles from La Morra), is directly across the valley from La Morra and enticingly in view from miles around. Here, too, are a number of restaurants (see our top choice below) and shops selling the village's rich red wines. Among these outlets is the **Castello di Barolo** ⭐ itself (© 0173-56-277; www.turismoinlanga.it), which houses a small wine museum, enoteca (where you can taste), and tourist office in its cavernous cellars. A tasting of three of Barolo's wines (all from the same year but different zones so you can more accurately compare labels) costs 5€ ($6). It's open Friday to Wednesday 10am to 12:30 and 3 to 6pm (closed Jan). Admission to the little wine museum is 3.50€ ($4).

Tiny **Novello** is a hilltop village about 15km (9¼ miles) south of Alba and located about 3km (2 miles) away from Barolo on well-signposted roads. It crowns the adjoining hilltop, offering some pleasant accommodations and yet more stunning views.

WHERE TO STAY

See "Visiting the Wine Villages," above, for information on how to get to the towns where the following hotels and restaurants are located.

Barbabuc ⭐   This charming and intimate new hotel, which wraps around a garden, lies behind the centuries-old facade of a house near the village square and is managed by the same private tourism consortium that owns nearby

Barolo castle. Walls of glass brick and open terraces fill the premises with air and light. Guest rooms are placed on different levels of a central staircase, ensuring privacy, and are simply furnished in a tasteful mix of contemporary Italian pieces and country antiques on terrazzo floors. A few even have third beds or hide-a-beds for families. Well-equipped bathrooms have corner stall showers. A roof terrace offers countryside views over the surrounding houses; downstairs, you'll find a handsome bar area and sitting room that opens to the pretty garden, an enoteca where local wines can be tasted, and an intimate little dining room where a lavish buffet breakfast is served.

Via Giordano 35, 12060 Novello. ☎ and fax **0173-731-430.** www.barbabuc.it. 9 units. 73€–88€ ($84–$101) double. Buffet breakfast 8€ ($9). AE, DC, MC, V. Closed Jan. **Amenities:** Bar; bike rental; concierge; car-rental desk; tour desk; room service (limited); laundry service; dry cleaning; whole hotel nonsmoking. *In room:* Hair dryer.

La Cascina del Monastero ★★ *(Finds)*   The main business at this delightful farm complex, just minutes away from La Morra toward Barolo (4km/2½ miles), is bottling wine and harvesting fruit. But Giuseppe and Velda di Grasso have converted part of the oldest and most character-filled building into a bed-and-breakfast. Guests can relax on a large covered terrace, furnished with wicker couches and armchairs, or on the grassy shores of a pond. A sumptuous breakfast of fresh cakes, yogurt, cheese, and salami is served in a vast brick-walled reception hall. The guest rooms, reached by a series of exterior brick staircases, have been smartly done with exposed timbers, golden-hued tile floors, and attractive antique bureaus, armoires, and brass beds. Bathrooms are sparkling new and quite luxurious, with state-of-the-art stall showers and luxuriously deep basins. The higher rate is for larger rooms, including one mini-apartment with kitchenette. Room renovations and the addition of a restaurant are planned for 2004.

Cascina Luciani 112a, Fraz. Annunziata 12064 La Morra (CN). ☎ and fax **0173-500-861.** www.cascinadel monastero.it. 10 units. 70€–80€ ($81–$92) double. Rates include breakfast. No credit cards. Free parking. Closed Jan–Feb. **Amenities:** Small outdoor children's pool; bike rental; small children's playground; room service (limited); laundry service; game room. *In room:* Kitchenette, coffeemaker, minibar, hair dryer, no phone.

WHERE TO DINE

La Cantinetta de Maurilio e Paolo PIEMONTESE   Two brothers, Maurilio and Paolo Chiappetto, do a fine job of introducing guests to the pleasures of the Piemontese table in their cozy dining room grouped around an open hearth (in nice weather, book ahead for a table out on the tiny back terrace). A seemingly endless stream of servings, which change daily, emerge from the kitchen: a wonderful country pâté; *bagna calda* (translated as "hot bath"), in which raw vegetables are dipped into a heated preparation of oil, anchovies, and garlic; ravioli in a truffle sauce; risotto with wild mushrooms; that funky giant egg-stuffed *raviolo* also found at Lalibera in Alba (see above); a thick slab of roast veal; a tender cut of beef; and salad made with wild herbs. The wonderful house wines come from the vines that run right up to the back door of this delightful restaurant (a bar/enoteca is up front if all you want is a glass or two).

Via Roma 33, Barolo. ☎ **0173-56-198.** Reservations recommended. Primi 7€ ($8); secondi 10€–12€ ($12–$14); tasting menu without wine 31€ ($36). AE, DC, MC, V. Fri–Wed 12:15–3pm; Fri–Tues 7:30–11pm. Closed Feb.

L'Osteria del Vignaiolo PIEMONTESE   Halfway up the road to hilltop La Morra in the village of Santa Maria (which is part of the town of La Morra), this stylish countryside restaurant draws a clientele from many of the surrounding villages as well as from Alba, about 13km (8 miles) away. Pale gold walls, richly hued tiled floors, and handsome furnishings achieve a sophisticated rustic ambience, and the kitchen adds flare to local favorites. Duck breast appears in a salad of fresh picked greens; wild mushrooms are served in many variations, perhaps lightly fried or grilled (porcini) and served with polenta. The *tortelli di zucca* (pumpkin-stuffed pasta pillows in a sauce of toasted hazelnuts) is flavorful and light. Veal appears thinly sliced in tagliatelle or, more traditionally, infused with herbs and simply grilled. Wines, of course, are local, many from Barolo, the lights of which you can see twinkling across the valley (especially if you snag one of the wrought-iron tables out on the flagstone terrace next to a hillside of grapevines).

Santa Maria 12, La Morra. ℂ 0173-50-335. Reservations recommended. Primi 7€ ($8); secondi 10€ ($12); tasting menu 29€ ($33). AE, MC, V. Fri–Tues 12:30–2:15pm and 7:45–9:15pm. Closed Jan 7–Feb 14 and Aug 15–31.

Ristorante Belvedere PIEMONTESE   The outlook from the baronial main room, built around a large brick hearth and perched high above vineyards that roll away in all directions, is in itself a pleasure and draws many diners here. When tour buses arrive to fill the back rooms and downstairs, service can turn brusque. But while the Belvedere is no longer the welcoming rustic retreat it once was, its moves toward refinement (classy table settings, complimentary Spumanti and crostini while you consider the menu, etc.) have been pulled off well, and the kitchen maintains the high standards that have made it one of the region's most popular restaurants. A wonderful salad of truffles and Parmesan cheese, and homemade ravioli in a mushroom sauce, are among the house specialties, which include many other pastas and risottos. Main courses lean heavily to meat, including a rich *petto di anatra* (duck breast), *coniglio farcito alle erbe aromatiche* (deboned rabbit stuffed with herbs), and *straccotto di vitello al vino Barolo,* a shank of veal braised with the local wine. The wine list is 83 pages long and has a table of contents, and the prices are surprisingly decent (keep in mind that this area's wines are among Italy's most expensive).

Piazza Castello 5, La Morra. ℂ 0173-50-190. Reservations recommended. Primi 8€–9€ ($9–$10); secondi 13€–14€ ($15–$16); fixed-price menu without wine 37€ ($43). AE, DC, MC, V. Tues–Sun 12:30–2pm; Tues–Sat 7:30–9pm. Closed Jan–Feb.

Vineria San Giorgio WINE BAR   Not only is this friendly wine bar in the center of La Morra, at the corner of Piazza Castello, but it also serves as the village social center, and the series of attractive rooms are filled with amiable chatter throughout the day and evening. Rough stone walls and vaulted brick ceilings provide just the right ambience in which to linger and enjoy the local wines (sold by the glass from 1€/$1.15) and such regional fare as salamis and cheeses, accompanied by homemade bread. Sandwiches are also available, as are three or four special daily dishes, usually including a delicious lasagna or other pasta dish.

Via Umberto I 1, La Morra. ℂ 0173-509-594. Light meals 1.50€–8€ ($1.75–$9). MC, V. Bar Tues–Sun 11am–2am (daily in Oct); kitchen Tues–Sun noon–4pm and 7–11pm.

3 Aosta & the Valle d'Aosta

Aosta: 113km (70 miles) NW of Turin, 184km (114 miles) NW of Milan; Courmayeur-Entrèves: 35km (22 miles) W of Aosta, 148km (92 miles) NW of Turin

Skiers, hikers, and fresh-air and scenery enthusiasts flock to this tiny mountainous region less than 2 hours by train or car north of Turin, eager to enjoy one of Italy's favorite Alpine playgrounds. At its best, the **Valle d'Aosta** fulfills its promise: Snowcapped peaks, among them the Matterhorn (Monte Cervino in Italian) and Mont Blanc (Monte Bianco), rise above the valley's verdant pastures and forests; waterfalls cascade into mountain streams; romantic castles cling to wooded hillsides.

Also plentiful in the Valle d'Aosta are crowds—especially in August, when the region welcomes hordes of vacationing Italians, and January through March, the height of the winter ski season—and one too many overdeveloped tourist centers to accommodate them. You would be best off coming at one of the nonpeak times, when you can enjoy the valley's beauty in relative peace and quiet.

Whenever you happen to find yourself in the Valle d'Aosta, three must-sees are the town of **Aosta** itself, with its Roman and medieval monuments set dramatically against the backdrop of the Alps (and a fine place to begin a tour of the surrounding mountains and valleys), and the natural wonders of **Parco Nazionale del Gran Paradiso.** If you are looking for drama, add to the itinerary the thrill of a cable car ride from fashionable ski resort **Courmayeur-Entrèves** over the shoulder of **Mont Blanc** to France. While much of the Valle d'Aosta is accessible by train or bus, you'll probably want a car to explore the quieter reaches of the region.

Of course, recreation, not sightseeing, is what draws many people to the Valle d'Aosta. Some of the best **downhill skiing,** accompanied by the best facilities, is on the runs at Courmayeur and Breuil-Cervínia (the Italian side and name of the Matterhorn). The Valle D'Aosta is also excellent for **cross-country skiing** and **hiking** (see the "Into the Great Outdoors" box, below).

AOSTA

GETTING THERE   By Train   Aosta is served by 13 trains a day to and from **Turin** (2 hr.); there are 11 trains a day to and from **Milan** (3 hr., with a change in Chivasso).

By Bus   Aosta's bus station, across the piazza and a bit to the right from the train station, handles about eight buses (only one or two direct; most change in Ivrea) to and from **Turin** daily; the trip takes 3 hours (2 hr. on the direct). Four to five daily buses also connect Aosta and **Milan** (2½–3½ hr.). Buses also connect Aosta with other popular spots in the valley, among them **Courmayeur,** where you can connect with a shuttle bus to the Palud cable car (see "Mont Blanc by Cable Car," later in this chapter) and **Cogne,** a major gateway to the Parco Nazionale del Gran Paradiso (see below). For information, call 𝄯 **0165-262-027.**

By Car   The A5 autostrada from Turin shoots up the length of the Valle d'Aosta en route to France and Switzerland via the Mont Blanc tunnel; there are numerous exits in the valley. The trip from Turin to Aosta normally takes about 1½ hours, but traffic can be heavy in the busy tourist months—especially in August, and from January through March, the height of the ski season.

VISITOR INFORMATION   The **tourist office** in Aosta, Piazza Chanoux 8 (𝄯 **0165-236-627;** www.regione.vda.it/turismo), dispenses a wealth of info on hotels, restaurants, and sights throughout the region, along with listings of campgrounds, maps of hiking trails, information about ski-lift tickets and special discounted ski packages, outlets for bike rentals, and rafting trips. It's open Monday through Saturday from 9am to 1pm and 3 to 8pm (closed Sun afternoons Oct–May).

FESTIVALS & MARKETS   Aosta celebrates it patron saint and warm winter days and nights with the **Fiera Sant'Orso** on the last 2 days of January. The festival fills the streets and involves dancing, drinking vast quantities of mulled wine, and perusing the local crafts pieces, such as lovely wood carvings and woven blankets, that vendors from throughout the Valle d'Aosta offer for sale. Aosta's other major event is the **Battaille des Reines (Battle of the Cows),** in which these mainstays of the local economy lock horns—the main event is held the third Sunday in October and preliminary heats take place throughout the year. Aosta's **weekly market** day is Tuesday, when stalls selling food, clothes, crafts, and household items fill the Piazza Cavalieri di Vittorio Veneto.

EXPLORING THE TOWN

This mountain town, surrounded by snowcapped peaks, is not only pleasant but it has soul—the product of a history that goes back to Roman times. While you're not going to find much in the line of pristine Alpine quaintness here in the Valle d'Aosta's busy tourist and economic center, you can spend some enjoyable time strolling past Roman ruins and medieval bell towers while checking out the chic shops that sell everything from Armani suits to locally made fontina cheese.

The "Rome of the Alps" sits majestically within its preserved walls, and the monuments of the empire make it easy to envision the days when Aosta was one of Rome's most important trading and military outposts. Two Roman gates arch gracefully across the Via Anselmo, Aosta's main thoroughfare: The **Porta Pretoria,** the western entrance to the Roman town, and the **Arco di Augusto** (sometimes called Arco Romano), the eastern entrance, built in A.D. 25 to commemorate a Roman victory over the Celts. A **Roman bridge** spans the River Buthier; just a few steps north of the Porta Pretoria you'll find the facade of the **Teatro Romano (Roman Theater)** and the ruins of the **amphitheater,** which once accommodated 20,000 spectators; the ruins of the forum are in an adjacent park. The theater and forum are open daily, in summer from 9:30am to noon and 2:30 to 6:30pm, in winter from 9:30am to noon and 2 to 4:30pm; admission is free. Architectural fragments from these monuments and a sizable collection of vessels and other objects unearthed during excavations are displayed in Aosta's **Archaeological Museum** at Piazza Roncas 12 (✆ **0165-238-680**); it's open daily from 9am to 7pm, and admission is free.

Behind the banal 19th-century facade of Aosta's **Duomo,** Piazza Giovanni XXIII (✆ **0165-40-251**), lie two remarkable treasures: an ivory diptych from A.D. 406 that depicts the Roman emperor Honorius, which is housed along with other precious objects in the treasury; and 12th-century mosaics on the floor of the choir and before the altar. Heavy-handed restorations cloud the fact that the church actually dates from the 10th century. It's open Monday through Saturday from 8am to 12:30pm and 2:30 to 5:30pm (though I've noticed they often just stay open all day), Sunday from 12:30 to 5:30pm. The treasury is open April through September, Monday through Saturday from 8am to 11:30am and 3 to 5:30pm, Sunday from 8 to 9:30am, 10:30 to 11:30am, and 3 to 5:30pm; October through March, Sunday from 8 to 9:30am, 10:30 to 11:30am, and 3 to 5:30pm. Admission to the treasury is 2.10€ ($2.40) for adults and .75€ (85¢) for children under age 10.

The **Collegiata dei Santi Pietro e Orso,** at the eastern edge of the old city off Via San Anselmo 9 (✆ **0165-262-026**), is a hodgepodge from the 6th through the 18th centuries. An 11th-century church was built over the original 6th-century church, and that in turn has been periodically enhanced with architectural embellishments representing every stylistic period from the Gothic through the baroque. In a room above the nave (the door on the left aisle marked AFFRESCHI OTTONIANI; search out sacristan or ring bell), the remains of

Into the Great Outdoors

Recreation, of course, is what draws many people to the Valle d'Aosta. You'll find some of the best **downhill skiing** and facilities on the runs at **Courmayeur, Breuil-Cervinia,** and in the **Valle di Cogne.** At the first two, you can expect to pay 26€ to 30€ ($30–$35) and up for daily lift passes. Cogne is a little less expensive, with daily passes running around 18€ ($21). Multiday passes, providing access to lifts and slopes of the entire valley, run 90€ ($104) for 3 days and 117€ ($135) for 4 days, with per-day rates sliding down a scale to 14 days at 319€ ($366). For more info, call ✆ **0165-238-871** or visit www.skivallee.it. Ski season starts in late November/early December and runs through April, if the snow holds out.

One money-saving option is to take one of the *settimane bianche* **(white-week) packages** that include room and board and unlimited skiing and are available at resorts throughout the Valle d'Aosta. You can expect to pay at least 270€ to 300€ ($310–$345) at Courmayeur, and 200€ to 225€ ($230–$259) at Cogne or one of the other less fashionable resorts. Contact the tourist board in Aosta for more information.

Cross-country skiing is superb around Cogne in the Parco Nazionale del Gran Paradiso, where there are more than 48km (30 miles) of trails. The Valle d'Aosta is also excellent **hiking** terrain, especially in July and August. For information about hiking in the Parco Nazionale del Gran Paradiso, ask at the tourist offices of Aosta and especially Cogne.

an 11th-century fresco cycle recounts the life of Christ and the Apostles on the bits of medieval church wall above the 15th-century vaults. The frescoes are open daily April to September from 9am to 7pm, October to March 10am to 5pm. The 12th-century cloisters are a fascinating display of Romanesque storytelling—40 columns are capped with carved capitals depicting scenes from the Bible and the life of Aosta's own Saint Orso.

SIDE TRIPS FROM AOSTA

CASTELLO DI FENIS (CASTLE OF FENIS) Built by the Challants, viscounts of Aosta throughout much of the Middle Ages, this castle (✆ **0165-764-263;** www.aostavalley.com), near the town of Fenis, is the most impressive and best preserved of the many castles perched on the hillsides above the Valle d'Aosta. From it, you can enjoy some fine views of the Alps and the valley below. One of the most appealing parts of a visit to Fenis is catching a glimpse into everyday life in a medieval castle—you can climb up to wooden loggias overlooking the courtyard and visit the cavernous kitchens. Alas, you cannot scamper among the ramparts, turrets, towers, and dungeons, thanks to a new Italian safety law.

March through June and September, the castle is open daily from 9am to 7pm; July and August hours are daily from 9am to 8pm; October through February hours are Wednesday through Monday from 10am to 5pm (to 6pm Sun). Requisite half-hour guided tours (Italian only) leave every 30 minutes. Come early; tours tend to fill up quickly in summer and you can't book them in advance. Admission is 5€ ($6) for adults and 3.50€ ($4.05) for students. The castle is 30km (19 miles) east of Aosta on route S26; there are 13 buses a day (only one, at 6:20am, on Sun from Aosta; the ride takes 30 min.).

BREUIL-CERVINIA& THE MATTERHORN   You don't come to Breuil-Cervínia to see the town, a banal collection of tourist facilities—the sight to see, and you can't miss it, is the **Matterhorn** (**Monte Cervino** in Italian) ✿. Its distinctive profile looms majestically above the valley, beckoning year-round skiers and those who simply want to savor a refreshing Alpine experience by ascending to its glaciers via cable car to the Plateau Rosa (24€/$28 round-trip; closed Sept 10 to mid-Oct). An excellent trail also ascends from **Breuil-Cervínia** up the flank of the mountain. After a moderately strenuous uphill trek of 90 minutes, you come to a gorgeous mountain lake, **Lac du Goillet** ✿, and from there it's another 90 minutes to the **Colle Superiore delle Cime Bianche** ✿, a plateau with heart-stopping views.

The **tourist office,** Via Carrel 29 (✆ **0166-949-136;** www.montecervino.it, www.breuil-cervinia.com, or www.cervinia.it), can provide information on other hikes, ski packages, and serious ascents to the top of the Matterhorn. Breuil-Cervínia is 54km (33 miles) northwest of Aosta via routes A5 and S406. **From Aosta,** you can take one of the Turin-bound trains and get off at Chatillon (20 min.), and continue from there on one of the seven daily buses to Breuil-Cervínia (1 hr.).

PILA   It's well worth the trip up the winding road 16km (10 miles) south from Aosta to this resort at 1,782m (5,940 ft.). The views are incredible. Aside from getting an eagle's-eye view of the valleys rolling away in all directions at your feet—and access to over a dozen trails around, and to the tops of, the surrounding mountains—you will also glimpse the peaks of Europe's two most spectacular mountains, Mont Blanc on the far left and the Matterhorn peeking up to the far right. Directly in front of you, the Gran Combin rises over Aosta to 4,271m (14,236 ft.). The little information office in back of the Pila gondola station (✆ **0165-521-045** or 0165-521-148; fax 0165-521-437; www.pila.it) has a good hiking map and is open Monday through Friday from 8am to noon and 1 to 5pm.

A gondola runs to Pila in 20 minutes (4.20€/$4.85 round-trip) from Aosta, June 28 through July 26 and August 25 to 31 daily from 8am to 12:15pm and 2 to 5pm (to 6pm July 26–Aug 24). It leaves from a large parking lot southwest of the train station (shortcut: take the *sottopassagio* passage under the tracks at the station to Via Paravera, turn right then take your first left). To drive, follow Via Ponte Suaz—next to the train station—south out of town.

PARCO NAZIONALE DEL GRAN PARADISO   The little town of Cogne is the most convenient gateway to one of Europe's finest parcels of unspoiled nature, the former hunting grounds of King Vittorio Emanuele that now comprise this vast and lovely national park. The park encompasses five valleys and a total of 3,626 sq. km (1,400 sq. miles) of forests and pastureland where many Alpine beasts roam wild, including the ibex, a long-horned goat, and the chamois, a small antelope, both of which have hovered near extinction in recent years.

Humans can roam these wilds via a vast network of well-marked trails. Among the few places where the hand of man intrudes ever so gently on nature is in a few scattered hamlets within the park borders and in the **Giardino Alpino Paradiso** (✆ **0165-74-147**), a stunning collection of rare Alpine fauna near the village of Valnontey, just 1.5km (1 mile) south of Cogne. It's open from June 10 through September daily from 10am to 6:30pm (5:30pm June and Sept); admission is 2.50€ ($2.90) for adults and 1€ ($1.15) for ages 12 to 18.

Visitor Information Cogne also offers some downhill skiing, but it is better regarded for its many cross-country skiing trails. The **tourist office** in Cogne, Piazza Chanoux 34–36 (© **0165-74-040;** www.cogne.org), provides a wealth of information on hiking and skiing trails and other outdoor activities in the park and elsewhere in the region; it's open Monday through Saturday from 9am to 12:30pm and daily from 3 to 6pm. You can also get info at www.pngp.it. Cogne is about 29km (18 miles) south of Aosta via S35 and S507; there are also seven buses a day to and from Aosta.

WHERE TO STAY

Many hotels in the Valle d'Aosta require that guests take their meals on the premises and stay 3 nights or more. However, outside of busy tourist times, hotels often have rooms to spare and are willing to be a little more liberal in their policies. Rates vary almost month by month; in general, expect to pay highest for a room in August and at Christmas and Easter, and the least for a room in the fall. For the best rates, check with the local tourist boards for information on *Settimane Bianche* (White Week) packages, all-inclusive deals that include room, board, and ski passes.

Belle Epoque *Value* The stucco exterior of this old building in a quiet corner of the historic center has a cozy Alpine look to it, but the same can't be said of the somewhat stark interior. What is appealing about this hotel is the family-run atmosphere and the price, appreciated all the more in this often-expensive resort region. Though there's no elevator, rooms are large enough but spartan, with the bare minimum of modern pieces scattered about, but some have balconies and newly installed, tidy little bathrooms. An equally serviceable trattoria occupies most of the ground floor; you can arrange a half-pension deal.

Via d'Avise 18, 11100 Aosta. © and fax **0165-262-276**. 14 units, 11 with bathroom. 41€–47€ ($47–$54) double without bathroom, 44€–57€ ($51–$66) double with bathroom. Breakfast 5.50€ ($6). AE, MC, V. **Amenities:** Restaurant; bar; room service (limited); babysitting. *In room:* A/C.

Bus The One of the nicest things about this newer hotel is its location, on a pleasant side street just a short walk from the center of Aosta. The Roman ruins and other sights are within a 5-minute walk, yet this quiet neighborhood has an almost rural feel to it. Downstairs you'll find a contemporary-style bar, restaurant, and breakfast area. Upstairs, the smallish guest rooms are comfortably furnished in a somewhat somber modern style that includes many wood-veneer touches and thin, worn carpeting. The bathrooms are serviceable, but suffer from the dreaded waffle towels. Since the hotel is taller than the surrounding houses, rooms on the upper floors overlook meadows and the surrounding mountains. Except at peak times, rooms are usually available without board. Fifteen rooms have A/C; if you prefer the opposite sensation, a sauna is downstairs.

Via Malherbes 18, 11100 Aosta. © **0165-236-958** or 0165-43-645. Fax 0165-236-962. www.netvallee.it/hotelbus. 39 units. 59€–86€ ($68–$99) double; half-board 49€–69€ ($56–$79) per person. Breakfast 8€ ($9). AE, DC, MC, V. **Amenities:** Valdostana restaurant; bar; tiny exercise room; sauna; room service (24-hr.); laundry service. *In room:* A/C (in 15 rooms), TV, minibar, hair dryer.

Milleluci *Finds* From its noticeably cooler perch on a hillside just above the town, this chaletlike hotel in a breezy garden offers pleasant views. Current owner Cristina's great-grandmother converted the family farm into a hotel 40 years ago, and it's been handed down from mother to daughter ever since. Downstairs, a large wood-beamed sitting area is grouped around an attractive hearth (always ablaze in winter) and woodsy bar. The spacious rooms (larger on the second floor; cozy on the first) sport some nice touches like traditional wood furnishings, beamed ceilings, canopied beds (in suites and in one double), rich fabrics, terrazzo floors, and handsome prints. All have spacious bathrooms with heated towel racks. Two suites are tucked under the eaves; another pair is going in on the second floor. The stupendous buffet breakfast alone would be reason to stay, all homemade cakes, freshly whipped cream, *frittata* wedges (eggs from their own chickens; veggies from the garden), Alpine cheeses, and more. In nice weather you can take breakfast on the wraparound terrace overlooking the town. By the end of 2004, they should have a small fitness room installed. While other hotels in town make no provision for parking (you'll have to find a space in the streets or find a local garage and pay a lot), Milleluci has it own little lot.

In Roppoz (off Via Porossan 1km/⅗ mile northeast of Arco di Augusto), 11100 Aosta. © 0165-23-5278. Fax 0165-235-284. www.hotelmilleluci.com. 31 units. 95€–100€ ($109–$115) double without balcony; 105€–110€ ($121–$127) double with balcony; 110€–120€ ($127–$138) double with a canopy bed; 200€ ($230) suite; 180€–200€ ($207–$230) adjoining rooms for 4. Rates include breakfast. AE, DC, MC, V. Free parking. **Amenities:** Outdoor pool (heated); Jacuzzi; sauna; playground; concierge; tour desk; courtesy car; room service (breakfast only); in-room massage; babysitting; nonsmoking rooms. *In room:* TV, VCR, fax (on request), dataport, minibar, hair dryer, safe.

Roma   Tucked into a cul-de-sac near the Porta Pretoria and close to the center of town, the Roma is named for the monuments of the empire that surround it. The paneled lobby and adjoining bar are pleasant places to relax, and, with their plaid carpet and furnishings, are a little cozier than the bright but crisply modern guest rooms upstairs.

Via Torino 7, 11100 Aosta. © 0165-41-000. Fax 0165-32-404. 38 units. 66€–75€ ($76–$86) double. Breakfast 6€ ($7). AE, DC, MC, V. Limited free parking is available. **Amenities:** Bar; room service (limited). *In room:* TV, dataport, hair dryer (some rooms).

WHERE TO DINE

This is the land of mountain food—hams and salamis are laced with herbs from Alpine meadows; creamy cornmeal polenta accompanies meals; a rich beef stew, *carbonada,* warms winter nights; and buttery fontina is the cheese of choice.

Caffè Nazionale CAFE   This lovely fixture on Aosta's main square dates from 1886, and little has changed since then. For an almost sacred experience, try taking your coffee and pastry in the frescoed room that was once a chapel of the dukes of Aosta.

Piazza Chanoux 9. © 0165-362-130. Pastries from 1€ ($1.15). AE, DC, MC, V. Tues–Sun 8am–2am.

Grotta Azzurra PIZZA/SOUTHERN ITALIAN   The best pizzeria in town also serves, as its name suggests, a bounty of fare from southern climes, along the lines of spaghetti with clam sauce. There is a wide selection of fresh fish, which makes this somewhat worn-looking trattoria popular with a local clientele. The pizzas emerge from a wood-burning oven and are often topped with fontina and other rich local cheeses and salamis.

Via Croix de Ville 97. © 0165-262-474. Primi 4€–9€ ($4.60–$10); secondi 5€–13€ ($6–$15); pizza 4€–8€ ($4.60–$9). Thurs–Tues (daily in summer) noon–2:30pm and 7–10pm. Closed July 10–27.

Taverna da Nando PIZZA/VALDOSTAN   On Aosta's main thoroughfare in the center of town, this popular basement eatery achieves a rustic ambience with stuccoed vault ceilings, traditional mountain furnishings, and warm (if excruciatingly slow) service. The kitchen, too, sticks to local traditions, serving such dishes as *fonduta* (a creamy fondue of fontina, milk, and eggs served atop polenta), *crepes à la Valdostana* (filled and topped with melted cheese), and *carbonada con polenta* (beef stew dished over polenta). There is also an excellent selection of grilled meats, pizzas, salads, and *bruschette*, as well as a wine list that includes many choices from the Valle d'Aosta's limited but productive vineyards and from Piedmont.

Via de Tillier 41. Ⓒ **0165-44-455.** Primi 5€–9€ ($6–$10); secondi 7€–13€ ($8–$15); pizza 4€–7€ ($4.60–$8); fixed-price menus 12€–28€ ($14–$32). AE, DC, MC, V. Tues–Sun noon–3pm and 7:15–10pm. Closed 15 days in late June/early July.

Trattoria Praetoria VALDOSTAN   This small, woody trattoria, one of the friendliest and best-priced in Aosta, takes its name from the nearby Roman gate and its menu from the surrounding countryside. This is the place to throw concerns about cholesterol to the wind and introduce your palate to Valdostan cuisine. Begin with *fonduta* (fondue) and follow it with *boudin* (spicy sausages served with potatoes) or *carbonada* (a hearty beef stew).

Via San Anselmo 9. Ⓒ **0165-44-356.** Reservations recommended. Primi 6.50€–8.50€ ($7–$10); secondi 7€–18€ ($8–$21). MC, V. Fri–Wed 12:15–2:30pm and 7:15–9:30pm. Closed 20 days in Oct.

COURMAYEUR-ENTREVES

The one-time mountain hamlet of **Courmayeur** is now the Valle d'Aosta's resort extraordinaire, a collection of traditional stone buildings, pseudo-Alpine chalets, and large hotels catering to a well-heeled international crowd of skiers. Even if you don't ski, you can happily while away the time sipping a grog while regarding the craggy bulk of Mont Blanc (*Monte Bianco* on this side of the border), which looms over this end of the Valle d'Aosta and forms the snowy barrier between Italy and France. The Mont Blanc tunnel—which makes it possible to zip into France in just 20 minutes— reopened in March 2002, 3 years after a devastating fire.

Entrèves, 3.2km (2 miles) north of Courmayeur, is the sort of place that the latter probably once was: a pleasant collection of stone houses and farm buildings surrounded by pastureland. Quaint as the village is in appearance, at its soul it is a worldly enclave with some nice hotels and restaurants catering to skiers and outdoor enthusiasts who prefer to spend time in the mountains in surroundings that are a little quieter than Courmayeur.

ESSENTIALS

GETTING THERE   By Bus   Thirteen daily buses connect Courmayeur with Aosta (1 hr.). At least hourly buses (more in summer; Ⓒ **0165-841-305**) run between Courmayeur's Piazzale Monte Bianco and Entrèves and La Palud (10 min.), just above Entrèves.

By Car   The A5 autostrada from Turin to the Mont Blanc tunnel passes Courmayeur; the trip from Aosta to Courmayeur on this much-used route takes less than half an hour (lots of time in tunnels; for scenery, take the parallel S26, about 1 hr.), and total travel time from Turin is less than 2 hours.

VISITOR INFORMATION   The **tourist office** in Courmayeur, Piazzale Monte Bianco 8 (Ⓒ **0165-842-060** or 0165-842-072; www.courmayeur.net or www.regione.vda.it/turismo), provides information on hiking, skiing, and other outdoor activities in the region, as well as hotel and restaurant listings. It's open late July to late August and Christmas to January 6 daily 9am to 1pm and 2:30 to 7pm; late April to late July and late August through November, Monday to Saturday 9am to 12:30 and 3 to 6:30pm, Sunday 9:30am to 12:30pm and 3 to 6pm; December 1 to 24 and January 7 to late April, Saturday and Sunday only, 9am to 1pm and 2:30 to 7pm.

Mont Blanc by Cable Car ★★★

One of the Valle d'Aosta's best experiences is to ride the series of cable cars from La Palud, just above Entrèves, across Mont Blanc to several ski stations in Italy and France and down into Chamonix, France. You make the trip in stages—first past two intermediate stops to the last aerie on Italian soil, **Punta Helbronner** (20 min. each way; 30.50€/$35 round-trip or 85€/$98 for a family pass valid for two adults and two children between ages 4 and 15). At 3,300m (11,000 feet), this ice-clad lookout provides stunning views of the Mont Blanc glaciers and the Matterhorn and other peaks looming in the distance. (In summer, you may want to hop off before you get to Punta Helbronner at **Pavillon Frety** and tour a pleasant botanic garden, Giardino Alpino Saussurea (© **333-446-2959**; www.saussurea.net), open daily June 24 to September 30; admission is 2.50€ ($2.90) or 1.50€ ($1.75) if you buy admission along with your cable car ticket.

For sheer drama, continue from Punta Helbronner to **Aiguille du Midi** ★★★ in France in a tiny gondola to experience the dramatic sensation of dangling more than 2,300m (7,544 ft.) in midair as you cruise above the Géant Glacier and the Vallée Blanche (30 min. each way; tack on another 18€/$20 round-trip). From Aiguille du Midi you can descend over more glaciers and dramatic valleys on the French flank of Mont Blanc to the resort town of **Chamonix** (50 min. each way; 39€/$45 round-trip). There's also a ticket that takes you on the whole series of cable cars and gondolas from Courmayeur all the way to Chamonix, France (about 30 min.; no passport required), then takes a bus back through the tunnel, for a total of 78€ ($90) for adults, 66€ ($76) ages 12 to 15, and 54€ ($62) ages 5 to 11. Buses back leave Chamonix at 9 and 10am, and 1:30, 3, 4, and 5:45pm.

Hours for these cable cars vary wildly, and service can be sporadic depending on weather conditions (winds often close the gondola between Helbronner and Aiguille du Midi), but in general they run every 20 minutes from 7:20am (8:20am in fall and spring) to 12:30pm and 2 to 5:30pm (all day long July 22–Aug 27; closed Nov 2–Dec 10). The last downward run is 5:30pm in summer and 4:30pm in winter. The Helbronner–Aiguille du Midi gondola is only open May through September. Note that kids ages 4 to 15 get 50% off the prices above, and seniors over 60 get a 10% discount. Hourly buses make the 10-minute run from Courmayeur to the cable car terminus at La Palud. For more info, call © **0165-89-925** (www.montebianco.com). For a report of weather at the top and on the other side, dial © **0165-89-961**.

A cheaper but far less dramatic way to cross over just one flank of Mont Blanc (but missing out on that thrilling 2.5km/1½mile dangle in the air while you cross a massive glacier field into France) is on the Courmayeur Monte Blanc Funivia, which leaves from a terminus in Entrèves and ascends to the Val Veny. The round-trip fare is 10€ ($11), with 20% off for those over 60 and free for kids under 1.3m (4 ft. 4 in.). Cars depart every 20 minutes from 9am to 12:50pm and 2:15 to 5:40pm; closed from late August/early September to late December.

WHERE TO STAY

Edelweiss 🌟 In winter the pine-paneled salons and cozy rooms of this chalet-style hotel near the center of town attract a friendly international set of skiers, and in summer many Italian families spend a month or two here at a time. The Roveyaz family extends a hearty welcome to all and provides modern mountain-style accommodations. (One wonders, however, why the contemporary bathrooms have heated towel racks but only flat, waffle-press towels that are so common in Europe.) Many rooms open onto terraces overlooking the mountains, and the nicest rooms are those on the top floor, tucked under the eaves. Basic, nonfussy meals are served in the cheerful main-floor dining room; you can arrange a half-board deal if you wish. The hotel recently opened a small exercise room.

Via Marconi 42, 11013 Courmayeur. ⓒ 0165-841-590. Fax 0165-841-618. www.albergoedelweiss.it. 30 units. 70€–100€ ($81–$115) double; half-board 45€–75€ ($52–$86) per person. Rates include breakfast. AE, DC, MC, V. Free parking. Closed Oct–Nov and May. **Amenities:** Aostan restaurant; exercise room; sauna; a few bikes for free; massage; laundry service; nonsmoking rooms; video games. *In room:* TV, hair dryer.

La Grange 🌟🌟 What may well be the most charming hotel in the Valle d'Aosta occupies a converted barn in the bucolic village of Entrèves and is ably managed by Bruna Berthold. None of the rooms are the same, though all are decorated with a pleasing smattering of antiques and rustic furnishings; some have balconies overlooking Mont Blanc, which quite literally hovers over the property. The stucco-walled, stone-floored lobby is a fine place to relax, with couches built around a corner hearth and a little bar area. A lavish buffet breakfast is served in a prettily paneled room off the lobby, and there is also an exercise room and a much-used sauna.

c.p. 75, 11013 Courmayeur-Entrèves. ⓒ 0165-869-733 (off season call 335-646-3533). Fax 0165-869-744. www.lagrange-it.com. 23 units. 80€–130€ ($92–$150) double; 100€–150€ ($115–$173) triple; 150€–230€ ($173–$265) suite. Rates include American breakfast. AE, DC, MC, V. Free parking. Closed May–June and Oct–Nov. **Amenities:** Bar; exercise room; sauna; bike rental; concierge; room service (limited); in-room massage; babysitting. *In room:* TV, dataport, minibar, hair dryer (ask at desk).

Pavillion 🌟 This first-class hotel offers a bit more warmth and personalized service than most large ski inns at Courmayeur. The modern lounges are decorated with wood sculptures and warmed by a copper-hooded fireplace, with sun terraces opening off the front. The rooms are all quite large; though larger ones do cost more, even the "standard"-size rooms are plenty, well, roomy. What you really should be concerned about is requesting one with a view of the Alps. They are all comfortably furnished with bland modern pieces and firm, genuine beds. The bathrooms are a bit cramped, however. Some suites are lofted with the bedroom upstairs. Oddly, the hotel's not well indicated. To find it, go into the heart of Courmayeur, veer right off the traffic circle, then at the signpost at the top of the brief hill, turn right toward "Pussey"; the hotel's a short way down on the left.

Strada Regionale 62, 11013 Courmayeur. ⓒ 0165-846-120. Fax 0165-846-122. 50 units. 125€–240€ ($144–$276) double; 200€–340€ ($230–$391) suite. AE, DC, MC, V. Parking 6€ ($7) in garage. Closed May

---

⎛Moments **Drinking with the Best of Them**

The **Caffè della Posta,** at Via Roma 51, Courmayeur (ⓒ **0165-842-272**), is Courmayeur's most popular spot for an après-ski grog. Since it opened 90 years ago, it has been welcoming the famous and not so famous into its series of cozy rooms, one of which is situated around an open hearth.

to mid-June and Oct–Nov. **Amenities:** 2 international restaurants; bar; indoor heated pool; discount on golf course 7km (4¼ miles) away; indoor and outdoor tennis courts in town; tiny exercise room; Jacuzzi; sauna; concierge; tour desk; room service (24-hr.); in-room massage; babysitting; laundry service; dry cleaning. *In room:* TV, dataport, minibar, hair dryer, safe.

WHERE TO DINE

La Brevna ★★ VALDOSTANA   This is a cozy Alpine hotel/restaurant with a devoted local following nestled in the center of the hamlet of Entrèves. They make all their own pasta to fill a seasonally changing menu of typical mountain ingredients put together in slightly creative ways. These include *stracetti* noodles in a goat ragù, herbed *gnocchetti* under a sauce of chopped seasonal vegetables, baked stream trout beside goat medallions and prunes, and steak in a spicy mustard sauce. They do great desserts as well, including a fantastic *tarte tatine* apple pie sided with vanilla gelato.

Loc. Entrèves. ✆ **0165-869-780.** Primi 9€ ($10); secondi 13€–19€ ($15–$22); fixed-price menu 30€ ($35) not including wine. AE, DC, MC, V. Tues–Sun 12:30–2pm and 7:30–9:30pm.

La Maison de Filippo ★★★ VALDOSTANA   The atmosphere at this popular and cheerful restaurant in Entrèves is delightfully country Alpine and the offerings so generous you may not be able to eat again for a week. Daily menus vary but often include an antipasto of mountain hams and salamis, a selection of pastas filled with wild mushrooms and topped with fontina and other local cheeses, and a sampling of fresh trout and game in season. Service is casual and friendly, and in summer you can choose between a table in the delightfully converted barnlike structure or on the flowery terrace.

Loc. Entrèves. ✆ **0165-869-797.** www.lamaison.com. Reservations required. Fixed-price menu 40€ ($46) not including wine. MC, V. Wed–Mon 12:30–2:30pm and 7:30–10:30pm. Closed June and Nov.

Ristorante La Palud SEAFOOD/VALDOSTANA   Come to this cozy restaurant, in the little cable-car settlement just outside Entrèves in the shadows of Mont Blanc, on Friday so that you can enjoy a wide selection of fresh fish brought up from Liguria. At any time, though, a table in front of the hearth is just the place to enjoy the specialties of the Valle d'Aosta: mountain hams, creamy *polenta concia* (with fontina cheese and butter folded in), and *cervo* (venison) in season. There is a selection of mountain cheeses for dessert, and the wine list borrows heavily from neighboring Piedmont but also includes some local vintages.

Strada la Palud 17, Courmayeur. ✆ **0165-89-169.** Primi 6€–8€ ($7–$9); secondi 8€–18€ ($9–$21); fixed-price menus 15€–23€ ($18–$27), the pricier one includes wine. AE, MC, V. Thurs–Tues noon–3:30pm and 7:30–10:30pm.

10

Liguria & the Italian Riviera

From the top of Tuscany to the French border, along the Ligurian and Mediterranean Seas, Italy follows a crescent-shape strip of seacoast and mountains that comprise the region of **Liguria.** The pleasures of this region are no secret. Ever since the 19th century, world-weary travelers have been heading for Liguria's resorts to enjoy balmy weather (ensured by the protective barrier of the Alps) and turquoise seas. Beyond the beach, the stones and tiles of fishing villages, small resort towns, and proud old port cities bake in the sun, and hillsides are fragrant with the scent of bougainvillea and pines.

Liguria is really two coasts: the beachier, more resort-oriented stretch west of Genoa known as the **Riviera di Ponente (Setting Sun),** and the rockier, more colorful fishing-village-filled stretch to the southeast of Genoa known as the **Riviera di Levante (Rising Sun).** Both are a mix of fishing villages, including the remote hamlets of the Cinque Terre, and fashionable resorts, many of which, like San Remo, have seen their heydays fade but continue to entice visitors with palm-fringed promenades and gentle ways.

The province's capital, Genoa, is the area's largest city by a long shot, an ancient center of commerce, and one of history's great maritime powers. However, though it is one of Italy's most historic places, it is also one of the least-visited cities in all of Italy. But don't judge the area by its capital: Genoa's port city squalor and its brusque and clamorous elements are a world apart from the easygoing and charming seaside villages and resorts that populate the province of which Genoa is capital.

REGIONAL CUISINE Anywhere you travel in this region, you will never be far from the sea. A truism, but a bit misleading, because seafood is not as plentiful as you might assume here in the heavily fished north. What is plentiful are *acciughe* **(anchovies),** and once you try them fresh and *marinate* (marinated in lemon) as part of an antipasto, you will never underestimate the culinary merits of this little fish again. More noticeable than fish are the many fresh vegetables that grow in patches clinging to the hillsides and find their way into tarts (the **torta pasqualina** is one of the most elaborate, with umpteen layers of pastry; some restaurants serve it year-round) and sauces, none more typical of Liguria than **pesto,** a simple and simply delicious concoction of basil, olive oil, pine nuts, and *parmigiano* ground together in a mortar and pestle (hence the name). It's often used to top *trenette:* a short, hand-rolled twist of pasta sort of like a 2-inch length of extra-thick spaghetti. Ligurians are also adept at making fast food, and there's no better light lunch or snack than a piece of **focaccia,** flatbread that's often topped with herbs or olives, or a *farinata,* a chickpea crepe that's served in wedges. Both are sold in bakeries and at small stands, making it easy to grab a bite before heading out to enjoy the other delights of the region.

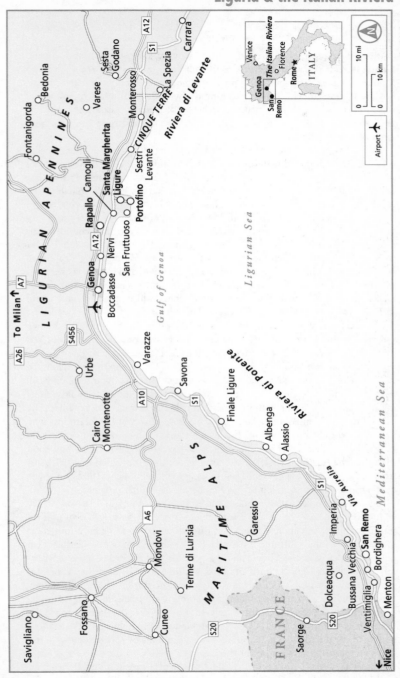

1 Genoa

142km (88 miles) S of Milan, 501km (311 miles) N of Rome, 194km (120 miles) E of Nice

With its dizzying mix of the old and the new, of sophistication and squalor, **Genoa (Genova)** is as multilayered as the hills it clings to. It was and is, first and foremost, a port city: an important maritime center for the Roman Empire, boyhood home of Christopher Columbus (whose much-restored house still stands near a section of the medieval walls), and, fueled by seafaring commerce that stretched all the way to the Middle East, one of the largest and wealthiest cities of Renaissance Europe.

Genoa began as a port of the ancient Ligurian people at least by the 6th century B.C., when it traded with the Greeks and Phoenicians. Genoa threw in its lot with Rome against Carthage and was destroyed for its loyalty in 205 B.C., but Rome rebuilt it. By the early Middle Ages, Genoa had become a formidable maritime power, conquering the surrounding coast and the mighty outlying islands of Corsica and Sardinia. Though all Mediterranean ports competed, the rivalry was particularly strident between neighbors Genoa and Pisa. After countless battles, Genoa soundly trounced its enemies at Meloria in 1284 (Pisa would never truly recover), after which Genoa's growth knew few bounds. She established colonies throughout North Africa and the Middle East, and made massive gains during the Crusades. With bigger success came new, bigger rivals, and Genoa locked commercial and military horns with Venice, which took the upper hand in 1380 with a naval victory at Chioggia. Though *La Superba*—"The Superb," a proud nickname given the city by Petrarch himself in 1358—nurtured its own powerful families, after Chioggia the city's power was broken, and Genoa was increasingly controlled by a series of French and Milanese kings and potentates.

In 1528 Genoese naval hero Andrea Doria led an insurrection that re-established local control, but the self-made government quickly turned tyrannical. Genoa's days at the top of the heap were ending. The locus of sea trade was rapidly shifting to Spain and eventually to its American colonies, a trend most dramatically exemplified by Genoa's most famous native son, Christopher Columbus, who had to travel to Spain to find the financial backing for his voyage of exploration across the Atlantic. By 1684 the French had reconquered the city, and soon thereafter the Austrians took control until 1746, then Napoléon in 1767. Austria tried again, failed, and Genoa set up a Ligurian Republic in 1802, but it was quickly subsumed into Piedmont, which became a French province.

Genoa's new links with Piedmont made its future, though, as it was deeply embroiled from early on in the Risorgimento, the 19th-century Italian unification movement. In simplest terms, the Risorgimento was built on a four-sided foundation: a king (Vittorio Emanuele II), a general (Giuseppe Garibaldi), a political leader (Camillo Cavour), and a political philosopher (Giuseppe Mazzini). Mazzini was Genoese born and bred, and in 1860 Garibaldi staged his single huge military push from this port city, the embarkation of the "Thousand" red-shirt soldiers who sailed to conquer and otherwise successfully bring all of the peninsula into the new Kingdom of Italy. In World War II the Allies bombed the heck out of this major port, but Genoa responded by rebuilding and expanding rapidly in the decades since, becoming once again a major Mediterranean port.

It's easy to capture glimpses of these former glory days on the narrow lanes and dank alleys of Genoa's portside Old Town, where treasure-filled palaces and fine marble churches stand next to laundry-draped tenements. In fact, life within the old medieval walls doesn't seem to have changed since the days when

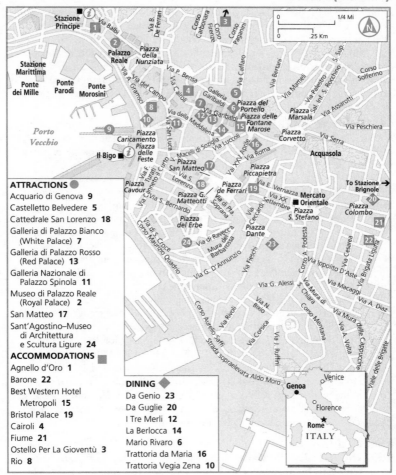

Genovese ships set sail to launch raids on the Venetians, crusaders embarked for the Holy Land, and Garibaldi shipped out to invade Sicily in the 19th-century struggle to unify Italy. The other Genoa, the modern city that stretches for miles along the coast and climbs the hills, is a city of international business, peaceful parks, and breezy belvederes from which you can enjoy fine views of this dingy yet colorful metropolis and the sea that continues to define its identity.

The city will also have to work hard to overcome the public-relations black eye it received when Genoa hosted the ill-fated G8 summit of 2001. After sweeping undesirables by the truckload into local prisons and welding 3.6m (12-ft.) iron barricades across the streets to seal off the historic center, Genoa was still deemed too dicey for the world leaders' safety, so the conferences were moved into luxury ships docked at the port. Meanwhile, the international protesters that swarm such high-level economics meetings swelled to as many as 80,000. They clashed with the 15,000 police and military forces, and things got ugly: Full rioting broke out, culminating in the police shooting and killing one Italian protester who was hefting a fire extinguisher and waving it toward a police truck.

Be prepared to deal with what is probably the seediest port city in Italy, however. Muggers, prostitutes, and heroin addicts positively teem throughout the back alleys—and plenty of main streets as well—all night *and* all day long; always stick to the widest, busiest, most major roads you can find. Genoa is, to say the least, probably not going to win "favorite bit of Italy" on your list, but it is worth a visit.

FESTIVALS & MARKETS In June, an ancient tradition continues when Genoa takes to the sea in the **Regatta Storica,** competing against crews from its ancient maritime rivals, Amalfi, Pisa, and Venice. The winner of the previous year's competition hosts the event, so your chances of witnessing the regatta during a June visit to Genoa depends on the fortunes of the previous year's boatmen.

Genoa adds a touch of culture to the summer season with an **International Ballet Festival** that attracts a stellar list of performers from around the world. Performances are held in the beautiful gardens of Villa Gropallo in outlying Nervi, a late-19th-century resort with lush parks and an animated seaside promenade. Contact the tourist office in Genoa for schedules and ticket information. (Frequent trains connect Genoa and Nervi in 10 min. and run about every 20 min.) The tourist office also keeps tabs of the summer concerts staged at different venues, many of them outdoors, around the city.

The **Mercato Orientale,** Genoa's sprawling indoor food market, evokes the days when ships brought back spices and other commodities from the ends of the earth. Still a boisterous affair and an excellent place to stock up on olives, herbs, fresh fruit, and other Ligurian products, it is held Monday through Saturday from 7am to 1pm and 3:30 to 7:30pm (closed Wed afternoons), with entrances on Via XX Settembre and Via Galata (about halfway between Piazza de Ferrari at the edge of the old city and Stazione Brignole). The district just north of the market (especially Via San Vincenzo and Via Colombo) is a gourmand's dream, with many bakeries, *pasticcerie* (pastry shops), and stores selling pasta and cheese, wine, olive oil, and other foodstuffs.

ESSENTIALS

GETTING THERE   By Plane Flights to and from most European capitals serve **Aeroporto Internazionale de Genova Cristoforo Colombo,** just 6.4km (4 miles) west of the city center (© 010-60-151 for the central line, 010-601-5410 for information; www.airport.genova.it). **Volabus no. 100 (© 010-558-2414)** connects the airport with Stazione Principe and Stazione Brignole, with buses running every half-hour from 6am to 10pm; buy tickets (2.05€/$2.40) on the bus. The nearest airports handling overseas flights are at Nice, 187km (116 miles) west just over the border with France, and Milan, 137km (85 miles) to the north; both cities are well connected to Genoa by superhighways and train service.

By Train An important thing for train travelers to know about Genoa is that the city has two major train stations, **Stazione Principe** (designated on timetables as Genova P.P.), near the old city on Piazza Acqua Verde, and **Stazione Brignole** (designated on timetables as Genova BR.), in the modern city on Piazza Verdi. Many trains, especially those on long-distance lines, service both stations; however, many trains stop only at one, making it essential that you know the station at which your train is scheduled to arrive and from which it will depart. Trains (free since they don't check tickets between the downtown stations) connect the two stations in just 5 minutes and run about every 15 minutes. City buses numbered 40 and 37 also run between the two train stations, leaving from the front of each station about every 10 minutes; you must allow at least 20 minutes for the connection on Genoa's crowded streets.

Genoa is the hub for trains serving the Italian Riviera, with trains arriving and departing for Ventimiglia on the French border about every half-hour, and **La Spezia,** at the eastern edge of Liguria, even more frequently, as often as every 15 minutes during peak times between 7am and 7pm (regional: 105 min.; high-speed: 1 hr.). Most of these trains make local stops at the coastal resorts (for those towns covered in this chapter, see each listing for connections with Genoa). Lots of trains connect Genoa with major Italian cities: **Milan** (one to three per hour; regional: 105 min.; high-speed: 90 min.), **Rome** (hourly; 4½–5½ hr.), **Turin** (one to two per hour; regional: 110 min.; high-speed: 90 min.), **Florence** (hourly but always with a change, usually at Pisa; 3 hr.), **Pisa** (hourly; regional: 3 hr.; high-speed: 1½–2 hr.).

By Bus An extensive bus network connects Genoa with other parts of Liguria, as well as other Italian and European cities, from the main bus station next to Stazione Principe. While it is easiest to reach seaside resorts by the trains that run up and down the coast, buses are the only link to many small towns in the region's hilly hinterlands. For tickets and information, contact **PESCI,** Piazza della Vittoria 94r (© **010-564-936**).

By Car Genoa is linked to other parts of Italy and to France by a convenient network of superhighways. The A10/A12 follows the coast and passes through dozens of tunnels to link Genoa with France to the west (Nice is less than 2 hr. away) and Pisa, about 1½ hours to the southeast. The A7 links Genoa with Milan, a little over an hour to the north.

By Ferry Port that it is, Genoa is linked to several other Mediterranean ports by ferry service (www.traghettigenova.it). Most boats leave and depart from the Stazione Marittima (© **010-256-682**), which is on a waterfront roadway, Via Marina D'Italia, about a 5-minute walk south of Stazione Principe. For service to and from the **Riviera Levante,** check with **Tigullio** (© **800-014-808;** www.traghettiportofino.it); there's once-daily service early July to late September.

VISITOR INFORMATION The **main tourist office** is near the aquarium on Via al Porto Antico (© **010-253-0671** or 010-248-711; fax 010-246-7658; www.apt.genova.it), open daily 9am to 1pm and 2 to 6pm. The agency also has branches at **Stazione Principe** (© **010-246-2633**), open Monday to Saturday 9:30am to 1pm and 2:30 to 6pm; **Cristoforo Colombo airport** (© **010-610-5247**), open Monday to Saturday 9:30am to 12:30pm and 1:30 to 5:30pm; and a seasonal one at the cruise terminal (© **010-246-3686**), whose hours vary year to year.

Tips **A Genoa Warning**

Even locals are wary of back streets in the old city, especially after dark and on midafternoons and Sundays, when shops are closed and streets tend to be deserted. Purse snatching, jewelry theft, and armed robberies are all too common. Also, **count your change** here. I've never had more people consistently try to rip me off (shops, restaurants, even the public parking garages) anywhere else in Italy.

CITY LAYOUT   Genoa extends for miles along the coast, with neighborhoods and suburbs tucked into valleys and climbing the city's many hills. Most sights of interest are in the **Old Town,** a fascinating jumble of old palazzos, laundry-festooned tenements, cramped squares, and tiny lanes and alleyways clustered on the eastern side of the old port. The city's two train stations are located on either side of the Old Town, known as **Caruggi;** as confusing as Genoa's topography is, wherever you are in the Old Town, you are only a short walk or bus or taxi ride from one of these two stations. **Stazione Principe** is the closest, just to the west; from **Piazza Aquaverde** in front of the station, follow **Via Balbi** through **Piazza della Nunziata** to **Via Cairoli,** which runs into Via Garibaldi (the walk will take about 15 min.). Palazzo-lined **Via Garibaldi** forms the northern flank of the Old Town and is the best place to begin your explorations. Many of the city's major museums and other major monuments are on and around this street, and from here you can descend into the warren of little lanes that lead through the cluttered heart of Caruggi down to the port.

From **Stazione Brignole,** walk straight across the broad, open, buildingless space to Piazza della Vittoria/Via Luigi Cadorna and turn right to follow broad **Via XX Settembre,** one of the city's major shopping avenues, due west for about 15 or 20 minutes to **Piazza de Ferrari,** which is on the eastern edge of the Old Town. From here, **Via San Lorenzo** will lead you past Genoa's cathedral and to the port, but if you want to use Via Garibaldi as your sightseeing base, continue north from the piazza on **Via XXV Aprile** to **Piazza delle Fontane Marose.** This busy square marks the eastern end of Via Garibaldi.

GETTING AROUND   Given Genoa's labyrinth of small streets (many of which can not be negotiated by taxi or bus), the only easy way to get around much of the city is **on foot.** This, however, can be a navigational feat that requires a good map. You can get a basic one for free at the tourist office, but it is woefully inadequate and lists only major arteries; purchase a more detailed map, preferably one with a good street index and a section showing the old city in detail, at a newsstand. Genovese are usually happy to direct visitors, but given the geography with which they are dealing, their instructions can be complicated. You should also be aware that Genoa's archaic street numbering system seems to have been designed to baffle tourists: Addresses in red (marked with an "r") generally indicate a commercial establishment; those in black are offices or residences. So, two buildings on the same street can have the same number, one in black, one in red.

By Bus   Bus tickets (1€/$1.15) are available at newsstands and at ticket booths, *tabacchi* (tobacconists, marked by a brown and white "T" sign), most newsstands, and at the train stations; look for the symbol **AMT** (© **010-254-3431;** www.amt.genova.it). You must stamp your ticket when you board a bus. Bus tickets can also be used on most of the funiculars and public elevators that climb the city's steep hills, which surround the ancient core of the town (Genoa's sprawl continues atop these hills and would probably continue right up them if they weren't so cliff-like steep). Day tickets cost 3€ ($3.45).

By Taxi   Metered taxis, which you can find at cab stands, are an especially convenient and safe way to get around Genoa at night—or by day, for that matter, if you are tired of navigating mazelike streets or trying to decipher the city's elaborate bus system. For instance, you may well want to consider taking a taxi from a restaurant in the old city to your hotel or to one of the train stations (especially Stazione Brignole, which is quite a bit farther). Cab stands at Piazza della Nunziata, Piazza Fontane Marose, and Piazza de Ferrari are especially convenient to the old city, or call a **radio taxi** at ℂ **010-5966.**

FAST FACTS: Genoa

Bookstores Genoa's best source for English-language books is **Feltrinelli,** Via XX Settembre 231-233r (ℂ **010-570-4818**; www.lafeltrinelli.it), though you'll also find some at **Bozzi,** Via Cairoli 4r (ℂ 010-248-1718).

Drugstores Pharmacies keep extended hours on a rotating basis; dial ℂ **192** to learn which ones are open late in a particular week. Several that are usually open overnight are **Pescetto,** Via Balbi 185r (ℂ **010-246-2697),** across from Stazione Principe; **Ghersi,** Corte Lambruschini 16 (ℂ **010-541-661**); and **Europa,** Corso Europa 676 (ℂ **010-397-615**).

Emergencies The general emergency number is ℂ **113.** If you require police assistance, call ℂ **118.** If you have car trouble, call ACI, Soccorso Stradale ℂ **116.** All of these are free calls.

Hospitals The **Ospedale San Martino,** Largo Rosanna Benzi 10 (ℂ **010-5551**), offers a variety of medical services.

Internet Nondove Internet Point, Corso Buenos Aires 2 (ℂ **010-589-990),** charges 5€ ($5.75) per hour and stays open daily from 9:30am to 7:30pm.

Laundry There is an Ondablu self-service laundromat at Via Gramsci 181r, open daily from 8am to 10pm.

Post Offices Genoa's main post office is at Piazza Dante 4 (ℂ **010-591-762**). This office, as well as those at the two train stations, the airport, and elsewhere around the city are open Monday through Saturday 8:10am to 7:40pm.

Travel Services **CTS,** Via San Vincenzo 117/R (ℂ **010-564-366** or 010-532-748), specializes in budget travel. It's open Monday to Friday 9am to 1pm and 2:30 to 6pm.

SEEING THE SIGHTS

Acquario di Genova (Aquarium of Genoa) ★★ *Kids*   Europe's largest aquarium is one of Genoa's biggest draws and a must-see for travelers with children. The structure alone is remarkable, resembling a ship and built alongside a pier in the old harbor (the aquarium is about a 15-min. walk from Stazione Principe and about 10 min. from Via Garibaldi). Inside, more than 50 aquatic displays realistically re-create Red Sea coral reefs, pools in the tropical rainforests of the Amazon River basin, and other marine ecosystems. These environments provide a pleasant home for sharks, seals, and just about every other known kind of sea creature, and even the displays are fun—one room is a forest of transparent columns eerily lit and filled with jellyfish; the playful seals and dolphins like to blow trick bubbles to entertain you; and there are small rays in a shallow pool that you can pet. All the descriptions are posted in English. There's also a 10-minute 3-D film on ocean life (ask for a sheet with the narration in English).

Ponte Spinola. ℂ **010-234-5678.** www.acquariodigenova.it. Admission 13€ ($14) adults, 7.50€ ($9) ages 4–12. Daily 9 am–11pm (Last admission 9:30pm). Bus: 1, 2, 3, 4, 5, 6, 7, 8, 12, 13, 14, or 15.

Cattedrale San Lorenzo ⭐   The austerity of this black-and-white-striped 12th-century structure is enlivened ever so slightly by the fanciful French Gothic carvings around the portal and the presence of two stone lions. A later addition is the campanile, completed in the 16th century and containing at one corner a beloved Genoa artifact—a sundial known as L'Arrotino (the knife grinder) for its utilitarian appearance. In the frescoed interior, chapels house two of Genoa's most notable curiosities: beyond the first pilaster on the right is a shell fired through the roof from a British ship offshore during World War II that never exploded, and in the Cappella di San Giovanni (left aisle), a 13th-century crypt contains what crusaders returning from the Holy Land claimed to be relics of John the Baptist. Fabled tableware of doubtful provenance appears to be a quirk of the adjoining treasury: The plate upon which Saint John's head was supposedly served to Salome, a bowl allegedly used at the Last Supper, and a bowl thought at one time to be the Holy Grail. The less fabled but nonetheless magnificent gold and bejeweled objects here reflect Genoa's medieval prominence as a maritime power. Entrance is only by guided tour; though the tours are only in Italian, you should take one anyway to get in and be able to look at what's inside.

Piazza San Lorenzo. ℂ 010-311-269. Admission to cathedral free; Treasury 5.50€ ($6) adults, 4.50€ ($5) seniors over 60 and students, 11€ ($12) family ticket for 2 adults and 2 children. Cathedral: Mon–Sat 9am–noon and 3–6pm. Treasury: by half-hour guided tour only (ask for one when you get there) Mon–Sat 9am–noon and 3–6pm. Bus: 1, 7, 8, 17, 18, 19, or 20.

Sant'Agostino—Museo di Architettura e Scultura Ligure (St. Augustine Museum of Ligurian Architecture and Sculpture) ⭐   The cloisters of the 13th-century church and monastery of Sant'Agostino (most of which, save its two cloisters and a campanile, were destroyed in World War II bombings) are the evocative setting for an eclectic and fascinating collection of architectural fragments and sculpture. Roman columns, statuary, and architectural debris from Genoa's churches are scattered in what seems to be random fashion throughout the grassy monastery gardens and in a few bare interior spaces. The treasures here are the panels from Giovanni Pisano's crypt for Margherita of Brabant, wife of the German emperor Henry IV. She died in Genoa in 1312 while en route to Rome for her husband's coronation as Holy Roman Emperor.

Piazza Sarzanno 35r. ℂ 010-251-1263 or 010-557-2057. Admission 3.10€ ($3.55), free for those under 18 or over 60 and for all on Sun. Tues–Fri 9am–7pm; Sat–Sun 10am–7pm. Bus: 17, 18, 19, 20, 30, 32, 33, 35, 37, 40, 41, 100, 605, 606, or 607.

Galleria di Palazzo Bianco (White Palace) ⭐⭐   One of Genoa's finest palaces, built of white stone by the powerful Grimaldi family in the 16th century and enlarged in the 18th century, houses the city's most notable collection of art. The paintings reflect the fine eye of the duchess of Galliera, who donated

---

Tips **A Money-Saving Tip**

Admission to all of Genoa's civic museums—Palazzo Bianco, Palazzo Rosso, Museo Sant'Agostino, and seven other minor museums around town—is free on Sunday. You can also buy a *Card Musei di Genova* (museum card) that's good for 1 entry to each of 20 museums across town (including all mentioned here). The museum card—sold at the admission offices—will also get you a small discount on admission to the city's aquarium. It costs 8€ ($9) for 1 day, 12€ ($14) for 3 days.

the palace and her art to the city in 1884. Her preference for painters of the northern schools, whom the affluent Genovese imported to decorate their palaces and paint their portraits, becomes strikingly obvious. Van Dyck and Rubens, both of whom came to Genoa in the early 17th century, are represented here with one painting each, as they are in the city's other major collections; one of the museum's most notable holdings is *Portrait of a Lady* by Lucas Cranach the Elder. The collection also includes works by other European and Italian masters (Filippino Lippi, Veronese, Palma il Giovanne, Caravaggio, Hans Memling, Jan Steen, Murillo, and Ribera), including several Genovese masters who were the catalyst for the city's flourishing art movements—an entire room is dedicated to the works of Bernardo Strozzi, whose early-17th-century school made Genoa an important force in the baroque movement. The palazzo was closed for restorations when we went to press and will reopen sometime in late 2004.

Via Garibaldi 11. ℂ 010-557-2057 or 010-557-2013. www.museige.liguriainrete.it/palazzobianco. Admission and hours yet to be established for when it reopens in 2004; as an indication, the old admission was 3.10€ ($3.55), free for those under 18 or over 60 and Sunday. It used to open Tues–Sat 9am–7pm; Sun 10am–7pm.

Museo di Palazzo Reale (Royal Palace) The Royal Palace takes its name from its 19th- to early-20th-century tenants, the Royal House of Savoy, who greatly altered the 17th-century palace built for the Balbi family. The Savoys endowed the sumptuous surroundings with ostentatious frippery, covered with elaborate 17th- and 18th-century stuccowork and frescoes, most in evidence in the hall of mirrors, the ballroom, and the throne room. The rooms are filled with the dusty accouterments of the Italian royalty which once lived here (or at least used it as a home when they occasionally passed through), and a lot of paintings by relative nobodies interspersed with a few by Tintoretto, Luca Giordano (in the crushed velvet throne room), and Van Dyck. The English placards explaining each room will help you identify them.

Via Balbi 10. ℂ 010-27-101. www.palazzorealegenova.it. Admission 4€ ($4.60) adults, 2€ ($2.30) ages 18–25, free for those under 18 or over 65. Or pay 6.50€ ($7) for a cumulative with Palazzo Spinola; free for those under 18 or over 65. Tues–Wed 9am–1:30pm; Thurs–Sun 9am–7pm. Bus: 20.

Galleria di Palazzo Rosso (Red Palace) Another lavish 17th-century palace now houses, as does its neighbor the Galleria di Palazzo Bianco (see above), a magnificent collection of art. Many of the works—including many lavish frescoes—were commissioned or acquired by the Brignole-Sale, an aristocratic family who once lived in this red-stone palace. Van Dyck painted two members of the clan, Pauline and Anton Giulio Brignole-Sale, and their full-length portraits are among the masterpieces in the second-floor portrait galleries, whose ceilings were frescoed by Gregorio de Ferrari and Domenico Piola. *La Cuoca,* widely considered to be the finest work of Genovese master Bernardo Strozzi, and works by many other Italian and European masters—Gudio Reni, Dürer, Titian, Guercino, and Veronese among them—hang in the first-floor galleries.

Via Garibaldi 18. ℂ 010-247-6351. www.museige.liguriainrete.it/palazzorosso. Admission 3.10€ ($3.55), free on Sun. Tues–Fri 9am–7pm; Sat–Sun 10am–7pm. Bus: 18, 19, 20, 30, 35, 37, 39, 40, 41, 42, or Volabus 100.

Galleria Nazionale di Palazzo Spinola ★ Another prominent Genovese family, the Spinolas, donated their palace and magnificent art collection to the city only recently, in 1958. One of the pleasures of viewing these works is seeing them amid the frescoed splendor in which the city's merchant/banking families once lived. As in Genoa's other art collections, you will find masterworks that range far beyond native artists like Strozzi and De Ferrari. In fact, perhaps the most memorable painting here is *Ecce Homo,* by the Sicilian master Antonello da Messina. Guido Reni and Luca Giordano are also well represented, as are Van Dyck (including his fragmentary *Portrait of Ansaldo Pallavicino* and four of the *Evangelists*) and other painters of the Dutch and Flemish schools, whom Genoa's wealthy burghers were so fond of importing to paint their portraits.

Piazza Pellicceria 1. (€) 010-270-5300. Admission 4€ ($4.60), or 6.50€ ($7) cumulative ticket with Palazzo Reale. Tues–Sat 8:30am–7:30pm; Sun 3–8pm. Bus: 1, 3, 7, 8, 18, 20, or 34.

HISTORIC SQUARES & STREETS

PIAZZA SAN MATTEO   This beautiful little square is the domain of the city's most acclaimed family, the seagoing Dorias, who ruled Genoa until the end of the 18th century. The church they built on the piazza in the 12th century, **San Matteo,** contains the crypt of the Dorias' most illustrious son, Andrea, and the cloisters are lined with centuries-old plaques heralding the family's many accomplishments, which included drawing up Genoa's constitution in 1529. The church is open Monday to Saturday 8am to noon and 4 to 5pm, and Sunday 4 to 5pm. The **Doria palaces** surround the church in a stunning array of loggias and black-and-white-striped marble facades denoting the homes of honored citizens—Andrea's at **no. 17,** Lamda's at **no. 15,** Branca's at **no. 14.** To get there, take bus no. 18, 19, 20, 30, 32, 33, 35, 37, 40, 41, 100, 605, 606, or 607.

VIA GARIBALDI ★★   Many of Genoa's museums and other sights are clustered on and around this street, one of the most beautiful in Italy, where Genoa's wealthy families built palaces in the 16th and 17th centuries. Aside from the art collections housed in the **Galleria di Palazzo Bianco** and **Galleria di Palazzo Rosso** (see above), the street contains a wealth of other treasures. The **Palazzo Podesta,** at no. 7, hides one of the city's most beautiful fountains in its courtyard, and the **Palazzo Turisi,** at no. 9, now housing municipal offices, proudly displays artifacts of famous Genoans: letters written by Christopher Columbus and the violin of Nicolo Paganini (which is still played on special occasions). Visitors are allowed free entry to the buildings when the offices are open: Monday through Friday 8:30am to noon and 1 to 4pm. To get there, take bus no. 19, 20, 30, 32, 33, 35, 36, 41, 42, 100, 605, or 606.

PIAZZA DANTE   Though most of the square is made of 1930s office buildings, one end is bounded by the twin round towers of the reconstructed **Porta Soprana,** a town gate built in 1155. The main draw, though, is the small **house** (rebuilt in the 18th century), still standing a bit incongruously in a tidy little park below the gate, said to have belonged to **Christopher Columbus's father,** who was a weaver and gatekeeper (whether young Christopher lived here is open to debate). Also in the tiny park are the reconstituted 12th-century **cloisters of Sant'Andrea,** a convent that was demolished nearby.

VISTAS & CRUISES

The **no. 33 bus** plies the scenic **Circonvallazione a Monte,** the corniche that hugs the hills and provides dizzying views over the city and the sea; you can board at Stazione Brignole or Stazione Principe.

From Piazza del Portello (off the eastern end of Via Garibaldi, just before the Galleria Garibaldi tunnel), an elevator carries you up to the **Castelletto Belvedere,** which offers stunning views and refreshing breezes and provides a handy break during sightseeing in the central city for just .30€ (35¢) each way, daily 6:40am to midnight.

A similar, view-affording climb is the one on the **Granarolo** funicular, a cog railway that leaves from Piazza del Principe, just behind the railway station of the same name, and ascends 300m (1,000 ft.) to Porto Granarolo, one of the gates in the city's 17th-century walls; there's a parklike belvedere in front (1€/$1.l5 each way or you can use a bus ticket; daily every 15 min. 6am–11:45pm).

An elevator lifts visitors to the top of **Il Bigo** (www.acquariodigenova.it/chi_ bigo.asp), the modernistic, mastlike tower that is the new landmark of Genoa, built to commemorate the Columbus quincentennial celebrations in 1992. The observation platform provides an eagle's-eye view of one of Europe's busiest ports for 3.30€ ($3.80) for adults, 2€ ($2.30) for children ages 3 to 12. It's open Tuesday to Sunday 10am to 5pm (Mar–May and Sept open until 6pm; June–Aug until 8pm).

Hour-long **harbor cruises** on one of the boats in the fleet of Cooperativa Battellieri dei Porto di Genova (✆ **010-265-712;** www.battellierigenova.it) provide a closer look at the bustle, along with close-up views of the **Lanterna,** the 108m-tall (360 ft.) lighthouse (tallest in Europe) built in 1544 at the height of Genoa's maritime might (you can ride to the top Sun afternoons only; visits leave from the Bigo at 2:30pm). Boats embark daily from Stazione Marittima, on the harbor, a short distance south of Stazione Principe, and the trip costs 6€ ($7).

WHERE TO STAY

Genoa is geared more to business than to tourism, and as a result, decent inexpensive rooms are scarce. On the other hand, just about the only time the town is booked solid is during its annual boat show, the world's largest, in October. Except for the ones we include below, avoid hotels in the old city, especially around the harbor—most are unsafe and prefer to accommodate guests by the hour.

VERY EXPENSIVE

Bristol Palace   The fantastic oval staircase and stained-glass dome of this converted late-19th-century palazzo set the tone for this oasis of comfort and calm in chaotic Genoa. It sits on the main shopping street 1 block off Genoa's main central piazza, halfway between the train station and the tangle of alleys that make up the historic center. Most rooms are modestly sized and carpeted, with a mix of modular and period pieces. A few choice ones along the front, though, are larger and airier, some with marvelous inlaid wood floors and Deco furnishings. The range for doubles below reflects a lower rate for the weekends.

Via XX Settembre 35, 16121 Genova. ✆ **010-592-541.** Fax 010-561-756. www.hotelbristolpalace.com. 133 units. 142€–190€ ($163–$219) standard double; 160€–350€ ($184–$403) superior double; 200€–350€ ($230–$403) executive double; 400€–900€ ($460–$1,035) suite. Buffet breakfast included. AE, DC, MC, V. Parking in garage 22€ ($25). **Amenities:** Italian restaurant; bar; bike rental; concierge; tour desk; car-rental desk; courtesy car (pay); room service (limited); in-room massage; babysitting; laundry service; dry cleaning (same day); nonsmoking rooms. *In room:* A/C, TV w/pay movies, VCR (on request), fax (on request), dataport, minibar, hair dryer.

EXPENSIVE

Best Western Hotel Metropoli   Facing a lovely historic square, just around the corner from the Via Garibaldi, the Metropoli brings modern amenities combined with a gracious ambience to the old city. No small part of the appeal of staying here is that many of the surrounding streets are open only to pedestrians, so you can step out of the hotel and avoid the onrush of traffic that plagues much of central Genoa. Guest rooms have somewhat banal and businesslike contemporary furnishings, but with double-pane windows and pleasing pastel fabrics, they provide an oasis of calm in this often unnerving city. They're renovating three or four rooms a year, and currently have the third, fourth, and fifth floors (there are 6 floors total) done. The style is more or less the same, but the furnishings are nicer; the biggest difference is in the newly refurbished bathrooms, now equipped with hair dryer, heated towel racks, and double sinks with lots of marble counter space.

Piazza delle Fontane Marose, 16123 Genova. (C) **010-246-8888.** Fax 010-246-8686. www.bestwestern.it/metropoli_ge. 48 units. 100€–180€ ($114–$207) double; 116€–198€ ($133–$228) triple. Lower rates during slow periods. Rates include buffet breakfast. AE, DC, MC, V. Parking 20€ ($23) in nearby garage. **Amenities:** Bar; bike rental; concierge; car-rental desk; room service (limited); laundry service; dry cleaning; nonsmoking rooms. *In room:* A/C, TV, dataport, minibar, hair dryer.

MODERATE

Agnello d'Oro   This converted convent enjoys a wonderful location—only a few short blocks from Stazione Principe yet on the edge of the old city. And the dead-end side street in front ensures peace and quiet. A few of the lower-floor rooms retain the building's original 16th-century character, with high (rooms numbered in teens) or vaulted (rooms numbered under 10) ceilings. Those upstairs have been completely renovated in crisp modern style, with warm-hued tile floors and mostly modular furnishings; the tiled bathrooms are new and spotless, though many have only curtainless tubs with hand-held nozzles. Singles all come with those lovely extra-wide "French-style" beds. Some top-floor rooms come with air-conditioning and the added charm of balconies and views over the Old Town and harbor (best from no. 56). The friendly proprietor dispenses wine, sightseeing tips, and breakfast in the cozy little bar off the lobby.

Via Monachette 6 (off Via Balbi), 16126 Genova. (C) **010-246-2084.** Fax 010-246-2327. www.hotelagnello doro.it. 25 units. 90€ ($104) double; 100€ ($115) triple. Ask about lower rates on weekends and Jan–Mar. Breakfast 7€ ($8). AE, DC, MC, V. Private parking 13€ ($15). **Amenities:** Restaurant (local cuisine); bar; concierge; room service (24-hr.); laundry service; nonsmoking rooms. *In room:* A/C (5th floor only), TV, hair dryer (some rooms).

INEXPENSIVE

Barone   Near Stazione Brignole, this family-run pensione occupies the high-ceilinged large rooms of what was once a grand apartment. And, a rarity in Genoa, it offers unusually pleasant accommodations at very reasonable rates. Marco, the young proprietor, affords a gracious welcome, pointing guests to nearby restaurants, telling them what not to miss, and joining them in the communal sitting room; self-service espresso is available around the clock. The rooms are indeed baronial in size (some can be set up with extra beds for families) and are reached by elegant halls hung with gilt mirrors and paintings. While the eclectic furnishings are a bit less grand, many retain lovely touches like a stuccoed ceiling here (in most, actually) or a chandelier there. The beds are firm and comfortable, the linens are fresh, and the TVs are hooked up with Telepiù (Italy's equivalent of HBO, with movies often in English), and the shared facilities are spotless. Two technically bathroomless accommodations also have a shower in the room, but you must share the hall toilets. Renovations to the communal bathrooms have now been completed, and there are plans to refurbish the guest rooms in 2004.

Via XX Settembre 2 (3rd floor), 16121 Genova. (C) and fax **010-587-578.** www.hotelsgiovani.com. 12 units, 1 with bathroom. 42€ ($48) double without bathroom; 47€ ($54) double with shower; 54€ ($62) double with bathroom; 54€ ($62) triple without bathroom; 63€ ($72) triple with shower; 72€ ($83) triple with bathroom; 70€ ($81) quad with bathroom; 80€ ($92) quad with shower. AE, DC, MC, V. Free parking in public lot nearby. **Amenities:** Bar. *In room:* TV w/pay movies, hair dryer (on request), safe (in 1 room).

Cairoli Location is a bonus at this pleasant family-run hotel on the third floor of an old building a little ways south of Stazione Principe and near the port, the aquarium, Via Garibaldi, and the sights of the old city. The small rooms are extremely pleasant, with tasteful modern furnishings and tidy little bathrooms; double-pane glass keeps street noise to a minimum. The friendly management leaves a little basket of snacks in your room (cookies, crackers, and Pringles) and has a soft spot for stray cats (four of them roam the place). In good weather you can relax on a terrace covered with potted plants (compact no. 9 opens onto it). Room 14 is perfect for families, with two twin beds in the first room and a double bed in a back room separated by a curtain.

Via Cairoli 14, 16124 Genova. (?) **010-246-1524.** Fax 010-246-7512. www.hotelcairoligenova.com. 12 units. 73€–88€ ($84–$101) double. Breakfast 8€ ($9). AE, DC, MC, V. Parking 14€ ($16) in nearby garage. Bus: 18, 19, 20, 30, 34, 35, 37, 39, 40, 41, or 100. **Amenities:** Concierge; tour desk; car-rental desk; room service (limited); laundry service; dry cleaning; nonsmoking rooms. *In room:* TV, dataport, minibar.

Fiume I don't include this choice as a memorable hotel experience. Rather, the Fiume is a serviceable budget option, clean, safe, and close to Stazione Brignole as well as to Genoa's intriguing Mercato Orientale food market and the profusion of food and wine shops around it. The desk staff in the brightly lit lobby can be brusquely efficient as they direct you to the rather run-down rooms, where the furnishings consist of little more than cotlike beds, tables, and functional chairs. Even so, everything—including shared facilities in the halls—is immaculate, and the travelers from around the world who stay here provide good company. This being a 19th-century palazzo, the second-floor rooms are more spacious with higher ceilings than those on the first floor (no elevator). All rooms save a few singles have a shower and sink in the room but toilets are shared, with the exception of in two doubles and two singles.

Via Fiume 9r, 16121 Genova. (?) **010-591-691.** Fax 010-570-2833. 20 units, all but a few singles with shower but only 4 with complete bathroom. 50€ ($58) double with shower, 55€ ($63) double with bathroom. No parking. AE, MC, V. *In room:* TV, hair dryer.

Ostello per la Gioventù Even if you feel you've outgrown hostelling, the quality of the accommodations and the pleasant surroundings here may convince you to take another stab at the experience. This one is fairly new and attractive, and affords some marvelous views over the city from its hillside perch about a kilometer (½ mile) from the terminal of the Righi funicular (which you can take downtown to the tiny piazza of Largo Zecca, the place to which you take the funicular, every 15–20 min. 6:40am to midnight for a regular 1€/$1.15 bus ticket). Families make out especially well here, in rooms with private bathrooms; other guests sleep four to eight in a room. There's a large terrace, a bar, a cheap cafeteria, TV room, and a laundromat. Plus, though the hostel is in a safe area well above the hustle and bustle of the city, it's only about 20 minutes to Stazione Brignole on the no. 40 bus, which makes the run about every 10 minutes. (From Stazione Principe, take bus 35 to Via Napoli, where you can change for the 40.)

Via Costanzi 120, 16136 Genova. (?) and fax **010-242-2457.** www.geocities.com/hostelge or www. ostellionline.com. 213 beds. 13€ ($15) per person in 8-bed dorm rooms; 14€ ($16) per person in family rooms with private bathroom for 3–5; 16€ ($18) per person in family double with private bathroom. IYH card required, or tack on extra 2.60€ ($2.95) per person. Rates include breakfast. No credit cards. Closed late Dec to Jan. Check-in 3:30pm–midnight. Curfew 12:30am. Bus: 40. **Amenities:** Restaurant; bar; game room; laundry service. *In room:* No phone.

Rio It's a bit of a dump, but at least it's a cheap, well-located dump. This hotel is wonderfully located amid the clamor and intrigue of the old city and just a few steps from the port and aquarium. In fact, the Rio provides just about the only decent accommodations so close to the old harbor area. (You'll want to keep your wits about you, though, when coming and going late at night.) The guest rooms tend to be large and are equipped with modern furnishings that do the job well enough, but bathrooms are hurting for an overhaul. *Tip:* upper floors have been renovated more recently, and tend to be a bit nicer. Genoa's convention facilities are nearby, so reservations are essential at periods when the city hosts one of its trade fairs (many are held in Oct).

Via Ponte Calvi 5 (off Via Gramsci), 16124 Genova. © 010-246-1594. Fax 010-247-6871. 42 units. 75€ ($86) double. Rates include breakfast. AE, MC, V. Parking 16€ ($18) in garage. **Amenities:** Bar. *In room:* TV, dataport, fridge (in some), hair dryer (in some).

WHERE TO DINE

Also don't miss out on the good food at classy wine bar **I Tre Merli,** recommended under "Genoa After Dark," below.

Da Genio GENOESE   One of Genoa's most beloved trattorias, handily situated near Piazza Dante in the old quarter, Da Genio is wonderfully animated. Local artists' works brighten the cozy dining rooms, which are almost always full of Genovese businesspeople and families who have been coming here for years. The assorted antipasti provide a nice introduction to local cuisine, with such specialties as stuffed sardines and *torte di verdure* (vegetable pie). While the menu usually includes a nice selection of fresh fish and some meat dishes (including delicious tripe or steak with porcini), you can also move on to some of the homey standbys the kitchen does so well, such as *spaghetti al sugo di pesce* (topped with a fish sauce) or an amazingly fresh *insalata di mare* (seafood salad)—though almost everyone starts off with Liguria's single most popular and famous traditional dish, *trenette al pesto* (see descriptions in "Regional Cuisine" on p. 368). The wine list includes a nice selection from Ligurian vineyards.

Salita San Leonardo 61r. © 010-588-463. Reservations recommended. Primi 7€–11€ ($8–$13); secondi 8.50€–14€ ($10–$16). AE, MC, V. Mon–Sat 12:30–3pm and 7:30–10pm. Closed Aug.

Da Guglie LIGURIAN   The busy kitchen here, with its open hearth, occupies a good part of this simple restaurant, which serves this neighborhood near Stazione Brignole with takeout fare from a counter and accommodates diners in a bare-bones little room off to one side. In fact, there's no attempt at all to provide a decorative ambience. The specials of the day (which often include octopus and other seafood) are displayed in the window; tell the cooks behind the counter what you want and they will bring it over to one of the oilcloth-covered tables when it's ready. Don't be shy about asking for a sampling of the reasonably priced dishes, because you could happily eat your way through all the Greatest Hits of Genovese cuisine here. *Farinata* (chick-pea crepes), focaccia with many different toppings, gnocchi with pesto, *riso di carciofi* (rice with artichokes), and other dishes are accompanied by Ligurian wines served by the glass or carafe.

Via San Vincenzo 64r. © 010-565-765. Primi 3.50€–7.50€ ($4.05–$9); secondi 5€–11€ ($6–$13). No credit cards. Daily noon–10pm.

La Berlocca GENOESE   Enrico Reboscio has turned this old pie and *farinata* shop into an oasis of good food in a somewhat seedy section of town. Service can be a bit slow in these two tiny rooms of small, sturdy wooden tables under stuccoed ceilings, but the seasonal Ligurian menu marrying sea and garden is delicious. I've enjoyed such dishes as *piccagge matte al pesto* (chestnut pasta with pesto), *taglierini neri con gamberi* (black pasta with crayfish and ginger), *stoccafisso* *accomodato alla genovese* (stockfish with potatoes, onions, pine nuts, and tomato sauce), and *filetto con mele, curry, e calvados* (a beef fillet in a curry made with apples and Calvados liqueur). There's a good wine selection, too.

Via dei Macelli di Soziglia 45r. ℃ **010-247-4162.** Primi 9€–13€ ($10–$15); secondi 15€–20€ ($17–$23). AE, DC, MC, V. Tues–Fri noon–3pm; Tues–Sun 7–11pm. Closed last week July to 3rd week Aug.

Mario Rivaro LIGURIAN/ITALIAN Wonderfully located amid the Renaissance splendor of the nearby Via Garibaldi, this old institution does a brisk business with a loyal clientele from nearby banks and consulates, especially at lunch and in the early evening. The decor is pleasantly reminiscent of a ship's cabin, with inlaid wood panels and long wooden tables lit by brass lanterns. Many of the attentive, white-jacketed waiters have worked here their entire careers. Ligurian classics such as *trenette al pesto con patate e fagiolini* (pasta with pesto, potatoes, and beans) and a *zuppa da pesce* made with local fish emerge from the kitchen, but the menu also ventures far beyond Genoa to include a wide range of pastas from other regions (many with tomato and cream sauces) and grilled meats.

Via di Portello 16r. ℃ **010-277-0054.** Reservations recommended. Primi 8€–10€ ($9–$12); secondi 9€–15€ ($10–$17); *menù turistico* 15€ ($17). AE, DC, MC, V. Mon–Sat noon–3:30pm and 6:30pm–12:30am.

Trattoria da Maria LIGURIAN Maria Mante is something of a local legend and for decades has turned out delicious meals from her busy kitchen, attended by relatives young and old. Her cooking and the congenial ambience of the two-floor restaurant in the old city near Piazza delle Fontane Marose draw a crowd of neighborhood residents, students, businesspeople, and tourists of all nationalities. This unlikely mix sits side by side at long tables covered with red- or blue-checked tablecloths and engages in animated conversation, while the staff hurries around them and shouts orders up and down the shaft of a dumbwaiter. Daily specials and the stupendously cheap fixed-price menu of the day—which often includes *minestrone alla Genovese, risotto buonissimo alla Genovese* (rice stirred with a sauce; they also feel secure labeling their creamy gelato *"buonissimo"*), *zuppe da pesce* (a rich fish soup you must try if it's available), and such simple main courses as a filet of fish sautéed in white wine or grilled sausages—are listed on sheets of paper posted to the shiny pale green walls. As befits a Genovese institution like this, the pasta with pesto sauce is especially delicious, as is *pansotti,* small ravioli covered with a walnut-cream sauce.

Fast Food, Genoa Style

Fast food is a Genovese specialty, and any number of storefronts all over the city disburse **focaccia,** the heavenly Ligurian flatbread often stuffed with cheese and topped with herbs, olives, onions, vegetables, or prosciutto. A favorite place for focaccia, and so close to Stazione Principe that you can stop in for a taste of this aromatic delicacy as soon as you step off the train, is **La Focacceria di Teobaldo** ✿, Via Balbi 115r (℃ **010-246-2294**), open daily 8am to 8pm; focaccia starts at .50€ (60¢) a slice.

Another Genovese favorite is *farinata,* a cross between a ravioli and a crepe made from chickpea flour that is stuffed with spinach and ricotta, lightly fried, and often topped with a cream-and-walnut sauce. Locals say this delicious concoction gets no better than it is at the two outlets of **Antica Sciamada,** Via Ravecca 19r (℃ **010-280-843**) and Via San Giorgio 14r, both open Monday through Saturday 9am to 7:30pm; prices from 2€ ($2.30) up.

Vico Testadoro 14r (just off Via XX Aprile). © 010-581-080. Primi 3€–3.50€ ($3.45–$4); secondi 4€–5.50€ ($4.60–$6); *menù turistico* 10€ ($12) with wine. MC, V. Sun and Tues–Fri 11:45am–2:15pm and 7–9:15pm; Mon 11:45am–2:45pm.

Trattoria Vegia Zena GENOESE   In the *centro storico* (historic center) near the old port (on an alley across from the aquarium), this lively, white-walled and wood-paneled room lives up to its name—dialect for Old Genoa—with expertly prepared Genovese dishes. Because the restaurant is very popular with Genovese from all over the city who consider this their favorite place to dine, you may well be asked to share one of the crowded tables with other diners. Pasta with pesto is excellent; follow it with a fine selection of fresh seafood.

Vico del Serriglio 15r. © 010-251-3332. Primi 6€–19€ ($7–$22); secondi 7.50€–25€ ($9–$29). MC, V. Mon–Sat noon–2:30pm; Tues–Sat 7:30–10pm.

PASTRY & GELATO

Antica Pasticceria Gelateria Klainguti ★★, on Piazza Soziglia 98r–100r (© 010-247-4552), is considered to be Genoa's best bakery, as well as its oldest—it was founded in 1828 by a Swiss family. One satisfied customer was the composer Giuseppe Verdi, who said the house's Falstaff (a sweet brioche) was better than his. This and a stupefying assortment of other pastries and chocolates, as well as light snacks (including panini), are served in a pretty rococo-style room or in the piazza out front. It's open daily 8am to 7pm.

Add **Banarama** at Via San Vincenzo 65r (© 010-581-130) to your explorations of the many food shops and markets in the neighborhood near Stazione Brignole. Is this the best gelato in Genoa? The jury is still out, but the creamy concoctions are indeed memorable. Just as good are the simple granites, shaved ice with fresh fruit flavorings. Open Monday to Saturday until 7:30pm. Just off the waterfront and near the fairgrounds, the simple, no-frills **Cremeria Augusto,** at Via Nino Bixio 5 (© 010-591-884), is almost a mandatory stop when taking a stroll through this part of the city. The house makes dozens of flavors of rich, delicious gelato fresh daily and it is marvelous, but the specialty is *crema,* a frozen egg custard. Open Sunday to Friday to 10pm.

GENOA AFTER DARK

The harbor area, much of which is unsafe even in broad daylight, is especially unseemly at night. Confine late-hour prowls in the old city to the well-trafficked streets around Piazza Fontane Marose and Piazza delle Erbe, where many bars and clubs are located anyway.

PERFORMING ARTS   Genoa has two major venues for culture: **Teatro Carlo Felice,** Piazza de Ferrari (© 010-589-329; www.carlofelice.it), which is home to Genoa's opera company and also hosts visiting companies; and the new (built in 2001 in a country where some theaters are over 500 years old) **Teatro della Corte** (© 010-534-2200; www.teatro-di-genova.it), on Piazza Borgo Pila near Stazione Brignole, which hosts concerts, dance events, and other cultural programs.

BARS & CLUBS   Open all day, **Brittania** at Vico Casana (just off Piazza De Ferrari) serves pints to homesick travelers from morning to night, but caters to a largely Italian crowd at night (© 010-294-878).

New Yorkers will recognize the name and chic ambience from the branch of **I Tre Merli Antica Cantina** at Vico Dietro il Coro della Maddalena 26r (© 010-247-4095; www.itremerli.it), which does a brisk business in Manhattan with several restaurants (three in SoHo, one uptown). Here in Genoa, I Tre Merli operates several *enotecas* (wine bars), and this one, with a location on a narrow street just off Via Garibaldi that makes it a safe nightspot in the old city, is delightful. A dark stone floor and walls of brick and stone provide a cozy setting, augmented by "refined country"–style tables and chairs. You can sample the wide selection of wines from throughout Italy by the glass, and there is a full bar. The half-dozen each of primi and secondi are refined Ligurian and, along with the cheese and salami platters, make this a good spot for a late-night meal; open Tuesday to Sunday 7pm to 1am.

Le Courbusier, Via San Donato 36 (© **010-246-8652**), opens early and closes late. This coffeehouse cum bar in the old quarter just west of Piazza delle Erbe is especially popular with students. The smoky room is perpetually busy, dispensing excellent coffee and sandwiches (from 3€/$3.45) as well as wine and spirits.

QUICK ESCAPES

Two seaside retreats within the city limits are Boccadasse and a little farther out, Nervi, both to the east of the city center and easily reached by public transportation. Take bus 41 from Stazione Principe or Piazza de Ferrari to Boccadasse (the trip takes 20–30 min., depending on traffic, and costs the same as a regular city bus ticket: 1€/$1.15) and bus 17 or one of the frequent trains from Stazione Brignole to Nervi (the train trip only takes 15 min.).

Once a quaint fishing village, **Boccadasse** has long since given way to some urban development. Even so, this bustling seaside community is still a pleasant corner of the city. Fishing boats and nets litter the shore, and the rocky seaside is lined with tall, colorful Ligurian houses, whose bottom floors now accommodate gelaterias, focaccerias, and simple restaurants with outdoor terraces.

Nervi was a fashionable resort a century ago, and it's still easy to see why. A 1.6km (1-mile) long seaside promenade affords stunning views of the sea, and elegant villas are surrounded by a lush profusion of flora. (Tempting as the waters are, you may want to refrain from a swim until you are a little farther away from Genoa, since the water is badly polluted—Italians don't go to the beach to swim, anyway, but to tan and socialize.) One of the most pleasant retreats in Genoa is Nervi's Parco Villa Grimaldi, where more than 2,000 varieties of roses bloom. Each July, Nervi hosts Genoa's International Ballet Festival (see "Festivals & Markets," earlier in this section).

2 The Riviera di Ponente: San Remo, Bordighera & More

San Remo: 140km (87 miles) W of Genoa, 59km (37 miles) E of Nice; Bordighera: 155km (96 miles) W of Genoa, 15km (9¹⁄₃ miles) W of San Remo, 45km (28 miles) E of Nice

SAN REMO

Gone are the days when Tchaikovsky and the Russian empress Maria Alexandranova joined a well-heeled mix of titled continental and British gentry in strolling along San Remo's palm-lined avenues. They left behind an onion-domed Orthodox church, a few grand hotels, and a snooty casino, but **San Remo** is a different sort of town these days. It's still the most cosmopolitan stop on the Riviera di Ponente (Setting Sun), as the stretch of coast west of Genoa is called, catering mostly to sun-seeking Italian families in the summer and elderly Romans and Milanese who come to enjoy the balmy temperatures in the winter.

In addition to the gentle ambience of days gone by, San Remo offers its visitors a long stretch of beach and a hilltop Old Town known as La Pigna. For cosmopolitan pleasures, the casino attracts a well-attired clientele willing to try their luck.

A Day at the Beach

Plunging into the Ligurian Sea in San Remo means spending some money. The pebbly beach below the Passeggiata dell'Imperatrice is lined with beach stations, where many visitors choose to spend their days: easy to do, since most provide showers, snack bars, and, of course, beach chairs, lounges, and umbrellas. Expect to spend at least 5€ ($6) for a basic lounge, up to 14€ ($16) for a more elaborate sun-bed arrangement with umbrella. *Note:* As is standard at most European resort towns without "public" sections of beach (which are usually not very nice anyway), you cannot go onto the beach without paying for at least a lounge chair.

San Remo is an excellent base from which to explore the rocky coast and Ligurian hills. So is Bordighera, a quieter resort just up the coast. With excellent train and bus connections, both are within easy reach of a full itinerary of fascinating stops, including Giardino Hanbury, one of Europe's most exquisite gardens; the fascinating prehistoric remains at Balzi Rossi; and Dolceacqua, perhaps the most enticing of all the inland Ligurian villages (for more information on these places, see below).

ESSENTIALS

GETTING THERE By Train There are trains almost hourly to and from **Genoa** (regional: 2½ hr.; high-speed: 1¾ hr.). There are two to three trains per hour connecting with **Bordighera** (13 min.). Trains from Genoa continue west for another 20 minutes to **Ventimiglia** on the French border. From Ventimiglia you can continue across the border on one of the hourly trains to **Nice,** 40 minutes west.

By Bus Riviera Trasporti buses (© **0184-592-706;** www.rivieratrasporti.it) run every 15 minutes between San Remo and **Bordighera** (20 min.). Almost as many buses continue on to **Ventimiglia** (40 min. from San Remo).

By Car The fastest driving route in and out of San Remo is the A10 autostrada, which follows the coast from the French border (20 min. away) to Genoa (about 45 min. away). The slower coast road, S1, cuts right through the center of town.

VISITOR INFORMATION The **APT tourist board** is at Largo Nuvoloni 1 (© **0184-571-571;** fax 0184-567-649; www.apt.rivieradeifiori.it or www.sanremonet.com), at the corner with Corso Imperatrice/Corso Matteotti (exit the train station, cross the street, and go to the left a few hundred feet). It's open Monday to Saturday 8am to 7pm and Sunday 9am to 1pm. In addition to a wealth of information on San Remo, the office also dispenses information on towns up and down the nearby coast, known as the Riviera dei Fiori.

FESTIVALS August 15, the **Feast of the Assumption,** is celebrated with special flair in San Remo, with the festival of Nostra Signora della Costa (our Lady of the Coast). The Virgin Mary allegedly saved a local sailor from drowning, and she is honored with fireworks and a procession in medieval garb to her shrine on a hillside high above the town.

Since the 1950s, the **Sanremo Festival** (in late Feb or early Mar) has been Italy's—and one of Europe's—premier music fests. It's sort of an Italian version of the Grammy Awards, only spread out over several days with far more live performances—by Italian pop stars, international headliners, and plenty of up-and-coming singers, songwriters, and bands. "Volare" was Sanremo's first-ever Best

Recording, and today if you peruse the CD collections of most Italian households (or, say, mine) you'll find at least a few of the yearly compilation albums the festival puts out. The festival has spawned many other contestlike celebrations of film and music (international folk to *musica lirica*) throughout the year, but this is the big one, booking hotels up and down the coast months in advance. Call the tourist office if you want to try to score tickets.

STROLLING AROUND TOWN

Though San Remo has a municipal bus system, you should be able to get anywhere you want to go on foot. The train station is on the seaside and divides the commercial part of town from the resort and beach area. The tourist board is just in front of the station and just beyond that is the onion-domed **Chiesa Russa** (© **0184-531-807**), more formally the Chiesa di Cristo Salvatore, where the Russian nobility who once favored San Remo worshipped. You can step inside for a view of dark, icon-enriched interior; open Tuesday to Sunday 9:30am to 12:30pm and 3:30 to 6:30pm; suggested donation .50€ (60¢).

To the left as you leave the station is the beginning of the palm-lined promenade, the **Passeggiata dell'Imperatrice,** which skirts the narrow pebbly strand between the train tracks and the busy coastal road, passing any number of cramped beach stations. One of the more pleasant stops along the way is the **Giardini Comunali Marsaglia** (signposted AUDITORIUM FRANCO ALFANO), a small but luxuriant hillside garden that bursts with exotic flora (open daily, dawn to dusk).

To the right of the station are the beginnings of Corso Roma and Corso Giacomo, San Remo's two main thoroughfares. Corso Giacomo will lead you past the **casino** (see below) and into the heart of the lively business district. Continue on that until it becomes Via Matteotti, which, after a block, runs into Piazza Colombo and the flower market. If you turn left (north) on Via Feraldi about midway down Corso Giacomo, you will find yourself in the charming older precincts of town. Continue through the Piazza degli Eroi Sanremesi to Piazza Mercato, where Via Monta leads into the old medieval quarter, **La Pigna.** The hill on which this fascinating district is located resembles a pinecone in its conical shape, hence the name. Aside from a few restaurants, La Pigna is today a residential quarter, with tall old houses that overshadow the narrow lanes that twist and turn up the hillside to the park-enclosed ruins of a **castle** at the top.

VISITING THE CASINO

Set intimidatingly atop a long flight of steps across from the train station— Corso degli Inglesi swoops around it off Corso Matteotti—San Remo's white palace of a casino (© **0184-5951**) not only lords over the center of town, it's also the hub of the local nightlife scene. You can't step foot inside without being

---

Is Board Necessary?

Many hotels offer room and board rates that include breakfast, lunch, and dinner (full board or full pension) or breakfast and one of these other two meals (half-board or half-pension). Only in the busy late July, early August, beach season do many require you to take these meals, however. If you can procure a room without the meal plan, do so—San Remo has many excellent restaurants, and this is not a place where you have to spend a lot for a good meal.

properly attired (jacket for gents Oct–June) and showing your passport. Monday to Thursday admission is free, but on weekends you must unburden yourself of 7.50€ ($8.65) to get in—and that's even before you hit the tables, which attract high rollers from the length of the Riviera. Gaming rooms are open daily 2:45pm to 3am (to 4am on weekends). Things are more relaxed in the rooms set aside for slot machines, where there is neither a dress code nor an entrance fee. It's open Sunday to Friday 10am to 2:30am and Saturday 2:30pm to 3am.

WHERE TO STAY
Very Expensive

Royal Hotel ★★★   San Remo's luxury inn of choice since 1872, the Bertolini family's Royal Hotel has been the preferred retreat of jet-setters passing through as well as the first place rock stars call for a suite during the San Remo music festival. The terraces of palms and flowers of its 1.6-hectare (4-acre) park leading up to its edifice from the main road blend seamlessly with the verdant public gardens next door, and the stucco-ceilinged bars and salons framed by granite ionic columns promise a cushy, elegant stay. The rooms are exceedingly comfortable and restrained, with rugs on the polished parquet and a floral-print theme. Each has a small sitting area of chairs and loveseats, real beds, and spacious new bathrooms. The shared door of neighboring corner rooms can be closed off to make family suites. The best accommodations, obviously, are those that enjoy the sea view from small terraces or small balconies; four floors have rooms facing all sides, but the tacked-on fifth-floor rooms all face the Ligurian Sea and distant Monaco. Of course, it wouldn't be "royal" if it didn't have a private beach across the road.

Corso Imperatrice 80, I-18038 San Remo. ℂ **0184-5391.** Fax 0184-661-445. www.royalhotelsanremo.com. 136 units. 198€–364€ ($228–$419) double; 234€–474€ ($269–$545) jr. suite; 330€–630€ ($380–$725) suite. Add 35€ ($40) for half-pension. Rates include breakfast. AE, DC, MC, V. Parking 10€ ($12) or 18€ ($21) in garage. Closed Oct 6–Dec 17. **Amenities:** 3 Italian/international restaurants (elegant dining room, terrace dining in summer, poolside lunch restaurant from Apr–Oct); 2 bars (1 at pool); large outdoor heated saltwater pool; minigolf at hotel; 18-hole golf course 5km (3 miles) away; outdoor tennis court; small exercise room; watersports equipment; bike rental; children's center (high season); concierge; secretarial services; salon; room service (24-hr.); babysitting on request; laundry service; same-day dry cleaning; nonsmoking rooms. *In room:* A/C, TV, minibar, hair dryer, safe.

Moderate

Paradiso ★   Three generations of the Gaiani family have run this former villa, set in a pretty garden above the seaside promenade, as a hotel since 1926. Since then, the original villa has been topped off with several extra floors of very pleasant guest rooms, many of which have flower-filled balconies overlooking the sea (rooms with balconies cost slightly more). An understated elegance characterizes these relaxing surroundings. Guest rooms are extremely well maintained to retain the sort of old-fashioned comfort that brings a loyal clientele back year after year for their month by the sea. Furnishings are a homey collection of old armoires, armchairs, and upholstered headboards, and the tiled bathrooms, with large sinks and bathtubs, are luxuriously commodious. Cocktails are served in the comfortable, elegantly furnished salon in the evenings, or in the nicely planted garden in good weather, and guests can take meals in an airy and newly renovated Liberty-style dining room. The owners recently added a pool and installed air-conditioning.

Via Roccasterone 12, 18038 San Remo. ℂ **0184-571-211.** Fax 0184-578-176. www.paradisohotel.it. 41 units. 104€–160€ ($120–$184) double. Half-board 75€–96€ ($86–$110) per person. Buffet breakfast included. AE, DC, MC, V. Parking 8€ ($9) in hotel garage. **Amenities:** Restaurant (Italian cuisine); bar; outdoor pool; bike rental; concierge; tour desk; car-rental desk; courtesy car; room service (24-hr.); babysitting; laundry service. *In room:* A/C, TV, dataport, minibar, hair dryer.

Villa Maria ★★   It's fairly easy to imagine San Remo's late 19th/early 20th century heyday in this charming hotel incorporating three villas on a flowery hillside above the casino. The promenade is only a short walk downhill, yet the hubbub of the resort seems miles away from this leafy residential district. A series of elegant salons and dining rooms with parquet floors, richly paneled ceilings, and crystal chandeliers spread across the ground floor, and many of these public rooms open to a nicely planted terrace. The bedrooms, too, retain the grandeur of the original dwellings, with silk-covered armchairs and antique beds; many have balconies facing the sea. The bathrooms have old-fashioned details such as tubs with hand-held shower nozzles. Since rooms vary considerably in size and decor, ask to look around before you settle on one that strikes your fancy.

Corso Nuvoloni 30, 18038 San Remo. © 0184-531-422. Fax 0184-531-425. 38 units, 36 with bathroom. 62€–111€ ($71–$128) double. Rates include continental breakfast. Half-board (required Easter, Christmas, and Aug 1–15) 51€–74€ ($59–$85) per person; full board 61€–89€ ($70–$102) per person. AE, DC, MC, V. **Amenities:** Restaurant (international cuisine); concierge; tour desk; car-rental desk; room service (limited); babysitting; laundry service; nonsmoking rooms. *In room:* TV, hair dryer.

Inexpensive

Al Dom   This rambling, dark, old-fashioned pensione near the casino, city center, and harbor occupies the second floor of a grand 19th-century apartment house. The rooms, basically but nicely furnished with modern pieces and floral bedspreads, are carved out of former salons and tucked into the closed-off ends of ballroom-size hallways; no. 5 has a large balcony over the street. Tiny bathrooms (some of them modular units that resemble the public facilities you find in Paris and other cities) have been appended wherever they might fit. So, be prepared for the unexpected: You may well find yourself staring up at an ornately plastered ceiling from a metal-frame bed crammed next to a marble fireplace. In short, the surroundings may not be stylish, but they are memorable, and the family that runs the pensione is friendly and always on hand to see that guests are comfortable.

Corso Mombello 13, 18038 San Remo. © 0184-501-460. 13 units. 40€–60€ ($46–$69) double. Breakfast included. No credit cards. **Amenities:** Restaurant. *In room:* TV, no phone.

Miramare Continental Palace ★ *Value*   The Miramare is a Liberty-style villa of sedate, faded elegance, and the only hotel on the shore side of the main road, but it is a 15-minute walk from the center. You really come for the setting, not the rooms, which are a bit small with modular furnishings and sea views. The hotel is set in a 1-hectare (2½-acre) park of flower-fringed palms and a mighty baobab tree. A pathway under the railroad tracks bounding one edge of the property (yes, trains are noisy, but infrequent) leads right onto the beach, and next door is an indoor lap swimming pool that's open to the public.

Corso Matuzia 9, 18038 San Remo. © 0184-667-601. Fax 0184-667-655. www.miramaresanremo.it. 59 units. 94€–154€ ($108–$177) double without sea view; 124€–196€ ($143–$225) double with sea view; 300€–500€ ($345–$575) suite. For half-board add 20€ ($23) per person; for full board in doubles add 18€ ($21); for full board in suites, add 53€ ($61) per person. Breakfast included. AE, DC, MC, V. **Amenities:** Italian/international/regional restaurant; bar; indoor heated seawater pool; golf course (6km/3¾ miles); concierge; tour desk; car-rental desk; room service (limited); babysitting; laundry service; dry cleaning; nonsmoking rooms. *In room:* TV, minibar, hair dryer.

Riviera   While convenient to the beach and other attractions, this family-run pensione, on the ground floor of a rather dire cement-cube hillside apartment house, is close to the center but just far enough off the beaten path to enjoy peace and quiet, and it often has rooms available when other places in town fill up. Oriental runners and attractive slip-covered furniture lend an air of elegance to the public areas. The guest rooms, most of which overlook the sea and the Old Town, are spacious and modestly but attractively furnished in modern style with an eye to comfort—beds are firm, there are ample surfaces on which to spread out belongings, and most of the bathrooms are up-to-date.

Corso degli Inglesi 86, 18038 San Remo. ℂ **0184-502-215.** Fax 0184-502-216. hotelriviera@ciaoweb.it. 14 units. 57€–83€ ($66–$95) double; 75€–115€ ($86–$132) suite. Breakfast 5€ ($6). For half pension, add 45€–65€ ($52–$75) per day. AE, DC, MC, V. Parking 2.50€ ($2.90) in hotel lot or 7€ ($8) in garage. Sometimes closed a few weeks in Nov and Mar. **Amenities:** Restaurant; bar; room service (limited). *In room:* TV, minibar, hair dryer.

Sole Mare ⭐ Don't let the location on a drab side street near the train station put you off. This cheerful pensione on the upper floors of an apartment house is a delight and offers its guests a friendly welcome along with some of the best-value lodgings in the resort area. A lounge, bar area, and dining room are airy and spacious and flooded with light, with gleaming white tile floors, blond-wood furniture, and doors leading out to a wide terrace. The large guest rooms are also cheerful and are equipped with the trappings of much more expensive hotels—pleasant modern furnishings and soothing pastel fabrics, TVs and mini-bars, small but modern and well-lit bathrooms—and almost all enjoy sea views, about half from wide balconies. Recent renovations included the installation of air-conditioning in 18 of the 21 rooms as well as construction of a new bar.

Via Carli 23, 18038 San Remo. ℂ **0184-577-105.** Fax 0184-532-778. www.solemarehotel.com. 21 units. 77€ ($89) double. Half-board (obligatory in Aug) 57€ ($66) per person if stay is at least 2 days; full board 62€ ($71) per person if stay is at least 3 days. Continental breakfast 6.20€ ($7). AE, DC, MC, V. **Amenities:** Restaurant (international cuisine); bar; concierge; room service (24-hr.); babysitting. *In room:* A/C (ask to be in one of the rooms with A/C if it's important to you), TV, minibar, hair dryer, safe.

WHERE TO DINE

Antica Trattoria Piccolo Mondo ⭐⭐ *Value* LIGURIAN The attentive staff will make you feel at home the moment you step into the perpetually crowded rooms of this decades-old trattoria on a narrow side street near the waterfront in the commercial district. The clientele is local, and they come here in droves to enjoy the comfortable atmosphere (which includes the furnishings installed when the restaurant opened in the 1920s) and the distinctly Ligurian fare—*verdura rip-iena* (fresh vegetables stuffed with rice and seafood), fresh fish, and *polpo con patate* (octopus with potatoes). The menu changes daily to incorporate what is fresh in the markets, but also includes excellent risottos, pasta dishes, and meat dishes that are standards. (The grilled veal chop topped with fresh mushrooms is delicious.)

Via Piave 7. ℂ **0184-509-012.** Reservations recommended. Primi 5.50€–8.50€ ($6–$10); secondi 7€–15€ ($8–$17). No credit cards. Tues–Sat 12:30–1:50pm and 7:30–9:30pm.

Cantine Sanremese LIGURIAN This cozy publike restaurant devoted to the local cuisine is firmly planted in the center of the modern town, as if to suggest that old San Remo traditions are not to be discarded. Patrons share tables as they enjoy the wide selections of wine by the glass (from 1.50€/$1.75) and sample the offerings that owner Renzo Morselli and his family prepare daily. The best way to dine here is to not order a whole meal, but to sample all the dishes that tempt you. These may include *sardemaira,* the local focaccia-like bread, *torta verde* (a quiche of fresh green vegetables), and many kinds of soups, including a minestrone thick with fresh vegetables and garnished with pesto.

Via Palazzo 7. ℂ 0184-572-063. Reservations recommended. Primi and secondi 7€–12€ ($8–$14). AE, MC, V. Tues–Sun 10am–3pm and 5–9:30pm. Closed last 10 days of June and all of Nov.

Il Mulattiere ★★ *Finds* LIGURIAN   Anyone who goes to San Remo should plan to visit this family-run trattoria in La Pigna, the oldest part of San Remo. Whether you come for lunch or dinner or just to enjoy a glass of wine, you'll probably first want to stroll around the surrounding quarter, an amazing warren of steep lanes clinging to the side of a hill. This two-floor eatery is as rich in character as its surroundings—the tables, covered with red-checked cloths, are overhung with antique farm implements (*Il Mulattiere* means "mule driver") and other rural artifacts. The menu is simple, featuring Ligurian specialties that change daily and often include delicious *crostini all'acciughe* (toasted bread topped with fresh anchovies), *zuppa al pomodoro* (a spicy soup of fresh tomatoes) or minestrone, and many fresh pastas. For a light meal, you can choose from an antipasto table laden with fresh vegetables and olives, and accompany it with a bowl of pasta.

Via Palma 11. ℂ 0184-502-662. Primi 4€–7.50€ ($4.60–$9); secondi 6€–8€ ($7–$9). Menù completo 9.50€ ($11) includes antipasto and a primo. No credit cards. Thurs–Tues noon–3pm and 7:30–10pm.

Ristorante da Giannino ★ LIGURIAN   With Anna in the kitchen and Giuseppe in the modern dining room, the Gasparini family runs one of the top (but also priciest) restaurants in town, down by the yachting port behind breezy picture windows. The menu is well balanced between surf and turf, and you can follow a *risotto* or *linguine ai frutti di mare* (rice or noodles richly studded with seafood) with *coniglio alle erbe* (rabbit roasted with fresh herbs), or catch of the day grilled or served under a cream sauce spiced with whole green peppercorns.

Corso Trento e Trieste 23. ℂ 0184-504-014. Reservations recommended. Primi 18€–25€ ($20–$29); secondi 22€–31€ ($25–$36); tasting menu 55€ ($63) without wine. AE, DC, MC, V. Tues–Sat noon–2pm; Mon–Sat 7:30–9:45pm.

Ristorante L'Airone ★ LIGURIAN/PIZZA   With its pale gold walls and green-hued tables and chairs, this delightful, friendly restaurant in a pedestrian-only section of the city center looks like it's been transported over the border from Provence. The food, though, is definitely Ligurian, with a wide selection of fresh pastas, including gnocchi in pesto sauce, followed perhaps by a *grigliata mista* of fresh fish or grilled sole. For a more casual meal, light-crusted pizzas emerge from a tiled oven in the rear. In good weather, meals are served in a small garden out back covered by a reed-thatched tent—and there are some tables on the (admittedly nothing special) piazza outside.

Piazza Eroi Sanremesi 12. ℂ 0184-531-469. Primi 6€–14€ ($7–$16); secondi 7€–17€ ($8–$20). Pizza 5€–9.50€ ($6–$11); menù turistico 13€ ($15) without wine; *menu degustazione* 31€ ($36) not including wine. DC, MC, V. Fri–Wed noon–2:30pm and 7:30–11:30pm.

THE CAFE & BAR SCENE

Agora Cafè, on Piazza San Siro (no phone), which faces San Remo's cathedral, makes no claim other than to be a comfortable watering hole, a function it performs very well. For footsore travelers, the terrace out front, facing the pretty stone piazza and cathedral of San Siro, is a welcome oasis. Sandwiches and other light fare are served late into the night, when an after-dinner crowd tends to make this one of the livelier spots in town. Closed Monday.

Wanderings through the center of town should include a stop at Giovanni Fabris's handsome wine bar **Enoteca Bacchus** ★★ (Via Roma 65; ℂ 0184-530-990), open Monday to Saturday 10am to 9pm. This is where you can also stock up on olive oil and other Ligurian foodstuffs. Wine is served by the glass at a sit-down bar or one of the small tables and you can accompany your libations with fresh focaccia, cheeses, vegetable tarts, and even such substantial fare as *buridda,* a dish of salted cod, tomatoes, and other vegetables.

BORDIGHERA

Known throughout Italy for its palm trees, **Bordighera** lays claim to the legend that the seeds of date palms carried across the sea from Egypt first took root in European soil here. To this day Bordighera has the honor of supplying its ubiquitous fronds to the Vatican for Palm Sunday services. The palm trees create a verdant canopy that extends up the hillside from the Mediterranean and the cluster of modern seaside development to the charming Old Town. Bordighera's other claim to fame is its enormous popularity with elderly Italian and British pensioners (its reputation as a getaway for retirees is similar to that of St. Petersburg in Florida). If you want glitter, you may be happier in San Remo; on the other hand, if you want to enjoy some peace and quiet and the same verdant vegetation that attracted Claude Monet, Bordighera may be just the stop for you.

ESSENTIALS

GETTING THERE   By Train   There are trains almost hourly to and from **Genoa** (regional: 2 hr. 20 min.; high-speed: 2 hr.), and two to three trains per hour connecting with **San Remo** (13 min.).

By Bus   Riviera Trasporti buses (© 0184-592-706; www.rivieratrasporti.it) run every 15 minutes between **San Remo** and Bordighera (20 min.). Buses also run between Bordighera and **Ventimiglia.**

By Car   You can take the A10 autostrada between Bordighera and San Remo, but the coast road, S1, is almost as fast. In fact, there is such a contiguous line of development along the route that you won't know where one town ends and the other begins.

VISITOR INFORMATION   The **tourist office** is at Via Vittorio Emanuele 172 (© 0184-262-322; fax 0184-264-455). It's open Monday to Saturday 8am to 7pm and Sunday 9am to 1pm (closed Sun Oct–May).

FESTIVALS & MARKETS   It's a sign of the pleasant nature of this resort that one of the major annual events is a **humor festival,** held in late August/early September. Stand-up comics perform along the streets and seaside promenade, humorous films are shown, and general merriment is presented. **Thursday morning's market** fills the Lungomare Argentina (see below) with stalls selling a bit of everything.

STROLLING AROUND TOWN

Lungomare Argentina is Bordighera's seaside promenade, and it extends for about a kilometer along a wide **beach;** the pebbly strand is public, so you can settle down anywhere you find a spot. If you want a more civilized beach experience, you can part with 5€ ($6) for a lounge at any number of beach stations. The promenade remains lively well past the height of the day, and it affords spectacular sunset views (since it faces west toward France's Côte d'Azur) that most of the town turns out to witness. The modern town, which in parts is unattractively developed, clusters around the seafront, with many businesses lining coastal route S1.

You need only head inland, though, to discover how lovely Bordighera is, with palm-fringed streets and pastel-colored villas hidden behind the walls of verdant gardens. The fortified **Old Town** ⭐, a picturesque cluster of ochre-colored stucco and red tile, is several hundred meters up the hillside from the sea. Aside from a few restaurants and a charming hotel (see below), there aren't specific attractions that draw visitors to town, rather it is the fusion of beauty of centuries-old architecture, charming ambience, and stunning views from the gardens that skirt the centuries-old walls. From here, you can also easily check out the sights surrounding nearby **Ventimiglia,** detailed in the next section.

WHERE TO STAY

Capo   The only hotel in the old city is a delightful pinkish structure surrounded by palm trees and an inviting terrace where many guests choose to spend most of their time. The hilltop location affords stunning views over the lower town and sea below, and there always seems to be a cooling breeze. Vaulted ceilings and colorful majolica-tile floors lend almost a Moorish look to the lobby, sitting rooms, and dining area, but once upstairs the decor becomes utilitarian, though not unpleasing. Furnishings in the largish guest rooms are 1960s-style modern, but unobtrusive enough not to be offensive. Bathrooms have not been updated for a while and tend to be small but are certainly adequate. The best features in the rooms are the shuttered doors that open to balconies and afford dazzling views up and down the coast. The one drawback here? The owners aren't particularly friendly, but this is still a desirable place to stay.

Via Al Capo 3, 18012 Bordighera. © **0184-261-558.** Fax 0184-262-463. 12 units. 80€ ($92) double. Breakfast 8€ ($9). AE, DC, MC, V. Free parking. Closed Nov and sometimes in Oct. **Amenities:** Restaurant; bar. *In room:* TV, minibar, hair dryer, safe.

Piccolo Lido ★★   This pink, sun-filled villa is at the end of the seafront promenade, with direct access to the pebbled beach but far enough away from the main seafront avenue and the center of things to provide a great deal of peace and quiet. The public rooms are airy and bright, opening onto terraces like the one on the second floor scattered with deck chairs that let you soak in the sun and sounds of the surf. Upstairs, the newly renovated rooms are bright and attractive, with white tile floors, pastel area rugs, and bright contemporary furnishings that include comfortable lounge chairs and some nice extras like round tables so you can dine in your room if you choose. Bathrooms are gleaming and modern, and nicely equipped with hair dryers and heated towel racks. The best rooms, of course, are those that open onto terraces overlooking the sea.

Lungomare Argentina 2, 18012 Bordighera. © **0184-261-297.** Fax 0184-262-316. www.hotelpiccololido.it. 33 units. 81€–141€ ($93–$162) double without sea view; 92€–141€ ($106–$162) double with sea view. Half and full board available for stays of 3 days or longer 66€–95€ ($76–$109). Rates include buffet breakfast. AE, DC, MC, V. Parking 12€ ($14) in garage. Closed late Oct to late Dec. **Amenities:** Restaurant (Italian cuisine); bar; children's center; concierge; room service (limited); babysitting; laundry service. *In room:* A/C, TV, minibar, hair dryer, safe.

WHERE TO DINE

Caffè Giglio CAFE   The most popular cafe in Bordighera seems to suit patrons of all stripes, whether they be British pensioners who sit on the terrace and sip tea, teenagers who stop on their way to the beach for a gelato (in 30 flavors, 1.50€/$1.75 and up), or night owls looking for a place to enjoy a glass of wine (not easy to do in this sleepy town). As a result, this is almost a mandatory stop for visitors interested in checking out the local scene. The more substantial fare includes sandwiches, salads, and crepes, which, depending on the filling, are served either as a meal or as a dessert.

Via Vittorio Emanuele 158. © **0184-261-530.** Panini and snacks from 2€ ($2.30). Tues–Fri 11am–3pm and 7pm–1am; Sat 11am–1am; Sun 3pm–1am.

Magiargé ★★ LIGURIAN   Recently expanded to two rooms, this attractive trattoria is lined with rustic cabinets that display the Ligurian wines and olive oils Magiargé offers for sale. These staples are shown to their best advantage in the delicious meals that emerge from the cramped kitchen. Only three or four pastas and main courses are prepared daily and are announced on a blackboard. Pasta selections usually include *trenette* or another pasta with a rich pesto sauce, and there is always a selection of fresh fish and one or two meat courses, often including a game hen cooked with local olives and fresh vegetables, a house specialty.

Piazza G. Viale. ✆ 0184-262-946. www.magiarge.it. Reservations recommended. Primi 8€ ($9); secondi 10€ ($12). AE, MC, V. Thurs–Tues noon–2:30pm and 8–10pm.

Piemontese ★ PIEMONTESE/SEAFOOD   Gino and Giuliana, the husband and wife proprietors, oversee things in both the kitchen and simply adorned dining room a few blocks off the seafront, serving up the cuisine of the nearby Piedmonte region. While the menu includes such classic Piemontese dishes as risotto cooked with Barolo wine and a rich *torta alla ricotta* (ricotta quiche), the offerings also suggest Liguria with their reliance on fresh seafood. Aside from simple but memorable grilled fish, there are also such delightful dishes as warm seafood salad and *tagliatelle al nero di seppia*, freshly made tagliatelle blackened with squid ink.

Via Roseto 8. ✆ 0184-261-651. Primi 5€–11€ ($6–$12); secondi 8.20€–19€ ($9–$22). AE, DC, MC, V. Wed–Mon 12:30–2:30pm and 7–10pm. Closed Nov 15–Dec 15.

VENTIMIGLIA

Ventimiglia is a quiet and somewhat unremarkable Italian town 11km (6¾ miles) from the French border and only minutes from Bordighera and San Remo. Although the town holds little of particular interest, the surrounding coast and hills boast a few of the most interesting sights along this stretch of coastline.

ESSENTIALS

GETTING THERE   By Train   There are one to three hourly trains from **Bordighera** and **San Remo** (7 min. on regional trains).

By Bus   Riviera Trasporti buses (✆ **0184-592-706**; www.rivieratrasporti.it) run every 15 minutes between **Bordighera** and Ventimiglia (10–30 min. depending on traffic).

By Car   Since traffic on the coastal S1 road can be extremely heavy approaching the French border, it's often faster to use the A10 autostrada from Bordighera or San Remo.

VISITOR INFORMATION   The **tourist office** is at Via Cavour 61 (✆ and fax **0184-351-183**). It's open Monday to Saturday 8am to 7pm and Sunday 9am to 1pm (closed Sun Oct–May).

FESTIVALS & MARKETS   July's **Battle of the Flowers** is fought by contestants vying to build the most elaborate float, three-dimensional sculptures whose surfaces are mosaics made up of thousands of flowers. **Friday morning's market** sells food, clothes, and all sorts of useful items in the park between Via Vittorio Veneto and the shoreline at Lungo Roia Girolamo Rossi and Passeggiata Oberdan.

SIGHTS IN TOWN

Sights in Ventimiglia are divided between the mostly modern, lower section of town, built after 1872 to service the new train station, and **Ventimiglia Alta,** a medieval town with a sweeping panorama from **Piazza Belvedere** ★ at the east end of Via Giuseppe Verdi. From here, turn up Via del Capo to reach the 11th-to 12th-century **Cattedrale dell'Assunta** and its octagonal **baptistery,** possibly built atop a temple to Juno. Via del Capo becomes palazzo-lined **Via Garibaldi.** At Piazza Fontana/Piazza del Canto, head to the back right corner to continue up Via Piedmont to Piazza Colletta and the isolated **Church of San Michele** ✪, the current version built around the 10th century using bits of ancient stones: The stoups and one of the crypt columns are Roman milestones, and two of the granite pillars in the crypt hail from a temple to Castor and Pollux.

Though today mostly modern, the more bustling **lower town** is actually built atop the remains of the ancient Roman border settlement of *Albintimilium,* which you can see a bit of at the far eastern end of main drag Corso Genova (the S1) in the splendidly preserved 2nd-century A.D., 5,000-seat **Roman theater** ✪, sandwiched between the road and the train tracks.

THE SURROUNDING SIGHTS

Giardino Hanbury (Hanbury Gardens), on the coast 6.5km (4 miles) east of Ventimiglia, is one of Europe's largest and most noted botanical collections. British merchant Sir Thomas Hanbury planted the gardens, which descend on terraces to the sea, in 1867 to nurture exotic species from five continents. As immensely important as the gardens were to the 19th-century study of botany, today they are a pleasure dome, a stunningly beautiful bower with heart-stopping views of the sea around every corner. The gardens (✆ **0184-229-507**) are open daily from the last Sunday in March through October (hours vary by season) and Thursday to Tuesday from November to the last Sunday in March 10am to 5pm. Last entry 1 hour before closing. Admission is 6€ ($7), or 15€ ($17) for a family ticket covering two parents and up to three kids under 18.

At **Balzi Rossi (Red Rocks;** ✆ **0184-38-113**), right on the French border 1.6km (1 mile) farther east along the coast from Giardino Hanbury, one of prehistoric Europe's most advanced Paleolithic cultures lived in cliff-side caves—first Neanderthals (80,000–35,000 years ago) and later Homo Sapiens (35,000–10,000 years ago). Restoration work should be finished by the time you read this, allowing visitors to once again visit several of the caves, the most interesting of which is Grotto del Cavglione, named for a horse etched on one of the walls. Most of the finds—including weapons, fertility figures (copies; the originals are in France), simple stone tools, five human skeletons, and even a bit of Homo erectus hip some 230,000 years old—are in the small Museo Preistorico split across two buildings. Many of the caves were damaged, and the only fossils once visible in situ destroyed, when the rail tunnels above were blown up during World War II. The caves and museum are open Tuesday to Sunday 8:30am to 7:30pm; admission is 2€ ($2.30), 1€ ($1.15) for ages 19 to 26, and free for those under 18 and over 65.

Another excursion from Ventimiglia takes you inland for 9.5km (6 miles) up the Val Nervia to **Dolceacqua,** a stone village that is as sweetly picturesque as its name implies it will be. The ruins of a 16th-century castle crown the collection of houses that climb from the banks of the river, spanned here by a single-arched medieval bridge. If you stumble into town at certain times of the year, you will find the locals engaged in strange revelries: On January 20 (St. Sebastian's Day), a man carrying a tree hung with communion hosts leads a procession through the streets; on August 15, costumed dancers celebrate Ferragosto.

From Ventimiglia, **Riviera Trasporti buses** (✆ **0184-592-706**; www.riviera trasporti.it), which leave from Via Cavour near the train station, make but a handful of daily runs (currently at 9:05am, 11:05am, 1:25pm, and 2:25pm) that stop first at the **Hanbury Gardens** (15 min.), then swing by the **Balzi Rossi** (30 min. from Ventimiglia) before returning to Ventimiglia. The stops aren't named after these sights, so be sure to let the driver know when you want to get off. To get back to Ventimiglia, hail the bus from the same stop where you got off.

There are also two direct buses (currently 7:05am and 12:05pm) from Ventimiglia to Balzi Rossi (15 min.), or you can stay on the **train** (usually only on local runs) past Ventimiglia to Menton-Garavan station (7 min. from Ventimiglia), from which Balzi Rossi is a 20- to 30-minute walk.

Ten buses a day leave Ventimiglia for **Dolceacqua** (20–30 min.).

WHERE TO STAY & DINE

When you're in town, you might want to grab a meal at **Marco Polo,** Passeggiata Felice Cavallotti 2 (© **0184-352-678**), with excellent Ligurian cooking, a good wine cellar, and outdoor tables right on the seaside promenade; meals average 45€ to 55€ ($52–$63) not including wine.

Hotel Ristorante La Riserva di Castel d'Appio ✦   There are plenty of narrow, switchbacked, two-lane roads in Italy, but the one up here may take the cake. The "castel" is actually a modern hotel, with modular furnishings and lurid chipped stone floors but fantastic coastal panoramas from the room balconies, most looking west over the French Riviera and Monte Carlo, some east over Italy. Recent renovations have added three junior suites with such a view. In a separate building are several rooms sharing common entranceways so you can have a family suite (though the owners may soon turn these into proper suites). A few ground-floor rooms lack the sweeping views but open onto small lawns as compensation. The restaurant is on a panoramic terrace next to the pool and billiards, foosball, and Ping-Pong tables. There's a pub with karaoke, but it only opens in the months when the hotel part is closed (Oct–Mar).

c.p. 108, 18039 Ventimiglia (IM). © **0184-229-533.** Fax 0184-229-712. www.lariserva.it. 23 units. 120€–130€ ($138–$150) double; 145€–156€ ($167–$179) triple; 190€–217€ ($219–$250) little apt for 3 people; 227€–248€ ($261–$285) little apt for 4 people; 248€–258€ ($285–$297) little apt for 5 people; 260€–280€ ($299–$322) jr. suite. Breakfast 8€ ($9). AE, DC, MC, V. Closed Oct–Mar. **Amenities:** Italian/international restaurant; bar; outdoor pool; bike rental; children's center; video arcade; concierge; tour desk; room service (limited); babysitting; nonsmoking rooms. *In room:* A/C, TV, dataport, minibar, hair dryer.

3 The Riviera di Levante: Camogli, Santa Margherita Ligure, Portofino & Rapallo

Camogli: 26km (16 miles) E of Genoa; Santa Margherita Ligure: 31km (19 miles) E of Genoa; Portofino: 38km (24 miles) E of Genoa; Rapallo: 37km (23 miles) E of Genoa

The coast east of Genoa, the **Riviera di Levante (Shore of the Rising Sun),** is more ruggedly beautiful than the Riviera Ponente, less developed, and hugged by mountains that plunge into the sea. Four of the coast's most appealing towns are within a few miles of one another, clinging to the shores of the Monte Portofino Promontory just east of Genoa: Camogli, Santa Margherita Ligure, Rapallo, and little Portofino.

CAMOGLI

Camogli (abbreviated from "Casa dei Mogli"—House of the Wives) was named for the women who held down the fort while their husbands went to sea for years on end. The little town remains delightfully unspoiled, an authentic Ligurian fishing port with tall, ochre-painted houses fronting the harbor and a nice swath of beach. Given also its excellent accommodations and eateries, Camogli is a lovely place to base yourself while exploring the Riviera Levante. This is also a restful retreat from which you can explore Genoa, which is only about 30 minutes away.

ESSENTIALS

GETTING THERE   By Train   One to three trains per hour ply the coastline, connecting Camogli with **Genoa** (30–45 min.), **Santa Margherita** (5 min.), and **Monterosso** (50–60 min.) and other Cinque Terre towns.

By Bus   There is at least one Tigullio ((©) **0185-288-835;** www.tigullio trasporti.it) bus an hour, often more, from **Santa Margherita;** since the bus must go around and not under the Monte Portofino Promontory, the trip takes quite a bit longer than the train—about half an hour.

By Boat   In summer, boats operated by Golfo Paradiso ((©) **0185-772-091;** www.golfoparadiso.it) sail from Camogli to **Portofino.**

By Car   The fastest route into the region is the A12 autostrada from Genoa; exit at Recco for Camogli (the trip takes less than half an hour). Route S1 along the coast from Genoa is much slower but more scenic.

VISITOR INFORMATION   The **tourist office** is across from the train station at Via XX Settembre 33 ((©) and fax **0185-771-066;** www.camogli.it or www.portofinocoast.it). It's open Monday to Saturday 9am to 12:30pm and 3:30 to 7pm (Mar–Oct it closes at noon and 6:30pm), Sunday 9am to 1pm.

FESTIVALS & MARKETS   Camogli throws a much-attended annual party, the **Sagra del Pesce** ⭐⭐, on the second Sunday of May, where the town fries up thousands of sardines in a 3.6m (12-ft.) diameter pan and passes them around for free—a practice that is accompanied by an annual outcry in the press about health concerns and even accusations that frozen fish is used. Even so, the beloved event is much attended.

The first Sunday of August, Camogli stages the lovely **Festa della Stella Maris.** A procession of boats sails to Punta Chiappa, a point of land about 1.5km (1 mile) down the coast, and releases 10,000 burning candles. Meanwhile, the same number of candles are set afloat from the Camogli beach. If currents are favorable, the burning candles will come together at sea, signifying a year of unity for couples who watch the spectacle.

EXPLORING THE TOWN

Camogli is clustered around its delightful waterfront, from which the town ascends via steep, stair-cased lanes to Via XX Settembre, one of the few streets in the town proper to accommodate cars (this is where the train station, tourist office, and many shops and other businesses are located). Adding to the charm of this setting is the fact that the oldest part of Camogli juts into the harbor on a little point (once an island) where ancient houses cling to the little **Castello Dragone** (now closed to the public) and the 12th-century **Basilica di Santa Maria Assunta** ((©) **0185-770-130**), with an impressively over-baroqued interior open daily 7:30am to noon and 3:30 to 7pm. Most visitors, though, seem drawn to the pleasant **seaside promenade** ⭐ that runs the length of the town. You can swim from the pebbly beach below, and should you feel your towel doesn't provide enough comfort, rent a lounge from one of the few beach stations for 5€ ($6).

WHERE TO STAY

Augusta *(Value)*   This is an acceptable alternative if the Camogliese (below) is full, and, more than a fallback, it's pleasant and convenient, with a handy location a short walk up a steep staircase from the harbor. The couple and their son who run this pensione also operate the ground-floor trattoria, which serves as a sitting room for the guest rooms upstairs and makes it easy to enjoy a cup of coffee or glass of wine. The rooms are extremely plain, with functional furnishings and drab decor slowly being spruced up (new modular units and wood floors in 2000), but they are large and clean, and have good-size bathrooms. You also get 15 minutes of free Internet access (in the reception area) per day. Ask for a room in front—those in back face the train tracks.

Via Schiaffino 100, 16032 Camogli. ⓒ 0185-770-592. www.htlaugusta.com. 14 units. 50€–78€ ($58–$90) double. Breakfast 6€ ($7) per person. Show your Frommer's guide for a discount (especially during slow periods). AE, DC, MC, V. Parking 13€ ($15). **Amenities:** Restaurant (local cuisine); bar; room service (limited). *In room:* TV, dataport.

Cenobio dei Dogi ★★   This Ligurian getaway sits just above the sea at one end of town and against the forested flank of Monte Portofino. The oldest part of the hotel incorporates an aristocratic villa dating from 1565; a chapel, still occasionally used as such, dates from the 17th century. Converted to a hotel in 1956, the premises now include several wings that wrap graciously around a garden on one side and a series of terraces facing the sea on the other. There's a pool and a private beach, and several airy salons, including a lovely bar and lounge area and a glass-enclosed breakfast room that hangs over the sea. The guest rooms vary considerably in size and shape, but all are furnished with a tasteful mix of reproduction writing desks, contemporary glass-top tables, and—especially in "standard"-category rooms—island-style furnishings (rattan, bent bamboo headboards, and the like). Many overlook the sea and have balconies, and a few have terraces that lead directly to the pool. In most rooms, the bathrooms have been redone with sizable counter space and luxurious fixtures.

Via Cuneo 34, 16032 Camogli. ⓒ 0185-7241. Fax 0185-772-796. www.cenobio.it. 106 units. 150€–203€ ($173–$233) standard double with garden view; 196€–281€ ($225–$323) standard double with sea view; 175€–244€ ($201–$281) superior double with garden view; 217€–311€ ($250–$358) superior double with sea view; 258€–348€ ($297–$400) jr. suite; 361€–425€ ($415–$489) suite. Rates include continental breakfast. Half-board supplement 35€ ($40) per person, full-board supplement 70€ ($81). AE, DC, MC, V. **Amenities:** 2 Ligurian/International restaurants (1 at beach); 2 bars; indoor pool; outdoor saltwater pool; 18-hole golf course (in Rapallo, 7km/4¼ miles away); outdoor tennis courts (lit); exercise room and sauna across the street; watersports equipment; bike rental; concierge; tour desk; car-rental desk; salon; room service (limited); massage (across the street); babysitting; laundry service; dry cleaning (48-hr.). *In room:* A/C, TV, dataport, minibar, hair dryer, safe.

La Camogliese ★★   A lot of Genovese come out to spend the weekend in this friendly, attractive little hotel near the waterfront, and they appreciate it for the same simple charms that will appeal to travelers from farther afield. (In fact, given the hotel's popularity, it's always a good idea to reserve, and it's essential on weekends.) Proprietor Bruno and his family extend guests a warm welcome, and are happy to help them navigate the logistics of visiting the different towns on the nearby coast (which is especially easy to do from here, since the hotel is at the bottom of a staircase that leads to the train station). Rooms are large, bright, and airy and decorated in modern furnishings that include comfortable beds. Some have balconies and, although the house isn't right on the waterfront, it faces a little river and is close enough to the beach that a slight twist of the head usually affords a view of the sea (best from corner room no. 16B). Bathrooms are small but adequate, and they remodeled the first floor in 2000 to add a breakfast room and overhaul the rooms on that level. They've also added several new beachfront rooms for 67€ to 77€ ($77–$89).

Additionally, the family runs the beachfront restaurant of the same name just down the road (see below).

Via Garibaldi 55, 16032 Camogli. ℭ **0185-771-402.** Fax 0185-774-024. www.lacamogliese.it. 22 **units.** 69€–77€ ($79–$89) double. 50€–55€ ($58–$63) half-board per person, 60€–65€ ($69–$75) full board per person. Rates include breakfast. AE, DC, MC, V. Parking 8€ ($9). **Amenities:** Outdoor pool; exercise room; concierge; salon; room service (limited); babysitting; laundry service. *In room:* TV, dataport, hair dryer, safe.

WHERE TO DINE

Bar Primula CAFE/LIGHT MEALS   Camogli's most fashionable bar is on the waterfront, and it seems as if just about anything goes here. Drinking is taken seriously, as self-proclaimed "Capo Barman" Renato Montanari is well known in his trade. You can also enjoy a light meal (a pasta dish and seafood plate or two are usually available, along with sandwiches, salads, and omelets), but many regulars come in for a cup of the delicious house espresso and dessert, which presents a difficult choice between the delicious ice cream and pastries (if you're torn, try the sumptuous Comogliese chocolate rum-ball–like concoction).

Via Garibaldi 140. ℭ **0185-770-351.** Sandwiches 3.50€–4€ ($4–$4.60); dishes and other light fare 6€– 10€ ($7–$12); gelato from 1.75€ ($2). AE, MC, V. Fri–Wed 9am–2am.

Ristorante La Camogliese ★★ SEAFOOD   You probably won't be surprised to find that the menu at this bright, seaside spot, perched over the beach on stilts, leans heavily to seafood. In fact, when the weather is pleasant and the windows that surround the dining room are open, you feel you are at sea (admittedly a sea with piped-in pop music). It's one of the most popular and appealing restaurants in town. The hearty fish soup for two is a meal in itself (at 20€/$23, it should be), as are any number of pastas topped with clam and other seafood sauces, and there is always a tempting array of fresh-fish entrees, caught that day, on hand as well.

Via Garibaldi 78. ℭ **0185-771-086.** Primi 6.50€–9.50€ ($7–$11); secondi 11€–21€ ($12–$24). AE, DC, MC, V. Oct–June Thurs–Tues 12:30–2:30pm and 7:30–10:30pm (daily July–Sept). Closed Nov.

A HOTEL BETWEEN CAMOGLI & SANTA MARGHERITA LIGURE

Hotel Portofino Kulm ★★   This grand old hotel slung in a skyscraping hammock of greenery in the midst of the Tigullio's parkland halfway between Camogli and Rapallo/Santa Margherita Ligure was opened in 1908, but for decades stood derelict until Camogli's Cenobio dei Dogi overhauled it to reopen in 2000. The long vistas sweep across the forest down to the Riviera north of the promontory toward Genoa in one direction, and in the other south over Santa Margherita Ligure down the coast toward the Cinque Terre. Many balconies and rooftop terraces take full advantage of the panoramas. The modest-size, carpeted rooms come with wrought-iron bedsteads, stylish furnishings, marble bathrooms, and queen-size beds. The best ones come with those sea views from balconies— though even many "garden view" rooms actually get a bit of sea in the vista. They host lots of conventions during the week, turning to a tourism-based clientele on the weekends. Four rooms are in a separate structure a smidgen higher up the driveway with even better views.

Viale Bernardo Gaggini 23 (6km/3¾ miles from Camogli on the over-mountain road to Santa Margherita Ligure), 16030 Ruta di Camogli, Portofino Vetta (GE). ℭ **0185-7361.** Fax 0185-776-622. www.portofino kulm.it. 77 units. 130€–176€ ($150–$202) double with park view; 155€–207€ ($178–$238) double with sea view; 171€–233€ ($197–$268) double with sea view and balcony. Rates include breakfast. AE, DC, MC, V. **Amenities:** International/Ligurian restaurant; bar; indoor heated pool; tiny exercise room (well, 2 Stairmasters); Jacuzzi; bike rental; concierge; tour desk; car-rental desk; courtesy car (shuttle to Camogli);

salon; room service (limited); massage; babysitting; laundry service; dry cleaning. *In room:* A/C, TV, data-port, minibar, hair dryer, safe.

SANTA MARGHERITA LIGURE

Santa Margherita had one brief moment in the spotlight, at the beginning of the 20th century when it was an internationally renowned retreat. Fortunately, the seaside town didn't let fame spoil its charm, and now that it's no longer as well known a destination as its glitzy neighbor Portofino, it might be the Mediterranean retreat of your dreams. A palm-lined harbor, nice beach, and a friendly ambience make Santa Margherita a fine place to settle down for a few days of sun and relaxation.

ESSENTIALS

GETTING THERE   By Train   Between two and three coastal trains per hour connect Santa Margherita with **Genoa** (regional: 35 min.; high-speed: 25 min.), **Camogli** (5 min.), Rapallo (3 min.), and **Monterosso** (regional: 55 min.; high-speed: 40 min.) of the Cinque Terre.

By Bus   There is at least one Tigullio (© **0185-288-834;** www.tigullio trasporti.it) bus an hour to **Camogli** (30–35 min.) and to **Rapallo** (10 min.), leaving from Piazza Vittorio Veneto. Buses also ply the stunningly beautiful coast road to **Portofino,** leaving every 20 minutes from the train station and Piazza Vittorio Veneto (25 min.).

By Boat   Tigullio ferries (© **0185-284-670;** www.traghettiportofino.it) make hourly trips to **Portofino** (15 min.) and **Rapallo** (15 min.). In summer there is a boat about 4 days a week to **Vernazza** in the Cinque Terre. Hours of service vary considerably with season; schedules are posted on the docks at Piazza Martiri della Liberta.

By Car   The fastest route into the region is the A12 autostrada from Genoa; the trip takes about half an hour. Route S1 along the coast from Genoa is much slower but more scenic.

VISITOR INFORMATION   The **tourist office** is near the harbor at Via XXV Aprile 2B (© **0185-287-485;** fax 0185-283-034; www.apttigullio.liguria.it). Summer hours are daily 9am to 12:30pm and 3 to 6pm; winter hours are Monday to Saturday 9am to 12:30pm and 2:30 to 5:30pm.

FESTIVALS & MARKETS   Santa Margherita's winters are delightfully mild, but even so, the town rushes to usher in spring with a **Festa di Primavera,** held on moveable dates in February. Like the Sagra del Pesce in neighboring Camogli, this festival also features food—in this case fritters are prepared on the beach and served around roaring bonfires. One of the more interesting daily spectacles in town is the **fish market** on Lungomare Marconi; this colorful event transpires from 8am to 12:30pm. On Fridays cars are banned from Corso Matteotti, Santa Margherita's major street for food shopping, turning the area into an open-air **food market.**

EXPLORING THE TOWN

Life in Santa Margherita centers around its palm-fringed **waterfront,** a pleasant string of marinas, docks for pleasure and fishing boats, and pebbly beaches. Landlubbers congregate in the cafes that spill out into the town's two seaside squares, Piazza Martiri della Liberta and Piazza Vittorio Veneto.

The station is on a hill above the waterfront, and a staircase in front of the entrance will lead you down into the heart of town. Santa Margherita's one landmark of note is its namesake **Basilica di Santa Margherita,** just off the seafront on Piazza Caprera. The church is open daily from 8am to noon and 3 to 7pm and is well worth a visit to view the extravagant, gilded, chandeliered interior.

WHERE TO STAY

Annabella   The nice proprietors manage to accommodate groups of just about any size in this old apartment that's been converted to an attractive pensione, with comfortable old modular furniture and whitewashed walls. Some of the rooms sleep up to four, and one family-style arrangement includes a large room with a double bed and a tiny room outfitted with bunk beds for children. None of the rooms have private bathrooms, but the four shared facilities are ample and hot water is plentiful. The proprietors' kids run the popular Cutty Sark pub/*paninocateca* near the train station at Via Roma 35.

Via Costasecca 10, 16038 Santa Margherita Ligure. © 0185-286-531. www.hotelannabella.com. 11 units, none with bathroom. 70€ ($81) double; 94€ ($108) triple; 115€ ($132) quad. Breakfast 4€ ($4.60). No credit cards. **Amenities:** Room service (breakfast only). *In room:* No phone.

Fasce ★★★   Aristide, whose grandmother built this small hotel, and his British wife, Jane, take great efforts to make their guests feel at home here—they do, after all, live here themselves along with his parents—and as a result they provide some of the most pleasant lodgings in Santa Margherita. Their hospitality includes the use of free bicycles, and a laundry service (15€/$17 for a wash and dry). If you stay 3 nights or longer, they'll give you a free Cinque Terre packet with train times and two free tickets to go all the way to Riomaggiore and back. The surroundings are lovely: A broad staircase leads into the flowery, courtyard-like entryway, off which there's a pleasant lobby and breakfast/bar area; a roof terrace affords lovely views of the sea and town. The guest rooms are large, bright, and modern in design, with cheerful white laminate furnishings and many thoughtful touches, such as copious amounts of storage space, shelves around the beds on which to place reading matter, and in-room safes. Four rooms have balconies, and three accommodations (the triples and a quad) have folding beds to make them perfect for families. With this many amenities at such reasonable prices, it's a good idea to reserve ahead.

Via Luigi Bozzo 3, 16038 Santa Margherita Ligure. © 0185-286-435. Fax 0185-283-580. www.hotelfasce.it. 16 units. 95€ ($109) double; 120€ ($138) triple; 140€ ($161) quad. Rates include breakfast. AE, DC, MC, V. Closed Dec 12–Mar 15. **Amenities:** Bar; free bike loans; concierge; tour desk; room service (until 11pm); laundry service; nonsmoking rooms. *In room:* TV, dataport, minibar, hair dryer, safe.

Gran Hotel Miramare ★★   This was one of the first grand hotels on this coast, converted in 1903 from a massive private villa a 10-minute walk from the town center along the road to Portofino. Rooms are enlivened by some modest stucco decorations on the walls and ceilings, from which hang chandeliers over parquet floors scattered with Persian rugs and slightly funky walnut and veneer furnishings. Several rooms have been completely redone in the last year. The first floor suite where Marconi stayed when conducting his radio experiments has been kept in 19th-century style, while fifth-floor suites are more modernized. A very steep, pretty park rises behind the hotel, from which a trail leads over the headland to Portofino (it also makes for a pleasant view if you don't get a room with that preferred sea view). There's a small, private pebble beach/beach terrace across the busy road.

Via Milite Ignoto, 16038 Santa Margherita Ligure (GE). © 0185-287-013. Fax 0185-284-651. www.grand hotelmiramare.it. 84 units. 230€–316€ ($265–$363) double; 370€–530€ ($426–$610) jr. suite; 480€–685€

($552–$788) suite. Rates include buffet breakfast. Add 35€ ($40) per person for half board. AE, DC, MC, V. **Amenities:** 2 restaurants (1 poolside lunch buffet; 1 international/regional); 2 bars (piano bar inside, pool bar); outdoor heated saltwater pool; 18-hole golf course (4km/2½ miles away); outdoor lit tennis courts (in town); exercise room nearby; sauna nearby; watersports equipment; bike rental (but you have to go pick it up from a rental shop in town); video arcade; concierge; tour desk; car-rental desk; courtesy car; small business center; room service (10€/$12 charge); in-room massage; babysitting; laundry service; dry cleaning. *In room:* A/C, TV, VCR (on request), fax (in 1 suite), dataport, minibar, hair dryer, safe.

Hotel Metropole 🌟🌟 *Kids*   This popular hotel sits on the road into town, just above the port and a 5-minute stroll into the center. Good planning made sure that no rooms overlook the busy road; all face the sea over a lovely shaded .6-hectare (1½-acre) garden blooming with flowers. Accommodations are split between the main, modern building and the far-preferable Villa Porticciolla, a dusty red Genoese villa right on the beach; the rooms are smaller, but they're graced with 19th-century stuccoes, and the sea laps practically right up against the building. (Once ensconced in the villa, many guests understandably decide to prolong their stay. So the owners can't guarantee you'll get a room there, even if you requested one in advance—if somebody decides to prolong their stay and you arrive when there are no rooms available in the villa, you'll have to stay in another part of the hotel.) Rooms in both buildings tend to be done up with parquet floors and furnishings in an antique-style natural wood finish or made up of bentwood and wicker. Bathrooms are a bit aged, but in good shape, all but one with tub and shower (that one has just a shower). Six rooms up on the far end of the garden (from where there are only glimpses of the sea through the palm fronds) have large terraces partly shaded by an arbor. All other guest rooms have large balconies. The fourth floor, added in 1999, is made up of junior suites and one double with sloped ceilings. Two suites on the lower floor of the main building open onto small private gardens. The management enjoys working with families; several rooms can be joined to make family suites, and there's day care at the beach with a separate area of sand just for the kiddies. The small private beach includes a curving sunbathing terrace and a private boat launch. Renovations planned for 2004 will add an outdoor swimming pool, small fitness room, and sauna to the Metropole.

Via Pagana 2, 16038 Santa Margherita Ligure (GE). (✆ **0185-286-134.** Fax 0185-283-495. www.metropole.it. 59 units. 130€–190€ ($150–$219) double; 150€–232€ ($173–$267) double with half-pension; 175€–256€ ($201–$294) triple; 205€–319€ ($236–$367) triple with half-pension; 180€–320 ($207–$368) jr. suite; 200€–362€ ($230–$416) jr. suite with half-pension. Rates include buffet breakfast. AE, DC, MC, V. Parking 18€ ($21) in private garage. **Amenities:** 2 restaurants (1 international/regional dining room; 1 beachside lunch restaurant); bar; private beach; outdoor swimming pool (in 2004); golf course (4km); small exercise room (in 2004); sauna (in 2004); watersports equipment; children's center (in summer); concierge; tour desk; car-rental desk; business center; room service (limited); in-room massage; babysitting; laundry service; dry cleaning (48-hr.). *In room:* A/C, TV, dataport, minibar, hair dryer, safe.

Nuova Riviera 🌟   The Sabini family acts as if its sunny, early-20th-century Liberty-style villa in a quiet neighborhood behind the town center was a private home and guests were old friends. Every room is different, and though eclectically furnished with pieces that look like they may have passed through a couple of generations of the family, most rooms retain the high-ceilinged elegance of days gone by and have a great deal more character than you're used to finding in rooms at this end of the budget scale; the best have expansive bay windows. Modular furnishings are mixed with antiques, the beds are springy (very springy), and a few rooms get balconies. New bathrooms were added to all but one room in 2000. There's a pretty garden out front and a homey, light-filled dining room where Signora Sabini serves breakfast with fresh-squeezed orange juice, and (in winter only) home-cooked dinners for 15€ to 25€ ($17–$29) not including wine.

Their **annex** nearby has four very nice, simple rooms—one a large triple with balcony—which share two bathrooms. They also rent out a ground-floor apartment with two double rooms, a living room, terrace, washing machine, and refrigerator for 880€ to 980€ ($1,012–$1,127) per week for four or five people. Credit cards aren't accepted at the annex; you'll have to use cash.

Via Belvedere 10–2, 16038 Santa Margherita Ligure. 𝒞 and fax **0185-287-403**. www.nuovariviera.com. 9 units in main house, 8 with bathroom; 4 units in B&B across the street, none with bathroom. In main house: 92€ ($106) double; 120€ ($138) triple; 146€ ($168) quad. In annex: 64€ ($74) double without bathroom; 90€ ($104) triple without bathroom; 680€–980€ ($782–$1,127) per week apt with kitchenette. Rates include breakfast. MC, V (only accepted at main hotel, and there's a slight discount for paying cash). **Amenities:** Restaurant (local cuisine, winter only); bar; laundry service; nonsmoking rooms. *In room:* TV, hair dryer, no phone.

WHERE TO DINE

Ristorante Il Faro 🅐🅐 ITALIAN/LIGURIAN   This cozy trattoria is run by Roberto Fabbro, who opened Santa Margherita Ligure's first *rosticceria* 40 years ago. They give you a glass of Spumanti and a bit of pizza to help you digest the menu, which runs the gamut from *penne all'arrabbiata* (pasta quills in a spicy-hot tomato sauce) and a *fritto misto* (a mix of seafood deep-fried) to *minestrone alla Genovese* (thick vegetable soup), *trenette al pesto*, and *pesce alla piastra* (grilled bream or sea bass). The best seating is at a few tables under the arcade out back.

Via Maragliano 24A. 𝒞 **0185-286-867**. Reservations recommended. Primi 8€–12€ ($9–$14); secondi 10€–12€ ($12–$14). Fixed-price menus 23€–30€ ($26–$35). AE, DC, MC, V. Wed–Mon 12:15–2:30pm and 7–10pm. Closed Nov.

Trattoria Baicin 🅐 LIGURIAN   The husband-and-wife owners, Piero and Carmela, make everything fresh daily, from fish soup to gnocchi, and still manage to find time to greet diners at the door of their cheerful trattoria just a few steps off the harbor. You can get a glimpse of the sea if you choose to sit at one of the tables out front, and the owner/cooks are most happy preparing fish, which they buy fresh every morning at the market just around the corner; the sole, simply grilled, is especially good here, and the *fritto misto di pesce* constitutes a memorable feast. You must begin a meal with one of the pastas made that morning, especially if *trofie alla Genovese* (a combination of gnocchi, potatoes, fresh vegetables, and pesto) is available. By ordering the tourist menu, you can get a nice sampling of the expertly prepared dishes served here.

Via Algeria 9. 𝒞 **0185-286-763**. Primi 4€–7.50€ ($4.60–$9); secondi 8.50€–17€ ($10–$19). Fixed-price menus 20€–22€ ($23–$25). AE, DC, MC, V. Tues–Sun noon–3pm and 7–10:30pm. Closed Jan.

Trattoria da Prezzi *Value* GENOVESE/LIGURIAN   The atmosphere in this cozy little restaurant in the center of town near the market is pleasantly casual. Two whitewashed, tile-floored rooms are usually filled with local workmen and businesspeople who invite newcomers to share a table when no other place is available. Service is minimal—the chef puts what he's prepared for the day on a table near the front door, you tell him what you want, and one of the staff brings it to the table when it's ready. Focaccia, *farinata,* and other Genovese specialties are usually on hand, as are at least one kind of soup (the minestrone is excellent), a chicken dish, and grilled fresh fish.

Via Cavour 21. 𝒞 **0185-285-303**. Primi 3.80€–6.40€ ($4.40–$7); secondi 2.90€–7.80€ ($3.35–$9). MC, V. Sun–Fri 11:45am–2:15pm and 6–9:15pm. Closed Dec 20–Jan 20.

An Excursion to San Fruttuoso

Much of the **Monte Portofino Promontory** can be approached only on foot or by boat (see below), making it a prime destination for hikers. If you want to combine some excellent exercise with the pleasure of glimpsing magnificent views of the sea through a lush forest, arm yourself with a map from the tourist offices in Camogli, Santa Margherita Ligure, Portofino, or Rapallo and set out for **Abbazia di San Fruttuoso** (© 0185-772-703). This medieval religious community, surrounded by a tiny six-house hamlet and pebbly beach, is about 2½ hours away from any of the above-mentioned towns (though Camogli and Portofino are closest, as they immediately flank the promontory on which it sits) by a not-too-strenuous inland hike, or 3½ hours away by a cliff-hugging trail. En route, you can clamor down well-posted paths that descend from the main path to visit San Rocco, San Niccolo, and Punta Chiappa, a string of fishing hamlets hugging the shore of the promontory.

Once you reach San Fruttuoso, you may well want to relax on the pebbly beach and enjoy a beverage or meal at one of the seaside bars. You can tour the stark interior of the abbey for 6€ ($7). It is open June to September daily 10am to 5:45pm; in May Tuesday to Sunday 10am to 5:45pm; March, April, and October Tuesday to Sunday 10am to 3:30pm; and December to February Saturday and Sunday 10am to 3:30pm. Note, though, that despite these official hours, it tends to close whenever the last boat (see below) leaves. The abbey is just a plain, evocatively simple medieval monastic complex with a stellar setting on the coast. There's nothing really to "see" except how the monks lived. Should you happen to have your scuba gear along, you can take the plunge to visit Christ of the Depths, a statue of Jesus erected 15m (50 ft.) beneath the surface to honor sailors lost at sea.

You can also visit San Fruttuoso with one of the **boats** that run almost every hour during the summer months from Camogli. A round-trip costs 8€ ($9) and takes about 30 minutes each way. For more information, contact Golfo Paradiso (© 0185-772-091; www.golfoparadiso.it). *Note:* You can also reach it by hourly (in summer) Tigullio boats (© 0185-284-670; www.traghettiportofino.it) from Portofino (20 min.; 8€/$9), Santa Margherita (35 min.; 12€/$13), and Rapallo (50 min.; 13€/$14).

PORTOFINO

Portofino is almost too beautiful for its own good—in almost any season, you'll be rubbing elbows on Portofino's harborside quays with day-tripping mobs who join Italian industrialists, international celebrities, and a lot of rich but not so famous folks who consider this little town to be the epicenter of the good life. If you make an appearance in the late afternoon when the crowds have thinned out a bit, you are sure to experience what remains so appealing about this enchanting place—its untouchable beauty.

ESSENTIALS
GETTING THERE   **By Train**   Get off in Santa Margherita (see above) and catch the bus.

By Bus   The Tigullio bus (© **0185-288-834;** www.tigulliotrasporti.it) leaves from the train station and Piazza Vittorio Veneto in **Santa Margherita** every 20 minutes and follows one of Italy's most beautiful coastal roads (25 min.). In Santa Margherita you can change for a bus to **Rapallo** (another 15 min.).

By Boat   The best way to arrive is to sail to Portofino on one of the Golfo Paradiso ferries (© **0185-772-091;** www.golfoparadiso.it) from **Camogli** or on one of the Tigullio ferries (© **0185-284-670;** www.traghettiportofino.it) from **Santa Margherita** or **Rapallo.**

By Car   On a summer visit you may encounter crowds even before you get into town, since traffic on the shore-hugging corniche from Santa Margherita, just a few miles down the coast of the promontory, can move at a snail's pace. In fact, given limited parking space in Portofino (© **0185-267-475;** visitors must pay obscene rates—4.50€/$5 per hour, 19€/$22 per day—to use the town garage), you would do well to leave your car in Santa Margherita and take the bus or boat.

VISITOR INFORMATION   Portofino's **tourist office** is at Via Roma 35 (©/fax **0185-269-024;** www.apttigullio.liguria.it). Summer hours are daily 10:30am to 1:30pm and 2 to 7:30pm; winter hours are Tuesday to Sunday 9:30am to 12:30pm and 2:30 to 5:30pm.

EXPLORING THE TOWN

The one thing that's free in Portofino is its scenery, which you can enjoy on an amble around the town. Begin with a stroll around the **harbor,** which—lined with expensive boutiques and eateries as it is—is stunningly beautiful, with colorful houses lining the quay and steep green hills rising behind them. One of the most scenic walks takes you uphill for about 10 minutes along a well-signposted path from the west side of town just behind the harbor to the **Chiesa di San Giorgio** (© **0185-269-337**), built on the site of a sanctuary Roman soldiers dedicated to the Persian god Mithras. It's open daily from 9am to 7pm.

From there, you'll want to continue uphill for a few minutes more to Portofino's **Castello Brown** (© **0185-267-101** or 0185-269-046), built to ward off invading Turks. You can step inside the walls to enjoy a lush garden and the views of the town and harbor below. The castle is open daily from 10am to 7pm (to 5pm Oct–Apr) and admission is 3.50€ ($4), free for those under 13. There are great views back over the town; for some lovely views on this stretch of coast and plenty of open sea before you, continue even higher up through lovely pine forests to the *faro* (lighthouse).

From Portofino, you can also set out for a longer hike on the paths that cross the **Monte Portofino Promontory** to the Abbazia di San Fruttuoso (see the "An Excursion to San Fruttuoso" box, above), about a 2-hour walk from Portofino. The tourist office provides maps.

WHERE TO STAY

Albergo Nazionale ★★ *Value*   It may be set smack in the middle of Portofino's harborfront square, amid some of the priciest real estate in Italy, but the Nazionale costs only one-third to one-half the price of its pricier neighbors (which is why it gets the "value" marker despite the 260€/$300 price tag). Decoration of the smallish to midsize rooms is minimal, but the pieces are a masterful mix of modern and antique, which adds to the relaxing elegance of the place. Several of the rooms are lofted suites with the bedroom upstairs. Only five rooms, all junior suites, enjoy views of the harbor.

Via Roma 8, 16034 Portofino (GE). © **0185-269-575.** Fax 0185-269-138. www.nazionalehotel.com. 12 units. 240€ ($276) double without sea view; 290€ ($334) jr. suite without sea view; 350€ ($403) jr. suite with sea view. Breakfast included. MC, V. Parking 18€ ($21). Closed mid-Dec to Mar. **Amenities:** Italian restaurant; bar; concierge; room service (limited); laundry service. *In room:* A/C, TV, minibar, hair dryer, safe.

Hotel Eden ★   Osta Ferruccio runs this cozy, beachy looking pensione in the heart of the tiny town, a long block up from the harbor. There are no views of the sea here, though those over the rooftops of the town itself are perfectly pleasant. The most sought-after room is no. 7, which comes with a small terrace. The rooms are simply furnished, with writing desks, good beds (some backed by wrought-iron bedsteads), floral wallpaper, and small but well-equipped bathrooms. There's a lovely small garden where Ligurian dishes are served in summer. It's also one of the few hotels here that's open year-round.

Vico Dritto 18, 16034 Portofino (GE). © **0185-269-091.** Fax 0185-269-047. www.hoteledenportofino.com. 12 units. 150€–250€ ($173–$288) double. Rates include breakfast. AE, DC, MC, V. Parking 19€ ($22) in nearby lot. **Amenities:** Ligurian restaurant; bar; concierge; tour desk; car-rental desk; babysitting; laundry service. *In room:* A/C, TV, hair dryer, safe.

Hotel Splendido/Splendido Mare ★★   This 19th-century villa grafted onto the remains of a 16th-century monastery has been a hotel since 1901, and since the early 1950s, one of those fabled retreats of the international rich and famous, of rock stars and Oscar winners. It's perched in a panoramic position atop the headland just before the last curve of the road into town (yes, it's a good 10-min. walk to Portofino harbor—and an uphill haul back—but there's a regular shuttle). Headshots of all the A-list stars from Hollywood's golden age who escaped here line the lounge off of which a terrace opens for drinks or dinner with a sea view. Many guests have been returning for 20 years or more, and stay for 6 weeks at a time. The spacious junior suites come with parquet floors, king-size beds, and antique-styled furnishings that hide the high-tech entertainment centers (TVs with DVD players that rise out automatically). Some come with a small terrace, and a few are set into the very private small building next door fronted by a grape arbor. A series of olive-lined, rosemary-scented paths wrap around the panoramic pool terrace and stretch along the hillside to various little lookouts. Though the Splendido closes down in winter, its sister Splendido Mare (eight doubles and eight suites on Portofino's harborfront piazzetta) stays open year-round.

Salita Baratta 16, 16034 Portofino (GE). © **800-237-1236** in the U.S., or 0185-267-801 in Italy. Fax 0185-267-806. www.splendido.orient-express.com. 66 units. At Hotel Splendido (all rates include half-board): 798€–916€ ($918–$1,053) standard double; 944€–1,142€ ($1,086–$1,313) double with sea view; 1,026€–1,246€ ($1,180–$1,433) double with sea view and balcony; 1,249€–1,470 ($1,436–$1,691) superior jr. suite; 1,420€–1,675€ ($1,633–$1,926) deluxe jr. suite; 1,570€–1,854€ ($1,805–$2,132) executive jr. suite; 1,577€–1,864€ ($1,814–$2,144) superior suite; 1,704€–2,016€ ($1,960–$2,318) deluxe suite; 1,854€–2,196€ ($2,132–$2,525) exclusive suite. At Splendido Mare (bed and breakfast only): 536€–594€ ($616–$683) standard double without sea view; 674€–741€ ($775–$852) standard double with sea view; 895€–984€ ($1,029–$1,132) jr. suite with sea view; 1,045€–1,150€ ($1,202–$1,323) jr. suite with sea view and balcony; 1,357€–1,537 ($1,561–$1,768) suite; 1,530€–1,733€ ($1,760–$1,993) Ava Gardner suite. Half-board supplement at Splendido Mare 73€ ($84) per person. Full American breakfast included. AE, DC, MC, V. Parking 21€ ($24) in garage. Closed Nov 12–Feb 28. **Amenities:** 2 restaurants (regional cuisine in an indoor/outdoor terrace dining room; poolside lunch buffet); bar (piano bar in the evening); outdoor heated seawater pool; 18-hole golf course in Rapallo; outdoor tennis courts; small exercise room; spa; sauna; watersports equipment; bike rental; concierge; tour desk; car-rental desk; courtesy car (down to Splendido Mare at the port); small business center; salon; room service (24-hr.); massage (in-room or at spa); babysitting; laundry service; same-day dry cleaning; video arcade. *In room:* A/C, TV w/free pay movies, VCR, fax (in jr. suites and suites), dataport, kitchenette (in a few jr. suites and suites), minibar, hair dryer, safe.

WHERE TO DINE

Portofino's charms come at a steep price. Its few hotels are expensive enough to put them in the "trip of a lifetime" category, and the harborside restaurants can take a serious chunk out of a vacation budget as well. I suggest you enjoy a light snack at a bar or one of the many shops selling focaccia and wait to dine in Santa Margherita or one of the other nearby towns.

La Gritta American Bar   James Jones called this snug little room the "nicest waterfront bar this side of Hong Kong." We're not sure your praise will go that far, but it is very attractive, very friendly, and far enough along the harborside quay to be a little less hectic than other establishments. Most patrons stop in for a (pricey) cocktail, coffee, or other libation (the floating terrace out front is perfect for a drink at sunset), but light fare, such as omelets and salads of tomatoes and mozzarella, are also available to provide a light and relatively affordable meal.

Calata Marconi 20. *C* **0185-269-126.** Salads and other light fare from about 7.50€ ($9). AE, MC, V. Fri–Wed noon–1am. Closed Nov.

Ristorante Puny ★★★   The gregarious owners make this the only restaurant in Portofino that treats you as more than just waddling bags of money. Right on the piazzetta, its tables enjoy views of the boats bobbing in the harbor and yachts having size contests beyond. Definitely book ahead to drink in those views and dig into *risotto al curry e gamberi* (curried rice embedded with tiny shrimp); *penne al puny* (pasta quills in a sauce of tomatoes, *pancetta* bacon, and mushrooms); fresh fish *al verde* (in a green sauce of parsley, lemon, and white wine) or *al sale* (baked under a thick salt crust); or *carne all'uccelleto* (diced veal sautéed in butter then cooked in white wine with bay leaves).

Piazza Martiri dell'Olivetta 5. *C* **0185-269-037.** Reservations highly recommended. Primi 8.50€–15€ ($10–$17); secondi 11€–22€ ($13–$25). No credit cards. Wed–Fri noon–3pm and 7–11pm.

RAPALLO

When you step out of Rapallo's busy train station, you may be put off by the traffic, blocks of banal apartment houses, and runaway development that in some places has given the resort the look of any other busy town. Keep walking, though, because at its heart Rapallo remains a gracious old seaside playground and port, and it's easy to see what drew the likes of Ezra Pound, Max Beerbohm, and D. H. Lawrence to take up residence here. Most of the town follows the sweep of a pretty harbor guarded by a medieval castle, and the gracious seafront promenade is cheerfully busy day and night.

ESSENTIALS

GETTING THERE   By Train   More than 30 trains a day connect Rapallo and **Genoa** (regional: 40 min.; high-speed: 30 min.). The same trains connect Rapallo with **Camogli** (10 min.), and **Santa Margherita** (3 min.), and **Monterosso** (regional: 50 min.; high-speed: 35 min.) at the north end of the Cinque Terre.

By Bus   At least one bus an hour runs between Rapallo and **Santa Margherita** (about 15 min.).

By Boat   Tigullio ferries (*C* **0185-284-670;** www.traghettiportofino.it) make hourly trips to **Portofino** (30 min.) via **Santa Margherita** (15 min.) from 9am to 4pm (hours of service vary considerably with season; schedules are posted on the docks).

By Car   The A12 autostrada connects Rapallo with Genoa and takes about half an hour. Route S1 along the coast from Genoa is much slower but more scenic.

VISITOR INFORMATION   The **tourist office** is at Lungomare Vittorio Veneto 7 ((C) **0185-230-346;** fax 0185-63-051; www.apttigullio.liguria.it) and is open Monday to Saturday 9:30am to 12:30pm and 2:30 to 5:30pm.

FESTIVALS & MARKETS   Rapallo is at its most exuberant July 1 to July 3, when it celebrates the **Madonna di Montallegro,** whose hilltop sanctuary crowns the town (see below). A famous icon of the Virgin is carried through the streets and a huge fireworks display culminates in the burning of the castle (a mock event, of course). Piazza IV Novembre/Via Gramsci is the site of a lively outdoor **food market** on Thursday mornings.

EXPLORING THE TOWN

From the train station, it's a walk of only about 5 minutes to the **waterfront** (follow Corso Italia to Piazza Canessa and the adjoining Piazza Cavour, and from there Via Cairoli to the harborside Piazza IV Novembre.) Dominating this perfect half-circle of a harbor is a **castle** built on a rocky outcropping reached by a causeway; it is open only for special exhibitions but the boulders around its base are usually teeming with sunbathers. Nearby, two other buildings reflect the fact that Rapallo enjoyed a long and prosperous existence before it became known as a retreat for pleasure seekers. The **Cathedral of Santi Gervasio e Protasio,** on Via Mazzini, was founded in the 6th century, and the leper house of **San Lorenzo** across the street dates from the Middle Ages. You can go inside the church, but not the leper house: It's just a medieval building to look at from the outside.

For striking views over the town and surrounding seacoast, make the ascent to the **Santuario di Montallegro** ((C) **0185-239-000**). You can take a bus from the train station (.75€/90¢) or an aerial cableway (funivia) from Via Castagneto on the eastern side of town. The funivia ((C) **0185-273-444**) operates daily every 30 minutes from 8am to sunset; the trip takes 7 minutes and costs 7€ ($8.05) round-trip. Inside this 16th-century church are some interesting frescoes and a curious Byzantine icon of the Virgin that allegedly flew here on its own from Dalmatia. The views over the sea and surrounding valleys are the main reason to come up here, though, and they are even more so from the summit of Monte Rosa, a short uphill hike away.

WHERE TO STAY

La Vela   This friendly, family-run pensione, about a block up from the seaside promenade and the center of town, is one of the better bargain choices in expensive Rapallo. The old-fashioned, high-ceilinged rooms open off cozy, homey sitting rooms. Accommodations are extremely comfortable, most are spacious, and they have brand-new cots, bland but serviceable modular furnishings, inlaid stone floors, and some nice practical touches like writing desks and lounge chairs. About half of the rooms have private bathrooms wedged into one corner; those that don't have sinks and bidets and share three commodious facilities in the hallway. All bathrooms, though, could stand an overhaul. Many of the rooms face a garden in the rear of the building, ensuring a good night's sleep, and in some rooms you can enjoy this quiet retreat from a large balcony. They won't take reservations for 1 night only, and since the phone must be manually switched over to receive faxes, please try to refrain from faxing after 6pm EST, which is the middle of the night in Italy! The hotel is connected with the excellent Ristorante Elite downstairs (see below), where you may well want to take most of your meals.

Via Milite Ignoto 21/7, 16035 Rapallo. (C) and fax **0185-50-551.** www.eliteristorante.it. 13 units, 6 with bathroom. 52€ ($59) double without bathroom, 57€ ($65) double with bathroom. Breakfast 3€ ($3.45). AE, DC, MC, V. Closed Nov. **Amenities:** Restaurant (Italian cuisine); bar; bike rental; car-rental desk. *In room:* TV.

Riviera ★★ The Gambero family has run this small hotel, which occupies an old villa on the waterfront, since 1939, and it is now in the capable hands of Claudio and Silvana. They have spent the past several years improving their property, with great attention to detail, especially in the guest rooms. New hardwood floors have been laid, and handsome wood desks and shelving units have been built to match. New double-pane windows keep noise from the seaside avenue out front to a minimum, and bathrooms have been redone with top-of-the-line fixtures. Many of the fine old touches remain, including small balconies off many of the rooms with vistas over the harbor. Three of the suites are perfect for families, consisting of two separate bedrooms and a shared bathroom off a hall, while the fourth is a single large corner room with three balconies, one off the double-sinked bathroom. A sunny terrace overlooking the sea extends from the new restaurant/breakfast room, where a generous buffet is served every morning and reasonable fixed-price menus (as well as a la carte) at mealtimes.

Piazza IV Novembre 2, 16035 Rapallo. © **0185-50-248.** Fax 0185-65-668. www.hotel-riviera.it. 20 units. 95€–110€ ($109–$127) double; 120€–145€ ($138–$167) double with sea view; 150€–165€ ($173–$190) suite. Rates include breakfast. AE, MC, V. Free parking. Closed Nov–Dec 23. **Amenities:** Restaurant; golf course (1km/²/₅ mile); tennis courts; bike rental; concierge; tour desk; car-rental desk; room service (limited); babysitting; laundry service. *In room:* A/C, TV, minibar, hair dryer, safe.

Rosa Bianca ★ *Finds* This small, lovely hotel is quiet, unassuming, and exceedingly personable, with friendly management and a perfect location right at the end of the main road at the port, with great views over the harbor and restaurant-lined promenade, all the way to the castle. Many of the smallish to midsize rooms are on corners with little semicircular balconies and are flooded with light. They're decorated with bentwood furnishings resting on somewhat tatty carpet, but the low beds lie on genuine box springs (a rarity in Italy). It's across, and down a bit, from the Riviera (above), but enjoys better views. The hoteliers just completed a massive renovation to rooms on the first floor, and further refurbishments are in the works.

Lungomare Vittorio Veneto 42, 16035 Rapallo (GE). © **0185-50-390.** Fax 0185-65-035. 18 units. 119€–180€ ($137–$207) double; 130€–180€ ($150–$207) suite. Rates include buffet breakfast. AE, DC, MC, V. **Amenities:** Bar; concierge; room service (24-hr.); in-room massage; babysitting; laundry service; same-day dry cleaning; nonsmoking rooms. *In room:* A/C, TV, fax, dataport, minibar, hair dryer.

WHERE TO DINE

O Bansin *Value* LIGURIAN This colorful and boisterous restaurant has been a Rapallo institution since 1907, and even though the new young owners have moved it a few blocks away from the marketplace and spruced it up a bit, they've kept the original respect for simplicity, low prices, and traditional Ligurian cuisine. Minestrone, *pasta al pesto* or *al Bansin* (with tomatoes, pesto, and cream), *polpette in umido* (stewed meatballs served with peas), and *sardine alla piastra* (roast sardines) are served without pomp and circumstance at communal tables in a plain interior room or, whenever warm enough, on the covered, semi-open deck out back. The service is as warm and friendly as the environs.

Via Venezia 105. © **0185-231-119.** Primi 5.20€–7.50€ ($6–$9); secondi 6€–18€ ($7–$21). Fixed-price menu at lunch (Mon–Fri) 10€ ($12) including wine. AE, DC, MC, V. Sun 12:30–2:30pm; Mon–Sat noon–2:30pm; Tues–Fri 7:30–9:30pm; Sat 7:30–10pm. Closed Oct 8–20.

Ristorante Elite ★ SEAFOOD This popular seafood restaurant is just up a busy avenue from the harbor, and the pleasant room, hung with paintings of local scenes, is a little less formal (and less overpriced) than the many seafood restaurants on the waterfront. The kitchen long ago won the approval of locals, who come here for the fresh fish of the day, which can follow such starters as seafood salad, a *risotto gamberetti e asparagi* (risotto with small prawns and fresh asparagus), or a *zuppe di pesce* (a hearty fish soup). Fresh fish can also be enjoyed on the fixed-price menus, veritable feasts that also include hot and cold seafood appetizers and a pasta course.

Via Milite Ignoto 19. ℂ 0185-50-551. Primi 4€–9€ ($4.60–$10); secondi 8€–21€ ($9–$24). Fixed-price "chef's menu" 31€ ($36) not including wine; *menù turistico* 18€ ($21) with wine. AE, DC, MC, V. Thurs–Tues (daily in summer) noon–2:30pm and 7:30–10pm. Closed Nov.

4 The Cinque Terre

Monterosso, the northernmost town of the Cinque Terre, 93km (58 miles) E of Genoa

Olive groves and vineyards clinging to hillsides, proud villages perched above the sea, hidden coves nestled at the foot of dramatic cliffs—the **Cinque Terre** is about as beautiful a coastline as you're likely to find in Europe. What's best about the Cinque Terre (named for the five neighboring towns of Monterosso, Vernazza, Corniglia, Manarola, and Riomaggiore) is what's *not* here—automobiles, large-scale development, or much else by way of 20th- and 21st-century interference. The pastimes in the Cinque Terre don't get much more elaborate than **walking** 🌟🌟🌟 from one lovely village to another along trails that afford spectacular vistas; plunging into the Mediterranean or basking in the sun on your own waterside boulder; and indulging in the tasty local food and wine.

Not too surprisingly, these charms have not gone unnoticed, and American tourism especially has positively exploded in the past 6 years or so. In summer (weekends are worst) you are likely to find yourself in a long procession of like-minded, English-speaking trekkers making their way down the coast or elbow to elbow with day-trippers from an excursion boat. Even so, the Cinque Terre still manages to escape the hubbub that afflicts so many coastlines, and even a short stay here is likely to reward you with one of the most memorable seaside visits of a lifetime.

ESSENTIALS

GETTING THERE **By Train** You often cannot coast directly into the Cinque Terre towns, as they are served only by the most local of train runs. You'll often find you must change trains in nearby **La Spezia** (one or two per hour; 8 min.) at the coast's south tip, or in **Pisa** (about six daily; 75 min.). This is true of the one or two trains per hour from **Rome** (total 4½–5 hr.) or the hourly ones from **Florence** (2½ hr.). There are one or two direct trains per hour from **Genoa** to La Spezia (1 hr. 40 min.); many more from Genoa require a change in Levanto or Sestri Levanto, both a bit farther north up the coast from Monterosso.

By Car The fastest route is via A12 autostrada from Genoa, exiting at the Corrodano exit for Monterosso. The trip from Genoa to Corrodano takes less than an hour, while the much shorter 9.3km (15-mile) trip from Corrodano to Monterosso (via Levanto) is made along a narrow road and can take about half that amount of time. Coming from the south or Florence, get off the A12 autostrada at La Spezia and follow CINQUE TERRE signs.

By Boat Navagazione Golfo dei Poeti (ℂ **0187-732-987** or 0187-730-336; www.navigazionegolfodeipoeti.it) runs erratic service from the **Riviera Levante towns**, as well as from **Genoa,** mid-June to mid-September, though these tend to be day cruises stopping for anywhere from 1 to 3 hours in Vernazza (see below

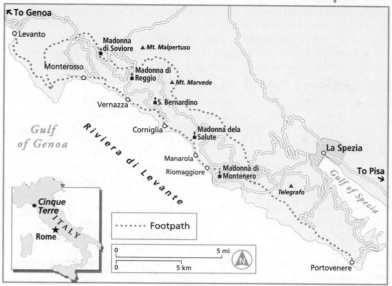

description) before returning (though you can usually talk them into not picking you up again for a day or three).

GETTING AROUND

By Foot The best way to link the Cinque Terre is to devote a whole day and hoof it along the trails. See "Exploring the Cinque Terre," below, for details.

By Train Local trains make frequent runs (2–3 per hour) between the five towns; some stop only in Monterosso and Riomaggiore, so check the posted "Partenze" schedule at the station first to be sure you're catching a local. One-way tickets between any two towns are available, including one version that is good for 6 hours of travel in one direction, meaning you can use it to town-hop—or you can buy a day ticket good for unlimited trips.

By Car A narrow, one-lane coast road hugs the mountainside above the towns, but all the centers are closed to cars; parking is difficult, and where possible, expensive.

There are public **parking** facilities as follows: Riomaggiore and Manarola both have small parking facilities just above their towns and minibuses to carry you and your luggage down. The cheapest option is the big open dirt lot right on the seafront in Monterosso. The priciest is the garage in Riomaggiore.

By Boat From the port in Monterosso, Navagazione Golfo dei Poeti (© **0187-732-987** or 0187-730-336; www.navigazionegolfodeipoeti.it) makes 8 to 10 trips a day between Manarola and Riomaggiore (a 25-min. trip), all stopping in Vernazza and half of them stopping in Manarola as well.

VISITOR INFORMATION The **tourist office** for the Cinque Terre is underneath the train station of Monterosso, Via Fegina 38 (© **0187-817-506;** fax 0187-817-825). It's open Easter to early November and again at Christmas daily 9:30 to 11:30am and 3:30 to 7:30pm. Even when it's closed or in the off season, posted outside the office is a rather handy display of phone numbers and other useful info, from hotels to ferries.

The commune of Riomaggiore (which also covers Manarola) maintains a Web site at www.riomaggiore.it. Other sites to visit include www.cinqueterrenet.com, www.cinqueterre.it, www.aptcinqueterre.sp.it, and www.monterossonet.com.

EXPLORING THE CINQUE TERRE

Aside from swimming and soaking in the atmosphere of unspoiled fishing villages, the most popular activity in the Cinque Terre is **hiking from one village to the next** ⭐ along centuries-old goat paths. Trails plunge through vineyards and groves of olive and lemon trees and hug seaside cliffs, affording heart-stopping views of the coast and the romantic little villages looming ahead in the distance. The well-signposted walks from village to village range in degree of difficulty and the length of time it takes to traverse them, but as a loose rule they get longer and steeper—and more rewarding—the farther north you go. Depending on your pace and how long you stop in each village for a fortifying glass of *sciacchetrà,* the local sweet wine, you can make the trip between Monterosso, at the northern end of the Cinque Terre, to Riomaggiore, at the southern end, in about 5 hours. You should decide whether you want to walk north to south or south to north. Walking south means tackling the worst trail first, which you may prefer since you'll get it out of the way and things will get easier as the day goes on and you start to tire. Heading north, the trail gets progressively harder between each town, so perhaps you might like this if you want to walk just until you get tired and then hop the train.

The walk from **Monterosso to Vernazza** is the most arduous and takes 1½ hours, on a trail that makes several steep ascents and descents (on the portion outside of Monterosso, you'll pass beneath funicular-like cars that transport grapes down the steep hillsides). The leg from **Vernazza to Corniglia** is also demanding and takes another 90 minutes, plunging into some dense forests and involving some lengthy ascents, but is among the prettiest and most rewarding stretches. Part of the path between **Corniglia and Manarola,** about 45 minutes apart, follows a level grade above a long stretch of beach, tempting you to break stride and take a dip. From **Manarola to Riomaggiore** it's easy going for about half an hour along a partially paved path known as the Via dell'Amore, so named for its romantic vistas (great to do at sunset).

Since all the villages are linked by rail, you can hike as many portions of the itinerary as you wish and take the train to your next destination. Trails also cut through the forested, hilly terrain inland from the coast, much of which is protected as a nature preserve; the tourist office in Monterosso can provide maps.

BEACHES The only sandy beach in the Cinque Terre is the crowded strand in **Monterosso,** on much of which you will be asked to pay 5€ ($6) per day for a chair, or 10€ to 15€ ($12–$17) per day for two chairs with umbrella.

Guvano Beach is a long, isolated pebbly strand that stretches just north of Corniglia and is popular with nudists (almost entirely men, many of whom are happy it's almost entirely men). You can clamber down to it from the Vernazza-Corniglia path, but the drop is steep and treacherous. A weird alternative route takes you through an unused train tunnel that you enter near the north end of Corniglia's train station. You must ring the bell at the gated entrance and wait for a custodian to arrive to unburden you of 2.50€ ($2.90), which is good for passage through the dank, dimly lit 1.6km (1-mile) long gallery that emerges onto the beach at the far end.

There's also a long, rocky beach to the south of **Corniglia,** and it is easily accessible by some quick downhill scrambles from the Corniglia to Manrola path. **Riomaggiore** has a tiny crescent-shaped pebble beach reached by a series of stone steps on the south side of the harbor. Everywhere else, you'll be swimming off piers or rocks.

MONTEROSSO

The Cinque Terre's largest village seems incredibly busy compared to its sleepier neighbors, but it's not without its charms. Monterosso is actually two towns—a bustling, character-filled Old Town built behind the harbor as well as a relaxed resort that stretches along the Cinque Terre's only **sand beach** and is home to the train station and the tiny regional tourist office (upon exiting the station, turn left and head through the tunnel for the Old Town; turn right for the newer town and Il Gigante restaurant; see below).

The region's most famous art treasure is here: housed in the **Convento dei Cappuccini,** perched on a hillock in the center of the Old Town, is a *Crucifixion* by Anthony Van Dyck, the Flemish master who worked for a time in nearby Genoa (you can visit the convent daily 9am–noon and 4–7pm). While you will find the most conveniences in citified Monterosso, you'll have a more rustic experience if you stay in one of the other four villages.

WHERE TO STAY

Albergo Amici ★★   The aptly named Amici is unpretentious and extremely friendly, reached by a curving marble staircase lined with flowerpots and facing a delightful garden. Although the hotel is not on the seafront (which is only a few minutes away by foot), there is a garden at the top of the property, many of the rooms overlook the town and the sea beyond, and the location on a narrow street in the Old Town ensures quiet. The rooms are simply but tastefully furnished in blond-wood contemporary pieces and open to balconies through French doors. All units have been equipped with air-conditioners, and now after 3 years the electric company has finally seen fit to provide the hotel with enough current to actually use them (ah, Italy!). Like most hotels in Monterosso, the Amici requires, from June 15 to September 15, that guests choose either half or full board. Meals, served in a cavernous dining room, are adequate, but you'd do well to opt for the half-board plan so you can sample other restaurants throughout the region. Once a week the Amici offers a candlelit dinner—ask when booking.

Via Buranco 36, 19016 Monterosso al Mare (SP). © 0187-817-544. Fax 0187-817-424. www.hotelamici.it. 40 units, 37 with bathroom in room (3 singles each have a private bathroom in hall). 95€–126€ ($109–$145) double with bathroom; 106€–136€ ($122–$156) double with half-board; 122€–152€ ($140–$175) double with full board. Buffet breakfast 8€ ($9). MC, V. Parking 9€ ($10) in nearby public lot. Closed Nov 3–Dec 22 and Jan 7 to around Feb 20. **Amenities:** Restaurant; bar; game room (billiards, Ping-Pong); children's center (Ping-Pong and billiards in garden); laundry service; dry cleaning. *In room:* A/C, TV, hair dryer, safe.

Hotel Pasquale ★ (Value)   The Pasquale gives you great views for the money. It's built into a cliff face—some of which shows through the walls inside—right at the port of the Old Town, so all rooms overlook the beach and sea. The green tile floors support mediocre beds and basic, built-in units. Rooms are midsize, but bathrooms are cramped, and some are showing mildew. Families will appreciate quad no. 3 with its two separate bedrooms. The entire hotel is nonsmoking, and the hoteliers recently added an elevator.

They also run the **Villa Steno,** 16 rooms at the top of the Old Town with views over the rooftops to the sea, which also has a few two-room units for families and small terraces with vistas. Rooms here are a bit larger, bathrooms just as cramped, and furnishing units newer, but a few rooms lack views. Prices are the same. The town is a 5- to 10-minute walk through a lemon grove away.

Via Fegina 4, 19016 Monterosso al Mare (SP). (✆ **0187-817-477**. Fax 0187-817-056. www.pasini.com. 15 units. 130€ ($150) double; 150€ ($173) triple; 170€ ($196) quad. Breakfast included. AE, MC, V. Closed Dec 6–26. **Amenities:** Bar; concierge; room service (only bar service); babysitting; laundry service; nonsmoking rooms (whole hotel). *In room:* A/C, TV, dataport, hair dryer.

WHERE TO DINE

All the towns in the Cinque Terre have little shops like **Enoteca Internazionale** 🌟🌟, where you can taste and purchase the local wines by the bottle, or simply enjoy a glass of Cinque Terre DOC (1.50€/$1.75) or *sciacchetrà* (3€/ $3.45) on the premises. The selection here, in the bustling part of old Monterosso, also includes olive oil pressed just down the street and jars of homemade pesto.

Focaccerio Il Frontoio SNACKS   Many patrons say this bustling shop, with a takeout counter and a few tables where you can dine on the premises, serves some of the best focaccia in Liguria. That's quite a claim, but suffice it to say that the freshly baked bread (especially when topped with fresh vegetables) is heavenly and provides one of the best fast meals around.

Via Gioberti 1 (off Via Roma). (✆ **0187-818-333**. Pizza and focaccia from 1€ ($1.15). No credit cards. Fri–Wed 9am–2pm and 4–7pm. Closed Oct–Mar.

Il Gigante SEAFOOD   This friendly, simple restaurant, a block off the waterfront in the newer part of town, serves some of the freshest and best-prepared seafood in the region—which is why so many residents of Genoa and nearby towns drive to Monterosso just to eat in one of the attractive rooms here. There is no set menu, but the offerings vary with the local catch. Staples, though, include the *zuppe di pesce,* which is almost legendary and starts off many a meal here, often followed by a huge platter of *fritto misto di pesce* (fried seafood). Book ahead, especially to sit in the garden out back.

Via IV Novembre 9. (✆ **0187-817-401**. Reservations recommended. Primi 5.20€–13€ ($6–$15); secondi 9€–18€ ($10–$21). AE, DC, MC, V. Daily noon–3pm and 6:30–10pm. Closed Nov and Tues in winter.

NIGHTLIFE

Monterosso's nightlife concentrates in the Old Town. Bookending the bocce-ball court between the elevated railroad tracks and the beach are a **free outdoor disco** Saturday nights in summer and, at the far end, **Bar Il Casello,** Lungo Ferrovia 70 (no phone), with outdoor tables and beer on tap. Under the railroad tracks and in town itself you'll find **Fast,** Via Roma 13 (no phone), a pub plastered with movie posters and serving the cheapest beer in town.

VERNAZZA

It's hard not to fall in love with this pretty village. Tall houses cluster around a natural harbor (where you can swim among the fishing boats) and beneath a **castle** built high atop a rocky promontory that juts into the sea (though this castle is nothing special, it's open Mar–Oct daily 10am–6:30pm; admission 1€/ $1.15). The center of town is waterside **Piazza Marconi,** itself a sea of cafe tables. The only Vernazza drawback is that too much good press has turned it into the Cinque Terre's ghetto of American tourists, in summer especially.

WHERE TO STAY

Besides the Barbara below, you can rent one of **Trattoria Gianni Franzi's** 23 rooms spread across two buildings; some come with a bathroom, some with excellent views up the coast, all with a steep climb up the stairlike streets of the town, then up the stairs within the building—but all are worth it. Rates are 58€ to 62€ ($67–$71) for a double without bathroom, 75€ ($86) for a double with bathroom, and 98€ ($113) for a triple with bathroom. Call ✆ **0187-821-003** or fax 0187-812-228 to book, or when you arrive in town stop by the trattoria's harborside bar at Piazza Marconi 5 (which is closed Wed except during the busy summer months). They're closed January 8 to March 8.

Albergo Barbara *Value*   This is the sort of place threatened by over-popularity and subsequent development of former backwaters like Vernazza: an exceedingly basic but clean and cheap hotel in an absolutely stellar location, in the center of the tiny harbor piazza with views over the fishing boats and Mediterranean. This pleasant, bare-bones pensione on the two upper floors of a tall old house on the waterfront is at the top of four flights of broad stone steps (63 of 'em), and from there, many of the rooms are reached by an additional climb up a ladderlike spiral staircase. These efforts are rewarded, however, by an eagle's-eye view of Vernazza's harbor from almost every room. While the accommodations are basic, they are not without charm, with a pleasant smattering of homey furniture, cool tile floors, and a sink. Guests share three clean and nicely equipped bathrooms. If no one answers the buzzer, step across the square to the Taverna del Capitano restaurant to ask about one of their rooms.

Piazza Marconi 30, 19018 Vernazza. ✆ **0187-812-398**. 9 units, none with bathroom. 55€ ($63) large double (nos. 8 and 9) with full sea view; 45€ ($52) smaller room upstairs with a sliver of a sea view; 43€ ($49) single or double without sea view; 10€ ($12) each additional person. No breakfast. No credit cards. Closed late Nov to mid-Feb. *In room:* No phone.

WHERE TO DINE

Al Castello *★* LIGURIAN   Operating as a bar all day and a restaurant at mealtimes, this establishment's reed-shaded terrace is set up against the medieval castle walls with pendulous fishing nets and stunning vertiginous views over Vernazza's cove. The food is nothing particularly special—though *penne al casello* (pesto mixed with cream and tomato sauce) or grilled fresh fish are fine—but that view is lovely, especially in the summertime around 7:30 to 8pm when you get to watch the sun set over the water. Service is very friendly; book ahead, especially in summer, for the best views. The only drawback: 10 minutes of endless stair climbing to get here.

Via Guidoni 56. ✆ **0187-812-296**. Primi 5.20€–9.50€ ($6–$11); secondi 8€–13€ ($9–$15). No credit cards. Thurs–Tues noon–2:30pm and 7 or 7:30–10pm. Closed Oct 26–Apr 24.

Gambero Rosso *★★* SEAFOOD/LIGURIAN   It would be hard to find a more pleasant way to take in the scene on Vernazza's lively harborside square than to do so while enjoying the tasting menu on the terrace at this excellent restaurant. You will also be content ordering one or two choices from the a la carte menu—either way, you can explore some hard to find dishes such as *acchiughe* (fresh anchovies) baked with onions and potatoes, *ravioli di pesci* (a delicate fish ravioli), and *muscoli ripieni* (*muscoli* is the Ligurian word for mussels, known as *cozze* elsewhere in Italy; here they are stuffed with fresh herbs). Another specialty, the *grigliata mista* of freshly caught fish, is excellent. Any meal should be followed by the house dessert, *sciacchetrà* (the local sweet wine) accompanied by homemade biscotti. The stone-walled, stone-floored, timbered-ceiling dining room is a pleasant alternative when the terrace is closed. If you're also looking for a place to stay, Gambero Rosso's owners also rent out four apartments.

Piazza Marconi 7. ℰ **0187-812-265.** Primi 7€–10€ ($8–$12); secondi 11€–22€ ($13–$25); tasting menu 30€–45€ ($35–$52). AE, DC, MC, V. Tues–Sun 12:30–4pm and 7:15–10:30pm. (sometimes open Mon in summer). Closed Dec 15–Mar 1.

CORNIGLIA

The quietest village in the Cinque Terre is isolated by its position midway down the coast, its hilltop location high above the open sea, and its little harbor. Whether you arrive by boat, train, or the trail from the south, you'll have to climb more than 300 steps to reach the village proper (if you arrive by trail from the north, you'll avoid these stairs unless you want to leave town to the south, when you'll have to descend them), which is an enticing maze of little walkways overshadowed by tall houses.

Once there, though, the views over the surrounding vineyards and up and down the coastline are stupendous—for the best outlook, walk to the end of the narrow main street to a belvedere that is perched between the sea and sky. More than these vistas, Corniglia is also the village most likely to offer you a glimpse into life in the Cinque Terre the way it was until a couple of decades ago.

WHERE TO STAY

Da Cecio ★★ *Finds* Proprietors Elia and Nunzio have converted the second floor of their old stone house in the countryside just 2 minutes outside Corniglia (on the road to Vernazza) to what we consider one of the Cinque Terre's most pleasant inns. The rooms are big, bright, and stylish with dark wood veneer headboards and furnishings. Most feature great views over the sea, olive groves, and the hilltop town (nos. 2 and 6 are on a corner with those vistas out both windows), and they all have modern bathrooms with good box showers and, in a few, marble sinks. The sun-drenched rooftop deck or flowery terrace downstairs (which at mealtimes serves as an outdoor dining room for the excellent restaurant; see below) is the perfect place to idle away an afternoon. If a room is not available here, one of the proprietors will take you down to one of their four pleasant rooms in the village. For breakfast, they'll send you to their nearby bar, which has tables set out on the village's tiny main piazza.

19010 Corniglia. ℰ **0187-812-043.** Fax 0187-812-138. 12 units (4 are in a *dipendenza* nearby). 60€ ($69) double. Breakfast 5€ ($6). MC, V. Closed Nov. **Amenities:** Ligurian restaurant (see review below); bar. *In room:* Hair dryer (putting in this year), no phone.

WHERE TO DINE

Bar Villagio Marino Europa BAR It would be hard to find a location more scenic than the one this simple outdoor bar enjoys, with stunning views up and down the coast from a hillside perch. Built to service guests at an attached bungalow village, the bar is also a welcome refuge for hikers on the Manarola–Corniglia path (at the Manarola end of the ramshackle tunnel of low buildings you pass through just beyond the Corniglia train station). The offerings don't get more elaborate than soda and beer, panini, and ice cream, but you will certainly want to stop here at least once on your treks up and the down the Cinque Terre to take in the view.

19010 Corniglia. ℰ **0187-812-279.** Snacks from 1€ ($1.15); sandwiches from 2.70€ ($3.10). Mid-May to mid-Oct daily 8am–midnight. Closed winter.

Osteria a Cantina de Mananan ★★ LIGURIAN The pleasure of being in hilltop Corniglia is well worth the trek up to town, especially if the visit includes a meal at this tiny restaurant carved into the stone cellars of an ancient house. Agostino and Marianne, the husband-and-wife owners and chefs, draw on age-old local recipes and use only the freshest ingredients in their preparations; the results, posted on a blackboard in the one handsome vaulted room furnished with granite tables, are wonderful. Fresh vegetables from gardens just outside the village are grilled and mixed with herbs and smoked mozzarella as a simple appetizer, or there's the variety in *antipasto misto mare,* which can be followed by any of the hand-rolled pastas topped with homemade pesto or porcini. You can continue in this nonmeat direction with a plate of mussels, grilled fish, or fresh anchovies stuffed with herbs, but the few meat dishes on the daily menu are also excellent—especially the *coniglio nostrano,* rabbit roasted in a white sauce. Local wines accompany the meals.

Via Fieschi 117, Corniglia. (C) **0187-821-166** or 0187-812-320. Reservations recommended. Primi 7.50€–8.50€ ($9–$10); secondi 8.50€–13€ ($10–$14). AE, DC, MC, V. Wed–Mon 12:30–2:30pm and 7:30–9:30pm. Closed Nov.

Ristorante Cecio ⭐ LIGURIAN   Like the inn upstairs, the stone-walled, wood-beamed dining room and flower-filled terrace overlooking olive groves provide extremely pleasant surroundings. A nice selection of simple, homemade fare emerges from the family-run kitchen, including fresh pasta with a rich pesto or walnut sauce or *alla scogliera,* topped with fresh clams and mussels. Meat and fish are grilled over an open hearth. Outside of peak meal times, you can sit on the terrace and enjoy the view over a beer or glass of the house wine.

Corniglia. (C) **0187-812-043.** Primi 6€–15€ ($7–$17); secondi 6€–18€ ($7–$21); fixed-price menu 20€ ($23). MC, V. Thurs–Tues (daily in summer) noon–3:30pm and 7–11pm. Closed Nov.

MANAROLA

Not as busy as nearby Riomaggiore or as quaint as its neighbor Corniglia, Manarola is a near-vertical cluster of tall houses that seems to rise piggyback up the hills on either side of the harbor. In fact, in a region with no shortage of heart-stopping views, one of the most amazing sights is the descent into the town of Manarola on the path from Corniglia: From this perspective, the hill-climbing houses seem to merge into one another to form a row of skyscrapers. Despite these urban associations, Manarola is a delightfully rural village where fishing and winemaking are big business. The region's major **wine cooperative,** Cooperativa Agricoltura di Riomaggiore, Manarola, Corniglia, Vernazza e Monterosso, made up of 300 local producers, is here; call (C) **0187-920-435** for information about tours of its modern (est. 1982) facilities.

WHERE TO STAY

Manarola's **Ostello 5 Terre** ((C) **0187-920-215;** fax 0187-920-218; www.cinque terre.net/ostello) has cheap sleeps: 16€ to 20€ ($18–$23) beds in six-bed dorm rooms or the same price per bed in four-bed family rooms with private bathroom—but you gotta rent the whole room. Breakfast costs 3.50€ ($4.05), dinner 12€ ($14). The hostel offers services such as kayak, bike, and snorkel rental, Internet access, and a cheap laundry. The only major drawback is the strict midnight curfew (1am in summer). It's closed January 6 to February 15 and November 4 to December 6.

Marina Piccola ⭐⭐   This cozy inn on the harbor in Manarola is a favorite with many travelers to the Cinque Terre, and it's easy to see why. Part of the premises, including the glass-enclosed seafood restaurant where you may be required to take half or full board in the busy summer months, is right on the water (plainer rooms but great views), and many of the guest rooms in the tall house across the street (nicer furnishings) have sea views as well. Decor is a cut above that of most inns in the region, and the welcoming lobby doubles as a sitting room, with divans wrapping around a fireplace. As one of the hotel's two buildings (the one above the restaurant) is right on the port, book ahead to be sure you get one of the rooms whose windows open onto fishing boats and the rocky shoals directly below and the Tyrrhenian Sea spread before you. Old prints, homey faded floor tiles, light pine-veneer furnishings, and a predominance of Santorini colors of white and pale blue lend the small but serviceable rooms a great amount of charm. Rooms in the other building (the next one up the hill, containing the hotel lobby) are done in more of a country style, with nicer nut-brown, heavy wooden furnishings, flower-edged wallpaper, and fancy scrolled headboards; even here about half the rooms get a sea view over, or around the side of, the pink stucco of the first building (better views as you go higher up, but no elevator). In 2002 they installed TVs and air-conditioning in both buildings. The aforementioned meals are excellent, a cut above most room and board fare. My only quibble with this otherwise pleasant hostelry is that the service can be somewhat scatterbrained, and occasionally downright unfriendly.

Via Discovolo 38, 19010 Manarola. © **0187-920-103.** Fax 0187-920-966. hotelmarinapiccola.com. 13 units. 100€ ($115) double. Half-board 80€ ($92) per person in double. Breakfast included. AE, DC, MC, V. Closed Nov. **Amenities:** Restaurant (local cuisine); bar. *In room:* A/C, TV.

WHERE TO DINE

Aristide ⭐ LIGURIAN   In this old house up the hill from the harbor (just below the train station), diners are accommodated on a couple of levels of small rooms as well as on a covered terrace across the street. Many of Aristide's patrons live in the Cinque Terre or take the train here from nearby La Spezia, because this long-standing trattoria is known for its heaping platters of grilled fish, *gamberoni* (jumbo prawns), and *frittura di mare* (a selection of fried seafood). The *antipasta di mare* includes a nice selection of octopus, clams, sardines, and other local catches and serves well as a lighter meal. The house's white wine is from the hills above the town, and if the owner is in a good mood, he may come around after your dinner proffering a complimentary glass of *sciacchetrà*, the local dessert wine.

Via Discovolo 290. © **0187-920-000.** Primi 4.20€–7€ ($4.85–$8); secondi 6€–18€ ($7–$21); fixed-price fish menu 36€ ($41) with wine. AE, DC, MC, V. Tues–Sun noon–2:30 and 7–9pm.

RIOMAGGIORE

Riomaggiore clings onto the vestiges of the Cinque Terre's rustic ways while making some concessions to the modern world. The old fishing quarter has expanded in recent years and Riomaggiore now has some sections of new houses and apartment blocks. This blend of the old and new works well—Riomaggiore is bustling and prosperous and makes the most of a lovely setting, with houses that cling to the hills that drop into the sea on either side of town. Many of the lanes end in seaside belvederes.

From the parking garage, follow the main drag down; from the train station, exit and turn right to head through the tunnel for the main part of town (or, from the station, take off left up the brick stairs to walk the Via dell'Amore to Manarola).

That tunnel and the main drag meet at the base of an elevated terrace that holds the train tracks. From here, a staircase leads down to a tiny fishing harbor off the left of which heads a rambling path that, after a few hundred meters, leads to a pleasant little **beach** of large pebbles.

WHERE TO STAY

Riomaggiore is a good bet for a room in a more genuine fishing-village Cinque Terre town (Monterosso is a bit more built-up), especially in the off season, as both inns remain open year-round, and Riomaggiore is home to two rental outfits that between them rent dozens of rooms and apartments across the village.

There are lots of folks renting out rooms illegally in the Cinque Terre (the rooms are fine—usually—and the price is right; it's just that they don't have the proper permits to do this and the properties are not inspected by the proper authorities). The people we've listed here, however, go to the trouble of filing the paperwork with the authorities and submitting themselves to oversight, which also means that by going through them, you'll be assured a certain guarantee of quality.

Brothers Luciano and Roberto **Fazioli,** Via Colombo 94 (② **0187-920-822;** fax 0187-920-904; robertofazioli@libero.it), rent about two dozen rooms and apartments all over town, operating out of a pink stripe–awninged shop front halfway down the main street. (One of them is likely to come out and greet you if you walk past the office carrying a bag.) While the rooms vary considerably in size, views, and furnishings, most have newly installed bathrooms and cooking facilities. One of our favorite rooms is on the top of a house in the oldest part of town, and opens onto a private rooftop terrace with views over Riomaggiore to the sea. Several choice apartments inhabit harborside houses, two on top floors with small terraces, another on the ground floor with a chic new kitchen, bathroom, and a sitting area from which you can hear the waves lapping against the rocks below. Some apartments have satellite TV, some terraces, some sea views. Call ahead or come early to luck into the perfect one. The office is open daily from 9am to 8pm. Room rates vary from 20€ to 60€ ($23–$69) per person depending on size and style of room (the pricier ones have sea views or are on the water), number of people, and how long you stay—but if you tell them you're a Frommer's reader and show them this book, you can get a 5% discount in high season, 10% discount in low season.

Like his friends Luciano and Roberto Fazioli, Mario Franceschetti runs a decent, above-board rental room business called **Mar Mar,** Via Colombo 25B (at the harbor end of town; ② and fax **0187-920-932;** www.marmar.5terre.com), handling eight apartments that sleep two to six people (35€–50€/$40–$58 per person, depending on how many are in the room), and six rooms in a nearby B&B (② **0187-920-773;** 65€–90€/$75–$104 for a double). Some of the rental units, and all the B&B rooms, come with TV and bathroom; some rental units have kitchenettes. Mar Mar's office, open daily from 8:30am to 12:30pm and 2:30 to 7pm, also offers Internet access at .10€ (10¢) per minute, and kayak rental for 3.50€ ($4.05) per hour for a one-seater, 8€ ($9) for a two-seater.

Locanda Ca dei Duxi   This is one of the more established outfits in the center, constantly expanding their little hospitality empire and offering more hotel-style amenities than most rental rooms around, spread across two "locandas" (the original six-room 18th-century building and a five-room inn across the street, which opened in summer 2001), three rental rooms, and several apartments. All of the midsize rooms are simple, with new modular furnishings, tile floors, and firm wood-slat beds. Room nos. 5 and 6 on the top floor have exposed beams and a bit of castle view.

They also rent three very simple **apartments** (which are part of the hotel rather than being in a separate building like most other Italian hotels that rent apartments) sleeping two to seven people (two bedrooms and a bunk-bed in the living room), with kitchenette and TV, small terrace over the main drag, and midget tubs in the bathrooms. They usually rent per week (though sometimes they will rent them on a daily basis during slow periods) at rates that boil down to 60€ to 80€ ($69–$92) per night, depending on the season and number of people.

Via Colombo 36/Via Pecunia 19, 19017 Riomaggiore (SP). ℂ **0187-920-036** or 338-841-8175. Fax 0187-920-036. www.duxi.it. 16 units, plus 3 in-house apts to let. 65€–110€ ($75–$127) double; 80€–130€ ($92–$150) triple; 90€–140€ ($104–$161) quad. Breakfast included. AE, DC, MC, V. Parking 7€ ($8) at hotel or 18€ ($21) in public lot. **Amenities:** Room service (breakfast). *In room:* A/C, TV, minibar, hair dryer (ask at desk), safe.

Villa Argentina　The only full-fledged hotel in Riomaggiore is in the newer section of town, on a hillside about a 5-minute walk (up a lot of stairs) from the center. This location affords astonishing views, which you can enjoy from most of the guest rooms, and provides a nice retreat from the tourist-crowded main street and harbor. A breezy, arbor-shaded terrace and a bar area decorated by local artists off the lobby are the places to relax. And, while the tile-floored rooms upstairs will not overwhelm you with their character, they are large and pleasant, if blandly furnished, with ceiling fans and (all except room nos. 4–6 and 10) balconies featuring views over the town to the sea. The hoteliers also offer apartments accommodating two to six people.

Via de Gaspari 187, 19017 Riomaggiore. ℂ and fax **0187-920-213**. www.hotelvillargentina.com. 15 units. 78€–106€ ($90–$122) double; 100€–120€ ($115–$138) triple; 90€ ($104) apt for 2 people, 180€ ($207) apt for 4 people, 270€ ($310) apt for 6 people. Breakfast 7€ ($8). MC, V. Parking 7.50€ ($9). **Amenities:** Ligurian restaurant nearby; bar; sauna (nearby); watersports equipment rentals; concierge; tour desk; salon (nearby); room service (24-hr.); laundry service; same-day dry cleaning. *In room:* TV, hair dryer, safe, no phone.

WHERE TO DINE

La Lanterna ⭐ SEAFOOD/LIGURIAN　From a table on the terrace here, perched only a few feet above Riomaggiore's snug harbor, you can hear the waves lap against the rocks and watch the local fishermen mend their nets. Seafood, of course, dominates the menu, with many unusual Ligurian-style dishes, such as *spaghetti al scoglio* (spaghetti with mussels and shrimp in a white wine sauce) or *spaghetti ai ricci di mare* (with sea urchins). The antipasto of shrimp, smoked tuna, and grilled swordfish is excellent and can suffice as an entree; you should, however, make room for one of the house specialties, *chiche*—homemade gnocchi filled with seafood and topped with a spicy tomato sauce.

Riomaggiore. ℂ **0187-920-589**. Primi 6€–7.50€ ($7–$9); secondi 9€–19€ ($10–$22); fixed-price menu without wine 25€ ($29). AE, DC, MC, V. Daily 11am–midnight. Closed Nov.

NIGHTLIFE

Riomaggiore's nightlife, such as it is, revolves around the **Bar Centrale,** smack in the middle of town at Via C. Colombo 144 (ℂ **0187-920-208**), with tables set under a roofed wooden deck in the middle of the main drag, Devil's Kiss beer on tap, and a cheap ISDN Internet connection (.10€/12¢ per min.; 3€/$3.45 for half an hour). It's open Tuesday to Sunday 7:30am to 1am.

Appendix A: Italy in Depth

Lord Byron called Italy his magnet; Robert Browning said Italy was engraved on his heart. Being poets, these fellows might have been given to hyperbole, but Italy does have a remarkably strong, and usually favorable, effect on visitors.

Part of the draw is Italy's cultural legacy—the country was, after all, the cradle of both ancient Rome and the Renaissance, two of the highest points of Western civilization. It's blessed with an endlessly varied and seductive scenery of azure seas, silvery olive groves, stony hill towns, snowcapped mountains, and colorful fishing villages. The cuisine only seems to get better from region to region, and an enormous emphasis is placed on hospitality. Most appealing of all is the emphasis Italians place on enjoying life—from strolling through town during the evening *passeggiata* to lingering over a 3-hour dinner—and they seem determined to ensure their visitors do the same.

But Italy isn't just a postcard: It has suffered its share of social and economic woes and has been riddled with political scandal. If you care to look, you'll find poverty, crime, unchecked urban development, and social injustice, just as there is in any other industrialized Western nation. But Italy offsets these realities with more grace notes than most other places manage, and in so doing rewards the traveler with a remarkable and enduring experience.

1 History 101: Italy Past & Present

In its 3,000 years of history, Italy has endured emperors and kings, duchies and despots, fools and knaves, popes and presidents. Italy has been a definer of democracy, has fallen prey to dictators, and has sagged into anarchy. Italy knows triumph, and it knows loss, but above all, it knows how to survive.

PREHISTORY & EARLY SETTLERS

Findings in caves around Isneria in the Abruzzi suggest that humans settled in Italy about a million years ago. Neanderthal man made a brief appearance, and Cro-Magnon, who knew how to fish and domesticate animals, showed up about 18,000 years ago.

Though prehistoric early cultural groups such as the Ligurians (Neolithic rulers of northwestern Italy—not just Liguria, but Piedmont and Lombardy as well—from 2400–1800 B.C.),

Dateline

- Prehistory. Neanderthal humans roam Italy; around 10,000 B.C., Cro-Magnon shows up.
- 1200 B.C. Etruscans begin to emigrate from Asia Minor, settling in Tuscany.
- 800 B.C. Greeks colonize Sicily and the peninsula's boot (collectively "Magna Graecia").
- 753 B.C. Romulus, says legend, founds Rome. In fact, Rome grows out of a strategically located shepherd village.
- 700 B.C. Etruscans rise in power, peaking in the 6th century B.C., and make Rome their capital.
- 509 B.C. Republic of Rome is founded; power is shared by two consuls.
- 494–450 B.C. Office of the Tribune established to defend plebeian rights. The Twelve Tablets stating basic rights are carved, the foundation of Roman law.

continues

Remedello (Copper Age folks centered around Brescia in 1800–1600 B.C.), Veneti (Bronze Age Illyrians settling the Veneto region around 1000 B.C.), and Villanovans (an influential Iron Age people of 1000–800 B.C. from the area around Bologna) inhabited parts of northern Italy, most of the peninsula's early action took place in central and southern Italy. Magna Graecia (Greater Greece) controlled Sicily and southern Italy all the way up to Naples. The Etruscans, probably a people who emigrated from Asia Minor between the 12th and 8th centuries B.C., settled into central Italy, ruling Tuscany, Umbria, and, as the Tarquin dynasty, acted as kings of a small Latin village, atop hills at a bend in the Tiber River, called Rome.

THE RISE OF ROME

Leaving aside the famous legend of a she-wolf nursing the abandoned twins Romulus and Remus (the former kills his brother and founds a village called Rome) and Virgil's *Aeneid* (Aeneas of Troy flees the burning city at the end of the Trojan War, makes his way to Romulus's little village, and turns it into an ancient superpower), Rome probably began as a collection of Latin and Sabine villages in the Tiber Valley. It was originally a kingdom ruled by the Etruscan Tarquin dynasty. In 509 B.C. the last Tarquin king raped the daughter of a powerful Roman. After the girl committed suicide, infuriated Romans ejected the king and established a republic ruled by two consuls (chosen from among the patrician elite) whose power was balanced by tribunes elected from among the plebian masses.

The young Roman Republic sent its military throughout the peninsula and by 279 B.C. ruled all of Italy. Rome's armies trampled Grecian colonies throughout the Mediterranean, and after a series of brutal wars defeated Carthage (present-day Tunisia), a rival sea power and once Rome's archenemy.

- **279 B.C.** Romans now rule all of the Italian peninsula.
- **146 B.C.** Rome defeats Tunisian power in Carthage; the Republic now controls Sicily, North Africa, Spain, Sardinia, Greece, and Macedonia.
- **100 B.C.** Julius Caesar born.
- **60 B.C.** Caesar, Pompey, and Crassus share power in the First Triumvirate.
- **51 B.C.** Caesar triumphs over Gaul (France).
- **44 B.C.** March 15, Caesar assassinated, leaving all to his nephew and heir, Octavian.
- **27 B.C.** Octavian, now Augustus, is declared emperor, beginning Roman Empire and 200 years of peace and prosperity.
- **A.D. 29 (or 33)** Jesus is crucified in Roman province of Judea.
- **64–100** Nero persecutes Christians; a succession of military commanders restore order; Trajan expands the empire.
- **200** Goths invade from the north; the empire begins to decline.
- **313** With the Edict of Milan, Emperor Constantine I grants Christians freedom of religion. By 324 it is declared the official religion. Constantine also establishes Constantinople as the eastern capital, splitting the empire in half.
- **410–76** Waves of northern barbarian tribes continue to overrun Italy and sack Rome itself, eventually setting up their own puppet "emperors."
- **476** Last emperor deposed; the empire falls; the Dark Ages begin.
- **590–604** Church asserts political control as Pope Gregory I "the Great" brings some stability to the peninsula.
- **774–800** Frankish king Charlemagne invades Italy and is crowned emperor by Pope Leo III. Upon his death, Italy dissolves into a series of small warring kingdoms.
- **962** Holy Roman Empire founded under Otto I, king of Saxony; serves as the temporal arm of the church's spiritual power.
- **11th century** Normans conquer southern Italy and introduce feudalism. The first Crusades are launched.
- **1309–77** Papacy abandons Rome for Avignon, France.

By 146 B.C., Rome controlled not only all of the Italian peninsula and Sicily but also North Africa, Spain, Sardinia, Greece, and Macedonia.

Still, Rome wanted more. It invaded Gaulish lands to the north and added what we now call France and Belgium to its realm. Rome even crossed the English Channel and conquered Britain all the way up to the Scottish Lowlands (Hadrian's Wall still stands as a testament to how far north the Roman army got). However, so much military success so distant from Rome itself resulted in a severely weakened home front. With war booty filling the coffers, Rome ended taxation on its citizens. So much grain poured in from North Africa that the Roman farmer couldn't find a market for his wheat and simply stopped growing it. The booty had an additional price tag: corruption. Senators advanced their own lots rather than the provinces ostensibly under their care. Plebeians clamored for a bigger share, and the slaves revolted repeatedly. More reforms appeased the plebes while the slaves were put down with horrific barbarity (one famous slave revolt, led by Spartacus, was stopped by capturing the slave army and crucifying it on crosses that lined both sides of the Via Appia from Rome and stretched for miles upon miles).

HAIL CAESAR!

At the end of the 2nd century B.C., the Republic, sped along by a corrupt Senate, was corroding into near-collapse. Julius Caesar—successful general, skilled orator, and shrewd politician—stepped in to help maintain control over Rome's vast territories, but from the day Caesar declared himself "dictator for life," Rome, as a republic, was finished. After sharing governmental power with others in a series of Triumvirates, Caesar became the sole consul in 44 B.C.

Caesar rose in popular influence partly by endearing himself to the lower

- **1350** The Black Death decimates Europe, reducing Italy's population by a third.
- **1450** City-states hold power; Venice controls much of the eastern Mediterranean. The Humanist movement rediscovers the art and philosophy of ancient Greece and gives rise to the artistic Renaissance.
- **ca. 1500** Peak of the High Renaissance. Italian artists working at the turn of the 15th century include Leonardo da Vinci, Michelangelo, Raphael, Botticelli, Giovanni Bellini, Mantegna, and Titian.
- **1519–27** Carlos I Hapsburg of Spain is crowned Holy Roman Emperor as Charles V in 1519. He wages war against the French, and the pope scurries back and forth, supporting first one side then the next as their wars are played out largely in Italy over Italian territories. In 1527 Charles V marches into Rome and sacks the city while Pope Clement VII escapes. Charles occupies nearly all of northern Italy, divvying it up amongst his followers.
- **1535** Francesco II Sforza of Milan dies, leaving the Duchy in Spanish Hapsburg hands.
- **1545–63** Council of Trent takes a hard line against the reformist Protestant movements sweeping Europe north of the Alps, launching the Counter-Reformation and, as an unexpected consequence, ultimately reducing the pope's power as a secular ruler of Europe to merely a prince of central Italy.
- **17th–18th centuries** Italy's darkest hour: Brigands control the countryside, the Austrians and Spanish everything else. By the mid–18th century, wealthy northern Europeans begin taking the Grand Tour, journeying to Italy to study ancient architecture and Italian old masters (as well as taking advantage of the sunny clime and low-cost living). Italy's tourism industry has begun.
- **1784** The French Revolution sparks Italian nationalism.
- **1796–1814** Napoléon sweeps through Italy, installing friends and relatives as rulers.

continues

classes through a lifelong fight against the corrupt Senate. As his power crested, he forced many immoral senators to flee Rome, introduced social reforms, inaugurated the first of many new public building programs in the center of Rome (still visible as the Forum of Caesar), and added Gaul (France) to the dying Republic. But Caesar's emphasis on the plebeians and their concerns (as well as his own thirst for power) did little to endear him to the old guard of patricians and senators. On March 15, 44 B.C., Caesar strolled out of the Baths of Pompey to meet Brutus, Cassius, and other "friends" who lay in wait with daggers hidden beneath their togas.

Caesar left everything to his nephew and heir, the 18-year-old Octavian. From the increasingly irrelevant Senate, Octavian eventually received the title Augustus, and from the people, lifetime tribuneship. And so Octavian became Emperor Augustus, sole ruler of Rome and most of the Western world.

THE EMPIRE

Augustus's long reign ushered in Pax Romana, 200 years of peace under Roman rule. The new emperor, who preferred to be called "First Citizen," reorganized the military and the provincial governments and reinstituted constitutional rule. Succeeding emperors weren't so virtuous: deranged Tiberius and Caligula, henpecked Claudius I, and Nero, who in A.D. 64 persecuted the Christians of Rome with a viciousness easily equal to the earlier slave repressions. Several of the military commanders who became emperors were exceptions to the tyrant mold. Late in the 1st century, Trajan expanded the empire's eastern boundaries and constructed great public works, including a vast series of markets (recently reopened to visitors in Rome).

At this peak, Rome knew amenities not to be enjoyed again in Europe until the 18th century. Citizens were

- 1814 Napoléon's defeat at Waterloo.
- 1830 Beginning of the Risorgimento political movement in Turin and Genoa, which will culminate in Italian nationalism, accompanied by a new Renaissance of literature and music.
- 1861 Kingdom of Italy is created under Vittorio Emanuele II, Savoy king of Piedmont (Piemonte), and united through the military campaign of General Garibaldi. Turin serves briefly as interim capital.
- 1870 Rome, last papal stronghold, falls to Garibaldi. Italy becomes a country, Rome its capital.
- Late 19th century Mass emigration to America and other foreign shores, though mostly from the impoverished, agricultural south.
- 1915 Italy enters World War I on Allied side.
- 1922 Mussolini marches on Rome and puts his Fascist Blackshirts in charge of the country, declaring himself prime minister.
- 1935 Mussolini defeats and annexes Ethiopia.
- 1939 Italy enters the war by signing an alliance with Nazi Germany.
- 1943 Italy switches sides as Allied troops push Nazis north up peninsula; by 1945, Mussolini and mistress executed by partisans, strung up at a Milan gas station and pelted with stones by the crowds.
- 1946 A national referendum narrowly establishes the Republic of Italy.
- 1950–93 Fifty changes of government were seen, but also the "economic miracle" that has made Italy the world's fifth leading economy.
- 1993–97 Series of disasters rock Italy's cultural roots: 1993 Mafia bombing of Florence's Uffizi Galleries; January 1996 fire at Venice's La Fenice opera house; April 1997 conflagration in Turin's cathedral; September 1997 earthquakes in Umbria, which destroyed priceless frescoes in Assisi.
- 1993–2000 Italy's Christian Democrat–controlled government dissolves amid corruption allegations. Silvio Berlusconi's right-wing coalition holds power for a few months, followed by center–left wing coalitions that introduce the most stable

privileged to have police protection, fire fighting, libraries, sanitation, huge public baths such as the Caracalla by the Appian Way, and even central heating and running water—if they could afford them.

The empire's decline began around A.D. 200. After sacking the city several times, Goths and other Germanic tribes set up their own leaders as emperors and were more interested in the spoils of an empire than in actually running one. And while Gibbon's famous opus *The Decline and Fall of the Roman Empire* takes up an entire bookshelf to explain Rome's downfall, in the end it all boils down to the fact that the empire had become just too big to manage.

After embracing Christianity in his famous 313 Edict of Milan, Emperor Constantine I tried to resolve the problem by moving the capital of the empire from Rome to the city of Byzantium (later renamed Constantinople and today known as Istanbul). The Roman empire was irrevocably split in half: a western Roman Empire comprising most of Europe and North Africa, and an eastern Roman Empire filling southeast Europe and the Near East.

CURTAIN GOING DOWN: THE DARK AGES

In 476, the last emperor (ironically, named Romulus) fell from power and the Roman Empire collapsed. It would be 1,500 years before Italy was once again united as a single nation. As the 6th century opened, Italy was in chaos.

governments in decades under prime ministers Romano Prodi, Massimo d'Alema, and Giuliano Amato.

- **2001** The first cases of BSE (mad cow disease) in Italy are confirmed; beef consumption plummets over 70%, and the government temporarily bans many kinds of steak on the bone. Media magnate (and the world's 29th richest man) Silvio Berlusconi—briefly prime minister in 1993 but brought down by professional and political scandals—gains control once again of the Italian government as part of a center-right coalition including the neo-Fascist Alleanza Nazionale party and the racist and separatist Lega del Nord, which wants to make northern Italy a new country called "Padania" with Milan as its capital (leaving Rome to govern the shrunken "Italy" of the south).

- **2002** January 1: Italy, along with most of western Europe, adopts the euro as its currency. January 2: Prices on everything skyrocket.

- **2003** Prime Minster Berlusconi, who through private media holdings and his government post controls 98% of Italian television (not to mention the country's largest publishing empire), and who in late 2002 fired his foreign minister and declared he himself would run that office, forces through legislation to protect him from being prosecuted for any crimes while in office—conveniently just as one of the many bribery cases that have been brought against him was about to come to a conclusion. Mussolini would have been proud.

Waves of barbarians from the north poured in while provincial nobles engaged in petty bickering and Rome became the personal fiefdom of the papacy. The Goths continued to rule the "Western Roman Empire" nominally from Ravenna, but were soon driven out by Constantinople. It was the Roman Catholic church, beginning with Pope Gregory I "the Great" late in the 6th century, that finally provided some stability. In 731 Pope Gregory II renounced Rome's nominal dependence on Constantinople and reoriented the Roman Catholic Church firmly toward Europe—in the process finalizing the empire's division into east and west.

During the Dark Ages, some inhabitants of the Veneto flatlands, seeking some degree of safety from the barbarian hordes, slowly moved out onto the islets of the north Adriatic's wide, marshy lagoon. The villages they founded eventually grew into the fairy-tale city of Venice. In 564 another Germanic tribe, called the

Hapsburgs

Though the Hapsburgs were never Italian, their imperial shenanigans frequently impacted northern Italy as they played out their power struggles with France on Italian battlefields, using Italian territories and duchies as pieces in a giant, prolonged, often bloody chess match. The Hapsburg name confuses some, though. It began with the 13th-century rulers of Swabia, in southern Germany. The family's main man in the early 16th century was Carlos of Ghent, who became king of Spain and, in 1519, changed his name to Holy Roman Emperor Charles V. When he abdicated in 1556, he left the Spanish crown to his heirs—the Spanish Hapsburgs—but left the family's Austrian/Bavarian lands, as well as the imperial title, to little brother Ferdinand I, whose heirs kept the title, and the Austro-Hungarian dynasty, for centuries.

Lombards, clambered over the Alps and swept through much of Italy, conquering a good two-thirds of the peninsula ruled from their base at Pavia. By 599 Pope Gregory I "the Great" had begun flexing the secular power of the papacy (beginning a policy that would eventually set the pope at the head of Europe's power structure), negotiating a peace between Constantinople and Italy's new Lombard rulers.

The Lombards weren't satisfied, though, and by 752 had conquered Ravenna itself. The pope cast around for a new ally against the Lombards and settled on the powerful king of another Barbarian tribe, Pepin the Short of the Franks. In 754 Pepin invades Italy and thrashes the Lombards; 20 years later his famous son Charlemagne follows suit. Not satisfied with merely the Lombard crown, the French king continued to Rome and convinces the pope to crown him as a new emperor, the so-called Holy Roman Emperor, on Christmas Day in the year 800. This new imperial office would become the plum of western European monarchies for nearly a millennium, and further helped cement the relationship between the papacy and the secular titular head of western Europe.

During the Middle Ages, northern Italy fragmented into a collection of city-states. The Lombards had to be content with a reduced duchy filling the Po Valley south of the Alps and Italy's large lakes, wedged between the eastern territory of the Republic of Venice and the western Duchy of Savoy in Piedmont as well as the coastal territory ruled by the maritime Republic of Genoa. Plenty of principalities, duchies, republics, and smaller city-states filled in the cracks, with Austrian Hapsburg rulers snaking their influence down the Adige River valley into the Dolomites, as well as across the eastern Alps to the coastline curving around the Northern Adriatic, founding the port of Trieste. This put them in constant conflict with the territories of Venice, and the line dividing the realms of Venice's Republican Doges and Austria's Hapsburg Emperors continued to shift, expand, and retreat well into the 20th century.

Meanwhile, the papacy's temporal power—the Papal States—slowly but inexorably shrank, eventually encompassing only Rome and portions of central Italy's provinces. Its political concerns turned to arguing with the German and Austrian emperors over the office of Holy Roman Emperor, which became increasingly irrelevant to daily affairs as the Renaissance dawned.

In the mid–14th century, the Black Death ravaged Europe, killing a third of Italy's population. Despite such setbacks, northern Italian cities grew wealthy from Crusade booty, trade with one another and with the Middle East, and banking. These wealthy principalities and pseudo-republics ruled by the merchant elite flexed their muscles in the absence of a strong central authority.

CURTAIN GOING UP: THE RENAISSANCE

The Renaissance peaked in the 15th century as northern cities bullied their way to city-state status. Even while warring constantly with one another to extend their territories, such ruling families as the Medicis in Florence, the Estes in Ferrara, and the Sforzas and Gonzagas in Milan grew incredibly rich and powerful.

The princes, popes, and merchant princes who ruled Italy's city-states, spurred on by the Humanist philosophical movement, collectively bankrolled the explosion of poetic and artistic expression we now call the Renaissance (see "Italy's Artistic Heritage" section, below). But with no clear political authority or unified military, Italy was easy pickings and by the mid–16th century, Spain, courtesy of Charles V, occupied nearly all of the country.

THE SECOND FALL

From the mid–16th century until the end of the 18th century, Italy suffered economic depression and foreign domination. As emphasis on world trade shifted away from the Mediterranean, Italy's influence diminished. Within Italy itself, Spanish Bourbons controlled the kingdoms of the south, the pope the center, and Austria and France fought over rule of the north, using Italy's realms—from the large Lombard duchy of Milan to tiny principalities like Mantua—as pawns in their power struggles. The only notable free state was the mighty Republic of Venice (though the extent of its landlubbing provinces in the Veneto, Dolomites [Dolomiti], and Friuli slowly shrank). These foreign overlords kept raising taxes, farming declined, the birthrate sank, and bandits proliferated. The 18th century is viewed as Italy's nadir. In fact, only Europe's eager ear for Italian music and eye for art and architecture kept the Italian profile haughty and its cultural patrimony resplendent.

It was the late-18th-century French Revolution and the arrival of Napoléon that lit Italy's nationalistic fire, although it would be the mid–19th century before the Risorgimento movement and a new king could spread the flame.

THE SECOND RISE: THE 19TH CENTURY

Italians initially gave Napoléon an exultant *benvenuto!* when he swept through the peninsula and swept out Italy's 18th-century political disasters (along with the Austrian army). But Napoléon, in the end, neither united Italy nor provided it with self-government—he merely set up his own friends and relatives as new princes and dukes. Many Italians, however, were fired up by the Napoleonic revolutionary rhetoric. The *Risorgimento* (resurgence) nationalist movement—an odd amalgam of radicals, moderate liberals, and Roman Catholic conservatives—struggled for 30 years to create a single, united Italy under a constitutional monarchy.

You'll find Risorgimento heroes' names recalled in streets and piazze throughout Italy: Giuseppe Mazzini provided the intellectual rigor for the movement; the political genius of noble-born Camillo Cavour engineered the underpinnings of the new nation (he served as its second prime minister); and General Giuseppe Garibaldi and his "Redshirt" soldiers did the legwork by conquering reluctant or foreign-controlled territories. In 1861 Vittorio Emanuele II of the southern French House of Savoy, previously king only of Piedmont and Liguria, became the first king of Italy. By 1871 Garibaldi finally defeated the papal holdout of Rome and the great city once again became capital of a unified Italy.

FINALLY, A NATION UNITED

A united nation? On paper, yes, but the old sectional differences remained. While there was rapid industrialization in the north, the south labored under the repressive neo-feudal agricultural ways of the late 19th century, creating a north/south division and mutual mistrust that still pervades Italian society. The north views the south as indolent, a welfare state sucking dry the money made in the industrial north; the south sees the north as elitist and arrogant, constantly proposing or enacting laws to keep the south economically depressed. Many southerners escaped economic hardship and political powerlessness by emigrating to the industrialized north, or to greener pastures abroad in the U.S., South America, or northern Europe.

Italy entered World War I on the Allied side in exchange for territorial demands, and to vanquish that old foe Austria. In the end the Austro-Hungarian Empire was defeated, but at the Paris Peace Conference, Italy was granted much less territory than had been promised (though it did receive Trieste), which compounded the country's problems. As southerners abandoned the country in droves, the economy stagnated, and what remained of Italy's world importance seemed to be fading rapidly, along came Benito Mussolini, promising to restore national pride and bring order out of the chaos.

FASCISM REIGNS

Mussolini marched on Rome in 1922, forced the king to make him premier, nicknamed himself Il Duce (the Duke), and quickly repressed all other political factions. He put his Fascist "Blackshirts" in charge of the entire country: schools, the press, industry, and labor. Seeking, as Italian despot-hopefuls throughout history have done, to endear himself to the general populace, Mussolini instituted a vast public works program, most of which eventually failed. Mussolini fancied himself a second Caesar and spent some time excavating the archaeological remains of ancient Rome—not always with the most stringent scientific methods—to help glorify his reign and lend it authority. The Great Depression of the 1930s made life considerably more difficult for Italians, and, to divert attention from his shortcomings as a ruler, Mussolini turned to foreign adventures, defeating and annexing Ethiopia in 1935.

Mussolini entered Italy into World War II as an Axis ally of the Nazis, but the Italian heart was not really in the war, and most Italians had little wish to pursue Hitler's anti-Semitic policies. Armed partisan resistance to the official government forces and to the Nazis remained strong. By 1945 the Italian people had had enough. They rose against Mussolini and the Axis, and the Fascists were disbanded. King Victor Emmanuel III, who had collaborated with the Fascists without much enthusiasm during the past 2 decades, appointed a new premier. At the end of the war, Mussolini and his mistress were pictured in the world press hanging by their heels at a Milanese gas station after being shot by partisans.

DEMOCRACY AT LAST

After the war, Italians narrowly voted to become a republic, and in 1946 a new republican constitution went into effect. Various permutations of the center-right Christian Democrat party ruled in a succession of more than 50 governments until 1993, when the entire government dissolved in a flurry of corruption and graft. The country's leaders were prosecuted (and many jailed) by what became known as the "Clean Hands" judges of Milan. The two main parties, the Christian Democrats and the Communists, both splintered in the aftermath, giving rise to some 16 major political parties and countless minor ones.

The parties formed various coalitions, leading to such strange political bed-fellows as the Forza Italia alliance, headed by media mogul Silvio Berlusconi, which filled the national power vacuum during 1994. It included both the nationalist Alleanza Nazionale party (the modern incarnation of the Fascist party) and the Lega del Nord, the separatist "Northern League" (originally the "Lombard League"), which wanted to split Italy in half, making Milan capital of a new country in the north called "Padania" and leaving Rome to govern the poor south. In 2000, though, the Lega changed its tune to become more palatable and is now calling for devolution, a decentralized government with more power going to individual regions.

In 1994 the center-left Olive Tree coalition swept the national elections and Italy enjoyed a novelty: 3 years of stable rule under the government of Prime Minister Romano Prodi, replaced by a center-left government of Massimo D'Alema. Interestingly, given the stereotype among fellow Europeans of Italy as a nation prone to graft and political chaos, Prodi—an economist before becoming prime minister and the man who reigned in Italy's debt to qualify the country for the European Union—was later named to head the European Commission to restore its status after a humiliating scandal.

By 2001 Berlusconi had fought off the dozens of legal charges of corruption (though courts in Spain, trying him for corporate crimes relating to his business relations in Iberia, found him guilty), and in April of that year, he and his right wing Forza Italia partners came back into power, just in time to shepherd Italy through the switch-over from the lira to the euro in 2002 (originally a left-wing initiative). Berlusconi continued to consolidate power through 2002 and 2003, introducing ever more legislation to protect himself and his interests from criminal investigations, as well as laws that would allow his private media company to control even more of the country's communications industry (which will be tough to accomplish, since through the trio of state-run RAI channels and his own Mediaset network, he already controls the six most popular of Italy's seven broadcast channels).

Politically, though, some things never change in Italy. The same mistrust among factions continues: Cities are still paranoid about their individuality and their rights, and the division between north and south is as sharp as ever. The Mafia had by the late 19th century become a kind of shadow government in the south, and to this day controls a staggering number of politicians (including senators and even prime ministers), national officials, and judges, providing one scandal after another.

Economically, it's a different story. The "economic miracle" of the north has worked around the political chaos (and often has even taken advantage of it) to make Italy the world's fifth largest economy. Even the south, while continuing to lag behind, isn't in the desperate straits it once was. The outsider looks and wonders how the country keeps going amid the political chaos, Byzantine bureaucracy, and deep regional differences. The Italian just shrugs and rolls his eyes. Italians have always excelled at getting by under difficult circumstances and making the most of any situation. If nothing else, they're masters at survival.

2 Italy's Artistic Heritage

When you mention art in Italy, most people's thoughts fly first to the Renaissance, to Giotto, Donatello, Michelangelo, Raphael, and Leonardo. But Italy's artistic heritage actually goes back at least 2,500 years.

ART 101
CLASSICAL: GREEKS, ETRUSCANS & ROMANS (5TH CENTURY B.C.–5TH CENTURY A.D.)

Today, all, or almost all, design roads lead to Milan. In the beginning, though, all roads led from Athens. What the **Greeks** identified early on that captured the hearts and minds of so many others was classical rendering of form. To the ancients, *classic* or *classical* simply meant perfection—of proportion, balance, harmony, and form. To the Greeks, man was the measure of perfection, an attitude lost in the Middle Ages and not rediscovered until the dawn of the Renaissance.

Although those early tourists to the Italian peninsula, the **Etruscans,** arrived with their own styles, by the 6th century B.C. they were borrowing heavily from the Greeks in their sculpture (and importing thousands of Attic painted vases). The **Romans,** in turn, copied heavily from the Greeks, often ad nauseum as they cranked out countless facsimiles of Greek sculptures to decorate Roman patrician homes and gardens. Bronze portraiture, a technique with Greek and Etruscan roots, was polished to photographic perfection.

Although painting got rather short shrift in ancient Rome (it was used primarily for decorative purposes), bucolic frescoes, the technique of painting on wet plaster, adorned the walls of the wealthy in Rome, though nothing significant survives in the north of Italy. Mosaics were rather better done, and survive the ages more intact, and you can see some of the best Roman mosaic flooring at the excavations of Aquileia in the Friuli.

BYZANTINE AND ROMANESQUE (5TH–13TH CENTURIES)

Artistic expression in the Dark Ages and early medieval Italy was largely church-related. Mass was recited in Latin, so to try to help explain the most important lessons to the illiterate masses, Biblical bas-reliefs around the churches' main doors, and wall paintings and altarpieces inside, told key tales to inspire faith in God and fear of sin (*Last Judgment*'s were favorites). Otherwise, decoration was spare, and what little existed was often destroyed, replaced, or covered over the centuries as tastes changed and cathedrals were remodeled.

The Byzantine style of painting and mosaic was very stylized and static, an iconographic tradition imported from the remnant eastern half of the Roman Empire centered at Byzantium (its major political outposts in Italy were Ravenna and Venice). Faces (and eyes) were almond-shaped with pointy little chins, noses long with a spoonlike depression at the top, and folds in robes (always Virgin Mary blue over red) represented by stylized cross-hatching in gold leaf.

Romanesque sculpture was somewhat more fluid, but still far from naturalistic, usually idiosyncratic and often wonderfully childlike in its narrative simplicity, frequently freely mixing Biblical scenes with the myths and motifs from local pagan traditions that were being slowly incorporated into early medieval Christianity. Romanesque art was seen as crude by most later periods and usually replaced or destroyed over the centuries; it survives mostly in scraps, innumerable column capitals and tympanums or carvings set above church doors all across Italy.

Some of the best major examples of this era in northern Italy include the astounding mosaics decorating San Marco cathedral in Venice, a late Byzantine church of domes and a glittering array of mosaics—though while the overall effect is indeed Byzantine, many of the mosaics are of various later dates. **Verona's San Zeno Maggiore** sports 48 relief panels on the bronze doors, one of the most important pieces of Romanesque sculpture in Italy, cast between the 9th and 11th centuries and flanked by strips of 12th-century stone reliefs.

Aosta's Collegiata dei Santi Pietro e Orso, on the edge of town, preserves part of an 11th-century fresco cycle and 40 remarkable 12th-century carved column capitals in the cloisters.

INTERNATIONAL GOTHIC (LATE 13TH–EARLY 15TH CENTURIES)

Late medieval Italian art continued to be largely ecclesiastical. Church facades and pulpits were festooned with statues and carvings. In both Gothic painting and sculpture, figures tended to be more natural than in the Romanesque (and the colors in painting more varied and rich), but highly stylized and rhythmic, the figures' features and gestures exaggerated for symbolic or emotional emphasis. In painting especially, late Gothic artists such as Giotto started introducing greater realism, a sense of depth, and more realistic emotion into their art, sowing the seeds of the Renaissance.

Without a doubt, **Giotto** (1266–1337) was the greatest Gothic artist, the man who lifted painting from its Byzantine funk and set it on the road to the realism and perspective of the Renaissance. His most renowned work is the fresco cycle of Assisi's Basilica di San Francesco, but arguably better (and more certain of its authorship) is Padua's (Padova's) outstanding **Scrovegni (Arena) Chapel.** The bulk of great Gothic art resides in Tuscany and Umbria, but Verona was blessed to have **Antonio Pisanello** (1395–1455), whose frescoes survive in Sant'Anastasia and San Fermo, and in Mantua (Mantova) at the Palazzo Ducale.

RENAISSANCE & MANNERISM (EARLY 15TH TO MID–17TH CENTURIES)

From the 14th to 16th centuries, the popularity of the Humanist movement in philosophy prompted princes and powerful prelates to patronize a generation of innovative young artists. These painters, sculptors, and architects were experimenting with new modes in art and breaking with static medieval traditions to pursue a greater degree of expressiveness and naturalism, using such techniques as linear perspective (actually pioneered by architect Brunelleschi and sculptors Donatello and Ghiberti). The term *Renaissance,* or "rebirth," was only later applied to this period in Florence, from which the movement spread to the rest of Italy and Europe.

Eventually the High Renaissance began to stagnate, producing vapid works of technical perfection but little substance. Several artists sought ways out of the downward spiral. Mannerism was the most interesting attempt, a movement that found its muse in the extreme torsion of Michelangelo's figures—in sculpture and painting—and his unusual use of oranges, greens, and other nontraditional colors, most especially in the Sistine Chapel ceiling. In sculpture, Mannerism produced twisting figures in exaggerated *contraposto* positioning.

This list of Renaissance giants merely scratches the surface of the masters Italy gave rise to in the 15th and 16th centuries.

Donatello (Donato Bardi; ca. 1386–1466) was the first full-fledged Renaissance sculptor, with a patented *schiacciato* technique of warping low relief surfaces and etching backgrounds in perspective to create a sense of deep space. His bronze and marble figures are some of the most expressive and psychologically probing of the Renaissance. Among his many innovations, this unassuming artist cast the first equestrian bronze since antiquity, the *Gattamelata* in Padua.

Leonardo da Vinci (1452–1519) was the original "Renaissance Man," dabbling his genius in a bit of everything from art to philosophy to science (on paper, he even designed machine guns and rudimentary helicopters). Little of his remarkable painting survives, however, as he often experimented with new pigment mixes that proved to lack the staying power of traditional materials. Leonardo invented such painterly effects as the fine haze of *sfumato,* "a moisture-laden atmosphere that delicately veils . . . forms." Unfortunately, the best example of this effect, his fresco of *The Last Supper* in Milan (1495–97), is sadly deteriorated, and even the ongoing multidecade restoration is saving but a shadow of the fresco's glory. See his *Portrait of a Musician* in Milan's Pinacoteca Ambrosiana for a better-preserved example.

Michelangelo Buonarotti (1475–1564), heavyweight contender for world's greatest artist ever, was a genius in sculpture, painting, architecture, and poetry. He marked the apogee of the Renaissance. A complex and difficult man—intensely jealous, probably manic-depressive, and certainly homosexual—Michelangelo enjoyed great fame in a life plagued by a series of never-ending projects commissioned by Pope Julius II—including Rome's Sistine Chapel frescoes. Michelangelo worshiped the male nude as the ultimate form and twisted the bodies of his figures (torsion) in different, often contradictory directions *(contraposto)* to bring out their musculature. When forced against his will to paint the Sistine Chapel, he broke almost all the rules and sent painting headlong in an entirely new direction—the Mannerist movement—marked by non-primary colors, Impressionistic shapes of light, and twisting muscular figures. While you'll have to go to Florence and Rome to see his greatest works, including the *David,* you can admire his final work (for free no less) in Milan, an oddly modern, elongated *Pietà* he was still working on when he died at age 89.

Raphael (Raffaello Sanzio; 1483–1520) is rightfully considered one of Western art's greatest draftsman. Raphael produced a body of work in his 37 short years that ignited European painters for generations to come. So it's only fitting that his only significant work in northern Italy, kept in Milan's Pinacoteca Ambrosiana, is a sketch, one for the *School of Athens,* the fresco of which graces the papal apartments of the Vatican, at once a celebration of Renaissance artistic precepts, the classical philosophers whose rediscovery spurred on the Renaissance, and Raphael's contemporaries (the various "philosophers" are actually portraits of Leonardo, Bramante, and Raphael himself—Michelangelo is not in the sketch, but was added in the painting).

All of the above artists hailed from central Italy. Now we get to some home-grown northern Italian talents. Though his father **Jacopo** (1400–71) and brother **Gentile** (1429–1507) were also fine practitioners of the family business (Jacopo really more from a Gothic vein, a student of Gentile da Fabriano and rival to Pisanello), it was **Giovanni Bellini** (1430–1516) who towered above them all with his painterly talent, limpid colors, sculptured forms, and complex compositions. Both he and his brother are best represented by works in Venice's Accademia and Palazzo Ducale as well as Milan's Pinacoteca di Brera. Giovanni Bellini's style and talent reverberated through Venetian art for generations; he himself taught the likes of Titian, Giorgione, Sebastiano del Piombo, and Palma il Vecchio.

Gentile and Giovanni had a sister, too, and as it happened she married a young painter named **Andrea Mantegna** (1431–1506). Mantegna excelled at three of the main tenets of Renaissance art: he was an early perfector of perspective (which

---

Fun Fact What's in a Name?

Many Italian artists came to be known by nicknames—usually based on the town from which they came—which are the names that we call them today. "Tintoretto" was called that because of his love of color ("*tinto*" in Italian). Leonardo had no official last name (he was the bastard son of a serving wench and her boss, a minor noble and landowner in the small town of Vinci), so everyone just called him "Leonardo from Vinci." Some also had silly nicknames, like Sandro Filipepi, better known to his buds as "Little Barrels"—or, in Italian, Botticelli.

---

he could warp masterfully), a keen observer of anatomy (which he modeled with sculptural exactitude), and he made careful studies of ancient architecture (the proportions and details of which he incorporated into his paintings). You'll find Mantegna's paintings throughout the region, from his early *Madonna and Child with Saints* altarpiece for Verona's San Zeno, to his work as court painter to the Gonzagas in Mantua (the Palazzo Ducale's *Camera degli Sposi*), to his unparalleled *Dead Christ,* considered the masterpiece of Milan's Pinacoteca di Brera (no small honor, considering the heavyweights inhabiting the premiere art gallery in northern Italy).

Titian (Tiziano Vecellio; 1485–1576) was the father of the Venetian High Renaissance, who imparted to the school his love of color and tonality and exploration of the effects of light on darkened scenes. In Venice you'll find his works everywhere, from canvases in the Accademia collections to altarpieces decorating churches such as the Frari to his early and famous *Battle* scene (1513) in the Palazzo Ducale's Sala del Maggior Consiglio.

After Titian, 16th-century Venetian art was dominated by two powerful talents, Paolo Veronese and **Tintoretto** (Jacopo Robusti; 1518–94). Tintoretto was something of a Venetian Mannerist, using a rapid, loose brushwork and a slightly somber, shadow-filled take on the tones of Titian's palette that together imparted a realism and vitality to his painting. Venice's Accademia has some works, of course, but his crowning glory is the Scuola Grande di San Rocco in Venice, for which he painted well over a dozen large-scale canvases. He also holds the honor of having produced (with the help of son Domenico) the largest oil painting in the world (6.9m by 24m/23 ft. by 79 ft.), the *Paradise* decorating the end wall of the Sala del Maggior Consiglio in the Palazzo Ducale in Mantua.

Verona-born **Paolo Veronese** (Paolo Caliari; 1528–88) has a much brighter, tighter style, and he loved crowding his canvases with hordes of extras straight out of 16th-century central casting. In fact, his broad inclusion of earthy details ran him afoul of the Counter-Reformation spirit of the times, and he only avoided incurring the church's wrath over the crowd of serving wenches and slave boys populating a *Last Supper* he painted by hastily retitling it *Feast in the House of Levi* (now in Venice's Accademia). The church of San Sebastiano boasts his ceiling frescoes, but it's Venice's Palazzo Ducale that bookends the career of Veronese (containing both his earliest paintings and one of his final ones). His earliest Venetian commissions (1553) were for paintings in the chambers where two groups in the highest echelon's of Venice's ruling body met, the Sala del Consiglio dei Dieci and the Sala dei Tre Capi del Consiglio. One of his final works (finished by his studio) was the huge *Apothesis of Venice* decorating the ceiling of the Sala del Maggior Consiglio. Veronese would be the main artist to inspire Tiepolo and others in Venice's next generation of baroque artists.

BAROQUE & ROCOCO (LATE 16TH–18TH CENTURIES)

The baroque is a more theatrical and decorative take on the Renaissance, mixing a kind of super-realism based on the peasant models and *chiaroscuro* (harsh light and exaggeratedly dark shadows) of Caravaggio with compositional complexity and explosions of dynamic fury, movement, color, and figures. Rococo is this later baroque art gone awry, frothy, and chaotic.

The baroque period produced many fine artists, but only a few true geniuses, and most of them (including Caravaggio and Bernini) worked in Rome and the south. **Giovanni Battista Tiepolo** (1696–1770) was by a long shot the best rococo artist there was, influenced by his Venetian late-Renaissance predecessors but also the Roman and Neapolitan baroque. His specialty was painting ceiling frescoes (and canvases meant to be placed in a ceiling) that opened up the space into frothy, cloud-filled Heavens of light, angels, and pale, sunrise colors. Though he painted many works for Veneto villas, including the sumptuous Villa Valmarana and Villa Pisani, he also spent much of his time traveling throughout Europe on long commissions (his work in Würzburg, Germany, enjoys distinction as the largest ceiling fresco in the world). His son **Giovanni Domenico Tiepolo** (1727–1804) carried on the family tradition in a Venice increasingly ruled by genre masters like **Antonio Canaletto** (1697–1738), whose ultra-realistic scenes of Venetian canals and palaces were snapped up by the collectors from across the Alps who began sniffing around Italy on their Grand Tour.

LATE 18TH CENTURY TO TODAY

After carrying the artistic church of innovation for over a millennium, Italy ran out of steam with the baroque, leaving countries such as France to develop the heights of neoclassicism (though Italy produced a few fine neoclassical sculptures) and late-19th-century Impressionism (Italians had their own version, called the *Macchiaioli*). Italy has not played an important role in late-19th/20th-century art, though it has produced a few great artists, all of whose works grace the excellent Pinacoteca di Brera, the Palazzo Reale, and the modern art gallery adjoining the Duomo, the Museo Civico d'Arte Contemporanea, all in Milan.

Antonio Canova (1757–1822) was Italy's top neoclassical sculptor, popular for his mythological figures and Bonaparte portraits (he even did both Napoléon and his sister Pauline as nudes); in addition to the Brera in Milan, you'll find his work in Venice's Museo Correr. **Giovanni Fattori** (1825–1908) was the best of the *Macchiaioli*, fond of battle scenes and landscapes populated by the Maremma's long-horned white cattle.

A sickly boy and only moderately successful in his short lifetime, **Amadeo Modigliani** (1884–1920) helped reinvent the portrait in painting and sculpture after he moved to Paris in 1906. He is famed for his elongated, mysterious heads and rapidly painted nudes. Check them out at Milan's Pinacoteca di Brera. **Giorgio de Chirico** (1888–1978) was the founder of freaky *metafisica,* "Metaphysical Painting," a forerunner of surrealism wherein figures and objects are stripped of their usual meaning through odd juxtapositions, warped perspective and reality, unnatural shadows, and other bizarre effects, and a general spatial emptiness. **Giorgio Morandi** (1890–1964) was influenced by *metafisica* in his eerily minimalist, highly modeled, quasi-monochrome still lifes. His paintings also decorate Turin's Galleria d'Arte Moderna.

Italian artists living in 1909 Paris made a spirited attempt to take the artistic initiative back into Italian hands, but what the **Futurist** movement's **Umberto Boccioni** (1882–1916) came up with was largely cubism with an element of movement added in (Duchamp-esque). **Gino Severini** (1883–1966) contributed a sophisticated take on color, which rubbed off on the core cubists as well. Both are represented at Milan's Pinacoteca di Brera and the Palazzo Reale.

ARCHITECTURE 101

While each architectural era has its own distinctive features, there are some elements, general floor plans, and terms common to many. Also, some features may appear near the end of one era and continue through several later ones.

From the Romanesque period on, most churches consist either of a single wide aisle, or a wide central nave flanked by two narrow aisles. The aisles are separated from the nave by a row of columns, or by square stacks of masonry called piers, usually connected by arches.

This main nave/aisle assemblage is usually crossed by a perpendicular corridor called a transept near the far, east end of the church so that the floor plan looks like a Latin Cross (shaped like a Crucifix). The shorter, east arm of the nave is the holiest area, called the chancel; it often houses the stalls of the choir and the altar. If the far end of the chancel is rounded off, we call it an apse. An ambulatory is a curving corridor outside the altar and choir area, separating it from the ring of smaller chapels radiating off the chancel and apse.

Some churches, especially after the Renaissance when mathematical proportion became important, were built on a Greek Cross plan, each axis the same length. By the baroque period, funky shapes became popular, with churches built in the round, or as ellipses, and so forth.

It's worth pointing out that very few buildings (especially churches) were built in only one particular style. These massive, expensive structures often took centuries to complete, during which time tastes would change and plans would be altered.

ANCIENT ROME (1ST CENTURY B.C.–4TH CENTURY A.D.)

The Romans made use of certain Greek innovations, particularly architectural ideas. The first to be adopted was post-and-lintel construction—essentially, a weight-bearing frame, like a door. Later came adaptation of Greek columns for supporting buildings, following the classical orders of Doric column capitals (the plain ones) on the ground floor, Ionic capitals (with the scrolls on either end) on the next level, and Corinthian capitals (flowering with acanthus leaves) on the top.

Romans thrived on huge complex problems for which they could produce organized, well-crafted solutions. Roman builders became inventive engineers, developing hoisting mechanisms and a specially trained workforce. They designed towns, built civic centers, raised grand temples and public baths, and developed the basilica, a rectangle supported by arches atop columns along both sides of the interior and with an apse at one or both ends. Basilicas were used for courts of justice, banking, and other commercial structures. The design was repeated all over the Roman world, beginning around the 1st century A.D. Later, early Christians adapted the architectural style for the first grand churches, still called basilicas.

Although marble is traditionally associated with Roman architecture, Roman engineers could also do wonders with bricks or even prosaic concrete. Their urban planning still stamps the street layouts of cities from **Aosta** (which preserves a gate and theater stage) to **Brescia** (with an ancient temple and theater remaining in the city center) to **Verona** (which preserves a magnificent ancient amphitheater still used for performances).

ROMANESQUE (A.D. 800–1300)

The Romanesque took its inspiration and rounded arches from ancient Rome (hence the name). Romanesque architects concentrated on building large churches with wide aisles to fit the masses who came both to hear the priests say Mass, but mainly to worship at the altars of various saints. But to support the weight of all that masonry, the walls had to be thick and solid (meaning they could be pierced only by few and rather small windows) resting on huge piers, giving Romanesque churches a dark, somber, mysterious, and often oppressive feeling.

The most identifiable Romanesque feature is rounded arches. These load-bearing architectural devices allowed the architects to open up wide naves and spaces, channeling all the weight of the stone walls and ceiling across the curve of the arch and down into the ground via the columns or pilasters. The style also made use of blind arcades, decorative bands of "filled-in" arches, the columns engaged in the wall and the arches' curves on top protruding mere inches. Set into each arch's curve is often a lozenge, a diamond-shaped decoration, often inlaid with colored marbles.

The **Basilica of Sant'Ambrogio in Milan** (11th–12th centuries) is festooned with the tiered loggias and arcades that would become hallmarks of the Lombard Romanesque.

GOTHIC (LATE 12TH–EARLY 15TH CENTURIES)

By the late 12th century, engineering developments—most significantly the pointed arch, which could bear a much heavier load than a rounded one—freed architects from the heavy, thick walls of Romanesque structures and allowed ceilings to soar, walls to thin, and windows to proliferate.

Instead of dark, somber, relatively unadorned Romanesque interiors that forced the eyes of the faithful toward the altar and its priest droning on in unintelligible Latin, the Gothic churchgoer's gaze was drawn up to high ceilings filled with light, a window unto heaven. The priests still gibbered in a dead language, but now peasants could "read" the Gothic comic books of colorful frescoes lining the walls and panels in stained-glass windows.

In addition to those pointy arches, another Gothic innovation was the famous flying buttress. These free-standing exterior pillars connected by graceful, thin arms of stone help channel the weight of the building and its roof out and down into the ground. To help counter the cross-forces involved in this engineering sleight of hand, the piers of buttresses were often topped by heavy pinnacles or statues. Inside, the general pointiness continues with cross vaults: The square patch of ceiling between four columns instead of being flat would arch up to a point in the center, creating four sail shapes, sort of like the underside of a pyramid with bulging faces. The X separating these four sails was often reinforced with ridges called ribbing. As the Gothic style progressed, four-sided cross-vaults would become six-, eight-, or multi-sided as architects played with the angles they could make. In addition, tracery—delicate, lacy spider webs of carved stone curly-cues—graced the pointy end of windows and just about any acute angle throughout the architecture.

The true, French-style Gothic only flourished in northern Italy, and the best example is **Milan's** massive **cathedral (Duomo),** a festival of pinnacles, buttresses, and pointy arches begun in the late 14th century. **Venice's I Frari** is a bit airier and boxier; **Padua's Basilica di Sant'Antonio** is largely Gothic, though its Romanesque facade and Byzantine domes try to throw you off. In palace architecture, the Venetians developed a distinctive style of insetting lacy, lithe, pointed marble windows with a distinct Eastern flair into pale pastel plaster walls. This is seen in countless palaces across **Venice,** but most strikingly in its most lavish: **Ca' d'Oro, Ca' Foscari,** and the model against which all were measured, the **Palazzo Ducale** itself.

RENAISSANCE (15TH–17TH CENTURIES)

As in painting, Renaissance architectural rules stressed proportion, order, classical inspiration, and mathematical precision to create unified, balanced structures. It was probably a Florentine architect, Filippo Brunelleschi, in the early 1400s, who first truly grasped the concept of "perspective," and provided artists with ground rules for creating the illusion of three dimensions on a flat surface.

The early Renaissance was truly codified by central Italian architects working in Florence and Rome, though influential early Florentine theorist **Leon Battista Alberti** (1404–72) built structures across Italy, including Sant'Andrea in Mantua. Urbino-born **Donato Bramante** (1444–1514), who would find fame in

Andrea Palladio—Father of Neoclassicism

Order, balance, elegance, harmony with the landscape, and a human scale are all apparent in the creations of architect **Andrea Palladio** (1508–80). Palladio was working as a stonemason and sculptor when, at 30, inspired by the design of ancient buildings he studied on trips to Rome, he turned his hand to architecture and applied the principles of classical proportion to Renaissance ideals of grace, symmetry, and functionality. Vicenza, the little city near Venice where Palladio lived as a boy and where he returned in his prime, is graced with many Palladian palazzi and a church as well as his Teatro Olimpico. In Venice he designed the churches of San Giorgio Maggiore and Redentore.

Palladio is best known, though, for the villas he built on the flat plains of the Veneto for Venetian nobles yearning to escape the cramped city. Nineteen of these villas still stand, including what may be his finest, **La Rotunda,** outside Vicenza. The design of this and Palladio's other villas—square, perfectly proportioned, elegant yet functional—may strike a note of familiarity with American and British visitors: Palladio influenced generations of architects who followed his lead when they designed neoclassical plantation houses in the American South and country estates in England, his "Palladian" style informing everything from British architecture to Thomas Jefferson's Monticello.

Other Palladio masterpieces include Vicenza's Palazzo della Ragione and Palazzo Valmarana (1566), and in the Veneto countryside around Vicenza the Villa Babaro and Villa Foscari. His final work is the Teatro Olimpico in Vicenza (1580), an attempt to reconstruct a Roman theater stage backdrop as described in ancient writings. He also designed the Venetian churches San Giorgio Maggiore (1565–1610) and Il Redentore.

Rome building St. Peter's, got his start in Milan by converting the older church of San Satiro and rebuilding the altar end of Santa Maria delle Grazie.

The undisputed master of the High Renaissance was **Andrea Palladio** (1508–80) from the Veneto, who worked in a much more strictly classical mode of columns, porticoes, pediments, and other ancient temple–inspired features (see the "Andrea Palladio—Father of Neoclassicism" box, below). In Venice **Jacopo Sansovino** (1486–1570) reigned supreme, his loggia and Libreria Sansoviniana lining St. Mark's Square becoming a cornerstone of the High Renaissance, to be copied and repeated in such far-flung architectural endeavors as the cast-iron facades in New York's SoHo district.

Raphael protégé **Giulio Romano** (1492–1546) designed Mantua's impressive **Palazzo Te; Galeazzo Alessi** (1512–72) was the premiere architect of Genoa's famed palaces, many of which are now museums.

BAROQUE & ROCOCO (17TH & 18TH CENTURIES)

More than any other movement, the **baroque** aimed toward a seamless meshing of architecture and art. The stuccoes, sculptures, and paintings were all carefully designed to complement each other—and the space itself—to create a unified whole. This whole was both aesthetic and narrative, the various art forms all working together to tell a single Biblical story (or, often, to subtly relate the deeds of the commissioning patron to great historic or Biblical events).

In the baroque, classical architecture is rewritten with curves, like a Renaissance where many of the crisp angles and ruler-straight lines are exchanged for curves of complex geometry and an interplay of concave and convex. The overall effect is to lighten the appearance of structures and add movement of line and vibrancy to the static look of the classical Renaissance.

Unlike the sometimes severe and austere designs of the Renaissance, the baroque was playful. Architects festooned structures and encrusted interiors with an excess of decorations intended to liven things up—lots of ornate stuccowork, pouty cherubs, airy frescoes, heavy gilding, twisting columns, multicolored marbles, and general frippery.

The baroque was also a movement of multiplying forms. The baroque asked why make do with one column when you can stack a half dozen partial columns on top of each other, slightly offset, until the effect is like looking at a single column though a fractured kaleidoscope? The baroque loved to pile up its forms and elements to create a rich, busy effect, breaking a pediment curve into segments so each would protrude further out than the last, or building up an architectural feature by stacking short sections of concave walls, each one curving to a different arc.

Rococo is the baroque gone awry into the grotesque, excessively complex and dripping with decorative tidbits.

The baroque flourished across Italy, but frankly little of it was truly inspired architecture. You'll find good examples in Venice's Santa Maria della Salute, and especially in Turin, from the Castellamonte-designed Piazza San Carlo to the great works of Guarino Guarini (San Lorenzo, Palazzo Carignano, the San Sidone chapel for the Holy Shroud in the cathedral) and Filippo Juvarra (Basilica di Superga, Palazzina di Stupinigi).

NEOCLASSICAL TO MODERN (18TH–21ST CENTURIES)

By the middle of the 18th century, as a backlash against the excesses of the baroque and rococo, architects, inspired by the rediscovery of Pompeii and other ancient sites, began turning to the austere simplicity and grandeur of the classical age and inaugurated a **neoclassical** style. The classical ideals of mathematical proportion and symmetry, first rediscovered during the Renaissance, are the hallmark of every classically styled era—a reinterpretation of ancient temples into buildings and massive colonnaded porticos. Northern Italy's two famed opera houses are both excellent neoclassical exercises: Milan's La Scala and Venice's La Fenice. Even though La Fenice is burned out and stands as a hollow shell, its still a good example, and, rest assured, it will be restored to its former neoclassical splendor . . . eventually. To see perhaps the best example of the chilliness the neoclassical style often entailed, pop into Padua's Caffè Pedrocchi for a cappuccino (interestingly, the architect, Giuseppe Japelli—who also worked in rococo and Palladian idioms—drew inspiration not just from Classical Greece/Rome, but also ancient Egypt).

Italy's take on the early-20th-century Art Nouveau movements was called **Liberty.** Like all Art Nouveau, decorators rebelling against the era of mass production stressed a craft uniqueness, creating asymmetrical, curvaceous designs based on organic inspiration (plants and flowers) and using wrought iron, stained glass, tile, and hand-painted wallpaper.

The **Industrial Age** of the late 19th/early 20th centuries brought with it the first genteel shopping malls of glass and steel girders, such as the famed Galleria in Milan. Mussolini made a spirited attempt to bring back ancient Rome in what can only be called **Fascist** architecture: Deco meets Caesar. Monumentally imposing and chillingly stark white marble structures are surrounded by classical-style statues. Fascist architecture still infests all corners of Italy, though most of the right-wing reliefs and the repeated engravings of "DVCE"—Mussolini's nickname for himself—have long since been chipped out. One of the best, easily accessible, oft-overlooked examples is Milan's massive train station (so if you're stuck with a long wait, wander outside to squint up at the weird Deco gargoyles and call your layover sightseeing).

Fitting into no style is Turin's truly odd **Mole Antonellina** (1863–97) designed as a synagogue but later put to various uses (currently, it is a film museum). Its squat brick base is topped by a steep cone supporting several layers of Greek temples piled one atop the other at right angles, capped off in turn by a needlelike spire at 166m (552 ft.).

Since then, Italy has mostly poured concrete and glass skyscrapers like the rest of us, though a few architects in the medium have stood out. The mid–20th century was dominated by Pier Luigi Nervi (1891–1979) and his reinforced concrete buildings, including Turin's Exposition Hall (1949). Italy's greatest living architect, Pritzker Prize–winning Renzo Piano (born 1937), lives in Paris, and most of his great commissions, including the Pompidou, are outside of Italy.

MUSIC 101

In the 14th century, Italy's music swept Europe. The country was an innovator in medieval music—**St. Ambrose,** bishop of Milan in the 4th century, introduced to the church the custom of singing liturgical chants. In the 12th century, **Guido d'Arezzo** developed the basis of the musical notation that we use today. Blind **Francesco Landini** introduced sophisticated, varied rhythms. And in the mid–16th century, the first violin appeared. Cremona lutists became the international standard bearers of fine instrument craftsmanship, and local son **Stradivari,** who learned his craft under the great master **Amati,** achieved a standard in violin design never improved upon.

Poets, who wanted a closer relationship between word and music, got their wish by the late 16th century. Until then, music had been but an incidental element in various entertainments, but a group in Florence wanted to adapt Greek drama, which they believed had been sung throughout, to a new kind of "musical drama." It came to be called "opera," a new form that caught on fast. The first great composer of opera was **Monteverdi,** of *Orfeo* fame, who's enjoying a new popularity today. Monteverdi managed to "translate human suffering into sound," lighting the way for succeeding generations of Italian composers.

Since Venice opened the first public opera house in 1637, it has continued to promote both operatic composers and productions. Venice's preeminent composer in the early 18th century was **Antonio Vivaldi,** who wrote more than 40 operas. The prolific **Scarlatti** (known mainly for his instrumental music) was also a composer of opera, turning out more than 100 in an exuberant rococo style. It's also possible that Scarlatti played some of his music on **Bartolomeo Cristofori's** 1709 invention the *pianoforte,* forerunner of the modern piano.

Italy has produced many fine composers, but **Giuseppe Verdi** was the unquestioned operatic master of the 19th century. Verdi, son of an innkeeper, understood dramatic form and wrote exquisite melodies, and his musicianship was unsurpassed. He achieved success early on with his third opera, *Nabucco,* a huge hit, then turned out *Rigiletto, Il Trovatore, Un Ballo in Maschera,* and *Aïda*—works that remain popular today. His powers continued unchecked as he grew older, maturing musically with such works as *Don Carlo* and his great *Otello* (written when the master was 73). At 80, he astonished the musical world with *Falstaff,* a masterpiece in *opera buffa* form, unlike anything he'd composed before.

Opera buffa was Italy's most popular operatic form in the early 19th century, works of comedy with more surface than depth in which, unlike grand opera, individual musical numbers alternate with spoken dialogue. Opera buffa had its origins in the wisecracking comedians who had long entertained at fairs. **Rossini's** charming *The Barber of Seville* and **Donizetti's** *Daughter of the Regiment* are examples of the form.

Rossini and Donizetti were also significant contributors to grand opera in the early and mid–19th century. **Puccini** came along a bit later, and his lyrical *La Bohème, Tosca,* and *Madama Butterfly* continue to please crowds. Well known to today's international audiences is American-born (with Italian parentage) **Gian-Carlo Menotti,** who has spent much of his life in Italy, and who is the composer of *Amahl and the Night Visitors* and creator of the huge Festival of Two Worlds music extravaganza in Spoleto, one of the world's top festivals for classical and instrumental music.

3 From the *Cucina Italiana:* Food & Wine

For Italians, eating is not just something to do for sustenance three times a day. Food is an essential ingredient of the Italian spirit, practically an art form in a culture that knows a lot about art. Even when Italy was a poor nation, it was said that poor Italians ate better than rich Germans or English or Americans.

Italians pay careful attention to the basics in both shopping and preparation. They know, for instance, which region produces the best onions or choicest peppers and when is the prime time of year to order porcini mushrooms, asparagus, truffles, or wild boar. If they're dining out, Italians expect the same care and pride they put into home cooking—and they get it. There are a lot of wonderful places to eat in Italy, from fancy *ristoranti* to more humble, homey trattorie and neighborhood joints called *osterie*.

MEALS

Prima colazione (breakfast) is treated lightly—a cappuccino and *cornetto* (croissant with a light sugar glaze) at the corner bar. There are exceptions: Many hotels, tired of hearing foreign guests grouse about the paltry morning offerings of this "continentale" breakfast, have taken to serving sumptuous buffets like those offered in the United States and north of the Alps, complete with ham, cheese, and sometimes eggs.

At the big meal of the day—be it *pranzo* (lunch) or *cena* (dinner)—portions on a plate may be smaller than visitors are accustomed to, but a traditional meal gets you four full courses: *antipasto, primo, secondo,* and *contorno.* The **antipasto** (appetizer) is often a platter of *salumi* (cold cuts), *bruschette,* or *crostini* (toasted or grilled bread topped with pâté or tomatoes) and/or vegetables prepared in oil or vinegar, or perhaps prosciutto and melon. Next is the **primo** (first course), which may be a *zuppa* or *miestra* (soup), pasta, *risotto* (arborio rice boiled to be thick and sticky, usually studded with some vegetables) or *polenta* (a cornmeal mush, often mixed with mushrooms or a dollop of meat ragù). The **secondo** (second course) is usually meat, fish, seafood, chicken, or game. To accompany it, you order a **contorno** (side dish) of vegetables or a salad. Traditionally, you won't find a pile of veggies next to your meat on the plate as in most American restaurants; however, a recent trend in Italian restaurants (especially ones that indulge in a more creative menu) is to include a side dish carefully chosen to complement your main course. At the end of the meal, dig into a **dolce** (dessert)—fruit, gelato (ice cream), tiramisù (sweetened, creamy mascarpone cheese atop espresso-soaked lady fingers), or *formaggio* (cheese) are traditionally offered.

Meals are usually accompanied by **wine** and a bottle of mineral water (*con gas* or *senza gas*/fizzy or still), and followed by an espresso. (One sure way to alienate an Italian waiter is to order cappuccino after dinner—it's usually drunk only in the morning.) Espresso is often followed by **grappa,** a fiery *digestivo* liqueur made from what's left over after the winemaking process.

RESTAURANTS

Traditionally, a *ristorante* (restaurant) is a bit formal and more expensive than a family-run *trattoria* or *osteria,* but the names are used almost interchangeably these days (trendy, expensive eateries often call themselves *osterie*, and little local joints may aggrandize themselves with the term *ristorante*).

To save money and grab a meal with Italians on their lunch break, pop in to a *tavola calda* (literally "hot table"), a kind of tiny cafeteria where a selection of pre-prepared hot dishes are sold by weight. A *rosticceria* is a *tavola calda* with roasting chickens in the window. Increasingly trendy **enoteche** (wine bars) usually offer ample platters of cheese and mixed *salumi* (cured meats) such as salami, prosciutto (salt-cured ham hock), *lardo* (salt-cured pork fat aged on marble slabs), and *mortadella* (bologna); most also offer a hot dish or two.

Any *bar* (a combo bar and cafe, where you go for your morning cappuccino, after-school ice cream, and evening aperitif) will also sell *panini* (sandwiches on a roll), *tramezzini* (giant tea sandwiches on sliced bread with the crusts cut off), and *piadine* (flatbread sandwiches).

Coffee All Day Long

Italians drink **caffè** (coffee) throughout the day, but only a little at a time and often while standing in a *bar*—remember, a "bar" in Italy is the place to go for your daily caffeine buzz. There's usually liquor available too, but it's the caffè that draws the customers.

Five types of coffee are popular in Italy. Plain old **caffè** is straight espresso in a demitasse, saturated with sugar and downed in one gulp. Espresso from a machine (as opposed to that made in the stove-top kettles most Italians use at home) is made by forcing steam through the tightly packed grounds, and despite popular perception, it actually contains less caffeine than typical American drip coffee; it's the rich taste that makes espresso seem so strong. **Cappuccino** is espresso mixed with hot milk and an overlay of foamy steamed milk, usually sipped for breakfast with a pastry and never as an after-dinner drink. "Stained" **Caffè macchiato** is espresso with a wee drop of steamed milk, while **latte macchiato** is the reverse, a glass of hot milk "stained" with a shot of espresso. **Caffè coretto** is espresso "corrected" with a shot of liquor. **Caffè Hag** is decaf. Most Italians hold in disdain the murky watered-down coffee that percolates in offices and kitchens across America, so if you want a big mug like the stuff at home, you'll have to order **caffè americano**.

PASTA

Aside from pizza, pasta is probably Italy's best-known export. It comes in two basic forms: *pastasciutta* (dry pasta), the kind most of us buy at the grocery store, and *pasta fresca* (fresh pasta) or *pasta fatto a mano* (handmade), the kind that most self-respecting establishments in Italy, even those of the most humble ilk, will probably serve.

Pastasciutta comes in long strands including *spaghetti, linguine,* and *trenette;* and in tubular *maccheroni* (macaroni) forms such as *penne* (pointed pasta quills) or *rigatoni* (fluted tubes), to name only a few. Pasta fresca is made in broad sheets, then cut into shapes used in lasagna, cannelloni, and the stuffed pastas tortelloni and ravioli or into noodles ranging from wide papparedelle to narrow fettuccine. If you sense that this isn't even a dent in the world of pasta, you're right: There are more than 600 pasta shapes in Italy.

ITALY'S REGIONAL CUISINES

Each Italian region has had thousands of years to develop its own culinary practices—and its own distinctive wines—and each still proudly sticks by its native dishes. What most Americans think of as Italian dishes is what Italian emigrants brought with them to the U.S., but the majority of those came from southern Italy, which is why when we think "Italian," we think of olive oil, pasta with tomato sauce, garlic, and pizza. Generally, though, northern Italian cooking uses a lot more cream and butter in sauces in addition to tomatoes. Also, pasta is not necessarily the first course of choice up north, often substituted by risotto (arborio rice boiled to be thick and sticky, usually studded with some vegetables) or polenta (a cornmeal mush, often mixed with mushrooms or a dollop of meat ragù).

VENICE & THE VENETO   Venice gained fame and fortune as the spice market of the world beginning in the 12th century (when Marco Polo visited the Orient), which may help account for the amazing ways local chefs dress up the scampi, crab, squid, and other creatures they pluck from the Adriatic. The Venetians also have raised that humble combination of liver and onions *(fegato alla veneziana)* to an irresistible level of haute cuisine, and have done the same with *risi e bisi* (rice and peas).

THE DOLOMITES   Dolomiti food is mountain food: rib-sticking and hearty, largely influenced by Austrian cuisine. Look for *speck* ham, *canederli* bread dumplings in thick broths, Wiener schnitzel, and *grostl* (hash made of veal, onions, and potatoes).

THE FRIULI   Alpine cuisine runs from the Tirolese influences of the Dolomites to Venetian specialties to Slovenian cuisine. They toss sauerkraut in their minestrone and call it *jota,* and serve up platters of everything from San Daniele prosciutto (the most delicate, expensive, and delicious in all of Italy) to *brovada* (a peasant dish of sausage, turnips, and grape skins).

LOMBARDY   Like other northern regions, Lombardy favors butter over olive oil and seems not to be overly concerned with cholesterol. A specialty is *osso buco,* sliced veal sautéed with the bone and marrow. A fine starter for any meal is the region's vegetable soup with rice and bacon, *minestrone alla milanese,* or a risotto made from arborio rice that grows on the region's low-lying plains and is often served in place of pasta. *Panettone,* the region's most popular dessert, is a local version of fruit cake that arrived from Vienna courtesy of Lombardy's 19th-century Austrian rulers. Austria also exported to Lombardy the breaded veal scallop of Wiener schnitzel, in Italy called *cotoletta alla Milanese.* Remember, too, that Lombardy is blessed with the Italian lakes, and trout and perch find their way into ravioli and other pasta dishes as well as simply sautéed as a secondo.

PIEDMONT & VALLE D'AOSTA   As befits these regions of cold winters, meat roasts and hearty soups are served, often accompanied by thick slabs of polenta. Piedmont is blessed with strong-flavored white truffles (the lovely town of Alba is Italy's truffle center), and they're used in a favorite local dish, *fonduta,* a fonduelike cheese dip mixed with milk and eggs. Piedmont is also home to Gorgonzola cheese.

LIGURIA   This is the homeland of the seafarers of Genoa, who brought back from the New World many cooking ingredients now taken for granted. What, for instance, would Italian cooking be without tomatoes, potatoes, or peppers? The sea-skirted region is also famous for its seafood, including a shellfish soup called *zuppa di datteri,* and for pesto, a pasta sauce of ground basil, pine nuts, and olive oil. To the world of bread, Liguria has contributed focaccia—flat, delicious, and often topped with herbs or, when eaten as a snack, with cheese and vegetables.

WINE

Italy, with the right kind of terrain and the perfect amounts of sun and rainfall, happens to be ideal for growing grapes. Centuries ago, the Etruscans had a hearty

Italian Wine Classifications

In 1963 Italy's wine was codified into two classifications: table wine and DOC. **DOC** *(Denominazione di Origine Controllata)* wines are merely those a government board guarantees have come from an official wine-producing area and meet the standard for carrying a certain name on the label. A *vino di tavola* **(table wine)** classification merely means a bottle doesn't fit the pre-established standards, and is no reflection of the wine's quality (see below).

In 1980 a new category was added. **DOCG** (the *G* stands for *Garantita*—guaranteed) is granted to wines with a certain subjective high quality. Traditionally, DOCG labels were merely the highest-profile wines that lobbied for the status (getting DOC and especially DOCG vastly improves reputations and, therefore, sales, though the costs of annually putting the wine up for testing are high). In 1992 the laws were rewritten and Italy's original six DOCG wines jumped to 15. Six of these are Tuscans.

Here's where things become a bit tricky. Though *vino di tavola* usually connotes a humble, simple, quaffable house wine from some indeterminate local producer (perhaps a local farmer's cooperative or even the restaurant owner's brother-in-law), in the 1980s and 1990s, this "table wine" classification was also co-opted by wine estates that wanted to experiment with grape mixtures and tinker with foreign varietals to create nontraditional but mighty wines. Problem is, these could never be called DOC or DOCG, which by law must follow strict formula guidelines. When many respectable producers started mixing varietals with French grapes like merlot, cabernet, and chardonnay to produce wines that, though complex and of high quality, don't fall into the conservative

wine industry, and the ancient Greeks bolstered it by transplanting their vine cuttings to Italy's southlands. And it was Italy, under the Romans, that first introduced the vine and its possibilities to France and Germany. Today, Italy exports more wine to the rest of the world than any other country. But there's plenty left at home from which to choose—more than 2,000 wines are produced in Italy.

Each region has different growing conditions, and so each has its own special wines. **Piedmont** is the north's premier wine region, known for its heavy reds, including Barolo, Barbaresco, Barbera, and Grignolino, as well as sparkling white Asti Spumanti. With these vineyards so close at hand, coastal **Liguria** hasn't developed many notable wines of its own save the white of Cinque Terre. The **Veneto** specializes in Valpolicella and Bardolino reds and, among whites, pinot grigio and Soave. The **Trentino** adds Tirolese varieties such as Traminer to cabernet, local wines such as Vernatsch, and pinot grigio, bianco, and nero. The **Friuli** masters the pinot grapes and cabernets as well, though local traditional wines Tocai, Verduzzo, and Malvasia are more unusual. **Lombardy** is not particularly known for its wines, though the area around Bergamo produces perfectly fine merlot, cabernet, pinot bianco, and pinto grigio in addition to local Valcalepio, and west of Brescia they bottle an excellent sparkling dry white wine

Index

See also Accommodations and Restaurant indexes, below.

RESTAURANTS

FROMMER'S® COMPLETE TRAVEL GUIDES

Alaska
Alaska Cruises & Ports of Call
Amsterdam
Argentina & Chile
Arizona
Atlanta
Australia
Austria
Bahamas
Barcelona, Madrid & Seville
Beijing
Belgium, Holland & Luxembourg
Bermuda
Boston
Brazil
British Columbia & the Canadian Rockies
Brussels & Bruges
Budapest & the Best of Hungary
California
Canada
Cancún, Cozumel & the Yucatán
Cape Cod, Nantucket & Martha's Vineyard
Caribbean
Caribbean Cruises & Ports of Call
Caribbean Ports of Call
Carolinas & Georgia
Chicago
China
Colorado
Costa Rica
Cuba
Denmark
Denver, Boulder & Colorado Springs
England
Europe
European Cruises & Ports of Call

Florida
France
Germany
Great Britain
Greece
Greek Islands
Hawaii
Hong Kong
Honolulu, Waikiki & Oahu
Ireland
Israel
Italy
Jamaica
Japan
Las Vegas
London
Los Angeles
Maryland & Delaware
Maui
Mexico
Montana & Wyoming
Montréal & Québec City
Munich & the Bavarian Alps
Nashville & Memphis
New England
New Mexico
New Orleans
New York City
New Zealand
Northern Italy
Norway
Nova Scotia, New Brunswick & Prince Edward Island
Oregon
Paris
Peru
Philadelphia & the Amish Country
Portugal

Prague & the Best of the Czech Republic
Provence & the Riviera
Puerto Rico
Rome
San Antonio & Austin
San Diego
San Francisco
Santa Fe, Taos & Albuquerque
Scandinavia
Scotland
Seattle & Portland
Shanghai
Sicily
Singapore & Malaysia
South Africa
South America
South Florida
South Pacific
Southeast Asia
Spain
Sweden
Switzerland
Texas
Thailand
Tokyo
Toronto
Tuscany & Umbria
USA
Utah
Vancouver & Victoria
Vermont, New Hampshire & Maine
Vienna & the Danube Valley
Virgin Islands
Virginia
Walt Disney World® & Orlando
Washington, D.C.
Washington State

FROMMER'S® DOLLAR-A-DAY GUIDES

Australia from $50 a Day
California from $70 a Day
England from $75 a Day
Europe from $70 a Day
Florida from $70 a Day
Hawaii from $80 a Day

Ireland from $60 a Day
Italy from $70 a Day
London from $85 a Day
New York from $90 a Day
Paris from $80 a Day

San Francisco from $70 a Day
Washington, D.C. from $80 a Day
Portable London from $85 a Day
Portable New York City from $90 a Day

FROMMER'S® PORTABLE GUIDES

Acapulco, Ixtapa & Zihuatanejo
Amsterdam
Aruba
Australia's Great Barrier Reef
Bahamas
Berlin
Big Island of Hawaii
Boston
California Wine Country
Cancún
Cayman Islands
Charleston
Chicago
Disneyland®
Dublin
Florence

Frankfurt
Hong Kong
Houston
Las Vegas
Las Vegas for Non-Gamblers
London
Los Angeles
Los Cabos & Baja
Maine Coast
Maui
Miami
Nantucket & Martha's Vineyard
New Orleans
New York City
Paris
Phoenix & Scottsdale

Portland
Puerto Rico
Puerto Vallarta, Manzanillo & Guadalajara
Rio de Janeiro
San Diego
San Francisco
Savannah
Seattle
Sydney
Tampa & St. Petersburg
Vancouver
Venice
Virgin Islands
Washington, D.C.

FROMMER'S® NATIONAL PARK GUIDES

Banff & Jasper
Family Vacations in the National Parks

Grand Canyon
National Parks of the American West
Rocky Mountain

Yellowstone & Grand Teton
Yosemite & Sequoia/Kings Canyon
Zion & Bryce Canyon

FROMMER'S® MEMORABLE WALKS

Chicago
London

New York
Paris

San Francisco

FROMMER'S® WITH KIDS GUIDES

Chicago
Las Vegas
New York City

Ottawa
San Francisco
Toronto

Vancouver
Washington, D.C.

SUZY GERSHMAN'S BORN TO SHOP GUIDES

Born to Shop: France
Born to Shop: Hong Kong,
  Shanghai & Beijing

Born to Shop: Italy
Born to Shop: London

Born to Shop: New York
Born to Shop: Paris

FROMMER'S® IRREVERENT GUIDES

Amsterdam
Boston
Chicago
Las Vegas
London

Los Angeles
Manhattan
New Orleans
Paris
Rome

San Francisco
Seattle & Portland
Vancouver
Walt Disney World®
Washington, D.C.

FROMMER'S® BEST-LOVED DRIVING TOURS

Britain
California
Florida
France

Germany
Ireland
Italy
New England

Northern Italy
Scotland
Spain
Tuscany & Umbria

HANGING OUT™ GUIDES

Hanging Out in England
Hanging Out in Europe

Hanging Out in France
Hanging Out in Ireland

Hanging Out in Italy
Hanging Out in Spain

THE UNOFFICIAL GUIDES®

Bed & Breakfasts and Country
  Inns in:
  California
  Great Lakes States
  Mid-Atlantic
  New England
  Northwest
  Rockies
  Southeast
  Southwest
Best RV & Tent Campgrounds in:
  California & the West
  Florida & the Southeast
  Great Lakes States
  Mid-Atlantic
  Northeast
  Northwest & Central Plains

Southwest & South Central
  Plains
  U.S.A.
Beyond Disney
Branson, Missouri
California with Kids
Central Italy
Chicago
Cruises
Disneyland®
Florida with Kids
Golf Vacations in the Eastern U.S.
Great Smoky & Blue Ridge Region
Inside Disney
Hawaii
Las Vegas
London
Maui

Mexio's Best Beach Resorts
Mid-Atlantic with Kids
Mini Las Vegas
Mini-Mickey
New England & New York with
  Kids
New Orleans
New York City
Paris
San Francisco
Skiing & Snowboarding in the West
Southeast with Kids
Walt Disney World®
Walt Disney World® for
  Grown-ups
Walt Disney World® with Kids
Washington, D.C.
World's Best Diving Vacations

SPECIAL-INTEREST TITLES

Frommer's Adventure Guide to Australia &
  New Zealand
Frommer's Adventure Guide to Central America
Frommer's Adventure Guide to India & Pakistan
Frommer's Adventure Guide to South America
Frommer's Adventure Guide to Southeast Asia
Frommer's Adventure Guide to Southern Africa
Frommer's Britain's Best Bed & Breakfasts and
  Country Inns
Frommer's Caribbean Hideaways
Frommer's Exploring America by RV
Frommer's Fly Safe, Fly Smart

Frommer's France's Best Bed & Breakfasts and
  Country Inns
Frommer's Gay & Lesbian Europe
Frommer's Italy's Best Bed & Breakfasts and
  Country Inns
Frommer's Road Atlas Britain
Frommer's Road Atlas Europe
Frommer's Road Atlas France
The New York Times' Guide to Unforgettable
  Weekends
Places Rated Almanac
Retirement Places Rated
Rome Past & Present

AOL Keyword: Travel

Booked aisle seat.

Reserved room with a view.

With a queen – no, make that a king-size bed.

With Travelocity, you can book your flights and hotels together, so you can get even better deals than if you booked them separately. You'll save time and money without compromising the quality of your trip. Choose your airline seat, search for alternate airports, pick your hotel room type, even choose the neighborhood you'd like to stay in.

Travelocity

Visit www.travelocity.com
or call 1-888-TRAVELOCITY

AOL Keyword: Travel

Fly. Sleep. Save.

Now you can book your flights and hotels together, so you can get even better deals than if you booked them separately.

Travelocity

Visit www.travelocity.com
or call 1-888-TRAVELOCITY

Travelocity,® Travelocity.com® and the Travelocity skyline logo are trademarks and/or service marks of Travelocity.com LP © 2003 Travelocity.com LP All rights rese